# Data Structures and Algorithms

## with Object-Oriented Design Patterns in C++

# WORLDWIDE SERIES IN COMPUTER SCIENCE

*SERIES EDITORS*    **Professor David Barron,** *Southampton University, UK*

**Professor Peter Wegner,** *Brown University, USA*

The Worldwide Series in Computer Science has been created to publish textbooks which both address and anticipate the needs of an ever-evolving curriculum, thereby shaping its future. It is designed for undergraduates majoring in Computer Science and practitioners who need to reskill. Its philosophy derives from the conviction that the discipline of computing needs to produce technically skilled engineers who will inevitably face, and possibly invent, radically new technologies throughout their future careers. New media will be used innovatively to support high-quality texts written by leaders in the field.

*Books in Series*    Winder, *Developing Java Software*

Kotonya & Sommerville, *Requirements Engineering*

Goodrich & Tamassia, *Data Structures and Algorithms in Java*

Reiss, *A Practical Introduction to Software Design with C++*

Preiss, *Data Structures and Algorithms with Object-Oriented Design Patterns in C++*

Ammeraal, *Computer Graphics for Java Programmers*

Ercegovac, *Introduction to Digital Systems*

# Data Structures and Algorithms
## with Object-Oriented Design Patterns in C++

**Bruno R. Preiss**
**B.A.Sc., M.A.Sc., Ph.D., P.Eng.**
*Associate Professor*
*Department of Electrical and Computer Engineering*
*University of Waterloo, Waterloo, Canada*

**John Wiley & Sons, Inc.**
*New York      Chichester      Weinheim      Brisbane      Singapore      Toronto*

Cover Photo: David Parker/Science Photo Library/Photo Researchers

METAFONT is a trademark of Addison Wesley Publishing Company.
SPARCstation, Solaris, and Java are registered trademarks of Sun Microsystems.
TEX is a trademark of the American Mathematical Society.
UNIX is a registered trademark of AT&T Bell Laboratories.

ACQUISITIONS EDITOR    Regina Brooks
MARKETING MANAGER    Katherine Hepburn
SENIOR PRODUCTION MANAGER    Lucille Buonocore
SENIOR PRODUCTION EDITOR    Monique Calello
SENIOR DESIGNER    Kevin Murphy
ILLUSTRATION COORDINATOR    Sigmund Malinowski

This book was set in Times Roman by Publication Services and printed and bound by
R.R. Donnelley & Sons / Crawfordsville. The cover was printed by Lehigh Press.

This book is printed on acid-free paper. ∞

The paper in this book was manufactured by a mill whose forest management programs include sustained
yield harvesting of its timberlands. Sustained yield harvesting principles ensure that the numbers of trees
cut each year does not exceed the amount of new growth.

*Library of Congress Cataloging in Publication Data:*
Preiss, Bruno R.
    Data structures and algorithms : with object-oriented design
patterns in C++ / Bruno R. Preiss.

        p.    cm.
    Includes index.
    ISBN 0-471-24134-2 (hardcover : alk. paper)
    1. Object-oriented programming (Computer science)    2. C++
(Computer program language)    3. Data structures (Computer science)
4. Computer algorithms.    I. Title.

QA76.64.P745    1999
005.1'17—dc21                                            98-18107
                                                        CIP

Printed in the United States of America

10 9 8 7 6 5 4 3 2

*To my children,*
*Anna Kristina,*
*Katherine Lila*
*and*
*Alexander Edgar*

# Preface

This book was motivated by my experience in teaching the course *E&CE 250: Algorithms and Data Structures* in the Computer Engineering program at the University of Waterloo. I have observed that the advent of *object-oriented methods* and the emergence of object-oriented *design patterns* has led to a profound change in the pedagogy of data structures and algorithms. The successful application of these techniques gives rise to a kind of cognitive unification: Ideas that are disparate and apparently unrelated seem to come together when the appropriate design patterns and abstractions are used.

This paradigm shift is both evolutionary and revolutionary. On the one hand, the knowledge base grows incrementally as programmers and researchers invent new algorithms and data structures. On the other hand, the proper use of object-oriented techniques requires a fundamental change in the way the programs are designed and implemented. Programmers who are well schooled in the procedural ways often find the leap to objects to be a difficult one.

## Goals

The primary goal of this book is to promote object-oriented design using C++ and to illustrate the use of the emerging *object-oriented design patterns*. Experienced object-oriented programmers find that certain ways of doing things work best and that these ways occur over and over again. The book shows how these patterns are used to create good software designs. In particular, the following design patterns are used throughout the text: *singleton, container, iterator, adapter,* and *visitor.*

Virtually all of the data structures are presented in the context of a *single, unified, polymorphic class hierarchy.* This framework clearly shows the *relationships* between data structures and it illustrates how polymorphism and inheritance can be used effectively. In addition, *algorithmic abstraction* is used extensively when presenting classes of algorithms. By using algorithmic abstraction, it is possible to describe a generic algorithm without having to worry about the details of a particular concrete realization of that algorithm.

A secondary goal of the book is to present mathematical tools *just in time*. Analysis techniques and proofs are presented as needed and in the proper context. In the past when the topics in this book were taught at the graduate level, an author could rely on students having the needed background in mathematics. However, because the book is targeted for second- and third-year students, it is necessary to fill in the background as needed. To the extent possible without compromising correctness, the presentation fosters intuitive understanding of the concepts rather than mathematical rigor.

## Approach

One cannot learn to program just by reading a book. It is a skill that must be developed by practice. Nevertheless, the best practitioners study the works of others and incorporate their observations into their own practice. I firmly believe that after learning the rudiments of program writing, students should be exposed to examples of complex, yet well-designed program artifacts so that they can learn about designing good software.

Consequently, this book presents the various data structures and algorithms as complete C++ program fragments. All the program fragments presented in this book have been extracted automatically from the source code files of working and tested programs.

The full functionality of the proposed draft ANSI standard C++ language is used in the examples—including *templates, exceptions,* and *run-time type information*[3]. It has been my experience that by developing the proper abstractions, it is possible to present the concepts as fully functional programs without resorting to *pseudo-code* or to hand-waving.

## Outline

This book presents material identified in the *Computing Curricula 1991* report of the ACM/IEEE-CS Joint Curriculum Task Force[38]. The book specifically addresses the following *knowledge units:* AL1: Basic Data structures, AL2: Abstract Data Types, AL3: Recursive Algorithms, AL4: Complexity Analysis, AL6: Sorting and Searching, and AL8: Problem-Solving Strategies. The breadth and depth of coverage is typical of what should appear in the second or third year of an undergraduate program in computer science/computer engineering.

In order to analyze a program, it is necessary to develop a model of the computer. Chapter 2 develops several models and illustrates with examples how these models predict performance. Both average-case and worst-case analyses of running time are considered. Recursive algorithms are discussed and it is shown how to solve a recurrence using repeated substitution. This chapter also reviews arithmetic and geometric series summations, Horner's rule, and the properties of harmonic numbers.

Chapter 3 introduces asymptotic (big-oh) notation and shows by comparing with Chapter 2 that the results of asymptotic analysis are consistent with models of higher fidelity. In addition to $O(\cdot)$, this chapter also covers other asymptotic notations ($\Omega(\cdot)$, $\Theta(\cdot)$ and $o(\cdot)$) and develops the asymptotic properties of polynomials and logarithms.

Chapter 4 introduces the *foundational data structures*—the array and the linked list. Virtually all the data structures in the rest of the book can be implemented using either one of these foundational structures. This chapter also covers multi-dimensional arrays and matrices.

Chapter 5 deals with abstraction and data types. It presents the recurring design patterns used throughout the text as well as a unifying framework for the data structures presented in the subsequent chapters. In particular, all of the data structures are viewed as *abstract containers*.

Chapter 6 discusses stacks, queues, and deques. This chapter presents implementations based on both foundational data structures (arrays and linked lists). Applications for stacks and queues and deques are presented.

Chapter 7 covers ordered lists, both sorted and unsorted. In this chapter, a list is viewed as a *searchable container*. Again several applications of lists are presented.

Chapter 8 introduces hashing and the notion of a hash table. This chapter addresses the design of hashing functions for the various basic data types as well as for the abstract data types described in Chapter 5. Both scatter tables and hash tables are covered in depth and analytical performance results are derived.

Chapter 9 introduces trees and describes their many forms. Both depth-first and breadth-first tree traversals are presented. Completely generic traversal algorithms based on the use of the *visitor* design pattern are presented, thereby illustrating the power of *algorithmic abstraction*. This chapter also shows how trees are used to represent mathematical expressions and illustrates the relationships between traversals and the various expression notations (prefix, infix, and postfix).

Chapter 10 addresses trees as *searchable containers*. Again, the power of *algorithmic abstraction* is demonstrated by showing the relationships between simple algorithms and balancing algorithms. This chapter also presents average case performance analyses and illustrates the solution of recurrences by telescoping.

Chapter 11 presents several priority queue implementations, including binary heaps, leftist heaps, and binomial queues. In particular this chapter illustrates how a more complicated data structure (leftist heap) extends an existing one (tree). Discrete-event simulation is presented as an application of priority queues.

Chapter 12 covers sets and multisets. Also covered are partitions and disjoint set algorithms. The latter topic illustrates again the use of algorithmic abstraction.

Techniques for dynamic storage management are presented in Chapter 13. This is a topic that is not found often in texts of this sort. However, the features of C++ which allow the user to redefine the **new** and **delete** operators make this topic approachable.

Chapter 14 surveys a number of algorithm design techniques. Included are brute-force and greedy algorithms, backtracking algorithms (including branch-and-bound), divide-and-conquer algorithms, and dynamic programming. An object-oriented approach based on the notion of an *abstract solution space* and an *abstract solver* unifies much of the discussion. This chapter also covers briefly random number generators, Monte Carlo methods, and simulated annealing.

Chapter 15 covers the major sorting algorithms in an object-oriented style based on the notion of an *abstract sorter*. Using the abstract sorter illustrates the relationships between the various classes of sorting algorithm and demonstrates the use of algorithmic abstractions.

Finally, Chapter 16 presents an overview of graphs and graph algorithms. Both depth-first and breadth-first graph traversals are presented. Topological sort is viewed as yet another special kind of traversal. Generic traversal algorithms based on the *visitor* design pattern are presented, once more illustrating *algorithmic abstraction*. This chapter also covers various shortest path algorithms and minimum-spanning-tree algorithms.

At the end of each chapter is a set of exercises and a set of programming projects. The exercises are designed to consolidate the concepts presented in the text. The programming projects generally require the student to extend the implementation given in the text.

## Suggested Course Outline

This text may be used in either a one-semester or a two-semester course. The course which I teach at Waterloo is a one-semester course that comprises 36 lecture hours on the following topics:

1.  Review of the fundamentals of programming in C++ and an overview of object-oriented programming with C++ (Appendix A). [4 lecture hours]
2.  Models of the computer, algorithm analysis, and asymptotic notation (Chapters 2 and 3). [4 lecture hours]
3.  Foundational data structures, abstraction, and abstract data types (Chapters 4 and 5). [4 lecture hours]
4.  Stacks, queues, ordered lists, and sorted lists (Chapters 6 and 7). [3 lecture hours]
5.  Hashing, hash tables, and scatter tables (Chapter 8). [3 lecture hours]
6.  Trees and search trees (Chapters 9 and 10). [6 lecture hours]
7.  Heaps and priority queues (Chapter 11). [3 lecture hours]
8.  Algorithm design techniques (Chapter 14). [3 lecture hours]
9.  Sorting algorithms and sorters (Chapter 15). [3 lecture hours]
10. Graphs and graph algorithms (Chapter 16). [3 lecture hours]

Depending on the background of students, a course instructor may find it necessary to review features of the C++ language. For example, an understanding of *templates* is required for the *foundational data structures* discussed in Chapter 4. Similarly, students need to understand the workings of *classes* and *inheritance* in order to understand the unifying class hierarchy discussed in Chapter 5.

## Online Course Materials

Additional material supporting this book can be found on the world wide web at the URL:

`http://www.pads.uwaterloo.ca/Bruno.Preiss/books/opus4`

In particular, you will find there the source code for all the program fragments in this book as well as an errata list.

Bruno R. Preiss
Waterloo, Canada
January 22, 1998

# Contents

**CHAPTER 1    Introduction**     1

   1.1    What This Book Is About     1

   1.2    Object-Oriented Design     1

   1.3    Object Hierarchies and Design Patterns     2

   1.4    The Features of C++ You Need to Know     3

   1.5    How This Book Is Organized     4

**CHAPTER 2    Algorithm Analysis**     6

   2.1    A Detailed Model of the Computer     7

   2.2    A Simplified Model of the Computer     22

   Exercises     31

   Programming Projects     33

**CHAPTER 3    Asymptotic Notation**     34

   3.1    An Asymptotic Upper Bound—Big Oh     34

   3.2    An Asymptotic Lower Bound—Omega     45

   3.3    More Notation—Theta and Little Oh     48

   3.4    Asymptotic Analysis of Algorithms     49

   Exercises     62

   Programming Projects     64

**CHAPTER 4    Foundational Data Structures**     66

   4.1    Dynamic Arrays     66

   4.2    Singly-Linked Lists     73

**xiii**

4.3   Multidimensional Arrays                                    85
Exercises                                                        93
Programming Projects                                             94

**CHAPTER 5   Data Types and Abstraction**                      **95**

5.1   Abstract Data Types                                        95
5.2   Design Patterns                                            96
Exercises                                                        122
Programming Projects                                             124

**CHAPTER 6   Stacks, Queues, and Deques**                      **126**

6.1   Stacks                                                     127
6.2   Queues                                                     142
6.3   Deques                                                     152
Exercises                                                        160
Programming Projects                                             161

**CHAPTER 7   Ordered Lists and Sorted Lists**                  **164**

7.1   Ordered Lists                                              164
7.2   Sorted Lists                                               186
Exercises                                                        198
Programming Projects                                             199

**CHAPTER 8   Hashing, Hash Tables, and Scatter Tables**        **201**

8.1   Hashing—The Basic Idea                                     201
8.2   Hashing Methods                                            204
8.3   Hash Function Implementations                              208
8.4   Hash Tables                                                218
8.5   Scatter Tables                                             225
8.6   Scatter Table using Open Addressing                        234
8.7   Applications                                               247
Exercises                                                        249
Programming Projects                                             251

# CHAPTER 9    Trees                                    253

    9.1   Basics                                    254

    9.2   *N*-ary Trees                             257

    9.3   Binary Trees                              261

    9.4   Tree Traversals                           262

    9.5   Expression Trees                          265

    9.6   Implementing Trees                        267

    Exercises                                      295

    Programming Projects                            297

# CHAPTER 10    Search Trees                            298

    10.1   Basics                                   298

    10.2   Searching a Search Tree                  300

    10.3   Average Case Analysis                    302

    10.4   Implementing Search Trees                308

    10.5   AVL Search Trees                         315

    10.6   *M*-Way Search Treees                    327

    10.7   B-Trees                                  335

    10.8   Applications                             346

    Exercises                                      346

    Programming Projects                            349

# CHAPTER 11    Heaps and Priority Queues               350

    11.1   Basics                                   351

    11.2   Binary Heaps                             353

    11.3   Leftist Heaps                            362

    11.4   Binomial Queues                          370

    11.5   Applications                             385

    Exercises                                      389

    Programming Projects                            390

# CHAPTER 12    Sets, Multisets, and Partitions         392

    12.1   Basics                                   393

    12.2   Array and Bit-Vector Sets                395

12.3   Multisets                                    401
12.4   Partitions                                   408
12.5   Applications                                 420
Exercises                                           423
Programming Projects                                424


# CHAPTER 13   Dynamic Storage Allocation: The Other Kind of Heap                                        426

13.1   Basics                                       426
13.2   Singly-Linked Free Storage                   432
13.3   Doubly-Linked Free Storage                   440
13.4   Buddy System for Storage Management           448
13.5   Applications                                 457
Exercises                                           460
Programming Projects                                461


# CHAPTER 14   Algorithmic Patterns and Problem Solvers   463

14.1   Brute-Force and Greedy Algorithms            463
14.2   Backtracking Algorithms                      467
14.3   Top-Down Algorithms: Divide-and-Conquer      476
14.4   Bottom-Up Algorithms: Dynamic Programming    486
14.5   Randomized Algorithms                        493
Exercises                                           504
Programming Projects                                507


# CHAPTER 15   Sorting Algorithms and Sorters       509

15.1   Basics                                       509
15.2   Sorting and Sorters                          510
15.3   Insertion Sorting                            513
15.4   Exchange Sorting                             518
15.5   Selection Sorting                            529
15.6   Merge Sorting                                539
15.7   A Lower Bound on Sorting                     544
15.8   Distribution Sorting                         546
15.9   Performance Data                             552

Exercises 555

Programming Projects 556

## CHAPTER 16   Graphs and Graph Algorithms    558

16.1    Basics    559

16.2    Implementing Graphs    567

16.3    Graph Traversals    577

16.4    Shortest-Path Algorithms    590

16.5    Minimum-Cost Spanning Trees    600

16.6    Application: Critical Path Analysis    609

Exercises    615

Programming Projects    618

## APPENDIX A    C++ and Object-Oriented Programming    619

A.1    Variables, Pointers, and References    619

A.2    Parameter Passing    622

A.3    Objects and Classes    625

A.4    Inheritance and Polymorphism    631

A.5    Templates    641

A.6    Exceptions    642

## APPENDIX B    Class Hierarchy Diagrams    645

## APPENDIX C    Character Codes    647

## Bibliography    648

## Index    651

# 1 | Introduction

## 1.1 What This Book Is About

This book is about the fundamentals of *data structures and algorithms*—the basic elements from which large and complex software artifacts are built. To develop a solid understanding of a data structure requires three things: First, you must learn how the information is arranged in the memory of the computer. Second, you must become familiar with the algorithms for manipulating the information contained in the data structure. And third, you must understand the performance characteristics of the data structure so that when called upon to select a suitable data structure for a particular application, you are able to make an appropriate decision.

This book also illustrates object-oriented design, and it promotes the use of common, object-oriented design patterns. The algorithms and data structures in the book are presented in the C++ programming language. Virtually all the data structures are presented in the context of a single class hierarchy. This commitment to a single design allows the programs presented in the later chapters to build upon the programs presented in the earlier chapters.

## 1.2 Object-Oriented Design

Traditional approaches to the design of software have been either *data oriented* or *process oriented*. Data-oriented methodologies emphasize the representation of information and the relationships between the parts of the whole. The actions which operate on the data are of less significance. On the other hand, process-oriented design methodologies emphasize the actions performed by a software artifact; the data are of lesser importance.

It is now commonly held that *object-oriented* methodologies are more effective for managing the complexity which arises in the design of large and complex software artifacts than either data-oriented or process-oriented methodologies. This is because data and processes are given equal importance. *Objects* are used to combine data with

1

the procedures that operate on that data. The main advantage of using objects is that they provide both *abstraction* and *encapsulation*.

### Abstraction

Abstraction can be thought of as a mechanism for suppressing irrelevant details while at the same time emphasizing relevant ones. An important benefit of abstraction is that it makes it easier for the programmer to think about the problem to be solved.

For example, *procedural abstraction* lets the software designer think about the actions to be performed without worrying about how those actions are implemented. Similarly, *data abstraction* lets the software designer think about the objects in a program and the interactions between those objects without having to worry about how those objects are implemented.

There are also many different *levels of abstraction*. The lower the levels of abstraction expose more of the details of an implementation, whereas the higher levels hide more of the details.

### Encapsulation

Encapsulation aids the software designer by enforcing *information hiding*. Objects *encapsulate* data and the procedures for manipulating that data. In a sense, the object *hides* the details of the implementation from the user of that object.

There are two very real benefits from encapsulation—*conceptual* and *physical* independence. Conceptual independence results from hiding the implementation of an object from the user of that object. Consequently, the user is prevented from doing anything with an object that depends on the implementation of that object. This is desirable because it allows the implementation to be changed without requiring the modification of the user's code.

Physical independence arises from the fact that the behavior of an object is determined by the object itself. The behavior of an object is not determined by some external entity. As a result, when we perform an operation on an object, there are no unwanted side effects.

## 1.3  Object Hierarchies and Design Patterns

There is more to object-oriented programming than simply encapsulating in an object some data and the procedures for manipulating those data. Object-oriented methods deal also with the *classification* of objects and they address the *relationships* between different classes of objects.

The primary facility for expressing relationships between classes of objects is *derivation*—new classes can be derived from existing classes. What makes derivation so useful is the notion of *inheritance*. Derived classes *inherit* the characteristics of the classes from which they are derived. In addition, inherited functionality can be overridden and additional functionality can be defined in a derived class.

A feature of this book is that virtually all the data structures are presented in the context of a single class hierarchy. In effect, the class hierarchy is a taxonomy of data structures. Different implementations of a given abstract data structure are all derived from the same abstract base class. Related base classes are in turn derived from classes that abstract and encapsulate the common features of those classes.

In addition to dealing with hierarchically related classes, experienced object-oriented designers also consider very carefully the interactions between unrelated classes. With experience, a good designer discovers the recurring patterns of interactions between objects. By learning to use these patterns, your object-oriented designs will become more flexible and reusable.

Recently, programmers have started to name the common design patterns. In addition, catalogs of the common patterns are now being compiled and published [14].

The following *object-oriented design patterns* are used throughout this text:

### Containers
A container is an object that holds within it other objects. A container has a capacity, it can be full or empty, and objects can be inserted and withdrawn from a container. In addition, a *searchable container* is a container that supports efficient search operations.

### Iterators
An *iterator* provides a means by which the objects within a container can be accessed one-at-a-time. All iterators share a common interface, and hide the underlying implementation of the container from the user of that container.

### Visitors
A visitor represents an operation to be performed on all the objects within a container. All visitors share a common interface, and thereby hide the operation to be performed from the container. At the same time, visitors are defined separately from containers. Thus, a particular visitor can be used with any container.

### Adapters
An *adapter* converts the interface of one class into the interface expected by the user of that class. This allows a given class with an incompatible interface to be used in a situation where a different interface is expected.

### Singletons
A singleton is a class of which there is only one instance. The class ensures that there is only one instance created and it provides a way to access that instance.

## 1.4　The Features of C++ You Need to Know

This book does not teach the basics of programming. It is assumed that you have taken an introductory course in programming and that you have learned how to write a program in C++. That is, you have learned the rules of C++ syntax and you have learned how to put together C++ statements in order to solve rudimentary programming problems. The following paragraphs describe more fully aspects of programming in C++ with which you should be familiar.

### Variables

You must be very comfortable with the notion of a variable as an abstraction for a region of a memory. A variable has attributes such as *name*, *type*, *value*, *address*, *size*, *lifetime*, and *scope*.

### Parameter Passing

There are two parameter passing mechanisms in C++: *pass-by-value* and *pass-by-reference*. Both of these methods are used extensively in this book. It is essential that you understand the behavioral difference between the two methods as well as the performance implications of using each of them.

### Pointers

Mastering the use of pointers is essential when programming in C++. The key to understanding pointers is to recognize that a pointer variable has exactly the same set of attributes as any other C++ variable. It is crucial that you keep straight the distinctions between the *value* of a pointer, the *address* of a pointer, and the object to which a pointer points.

### Classes and Objects

A C++ class encapsulates a set of values and a set of operations. The values are represented by the member variables of the class and the operations by the member functions of the class. In C++ a class definition introduces a new *type*. The instances of a class type are called objects. You should understand the special role of the constructor and the destructor member functions of a class, and, in particular, you should know when the C++ compiler invokes each of them.

### Inheritance

In C++ one class may be derived from another. The derived class *inherits* all the member variables and the member functions of the base class or classes. In addition, inherited member functions can be overridden in the derived class and new member variables and functions can be defined. You should understand how the compiler determines the code to execute when a particular member function is called.

### Other Features

This book makes use of other C++ features such as templates, exceptions, and run-time type information. You can learn about these topics as you work your way through the book.

## 1.5  How This Book Is Organized

### Models and Asymptotic Analysis

To analyze the performance of an algorithm, we need to have a model of the computer. Chapter 2 presents a series of three models, each one less precise but easier to use than its predecessor. These models are similar, in that they require a careful accounting of the operations performed by an algorithm.

Next, Chapter 3 presents *asymptotic analysis*. This is an extremely useful mathematical technique because it simplifies greatly the analysis of algorithms. Asymptotic analysis obviates the need for a detailed accounting of the operations performed by an algorithm, yet at the same time gives a very general result.

### Foundational Data Structures

When implementing a data structure, we must decide first whether to use an *array* or a *linked list* as the underlying organizational technique. For this reason, the array and the linked list are called *foundational data structures*. Chapter 4 also covers multidimensional arrays and matrices.

### Abstract Data Types and the Class Hierarchy

Chapter 5 introduces the notion of an *abstract data type*. All of the data structures discussed in this book are presented as instances of various abstract data types. Chapter 5 also introduces the class hierarchy as well as the various related concepts such as *iterators* and *visitors*.

### Data Structures

Chapter 6 covers *stacks*, *queues*, and *deques*. *Ordered lists* and *sorted lists* are presented in Chapter 7. The concept of hashing is introduced in Chapter 8. This chapter also covers the design of hash functions for a number of different object types. Finally, *hash tables* and *scatter tables* are presented.

Trees and search trees are presented in Chapters 9 and 10. Trees are one of the most important nonlinear data structures. Chapter 9 also covers the various tree traversals, including depth-first traversal and breadth-first traversal. Chapter 11 presents *priority queues* and Chapter 12 covers *sets*, *multisets*, and *partitions*.

An essential element of the C++ run-time system is the pool of dynamically allocated storage. Chapter 13 presents a number of different approaches for implementing storage pools, in the process illustrating the actual costs associated with dynamic storage allocation.

### Algorithms

The last three chapters of the book focus on algorithms, rather than data structures. Chapter 14 is an overview of various algorithmic patterns. By introducing the notion of an abstract problem solver, we show how many of the patterns are related. Chapter 15 uses a similar approach to present various sorting algorithms. That is, we introduce the notion of an abstract sorter and show how the various sorting algorithms are related.

Finally, Chapter 16 gives a brief overview of the subject of graphs and graph algorithms. This chapter brings together various algorithmic techniques from Chapter 14 with the class hierarchy discussed in the earlier chapters.

# 2 | Algorithm Analysis

What is an algorithm, and why do we want to analyze one? An algorithm is "a ... step-by-step procedure for accomplishing some end."[9] An algorithm can be given in many ways. For example, it can be written down in English (or French, or any other "natural" language). However, we are interested in algorithms which have been precisely specified using an appropriate mathematical formalism, such as a programming language.

Given such an expression of an algorithm, what can we do with it? Well, obviously we can run the program and observe its behavior. This is not likely to be very useful or informative in the general case. If we run a particular program on a particular computer with a particular set of inputs, then all we know is the behavior of the program in a single instance. Such knowledge is anecdotal and we must be careful when drawing conclusions based upon anecdotal evidence.

In order to learn more about an algorithm, we can "analyze" it. By this we mean to study the specification of the algorithm and to draw conclusions about how the implementation of that algorithm—the program—will perform in general. But what can we analyze? We can determine

- the running time of a program as a function of its inputs;
- the total or maximum memory space needed for program data;
- the total size of the program code;
- whether the program correctly computes the desired result;
- the complexity of the program—e.g., how easy is it to read, understand, and modify; and,
- the robustness of the program—e.g., how well does it deal with unexpected or erroneous inputs?

In this text, we are concerned primarily with the running time. We also consider the memory space needed to execute the program. There are many factors that affect the running time of a program. Among these are the algorithm itself, the input data, and the computer system used to run the program. The performance of a computer is determined by

- the hardware:
  - processor used (type and speed),
  - memory available (cache and RAM), and
  - disk available;
- the programming language in which the algorithm is specified;
- the language compiler/interpreter used; and
- the computer operating system software.

A detailed analysis of the performance of a program which takes all of these factors into account is very difficult and time-consuming. Furthermore, such an analysis is not likely to have lasting significance. The rapid pace of change in the underlying technologies means that results of such analyses are not likely to be applicable to the next generation of hardware and software.

In order to overcome this shortcoming, we devise a "model" of the behavior of a computer with the goals of simplifying the analysis while still producing meaningful results. The next section introduces the first in a series of such models.

## 2.1 A Detailed Model of the Computer

In this section we develop a detailed model of the running time performance of C++ programs. This model is independent of the underlying hardware and system software. Rather than analyze the performance of a particular, arbitrarily chosen physical machine, we consider the implementation of the C++ programming language as a kind a "virtual C++ machine" (see Figure 2.1).

A direct consequence of this approach is that we lose some fidelity—the resulting model will not be able to accurately predict the performance of all possible hardware/software systems. On the other hand, we shall see that the resulting model is still rather complex and rich in detail.

### 2.1.1 The Basic Axioms

The running time performance of the C++ virtual machine is given by a set of axioms which we shall now postulate. For now we consider only operations on integers. The first axiom addresses the running time of simple variable references:

**Axiom 2.1**
*The time required to fetch an integer operand from memory is a constant, $\tau_{fetch}$, and the time required to store an integer result in memory is a constant, $\tau_{store}$.*

**FIGURE 2.1**
Virtual C++ machine.

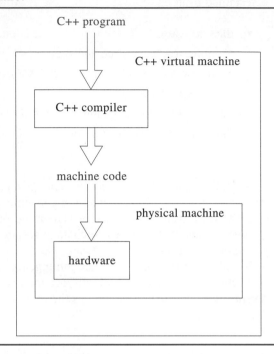

According to Axiom 2.1, the assignment statement

```
y = x;
```

has running time $\tau_{\text{fetch}} + \tau_{\text{store}}$. That is, the time taken to fetch the value of variable **x** is $\tau_{\text{fetch}}$ and the time taken to store the value in variable **y** is $\tau_{\text{store}}$.

We shall apply Axiom 2.1 to manifest constants too: The assignment

```
y = 1;
```

also has running time $\tau_{\text{fetch}} + \tau_{\text{store}}$. To see why this should be the case, consider that the constant typically needs to be stored in the memory of the computer, and we can expect the cost of fetching it to be the same as that of fetching any other operand.

The next axiom addresses the running time of simple arithmetic operations on integers:

**Axiom 2.2**
*The times required to perform elementary operations on integers, such as addition, subtraction, multiplication, division, and comparison, are all constants. These times are denoted by $\tau_{+}$, $\tau_{-}$, $\tau_{\times}$, $\tau_{\div}$, and $\tau_{<}$, respectively.*

According to Axiom 2.2, all the simple operations on integers can be accomplished in a fixed amount of time. In order for this to be feasible, the number of bits used to represent an integer must be fixed. Typically, between 16 and 64 bits are used to represent an integer. It is precisely because the number of bits used is fixed that we can say that the running times are also fixed. If arbitrarily large integers are allowed, then the basic arithmetic operations can take an arbitrarily long amount of time.

By applying Axioms 2.1 and 2.2, we can determine that the running time of a statement like

```
y = y + 1;
```

is $2\tau_{\text{fetch}} + \tau_+ + \tau_{\text{store}}$. This is because we need to fetch two operands, $\mathbf{y}$ and $\mathbf{1}$; add them; and store the result back in $\mathbf{y}$.

C++ syntax provides several alternative ways to express the same computation:

```
y += 1;
++y;
y++;
```

We shall assume that these alternatives require exactly the same running time as the original statement.

The third basic axiom addresses the function call/return overhead:

### Axiom 2.3
*The time required to call a function is a constant, $\tau_{\text{call}}$, and the time required to return from a function is a constant, $\tau_{\text{return}}$.*

When a function is called, certain housekeeping operations need to be performed. Typically this includes saving the return address so that program execution can resume at the correct place after the call, saving the state of any partially completed computations so that they may be resumed after the call, and the allocation of a new execution context (stack frame or activation record) in which the called function can be evaluated. Conversely, on the return from a function, all of this work is undone. While the function call/return overhead may be rather large, nevertheless it entails a constant amount of work.

In addition to the function call/return overhead, additional overhead is incurred when parameters are passed to the function:

### Axiom 2.4
*The time required to pass an integer argument to a function or procedure is the same as the time required to store an integer in memory, $\tau_{\text{store}}$.*

The rationale for making the overhead associated with parameter passing the same as the time to store a value in memory is that the passing of an argument is conceptually the same as assignment of the actual parameter value to the formal parameter of the function.

According to Axiom 2.5, the running time of the statement

```
y = f (x);
```

would be $\tau_{\text{fetch}} + 2\tau_{\text{store}} + \tau_{\text{call}} + T_{\mathbf{f(x)}}$, where $T_{\mathbf{f(x)}}$ is the running time of function $\mathbf{f}$ for input $\mathbf{x}$. The first of the two stores is due to the passing of the parameter $\mathbf{x}$ to the function $\mathbf{f}$; the second arises from the assignment to the variable $\mathbf{y}$.

### 2.1.2 A Simple Example—Arithmetic Series Summation

In this section we apply Axioms 2.1, 2.2, and 2.3 to the analysis of the running time of a program to compute the following simple arithmetic series summation

$$\sum_{i=1}^{n} i.$$

The algorithm to compute this summation is given in Program 2.1.

The executable statements in Program 2.1 comprise lines 3–6. Table 2.1 gives the running times of each of these statements.

Note that the **for** statement on line 4 of Program 2.1 has been split across three lines in Table 2.1. This is because we analyze the running time of each of the elements of a **for** statement separately. The first element, the *initialization code,* is executed once

---

**PROGRAM 2.1**
Program to compute $\sum_{i=1}^{n} i$

```
1   unsigned int Sum (unsigned int n)
2   {
3       unsigned int result = 0;
4       for (unsigned int i = 1; i <= n; ++i)
5           result += i;
6       return result;
7   }
```

---

**TABLE 2.1**
Computing the Running Time of Program 2.1

| Statement | Time | Code |
|:---:|:---:|:---|
| 3 | $\tau_{\text{fetch}} + \tau_{\text{store}}$ | `result = 0` |
| 4a | $\tau_{\text{fetch}} + \tau_{\text{store}}$ | `i = 1` |
| 4b | $(2\tau_{\text{fetch}} + \tau_{<}) \times (n+1)$ | `i <= n` |
| 4c | $(2\tau_{\text{fetch}} + \tau_{+} + \tau_{\text{store}}) \times n$ | `++i` |
| 5 | $(2\tau_{\text{fetch}} + \tau_{+} + \tau_{\text{store}}) \times n$ | `result += i` |
| 6 | $\tau_{\text{fetch}} + \tau_{\text{return}}$ | `return result` |
| TOTAL | $(6\tau_{\text{fetch}} + 2\tau_{\text{store}} + \tau_{<} + 2\tau_{+}) \times n$ $+ (5\tau_{\text{fetch}} + 2\tau_{\text{store}} + \tau_{<} + \tau_{\text{return}})$ | |

before the first iteration of the loop. The second element, the *loop termination test,* is executed before each iteration of the loop begins. Altogether, the number of times the termination test is executed is one more than the number of times the loop body is executed. Finally, the third element, the *loop counter increment step,* is executed once per loop iteration.

Summing the entries in Table 2.1 we get that the running time, $T(n)$, of Program 2.1 is

$$T(n) = t_1 + t_2 n \qquad (2.1)$$

where $t_1 = 5\tau_{\text{fetch}} + 2\tau_{\text{store}} + \tau_< + \tau_{\text{return}}$ and $t_2 = 6\tau_{\text{fetch}} + 2\tau_{\text{store}} + \tau_< + 2\tau_+$.

### 2.1.3 Array Subscripting Operations

We now address the question of accessing the elements of an array of data. In general, the elements of a one-dimensional array are stored in consecutive memory locations. Therefore, given the address of the first element of the array, a simple addition suffices to determine the address of an arbitrary element of the array.

**Axiom 2.5**
*The time required for the* address calculation *implied by an array subscripting operation, e.g.,* a[i], *is a constant,* $\tau_{[\cdot]}$. *This time does not include the time to compute the subscript expression, nor does it include the time to access (i.e., fetch or store) the array element.*

By applying Axiom 2.5, we can determine that the running time for the statement

```
y = a [i];
```

is $3\tau_{\text{fetch}} + \tau_{[\cdot]} + \tau_{\text{store}}$. Three operand fetches are required: the first to fetch **a**, the base address of the array; the second to fetch **i**, the index into the array; and the third to fetch array element **a[i]**.

### 2.1.4 Another Example—Horner's Rule

In this section we apply Axioms 2.1, 2.2, 2.3, and 2.4 to the analysis of the running time of a program which evaluates the value of a polynomial. That is, given the $n + 1$ coefficients $a_0, a_1, \ldots, a_n$, and a value $x$, we wish to compute the following summation

$$\sum_{i=0}^{n} a_i x^i.$$

The usual way to evaluate such polynomials is to use Horner's rule, which is an algorithm to compute the summation without requiring the computation of arbitrary

---

**PROGRAM 2.2**
Program to compute $\sum_{i=0}^{n} a_i x^i$ using Horner's rule

---

```
1   int Horner (int a [], unsigned int n, int x)
2   {
3       int result = a [n];
4       for (int i = n - 1; i >= 0; --i)
5           result = result * x + a [i];
6       return result;
7   }
```

---

**TABLE 2.2**
Computing the Running Time of Program 2.2

| Statement | Time |
|:---:|:---:|
| 3 | $3\tau_{\text{fetch}} + \tau_{[\cdot]} + \tau_{\text{store}}$ |
| 4a | $2\tau_{\text{fetch}} + \tau_{-} + \tau_{\text{store}}$ |
| 4b | $(2\tau_{\text{fetch}} + \tau_{<}) \times (n + 1)$ |
| 4c | $(2\tau_{\text{fetch}} + \tau_{-} + \tau_{\text{store}}) \times n$ |
| 5 | $(5\tau_{\text{fetch}} + \tau_{[\cdot]} + \tau_{+} + \tau_{\times} + \tau_{\text{store}}) \times n$ |
| 6 | $\tau_{\text{fetch}} + \tau_{\text{return}}$ |
| TOTAL | $(9\tau_{\text{fetch}} + 2\tau_{\text{store}} + \tau_{<} + \tau_{[\cdot]} + \tau_{+} + \tau_{\times} + \tau_{-}) \times n$ <br> $+ (8\tau_{\text{fetch}} + 2\tau_{\text{store}} + \tau_{[\cdot]} + \tau_{-} + \tau_{<} + \tau_{\text{return}})$ |

powers of $x$. The algorithm to compute this summation is given in Program 2.2. Table 2.2 gives the running times of each of the executable statements in Program 2.2.

Summing the entries in Table 2.2 we get that the running time, $T(n)$, of Program 2.2 is

$$T(n) = t_1 + t_2 n \tag{2.2}$$

where $t_1 = 8\tau_{\text{fetch}} + 2\tau_{\text{store}} + \tau_{[\cdot]} + \tau_{-} + \tau_{<} + \tau_{\text{return}}$ and $t_2 = 9\tau_{\text{fetch}} + 2\tau_{\text{store}} + \tau_{<} + \tau_{[\cdot]} + \tau_{+} + \tau_{\times} + \tau_{-}$.

## 2.1.5  Analyzing Recursive Functions

In this section we analyze the performance of a recursive algorithm which computes the factorial of a number. Recall that the factorial of a non-negative integer $n$, written $n!$, is defined as

$$n! = \begin{cases} 1 & n = 0, \\ \prod_{i=1}^{n} i & n > 0. \end{cases} \tag{2.3}$$

However, we can also define factorial *recursively* as follows:

$$n! = \begin{cases} 1 & n = 0, \\ n \times (n-1)! & n > 0. \end{cases}$$

It is this latter definition which leads to the algorithm given in Program 2.3 to compute the factorial of $n$. Table 2.3 gives the running times of each of the executable statements in Program 2.3.

Notice that we had to analyze the running time of the two possible outcomes of the conditional test on line 3 separately. Clearly, the running time of the program depends on the result of this test.

Furthermore, the function **Factorial** calls itself recursively on line 6. Therefore, in order to write down the running time of line 6, we need to know the running time, $T(\cdot)$, of **Factorial**. But this is precisely what we are trying to determine in the first place! We escape from this catch-22 by assuming that we already know what is the function $T(\cdot)$, and that we can make use of that function to determine the running time of line 6.

By summing the columns in Table 2.3 we get that the running time of Program 2.3 is

$$T(n) = \begin{cases} t_1 & n = 0, \\ T(n-1) + t_2 & n > 0, \end{cases} \tag{2.4}$$

---

**PROGRAM 2.3**
Recursive program to compute $n!$

```
1   unsigned int Factorial (unsigned int n)
2   {
3       if (n == 0)
4           return 1;
5       else
6           return n * Factorial (n - 1);
7   }
```

---

**TABLE 2.3**
Computing the Running Time of Program 2.3

| | Time | |
|---|---|---|
| Statement | $n = 0$ | $n > 0$ |
| 3 | $2\tau_{\text{fetch}} + \tau_<$ | $2\tau_{\text{fetch}} + \tau_<$ |
| 4 | $\tau_{\text{fetch}} + \tau_{\text{return}}$ | — |
| 6 | — | $3\tau_{\text{fetch}} + \tau_- + \tau_{\text{store}} + \tau_\times$ $+ \tau_{\text{call}} + \tau_{\text{return}} + T(n-1)$ |

where $t_1 = 3\tau_{\text{fetch}} + \tau_< + \tau_{\texttt{return}}$ and $t_2 = 5\tau_{\text{fetch}} + \tau_< + \tau_- + \tau_{\text{store}} + \tau_\times + \tau_{\text{call}} + \tau_{\texttt{return}}$. This kind of equation is called a *recurrence relation* because the function is defined in terms of itself recursively.

### Solving Recurrence Relations—Repeated Substitution

In this section we present a technique for solving a recurrence relation such as Equation 2.4 called *repeated substitution*. The basic idea is this: Given that $T(n) = T(n-1) + t_2$, then we may also write $T(n-1) = T(n-2) + t_2$, provided $n > 1$. Since $T(n-1)$ appears in the right-hand side of the former equation, we can substitute for it the entire right-hand side of the latter. By repeating this process we get

$$
\begin{aligned}
T(n) &= T(n-1) + t_2 \\
&= (T(n-2) + t_2) + t_2 \\
&= T(n-2) + 2t_2 \\
&= (T(n-3) + t_2) + 2t_2 \\
&= T(n-3) + 3t_2 \\
&\;\;\vdots
\end{aligned}
$$

The next step takes a little intuition: We must try to discern the pattern which is emerging. In this case it is obvious:

$$
T(n) = T(n-k) + kt_2,
$$

where $1 \le k \le n$. Of course, if we have doubts about our intuition, we can always check our result by induction:

**Base Case**  Clearly the formula is correct for $k = 1$, since $T(n) = T(n-k) + kt_2 = T(n-1) + t_2$.

**Inductive Hypothesis**  Assume that $T(n) = T(n-k) + kt_2$ for $k = 1, 2, \ldots, l$. By this assumption

$$
T(n) = T(n-l) + lt_2. \tag{2.5}
$$

Note also that using the original recurrence relation we can write

$$
T(n-l) = T(n-l-1) + t_2 \tag{2.6}
$$

for $l \le n$. Substituting Equation 2.5 in the right-hand side of Equation 2.6 gives

$$
\begin{aligned}
T(n) &= T(n-l-1) + t_2 + lt_2 \\
&= T(n - (l+1)) + (l+1)t_2.
\end{aligned}
$$

Therefore, by induction on $l$, our formula is correct for all $0 \le k \le n$.

So, we have shown that $T(n) = T(n - k) + kt_2$, for $1 \le k \le n$. Now, if $n$ was known, we would repeat the process of substitution until we got $T(0)$ on the right-hand side. The fact that $n$ is unknown should not deter us—we get $T(0)$ on the right-hand side when $n - k = 0$. That is, $k = n$. Letting $k = n$ we get

$$
\begin{aligned}
T(n) &= T(n - k) + kt_2 \\
&= T(0) + nt_2 \\
&= t_1 + nt_2
\end{aligned}
\tag{2.7}
$$

where $t_1 = 3\tau_{\text{fetch}} + \tau_< + \tau_{\text{return}}$ and $t_2 = 5\tau_{\text{fetch}} + \tau_< + \tau_- + \tau_{\text{store}} + \tau_\times + \tau_{\text{call}} + \tau_{\text{return}}$.

### 2.1.6 Yet Another Example—Finding the Largest Element of an Array

In this section we consider the problem of finding the largest element of an array. That is, given an array of $n$ non-negative integers, $a_0, a_1, \ldots, a_{n-1}$, we wish to find

$$
\max_{0 \le i < n} a_i.
$$

The straightforward way of solving this problem is to perform a *linear search* of the array. The linear search algorithm is given in Program 2.4, and the running times for the various statements are given in Table 2.4.

With the exception of line 6, the running times follow simply from Axioms 2.1, 2.2, and 2.5. In particular, note that the body of the loop is executed $n - 1$ times. This means that the conditional test on line 5 is executed $n - 1$ times. However, the number of times line 6 is executed depends on the data in the array and not just $n$.

If we consider that in each iteration of the loop body, the variable **result** contains the largest array element seen so far, then line 6 will be executed in the $i$th iteration of

---

**PROGRAM 2.4**
Linear search to find $\max_{0 \le i < n} a_i$

```
1   unsigned int FindMaximum (unsigned int a [], unsigned int n)
2   {
3       unsigned int result = a [0];
4       for (unsigned int i = 1; i < n; ++i)
5           if (a [i] > result)
6               result = a [i];
7       return result;
8   }
```

**TABLE 2.4**
Computing the Running Time of Program 2.4

| Statement | Time |
|---|---|
| 3 | $3\tau_{\text{fetch}} + \tau_{[\cdot]} + \tau_{\text{store}}$ |
| 4a | $\tau_{\text{fetch}} + \tau_{\text{store}}$ |
| 4b | $(2\tau_{\text{fetch}} + \tau_<) \times n$ |
| 4c | $(2\tau_{\text{fetch}} + \tau_+ + \tau_{\text{store}}) \times (n-1)$ |
| 5 | $(4\tau_{\text{fetch}} + \tau_{[\cdot]} + \tau_<) \times (n-1)$ |
| 6 | $(3\tau_{\text{fetch}} + \tau_{[\cdot]} + \tau_{\text{store}}) \times ?$ |
| 7 | $\tau_{\text{fetch}} + \tau_{\text{store}}$ |

the loop only if $a_i$ satisfies the following

$$a_i > \left( \max_{0 \le j < i} a_j \right).$$

Thus, the running time of Program 2.4, $T(\cdot)$, is a function not only of the number of elements in the array, $n$, but also of the actual array values, $a_0, a_1, \ldots, a_{n-1}$. Summing the entries in Table 2.4 we get

$$T(n, a_0, a_1, \ldots, a_{n-1}) = t_1 + t_2 n + \sum_{\substack{i=1 \\ a_i > (\max_{0 \le j < i} a_j)}}^{n-1} t_3$$

where

$$t_1 = 2\tau_{\text{store}} - \tau_{\text{fetch}} - \tau_+ - \tau_<$$
$$t_2 = 8\tau_{\text{fetch}} + 2\tau_< + \tau_{[\cdot]} + \tau_+ + \tau_{\text{store}}$$
$$t_3 = 3\tau_{\text{fetch}} + \tau_{[\cdot]} + \tau_{\text{store}}.$$

While this result may be correct, it is not terribly useful. In order to determine the running time of the program we need to know the number of elements in the array, $n$, and we need to know the values of the elements in the array, $a_0, a_1, \ldots, a_{n-1}$. Even if we know these data, it turns out that in order to compute the running time of the algorithm, $T(n, a_0, a_1, \ldots, a_{n-1})$, we actually have to solve the original problem!

### 2.1.7 Average Running Times

In the previous section, we found the function, $T(n, a_0, a_1, \ldots, a_{n-1})$, which gives the running time of Program 2.4 as a function both of number of inputs, $n$, and of the actual input values. Suppose instead we are interested in a function $T_{\text{average}}(n)$ which gives the running time *on average* for $n$ inputs, regardless of the values of those inputs. In other words, if we run Program 2.4 a large number of times on a selection of random inputs of length $n$, what will the average running time be?

We can write the sum of the running times given in Table 2.4 in the following form:

$$T_{\text{average}}(n) = t_1 + t_2 n + \sum_{i=1}^{n-1} p_i t_3 \tag{2.8}$$

where $p_i$ is the probability that line 6 of the program is executed. The probability $p_i$ is given by

$$p_i = P\left[a_i > \left(\max_{0 \le j < i} a_j\right)\right].$$

That is, $p_i$ is the probability that the $i$th array entry, $a_i$, is larger than the maximum of all the preceding array entries, $a_0, a_1, \ldots, a_{i-1}$.

In order to determine $p_i$, we need to know (or to assume) something about the distribution of input values. For example, if we know a priori that the array passed to the function **FindMaximum** is ordered from smallest to largest, then we know that $p_i = 1$. Conversely, if we know that the array is ordered from largest to smallest, then we know that $p_i = 0$.

In the general case, we have no a priori knowledge of the distribution of the values in the input array. In this case, consider the $i$th iteration of the loop. In this iteration $a_i$ is compared with the maximum of the $i$ values, $a_0, a_1, \ldots, a_{i-1}$ preceding it in the array. Line 6 of Program 2.4 is only executed if $a_i$ is the largest of the $i + 1$ values $a_0, a_1, \ldots, a_i$. All things being equal, we can say that this will happen with probability $1/(i + 1)$. Thus

$$p_i = P\left[a_i > \left(\max_{0 \le j < i} a_j\right)\right] \tag{2.9}$$
$$= \frac{1}{i + 1}.$$

Substituting this expression for $p_i$ in Equation 2.8 and simplifying the result we get

$$T_{\text{average}}(n) = t_1 + t_2 n + \sum_{i=1}^{n-1} p_i t_3$$
$$= t_1 + t_2 n + t_3 \sum_{i=1}^{n-1} \frac{1}{i + 1}$$
$$= t_1 + t_2 n + t_3 \left(\sum_{i=1}^{n} \frac{1}{i} - 1\right)$$
$$= t_1 + t_2 n + t_3 (H_n - 1) \tag{2.10}$$

where $H_n = \sum_{i=1}^{n} \frac{1}{i}$, is the $n$th *harmonic number*.

### 2.1.8  About Harmonic Numbers

The series $1, \frac{1}{2}, \frac{1}{3}, \frac{1}{4}, \ldots$ is called the *harmonic series,* and the summation

$$H_n = \sum_{i=1}^{n} \frac{1}{i}$$

gives rise to the series of *harmonic numbers,* $H_1, H_2, \ldots.$ As it turns out, harmonic numbers often creep into the analysis of algorithms. Therefore, we should understand a little bit about how they behave.

A remarkable characteristic of harmonic numbers is that, even though as $n$ gets large and the difference between consecutive harmonic numbers gets arbitrarily small ($H_n - H_{n-1} = \frac{1}{n}$), *the series does not converge!* That is, $\lim_{n \to \infty} H_n$ does not exist. In other words, the summation $\sum_{i=1}^{\infty} \frac{1}{i}$ goes off to infinity, but just barely.

Figure 2.2 helps us to understand the behavior of harmonic numbers. The smooth curve in this figure is the function $y = 1/x$. The descending staircase represents the function $y = 1/\lfloor x \rfloor$.[1] That is, for $i \le x < (i + 1)$, $y = 1/i$, for $i = 1, 2, \ldots.$

Notice that the area under the staircase between 1 and $n$ for any integer $n > 1$ is given by

$$\int_1^n \frac{1}{\lfloor x \rfloor} dx = \sum_{i=1}^{n-1} \frac{1}{i} = H_{n-1}.$$

---

**FIGURE 2.2**
Computing harmonic numbers.

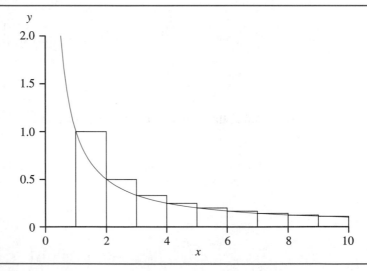

---

[1]The notation $\lfloor \cdot \rfloor$ denotes the *floor function,* which is defined as follows: For any real number $x$, $\lfloor x \rfloor$ is the greatest integer less than or equal to $x$. While we are on the subject, there is a related function, the *ceiling function,* written $\lceil \cdot \rceil$. For any real number $x$, $\lceil x \rceil$ is the smallest integer greater than or equal to $x$.

Thus, if we can determine the area under the descending staircase in Figure 2.2, we can determine the values of the harmonic numbers.

As an approximation, consider the area under the smooth curve $y = 1/x$:

$$\int_1^n \frac{1}{x} dx = \left. \ln x \right|_1^n$$

$$= \ln(n).$$

Thus, $H_{n-1}$ is approximately $\ln n$ for $n > 1$.

If we approximate $H_{n-1}$ by $\ln n$, the error in this approximation is equal to the area between the two curves. In fact, the area between these two curves is such an important quantity that it has its own symbol, $\gamma$, which is called *Euler's constant*. The following derivation indicates a way in which to compute Euler's constant:

$$\gamma = \lim_{n \to \infty} (H_{n-1} - \ln n)$$

$$= \sum_{i=1}^{\infty} \left( \int_i^{i+1} (\frac{1}{i} - \frac{1}{x}) dx \right)$$

$$= \sum_{i=1}^{\infty} \left( \frac{1}{i} \int_i^{i+1} 1 dx - \int_i^{i+1} \frac{1}{x} dx \right)$$

$$= \sum_{i=1}^{\infty} \left( \frac{1}{i} - \ln \left( \frac{i+1}{i} \right) \right)$$

$$\approx 0.577\,215.$$

A program to compute Euler's constant on the basis of this derivation is given in Program 2.5. While this is not necessarily the most accurate or most speedy way to compute Euler's constant, it does give the correct result to six significant digits.

---

**PROGRAM 2.5**
Program to compute $\gamma$

---

```
1   #include <iostream>
2   #include <cmath>
3
4   int main (int, char* [])
5   {
6       double result = 0;
7       for (unsigned long int i = 1; i <= 500000; ++i)
8           result += 1./i - std::log ((i + 1.)/i);
9       cout << "gamma = " << result << endl;
10      return 0;
11  }
```

So, with Euler's constant in hand, we can write down an expression for the $(n-1)$th harmonic number:

$$H_{n-1} = \ln n + \gamma - \epsilon_n \tag{2.11}$$

where $\epsilon_n$ is the error introduced by the fact that $\gamma$ is defined as the difference between the curves on the interval $[1, +\infty)$, but we only need the difference on the interval $[1, n]$. As it turns out, it can be shown (but not here), that there exists a constant $K$ such that for large enough values of $n$, $|\epsilon_n| < K/n$.[2]

Since the error term is less than $1/n$, we can add $1/n$ to both sides of Equation 2.11 and still have an error which goes to zero as $n$ gets large. Thus, the usual approximation for the harmonic number is

$$H_n \approx \ln n + \gamma.$$

We now return to the question of finding the average running time of Program 2.4, which finds the largest element of an array. We can now rewrite Equation 2.10 to give

$$
\begin{aligned}
T_{\text{average}}(n) &= t_1 + t_2 n + t_3(H_n - 1) \\
&\approx t_1 + t_2 n + t_3(\ln n + \gamma - 1) \\
&\approx (t_1 + t_3(\gamma - 1)) + t_2 n + t_3 \ln n.
\end{aligned}
$$

### 2.1.9  Best-Case and Worst-Case Running Times

In Section 2.1.7 we derived the average running time of Program 2.4 which finds the largest element of an array. In order to do this we had to determine the probability that a certain program statement is executed. To do this, we made an assumption about the *average* input to the program.

The analysis can be significantly simplified if we simply wish to determine the *worst case* running time. For Program 2.4, the worst-case scenario occurs when line 6 is executed in every iteration of the loop. We saw that this corresponds to the case in which the input array is ordered from smallest to largest. In terms of Equation 2.8, this occurs when $p_i = 1$. Thus, the worst-case running time is given by

$$
\begin{aligned}
T_{\text{worst case}}(n) &= t_1 + t_2 n + \left. \sum_{i=1}^{n-1} p_i t_3 \right|_{p_i = 1} \\
&= t_1 + t_2 n + t_3 \sum_{i=1}^{n-1} 1 \\
&= t_1 + t_2 n + t_3(n - 1) \\
&= (t_1 - t_3) + (t_2 + t_3) \times n.
\end{aligned}
$$

---

[2] In fact, we would normally write $\epsilon_n = O(\frac{1}{n})$, but we have not yet seen the $O(\cdot)$ notation which is introduced in Chapter 3.

Similarly, the *best-case* running time occurs when line 6 is never executed. This corresponds to the case in which the input array is ordered from largest to smallest. This occurs when $p_i = 0$ and best-case running time is

$$T_{\text{best case}}(n) = t_1 + t_2 n + \left. \sum_{i=1}^{n-1} p_i t_3 \right|_{p_i = 0}$$

$$= t_1 + t_2 n.$$

In summary, we have the following results for the running time of Program 2.4:

$$T(n, a_0, a_1, \ldots, a_{n-1}) = t_1 + t_2 n + \sum_{\substack{i=1 \\ a_i > \left( \max_{0 \le j < i} a_j \right)}}^{n-1} t_3$$

$$T_{\text{average}}(n) \approx (t_1 + t_3(\gamma - 1)) + t_2 n + t_3 \ln n$$

$$T_{\text{worst case}}(n) = (t_1 - t_3) + (t_2 + t_3) \times n$$

$$T_{\text{best case}}(n) = t_1 + t_2 n.$$

### 2.1.10 The Last Axiom

In this section we state the last axiom we need for our detailed model of the C++ virtual machine. This axiom addresses the time required to allocate and to free dynamically allocated storage:

**Axiom 2.6**
*The time required to allocate a fixed amount of storage from the heap using* operator new *is a constant,* $\tau_{\text{new}}$. *This time does not include any time required for initialization of the storage. Similarly, the time required to return a fixed amount of storage to the heap using* operator delete *is a constant,* $\tau_{\text{delete}}$. *This time does not include any time spent cleaning up the storage before it is returned to the heap.*

By applying Axioms 2.1 and 2.6, we can determine that the running time of the statement

```
int* ptr = new int;
```

is $\tau_{\text{new}} + \tau_{\text{store}}$. Similarly, the running time of

```
delete ptr;
```

is $\tau_{\text{fetch}} + \tau_{\text{delete}}$.

## 2.2 A Simplified Model of the Computer

The detailed model of the computer given in the previous section is based on a number of different timing parameters—$\tau_{\text{fetch}}$, $\tau_{\text{store}}$, $\tau_+$, $\tau_-$, $\tau_\times$, $\tau_\div$, $\tau_<$, $\tau_{\text{call}}$, $\tau_{\text{return}}$, $\tau_{\text{new}}$, $\tau_{\text{delete}}$, and $\tau_{[\cdot]}$. While it is true that a model with a large number of parameters is quite flexible and therefore likely to be a good predictor of performance, keeping track of the all of the parameters during the analysis is rather burdensome.

In this section, we present a simplified model which makes the performance analysis easier to do. The cost of using the simplified model is that it is likely to be a less accurate predictor of performance than the detailed model.

Consider the various timing parameters in the detailed model. In a real machine, each of these parameters will be a multiple of the basic clock period of the machine. The clock frequency of a modern computer is typically between 100 and 500 MHz. Therefore, the clock period is typically between 2 and 10 ns. Let the clock period of the machine be $T$. Then each of the timing parameters can be expressed as an integer multiple of the clock period. For example, $\tau_{\text{fetch}} = k_{\text{fetch}}T$, where $k_{\text{fetch}} \in \mathbb{Z}$, $k_{\text{fetch}} > 0$.

The simplified model eliminates all of the arbitrary timing parameters in the detailed model. This is done by making the following two simplifying assumptions:

- All timing parameters are expressed in units of clock cycles. In effect, $T = 1$.
- The proportionality constant, $k$, for all timing parameters is assumed to be the same: $k = 1$.

The effect of these two assumptions is that we no longer need to keep track of the various operations separately. To determine the running time of a program, we simply count the total number of cycles taken.

### 2.2.1 An Example—Geometric Series Summation

In this section we consider the running time of a program to compute the following *geometric series summation*. That is, given a value $x$ and non-negative integer $n$, we wish to compute the summation

$$\sum_{i=0}^{n} x^i.$$

An algorithm to compute this summation is given in Program 2.6.

Table 2.5 gives the running time, as predicted by the simplified model, for each of the executable statements in Program 2.6.

In order to calculate the total cycle counts, we need to evaluate the two series summations $\sum_{i=0}^{n}(i + 1)$ and $\sum_{i=0}^{n} i$. Both of these are *arithmetic series summations*. In the next section we show that the sum of the series $1, 2, \ldots, n$ is $n(n + 1)/2$. Using this result we can sum the cycle counts given in Table 2.5 to arrive at the total running time of $\frac{11}{2}n^2 + \frac{47}{2}n + 27$ cycles.

**PROGRAM 2.6**
Program to compute $\sum_{i=0}^{n} x^i$

```
1    int GeometricSeriesSum (int x, unsigned int n)
2    {
3        int sum = 0;
4        for (unsigned int i = 0; i <= n; ++i)
5        {
6            int prod = 1;
7            for (unsigned int j = 0; j < i; ++j)
8                prod *= x;
9            sum += prod;
10       }
11       return sum;
12   }
```

**TABLE 2.5**
Computing the Running Time of
Program 2.6

| Statement | Time |
|:---:|:---:|
| 3 | 2 |
| 4a | 2 |
| 4b | $3(n + 2)$ |
| 4c | $4(n + 1)$ |
| 6 | $2(n + 1)$ |
| 7a | $2(n + 1)$ |
| 7b | $3\sum_{i=0}^{n}(i + 1)$ |
| 7c | $4\sum_{i=0}^{n} i$ |
| 8 | $4\sum_{i=0}^{n} i$ |
| 9 | $4(n + 1)$ |
| 11 | 2 |
| TOTAL | $\frac{11}{2}n^2 + \frac{47}{2}n + 27$ |

### 2.2.2 About Arithmetic Series Summation

The series, 1, 2, 3, 4, . . ., is an *arithmetic series* and the summation

$$S_n = \sum_{i=1}^{n} i$$

is called the *arithmetic series summation*.

The summation can be solved as follows: First, we make the simple variable substitution $i = n - j$:

$$\sum_{i=1}^{n} i = \sum_{n-j=1}^{n} (n - j)$$

$$= \sum_{j=0}^{n-1} (n - j)$$

$$= \sum_{j=0}^{n-1} n - \sum_{j=0}^{n-1} j$$

$$= n \sum_{j=0}^{n-1} 1 - \sum_{j=1}^{n} j + n. \tag{2.12}$$

Note that the term in the first summation in Equation 2.12 is independent of $j$. Also, the second summation is identical to the left-hand side. Rearranging Equation 2.12, and simplifying gives

$$2 \sum_{i=1}^{n} i = n \sum_{j=0}^{n-1} 1 + n$$

$$= n^2 + n$$

$$= n(n + 1)$$

$$\sum_{i=1}^{n} i = \frac{n(n + 1)}{2}.$$

There is, of course, a simpler way to arrive at this answer. Consider the series, $1, 2, 3, 4, \ldots, n$, and suppose $n$ is even. The sum of the first and last element is $n + 1$. So too is the sum of the second and second-last element, and the third and third-last element, etc., and there are $n/2$ such pairs. Therefore, $S_n = \frac{n}{2}(n + 1)$.

And if $n$ is odd, then $S_n = S_{n-1} + n$, where $n - 1$ is even. So we can use the previous result for $S_{n-1}$ to get $S_n = \frac{n-1}{2}n + n = n(n + 1)/2$.

## 2.2.3 Example—Geometric Series Summation Again

In this example we revisit the problem of computing a *geometric series summation*. We have already seen an algorithm to compute this summation in Section 2.2.1 (Program 2.6). This algorithm was shown to take $\frac{11}{2}n^2 + \frac{47}{2}n + 27$ cycles.

The problem of computing the geometric series summation is identical to that of computing the value of a polynomial in which all of the coefficients are one. This suggests that we could make use of *Horner's rule* as discussed in Section 2.1.4. An algorithm to compute a geometric series summation using Horner's rule is given in Program 2.7.

**PROGRAM 2.7**
Program to compute $\sum_{i=0}^{n} x^i$ using Horner's rule

```
1   int GeometricSeriesSum (int x, unsigned int n)
2   {
3       int sum = 0;
4       for (unsigned int i = 0; i <= n; ++i)
5           sum = sum * x + 1;
6       return sum;
7   }
```

**TABLE 2.6**
Computing the Running
Time of Program 2.7

| Statement | Time |
|-----------|------|
| 3 | 2 |
| 4a | 2 |
| 4b | $3(n + 2)$ |
| 4c | $4(n + 1)$ |
| 5 | $6(n + 1)$ |
| 6 | 2 |
| TOTAL | $13n + 22$ |

The executable statements in Program 2.7 comprise lines 3–6. Table 2.6 gives the running times, as given by the simplified model, for each of these statements.

In Programs 2.6 and 2.7 we have seen two different algorithms to compute the same geometric series summation. We determined the running time of the former to be $\frac{11}{2}n^2 + \frac{47}{2}n + 27$ cycles and of the latter to be $13n + 22$ cycles. In particular, note that for all non-negative values of $n$, $(\frac{11}{2}n^2 + \frac{47}{2}n + 27) > 13n + 22$. Hence, according to our simplified model of the computer, Program 2.7, which uses Horner's rule, *always* runs faster than Program 2.6!

## 2.2.4  About Geometric Series Summation

The series, $1, a, a^2, a^3, \ldots$, is a *geometric series* and the summation

$$S_n = \sum_{i=0}^{n} a^i$$

is called the *geometric series summation*.

The summation can be solved as follows: First, we make the simple variable substitution $i = j - 1$:

$$\sum_{i=0}^{n} a^i = \sum_{j-1=0}^{n} a^{j-1} = \frac{1}{a} \sum_{j=1}^{n+1} a^j$$

$$= \frac{1}{a} \left( \sum_{j=0}^{n} a^j + a^{n+1} - 1 \right). \tag{2.13}$$

Note that the summation which appears on the right is identical to the left-hand side. Rearranging Equation 2.13, and simplifying gives

$$\sum_{i=0}^{n} a_i = \frac{a^{n+1} - 1}{a - 1}. \tag{2.14}$$

## 2.2.5   Example—Computing Powers

In this section we consider the running time to raise a number to a given integer power. That is, given a value $x$ and non-negative integer $n$, we wish to compute the $x^n$. A naive way to calculate $x^n$ would be to use a loop such as

```
int result = 1;
for (unsigned int i = 0; i <= n; ++i)
    result *= x;
```

While this may be fine for small values of $n$, for large values of $n$ the running time may become prohibitive. As an alternative, consider the following recursive definition

$$x^n = \begin{cases} 1 & n = 0, \\ (x^2)^{\lfloor n/2 \rfloor} & n > 0, n \text{ is even}, \\ x(x^2)^{\lfloor n/2 \rfloor} & n > 0, n \text{ is odd}. \end{cases} \tag{2.15}$$

For example, using Equation 2.15, we would determine $x^{32}$ as follows:

$$x^{32} = \left( \left( \left( \left( x^2 \right)^2 \right)^2 \right)^2 \right)^2,$$

which requires a total of five multiplication operations. Similarly, we would compute $x^{31}$ as follows:

$$x^{31} = \left( \left( \left( \left( x^2 \right) x \right)^2 x \right)^2 x \right)^2 x,$$

which requires a total of eight multiplication operations.

**PROGRAM 2.8**
Program to compute $x^n$

```
1  int Power (int x, unsigned int n)
2  {
3      if (n == 0)
4          return 1;
5      else if (n % 2 == 0) // n is even
6          return Power (x * x, n / 2);
7      else // n is odd
8          return x * Power (x * x, n / 2);
9  }
```

**TABLE 2.7**
Computing the Running Time of Program 2.8

| | | Time | |
| --- | --- | --- | --- |
| Statement | $n = 0$ | $n > 0$<br>$n$ Is Even | $n > 0$<br>$n$ Is Odd |
| 3 | 3 | 3 | 3 |
| 4 | 2 | — | — |
| 5 | | 5 | 5 |
| 6 | — | $10 + T(\lfloor n/2 \rfloor)$ | — |
| 8 | — | — | $12 + T(\lfloor n/2 \rfloor)$ |
| TOTAL | 5 | $18 + T(\lfloor n/2 \rfloor)$ | $20 + T(\lfloor n/2 \rfloor)$ |

A recursive algorithm to compute $x^n$ based on the direct implementation of Equation 2.15 is given in Program 2.8. Table 2.7 gives the running time, as predicted by the simplified model, for each of the executable statements in Program 2.8.

By summing the columns in Table 2.7 we get the following recurrence for the running time of Program 2.8

$$T(n) = \begin{cases} 5 & n = 0 \\ 18 + T(\lfloor n/2 \rfloor) & n > 0, n \text{ is even,} \\ 20 + T(\lfloor n/2 \rfloor) & n > 0, n \text{ is odd.} \end{cases} \qquad (2.16)$$

As the first attempt at solving this recurrence, let us suppose that $n = 2^k$ for some $k > 0$. Clearly, since $n$ is a power of two, it is even. Therefore, $\lfloor n/2 \rfloor = n/2 = 2^{k-1}$.

For $n = 2^k$, Equation 2.16 gives

$$T(2^k) = 18 + T(2^{k-1}), \quad k > 0.$$

This can be solved by repeated substitution:

$$
\begin{aligned}
T(2^k) &= 18 + T(2^{k-1}) \\
&= 18 + 18 + T(2^{k-2}) \\
&= 18 + 18 + 18 + T(2^{k-3}) \\
&\vdots \\
&= 18j + T(2^{k-j}).
\end{aligned}
$$

The substitution stops when $k = j$. Thus,

$$
\begin{aligned}
T(2^k - 1) &= 18k + T(1) \\
&= 18k + 20 + T(0) \\
&= 18k + 20 + 5 \\
&= 18k + 25.
\end{aligned}
$$

Note that if $n = 2^k$, then $k = \log_2 n$. In this case, running time of Program 2.8 is $T(n) = 18 \log_2 n + 25$.

The preceding result is, in fact, the best case—in all but the last two recursive calls of the function, $n$ was even. Interestingly enough, there is a corresponding worst-case scenario. Suppose $n = 2^k - 1$ for some value of $k > 0$. Clearly $n$ is odd, since it is one less than $2^k$ which is a power of two and even. Now consider $\lfloor n/2 \rfloor$:

$$
\begin{aligned}
\lfloor n/2 \rfloor &= \lfloor (2^k - 1)/2 \rfloor \\
&= (2^k - 2)/2 \\
&= 2^{k-1} - 1.
\end{aligned}
$$

Hence, $\lfloor n/2 \rfloor$ is also odd!

For example, suppose $n$ is 31 ($2^5 - 1$). To compute $x^{31}$, Program 2.8 calls itself recursively to compute $x^{15}$, $x^7$, $x^3$, $x^1$, and finally, $x^0$—all but the last of which are odd powers of $x$.

For $n = 2^k - 1$, Equation 2.16 gives

$$
T(2^k - 1) = 20 + T(2^{k-1} - 1), \quad k > 1.
$$

Solving this recurrence by repeated substitution we get

$$
\begin{aligned}
T(2^k - 1) &= 20 + T(2^{k-1} - 1) \\
&= 20 + 20 + T(2^{k-2} - 1) \\
&= 20 + 20 + 20 + T(2^{k-3} - 1) \\
&\vdots \\
&= 20j + T(2^{k-j} - 1).
\end{aligned}
$$

**TABLE 2.8**
Recursive Calls Made in Program 2.8

| $n$ | $\lfloor \log_2 n \rfloor + 1$ | Powers Computed Recursively |
|-----|-------------------------------|------------------------------|
| 1 | 1 | 1, 0 |
| 2 | 2 | 2, 1, 0 |
| 3 | 2 | 3, 1, 0 |
| 4 | 3 | 4, 2, 1, 0 |
| 5 | 3 | 5, 2, 1, 0 |
| 6 | 3 | 6, 3, 1, 0 |
| 7 | 3 | 7, 3, 1, 0 |
| 8 | 4 | 8, 4, 2, 1, 0 |

The substitution stops when $k = j$. Thus,

$$T(2^k - 1) = 20k + T(2^0 - 1)$$
$$= 20k + 5.$$

Note that if $n = 2^k - 1$, then $k = \log_2(n + 1)$. In this case, running time of Program 2.8 is $T(n) = 20 \log_2(n + 1) + 5$.

Consider now what happens for an arbitrary value of $n$. Table 2.8 shows the recursive calls made by Program 2.8 in computing $x^n$ for various values of $n$.

By inspection we determine that the number of recursive calls made in which the second argument is nonzero is $\lfloor \log_2 n \rfloor + 1$. Furthermore, depending on whether the argument is odd or even, each of these calls contributes either 18 or 20 cycles. The pattern emerging in Table 2.7 suggests that, on average just as many of the recursive calls result in an even number as result in an odd one. The final call (zero argument) adds another five cycles. So, on average, we can expect the running time of Program 2.8 to be

$$T(n) = 19(\lfloor \log_2 n \rfloor + 1) + 5. \tag{2.17}$$

### 2.2.6   Example—Geometric Series Summation Yet Again

In this example we consider the problem of computing a *geometric series summation* for the last time. We have already seen two algorithms to compute this summation in Sections 2.2.1 and 2.2.3 (Programs 2.6 and 2.7).

An algorithm to compute a geometric series summation using the closed-form expression (Equation 2.14) is given in Program 2.9. This algorithm makes use of Program 2.8 to compute $x^{n+1}$.

To determine the average running time of Program 2.9 we will make use of Equation 2.17, which gives the average running time for the **Power** function which is called on line 5. In this case, the arguments are $x$ and $n + 1$, so the running time of the call to

---

**PROGRAM 2.9**
Program to compute $\sum_{i=0}^{n} x^i$ using the closed-form expression

---

```
1    int Power (int, unsigned int);
2
3    int GeometricSeriesSum (int x, unsigned int n)
4    {
5        return (Power (x, n + 1) - 1) / (x - 1);
6    }
```

---

**TABLE 2.9**
Running Times of Programs 2.6, 2.7, and 2.9

| Program | $T(n)$ |
|---------|--------|
| Program 2.6 | $(\frac{11}{2}n^2 + \frac{47}{2}n + 27)$ |
| Program 2.7 | $13n + 22$ |
| Program 2.9 | $19(\lfloor \log_2(n + 1) \rfloor + 1) + 18$ |

---

**FIGURE 2.3**
Plot of running time versus $n$ for Programs 2.6, 2.7, and 2.9.

---

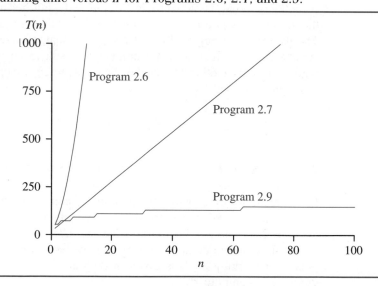

**Power** is $19(\lfloor\log_2(n+1)\rfloor + 1) + 5$. Adding to this the additional work done on line 5 gives the average running time for Program 2.9:

$$T(n) = 19(\lfloor\log_2(n+1)\rfloor + 1) + 18.$$

The running times of the three programs which compute the geometric series summation presented in this chapter are tabulated in Table 2.9 and are plotted for $1 \leq n \leq 100$ in Figure 2.3. Figure 2.3 shows that, according to our simplified model of the computer, for $n < 4$, Program 2.7 has the best running time. However, as $n$ increases, Program 2.9 is clearly the fastest of the three and Program 2.6 is the slowest for all values of $n$.

## Exercises

**2.1** Determine the running times predicted by the detailed model of the computer given in Section 2.1 for each of the following program fragments:

a.
```
for (unsigned int i = 0; i < n; ++i)
    ++k;
```

b.
```
for (unsigned int i = 1U; i < n; i *= 2U)
    ++k;
```

c.
```
for (unsigned int i = n - 1U; i != 0; i /= 2U)
    ++k;
```

d.
```
for (unsigned int i = 0; i < n; ++i)
    if (i % 2 == 0)
        ++k;
```

e.
```
for (unsigned int i = 0; i < n; ++i)
    for (unsigned int j = 0; j < n; ++j)
        ++k;
```

f.
```
for (unsigned int i = 0; i < n; ++i)
    for (unsigned int j = i; j < n; ++j)
        ++k;
```

g.
```
for (unsigned int i = 0; i < n; ++i)
    for (unsigned int j = 0; j < i * i; ++j)
        ++k;
```

**2.2** Repeat Exercise 2.1, this time using the simplified model of the computer given in Section 2.2.

**2.3**   Prove by induction the following summation formulas:

a.   $\displaystyle\sum_{i=0}^{n} i = \frac{n(n+1)}{2}$

b.   $\displaystyle\sum_{i=0}^{n} i^2 = \frac{n(n+1)(2n+1)}{6}$

c.   $\displaystyle\sum_{i=0}^{n} i^3 = \frac{n^2(n+1)^2}{4}$

**2.4**   Evaluate each of the following series summations:

a.   $\displaystyle\sum_{i=0}^{n} 2^i$

b.   $\displaystyle\sum_{i=0}^{n} \left(\frac{1}{2}\right)^i$

c.   $\displaystyle\sum_{i=0}^{\infty} \left(\frac{1}{2}\right)^i$

d.   $\displaystyle\sum_{i=-\infty}^{n} 2^i$

**2.5**   Show that $\sum_{i=0}^{\infty} a^i = \frac{1}{1-a}$, for $0 \le a < 1$. **Hint:** Let $S_n = \sum_{i=0}^{n} a^i$ and show that $\lim_{n\to\infty}(S_n - aS_n) = 1$.

**2.6**   Show that $\sum_{i=0}^{\infty} i/2^i = 2$. **Hint:** Let $S_n = \sum_{i=0}^{n} i/2^i$ and show that the difference $2S_n - S_n$ is (approximately) a geometric series summation.

**2.7**   Solve each of the following recurrences by repeated substitution:

a.   $T(n) = \begin{cases} 1 & n = 0, \\ T(n-1) + 1 & n > 0. \end{cases}$

b.   $T(n) = \begin{cases} 1 & n \le a, a > 0, \\ T(n-a) + 1 & n > a. \end{cases}$

c.   $T(n) = \begin{cases} 1 & n = 0, \\ 2T(n-1) + 1 & n > 0. \end{cases}$

d.   $T(n) = \begin{cases} 1 & n = 0, \\ 2T(n-1) + n & n > 0. \end{cases}$

e.   $T(n) = \begin{cases} 1 & n = 1, \\ T(n/2) + 1 & n > 1. \end{cases}$

f.   $T(n) = \begin{cases} 1 & n = 1, \\ 2T(n/2) + 1 & n > 1. \end{cases}$

g.   $T(n) = \begin{cases} 1 & n = 1, \\ 2T(n/2) + n & n > 1. \end{cases}$

# Programming Projects

**2.1** Write a nonrecursive routine to compute the factorial of $n$ according to Equation 2.3. Calculate the running time predicted by the detailed model given in Section 2.1 and the simplified model given in Section 2.2.

**2.2** Write a nonrecursive routine to compute $x^n$ according to Equation 2.15. Calculate the running time predicted by the detailed model given in Section 2.1 and the simplified model given in Section 2.2.

**2.3** Write a program that determines the values of the timing parameters of the detailed model ($\tau_{fetch}$, $\tau_{store}$, $\tau_+$, $\tau_-$, $\tau_\times$, $\tau_\div$, $\tau_<$, $\tau_{call}$, $\tau_{return}$, $\tau_{new}$, $\tau_{delete}$, and $\tau_{[\cdot]}$) for the machine on which it is run.

**2.4** Using the program written for Project 2.3, determine the timing parameters of the detailed model for your computer. Then, measure the actual running times of Programs 2.1, 2.2, and 2.3 and compare the measured results with those predicted by Equations 2.1, 2.2, and 2.7, respectively.

**2.5** Given a sequence of $n$ integers, $\{a_0, a_1, \ldots, a_{n-1}\}$, and a small positive integer $k$, write an algorithm to compute

$$\sum_{i=0}^{n-1} 2^{ki} a_i,$$

*without multiplication.* **Hint:** Use Horner's rule and bitwise shifts.

**2.6** Verify Equation 2.9 experimentally as follows: Generate a large number of random sequences of length $n$, $\{a_0, a_1, a_2, \ldots, a_{n-1}\}$. For each sequence, test the hypothesis that the probability that $a_i$ is larger than all its predecessors in the sequence is $p_i = 1/(i + 1)$. (For a good source of random numbers, see Section 14.5.1).

# 3 | Asymptotic Notation

Suppose we are considering two algorithms, $A$ and $B$, for solving a given problem. Furthermore, let us say that we have done a careful analysis of the running times of each of the algorithms and determined them to be $T_A(n)$ and $T_B(n)$, respectively, where $n$ is a measure of the problem size. Then it should be a fairly simple matter to compare the two functions $T_A(n)$ and $T_B(n)$ to determine which algorithm is *the best*!

But is it really that simple? What exactly does it mean for one function, say $T_A(n)$, to be *better than* another function, $T_B(n)$? One possibility arises if we know the problem size a priori. For example, suppose the problem size is $n_0$ and $T_A(n_0) < T_B(n_0)$. Then clearly algorithm $A$ is better than algorithm $B$ for problem size $n_0$.

In the general case, we have no a priori knowledge of the problem size. However, if it can be shown, say, that $\forall n \geq 0 : T_A(n) \leq T_B(n)$, then algorithm $A$ is better than algorithm $B$ regardless of the problem size.

Unfortunately, we usually don't know the problem size beforehand, nor is it true that one of the functions is less than or equals the other over the entire range of problem sizes. In this case, we consider the *asymptotic* behavior of the two functions for very large problem sizes.

## 3.1 An Asymptotic Upper Bound—Big Oh

In 1892, P. Bachmann invented a notation for characterizing the asymptotic behavior of functions. His invention has come to be known as *big oh notation*.

### Definition 3.1 (Big Oh)
*Consider a function $f(n)$ which is non-negative for all integers $n \geq 0$. We say that "$f(n)$ is big oh $g(n)$," which we write $f(n) = O(g(n))$, if there exists an integer $n_0$ and a constant $c > 0$ such that for all integers $n \geq n_0$, $f(n) \leq cg(n)$.*

**34**

### 3.1.1  A Simple Example

Consider the function $f(n) = 8n + 128$ shown in Figure 3.1. Clearly, $f(n)$ is non-negative for all integers $n \geq 0$. We wish to show that $f(n) = O(n^2)$. According to Definition 3.1, in order to show this we need to find an integer $n_0$ and a constant $c > 0$ such that for all integers $n \geq n_0$, $f(n) \leq cn^2$.

It does not matter what the particular constants are—as long as they exist! E.g., suppose we choose $c = 1$. Then

$$f(n) \leq cn^2 \Rightarrow 8n + 128 \leq n^2$$
$$\Rightarrow 0 \leq n^2 - 8n - 128$$
$$\Rightarrow 0 \leq (n - 16)(n + 8).$$

Since $(n+8) > 0$ for all values of $n \geq 0$, we conclude that $(n_0 - 16) \geq 0$. I.e., $n_0 = 16$.

So, we have that for $c = 1$ and $n_0 = 16$, $f(n) \leq cn^2$ for all integers $n \geq n_0$. Hence, $f(n) = O(n^2)$. Figure 3.1 clearly shows that the function $f(n) = n^2$ is greater than the function $f(n) = 8n + 128$ to the right of $n = 16$.

Of course, there are many other values of $c$ and $n_0$ that will do. For example, $c = 2$ and $n_0 = 2 + 4\sqrt{17} \approx 10.2$ will do, as will $c = 4$ and $n_0 = 1 + \sqrt{33} \approx 6.7$. (See Figure 3.1)

### 3.1.2  Big Oh Fallacies and Pitfalls

Unfortunately, the way we write big oh notation can be misleading to the naïve reader. This section presents two fallacies which arise because of a misinterpretation of the notation.

---

**FIGURE 3.1**
Showing that $f(n) = 8n + 128 = O(n^2)$.

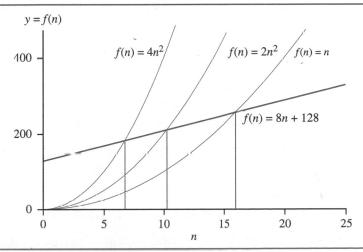

**Fallacy 3.1**
*Given that $f_1(n) = O(g(n))$ and $f_2(n) = O(g(n))$, then $f_1(n) = f_2(n)$.*

Consider these equations:

$$f_1(n) = h(n^2)$$
$$f_2(n) = h(n^2).$$

Clearly, it is reasonable to conclude that $f_1(n) = f_2(n)$.
  However, consider these equations:

$$f_1(n) = O(n^2)$$
$$f_2(n) = O(n^2).$$

It *does not* follow that $f_1(n) = f_2(n)$. For example, $f_1(n) = n$ and $f_2(n) = n^2$ are both $O(n^2)$, but they are not equal.

**Fallacy 3.2**
*If $f(n) = O(g(n))$, then $g(n) = O^{-1}(f(n))$.*

Consider functions $f$, $g$, and $h$, such that $f(n) = h(g(n))$. It is reasonable to conclude that $g(n) = h^{-1}(f(n))$ provided that $h(\cdot)$ is an invertible function. However, while we may write $f(n) = O(h(n))$, the equation $g(n) = O^{-1}(f(n))$ is nonsensical and meaningless. Big oh is not a mathematical function, so it has no inverse!
  The reason for these difficulties is that we should read the notation $f(n) = O(n^2)$ as "$f(n)$ is big oh $n$ squared" not "$f(n)$ equals big oh of $n$ squared." The equal sign in the expression does not really denote mathematical equality! And the use of the functional form, $O(\cdot)$, does not really mean that $O$ is a mathematical function!

### 3.1.3   Properties of Big Oh

In this section we examine some of the mathematical properties of big oh. In particular, suppose we know that $f_1(n) = O(g_1(n))$ and $f_2(n) = O(g_2(n))$.

- What can we say about the asymptotic behavior of the *sum* of $f_1(n)$ and $f_2(n)$? (Theorems 3.1 and 3.2)
- What can we say about the asymptotic behavior of the *product* of $f_1(n)$ and $f_2(n)$? (Theorems 3.3 and 3.4)
- How are $f_1(n)$ and $g_2(n)$ related when $g_1(n) = f_2(n)$? (Theorem 3.5)

The first theorem addresses the asymptotic behavior of the sum of two functions whose asymptotic behaviors are known:

**Theorem 3.1**
*If $f_1(n) = O(g_1(n))$ and $f_2(n) = O(g_2(n))$, then*

$$f_1(n) + f_2(n) = O(\max(g_1(n), g_2(n))).$$

**Proof**   By Definition 3.1, there exist two integers, $n_1$ and $n_2$, and two constants $c_1$ and $c_2$, such that $f_1(n) \leq c_1 g_1(n)$ for $n \geq n_1$ and $f_2(n) \leq c_2 g_2(n)$ for $n \geq n_2$.

Let $n_0 = \max(n_1, n_2)$ and $c_0 = 2\max(c_1, c_2)$. Consider the sum $f_1(n) + f_2(n)$ for $n \geq n_0$:

$$
\begin{aligned}
f_1(n) + f_2(n) &\leq c_1 g_1(n) + c_2 g_2(n), \quad n \geq n_0 \\
&\leq c_0(g_1(n) + g_2(n))/2 \\
&\leq c_0 \max(g_1(n), g_2(n)).
\end{aligned}
$$

Thus, $f_1(n) + f_2(n) = O(\max(g_1(n), g_2(n)))$.

---

According to Theorem 3.1, if we know that functions $f_1(n)$ and $f_2(n)$ are $O(g_1(n))$ and $O(g_2(n))$, respectively, the *sum* $f_1(n) + f_2(n)$ is $O(\max(g_1(n), g_2(n)))$. The meaning of $\max(g_1(n), g_2(n))$ in this context is the *function h(n)* where $h(n) = \max(g_1(n), g_2(n))$ for integers all $n \geq 0$.

For example, consider the functions $g_1(n) = 1$ and $g_2(n) = 2\cos^2(n\pi/2)$. Then

$$
\begin{aligned}
h(n) &= \max(g_1(n), g_2(n)) \\
&= \max(1, 2\cos^2(n\pi/2)) \\
&= \begin{cases} 1 & n \text{ is even,} \\ 2 & n \text{ is odd.} \end{cases}
\end{aligned}
$$

Theorem 3.2 helps us simplify the asymptotic analysis of the sum of functions by allowing us to drop the max required by Theorem 3.1 in certain circumstances:

**Theorem 3.2**

*If $f(n) = f_1(n) + f_2(n)$ in which $f_1(n)$ and $f_2(n)$ are both non-negative for all integers $n \geq 0$ such that $\lim_{n \to \infty} f_2(n)/f_1(n) = L$ for some limit $L \geq 0$, then $f(n) = O(f_1(n))$.*

**Proof**   According to the definition of limits, the notation

$$
\lim_{n \to \infty} \frac{f_2(n)}{f_1(n)} = L
$$

means that, given any arbitrary positive value $\epsilon$, it is possible to find a value $n_0$ such that for all $n \geq n_0$

$$
\left| \frac{f_2(n)}{f_1(n)} - L \right| \leq \epsilon.
$$

Thus, if we chose a particular value, say $\epsilon_0$, then there exists a corresponding $n_0$ such that

$$\left| \frac{f_2(n)}{f_1(n)} - L \right| \leq \epsilon_0, \quad n \geq n_0$$

$$\frac{f_2(n)}{f_1(n)} - L \leq \epsilon_0$$

$$f_2(n) \leq (\epsilon_0 + L) f_1(n).$$

Consider the sum $f(n) = f_1(n) + f_2(n)$:

$$
\begin{aligned}
f(n) &= f_1(n) + f_2(n) \\
&\leq c_1 f_1(n) + c_2 f_2(n) \\
&\leq c_1 f_1(n) + c_2(\epsilon_0 + L) f_1(n), \quad n \geq n_0 \\
&\leq c_0 f_1(n)
\end{aligned}
$$

where $c_0 = c_1 + c_2(\epsilon_0 + L)$. Thus, $f(n) = O(f_1(n))$.

---

Consider a pair of functions $f_1(n)$ and $f_2(n)$, which are known to be $O(g_1(n))$ and $O(g_2(n))$, respectively. According to Theorem 3.1, the sum $f(n) = f_1(n) + f_2(n)$ is $O(\max(g_1(n), g_2(n)))$. However, Theorem 3.2 says that, if $\lim_{n \to \infty} f_2(n)/f_1(n)$ exists, then the sum $f(n)$ is simply $O(f_1(n))$, which, by the transitive property (see Theorem 3.5), is $O(g_1(n))$.

In other words, if the ratio $f_1(n)/f_2(n)$ asymptotically approaches a constant as $n$ gets large, we can say that $f_1(n) + f_2(n)$ is $O(g_1(n))$, which is often a lot simpler than $O(\max(g_1(n), g_2(n)))$.

Theorem 3.2 is particularly useful result. Consider $f_1(n) = n^3$ and $f_2(n) = n^2$.

$$
\begin{aligned}
\lim_{n \to \infty} \frac{f_2(n)}{f_1(n)} &= \lim_{n \to \infty} \frac{n^2}{n^3} \\
&= \lim_{n \to \infty} \frac{1}{n} \\
&= 0.
\end{aligned}
$$

From this we can conclude that $f_1(n) + f_2(n) = n^3 + n^2 = O(n^3)$. Thus, Theorem 3.2 suggests that the sum of a series of powers of $n$ is $O(n^m)$, where $m$ is the largest power of $n$ in the summation. We will confirm this result in Section 3.1.4.

The next theorem addresses the asymptotic behavior of the product of two functions whose asymptotic behaviors are known.

### Theorem 3.3

*If $f_1(n) = O(g_1(n))$ and $f_2(n) = O(g_2(n))$, then*

$$f_1(n) \times f_2(n) = O(g_1(n) \times g_2(n)).$$

**Proof**  By Definition 3.1, there exist two integers, $n_1$ and $n_2$, and two constants, $c_1$ and $c_2$, such that $f_1(n) \leq c_1 g_1(n)$ for $n \geq n_1$ and $f_2(n) \leq c_2 g_2(n)$ for $n \geq n_2$. Furthermore, by Definition 3.1, $f_1(n)$ and $f_2(n)$ are both non-negative for all integers $n \geq 0$. Let $n_0 = \max(n_1, n_2)$ and $c_0 = c_1 c_2$. Consider the product $f_1(n) \times f_2(n)$ for $n \geq n_0$:

$$f_1(n) \times f_2(n) \leq c_1 g_1(n) \times c_2 g_2(n), \quad n \geq n_0$$
$$\leq c_0(g_1(n) \times g_2(n)).$$

Thus, $f_1(n) \times f_2(n) = O(g_1(n) \times g_2(n))$.

---

Theorem 3.3 describes a simple, but extremely useful property of big oh. Consider the functions $f_1(n) = n^3 + n^2 + n + 1 = O(n^3)$ and $f_2(n) = n^2 + n + 1 = O(n^2)$. By Theorem 3.3, the asymptotic behavior of the product $f_1(n) \times f_2(n)$ is $O(n^3 \times n^2) = O(n^5)$. That is, we are able to determine the asymptotic behavior of the product without having to go through the gory details of calculating that $f_1(n) \times f_2(n) = n^5 + 2n^4 + 3n^3 + 3n^2 + 2n + 1$.

The next theorem is closely related to the preceding one in that it also shows how big oh behaves with respect to multiplication.

## Theorem 3.4

*If $f_1(n) = O(g_1(n))$ and $g_2(n)$ is a function whose value is non-negative for integers $n \geq 0$, then*

$$f_1(n) \times g_2(n) = O(g_1(n) \times g_2(n)).$$

**Proof**  By Definition 3.1, there exist integers $n_0$ and constant $c_0$ such that $f_1(n) \leq c_0 g_1(n)$ for $n \geq n_0$. Since $g_2(n)$ is never negative,

$$f_1(n) \times g_2(n) \leq c_0 g(n) \times g_2(n), \quad n \geq n_0.$$

Thus, $f_1(n) \times g_2(n) = O(g_1(n) \times g_2(n))$.

---

Theorem 3.4 applies when we multiply a function, $f_1(n)$, whose asymptotic behavior is known to be $O(g_1(n))$, by another function $g_2(n)$. The asymptotic behavior of the result is simply $O(g_1(n) \times g_2(n))$.

One way to interpret Theorem 3.4 is that it allows us to do the following mathematical manipulation:

$$f_1(n) = O(g_1(n)) \Rightarrow f_1(n) \times g_2(n) = O(g_1(n)) \times g_2(n)$$
$$\Rightarrow f_1(n) \times g_2(n) = O(g_1(n) \times g_2(n)).$$

That is, Fallacy 3.1 notwithstanding, we can multiply both sides of the "equation" by $g_2(n)$ and the "equality" still holds. Furthermore, when we multiply $O(g_1(n))$ by $g_2(n)$, we simply bring the $g_2(n)$ inside the $O(\cdot)$.

The last theorem in this section introduces the *transitive property* of big oh:

**Theorem 3.5 (Transitive Property)**
*If $f(n) = O(g(n))$ and $g(n) = O(h(n))$ then $f(n) = O(h(n))$.*

**Proof**   By Definition 3.1, there exist two integers, $n_1$ and $n_2$ and two constants $c_1$ and $c_2$ such that $f(n) \leq c_1 g(n)$ for $n \geq n_1$ and $g(n) \leq c_2 h(n)$ for $n \geq n_2$. Let $n_0 = \max(n_1, n_2)$ and $c_0 = c_1 c_2$. Then

$$
\begin{aligned}
f(n) &\leq c_1 g(n), \quad n \geq n_1 \\
&\leq c_1 c_2 h(n), \quad n \geq n_0 \\
&\leq c_0 h(n).
\end{aligned}
$$

Thus, $f(n) = O(h(n))$.

---

The transitive property of big oh is useful in conjunction with Theorem 3.2. Consider $f_1(n) = 5n^3$ which is clearly $O(n^3)$. If we add to $f_1(n)$ the function $f_2(n) = 3n^2$, then by Theorem 3.2, the sum $f_1(n) + f_2(n)$ is $O(f_1(n))$ because $\lim_{n \to \infty} f_2(n)/f_1(n) = 0$. I.e., $f_1(n) + f_2(n) = O(f_1(n))$. The combination of the fact that $f_1(n) = O(n^3)$ *and* the transitive property of big oh, allows us to conclude that the sum is $O(n^3)$.

### 3.1.4   About Polynomials

In this section we examine the asymptotic behavior of polynomials in $n$. In particular, we will see that as $n$ gets large, the term involving the highest power of $n$ will dominate all the others. Therefore, the asymptotic behavior is determined by that term.

**Theorem 3.6**
*Consider a polynomial in n of the form*

$$
\begin{aligned}
f(n) &= \sum_{i=0}^{m} a_i n^i \\
&= a_m n^m + a_{m-1} n^{m-1} + \cdots + a_2 n^2 + a_1 n + a_0
\end{aligned}
$$

*where $a_m > 0$. Then $f(n) = O(n^m)$.*

**Proof**   Each of the terms in the summation is of the form $a_i n^i$. Since $n$ is non-negative, a particular term will be negative only if $a_i < 0$. Hence, for each term in the summation, $a_i n^i \leq |a_i| n^i$. Recall too that we have stipulated that the coefficient of the largest power of $n$ is positive, i.e., $a_m > 0$.

$$f(n) \leq \sum_{i=0}^{m} |a_i| n^i$$

$$\leq n^m \sum_{i=0}^{m} |a_i| n^{i-m}, \quad n \geq 1$$

$$\leq n^m \sum_{i=0}^{m} |a_i| \frac{1}{n^{m-i}}.$$

Note that for integers $n \geq 1$, $1/(n^{m-i}) \leq 1$ for $0 \leq i \leq m$. Thus

$$f(n) \leq \underbrace{n^m \underbrace{\sum_{i=0}^{m} |a_i|}_{c}}_{g(n)}, \quad n \geq \underbrace{1}_{n_0}. \tag{3.1}$$

From Equation 3.1 we see that we have found the constants $n_0 = 1$ and $c = \sum_{i=0}^{m} |a_i|$, such that for all $n \geq n_0$, $f(n) = \sum_{i=0}^{n} a_i n^m \leq c n^m$. Thus, $f(n) = O(n^m)$.

This property of the asymptotic behavior of polynomials is used extensively. In fact, whenever we have a function, which is a polynomial in $n$, $f(n) = a_m n^m + a_{m-1} n^{m-1} + \cdots + a_2 n^2 + a_1 n + a_0$ we will immediately "drop" the less significant terms (i.e., terms involving powers of $n$ which are less than $m$), as well as the leading coefficient, $a_m$, to write $f(n) = O(n^m)$.

### 3.1.5 About Logarithms

In this section we determine the asymptotic behavior of logarithms. Interestingly, despite the fact that $\log n$ diverges as $n$ gets large, $\log n < n$ for all integers $n \geq 0$. Hence, $\log n = O(n)$. Furthermore, as the following theorem will show, $\log n$ raised to any integer power $k \geq 1$ is still $O(n)$.

**Theorem 3.7**
*For every integer $k \geq 1$, $\log^k n = O(n)$.*

**Proof**  This result follows immediately from Theorem 3.5 and the observation that for all integers $k \geq 1$,

$$\lim_{n \to \infty} \frac{\log^k n}{n} = 0. \tag{3.2}$$

This observation can be proved by the following induction.

**Base Case**    Consider the limit

$$\lim_{n\to\infty} \frac{\log^k n}{n}$$

for the case $k = 1$. Using L'Hôpital's rule[1] we see that

$$\lim_{n\to\infty} \frac{\log n}{n} = \lim_{n\to\infty} \frac{1}{n} \cdot \frac{1}{\ln 10}$$
$$= 0$$

**Inductive Hypothesis**    Assume that Equation 3.2 holds for $k = 1, 2, \ldots, m$. Consider the case $k = m + 1$. Using L'Hôpital's rule we see that

$$\lim_{n\to\infty} \frac{\log^{m+1} n}{n} = \lim_{n\to\infty} \frac{m\log^m n \times \dfrac{1}{n\ln 10}}{1}$$
$$= \frac{m}{\ln 10} \lim_{n\to\infty} \frac{\log^m n}{n}$$
$$= 0$$

Therefore, by induction on $m$, Equation 3.2 holds for all integers $k \geq 1$.

---

For example, using this property of logarithms together with the rule for determining the asymptotic behavior of the product of two functions (Theorem 3.3), we can determine that since $\log n = O(n)$, then $n \log n = O(n^2)$.

### 3.1.6    Tight Big Oh Bounds

Big oh notation characterizes the asymptotic behavior of a function by providing an upper bound on the rate at which the function grows as $n$ gets large. Unfortunately, the notation does not tell us how close the actual behavior of the function is to the bound. That is, the bound might be very close (tight) or it might be overly conservative (loose).

The following definition tells us what makes a bound tight, and how we can test to see whether a given asymptotic bound is the best one available.

---

[1]Guillaume François Antoine de L'Hôpital, marquis de Sainte-Mesme, is known for his rule for computing limits which states that if $\lim_{n\to\infty} g(n) = \infty$ and $\lim_{n\to\infty} h(n) = \infty$, then

$$\lim_{n\to\infty} \frac{g(n)}{h(n)} = \lim_{n\to\infty} \frac{g'(n)}{h'(n)},$$

where $f'(n)$ and $g'(n)$ are the first derivatives with respect to $n$ of $f(n)$ and $g(n)$, respectively. The rule is also effective if $\lim_{n\to\infty} g(n) = 0$ and $\lim_{n\to\infty} h(n) = 0$.

**Definition 3.2 (Tightness)**
*Consider a function $f(n) = O(g(n))$. If for every function $h(n)$ such that $f(n) = O(h(n))$ it is also true that $g(n) = O(h(n))$, then we say that $g(n)$ is a tight asymptotic bound on $f(n)$.*

For example, consider the function $f(n) = 8n + 128$. In Section 3.1.1, it was shown that $f(n) = O(n^2)$. However, since $f(n)$ is a polynomial in $n$, Theorem 3.6 tells us that $f(n) = O(n)$. Clearly $O(n)$ is a tighter bound on the asymptotic behavior of $f(n)$ than is $O(n^2)$.

By Definition 3.2, in order to show that $g(n) = n$ is a tight bound on $f(n)$, we need to show that for every function $h(n)$ such that $f(n) = O(h(n))$, it is also true that $g(n) = O(h(n))$.

We will show this result using proof by contradiction: Assume that $g(n)$ is *not* a tight bound for $f(n) = 8n + 128$. Then there exists a function $h(n)$ such that $f(n) = 8n + 128 = O(h(n))$, but for which $g(n) \neq O(h(n))$. Since $8n + 128 = O(h(n))$, by the definition of big oh there exist positive constants $c$ and $n_0$ such that $\forall n \geq n_0$ : $8n + 128 \leq ch(n)$.

Clearly, for all $n \geq 0, n \leq 8n + 128$. Therefore, $g(n) \leq ch(n)$. But then, by the definition of big oh, we have that $g(n) = O(h(n))$—a contradiction! Therefore, the bound $f(n) = O(n)$ is a tight bound.

## 3.1.7   More Big Oh Fallacies and Pitfalls

The purpose of this section is to dispel some common misconceptions about big oh. The next fallacy is related to the selection of the constants $c$ and $n_0$ used to show a big oh relation.

**Fallacy 3.3**
*Consider non-negative functions $f(n)$, $g_1(n)$, and $g_2(n)$, such that $f(n) = g_1(n) \times g_2(n)$. Since $f(n) \leq cg_1(n)$ for all integers $n \geq 0$ if $c = g_2(n)$, then by Definition 3.1 $f(n) = O(g_1(n))$.*

This fallacy often results from the following line of reasoning: Consider the function $f(n) = n \log n$. Let $c = \log n$ and $n_0 = 1$. Then $f(n)$ must be $O(n)$, since $\forall n \geq n_0$ : $f(n) \leq cn$. However, this line of reasoning is false because according to Definition 3.1, $c$ must be a *positive constant*, not a function of $n$.

The next fallacy involves a misunderstanding of the notion of the *asymptotic upper bound*.

**Fallacy 3.4**
*Given non-negative functions $f_1(n)$, $f_2(n)$, $g_1(n)$, and $g_2(n)$, such that $f_1(n) = O(g_1(n))$, $f_2(n) = O(g_2(n))$, and for all integers $n \geq 0$, $g_1(n) < g_2(n)$, then $f_1(n) < f_2(n)$.*

This fallacy arises from the following line of reasoning: Consider the function $f_1(n) = O(n^2)$ and $f_2(n) = O(n^3)$. Since $n^2 \leq n^3$ for all values of $n \geq 1$, we might be tempted to conclude that $f_1(n) \leq f_2(n)$. In fact, such a conclusion is erroneous. For example, consider $f_1(n) = n$ and $f_2(n) = n^2 + 1$. Clearly, the former is $O(n^2)$ and the latter is $O(n^3)$. Clearly too, $f_2(n) \geq f_1(n)$ for all values of $n \geq 0$!

The previous fallacy essentially demonstrates that while we may know how the asymptotic upper bounds on two functions are related, we don't necessarily know, in general, the relative behavior of the two bounded functions.

This fallacy often arises in the comparison of the performance of algorithms. Suppose we are comparing two algorithms, $A$ and $B$, to solve a given problem and we have determined that the running times of these algorithms are $T_A(n) = O(g_1(n))$ and $T_B(n) = O(g_2(n))$, respectively. Fallacy 3.4 demonstrates that it is an error to conclude from the fact that $\forall n \geq 0 : g_1(n) \leq g_2(n)$ that algorithm $A$ will solve the problem faster than algorithm $B$ for all problem sizes.

But what about any one specific problem size? Can we conclude that for a given problem size, say $n_0$, that algorithm $A$ is faster than algorithm $B$? The next fallacy addresses this issue.

### Fallacy 3.5

*Given non-negative functions $f_1(n)$, $f_2(n)$, $g_1(n)$, and $g_2(n)$, such that $f_1(n) = O(g_1(n))$, $f_2(n) = O(g_2(n))$, and for all integers $n \geq 0$, $g_1(n) < g_2(n)$, there exists an integer $n_0$ for which then $f_1(n_0) < f_2(n_0)$.*

This fallacy arises from a similar line of reasoning as the preceding one. Consider the function $f_1(n) = O(n^2)$ and $f_2(n) = O(n^3)$. Since $n^2 \leq n^3$ for all values of $n \geq 1$, we might be tempted to conclude that there exists a value $n_0$ for which $f_1(n_0) \leq f_2(n_0)$. Such a conclusion is erroneous. For example, consider $f_1(n) = n^2 + 1$ and $f_2(n) = n$. Clearly, the former is $O(n^2)$ and the latter is $O(n^3)$. Clearly, too, since $f_2(n) \geq f_1(n)$ for all values of $n \geq 0$, there does not exist any value $n_0 \geq 0$ for which $f_1(n_0) \leq f_2(n_0)$.

The final fallacy shows that not all functions are *commensurate*.

### Fallacy 3.6

*Given two non-negative functions $f(n)$ and $g(n)$, then either $f(n) = O(g(n))$ or $g(n) = O(f(n))$.*

This fallacy arises from thinking that the relation $O(\cdot)$ is like $\leq$ and can be used to compare any two functions. However, not all functions are commensurate.[2] Consider the following functions:

$$f(n) = \begin{cases} n & n \text{ is even,} \\ 0 & n \text{ is odd.} \end{cases}$$

$$g(n) = \begin{cases} 0 & n \text{ is even,} \\ n & n \text{ is odd.} \end{cases}$$

Clearly, there does not exist a constant $c$ for which $f(n) \leq cg(n)$ for any even integer $n$, since the $g(n)$ is zero and $f(n)$ is not. Conversely, there does not exist a constant $c$

---

[2]Functions which are commensurate are functions which can be compared one with the other.

**TABLE 3.1**
The Names of Common Big Oh Expressions

| Expression | Name |
| --- | --- |
| $O(1)$ | constant |
| $O(\log n)$ | logarithmic |
| $O(\log^2 n)$ | log squared |
| $O(n)$ | linear |
| $O(n \log n)$ | $n \log n$ |
| $O(n^2)$ | quadratic |
| $O(n^3)$ | cubic |
| $O(2^n)$ | exponential |

for which $g(n) \leq c f(n)$ for any odd integer $n$, since the $f(n)$ is zero and $g(n)$ is not. Hence, neither $f(n) = O(g(n))$ nor $g(n) = O(f(n))$ is true.

### 3.1.8 Conventions for Writing Big Oh Expressions

Certain conventions have evolved which concern how big oh expressions are normally written:

- First, it is common practice when writing big oh expressions to drop all but the most significant terms. Thus, instead of $O(n^2 + n \log n + n)$ we simply write $O(n^2)$.
- Second, it is common practice to drop constant coefficients. Thus, instead of $O(3n^2)$, we simply write $O(n^2)$. As a special case of this rule, if the function is a constant, instead of, say O(1024), we simply write $O(1)$.

Of course, in order for a particular big oh expression to be the most useful, we prefer to find a *tight* asymptotic bound (see Definition 3.2). For example, while it is not wrong to write $f(n) = n = O(n^3)$, we prefer to write $f(n) = O(n)$, which is a tight bound.

Certain big oh expressions occur so frequently that they are given names. Table 3.1 lists some of the commonly occurring big oh expressions and the usual name given to each of them.

## 3.2 An Asymptotic Lower Bound—Omega

The big oh notation introduced in the preceding section is an asymptotic *upper bound*. In this section, we introduce a similar notation for characterizing the asymptotic behavior of a function, but in this case it is a *lower bound*.

### Definition 3.3 (Omega)
*Consider a function $f(n)$, which is non-negative for all integers $n \geq 0$. We say that "$f(n)$ is omega $g(n)$," which we write $f(n) = \Omega(g(n))$, if there exists an integer $n_0$ and a constant $c > 0$ such that for all integers $n \geq n_0$, $f(n) \geq cg(n)$.*

The definition of omega is almost identical to that of big oh. The only difference is in the comparison—for big oh it is $f(n) \leq cg(n)$; for omega, it is $f(n) \geq cg(n)$. All of the same conventions and caveats apply to omega as they do to big oh.

### 3.2.1   A Simple Example

Consider the function $f(x) = 5n^2 - 64n + 256$, which is shown in Figure 3.2. Clearly, $f(n)$ is non-negative for all integers $n \geq 0$. We wish to show that $f(n) = \Omega(n^2)$. According to Definition 3.3, in order to show this we need to find an integer $n_0$ and a constant $c > 0$ such that for all integers $n \geq n_0$, $f(n) \geq cn^2$.

As with big oh, it does not matter what the particular constants are—as long as they exist! For example, suppose we choose $c = 1$. Then

$$f(n) \geq cn^2 \Rightarrow 5n^2 - 64n + 256 \geq n^2$$
$$\Rightarrow 4n^2 - 64n + 256 \geq 0$$
$$\Rightarrow 4(n - 8)^2 \geq 0.$$

Since $(n - 8)^2 > 0$ for all values of $n \geq 0$, we conclude that $n_0 = 0$.

So, we have that for $c = 1$ and $n_0 = 0$, $f(n) \geq cn^2$ for all integers $n \geq n_0$. Hence, $f(n) = \Omega(n^2)$. Figure 3.2 clearly shows that the function $f(n) = n^2$ is less than the function $f(n) = 5n^2 - 64n + 256$ for all values of $n \geq 0$. Of course, there are many other values of $c$ and $n_0$ that will do. For example, $c = 2$ and $n_0 = 16$.

**FIGURE 3.2**
Showing that $f(n) = 4n^2 - 64n + 288 = \Omega(n^2)$.

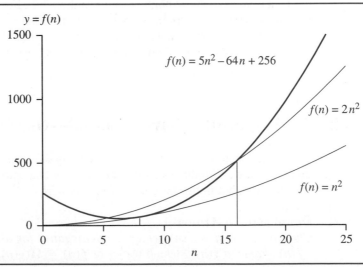

### 3.2.2 About Polynomials Again

In this section we reexamine the asymptotic behavior of polynomials in $n$. In Section 3.1.4 we showed that $f(n) = O(n^m)$. That is, $f(n)$ grows asymptotically no more quickly than $n^m$. This time we are interested in the asymptotic lower bound rather than the asymptotic upper bound. We will see that as $n$ gets large, the term involving $n^m$ also dominates the lower bound in the sense that $f(n)$ grows asymptotically *as quickly* as $n^m$. That is, that $f(n) = \Omega(n^m)$.

### Theorem 3.8
*Consider a polynomial in n of the form*

$$f(n) = \sum_{i=0}^{m} a_i n^i$$

$$= a_m n^m + a_{m-1} n^{m-1} + \cdots + a_2 n^2 + a_1 n + a_0$$

*where $a_m > 0$. Then $f(n) = \Omega(n^m)$.*

**Proof**   We begin by taking the term $a_m n^m$ out of the summation:

$$f(n) = \sum_{i=0}^{m} a_i n^i$$

$$= a_m n^m + \sum_{i=0}^{m-1} a_i n^i$$

Since, $n$ is a non-negative integer and $a_m > 0$, the term $a_m n^m$ is positive. For each of the remaining terms in the summation, $a_i n^i \geq -|a_i| n^i$. Hence

$$f(n) \geq a_m n^m - \sum_{i=0}^{m-1} |a_i| n^i$$

$$\geq a_m n^m - n^{m-1} \sum_{i=0}^{m-1} |a_i| n^{i-(m-1)}, \quad n \geq 1$$

$$\geq a_m n^m - n^{m-1} \sum_{i=0}^{m-1} |a_i| \frac{1}{n^{(m-1)-i}}.$$

Note that for integers $n \geq 1$, $1/(n^{(m-1)-i}) \leq 1$ for $0 \leq i \leq (m-1)$. Thus

$$f(n) \geq a_m n^m - n^{m-1} \sum_{i=0}^{m-1} |a_i|, \quad n \geq 1$$

$$\geq n^m \left( a_m - \frac{1}{n} \sum_{i=0}^{m-1} |a_i| \right).$$

Consider the term in parentheses on the right. What we need to do is to find a positive constant $c$ and an integer $n_0$ so that for all integers $n \geq n_0$ this term is greater than or equal to $c$:

$$a_m - \frac{1}{n}\sum_{i=0}^{m-1}|a_i| \geq a_m - \frac{1}{n_0}\sum_{i=0}^{m-1}|a_i|$$

We choose the value $n_0$ for which the term is greater than zero:

$$a_m - \frac{1}{n_0}\sum_{i=0}^{m-1}|a_i| > 0$$

$$n_0 > \frac{1}{a_m}\sum_{i=0}^{m-1}|a_i|$$

The value $n_0 = \left\lceil \frac{1}{a_m}\sum_{i=0}^{m-1}|a_i| \right\rceil + 1$ will suffice! Thus

$$f(n) \geq \underbrace{n^m}_{g(n)} \underbrace{\left(a_m - \frac{1}{n_0}\sum_{i=0}^{m-1}|a_i|\right)}_{c}, \quad n \geq n_0 \tag{3.3}$$

$$n_0 = \left\lceil \frac{1}{a_m}\sum_{i=0}^{m-1}|a_i| \right\rceil + 1.$$

From Equation 3.3 we see that we have found the constants $n_0$ and $c$, such that for all $n \geq n_0$, $f(n) = \sum_{i=0}^{n}a_i n^m \geq c n^m$. Thus, $f(n) = \Omega(n^m)$.

---

This property of the asymptotic behavior of polynomials is used extensively. In fact, whenever we have a function which is a polynomial in $n$, $f(n) = a_m n^m + a_{m-1}n^{m-1} + \cdots + a_2 n^2 + a_1 n + a_0$, we will immediately "drop" the less significant terms (i.e., terms involving powers of $n$ which are less than $m$), as well as the leading coefficient, $a_m$, to write $f(n) = \Omega(n^m)$.

## 3.3   More Notation—Theta and Little Oh

This section presents two less commonly used forms of asymptotic notation. They are

- A notation, $\Theta(\cdot)$, to describe a function which is both $O(g(n))$ and $\Omega(g(n))$, for the same $g(n)$. (Definition 3.4)
- A notation, $o(\cdot)$, to describe a function which is $O(g(n))$ but not $\Theta(g(n))$, for the same $g(n)$. (Definition 3.5)

### Definition 3.4 (Theta)
*Consider a function $f(n)$ which is non-negative for all integers $n \geq 0$. We say that "$f(n)$ is theta $g(n)$," which we write $f(n) = \Theta(g(n))$, if and only if $f(n)$ is $O(g(n))$ and $f(n)$ is $\Omega(g(n))$.*

Recall that we showed in Section 3.1.4 that a polynomial in $n$, say $f(n) = a_m n^m + a_{m-1} n^{m-1} + \cdots + a_2 n^2 + a_1 n + a_0$, is $O(n^m)$. We also showed in Section 3.2.2 that such a polynomial is $\Omega(n^m)$. Therefore, according to Definition 3.4, we will write $f(n) = \Theta(n^m)$.

### Definition 3.5 (Little Oh)
*Consider a function $f(n)$ which is non-negative for all integers $n \geq 0$. We say that "$f(n)$ is little oh $g(n)$," which we write $f(n) = o(g(n))$, if and only if $f(n)$ is $O(g(n))$ but $f(n)$ is not $\Theta(g(n))$.*

Little oh notation represents a kind of *loose asymptotic bound* in the sense that if we are given that $f(n) = o(g(n))$, then we know that $g(n)$ is an asymptotic upper bound since $f(n) = O(g(n))$, but $g(n)$ is *not* an asymptotic lower bound since $f(n) = O(g(n))$ and $f(n) \neq \Theta(g(n))$ implies that $f(n) \neq \Omega(g(n))$.[3]

For example, consider the function $f(n) = n + 1$. Clearly, $f(n) = O(n^2)$. Clearly too, $f(n) \neq \Omega(n^2)$, since no matter what $c$ we choose, for large enough $n$, $cn^2 \geq n + 1$. Thus, we may write $f(n) = n + 1 = o(n^2)$.

## 3.4  Asymptotic Analysis of Algorithms

The previous chapter presents a detailed model of the computer which involves a number of different timing parameters—$\tau_{fetch}$, $\tau_{store}$, $\tau_+$, $\tau_-$, $\tau_\times$, $\tau_\div$, $\tau_<$, $\tau_{call}$, $\tau_{return}$, $\tau_{new}$, $\tau_{delete}$, and $\tau_{[\cdot]}$. We show that keeping track of the details is messy and tiresome. So we simplify the model by measuring time in clock cycles, and by assuming that each of the parameters is equal to one cycle. Nevertheless, keeping track of and carefully counting all the cycles is still a tedious task.

In this chapter we introduce the notion of asymptotic bounds, principally big oh, and examine the properties of such bounds. As it turns out, the rules for computing and manipulating big oh expressions greatly simplify the analysis of the running time of a program when all we are interested in is its asymptotic behavior.

For example, consider the analysis of the running time of Program 3.1, which is just Program 2.2 again, an algorithm to evaluate a polynomial using Horner's rule.

Table 3.2 shows the running time analysis of Program 3.1 done in three ways—a detailed analysis, a simplified analysis, and an asymptotic analysis. In particular, note that all three methods of analysis are in agreement: Statements 3, 4a, and 6 execute

---

[3]This notion of the looseness (tightness) of an asymptotic bound is related to, but not exactly the same as, that given in Definition 3.2.

**PROGRAM 3.1**
Program 2.2 again

```
1   int Horner (int a [], unsigned int n, int x)
2   {
3       int result = a [n];
4       for (int i = n - 1; i >= 0; --i)
5           result = result * x + a [i];
6       return result;
7   }
```

**TABLE 3.2**
Computing the Running Time of Program 3.1

| Statement | Detailed Model | Simple Model | Big Oh |
|-----------|----------------|--------------|--------|
| 3 | $3\tau_{\text{fetch}} + \tau_{[\cdot]} + \tau_{\text{store}}$ | 5 | $O(1)$ |
| 4a | $2\tau_{\text{fetch}} + \tau_- + \tau_{\text{store}}$ | 4 | $O(1)$ |
| 4b | $(2\tau_{\text{fetch}} + \tau_<) \times (n + 1)$ | $3n + 3$ | $O(n)$ |
| 4c | $(2\tau_{\text{fetch}} + \tau_- + \tau_{\text{store}}) \times n$ | $4n$ | $O(n)$ |
| 5 | $(5\tau_{\text{fetch}} + \tau_{[\cdot]} + \tau_+ + \tau_\times + \tau_{\text{store}}) \times n$ | $9n$ | $O(n)$ |
| 6 | $\tau_{\text{fetch}} + \tau_{\text{return}}$ | 2 | $O(1)$ |
| TOTAL | $(9\tau_{\text{fetch}} + 2\tau_{\text{store}} + \tau_< + \tau_{[\cdot]}$ $+ \tau_+ + \tau_\times + \tau_-) \times n$ $+ (8\tau_{\text{fetch}} + 2\tau_{\text{store}} + \tau_{[\cdot]} + \tau_- + \tau_< + \tau_{\text{return}})$ | $16n + 14$ | $O(n)$ |

in a constant amount of time; 4b, 4c, and 5 execute in an amount of time which is proportional to $n$, plus a constant.

The most important observation to make is that, regardless of what the actual constants are, the asymptotic analysis always produces the same answer! Since the result does not depend on the values of the constants, the asymptotic bound tells us something fundamental about the running time of the algorithm. And this fundamental result *does not depend on the characteristics of the computer and compiler actually used to execute the program*!

Of course, you don't get something for nothing. While the asymptotic analysis may be significantly easier to do, all that we get is an upper bound on the running time of the algorithm. In particular, we know nothing about the *actual* running time of a particular program. (Recall Fallacy 3.3 and 3.4.)

### 3.4.1   Rules for Big Oh Analysis of Running Time

In this section we present some simple rules for determining a big-oh upper bound on the running time of the basic compound statements in a C++ program.

### Rule 3.1 (Sequential Composition)
*The worst-case running time of a sequence of C++ statements such as*

$S_1$ ;
$S_2$ ;
$\vdots$
$S_m$ ;

*is $O(\max(T_1(n), T_2(n), \ldots, T_m(n)))$, where the running time of $S_i$, the $i^{th}$ statement in the sequence, is $O(T_i(n))$.*

Rule 3.1 follows directly from Theorem 3.1. The total running time of a sequence of statements is equal to the sum of the running times of the individual statements. By Theorem 3.1, when computing the sum of a series of functions it is the largest one (the max) that determines the bound.

### Rule 3.2 (Iteration)
*The worst-case running time of a C++ **for** loop such as*

```
for  (S₁ ;  S₂ ;  S₃ )
        S₄ ;
```

*is $O(\max(T_1(n), T_2(n) \times (I(n) + 1), T_3(n) \times I(n), T_4(n) \times I(n)))$, where the running time of statement $S_i$ is $O(T_i(n))$, for $i = 1, 2, 3,$ and $4$, and $I(n)$ is the number of iterations executed in the worst case.*

Rule 3.2 appears somewhat complicated due to the semantics of the C++ **for** statement. However, it follows directly from Theorem 3.4. Consider the following simple *counted do loop*.

```
for (int i = 0; i < n; ++i)
        S₄ ;
```

Here $S_1$ is **int i = 0**, so its running time is constant ($T_1(n) = 1$); $S_2$ is **i < n**, so its running time is constant ($T_2(n) = 1$); and $S_3$ is **++i**, so its running time is constant ($T_3(n) = 1$). Also, the number of iterations is $I(n) = n$. According to Rule 3.2, the running time of this is $O(\max(1, 1 \times (n + 1), 1 \times n, T_4(n) \times n))$, which simplifies to $O(\max(n, T_4(n) \times n))$. Furthermore, if the loop body *does anything at all*, its running time must be $T_4(n) = \Omega(1)$. Hence, the loop body will dominate the calculation of the maximum, and the running time of the loop is simply $O(n \times T_4(n))$.

If we don't know the exact number of iterations executed, $I(n)$, we can still use Rule 3.2 provided we have an upper bound, $I(n) = O(f(n))$, on the number of iterations executed. In this case, the running time is $O(\max(T_1(n), T_2(n) \times (f(n) + 1), T_3(n) \times f(n), T_4(n) \times f(n)))$.

**Rule 3.3 (Conditional Execution)**
*The worst-case running time of a C++ if-then-else such as*

```
if (S₁)
    S₂ ;
else
    S₃ ;
```

*is $O(\max(T_1(n), T_2(n), T_3(n)))$ the running time of statement $S_i$ is $O(T_i(n))$, for $i = 1, 2, 3$.*

Rule 3.3 follows directly from the observation that the total running time for an if-then-else statement will never exceed the sum of the running time of the conditional test, $S_1$, plus the larger of the running times of the *then part*, $S_2$, and the *else part*, $S_3$.

## 3.4.2   Example—Prefix Sums

In this section we will determine a tight big oh bound on the running time of a program to compute the series of sums $S_0, S_1, \ldots, S_{n-1}$, where

$$S_j = \sum_{i=0}^{j} a_i.$$

An algorithm to compute this series of summations is given in Program 3.2. Table 3.3 summarizes the running time calculation.

Usually the easiest way to analyze a program which contains nested loops is to start with the body of the innermost loop. In Program 3.2, the innermost loop comprises lines 6 and 7. In all, a constant amount of work is done—this includes the loop body (line 7), the conditional test (line 6b) and the incrementing of the loop index (line 6c).

---

**PROGRAM 3.2**
Program to compute $\sum_{i=0}^{j} a_i$ for $0 \leq j < n$

---

```
1   void PrefixSums (int a [], unsigned int n)
2   {
3       for (int j = n - 1; j >= 0; --j)
4       {
5           int sum = 0;
6           for (unsigned int i = 0; i <= j; ++i)
7               sum += a[i];
8           a [j] = sum;
9       }
10  }
```

---

**TABLE 3.3**
Computing the Running Time of Program 3.2

| Statement | Time |
|-----------|------|
| 3a | $O(1)$ |
| 3b | $O(1) \times O(n)$ iterations |
| 3c | $O(1) \times O(n)$ iterations |
| 5 | $O(1) \times O(n)$ iterations |
| 6a | $O(1) \times O(n)$ iterations |
| 6b | $O(1) \times O(n^2)$ iterations |
| 6c | $O(1) \times O(n^2)$ iterations |
| 7 | $O(1) \times O(n^2)$ iterations |
| 8 | $O(1) \times O(n)$ iterations |
| TOTAL | $O(n^2)$ |

For a given value of $j$, the innermost loop is done a total $j + 1$ times. And since the outer loop is done for $j = n - 1, n - 2, \ldots, 0$, in the worst case, the innermost loop is done $n$ times. Therefore, the contribution of the inner loop to the running time of one iteration of the outer loop is $O(n)$.

The rest of the outer loop (lines 3, 5, and 8) does a constant amount of work in each iteration. This constant work is dominated by the $O(n)$ of the inner loop. The outer loop does exactly $n$ iterations. Therefore, the total running time of the program is $O(n^2)$.

But is this a tight big oh bound? We might suspect that it is not, because of the worst-case assumption we made in the analysis concerning the number of times the inner loop is executed. The innermost loop is done exactly $j + 1$ times for $j = n - 1, n - 2, \ldots, 0$. However, we did the calculation assuming the inner loop is done $O(n)$ times, in each iteration of the outer loop. Unfortunately, in order to determine whether our answer is a tight bound, we must determine more precisely the actual running time of the program.

However, there is one approximate calculation that we can easily make. If we observe that the running time will be dominated by the work done in the innermost loop, and that the work done in one iteration of the innermost loop is constant, then all we need to do is to determine exactly the number of times the inner loop is actually executed. This is given by

$$\sum_{j=0}^{n-1} j + 1 = \sum_{j=1}^{n} j$$
$$= \frac{n(n + 1)}{2}$$
$$= \Theta(n^2)$$

Therefore, the result $T(n) = O(n^2)$ is a tight, big oh bound on the running time of Program 3.2.

### 3.4.3    Example—Fibonacci Numbers

In this section we will compare the asymptotic running times of two different programs that both compute Fibonacci numbers.[4] The *Fibonacci numbers* are the series of numbers $F_0, F_1, \ldots$, given by

$$F_n = \begin{cases} 0 & n = 0, \\ 1 & n = 1, \\ F_{n-1} + F_{n-2} & n \geq 2. \end{cases} \tag{3.4}$$

Fibonacci numbers are interesting because they seem to crop up in the most unexpected situations. However, in this section, we are merely concerned with writing an algorithm to compute $F_n$ given $n$.

Fibonacci numbers are easy enough to compute. Consider the sequence of Fibonacci numbers

$$0, 1, 1, 2, 3, 5, 8, 13, 21, 34, \ldots$$

The next number in the sequence is computed simply by adding together the last two numbers—in this case it would be $55 = 21 + 34$. Program 3.3 is a direct implementation of this idea. The running time of this algorithm is clearly $O(n)$, as shown by the analysis in Table 3.4.

Recall that the Fibonacci numbers are defined recursively: $F_n = F_{n-1} + F_{n-2}$. However, the algorithm used in Program 3.3 is nonrecursive—it is *iterative*. What happens

---

**PROGRAM 3.3**
Nonrecursive program to compute Fibonacci numbers

```
1   unsigned int Fibonacci (unsigned int n)
2   {
3       int previous = -1;
4       int result = 1;
5       for (unsigned int i = 0; i <= n; ++i)
6       {
7           int const sum = result + previous;
8           previous = result;
9           result = sum;
10      }
11      return result;
12  }
```

---

[4]Fibonacci numbers are named in honor of Leonardo Pisano (Leonardo of Pisa), the son of Bonaccio (in Latin, *Filius Bonaccii*), who discovered the series in 1202.

**TABLE 3.4**
Computing the Running Time of Program 3.3

| Statement | Time |
|---|---|
| 3 | $O(1)$ |
| 4 | $O(1)$ |
| 5a | $O(1)$ |
| 5b | $O(1) \times (n + 2)$ iterations |
| 5c | $O(1) \times (n + 1)$ iterations |
| 7 | $O(1) \times (n + 1)$ iterations |
| 8 | $O(1) \times (n + 1)$ iterations |
| 9 | $O(1) \times (n + 1)$ iterations |
| 11 | $O(1)$ |
| TOTAL | $O(n)$ |

if instead of using the iterative algorithm, we use the definition of Fibonacci numbers to implement directly a recursive algorithm? Such an algorithm is given in Program 3.4, and its running time is summarized in Table 3.5.

From Table 3.5 we find that the running time of the recursive Fibonacci algorithm is given by the recurrence

$$T(n) = \begin{cases} O(1) & n < 2, \\ T(n - 1) + T(n - 2) + O(1) & n > 2. \end{cases}$$

But how do you solve a recurrence containing big oh expressions?

It turns out that there is a simple trick we can use to solve a recurrence containing big oh expressions *as long as we are only interested in an asymptotic bound on the result.* Simply drop the $O(\cdot)$s from the recurrence, solve the recurrence, and put the $O(\cdot)$ back! In this case, we need to solve the recurrence

$$T(n) = \begin{cases} 1 & n < 2, \\ T(n - 1) + T(n - 2) + 1 & n \geq 2. \end{cases}$$

**PROGRAM 3.4**
Recursive program to compute Fibonacci numbers

```
1   Unsigned int Fibonacci (unsigned int n)
2   {
3       if (n == 0 || n == 1)
4           return n;
5       else
6           return Fibonacci (n - 1U) + Fibonacci (n - 2U);
7   }
```

**TABLE 3.5**
Computing the Running Time of Program 3.4

| Statement | Time | |
| | $n < 2$ | $n \geq 2$ |
| --- | --- | --- |
| 3 | $O(1)$ | $O(1)$ |
| 4 | $O(1)$ | — |
| 6 | — | $T(n-1) + T(n-2) + O(1)$ |
| TOTAL | $O(1)$ | $T(n-1) + T(n-2) + O(1)$ |

In the previous chapter, we used successfully repeated substitution to solve recurrences. However, in the previous chapter, all of the recurrences only had one instance of $T(\cdot)$ on the right-hand side—in this case there are two. There is something interesting about this recurrence: It looks very much like the definition of the Fibonacci numbers. In fact, we can show by induction on $n$ that $\forall n \geq 0 : T(n) \geq F_{n+1}$.

**Proof**   (By induction).

**Base Case**   There are two base cases:

$$T(0) = 1, \quad F_1 = 1 \Rightarrow T(0) \geq F_1, \text{ and}$$
$$T(1) = 1, \quad F_2 = 1 \Rightarrow T(1) \geq F_2.$$

**Inductive Hypothesis**   Suppose that $T(n) \geq F_{n+1}$ for $n = 0, 1, 2, \ldots, k$ for some $k \geq 1$. Then

$$\begin{aligned}
T(k + 1) &= T(k) + T(k-1) + 1 \\
&\geq F_{k+1} + F_k + 1 \\
&\geq F_{k+2} + 1 \\
&\geq F_{k+2}.
\end{aligned}$$

Hence, by induction on $k$, $T(n) \geq F_{n+1}$ for all $n \geq 0$.

So, we can now say with certainty that the running time of the recursive Fibonacci algorithm, Program 3.4, is $T(n) = \Omega(F_{n+1})$. But is this good or bad? The following theorem shows us how bad this really is!

**Theorem 3.9 (Fibonacci numbers)**
*The Fibonacci numbers are given by the closed form expression*

$$F_n = \frac{1}{\sqrt{5}}(\phi^n - \hat{\phi}^n) \tag{3.5}$$

*where $\phi = (1 + \sqrt{5})/2$ and $\hat{\phi} = (1 - \sqrt{5})/2$.*

**Proof**   (By induction).

**Base Case**   There are two base cases:

$$F_0 = \frac{1}{\sqrt{5}}(\phi^0 - \hat{\phi}^0)$$

$$= 0$$

$$F_1 = \frac{1}{\sqrt{5}}(\phi^1 - \hat{\phi}^1)$$

$$= \frac{1}{\sqrt{5}}((1 + \sqrt{5})/2) - (1 - \sqrt{5})/2)$$

$$= 1$$

**Inductive Hypothesis**   Suppose that Equation 3.5 holds for $n = 0, 1, 2, \ldots, k$ for some $k \geq 1$. First, we make the following observation:

$$\phi^2 = ((1 + \sqrt{5})/2)^2$$

$$= 1 + (1 + \sqrt{5})/2$$

$$= 1 + \phi.$$

Similarly,

$$\hat{\phi}^2 = ((1 - \sqrt{5})/2)^2$$

$$= 1 + (1 - \sqrt{5})/2$$

$$= 1 + \hat{\phi}.$$

Now, we can show the main result:

$$F_{n+1} = F_n + F_{n-1}$$

$$= \frac{1}{\sqrt{5}}(\phi^n - \hat{\phi}^n) + \frac{1}{\sqrt{5}}(\phi^{n\,1} - \hat{\phi}^{n\,1})$$

$$= \frac{1}{\sqrt{5}}(\phi^{n-1}(1 + \phi) - \hat{\phi}^{n-1}(1 + \hat{\phi}))$$

$$= \frac{1}{\sqrt{5}}(\phi^{n-1}\phi^2 - \hat{\phi}^{n-1}\hat{\phi}^2)$$

$$= \frac{1}{\sqrt{5}}(\phi^{n+1} - \hat{\phi}^{n+1})$$

Hence, by induction, Equation 3.5 correctly gives $F_n$ for all $n \geq 0$.

**FIGURE 3.3**
Actual running times of Programs 3.3 and 3.4.

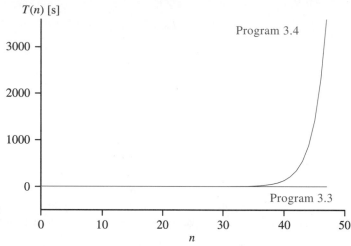

Theorem 3.9 gives us that $F_n = \frac{1}{\sqrt{5}}(\phi^n - \hat{\phi}^n)$ where $\phi = (1 + \sqrt{5})/2$ and $\hat{\phi} = (1 - \sqrt{5})/2$. Consider $\hat{\phi}$. A couple of seconds with a calculator should suffice to convince you that $|\hat{\phi}| < 1$. Consequently, as $n$ gets large, $|\hat{\phi}^n|$ is vanishingly small. Therefore, $F_n \geq \phi^n - 1$. In asymptotic terms, we write $F_n = \Omega(\phi^n)$. Now, since $\phi \approx 1.62 > (3/2)$, we can write that $F_n = \Omega((3/2)^n)$.

Returning to Program 3.4, recall that we have already shown that its running time is $T(n) = \Omega(F_{n+1})$. And since $F_n = \Omega((3/2)^n)$, we can write that $T(n) = \Omega((3/2)^{n+1}) = \Omega((3/2)^n)$. That is, the running time of the recursive Fibonacci program grows *exponentially* with increasing $n$. And that is really bad in comparison with the linear running time of Program 3.3!

Figure 3.3 shows the actual running times of both the non-recursive and recursive algorithms for computing Fibonacci numbers.[5] Because 32-bit unsigned integers are used, it is only possible to compute Fibonacci numbers up to $F_{47} = 2\,971\,215\,073$ before overflowing.

The graph shows that up to about $n = 35$, the running times of the two algorithms are comparable. However, as $n$ increases past 40, the exponential growth rate of Program 3.4 is clearly evident. In fact, the actual time taken by Program 3.4 to compute $F_{47}$ was in excess of one hour!

---

[5]These running times were measured on a Sun SPARCstation 5, Model 85, which has an 85 MHz clock, and 32MB RAM. The programs were compiled using the SPARCompiler C++ 4.1 compiler, and run under the Solaris 2.3 operating system. The times shown are user CPU times, measured in seconds.

### 3.4.4 Example—Bucket Sort

So far all of the asymptotic running time analyses presented in this chapter have resulted in tight big oh bounds. In this section we consider an example which illustrates that a cursory big oh analysis does not always result in a tight bound on the running time of the algorithm.

In this section we consider an algorithm to solve the following problem: Sort an array of $n$ integers $a_0, a_1, \ldots, a_{n-1}$, each of which is known to be between 0 and $m - 1$ for some fixed $m$. I.e., $\forall i = 0, 1, \ldots, n - 1 : 0 \leq a_i < m$. An algorithm for solving this problem, called a *bucket sort*, is given in Program 3.5.

A bucket sort works as follows: An array of $m$ counters, or *buckets*, is used. Each of the counters is set initially to zero. Then, a pass is made through the input array, during which the buckets are used to keep a count of the number of occurrences of each value between 0 and $m - 1$. Finally, the sorted result is produced by first placing the required number of zeroes in the array, then the required number of ones, followed by the twos, and so on, up to $m - 1$.

The analysis of the running time of Program 3.5 is summarized in Table 3.6. Clearly, the worst-case running time of the first loop (lines 7–8) is $O(m)$ and that of the second loop (lines 9–10) is $O(n)$.

Consider nested loops on lines 11–13. Exactly $m$ iterations of the outer loop are done—the number of iterations of the outer loop is fixed. But the number of iterations of the inner loop depends on `bucket [j]`—the value of the counter. Since there are $n$ numbers in the input array, in the worst case a counter may have the value $n$. Therefore, the running time of lines 11–13 is $O(mn)$ and this running time dominates all the others, so the running time of Program 3.5 is $O(mn)$. (This is the *cursory analysis* column of Table 3.6).

---

**PROGRAM 3.5**
Bucket sort

---

```
1   unsigned int const m = ?;
2
3   void BucketSort (unsigned int a [], unsigned int n)
4   {
5       int buckets [m];
6
7       for (unsigned int j = 0; j < m; ++j)
8           buckets [j] = 0;
9       for (unsigned int i = 0; i < n; ++i)
10          ++buckets [a [i]];
11      for (unsigned int i = 0, j = 0; j < m; ++j)
12          for (unsigned int k = buckets [j]; k > 0; --k)
13              a [i++] = j;
14  }
```

**TABLE 3.6**
Computing the Running Time of Program 3.5

| | Time | |
|---|---|---|
| Statement | Cursory Analysis | Careful Analysis |
| 7–8 | $O(m)$ | $O(m)$ |
| 9–10 | $O(n)$ | $O(n)$ |
| 11–13 | $O(mn)$ | $O(m + n)$ |
| TOTAL | $O(mn)$ | $O(m + n)$ |

Unfortunately, this time our analysis has not produced a tight bound. To see why this is the case, we must consider the operation of Program 3.5 more carefully. In particular, since we are sorting $n$ items, the final answer will only contain $n$ items. Therefore, line 13 will be executed exactly $n$ times—not $mn$ times, as the cursory result suggests.

Consider the inner loop at line 12. During the $j^{\text{th}}$ iteration of the outer loop, the inner loop does `bucket[`$j$`]` iterations. Therefore, the conditional test at line 12b is done `bucket[`$j$`]`+1 times. Therefore, the total number of times the conditional test is done is

$$\sum_{j=0}^{m-1}(\texttt{bucket}[j] + 1) = \sum_{j=0}^{m-1}\texttt{bucket}[j] + \sum_{j=0}^{m-1}1$$
$$= n + m.$$

So, the running time of lines 11–13 is $O(m + n)$, and therefore running time of Program 3.5 is $O(m + n)$. (This is the *careful analysis* column of Table 3.6.)

### 3.4.5   Reality Check

"Asymptotic analysis is nice in theory," you say, "but of what practical value is it when I don't know the values of $c$ and $n_0$ are?" Fallacy 3.3 and 3.4 showed us that if we have two programs, $A$ and $B$, that solve a given problem, whose running times are, say, $T_A = O(n^2)$ and $T_B = O(n^3)$, we cannot conclude in general that we should use algorithm $A$ rather than algorithm $B$ to solve a particular instance of the problem. Even if the bounds are both known to be tight, we still don't have enough information. What we do know for sure is that *eventually*, for large enough $n$, program $A$ is the better choice.

In practice we need not be so conservative. It is almost always the right choice to select program $A$. To see why this is the case, consider the times shown in Table 3.7. This table shows the running times computed for a very conservative scenario. We assume that the constant of proportionality, $c$, is one cycle of a 100 MHz clock. This table shows the running times we can expect even if only one instruction is done for each element of the input.

**TABLE 3.7**
Actual Lower Bounds Assuming a 100 Mhz Clock, $c = 1$ Cycle
and $n_0 = 0$

|  | $n = 1$ | $n = 8$ | $n = 1K$ | $n = 1024K$ |
|---|---|---|---|---|
| $\Omega(1)$ | 10 ns | 10 ns | 10 ns | 10 ns |
| $\Omega(\log n)$ | 10 ns | 30 ns | 100 ns | 200 ns |
| $\Omega(n)$ | 10 ns | 80 ns | 10.2 $\mu$s | 10.5 ms |
| $\Omega(n \log n)$ | 10 ns | 240 ns | 10.2 $\mu$s | 210 ms |
| $\Omega(n^2)$ | 10 ns | 640 ns | 102 $\mu$s | 3.05 hours |
| $\Omega(n^3)$ | 10 ns | 5.12 $\mu$s | 10.7 s | 365 years |
| $\Omega(2^n)$ | 10 ns | 2.56 $\mu$s | $10^{293}$ years | $10^{10^5}$ years |

## 3.4.6 Checking Your Analysis

Having made an asymptotic analysis of the running time of an algorithm, how can you verify that the implementation of the algorithm performs as predicted by the analysis? The only practical way to do this is to conduct an experiment—write out the algorithm in the form of a computer program, compile and execute the program, and measure its actual running time for various values of the parameter, $n$ say, used to characterize the size of the problem.

However, several difficulties immediately arise:

- How do you compare the results of the analysis which, by definition, only applies asymptotically, i.e., as $n$ gets arbitrarily large, with the actual running time of a program which, of necessity, must be measured for fixed and finite values of $n$?

- How do you explain it when the results of your analysis do not agree with the observed behavior of the program?

Suppose you have conducted an experiment in which you measured the actual running time of a program, $T(n)$, for a number of different values of $n$. Furthermore, suppose that on the basis of an analysis of the algorithm you have concluded that the worst-case running time of the program is $O(f(n))$. How do you tell from the measurements made that the program behaves as predicted?

One way to do this follows directly from the definition of big oh: $\exists c > 0 : T(n) \leq cf(n), \forall n \geq n_0$. This suggests that we should compute the ratio $T(n)/f(n)$ for each of value of $n$ in the experiment and observe how the ratio behaves as $n$ increases. If this ratio diverges, then $f(n)$ is probably too small; if this ratio converges to zero, then $f(n)$ is probably too big; and if the ratio converges to a constant, then the analysis is probably correct.

What if $f(n)$ turns out too large? There are several possibilities:

- The function $f(n)$ is not a *tight* bound. I.e., the analysis is still correct, but the bound is not the tightest bound possible.

- The analysis was for the *worst case* but the worst case did not arise in the set of experiments conducted.
- A mistake was made, and the analysis is wrong.

## Exercises

**3.1**  Consider the function $f(n) = 3n^2 - n + 4$. Using Definition 3.1 show that $f(n) = O(n^2)$.

**3.2**  Consider the function $f(n) = 3n^2 - n + 4$. Using Definition 3.3 show that $f(n) = \Omega(n^2)$.

**3.3**  Consider the functions $f(n) = 3n^2 - n + 4$ and $g(n) = n \log n + 5$. Using Theorem 3.2 show that $f(n) + g(n) = O(n^2)$.

**3.4**  Consider the functions $f(n) = \sqrt{n}$ and $g(n) = \log n$. Using Theorem 3.2 show that $f(n) + g(n) = O(\sqrt{n})$.

**3.5**  For each pair of functions, $f(n)$ and $g(n)$, in the following table, indicate if $f(n) = O(g(n))$ and if $g(n) = O(f(n))$.

| $f(n)$ | $g(n)$ |
|---|---|
| $10n$ | $n^2 - 10n$ |
| $n^3$ | $n^2 \log n$ |
| $n \log n$ | $n + \log n$ |
| $\log n$ | $\sqrt[k]{n}$ |
| $\ln n$ | $\log n$ |
| $\log(n + 1)$ | $\log n$ |
| $\log \log n$ | $\log n$ |
| $2^n$ | $10^n$ |
| $n^m$ | $m^n$ |
| $\cos(n\pi/2)$ | $\sin(n\pi/2)$ |
| $n^2$ | $(n \cos n)^2$ |

**3.6**  Show that the Fibonacci numbers (see Equation 3.4) satisfy the identities

$$F_{2n-1} = (F_n)^2 + (F_{n-1})^2$$
$$F_{2n} = (F_n)^2 + 2F_n F_{n-1}$$

for $n \geq 1$.

**3.7**  Prove each of the following formulas:

a.  $\displaystyle\sum_{i=0}^{n} i = O(n^2)$

**b.** $\displaystyle\sum_{i=0}^{n} i^2 = O(n^3)$

**c.** $\displaystyle\sum_{i=0}^{n} i^3 = O(n^4)$

**3.8**   Show that $\sum_{i=0}^{n} a^i = O(1)$, where $0 \le a < 1$ and $n \ge 0$.

**3.9**   Show that $\sum_{i=1}^{n} \frac{1}{i} = O(\log n)$.

**3.10**   Solve each of the following recurrences:

**a.**  $T(n) = \begin{cases} O(1) & n = 0, \\ aT(n-1) + O(1) & n > 0, \quad a > 1. \end{cases}$

**b.**  $T(n) = \begin{cases} O(1) & n = 0, \\ aT(n-1) + O(n) & n > 0, \quad a > 1. \end{cases}$

**c.**  $T(n) = \begin{cases} O(1) & n = 1, \\ aT(\lfloor n/a \rfloor) + O(1) & n > 1, \quad a \ge 2. \end{cases}$

**d.**  $T(n) = \begin{cases} O(1) & n = 1, \\ aT(\lfloor n/a \rfloor) + O(n) & n > 1, \quad a \ge 2. \end{cases}$

**3.11**   Derive tight, big oh expressions for the running times of Programs 2.1, 2.2, 2.3, 2.4, 2.6, 2.7, 2.8, and 2.9.

**3.12**   Consider the C++ program fragments given below. Assume that **n**, **m**, and **k** are **unsigned int**s and that the functions **e**, **f**, **g**, and **h** have the following characteristics:

- The worst case running time for **e(n,m,k)** is $O(1)$, and it returns a value between 1 and $(n + m + k)$.
- The worst case running time for **f(n,m,k)** is $O(n + m)$.
- The worst case running time for **g(n,m,k)** is $O(m + k)$.
- The worst case running time for **h(n,m,k)** is $O(n + k)$.

Determine a tight, big oh expression for the worst-case running time of each of the following program fragments:

**a.**
```
f (n, 10, 0);
g (n, m, k);
h (n, m, 1000000);
```

**b.**
```
for (unsigned int i = 0; i < n; ++i)
    f (n, m, k);
```

**c.**
```
for (unsigned int i = 0; i < e (n, 10, 100); ++i)
    f (n, 10, 0);
```

**d.**
```
for (unsigned int i = 0; i < e (n, m, k); ++i)
    f (n, 10, 0);
```

e.
```
for (unsigned int i = 0; i < n; ++i)
    for (unsigned int j = i; j < n; ++j)
        f (n, m, k);
```

**3.13**  Consider the following C++ program fragment. What value does **f** compute? (Express your answer as a function of *n*). Give a tight, big oh expression for the worst-case running time of the function **f**.

```
unsigned int f (unsigned int n)
{
    unsigned int sum = 0;
    for (unsigned int i = 1; i <= n; ++i)
        sum = sum + i;
    return sum;
}
```

**3.14**  Consider the following C++ program fragment. (The function **f** is given in Exercise 3.13). What value does **g** compute? (Express your answer as a function of *n*). Give a tight, big oh expression for the worst-case running time of the function **g**.

```
unsigned int g (unsigned int n)
{
    unsigned int sum = 0;
    for (unsigned int i = 1; i <= n; ++i)
        sum = sum + i + f (i);
    return sum;
}
```

**3.15**  Consider the following C++ program fragment. (The function **f** is given in Exercise 3.13 and the function **g** is given in Exercise 3.14). What value does **h** compute? (Express your answer as a function of *n*). Give a tight, big oh expression for the worst-case running time of the function **h**.

```
unsigned int h (unsigned int n)
    { return f (n) + g (n); }
```

## Programming Projects

**3.1**  Write a C++ function that takes a single integer argument *n* and has a worst-case running time of $O(n)$.

**3.2**  Write a C++ function that takes a single integer argument *n* and has a worst-case running time of $O(n^2)$.

**3.3** Write a C++ function that takes two integer arguments $n$ and $k$ and has a worst-case running time of $O(n^k)$.

**3.4** Write a C++ function that takes a single integer argument $n$ and has a worst-case running time of $O(\log n)$.

**3.5** Write a C++ function that takes a single integer argument $n$ and has a worst-case running time of $O(n \log n)$.

**3.6** Write a C++ function that takes a single integer argument $n$ and has a worst-case running time of $O(2^n)$.

**3.7** The generalized Fibonacci numbers of order $k \geq 2$ are given by

$$F_n^{(k)} = \begin{cases} 0 & 0 \leq n < k - 1, \\ 1 & n = k - 1, \\ \sum_{i=1}^{k} F_{n-i}^{(k)} & n \geq k. \end{cases} \tag{3.6}$$

Write both *recursive* and *non-recursive* functions that compute $F_n^{(k)}$. Measure the running times of your algorithms for various values of $k$ and $n$.

# 4 | Foundational Data Structures

In this book we consider a variety of *abstract data types* (ADTs), including stacks, queues, deques, ordered lists, sorted lists, hash and scatter tables, trees, priority queues, sets and graphs. In just about every case, we have the option of implementing the ADT using an array or using some kind of linked data structure.

Because they are the base upon which almost all of the ADTs are built, we call the *array* and the *linked list* the *foundational data structures*. It is important to understand that we do not view the array or the linked list as ADTs, but rather as alternatives for the implementation of ADTs.

In this chapter we discuss in detail the implementation of two classes, `Array<T>` and `LinkedList<T>`, that embody the foundational data structures. It is important to become familiar with these classes, as they are used extensively throughout the remainder of the book.

## 4.1 Dynamic Arrays

Probably the most common way to aggregate data is to use an array. While the C++ programming language does indeed provide built-in support for arrays, that support is not without its shortcomings. Arrays in C++ are not first-class data types. There is no such thing as an array-valued expression. Consequently, you cannot use an array as an actual value parameter of a function; you cannot return an array value from a function; you cannot assign one array to another. (Of course, you *can* do all of these things with a *pointer* to an array). In addition, array subscripts range from zero to $N - 1$, where $N$ is the array size, and there is no bounds checking of array subscript expressions. And finally, the size of an array is static and fixed at compile time, unless dynamic memory allocation is explicitly used by the programmer.

Some of these characteristics of arrays are due in part to the fact that in C++, given a pointer, `T* ptr`, to some type, `T`, it is not possible to tell, just from the pointer itself,

**FIGURE 4.1**
Memory representation of array objects.

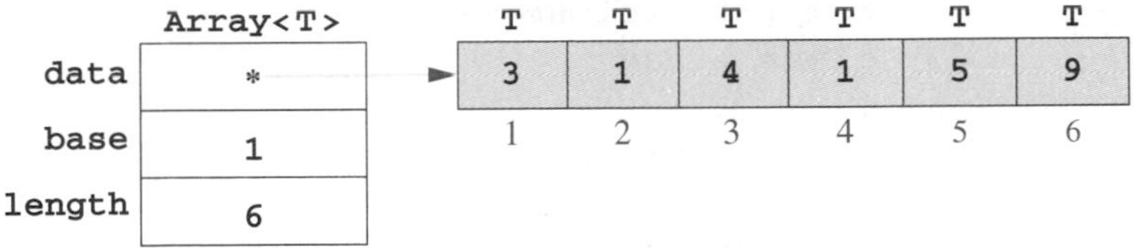

whether it points to a single instance of a variable of type **T** or to an array of variables of type **T**. Furthermore, even if we know that the pointer points to an array, we cannot determine the actual number of elements in that array.

It is primarily to address these deficiencies that we introduce the **Array** object which is implemented as a generic class. Figure 4.1 illustrates how the **Array** object is represented in the memory of the computer. Two structures are used. The first is a structure which comprises three fields—**data**, **base**, and **length**. The member variable **data** is a pointer to the array data. Variables **base** and **length** are used in the array subscript calculation. The second structure comprises contiguous memory locations which hold the array elements. In the implementation given below, this second structure is allocated dynamically.

The C++ declaration of the **Array<T>** class template is given in Program 4.1. The **Array<T>** class has three protected member variables, **data**, **base**, and **length**; constructors; destructor; and various member functions. The number of member functions has been kept to the bare minimum in this example—in the "real world" you can expect that such a class would contain many more useful member functions.

On the basis of Program 4.1, we can now calculate the total storage required to represent **Array<T>** objects. Let $S(n)$ be the total storage (memory) needed to represent an **Array<T>** object which includes $n$ array elements of type **T**. $S(n)$ is given by

$$S(n) = \texttt{sizeof(Array<T>)} + n\texttt{sizeof(T)}$$
$$= \texttt{sizeof(T*)} + 2\texttt{sizeof(unsigned int)} + n\texttt{sizeof(T)},$$

where the function **sizeof(X)** is the number of bytes used for the memory representation of an instance of an object of type **X**.

In C++, the sizes of the basic (built-in) data types are fixed constants. So too are the sizes of all pointers. Hence, **sizeof(T*)** $= O(1)$ and **sizeof(unsigned int)** $= O(1)$. Therefore,

$$S(n) = n\texttt{sizeof(T)} + O(1).$$

Unfortunately, since **Array<T>** is a generic class, we have no a priori knowledge of the amount of storage used by an object of type **T**. However, if we assume that the amount of storage used by an object of type **T** is a fixed constant, then $S(n) = O(n)$.

**PROGRAM 4.1**
Array<T> class definition

```
1   template <class T>
2   class Array
3   {
4   protected:
5       T* data;
6       unsigned int base;
7       unsigned int length;
8   public:
9       Array ();
10      Array (unsigned int, unsigned int = 0);
11      ~Array ();
12
13      Array (Array const&);
14      Array& operator = (Array const&);
15
16      T const& operator [] (unsigned int) const;
17      T& operator [] (unsigned int);
18
19      T const* Data () const;
20      unsigned int Base () const;
21      unsigned int Length () const;
22
23      void SetBase (unsigned int);
24      void SetLength (unsigned int);
25  };
```

### 4.1.1 Default Constructor

The *default constructor* for an object of class **T** is the function **T::T()**. That is, it is the constructor which takes no arguments. The definition of the **Array<T>** default destructor is given in Program 4.2. The default constructor allocates a zero-length array of elements of type **T** and sets the fields **base** and **length** to zero. Clearly, the running time of this routine is $O(1)$.

### 4.1.2 Array Constructor

In this section we consider the **Array<T>** class constructor which takes two numeric arguments of type **unsigned int**. The definition of this constructor is given in Program 4.3. Given argument values $m$ and $n$, the constructor first allocates an array of $n$ elements of type **T** using **operator new**, and then sets the **length** field to $n$ and the **base** field to $m$. The running time is a constant plus the time do the array allocation.

---

**PROGRAM 4.2**
`Array<T>` class default constructor definition

---

```
1  template <class T>
2  Array<T>::Array () :
3      data (new T [0]),
4      base (0),
5      length (0)
6      {}
```

---

---

**PROGRAM 4.3**
`Array<T>` class constructor definition

---

```
1  template <class T>
2  Array<T>::Array (unsigned int n, unsigned int m) :
3      data (new T [n]),
4      base (m),
5      length (n)
6      {}
```

---

In C++, when an array is allocated, two things happen. First, memory is allocated for the array from the free store, known as the *heap*. Second, each element of the array is initialized by calling its default constructor.

For now, we shall assume that the first step in the dynamic allocation—the allocation of space in the heap—takes a constant amount of time. In fact, when we look at how the heap is implemented we will see that this assumption does not always hold (see Chapter 13). Suppose that the running time of the default constructor for objects of type `T` is given by $\mathcal{T}\langle \texttt{T::T()} \rangle$. Then, the time to initialize an array of size $n$ is $T(n) = n\mathcal{T}\langle \texttt{T::T()} \rangle + O(1)$.

There is a special case to consider: The behavior of the default constructor for the C++ built-in types (`int`, `char`, ..., and pointers thereto) is to do nothing! So, if `T` is a built-in type, $\mathcal{T}\langle \texttt{T::T()} \rangle = 0$. In this case, the running time for the `Array<T>` constructor is simply $T(n) = O(1)$, regardless of the value $n$.

### 4.1.3 Copy Constructor

The *copy constructor* for an object of class `T` is the function `T::T(T const&)`. That is, it is the constructor for objects of class `T` which takes as its single argument a reference to another object of class `T`. This constructor builds a *copy* of the object passed by reference—hence the name *copy constructor*.

Copy constructors play a crucial rôle in C++ programs. For example, the copy constructor is called automatically by the compiler to pass the value of an actual parameter used in a function call to the formal parameter used in the function definition.

---

**PROGRAM 4.4**
Array<T> class copy constructor definition

---

```
1   template <class T>
2   Array<T>::Array (Array<T> const& array) :
3       data (new T [array.length]),
4       base (array.base),
5       length (array.length)
6   {
7       for (unsigned int i = 0; i < length; ++i)
8           data [i] = array.data [i];
9   }
```

---

Similarly, the copy constructor is called automatically by the compiler to pass the return value from a function back to the caller.

Program 4.4 shows a simple, though perhaps somewhat naïve implementation for the copy constructor of **Array<T>** class objects. To determine its running time, we need to consider carefully the execution of this function.

First, the required amount of memory is allocated by **operator new**. As discussed above, this involves finding space in the heap, which we assume takes constant time; and then initializing the elements of the array using the default constructor for objects of type **T**, which takes $n\mathcal{T}\langle\text{T::T()}\rangle + O(1)$. Next, the **length** field is set to the correct value, which takes constant time.

Finally, the body of the **Array<T>** constructor is a loop which copies one-by-one the elements of the input array to the newly allocated array. How this copy will actually be done depends on the type **T**. We shall assume that the running time of this assignment is the same as that of the copy constructor for objects of type **T**.[1] Then, the running time of the main loop of the **Array<T>** constructor is $n\mathcal{T}\langle\text{T::T(T\&)}\rangle + O(1)$. where $\mathcal{T}\langle\text{T::T(T\&)}\rangle$ is the time taken by the copy constructor for objects of type **T**.

Altogether, the running time of the copy constructor for **Array<T>** is $T(n) = n\mathcal{T}\langle\text{T::T()}\rangle + n\mathcal{T}\langle\text{T::T(T\&)}\rangle + O(1)$, where $n$ is the size of the array being copied. In the case where **T** is one of the built-in types, $\mathcal{T}\langle\text{T::T()}\rangle = 0$ and $\mathcal{T}\langle\text{T::T(\&T)}\rangle = O(1)$, which gives the simple and obvious result, $T(n) = O(n)$.

## 4.1.4   Destructor

Program 4.5 shows the definition of the **Array<T>** destructor. The destructor simply invokes **operator delete** to deallocate the storage used by the array elements. In C++ two things happen when an array is deallocated. First, the destructor for each element of the array is called one-by-one. Second, the memory space used by the array is returned to the free store (heap).

---

[1] This is not an unrealistic assumption. In the absence of a user-defined overloading of the assignment operator, the default behavior for assignment is to copy one-by-one the data members of the object of type **T**.

---

**PROGRAM 4.5**
`Array<T>` class destructor definition

---

```
1  template <class T>
2  Array<T>::~Array ()
3      { delete [] data; }
```

---

---

**PROGRAM 4.6**
`Array<T>` class accessor function definitions

---

```
1   template <class T>
2   T const* Array<T>::Data () const
3       { return data; }
4
5   template <class T>
6   unsigned int Array<T>::Base () const
7       { return base; }
8
9   template <class T>
10  unsigned int Array<T>::Length () const
11      { return length; }
```

---

If the running time of the destructor for an object of type **T** is $\mathcal{T}\langle \mathtt{T::T()} \rangle$, and assuming the time to return memory to the free store is a constant, the running time for the **Array<T>** destructor is $T(n) = n\mathcal{T}\langle \mathtt{T::T()} \rangle + O(1)$. In C++ the default behavior of the destructor for a built-in types is to do nothing. Therefore, in the case where **T** is a built-in type, $T(n) = O(1)$.

## 4.1.5  Array Member Functions

Program 4.6 defines three **Array<T>** class member functions. The three functions **Data**, **Base**, and **Length** provide a means for the user to *inspect* the contents of the **Array<T>** object.

The functions **Data**, **Base**, and **Length**, are **const** member functions As such, they provide *read-only access* to the contents of the **Array<T>** object. Such functions are sometimes called *member variable accessors*. Clearly, the running times of each of these functions is a constant, that is $T(n) = O(1)$

## 4.1.6  Array Subscripting Operator

Program 4.7 defines two functions, each of which overloads the array subscripting operation. The purpose of overloading **operator[]** is to allow arbitrary subscript ranges and to provide array bounds-checking. The array subscripting operator, **operator[]**

**PROGRAM 4.7**
`Array<T>` class subscripting function definitions

```
1   template <class T>
2   T const& Array<T>::operator [] (unsigned int position) const
3   {
4       unsigned int const offset = position - base;
5       if (offset >= length)
6           throw out_of_range ("invalid position");
7       return data [offset];
8   }
9
10  template <class T>
11  T& Array<T>::operator [] (unsigned int position)
12  {
13      unsigned int const offset = position - base;
14      if (offset >= length)
15          throw out_of_range ("invalid position");
16      return data [offset];
17  }
```

is provided in two forms. One which operates on a **const** array object and returns a **const** reference to an object of type **T**; and another which does the same for non-**const** objects. The code in both instances is identical. The **position** argument is checked and then a reference to the selected item is returned. In the event of an array-bounds error, an **out_of_range**[2] *exception* is thrown.

We will assume that in a bug-free program there will never be an array-bounds error. Therefore, the running time of **operator[]** is a constant. That is, $T(n) = O(1)$. This is, after all, the sole reason for using an array—the time it takes to access the *i*th element of the array is a constant!

### 4.1.7   Resizing an Array

The definitions for the **SetBase** and **SetLength** member functions of the **Array<T>** class are given in Program 4.8. The **SetBase** function simply modifies the **base** field as required. The **SetLength** function provides a means to change the size of an array at run time. This function can be used both to increase and to decrease the size of an array.

The running time of this algorithm depends on two parameters. If $n$ is the original size of the array and $m$ is the new size of the array, then the running time of **Resize** is $T(m, n) = m\mathcal{T}\langle\texttt{T::T()}\rangle + \min(m, n) \times \mathcal{T}\langle\texttt{T::T()}\rangle + n\mathcal{T}\langle\texttt{T::T()}\rangle + O(1)$. This is because the program first allocates and initializes a new array of size $m$; then it copies at most $\min(m, n)$ elements from the old array to the new array; and then it deletes the old

---

[2]The **out_of_range** exception is defined in the C++ standard library.

**PROGRAM 4.8**
Array<T> class SetBase and SetLength member function definitions

```
1   template <class T>
2   void Array<T>::SetBase (unsigned int newBase)
3       { base = newBase; }
4
5   template <class T>
6   void Array<T>::SetLength (unsigned int newLength)
7   {
8       T* const newData = new T [newLength];
9       unsigned int const min =
10          length < newLength ? length : newLength;
11      for (unsigned int i = 0; i < min; ++i)
12          newData [i] = data [i];
13      delete [] data;
14      data = newData;
15      length = newLength;
16  }
```

array. And in the case where T is a built in C++ data type, this simplifies to $T(m, n) = \min(m, n) \times \mathcal{T}\langle\text{T::T(T\&)}\rangle + O(1)$.

## 4.2 Singly-Linked Lists

The singly-linked list is the most basic of all the pointer-based data structures. A singly-linked list is simply a sequence of dynamically allocated storage elements, each containing a pointer to its successor. Despite this obvious simplicity, there are myriad implementation variations. Figure 4.2 shows several of the most common singly-linked list variants.

The basic singly-linked list is shown in Figure 4.2(a). Each element of the list contains a pointer to its successor; the last element contains a null pointer. A pointer to the first element of the list, labeled **head** in Figure 4.2(a), is used to keep track of the list.

The basic singly-linked list is inefficient in those cases when we wish to add elements to both ends of the list. While it is easy to add elements at the head of the list, to add elements at the other end (the *tail*) we need to locate the last element. If the basic singly-linked list is used, the entire list needs to be traversed in order to find its tail.

Figure 4.2(b) shows a way to make adding elements to the tail of a list more efficient. The solution is to keep a second pointer, **tail**, which points to the last element of the list. Of course, this time efficiency comes at the cost of the additional space used to store the **tail** pointer.

The singly-linked lists labeled (c) and (d) in Figure 4.2 illustrate two common programming tricks. The list (c) has an extra element at the head of the list called a *sentinel*. This element is never used to hold data and it is always present. The principal

**FIGURE 4.2**
Singly-linked list variations.

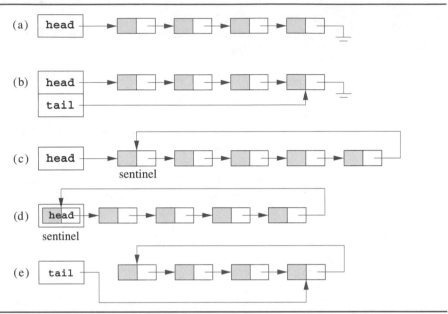

advantage of using a sentinel is that it simplifies the programming of certain operations. For example, since there is always a sentinel standing guard, we never need to modify the **head** pointer. Of course, the disadvantage of a sentinel such as that shown in (c) is that extra space is required, and the sentinel needs to be created when the list is initialized.

The list (c) is also a *circular list*. Instead of using a null pointer to demarcate the end of the list, the pointer in the last element points to the sentinel. The advantage of this programming trick is that insertion at the head of the list, insertion at the tail of the list, and insertion at an arbitrary position of the list are all identical operations.

Figure 4.2(d) shows a variation of a singly-linked list using a sentinel in which instead of keeping a pointer to the sentinel, the sentinel itself serves as the handle for the list. This variant eliminates the need to allocate storage for the sentinel separately.

Of course, it is also possible to make a circular, singly-linked list that does not use a sentinel. Figure 4.2(e) shows a variation in which a single pointer is used to keep track of the list, but this time the pointer, **tail**, points to the last element of the list. Since the list is circular in this case, the first element follows the last element of the list. Therefore, it is relatively simple to insert both at the head and at the tail of this list. This variation minimizes the storage required, at the expense of a little extra time for certain operations.

Figure 4.3 illustrates how the empty list (i.e., the list containing no list elements) is represented for each of the variations given in Figure 4.3. Notice that the sentinel is always present in those list variants which use it. On the other hand, in the list variants which do not use a sentinel, null pointers are used to indicate the empty list.

**FIGURE 4.3**
Empty singly-linked lists.

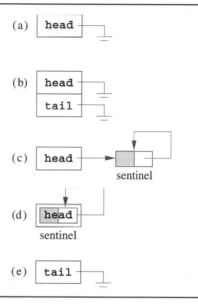

The list variant (*b*) introduces a potential source of very subtle programming errors. A conservative programmer would insist that *both* the **head** and **tail** pointers must be null. However, a clever programmer might realize that it is sufficient to require only that the **head** pointer be null in the case of an empty list. Since the **tail** pointer is not used when the list is empty, its value may be left undefined. Of course, if that is the case, extreme care must be taken to ensure that the **tail** pointer is never used when the **head** pointer is null.

In the following sections we will present the implementation details of a generic singly-linked list. We have chosen to present variation (*b*)—the one which uses a head and a tail pointer—since it supports append and prepend operations efficiently. While linked lists which use a sentinel do present some interesting time efficiencies, we have chosen not to use a sentinel because the use of a sentinel is essentially a programming trick. Also, from an object-oriented perspective, the use of a sentinel introduces some semantic difficulties. For example, if each element of the list contains an object of type **T**, and we create a list to hold exactly *n* elements, it might be reasonable to expect that **T**'s constructor is called only *n* times. However, when using a sentinel, $n + 1$ objects of type **T** are actually created—the extra one being the sentinel itself. Thus, the constructor of **T** objects is called $n + 1$ times which may not be at all what the programmer expects

## 4.2.1   An Implementation

Figure 4.4 illustrates the the singly-linked list scheme we have chosen to implement. Two structures are used. The elements of the list are represented using a structure which

**FIGURE 4.4**
Memory representation of linked list objects.

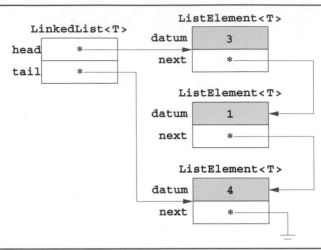

comprises two fields—**datum** and **next**. The former holds the a single data item; the latter is a pointer to the next array element. The main structure also comprises two fields—**head** and **tail**, which contain pointers to the first and last list elements, respectively.

Program 4.9 gives the declaration of the **LinkedList<T>** and **ListElement<T>** class templates. The **ListElement<T>** class is used to represent the elements of a linked list. It has two private member variables, **datum** and **next**; a private constructor; and two public accessor functions.

A **LinkedList<T>** class object has two protected member variables, **head** and **tail**, several constructors, a destructor, and various other member functions.

We can calculate the total storage required, $S(n)$, to hold a linked list of $n$ items from the class definitions given in Program 4.9 as follows:

$$S(n) = \texttt{sizeof(LinkedList<T>)} + n\texttt{sizeof(ListElement<T>)}$$
$$= 2\texttt{sizeof(ListElement<T>*)}$$
$$+ n(\texttt{sizeof(T)} + \texttt{sizeof(ListElement<T>*)})$$
$$= (n + 2)\texttt{sizeof(ListElement<T>*)} + n\texttt{sizeof(T)}$$

Since **LinkedList<T>** and **ListElement<T>** are generic classes, we have no a priori knowledge of the amount of storage used by an object of type **T**. However, it is often reasonable to assume that **sizeof(T)** $= O(1)$.[3] And since a pointer requires a

---

[3] Actually, in C++ it is not possible to have a data type **T** for which **sizeof(T)** $= 0$. While C expressly forbids an empty **struct** declaration, i.e., one which contains no data members **fields**, such declarations are permissible and quite common in C++ programs. However, the draft standard specifically says that even though an *empty* **struct** or **class** declaration is legal, it shall always be the case that **sizeof(class T)** $> 0$!

**PROGRAM 4.9**
`LinkedList<T>` and `ListElement<T>` class definitions

```
1   template <class T>
2   class LinkedList;
3
4   template <class T>
5   class ListElement
6   {
7       T datum;
8       ListElement* next;
9
10      ListElement (T const&, ListElement*);
11  public:
12      T const& Datum () const;
13      ListElement const* Next () const;
14
15      friend LinkedList<T>;
16  };
17
18  template <class T>
19  class LinkedList
20  {
21      ListElement<T>* head;
22      ListElement<T>* tail;
23  public:
24      LinkedList ();
25      ~LinkedList ();
26
27      LinkedList (LinkedList const&);
28      LinkedList& operator = (LinkedList const&);
29
30      ListElement<T> const* Head () const;
31      ListElement<T> const* Tail () const;
32      bool IsEmpty () const;
33      T const& First () const;
34      T const& Last () const;
35
36      void Prepend (T const&);
37      void Append (T const&);
38      void Extract (T const&);
39      void Purge ();
40      void InsertAfter (ListElement<T> const*, T const&);
41      void InsertBefore (ListElement<T> const*, T const&);
42  };
```

**PROGRAM 4.10**
ListElement<T> class member function definitions

```
1   template <class T>
2   ListElement<T>::ListElement (
3       T const& _datum, ListElement<T>* next) :
4       datum (_datum), next (_next)
5       {}
6
7   template <class T>
8   T const& ListElement<T>::Datum () const
9       { return datum; }
10
11  template <class T>
12  ListElement<T> const* ListElement<T>::Next () const
13      { return next; }
```

constant amount of space, $S(n) = n$ `sizeof(T)` $+ O(n)$. If we assume that the amount of storage used by an object of type **T** is $O(1)$, then $S(n) = O(n)$.

### 4.2.2 List Elements

The definitions of the member functions of the **ListElement<T>** class are given in Program 4.10. Altogether, there are three functions—a constructor and two accessors.

The constructor simply initializes the member variable to the passed values. The running time of the constructor is $\mathcal{T}\langle \text{T::T(T\&)} \rangle + O(1)$, where $\mathcal{T}\langle \text{T::T(T\&)} \rangle$ is the running time of the copy constructor for objects of class **T**. Assigning a value to the **next** field takes a constant amount of time.

The two accessor functions, **Datum** and **Next**, simply return the values of the corresponding member variables. Clearly, the running times of each of these functions is $O(1)$. Note that if **Datum** had been defined as returning a **T**, rather than a *reference* to **T**, the assumption of constant running time would not be valid.

### 4.2.3 Default Constructor

The code for the default **LinkedList<T>** constructor is given in Program 4.11. This routine simply constructs the representation of an empty linked list as shown in Figure 4.4(*b*). That is, both the **head** and **tail** pointers are set to zero. The running time of the default constructor is clearly constant. That is, $T(n) = O(1)$.

### 4.2.4 Destructor and Purge Member Function

Program 4.12 gives the code for the destructor and the **Purge** member function of the **LinkedList<T>** class. In the general case, when the destructor is invoked, we cannot

---

**PROGRAM 4.11**
LinkedList<T> class default constructor definition

```
1  template <class T>
2  LinkedList<T>::LinkedList () :
3      head (0),
4      tail(0)
5      {}
```

---

---

**PROGRAM 4.12**
LinkedList<T> class destructor and Purge member function definitions

```
1   template <class T>
2   void LinkedList<T>::Purge ()
3   {
4       while (head != 0)
5       {
6           ListElement<T>* const tmp = head;
7           head = head->next;
8           delete tmp;
9       }
10      tail = 0;
11  }
12
13  template <class T>
14  LinkedList<T>::~LinkedList ()
15      { Purge (); }
```

---

expect the list to be empty. Therefore, it is the responsibility of the destructor to first release any LinkedList<T>s which have been allocated and linked into the list. And this is precisely what the Purge member function does.

The main loop of the Purge function simply traverses all the elements of linked list, deleting each of them one-by-one. Note that the body of the loop has been carefully written so as to determine the new value of **head**, before deleting the current list element. For example, the following loop body is the *wrong* way to do it:

```
while (head != 0)
{
    delete head;
    head = head->next; // Wrong.  Don't do this.
}
```

---

**PROGRAM 4.13**
LinkedList<T> class accessor function definitions

---

```
1   template <class T>
2   ListElement<T> const* LinkedList<T>::Head () const
3       { return head; }
4
5   template <class T>
6   ListElement<T> const* LinkedList<T>::Tail () const
7       { return tail; }
8
9   template <class T>
10  bool LinkedList<T>::IsEmpty () const
11      { return head == 0; }
```

---

The problem with the code fragment above is that the **head** pointer is dereferenced *after* the object to which it points has been deleted. While this code might actually work fortuitously for some compilers on some machines under some operating systems, it is invalid and illegal.

### 4.2.5   Accessors

Three **LinkedList<T>** class member variable accessors are defined in Program 4.13. The member functions **Head** and **Tail** provide read-only access to the corresponding data members of **LinkedList<T>**. The function **IsEmpty** returns a Boolean result which indicates whether the list is empty. Clearly, the running time of the of the accessors is $O(1)$.

### 4.2.6   **First** and **Last** Functions

Two more **LinkedList<T>** class object accessors are defined in Program 4.14. The **First** member function returns a **const** reference to the first list element. Similarly, the **Last** member function returns a **const** reference to the last list element.

The code for both functions is almost identical. In the event that the list is empty, a **domain_error**[4] *exception* is thrown. An exception is thrown because if the list is empty, it is not possible even to create a return value—there is no **T** object instance to which to refer!

We will assume that in a bug-free program, neither the **First** nor the **Last** functions will be called for an empty list. In that case, the running time of each of theses functions is constant. That is, $T(n) = O(1)$.

---

[4]The **domain_error** exception is defined in the C++ standard library.

**PROGRAM 4.14**
`LinkedList<T>` class `First` and `Last` function definitions

```
1   template <class T>
2   T const& LinkedList<T>::First () const
3   {
4       if (head == 0)
5           throw domain_error ("list is empty");
6       return head->datum;
7   }
8
9   template<class T>
10  T const& LinkedList<T>::Last () const
11  {
12      if (tail == 0)
13          throw domain_error ("list is empty");
14      return tail->datum;
15  }
```

### 4.2.7 Prepend

To *prepend* an element to a linked list is to insert that element in front of the first element of the list. The prepended list element becomes the new head of the list. Program 4.15 gives the algorithm for the `Prepend` member function of the `LinkedList<T>` class.

The `Prepend` function first allocates a new `ListElement<T>`. Its `datum` field is initialized with the value to be prepended to the list, `item`; and the `next` field is made to point to the first element of the existing list by initializing it with the value of the current `head` pointer. If the list is initially empty, both `head` and `tail` are made to point at the new element. Otherwise, just `head` needs to be updated.

Note, `operator new` calls the constructor for objects of class `ListElement<T>`. In Section 4.2.2 the running time of the constructor was determined to be $\mathcal{T}\langle \texttt{T::T(T\&)} \rangle +$

**PROGRAM 4.15**
`LinkedList<T>` class `Prepend` function definition

```
1   template <class T>
2   void LinkedList<T>::Prepend (T const& item)
3   {
4       ListElement<T>* const tmp = new ListElement<T> (item, head);
5       if (head == 0)
6           tail = tmp;
7       head = tmp;
8   }
```

$O(1)$. And since the body of the **Prepend** function adds only a constant amount of work, the running time of the **Prepend** function is also $\mathcal{T}\langle\text{T::T(T\&)}\rangle + O(1)$. If **T** is one of the built-in types, then its copy constructor does a constant amount of work, and the running time of **Prepend** simplifies to $O(1)$.

### 4.2.8 Append

The **Append** function, the definition of which is given in Program 4.16, adds a new **ListElement<T>** at the tail-end of the list. The appended element becomes the new tail of the list.

The **Append** function first allocates a new **ListElement<T>**. Its **datum** field is initialized with the value to be appended, and the **next** field is set to zero. If the list is initially empty, both **head** and **tail** are made to point at the new element. Otherwise, the new element is appended to the existing list, and the just **tail** pointer is updated.

The running time analysis of the **Append** function is essentially the same as for **Prepend**. That is, the running time is $\mathcal{T}\langle\text{T::T(T\&)}\rangle + O(1)$. And if **T** is one of the built-in types, the running time simplifies to $O(1)$.

### 4.2.9 Copy Constructor and Assignment Operator

The code for the copy constructor and assignment operator (**operator=**) of the **LinkedList<T>** class is given in Program 4.17. These functions are similar in that they both build a copy of a given list. The copy constructor first initializes the member variables to represent the empty list. Then, it traverses the referenced list one-by-one, calling the **Append** function to append the items of the referenced list to the list begin constructed.

In Section 4.2.8 the running time for the **Append** function was determined to be $\mathcal{T}\langle\text{T::T(T\&)}\rangle + O(1)$. If the resulting list has $n$ elements, the **Append** function will

---

**PROGRAM 4.16**
**LinkedList<T>** class **Append** function definition

```
1   template <class T>
2   void LinkedList<T>::Append (T const& item)
3   {
4       ListElement<T>* const tmp = new ListElement<T> (item, 0);
5       if (head == 0)
6           head = tmp;
7       else
8           tail->next = tmp;
9       tail = tmp;
10  }
```

---

**PROGRAM 4.17**
LinkedList<T> class copy constructor definition

---

```
1   template <class T>
2   LinkedList<T>::LinkedList (LinkedList<T> const& linkedList) :
3       head (0),
4       tail (0)
5   {
6       ListElement<T> const* ptr;
7       for (ptr = linkedList.head; ptr != 0; ptr = ptr->next)
8           Append (ptr->datum);
9   }
10
11  template <class T>
12  LinkedList<T>& LinkedList<T>::operator = (
13      LinkedList<T> const& linkedList)
14  {
15      if (&linkedList != this)
16      {
17          Purge ();
18          ListElement<T> const* ptr;
19          for (ptr = linkedList.head; ptr != 0; ptr = ptr->next)
20              Append (ptr->datum);
21      }
22      return *this;
23  }
```

---

be called $n$ times. Therefore, the running time of the copy constructor is $T(n) = n\mathcal{T}\langle\text{T::T(T\&)}\rangle + O(n)$. If **T** is one of the built-in types, $\mathcal{T}\langle\text{T::T(T\&)}\rangle = O(1)$. As a result, the running time of the copy constructor would be $T(n) = O(n)$.

The assignment operator first calls **Purge** to make sure that the list to which new contents are being assigned is empty. It then builds a copy of the given list in the same way as discussed above for the copy constructor. The running time is equal to that of the **Purge** function plus that of the copy constructor.

### 4.2.10 Extract

In this section we consider the **Extract** member function of the **LinkedList<T>** class. The purpose of this function is to delete the specified element from the linked list.

The element to be deleted is identified by its value. The **Extract** function searches sequentially for the item to be deleted. In the absence of any a priori knowledge, we do not know in which list element the item to be deleted will be found. In fact, the specified item may not even appear in the list!

If we assume that the item to be deleted *is* in the list, and if we assume that there is an equal probability of finding it in each possible position, then on average we will need to search halfway through the list before the item to be deleted is found. In the worst case, the item will be found at the tail—assuming it is in the list.

If the item to be deleted does not appear in the list, the algorithm shown in Program 4.18 throws a **domain_error** exception. A simpler alternative might be to do nothing—after all, if the item to be deleted is not in the list, then we are already done! However, attempting to delete an item which is not there is more likely to indicate a logic error in the programming. This is why an exception is thrown.

In order to determine the running time of the **Extract** function, we first need to determine the time to find the element to be deleted. And to determine that, we need to know the running time for the comparison on line 8. Unfortunately, since **LinkedList<T>** is a generic class, we don't know in general what the running time of the comparison will be. So we need to introduce yet another variable to represent this unknown. Let $\mathcal{T}\langle \texttt{op==(T\&,T\&)} \rangle$ be the time required to determine if two objects of type **T** are equal.

If the item to be deleted *is not* in the list, then the running time of Program 4.18 up to the point where it throws the exception (line 12) is $T(n) = n\mathcal{T}\langle \texttt{op==(T\&,T\&)} \rangle + O(1)$, which simplifies to $T(n) = O(n)$ if $\mathcal{T}\langle \texttt{op==(T\&,T\&)} \rangle = O(1)$.

Now consider what happens if the item to be deleted *is* found in the list. In the worst case the item to be deleted is at the tail. Thus, the running time to find the

---

**PROGRAM 4.18**
LinkedList<T> class **Extract** function definition

---

```
1   template <class T>
2   void LinkedList<T>::Extract (T const& item)
3   {
4       ListElement<T>* ptr = head;
5       ListElement<T>* prevPtr = 0;
6       while (ptr != 0 && ptr->datum != item)
7       {
8           prevPtr = ptr;
9           ptr = ptr->next;
10      }
11      if (ptr == 0)
12          throw invalid_argument ("item not found");
13      if (ptr == head)
14          head = ptr->next;
15      else
16          prevPtr->next = ptr->next;
17      if (ptr == tail)
18          tail = prevPtr;
19      delete ptr;
20  }
```

element is $n\mathcal{T}\langle \text{op==(T\&,T\&)} \rangle + O(1)$ in the worst case. Deleting the element from the list once it has been found is a short sequence of relatively straightforward pointer manipulations. These manipulations can be done in constant time. Finally, the list element, having been unlinked from the list, is returned to the free store. So, the total running time is $T(n) + n\mathcal{T}\langle \text{op==(T\&,T\&)} \rangle + \mathcal{T}\langle \text{T::~T()} \rangle + O(1)$. For a built-in type, $\mathcal{T}\langle \text{op==(T\&,T\&)} \rangle = O(1)$ and $\mathcal{T}\langle \text{T::~T()} \rangle = 0$, which gives the running time $T(n) = O(n)$.

### 4.2.11 `InsertAfter` and `InsertBefore`

The functions `InsertAfter` and `InsertBefore` both take two arguments. The first is a pointer to an element of the linked list, and the second is a reference to the item to be inserted into the list. The item is inserted either in front of or immediately following the indicated list element. Program 4.19 gives the code for the `InsertAfter` and `InsertBefore` member functions.

The `InsertAfter` member function is almost identical to `Append`. Whereas `Append` inserts an item after the tail, `InsertAfter` inserts an item after an arbitrary list element. Nevertheless, the running time of `InsertAfter` is identical to that of `Append`, i.e., it is $\mathcal{T}\langle \text{T::T(T\&)} \rangle + O(1)$.

To insert a new item *before* a given list element, it is necessary to traverse the linked list starting from the head to locate the list element that precedes the given list element. In the worst case, the given element is at the tail of the list and the entire list needs to be traversed. Therefore, the running time of the `InsertBefore` member function is $\mathcal{T}\langle \text{T::T(T\&)} \rangle + O(n)$.

## 4.3 Multidimensional Arrays

A *multidimensional array* of dimension $n$ (i.e., an $n$-dimensional array or simply $n$D array) is a collection of items which is accessed via $n$ subscript expressions. For example, the $(i, j)$th element of the two-dimensional array **x** is accessed by writing `x[i][j]`.

The C++ programming language provides built-in support for multidimensional arrays. However, the built-in multidimensional arrays suffer the same indignities that simple one-dimensional arrays do: Arrays in C++ are not first-class data types. There is no such thing as an array-valued expression. Consequently, you cannot use an array as an actual value parameter of a function; you cannot return an array value from a function; and, you cannot assign one array to another. The subscript ranges all start at zero, and there is no bounds checking of array subscript expressions. Finally, the size of an array is static and fixed at compile time, unless dynamic memory allocation is explicitly used by the programmer.

In order to illustrate how these deficiencies of the C++ built-in multidimensional arrays can be overcome, we will examine the implementation of a two-dimensional array class, **Array2D**, that is based on the one-dimensional array class discussed in Section 4.1.

**PROGRAM 4.19**
LinkedList<T> class `InsertAfter` and `InsertBefore` function definitions

```
1   template <class T>
2   void LinkedList<T>::InsertAfter (
3       ListElement<T> const* arg, T const& item)
4   {
5       ListElement<T>* ptr = const_cast<ListElement<T>*> (arg);
6       if (ptr == 0)
7           throw invalid_argument ("invalid position");
8       ListElement<T>* const tmp =
9           new ListElement<T> (item, ptr->next);
10      ptr->next = tmp;
11      if (tail == ptr)
12          tail = tmp;
13  }
14
15  template <class T>
16  void LinkedList<T>::InsertBefore (
17      ListElement<T> const* arg, T const& item)
18  {
19      ListElement<T>* ptr = const_cast<ListElement<T>*> (arg);
20      if (ptr == 0)
21          throw invalid_argument ("invalid position");
22      ListElement<T>* const tmp = new ListElement<T> (item, ptr);
23      if (head == ptr)
24          head = tmp;
25      else
26      {
27          ListElement<T>* prevPtr = head;
28          while (prevPtr != 0 && prevPtr->next != ptr)
29              prevPtr = prevPtr->next;
30          if (prevPtr == 0)
31              throw invalid_argument ("invalid position");
32          prevPtr->next = tmp;
33      }
34  }
```

### 4.3.1 Array Subscript Calculations

The memory of a computer is essentially a one-dimensional array—the memory address is the array subscript. Therefore, the most natural way to implement a multidimensional array is to store its elements in a one-dimensional array. In order to do this, we need a mapping from the $n$ subscript expressions used to access an element of the multidimensional array to the one subscript expression used to access the one-dimensional array. For example, suppose we have a two-dimensional array of elements of type **T**, **T a[2][3]**, the elements of which are to be stored in a one-dimensional array, **T b[20]**. Then we need to determine which element of **b**, say **b[k]**, will be accessed given a reference of the form **a[i][j]**. That is, we need the mapping $f$ such that $\mathbf{k} = f(\mathbf{i}, \mathbf{j})$.

The mapping function determines the way in which the elements of the array are stored in memory. The most common way to represent an array is in *row-major order*, also known as *lexicographic order*, For example, consider the 2D array **T a[2][3]**. The row-major layout of this array is shown in Figure 4.5.

In row-major layout, it is the right-most subscript expression (the column index) that increases the fastest. As a result, the elements of the rows of the matrix end up stored in contiguous memory locations. In Figure 4.5, the array is stored starting from address $a$. The first element of the first row is a address $a + 0 \times \mathbf{sizeof(T)} = a$. The first element of the second row is at address $a + 3 \times \mathbf{sizeof(T)}$, since there are **3** elements in each row.

We can now generalize this to an arbitrary $n$-dimensional array. Suppose we have an $n$D array declared as **T a[$s_1$][$s_2$][$\cdots$][$s_n$]**. Furthermore, let $a$ be the starting address of the array. Then, the address of the element **a[$i_1$][$i_2$][$\cdots$][$i_n$]** is given by

$$a + \mathbf{sizeof(T)} \times \sum_{j=1}^{n} \delta_j i_j \tag{4.1}$$

where

$$\delta_j = \begin{cases} 1 & j = n, \\ \prod_{k=j+1}^{n} s_k & 1 \le j < n. \end{cases}$$

The running time required to calculate the address appears to be $O(n^2)$ since the address is the sum of $n$ terms and for each term we need to compute $\delta_j$, which requires

**FIGURE 4.5**
Row-major order layout of a 2D array.

| address | value |
|---|---|
| $+0 \times$ **sizeof(T)** | **a[0][0]** |
| $+1 \times$ **sizeof(T)** | **a[0][1]** |
| $+2 \times$ **sizeof(T)** | **a[0][2]** |
| $+3 \times$ **sizeof(T)** | **a[1][0]** |
| $+4 \times$ **sizeof(T)** | **a[1][1]** |
| $+5 \times$ **sizeof(T)** | **a[1][2]** |

$O(n)$ multiplications in the worst case. However, the address calculation can in fact be done in $O(n)$ time using the following algorithm:

```
unsigned int product = 1;
T* address = a;
for (int j = n; j >= 1; --j)
{
    address += product * i_j ;
    product *= s_j ;
}
```

This algorithm makes subtle use of the way that address arithmetic is done in C++ . Since the variable **address** is of type **T\***, it is not necessary to scale the computation by **sizeof(T)**. In C++ whenever an integer value is added to a pointer variable, it is automatically scaled by the compiler before the addition.

---

**PROGRAM 4.20**
**Array2D<T>** and **Array2D<T>::Row** class definitions

```
1   template <class T>
2   class Array2D
3   {
4   protected:
5       unsigned int numberOfRows;
6       unsigned int numberOfColumns;
7       Array<T> array;
8   public:
9       class Row
10      {
11          Array2D& array2D;
12          unsigned int const row;
13      public:
14          Row (Array2D& _array2D, unsigned int _row) :
15              array2D (_array2D), row (_row) {}
16          T& operator [] (unsigned int column) const
17              { return array2D.Select (row, column); }
18      };
19
20      Array2D (unsigned int, unsigned int);
21      T& Select (unsigned int, unsigned int);
22      Row operator [] (unsigned int);
23  };
```

---

### 4.3.2 Two-Dimensional Array Implementation

In this section we illustrate the implementation of a multidimensional array by giving the code for a generic two-dimensional array class, **Array2D<T>**, which is derived from the **Array<T>** class discussed in Section 4.1. The declaration of the **Array2D<T>** class template is shown in Program 4.20.

Objects of the **Array2D<T>** class contain three member variables—**numberOfRows**, **numberOfColumns**, and **array**. The first two record the dimensions of the array. The last is an instance of the one-dimensional array object discussed in Section 4.1.

The definitions of the **Array2D<T>** class member functions are given in Program 4.21. The constructor takes two arguments, $m$ and $n$, which are the desired dimensions of the array. It calls the **Array<T>** class constructor to build a one-dimensional array of size $mn$. Using the result from Section 4.1.2, it can be shown that the running time for the **Array2D<T>** constructor is $mn\mathcal{T}\langle {\tt T::T()}\rangle + O(1)$.

The **Select** function takes two arguments, $i$ and $j$, and returns a reference to the $(i, j)$th element of the array. In the previous section we saw that the running time for the array subscripting calculation in an $k$-dimensional array is $O(k)$. For a two-dimensional array, $k = 2$. Therefore, the running time for the subscript calculation is $O(2) = O(1)$.

---

**PROGRAM 4.21**
Array2D<T> class member functions

---

```
1   template <class T>
2   Array2D<T>::Array2D (unsigned int m, unsigned int n) :
3       numberOfROws (m),
4       numberOfColumns (n),
5       array (m * n)
6       {}
7
8   template <class T>
9   T& Array2D<T>::Select (unsigned int i, unsigned int j)
10  {
11      if (i >= numberOfRows)
12          throw out_of_range ("invalid row");
13      if (j >= numberOfColumns)
14          throw out_of_range ("invalid column");
15      return array [i * numberOfColumns + j];
16  }
17
18  template <class T>
19  Array2D<T>::Row Array2D<T>::operator [] (unsigned int row)
20      { return Row (*this, row); }
```

---

### 4.3.3   Multidimensional Subscripting in C++

When accessing the elements of a multidimensional array, programmers usually prefer to use the C++ array subscripting operator rather than call a member function explicitly. This is because it is much more convenient to write `a[i][j]` than to write `a.Select(i,j)`. However, C++ does not directly support the overloading of multidimensional array subscripting. For example, an experienced Fortran programmer would expect to be able to write `a[i,j]` and to overload `operator[](int,int)`. Alas, neither of these things is valid in C++ .

The solution to this problem is to do the subscripting in two steps. Consider the reference `a[i][j]`. In C++ this is equivalent to

```
a.operator[] (i).operator[] (j) .
```

In effect, the first subscripting operator selects the *i*th row, and then the second subscripting operator picks the *j*th element of that row.

Program 4.20 gives a framework for implementing the two-step process in C++ , Two object classes are declared—`Array2D<T>` and the nested class `Row`. The latter class is used to represent a reference to a particular row of a given two-dimensional array.

In Program 4.20 we see that `operator[]` for `Array2D<T>` objects returns an object of type `Array2D<T>::Row`. The purpose of a `Row` object is to "remember" both the array and the row of that array that is being accessed—its data members are a reference to the accessed array, and the row number.

There is also a subscripting operator defined for `Row` class objects. This one uses the remembered row number together with the given column number to call the `Select` function on the appropriate array.

The definition of the `Array2D<T>` subscripting member function, `operator[]`, is given in Program 4.21. This function simply constructs an instance of the `Array2D<T>::Row` class. Clearly, the running time of this function is $O(1)$.

Given the `Array2D<T>` class we are able to write code such as the following:

```
Array2D<int> a (4, 5);
for (int i = 0; i < 4; ++i)
    for (int j = 0; j < 5; ++j)
        a[i][j] = 0;
```

which declares a $4 \times 5$ array of integers, and initializes all of the elements with the value zero.

### 4.3.4   Example—Canonical Matrix Multiplication

Given an $m \times n$ matrix $A$ and an $n \times p$ matrix $B$, the product $C = AB$ is an $m \times p$ matrix. The elements of the result matrix are given by

$$c_{i,j} = \sum_{k=0}^{n-1} a_{i,k} b_{k,j}. \tag{4.2}$$

Accordingly, in order to compute the produce matrix, C, we need to compute $mp$ summations each of which is the sum of $n$ product terms.

To represent matrices we use the **Matrix<T>** class shown in Program 4.22. This class simply extends the **Array2D<T>** class by adding declarations for the various operations on matrices.

An algorithm to compute the matrix product is given in Program 4.23 . The algorithm given is a direct implementation of Equation 4.2.

The matrix multiplication routine in Program 4.23 overloads the multiplication operator, **operator\***, as a member function of the **Matrix<T>** class. As a result it takes a single argument, **arg**, which is a **const** reference to a matrix. The routine computes a result matrix which is the produce of **\*this** and **arg**.

In C++ there are two ways to overload **operator\***. The first is to define a non-member function

```
Matrix<T> operator * (Matrix<T> const&, Matrix<T> const&);
```

which takes two arguments, both of them **const** references to **Matrix<T>** objects, and produces a result of type **Matrix<T>**. The second way is to declare a **const** member function of class **Matrix<T>** called

```
Matrix<T> Matrix<T>::operator * (Matrix<T> const&) const;
```

which takes as its single argument a **const** reference to a **Matrix<T>** class object.

There are pros and cons associated with each approach. The former approach requires the function to be declared a **friend** of the **Matrix<T>** class and any of the classes from which it may be derived if access to the **protected** members of those classes is needed in the implementation. On the other hand, in this approach, the operands are treated symmetrically with respect to implicit *type coercion*.

---

**PROGRAM 4.22**
**Matrix<T>** class definition

---

```
1   template <class T>
2   class Matrix : public Array2D<T>
3   {
4   public:
5       Matrix (unsigned int, unsigned int);
6       Matrix operator * (Matrix const&) const;
7       Matrix operator + (Matrix const&) const;
8   };
```

---

---

**PROGRAM 4.23**
Matrix<T> class multiplication operator definition

---

```
1   template <class T>
2   Matrix<T> Matrix<T>::operator * (Matrix<T> const& arg) const
3   {
4       if (numberOfColumns != arg.numberOfRows)
5           throw invalid_argument ("incompatible matrices");
6       Matrix<T> result (numberOfRows, arg.numberOfColumns);
7       for (unsigned int i = 0; i < numberOfRows; ++i)
8       {
9           for (unsigned int j = 0; j < arg.numberOfColumns; ++j)
10          {
11              T sum = 0;
12              for (unsigned int k = 0; k < numberOfColumns; ++k)
13                  sum += (*this) [i][j] * arg [k][j];
14              result [i][j] = sum;
15          }
16      }
17      return result;
18  }
```

---

The latter approach has been chosen for the implementation of the matrix multi-plication operator since **Matrix<T>** is a derived class and the implementation of the operator requires access to **protected** members of the base class.

To determine the running time of Program 4.23, we need to make some assumptions about the running times for assignment, addition, and multiplication of objects of type **T**. For simplicity, we shall assume that these are all constant. We will also assume that the dimensions of the matrices to be multiplied are $m \times n$ and $n \times p$.

The algorithm begins by checking to see that the matrices to be multiplied have compatible dimensions. That is, the number of columns of the first matrix must be equal to the number of rows of the second one. This check takes $O(1)$ time in the worst case.

Next a matrix in which the result will be formed is constructed (line 6). The running time for this is $mp\mathcal{T}\langle \texttt{T::T()} \rangle + O(1)$. If **T** is one of the built-in types whose constructor does nothing, this running time reduces to $O(1)$.

For each value of $i$ and $j$, the innermost loop (lines 12–13) does $n$ iterations. Each iteration takes a constant amount of time, assuming assignment, addition, and multipli-cation of type **T** objects each take a constant amount of time.

The body of the middle loop (lines 9–15) takes time $O(n)$ for each value of $i$ and $j$. The middle loop is done for $p$ iterations, giving the running time of $O(np)$ for each value of $i$. Since the outer loop does $m$ iterations, its overall running time is $O(mnp)$.

Finally, the result matrix is returned on line 17. The return involves a call to the copy constructor for **Matrix<T>** class objects. In fact, no such constructor has been declared for **Matrix<T>** class objects. The default behavior of C++ in this case is to create a *default copy constructor* for **Matrix\<T>** class objects. In C++ the behavior of the default copy constructor for objects of class **X** is to call the copy constructor for the each of the base classes from which the class **X** may be derived and then to copy the data members of **X** one-by-one using their respective copy constructors. Since the **Matrix\<T>** class is derived from the **Array2D\<T>** class and since the **Matrix\<T>** class has no data members, the running time of this default copy constructor is equal to the running time of the copy constructor for **Array2D\<T>** class objects (see Section 4.1.3). Hence the running time of line 18 is $mp\mathcal{T}\langle \text{T::T(T\&)} \rangle + O(1)$. Assuming that $\mathcal{T}\langle \text{T::T(T\&)} \rangle = 1$, we get $O(mp)$.

In summary, we have shown that lines 4–5 are $O(1)$; line 6 is $O(mp)$; lines 7–16 are $O(mnp)$; and line 17 is $O(mp)$. Therefore, the running time of the canonical matrix multiplication algorithm is $O(mnp)$.

## Exercises

**4.1**

    **a.** How much space does the **Array\<T>** class declared in Program 4.1 use for an array of integers of length $N$?

    **b.** How much space does the **LinkedList\<T>** class declared in Program 4.9 use to store a list of $n$ integers?

    **c.** For what value of $N/n$ do the two classes use the same amount of space?

**4.2** The array subscripting operators defined in Program 4.7 only test whether **offset** $\geq$ **length**, but do not test whether **offset** $< 0$. Explain why the second test is not required in this implementation.

**4.3** The **SetBase** member function of the **Array\<T>** class defined in Program 4.6 simply changes the value of the **base** member variable. As a result, after the base is changed, all the array elements appear to have moved. How might the routine be modified so that the elements of the array don't change their apparent locations when the base is changed?

**4.4** Write the C++ code for the assignment operator of the **Array\<T>** class declared in Program 4.1.

**4.5** Which routines are affected if we drop the **tail** member variable from the **LinkedList\<T>** class declared in Program 4.9? Determine new running times for the affected routines.

**4.6** How does the implementation of the **Prepend** function of the **LinkedList\<T>** class defined in Program 4.15 change when a circular list with a sentinel is used as shown in Figure 4.2(*c*).

**4.7** How does the implementation of the **Append** function of the **LinkedList\<T>** class defined in Program 4.16 change when a circular list with a sentinel is used as shown in Figure 4.2(*c*).

**4.8** Consider the assignment operator for the **LinkedList<T>** class given in Program 4.17. What is the purpose of the test **&linkedlist != this** on line 15?

**4.9** Equation 4.1 is only correct if the subscript ranges in each dimension start at zero. How does the formula change when each dimension is allowed to have an arbitrary subscript range?

**4.10** The alternative to *row-major* layout of of multidimensional arrays is called *column-major order*. In column-major layout the left-most subscript expression increases fastest. For example, the elements of the columns of a two-dimensional matrix end up stored in contiguous memory locations. Modify Equation 4.1 to compute the correct address for column-major layout.

**4.11** We wish to add an **operator+** member function to the **Matrix<T>** class declared in Program 4.22 that does the usual matrix addition. Write the C++ code for this member function.

# Programming Projects

**4.1** Complete the implementation of the **Array<T>** class declared in Program 4.1. Write a test suite to verify all of the functionality. Try to exercise every line of code in the implementation.

**4.2** Complete the implementation of the **LinkedList<T>** class declared in Program 4.9. Write a test suite to verify all of the functionality. Try to exercise every line of code in the implementation.

**4.3** Change the implementation of the **LinkedList<T>** class declared in Program 4.9 by removing the **tail** member variable, that is, implement the singly-linked list variant shown in Figure 4.2(*a*). Write a test suite to verify all of the functionality. Try to exercise every line of code in the implementation.

**4.4** Change the implementation of the **LinkedList<T>** class declared in Program 4.9 so that it uses a circular, singly-linked list with a sentinel as shown in Figure 4.2(*c*). Write a test suite to verify all of the functionality. Try to exercise every line of code in the implementation.

**4.5** The **Array2D<T>** class declared in Program 4.20 only supports subscript ranges starting at zero. Modify the implementation to allow an arbitrary subscript base in each dimension.

**4.6** Design an implement a three-dimensional array class **Array3D<T>** based on the two-dimensional class **Array2D<T>** declared in Program 4.20.

**4.7** A row vector is a $1 \times n$ matrix and a column vector is an $n \times 1$ matrix. Define and implement classes **RowVector<T>** and **ColumnVector<T>** as classes derived from the base class **Array2D<T>**.

# 5 | Data Types and Abstraction

It is said that "computer science is [the] science of *abstraction*[2]." But what exactly is abstraction? Abstraction is "the idea of a quality thought of apart from any particular object or real thing having that quality"[9]. For example, we can think about the size of an object without knowing what that object is. Similarly, we can think about the way a car is driven without knowing its model or make.

Abstraction is used to suppress irrelevant details while at the same time emphasizing relevant ones. The benefit of abstraction is that it makes it easier for the programmer to think about the problem to be solved.

## 5.1 Abstract Data Types

A variable in a procedural programming language such as Fortran, Pascal, C, and C++ is an abstraction. The abstraction comprises a number of *attributes*—name, address, value, lifetime, scope, type, and size. Each attribute has an associated value. For example, if we declare an integer variable in C++, `int x`, we say that the name attribute has value `"x"` and that the type attribute has value `"int"`.

Unfortunately, the terminology can be somewhat confusing: The word "value" has two different meanings—in one instance it denotes one of the attributes, and in the other it denotes the quantity assigned to an attribute. For example, after the assignment statement `x = 5`, the *value attribute* has the *value* five.

The *name* of a variable is the textual label used to refer to that variable in the text of the source program. The *address* of a variable denotes is location in memory. The *value* attribute is the quantity which that variable represents.[1] The *lifetime* of a variable is

---

[1]The *address* attribute is sometimes called its *l-value* and the *value* attribute is sometimes called its *r-value*. This terminology arises from considering the semantics of an assignment statement such as `y = x`. The meaning of such a statement is "take the *value* of variable `x` and store it in memory at the *address* of variable `y`." So, when a variable appears on the right-hand side of an assignment, we use its r-value; and when it appears on the left-hand side, we use its l-value.

the interval of time during the execution of the program in which the variable is said to exist. The *scope* of a variable is the set of statements in the text of the source program in which the variable is said to be *visible*. The *type* of a variable denotes the set of values which can be assigned to the *value* attribute and the set of operations which can be performed on the variable. Finally, the *size* attribute denotes the amount of storage required to represent the variable.

The process of assigning a value to an attribute is called *binding*. When a value is assigned to an attribute, that attribute is said to be *bound* to the value. Depending on the semantics of the programming language, and on the attribute in question, the binding may be done statically by the compiler or dynamically at run time. For example, in C++ the *type* of a variable is determined at compile time—*static binding*. On the other hand, the *value* of a variable is usually not determined until run time—*dynamic binding*.

In this chapter we are concerned primarily with the *type* attribute of a variable. The type of a variable specifies two sets:

- a set of values
- a set of operations

For example, when we declare a variable, say $x$, of type `int`, we know that $x$ can represent an integer in the range $[-2^{31}, 2^{31} - 1]$ (assuming 32-bit integers) and that we can perform operations on $x$ such as addition, subtraction, multiplication, and division.

The type `int` is an *abstract data type* in the sense that we can think about the qualities of an `int` apart from any real thing having that quality. In other words, we don't need to know *how* `int`s are represented nor how the operations are implemented to be able to use them or reason about them.

In designing *object-oriented* programs, one of the primary concerns of the programmer is to develop an appropriate collection of abstractions for the application at hand, and then to define suitable abstract data types to represent those abstractions. In so doing, the programmer must be conscious of the fact that defining an abstract data type requires the specification of *both* a set of values and a set of operations on those values.

Indeed, it has been only since the advent of the so-called *object-oriented programming languages* that the we see programming languages which provide the necessary constructs to properly declare abstract data types. For example, in C++, the `class` construct is the means by which both a set of values and an associated set of operations are declared. Compare this with the `struct` construct of C or Pascal's `record`, which only allows the specification of a set of values!

## 5.2  Design Patterns

An experienced programmer is like a concert musician—she has mastered a certain *repertoire* of pieces which she is prepared to play at any time. For the programmer, the repertoire comprises a set of abstract data types with which she is familiar and which she is able to use in her programs as the need arises.

The chapters following this present a basic repertoire of abstract data types. In addition to defining the abstractions, we show how to implement them in C++ and we analyze the performance of the algorithms.

The repertoire of basic abstract data types has been designed as a hierarchy of C++ classes. This section presents an overview of the class hierarchy and lays the groundwork for the following chapters.

## 5.2.1   Class Hierarchy

The C++ class hierarchy which is used to represent the basic repertoire of abstract data types is shown in Figure 5.1. Two kinds of classes are shown in Figure 5.1; *abstract C++ classes,* which look like this **Abstract Class** , and *concrete C++ classes,* which look like this Concrete Class . Lines in the figure indicate derivation; base classes always appear to the left of derived classes.

An *abstract class* is a class which specifies an *interface* only. It is not possible to create object instances of abstract classes. In C++ an abstract class typically has one or more *pure virtual member functions*. A *pure* virtual member function declares an interface only—there is no implementation defined. In effect, the interface specifies the set of operations without specifying the implementation.

An abstract class is intended to be used a the *base class* from which other classes are *derived*. Declaring the member functions *virtual* makes it possible to access the implementations provided by the derived classes through the base class interface. Consequently, we don't need to know how a particular object instance is implemented, nor do we need to know of which derived class it is an instance.

This design pattern uses the idea of *polymorphism*. Polymorphism literally means "having many forms." The essential idea is that a single, common abstraction is used to define the set of values and the set of operations—the abstract data type. This interface is embodied in the C++ abstract class definition. Then, various different implementations (*many forms*) of the abstract data type can be made. This is done in C++ by deriving concrete classes from the abstract base class.

The remainder of this section presents the top levels of the class hierarchy which are shown in Figure 5.2. The top levels define those attributes of objects which are common to all the classes in the hierarchy. The lower levels of the hierarchy (i.e., those derived from the **Container** class) are presented in subsequent chapters where the abstractions are defined and various implementations of those abstractions are elaborated.

## 5.2.2   Objects

The abstract class at the top of the class hierarchy is called **Object**. With the exception of the **Ownership** class, all the other classes in the hierarchy are derived from this class. Program 5.1 gives the declaration of the **Object** class. Altogether only six member functions are declared: the destructor, **IsNull**, **Hash**, **Put**, **Compare**, and **CompareTo**.

**FIGURE 5.1**
Object class hierarchy.

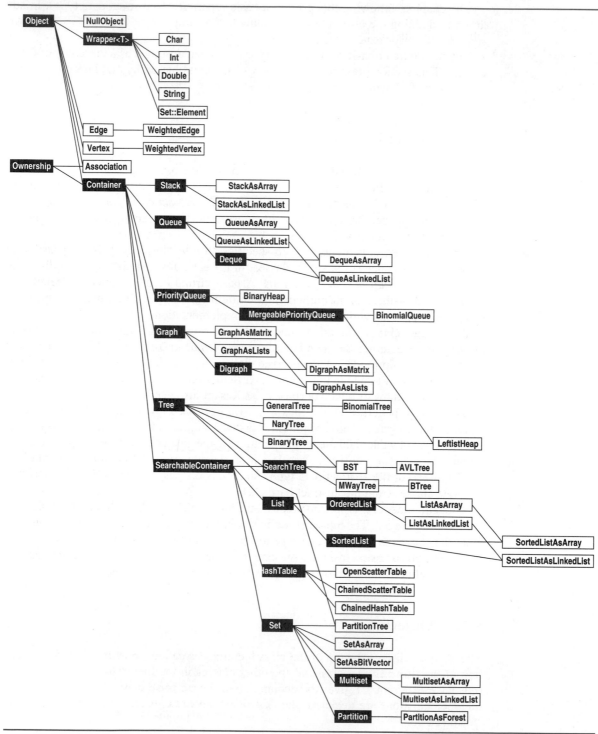

**FIGURE 5.2**
Object class hierarchy.

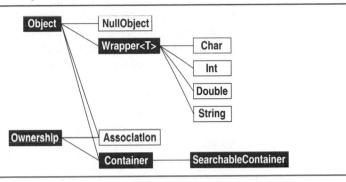

**PROGRAM 5.1**
Object class definition

```
 1   class Object
 2   {
 3   protected:
 4        virtual int CompareTo (Object const&) const = 0;
 5   public:
 6        virtual ~Object ();
 7        virtual bool IsNull () const;
 8        virtual int Compare (Object const&) const;
 9        virtual HashValue Hash () const = 0;
10        virtual void Put (ostream&) const = 0;
11   };
```

The **Object** class destructor is declared **virtual**. It is essential to declare it so, because **Object** is an abstract class, and instances of derived class objects are very likely to be accessed through the base class interface. In particular, it is necessary for the destructor of the derived class to be called through the base class interface—this is precisely what the **virtual** keyword achieves.

The **IsNull** function is a pure virtual member function which returns a Boolean value. This function is used in conjunction with the **NullObject** concrete class described in Section 5.2.3. The **IsNull** function shall return **false** for all object instances derived from **Object** except if the object instance is the **NullObject**. We will see later that certain functions return object references. For example, a function which searches through a data structure for a particular object returns a reference to that object if it is found. If the object is not found, the search returns a reference to the **NullObject** instance. By using the **IsNull** function, the programmer can test whether the search was successful. This is analogous to the **NULL** pointer in the C programming language and to the pointer value **0** in C++.

The **Hash** function is a pure virtual member function which returns a **HashValue**. The **Hash** function is used in the implementation of hash tables which are discussed in Chapter 8. We have put the **Hash** function in the **Object** class interface, so that it is possible to store any object derived from **Object** in a hash table. What the **Hash** function computes is unspecified. The only requirement is that it is *idempotent;* that is, given an object instance **obj**, **obj.Hash()** does not modify the object in any way, and as long as **obj** is not modified in the interim, repeated calls always give exactly the same result.

Two functions for comparing objects are declared—**Compare** and **CompareTo**. **Compare** is a public member function that takes a **const** reference to **Object** and returns an **int**. Given two objects **obj1** and **obj2**, calling **obj1.Compare (obj2)** *compares* the value of **obj1** with the value of **obj2**. The result is equal to zero if **obj1=obj2**; less than zero if **obj1<obj2**; and, greater than zero if **obj1>obj2**.

It is not necessary that the two objects compared using **Compare** have the same type. As long as they are instances of classes derived from **Object**, they can be compared. The **Compare** function is used in the overloading of the comparison operators **operator==, operator!=, operator<, operator<=, operator>**, and **operator>=**, as shown in Program 5.2.

The second comparison function, **CompareTo**, is a pure virtual function. An implementation for this function must be given in every concrete class derived from **Object**.

---

**PROGRAM 5.2**
Object operator definitions

---

```
1   inline bool operator == (Object const& left, Object const& right)
2       { return left.Compare (right) == 0; }
3
4   inline bool operator != (Object const& left, Object const& right)
5       { return left.Compare (right) != 0; }
6
7   inline bool operator <= (Object const& left, Object const& right)
8       { return left.Compare (right) <= 0; }
9
10  inline bool operator < (Object const& left, Object const& right)
11      { return left.Compare (right) < 0; }
12
13  inline bool operator >= (Object const& left, Object const& right)
14      { return left.Compare (right) >= 0; }
15
16  inline bool operator > (Object const& left, Object const& right)
17      { return left.Compare (right) > 0; }
18
19  inline ostream& operator << (ostream& s, Object const& object)
20      { object.Put (s); return s; }
```

---

The purpose of this function is to compare two objects that are both instances of the same derived class.

The purpose of the **Put** member function of the **Object** class is to output a human-readable representation of the object on the specified output stream. The **Put** function is a pure virtual function. However, since it has the side effect of output, it is not strictly idempotent. Nevertheless, it is a **const** member function which means that calling the **Put** member function does not modify the object in any way. The use of the **Put** in the overloading of the **ostream** insertion operator, **operator<<**, is shown in Program 5.2.

The use of polymorphism in the way shown gives the programmer enormous leverage. The fact that almost all objects will be derived from the **Object** base class, together with the fact that the **Put** and **CompareTo** member functions are virtual functions, ensures that the overloaded operators work as we expect for all derived class instances.

### Implementation

Only three functions need to be implemented to complete the definition of the **Object** class. These are shown in Program 5.3.

The **Object** class destructor is trivial. Since there are no member variables, nothing remains to be cleaned up. It is necessary to define the destructor in any event. As explained above, the destructor needs to be **virtual** because in C++ there is no such thing as a pure virtual destructor.

The implementation of the **IsNull** member function is trivial. It simply returns the Boolean value **false**.

---

**PROGRAM 5.3**
**Object** class member function definitions

```
1   #include <typeinfo>
2
3   Object::~Object ()
4       {}
5
6   bool Object::IsNull () const
7       { return false; }
8
9   int Object::Compare (Object const& object) const
10  {
11      if (typeid (*this) == typeid (object))
12          return CompareTo (object);
13      else if (typeid (*this).before (typeid (object)))
14          return -1;
15      else
16          return 1;
17  }
```

---

The `Compare` member function makes use of *run-time type information* to ensure that the `CompareTo` member function is only invoked for objects which are of the same class. For objects which are not instances of the same class, the `before` function is used to order those objects based on their types. The C++ run-time library provides an implementation for the `before` function which returns true if the left-hand type precedes the right-hand type in the implementation's collation order.

### 5.2.3 The `NullObject` Singleton Class

The declaration of the `NullObject` class is given in Program 5.4. The `NullObject` class is a concrete class derived from the `Object` abstract base class. The `NullObject` class is also a *singleton* class, that is, it is a class of which there will only ever be exactly one instance. The one instance is in fact a static member variable of the class itself. In order to ensure that no other instances can be created, the default constructor is declared to be a private member function. The static member function `Instance` returns a reference to the one and only `NullObject` instance.

**Implementation**

Program 5.5 shows how the member functions of the `NullObject` class are defined. The most important characteristic of the `NullObject` class is that its `IsNull` member function returns the value `true`.

The remaining functions are trivial: The constructor does nothing; the two member functions `Hash` and `CompareTo` both return zero; and the `Put` function simply prints "`NullObject`". Finally, the `Instance` static member function returns a reference to the static member variable `instance` which is the one and only instance of the `NullObject` class.

### 5.2.4 Object Wrappers for the Built-In Types

One of the design goals of the C++ language is to treat user-defined data types and the built-in data types as equally as possible. However, the built-in data types of C++ do have one shortcoming with respect to user-defined ones—a built-in data type cannot be used as the base class from which other classes are derived. For example, it is not possible to write:

```
class D : public int // Wrong!
```

Consequently, it is not possible to extend the functionality of a built-in type using inheritance.

The usual design pattern for dealing with this deficiency is to put instances of the built-in types inside a *wrapper* class and to use the wrapped objects in place of the built-in types. Program 5.6 illustrates this idea. The class `Wrapper<T>` is a concrete class which is derived from the abstract base class `Object`. It is also a generic class, the purpose of which is to encapsulate an object of type `T`. Each instance of the `Wrapper<T>` class contains a single member variable of type `T` called `datum`.

**PROGRAM 5.4**
NullObject class definition

```
1   class NullObject : public Object
2   {
3       static NullObject instance;
4
5       NullObject ();
6   protected:
7       int CompareTo (Object const&) const;
8   public:
9       bool IsNull () const;
10      HashValue Hash () const;
11      void Put (ostream& s) const;
12
13      static NullObject& Instance ();
14  };
```

**PROGRAM 5.5**
NullObject class member function definitions

```
1   NullObject NullObject::instance;
2
3   NullObject::NullObject ()
4       {}
5
6   bool NullObject::IsNull () const
7       { return true; }
8
9   int NullObject::CompareTo (Object const&) const
10      { return 0; }
11
12  HashValue NullObject::Hash () const
13      { return 0; }
14
15  void NullObject::Put (ostream& s) const
16      { s << "NullObject"; }
17
18  NullObject& NullObject::Instance ()
19      { return instance; }
```

**PROGRAM 5.6**
Wrapper<T> class definition

```
1   template <class T>
2   class Wrapper : public Object
3   {
4   protected:
5       T datum;
6
7       int CompareTo (Object const&) const;
8   public:
9       Wrapper ();
10      Wrapper (T const&);
11      Wrapper& operator = (T const&);
12      operator T const& () const;
13      HashValue Hash () const;
14      void Put (ostream&) const;
15  };
```

**Implementation**

The implementation of the Wrapper<T> class member functions is shown in Program 5.7. The Wrapper<T> class default constructor simply initializes the member variable datum using its default constructor. A second constructor takes as its lone argument a const reference to an object of type T and copies that value to the member variable datum. In effect, the constructor *wraps* its argument.

A type-cast operator is defined, operator T const&, which converts from an object of type Wrapper<T> to a const reference to an object of type T. In effect, the type-cast operator *unwraps* the contained object! This, together with the automatic type coercion rules of C++, makes it possible to use the wrapped object in the same context in which the unwrapped object is expected.

The Hash member function of the Wrapper<T> class simply calls the global (nonmember) function, ::Hash(T). In effect, we have punted on the implementation of the Hash function. The implementation of a suitable hash function for an object of type T depends on the actual type used. However, the Wrapper<T> class is generic—we don't know what T is. Hash functions are discussed in Chapter 8.

The CompareTo function takes as its lone argument a const reference to Object. It uses the dynamic_cast operator to convert the argument to the type Wrapper<T>. In C++, the dynamic cast will succeed only if the type of the referenced actually is Wrapper<T>. Otherwise a bad_cast exception is thrown. The CompareTo member function is implemented in the same way as the Hash member function, that is, it calls the global (nonmember) function ::Compare to do the actual comparison.

The implementation of the Put member function is trivial. It simply inserts datum into the given ostream using operator<<. Again, this assumes that the operator has already been defined for objects of type T.

---

**PROGRAM 5.7**

`Wrapper<T>` class member function definitions

---

```
1   template <class T>
2   Wrapper<T>::Wrapper () :
3       datum ()
4       {}
5
6   template <class T>
7   Wrapper<T>::Wrapper (T const& d) :
8       datum (d)
9       {}
10
11  template <class T>
12  Wrapper<T>& Wrapper<T>::operator = (T const& d)
13  {
14      datum = d;
15      return *this;
16  }
17
18  template <class T>
19  Wrapper<T>::operator T const& () const
20      { return datum; }
21
22  template <class T>
23  int Wrapper<T>::CompareTo (Object const& obj) const
24  {
25      Wrapper<T> const& arg =
26          dynamic_cast<Wrapper<T> const&> (obj);
27      return ::Compare (datum, arg.datum);
28  }
29
30  template <class T>
31  void Wrapper<T>::Put (ostream& s) const
32      { s << datum; }
```

---

Program 5.8 uses the `Wrapper<T>` class defined above to define the `Int`, `Char`, `Double`, and `String` object classes which simply encapsulate variables of type `int`, `char`, `double`, and `string`, respectively.

These declarations require the existence of suitable `::Compare` and `::Hash` functions. For example, the `Int` class definition requires the existence of a `Compare (int,int)` and a `Hash(int)` function. Hash functions are described in Chapter 8. The implementation of a suitable compare function is left as a project for the reader (Project 5.1).

**PROGRAM 5.8**
Int, Char, Double and String class definitions

```
1   typedef Wrapper<int> Int;
2   typedef Wrapper<char> Char;
3   typedef Wrapper<double> Double;
4   typedef Wrapper<std::string> String;
```

### 5.2.5 Containers

The **Container** class abstracts the notion of a container—an object that holds within it other objects. A container is itself an object. Therefore, the **Container** class is derived from the **Object** class. A consequence of this is that containers can be held in other containers!

The declaration of the **Container** class is given in Program 5.9. Notice that the **Container** declaration uses *multiple inheritance*. It is derived from two base classes, **Object** and **Ownership**. We have already seen the definition of the **Object** class. The **Ownership** class is defined in Section 5.2.10.

The **Container** class is an *abstract base class*. It is intended to be used as the base class from which concrete container realizations are derived. The **Container** class public interface comprises eight virtual member functions—**Count**, **IsEmpty**, **IsFull**, **Hash**, **Put**, **NewIterator**, **Purge**, and **Accept**. Default implementations are provided for the first six; the last two are pure virtual member functions.

**PROGRAM 5.9**
Container class definition

```
1   class Container : public virtual Object, public virtual Ownership
2   {
3   protected:
4       unsigned int count;
5
6       Container ();
7   public:
8       virtual unsigned int Count () const;
9       virtual bool IsEmpty () const;
10      virtual bool IsFull () const;
11      virtual HashValue Hash () const;
12      virtual void Put (ostream&) const;
13      virtual Iterator& NewIterator () const;
14
15      virtual void Purge () = 0;
16      virtual void Accept (Visitor&) const = 0;
17  };
```

A single member variable, `count`, is declared. This variable is used to keep track of the number of objects held in the container. The `count` field is set initially to zero. It is the responsibility of the derived class to update this field as required.

The `Count` member function is an accessor that returns the number of items contained in the container. The `IsEmpty` and `IsFull` functions are Boolean-valued accessors which indicate whether a given container is empty or full, respectively. The `Hash` function is used in conjunction with hash tables as discussed in Chapter 8 and the `Put` function inserts a human-readable representation of the container and its contents in a specified output stream. The purpose of the `Purge` function is to remove all the objects from a container, making it empty.

In order to describe the remaining two member functions, `Accept` and `New-Iterator`, we need to become familiar first with the concepts of a visitor and an iterator, as well as with the `Visitor` and `Iterator` classes which embody these concepts. Visitors are discussed in Section 5.2.6, and iterators are discussed in Section 5.2.7.

Program 5.10 gives code that defines the `Container` class constructor as well as the default behaviors for several of the member functions. The three functions `Count`, `IsEmpty`, and `IsFull` are member variable accessors—they are idempotent `const` member functions which provide information about the status of the container.

The `Count` function simply returns the value of the `count` member variable. The `IsEmpty` function is a Boolean valued accessor which returns the value `true` if the container is empty, i.e., it contains no objects. Notice that the `IsEmpty` function does not directly access the `count` field; instead it calls `Count`, which is a virtual function.

In some cases, a container is implemented in a way which makes its capacity finite. When this is the case, it is necessary to be able to determine when the container is full. The `IsFull` function is a Boolean-valued accessor which returns the value `true` if the container is full. However, the default version always returns `false`.

---

**PROGRAM 5.10**
`Container` class member function definitions

---

```
1   Container::Container () :
2       count (0)
3       {}
4
5   unsigned int Container::Count () const
6       { return count; }
7
8   bool Container::IsEmpty () const
9       { return Count () == 0; }
10
11  bool Container::IsFull () const
12      { return false; }
```

---

Default behaviors are also provided by the **Container** class for the **Hash** and **Put** operations. The implementation of the **Put** function is discussed in the following section. The **Hash** function is given in Chapter 8.

### 5.2.6 Visitors

The **Container** class described in the preceding section interacts closely with the **Visitor** class shown in Program 5.11. In particular, the **Accept** member function of the **Container** class takes as its lone argument a reference to a **Visitor**.

But what is a visitor? As shown in Program 5.11, a visitor is an object that has the two member functions **Visit** and **IsDone**. Of these, the **Visit** function is the most interesting. The **Visit** function takes as its lone argument a reference to an **Object** instance.

The interaction between a container and a visitor goes like this. The container is passed a reference to a visitor by calling the container's **Accept** member function. That is, the container "accepts" the visitor. What does a container do with a visitor? It calls the **Visit** member function of that visitor one-by-one for each object contained in the container.

The interaction between a **Container** and its **Visitor** is best understood by considering an example. The following code fragment gives the design framework for the implementation of the **Accept** function in some concrete class, say **SomeContainer**, which is derived from the abstract base class **Container**:

```
void SomeContainer::Accept (Visitor& visitor) const
{
    for each Object i in this container
    {
        visitor.Visit (i);
    }
}
```

The **Accept** function calls **Visit** for each object i in the container. Since the class **Visitor** is an abstract base class which does not provide an implementation for the

---

**PROGRAM 5.11**
**Visitor** class definition

---

```
1  class Visitor
2  {
3  public:
4      virtual void Visit (Object&) = 0;
5      virtual bool IsDone () const
6          { return false; }
7  };
```

`Visit` operation, what the visitor actually does with an object depends on the type of visitor used.

Suppose that we want to print all of the objects in the container. One way to do this is to create a `PrintingVisitor` which prints every object it visits, and then to pass the visitor to the container by calling the `Accept` member function. The following code shows how we can declare the `PrintingVisitor` class which prints an object on the standard output stream, `cout`.

```
class PrintingVisitor : public Visitor
{
public:
    void Visit (object& object)
        { cout << object; }
};
```

Finally, given a container `c` that is an instance of a concrete container class `Some-Container` which is derived from the abstract base class `Container`, we can call the `Accept` function as follows:

```
SomeContainer c;
PrintingVisitor v;
c.Accept (v);
```

The effect of this call is to call the `Visit` member function of the visitor for each object in the container.

### The `IsDone` Member Function

As shown in Program 5.11, the `Visitor` class interface also includes the member function `IsDone`. The `IsDone` member function is an accessor which is used to determine whether a visitor has finished its work. That is, the `IsDone` member function returns the boolean value `true` if the visitor "is done."

The idea is this: Sometimes a visitor does not need to visit all the objects in a container. That is, in some cases, the visitor may have finished its task after having visited only some of the objects. The `IsDone` member function can be used by the container to terminate the `Accept` function like this:

```
void SomeContainer::Accept (Visitor& visitor) const
{
    for each Object i in this container
    {
        if (visitor.IsDone ())
            return;
        visitor.Visit (i);
    }
}
```

To illustrate the usefulness of **IsDone**, consider a visitor which visits the objects in a container with the purpose of finding the first object that matches a given object. Having found the first matching object in the container, the visitor is done and does not need to visit any more contained objects.

The following code fragment defines a visitor which finds the first object in the container that matches a given object.

```
class MatchingVisitor : public Visitor
{
    Object const& target;
    Object* found;
public:
    MatchingVisitor (Object const& object) :
        target (object), found (0)
        {}
    void Visit (Object& object)
    {
        if (found == 0 && object == target)
            found = &object;
    }
    bool IsDone ()
        { return found != 0; }
};
```

The constructor of the **MatchingVisitor** visitor takes a reference to an **Object** instance that is the target of the search. That is, we wish to find an object in a container that matches the target. For each object the **MatchingVisitor** visitor visits, it compares that object with the target and makes **found** point at that object if it matches. Clearly, the **MatchingVisitor** visitor is done when the **found** pointer is nonzero.

Suppose we have a container **c** that is an instance of a concrete container class, **SomeContainer**, which is derived from the abstract base class **Container**; and an object **x** that is an instance of a concrete object class, **SomeObject**, which is derived from the abstract base class **Object**. Then, we can use the **MatchingVisitor** visitor as follows:

```
SomeContainer c;
SomeObject x;
MatchingVisitor v (x);
c.Accept (v);
```

The observant reader will have noticed in Program 5.11 that the **Visit** member function of the abstract **Visitor** class is a *pure* virtual function, whereas the **IsDone** function is not. It turns out that it is convenient to define a default implementation for the **IsDone** function that always returns **false**.

### Container Class Default `Put` Member Function

Program 5.12 gives the definition of the default `Put` function for containers. Recall that the `Put` function is a virtual function inherited by the `Container` class from the abstract base class `Object`. A default `Put` function is provided to simplify the implementation of classes derived from the `Container` class. The default behavior is to print out the name of the class and then to print each of the elements in the container, by using the `Accept` member function with the visitor `PuttingVisitor`.

This implementation makes use of *run-time type information* to determine the name of the class. The C++ operator `typeid` returns a reference to an instance of the `type_info` class which is defined in the standard header file `typeinfo`. This class has member function, `name()`, which returns a pointer to a character string that contains the name of the class.

---

**PROGRAM 5.12**
`Container` class `Put` function definition

---

```
1   # include <typeinfo>
2
3   class PuttingVisitor : public Visitor
4   {
5       ostream& stream;
6       bool comma;
7   public:
8       PuttingVisitor (ostream& s) : stream (s), comma (false)
9           {}
10      void Visit (Object& object)
11      {
12          if (comma)
13              stream << ", ";
14          stream << object;
15          comma = true;
16      }
17  };
18
19  void Container::Put (ostream& s) const
20  {
21      PuttingVisitor visitor (s);
22
23      s << typeid (*this).name () << " {";
24      Accept (visitor);
25      s << "}";
26  }
```

---

### 5.2.7 Iterators

In this section we introduce an abstraction called an *iterator*. An iterator provides a means for visiting one-by-one all the objects in a container. Iterators are an alternative to using the visitors described in Section 5.2.6. The basic idea is that for every concrete container class we will also implement a related concrete iterator derived from an abstract **Iterator** class.

Program 5.13 gives the declaration of the abstract **Iterator** class. It defines an interface comprised of a virtual destructor and four pure virtual member functions—**Reset, IsDone** and two overloaded operators.

The **Iterator** class is intended to be used as the base class from which other classes are derived in a polymorphic class hierarchy. Consequently, the destructor is declared as a virtual member function. Since the **Iterator** class is an abstract class which has no member variables, the behavior of the destructor trivial—it does nothing.

In addition to the destructor, the **Iterator** class interface comprises the **Reset** and **IsDone** functions and two overloaded operators—**operator*** and **operator++**. In order to understand the desired semantics, it is best to consider first an example which illustrates the use of an iterator.

Consider the implementation of a concrete container class, say **SomeContainer**, which is derived from the abstract base class **Container**. Associated with this container class is a concrete iterator, say **SomeIterator**, which is derived from the abstract base class **Iterator**. The following code fragment serves to illustrate the use of the iterator to visit one-by-one the objects contained in the container:

```
SomeContainer c;
Iterator& i = c.NewIterator ();
while (!i.IsDone ()) {
    cout << *i << endl;
    ++i;
}
delete &i;
```

**PROGRAM 5.13**
**Iterator** class definition

```
1   class Iterator
2   {
3   public:
4       virtual ~Iterator ();
5       virtual void Reset () = 0;
6       virtual bool IsDone () const = 0;
7       virtual Object& operator * () const = 0;
8       virtual void operator ++ () = 0;
9   };
```

The **NewIterator** function of the **SomeContainer** class is defined as follows:

```
Iterator& SomeContainer::NewIterator () const
    { return *new SomeIterator (*this); }
```

That is, given an instance **c** of **SomeContainer**, the call

```
c.NewIterator ();
```

results in the creation of a new instance of **SomeIterator** associated with container **c**.

In order to have the desired effect, the member functions **IsDone, operator\*,** and **operator++**, must have the following behaviors:

IsDone   The IsDone member function is called in the loop-termination test of the **while** statement. The **IsDone** function returns **false** if the iterator still refers to an object in the container, and **true** when the container has been exhausted. That is, if all of the contained objects have been visited.

operator\*   The pointer dereferencing operator, **operator\***, is used to access the object to which the iterator currently refers. If this function is called when the container has been exhausted, a reference to the **NullObject** instance is returned.

operator++   The pre-increment operator is used to advance the iterator to the next object in the container. If the container is exhausted, the increment operator has no effect on the iterator.

Given these semantics for the iterator operators, the program fragment shown above systematically visits all of the objects in the container and prints each one on its own line of the standard output file.

After an iterator has exhausted all the contained objects, it can be reset via the **Reset** function and used again like this:

```
Iterator& i = c.NewIterator ();
while (!i.IsDone ()) {
    cout << *i << endl;
    ++i;
}
i.Reset ()
while (!i.IsDone ()) {
    cout << *i << endl;
    ++i;
}
delete &i;
```

One of the advantages of using an iterator object which is separate from the container is that it is possible then to have more than one iterator associated with a given container. This provides greater flexibility than possible using a visitor, since only one visitor can be accepted by the container at any given time. For example, consider the following code fragment:

```
SomeContainer c;
Iterator& i = c.NewIterator ();
while (!i.IsDone ()) {
    Iterator& j = c.NewIterator ();
    while (!j.IsDone ()) {
        if (*i == *j)
            cout << *i << endl;
        ++j
    }
    delete &j;
    ++i;
}
delete &i;
```

This code compares all pairs of objects, $(i, j)$, in the container and prints out those which are equal.

A certain amount of care is required when defining and using iterators. In order to simplify the implementation of iterators, we shall assume that while an iterator is in use, the associated container will not be modified. Specifically, this means that no non-**const** member function of the associated container may be called. In particular, this also means that the container must not be deleted while an iterator is in use!

### 5.2.8 The NullIterator Class

A **NullIterator** is a concrete iterator that does nothing. As discussed in Section 5.2.5, every container has a **NewIterator** member function that returns a reference to an iterator instance. If a particular concrete container class does not provide an

---

**PROGRAM 5.14**
**NullIterator** class definition

```
1   class NullIterator : public Iterator
2   {
3   public:
4       NullIterator ();
5       void Reset ();
6       bool IsDone () const;
7       Object& operator * () const;
8       void operator ++ ();
9   };
```

---

associated iterator class, its **NewIterator** member function returns a reference to a **NullIterator**. Program 5.14 gives the declaration of the **NullIterator** class.

Because it is a concrete class, **NullIterator** provides implementations for all the pure virtual member functions of the **Iterator** class. As shown in Program 5.15, the implementation is trivial: The **IsDone** member function always returns **true**; the **operator\*** member function always returns a reference to the **NullObject** instance; and the remaining functions do nothing at all.

The default behavior of the **NewIterator** function of the **Container** class is to return a reference to a new **NullIterator** instance as shown in Program 5.16.

### 5.2.9 Direct versus Indirect Containment

The notion of a container as an object which contains other objects is introduced in Section 5.2.5. Conspicuous by their absence from the interface are member functions for putting objects into the container and for taking objects out of the container. As it turns out, the particular forms of the functions required depend on the type of container implemented. Therefore, we have left the specification of those functions for the classes which are derived from the **Container** base class.

---

**PROGRAM 5.15**
**NullIterator** class member function definitions

```
1   NullIterator::NullIterator ()
2       {}
3
4   void NullIterator::Reset ()
5       {}
6
7   bool NullIterator::IsDone () const
8       { return true; }
9
10  Object& NullIterator::operator * () const
11      { return NullObject::Instance (); }
12
13  void NullIterator::operator ++ ()
14      {}
```

---

**PROGRAM 5.16**
**Container** class **NewIterator** member function definition

```
1   Iterator& Container::NewIterator () const
2       { return *new NullIterator (); }
```

---

Another reason for leaving these matters unspecified is that we have not yet defined what it means for one object to be contained within another! We have two options:

1. **Direct containment** When an object is put into a container, a *copy* of that object is made in the container.
2. **Indirect containment** When an object is put into a container, a *pointer* to that object is kept in the container.

The main advantage of using direct containment is its simplicity. It is easy to understand and easy to implement. However, it does suffer some problems. First, if the objects which are to be put into a container are large, i.e., if they occupy a large amount of memory space, the copying of the objects is likely to be both time-consuming and space-consuming. Second, an object cannot be contained in more than one container at a time. Third, a container cannot contain itself.

The indirect containment approach addresses these three concerns. By keeping a pointer to the contained object rather than a copy of the contained object, it is not necessary to copy the object when it is put into the container—this saves time and space. By keeping pointers to the contained objects, it is possible to put a pointer to the same object into several different containers. Finally, it is possible to put the pointer to a container into the container itself.

The indirect containment approach is not without disadvantages, the principal disadvantage being that for every access to a contained object it is necessary to dereference a pointer. This adds a constant overhead to such accesses. Despite the disadvantages, the `Container` classes presented in the following chapters are all implemented using indirect containment.

## 5.2.10   Ownership of Contained Objects

A matter that is closely related to the containment of objects is the *ownership* of objects. Ownership is important because it is the owner of an object that ensures that the object's destructor is called and that any storage dynamically allocated for the object is freed when the object is no longer needed.

The ownership of contained objects is clear when direct containment is used. Since the container makes a copy of any object put into the container, it is the container that is responsible for deleting the copy when it is longer needed. In particular, the destructor for the container would normally delete all contained objects.

Unfortunately, the issue of ownership is not as clear when indirect containment is used. Indirect containment means that when an object is put into a container, it is a pointer to that object which is recorded in the container. This implies that the object was initially created outside of the container. The question then becomes, should the container delete the object when the time comes to clean up or should the deletion be done outside of the container?

If we assume that it is the responsibility of the container to delete the contained objects, then we must make sure that the only objects put into a container are objects whose storage was dynamically allocated. This is because as the owner of the object, the container must delete the object when the time comes to clean up. But, given a pointer to an object, it is not possible for the container to know whether the object to which it points has been dynamically allocated or whether it is actually a statically allocated global variable or a stack allocated local variable.

Another consequence of assigning the ownership of objects to a container is that things become complicated when an object is put into two or more different containers, as well as when a given object is put into the same container more than once. The problem is that an object inserted in more than one container has more than one owner. In order to ensure that the object is only deleted once, we would have to extract the pointer from all but one of the containers before deleting them.

On the other hand, if we assume that it is not the responsibility of the container to delete contained objects, then the responsibility to clean up falls on the user of the container. In order to ensure that all contained objects are properly deleted, it is necessary to extract all of the contained objects from a container before deleting the container itself.

The solution to this dilemma is to support both paradigms, that is, make it possible for the user of a container to specify whether that container is to be the owner of its objects. The **Ownership** class given in Program 5.17 does precisely that.

The **Ownership** class encapsulates a single Boolean variable, **isOwner**, which records whether the container is the owner of the contained objects. By default, the **isOwner** field is set to **true** in the constructor. Two member functions, **AssertOwnership** and **RescindOwnership**, provide a means for the user of a container to change the state of the **isOwner** datum. The **IsOwner** accessor reveals the current ownership status.

---

**PROGRAM 5.17**
Ownership class definition

---

```
1   class Ownership
2   {
3       bool isOwner;
4   protected:
5       Ownership () : isOwner (true)
6           {}
7       Ownership (Ownership& arg) : isOwner (arg.isOwner)
8           { arg.isOwner = false; }
9   public:
10      void AssertOwnership ()
11          { isOwner = true; }
12      void RescindOwnership ()
13          { isOwner = false; }
14      bool IsOwner () const
15          { return isOwner; }
16  };
```

---

The behavior of the copy constructor is subtle: It transfers ownership status from the original container to the copy. This behavior is useful because it simplifies the task of returning a container as the result of a function.

In its declaration in Program 5.9 we saw that the **Container** class was derived both from the **Object** base class *and* from the **Ownership** class. Therefore, all containers have ownership associated with them.

The following code fragment gives the design framework for the implementation of the **Purge** member function in some concrete class, say **SomeContainer**, which is derived from the abstract base class **Container**:

```
void SomeContainer::Purge ()
{
    if (IsOwner ())
    {
        for each Object i in this container
        {
            delete &i;
        }
    }
    Now clean up the container itself.
}
```

---

**PROGRAM 5.18**
Association class definition

---

```
1   class Association : public Object, public Ownership
2   {
3   protected:
4       Object* key;
5       Object* value;
6
7       int CompareTo (Object const&) const;
8   public:
9       Association (Object&);
10      Association (Object&, Object&);
11      ~Association ();
12
13      Object& Key () const;
14      Object& Value () const;
15
16      HashValue Hash () const;
17      void Put (ostream&) const;
18   };
```

---

The container calls its own **IsOwner** member function to determine whether it is the owner of its contained objects. Then, and only if it is the owner, the contained objects are deleted. Given the **Purge** function, the implementation of the destructor is trivial:

```
SomeContainer::~SomeContainer ()
    { Purge (); }
```

## 5.2.11 Associations

An association is an ordered pair of objects. The first element of the pair is called the *key;* the second element is the *value* associated with the given key. Associations are useful for storing information in a database for later retrieval. For example, a database can be viewed as a collection of key-and-value pairs. The information associated with a given key is retrieved from the database by searching the database for the ordered pair in which the key matches the given key.

An association is like a container in that it contains two objects—the key and the value. On the other hand, an association is fundamentally different from a container since the contained objects are treated very differently. Normally, the objects in a container are not distinguished one from another. In an association, the two contained objects are distinct—one of them is *the key* and the other is a value *associated with* the key.

Program 5.18 gives the declaration of the concrete object class **Association**. The declaration of the **Association** class is like that of the **Container** class in that both of them are derived from the same set of base classes—**Object** and **Ownership**.

An association has two member variables, **key** and **value**, both of which are of type *pointer* to **Object**. Since pointers are used, the **Association** class implements *indirect containment.*

### Implementation

Two constructors and the destructor are defined in Program 5.19. The first constructor takes as its lone argument a reference to an **Object**. It makes the **key** member variable point at the specified object and sets the **value** pointer to zero. The second constructor takes two arguments—both of them a reference to an **Object**. The **key** and **value** member variables are made to point at the corresponding objects.

The destructor follows the general framework for the destructor of a class derived from **Ownership**. If the association is the owner of the contained key and value, then those objects must be deleted by the destructor.

The remaining member functions of the **Association** class are defined in Program 5.20. The first two, **Key** and **Value**, are member variable accessors. The former returns a reference to the key object obtained by dereferencing the **key** member variable; the latter, a reference to the value object obtained by dereferencing the **value** member variable.

The **CompareTo** function is one place where an association distinguishes between the key and the value. The **CompareTo** function only operates on the key. The

---

**PROGRAM 5.19**
`Association` class constructor and destructor

---

```
1   Association::Association (Object& _key) :
2       key (&_key),
3       value (0)
4       {}
5
6   Association::Association (Object& _key, Object& _value) :
7       key (&_key),
8       value (&_value)
9       {}
10
11  Association::~Association ()
12  {
13      if (IsOwner ())
14      {
15          delete key;
16          delete value;
17      }
18  }
```

---

`CompareTo` function takes as its lone argument a `const` reference to `Object`. It uses the `dynamic_cast` operator to convert the argument to an `Association`. The result of the comparison is based solely on the keys of the objects—the values have no rôle in the comparison.

Finally, the purpose of the `Put` member function is to print out a representation of the association. The implementation is trivial and needs no further explanation.

### 5.2.12 Searchable Containers

A *searchable container* is an extension of the container abstraction. It adds to the interface provided for containers functions for putting objects in and taking objects out, for testing whether a given object is in the container, and a routine to search the container for a given object.

The declaration of the `SearchableContainer` class is shown in Program 5.21. The `SearchableContainer` class is an abstract class derived from the abstract base class `Container`. It adds four more pure virtual member functions to the inherited abstract interface.

The `IsMember` function is a Boolean-valued function which takes as its lone argument a `const` reference to `Object`. The purpose of this routine is to test whether the given object instance is in the container. In effect, the routine searches the container for a pointer to the given object.

**PROGRAM 5.20**
Association class member functions

```
1   Object& Association::Key () const
2       { return *key; }
3
4   Object& Association::Value () const
5   {
6       if (value == 0)
7           return NullObject::Instance ();
8       else
9           return *value;
10  }
11
12  int Association::CompareTo (Object const& object) const
13  {
14      Association const& association =
15          dynamic_cast<Association const&> (object);
16      return Key ().Compare (association.Key ());
17  }
18
19  void Association::Put (ostream& s) const
20  {
21      s << "Association {" << *key;
22      if (value != 0)
23          s << ", " << *value;
24      s << "}";
25  }
```

**PROGRAM 5.21**
SearchableContainer class definition

```
1   class SearchableContainer : public virtual Container
2   {
3   public:
4       virtual bool IsMember (Object const&) const = 0;
5       virtual void Insert (Object&) = 0;
6       virtual void Withdraw (Object&) = 0;
7       virtual Object& Find (Object const&) const = 0;
8   };
```

The purpose of the **Insert** member function is to put an object into the container. The **Insert** function takes as its argument a reference to **Object**. Remember, we have chosen to implement containers using indirect containment. In addition, it depends on the ownership status of the container whether it will delete the objects it contains.

The **Withdraw** function is used to remove an object from a container. The lone argument is a reference to the object to be removed. After an object has been removed from a container, the container no longer owns that object. In any event, the container never deletes an object which is removed from the container.

The final member function, **Find**, is used to locate an object in a container and to return a reference to that object. In this case, it is understood that the search is to be done using the object comparison functions. That is, the routine is *not* to be implemented as a search of the container for a pointer to the given object but rather as a search of the container for an object which compares equal to the given object.

There is an important subtlety in the semantics of **Find**. The search is not for the given object, but rather for an object which compares equal to the given object. These semantics are particularly useful when using associations. Recall that two associations will compare equal if their keys compare equal—the values may be different.

In the event that the **Find** function fails to find an object equal to the specified object, then it will return a reference to the **NullObject** instance. Therefore, the user of the **Find** function should test whether the object which is returned is the **NullObject** instance by calling the **IsNull()** member function.

The **Find** function does *not* remove the object it finds from the container. Therefore, a container which owns its contained objects retains ownership of the result of the search. An explicit call of the **Withdraw** function is needed to actually remove the object from the container.

# Exercises

5.1 Specify the set of values and the set of operations provided by each of the following C++ built-in data types:

a. `char`

b. `int`

c. `double`

d. `string`

5.2 What are the features of C++ that facilitate the creation of *user-defined* data types.

5.3 Explain how each of the following C++ features supports *polymorphism:*

a. operator overloading

b. templates

c. inheritance

**5.4** Suppose we define two concrete classes, **A** and **B**, both of which are derived from the **Object** class declared in Program 5.1. Furthermore, let **a** and **b** be instances of classes **A** and **B** (respectively) declared as follows:

```
class A : public Object { ... };
class B : public Object { ... };
A a;
B b;
```

Give the sequence of functions called in order to evaluate a comparison such as "**a<b**". Is the result of the comparison **true** or **false**? Explain.

**5.5** Consider the **Wrapper<T>** class defined in Program 5.6. Explain the operation of the following program fragment:

```
int i = 5;
Wrapper<int> j = 7;
i = j;
j = i;
```

**5.6** There are three ways to test whether a given object instance, **obj**, is the null object:

a. **obj.IsNull ()**

b. **obj == NullObject::Instance ()**, and

c. **&obj == &(NullObject::Instance ())**.

Discuss the relative merits of each approach.

**5.7** Let **c** be an instance of some concrete class derived from the **Container** class given in Program 5.9. Explain how the statement

```
cout << c;
```

prints the contents of the container on the standard output stream, **cout**.

**5.8** Suppose we have a container **c** (i.e., an instance of some concrete class derived from the **Container** class defined in Program 5.9) which among other things happens to contain itself. Is it permissible for **c** to own the objects it contains? What happens when **c**'s destructor runs if it owns the objects it contains.

**5.9** Iterators and visitors provide two ways to do the same thing—to visit one-by-one all the objects in a container. Give an implementation for the **Accept** function of the **Container** class that uses an iterator.

**5.10** Is it possible to implement an iterator using a visitor? Explain.

**5.11** Suppose we have a container which we know contains only instances of the **Int** class defined in Program 5.8. Design a **Visitor** which computes the sum of all the integers in the container.

**5.12** Explain what the following visitor does and why it is a horribly bad idea:

```
class DeletingVisitor : public Visitor
{
public:
    void Visit (Object& object)
        { delete &object; }
};
```

**5.13** Consider the following pair of **Association**s:

```
Association a (*new Int (3), *new Int (4));
Association b (*new Int (3));
```

Give the sequence of functions called in order to evaluate a comparison such as "a==b". Is the result of the comparison **true** or **false**? Explain.

# Programming Projects

**5.1** Design and implement suitable **Compare** functions for the C++ built-in types **int**, **char**, **double**, and **string** so that they may be wrapped using the **Wrapper<T>** class declared in Program 5.6.

**5.2** Using *visitors,* devise implementations for the **IsMember** and **Find** member functions of the **SearchableContainer** class declared in Program 5.21.

**5.3** Using *iterators,* devise implementations for the **IsMember** and **Find** member functions of the **SearchableContainer** class declared in Program 5.21.

**5.4** Devise a scheme using visitors whereby all of the objects contained in one searchable container can be removed from it and transferred to another container.

**5.5** A *bag* is a simple container that can hold a collection of objects. Design and implement a concrete class called **Bag** derived from the **SearchableContainer** class declared in Program 5.21. Use the **Array<T>** class given in Chapter 4 to keep track of the contents of the bag.

**5.6** Repeat Project 5.5, this time using the **LinkedList<T>** class given in Chapter 4.

**5.7** Ownership is all or nothing—a container owns all the object it contains or none of them. However, sometimes it is useful for an association to be the owner of the key but not of the associated value. Design and implement a class called **Assoc** which has this characteristic. Derive the class **Assoc** from the class **Association** given in Program 5.18.

**5.8** The *Java* programming language provides the notion of an *enumeration* as the means to iterate through the objects in a container. In C++ we can define enumerations like this:

```
class Enumeration
{
public:
    virtual bool hasMoreElements () const = 0;
    virtual Object& nextElement () = 0;
};
```

Given an enumeration **e** for some container **c**, the contents of **c** can be printed like this:

```
while (e.hasMoreElements ())
    cout << e.nextElement () << endl;
```

Devise a wrapper class to encapsulate an iterator and provide the functionality of an enumeration.

# 6 | Stacks, Queues, and Deques

In this chapter we consider several related abstract data types—stacks, queues, and deques. Each of these can be viewed as a pile of items. What distinguishes each of them is the way in which items are added to or removed from the pile.

In the case of a *stack,* items are added to and removed from the top of the pile. Consider the pile of papers on your desk. Suppose you add papers only to the top of the pile or remove them only from the top of the pile. At any point, the only paper that is visible is the one on top. What you have is a *stack.*

Now suppose your boss comes along and asks you to immediately complete a form. You stop doing whatever it is you are doing, and place the form on top of your pile of papers. When you have filled-out the form, you remove it from the top of the stack and return to the task you were working on before your boss interrupted you. This example illustrates that a *stack* can be used to keep track of partially completed tasks.

A *queue* is a pile in which items are added at one end and removed from the other. In this respect, a queue is like the line of customers waiting to be served by a bank teller. As customers arrive, they join the end of the queue while the teller serves the customer at the head of the queue. As a result, a *queue* is used when a sequence of activities must be done on a *first-come, first-served* basis.

Finally, a *deque* extends the notion of a queue. In a deque, items can be added to or removed from either end of the queue. In a sense, a deque is the more general abstraction of which the stack and the queue are just special cases.

Figure 6.1 shows the elements of the class hierarchy described in this chapter. Separate abstract classes are defined to represent stacks, queues, and deques. This chapter presents both an array-based and pointer-based implementation for each of these abstractions.

**FIGURE 6.1**
Object class hierarchy.

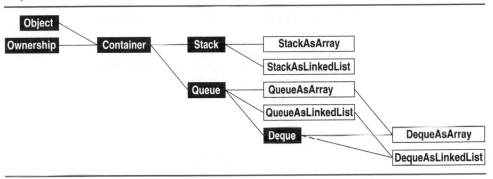

# 6.1 Stacks

The simplest of all the containers is a *stack*. A stack is a container which provides exactly one function, **Push**, for putting objects into the container; and one function, **Pop**, for taking objects out of the container. Figure 6.2 illustrates the basic idea.

Objects which are stored in stack are kept in a pile. The last item put into the stack is at the top. When an item is pushed into a stack, it is placed at the top of the pile. When an item popped, it is always the top item that is removed. Since it is always the last item

**FIGURE 6.2**
Basic stack operations.

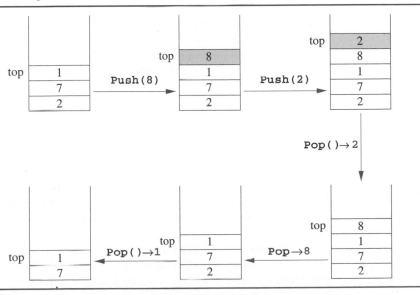

---

**PROGRAM 6.1**
Stack class definition

---

```
1  class Stack : public virtual Container
2  {
3  public:
4      virtual Object& Top () const = 0;
5      virtual void Push (Object&) = 0;
6      virtual Object& Pop () = 0;
7  };
```

---

to be put into the stack that is the first item to be removed, a stack is a *last-in, first-out* (*LIFO*) data structure.

In addition to the Push and Pop operations, the typical stack implementation also provides an accessor called Top which returns the item at the top of the stack without removing it from the stack.

Program 6.1 gives the Stack abstract class definition. The Stack class is derived from the Container class. Hence, its interface comprises all of the member functions inherited from the base class plus the three member functions Push, Pop, and Top. Notice also that the Stack class is an abstract class. The functions Push, Pop, and Top are declared as pure virtual functions.

When implementing a data structure, the first issue to be addressed is to select the foundational data structure(s) to use. Often, the choice is between an array-based implementation and a pointer-based implementation. The next two sections show an array-based implementation of stacks which uses the Array<T> class introduced in Chapter 4 and a pointer-based implementation which uses the LinkedList<T> class.

## 6.1.1 Array Implementation

This section describes an array-based implementation of stacks. Program 6.2 gives the declaration of the StackAsArray class. The StackAsArray class is a concrete object class. Therefore, its definition provides an implementation for all of the inherited member functions which are pure in the base class definition. Most of the function prototypes have been elided from Program 6.2 for the sake of brevity.

### Member Variables
The StackAsArray class definition contains one member variable—array. The variable array is declared by instantiating the Array<T> class template with T=Object*, that is, array is an array of pointers to Objects. The use of pointers is in keeping with the design decision to implement containers using indirect storage.

### Constructor and Destructor
The definitions of the StackAsArray class constructor and destructor are given in Program 6.3. The constructor takes a single parameter, size, which specifies the

**PROGRAM 6.2**
StackAsArray class definition

```
1   class StackAsArray : public Stack
2   {
3       Array<Object*> array;
4
5       class Iter;
6   public:
7       StackAsArray (unsigned int);
8       // ...
9       friend class Iter;
10  };
11
12  class StackAsArray::Iter : public Iterator
13  {
14      StackAsArray const& stack;
15      unsigned int position;
16  public:
17      Iter (StackAsArray const&);
18      // ...
19  };
```

**PROGRAM 6.3**
StackAsArray class constructor, destructor, and Purge member function definitions

```
1   StackAsArray::StackAsArray (unsigned int size) :
2       array (size)
3       {}
4
5   void StackAsArray::Purge ()
6   {
7       if (IsOwner ())
8       {
9           for (unsigned int i = 0; i < count; ++i)
10              delete array [i];
11      }
12      count = 0;
13  }
14
15  StackAsArray::~StackAsArray ()
16      { Purge (); }
```

maximum number of items that can be stored in the stack. The variable **array** is initialized to be an array of length **size**. Its constructor requires $O(1)$ time to construct an array of pointers. Therefore, the total running time for the **StackAsArray** constructor is $O(1)$.

The **StackAsArray** destructor simply calls the **Purge** member function. The behavior of the **Purge** function depends on whether the stack (as a container) is the owner of the contained objects. If it is the owner, then the contained objects must be deleted by the **Purge** function. In this case, the **Purge** function deletes one-by-one the first **count** elements of the array. In general, because of the polymorphic implementation of **Objects**, we cannot know the running time to delete the array elements. However, if we assume that the destructors for all the objects run in constant time, the total running time for the **Purge** function is $O(n)$, where $n =$ **count**, i.e., $n$ is the number of elements in the stack.

### Push, Pop, and Top Member Functions

Program 6.4 defines the **Push**, **Pop**, and **Top**, member functions of the **StackAsArray** class. The first of these, **Push**, adds an element to the stack. It takes as its lone argument a reference to the **Object** to be pushed onto the stack.

The **Push** function first checks to see if there is room left in the stack. If no room is left, it throws a **domain_error** exception. Otherwise, it simply puts a pointer to

---

**PROGRAM 6.4**
StackAsArray class Push, Pop, and Top member function definitions

```
1   void StackAsArray::Push (Object& object)
2   {
3       if (count == array.Length ())
4           throw domain_error ("stack is full");
5       array [count++] = &object;
6   }
7
8   Object& StackAsArray::Pop ()
9   {
10      if (count == 0)
11          throw domain_error ("stack is empty");
12      return *array [--count];
13  }
14
15  Object& StackAsArray::Top () const
16  {
17      if (count == 0)
18          throw domain_error ("stack is empty");
19      return *array [count - 1U];
20  }
```

the object into the array, and then increases the `count` variable by one. In a correctly functioning program, stack overflow should not occur. If we assume that overflow does not occur, the running time of the `Push` function is clearly $O(1)$.

The `Pop` function removes an item from the stack and returns a reference to that item. If the stack is the owner of its contained objects, then when an item is removed from the stack, that item ceases to be owned by the stack. Consequently, the `Pop` function never invokes `operator delete`. The `Pop` function first checks to see if the stack is empty. If the stack is empty, it throws a `domain_error` exception. Otherwise, it simply decreases `count` by one and returns a reference to the item found at the top of the stack. In a correctly functioning program, stack underflow will not occur normally. The running time of the `Pop` function is $O(1)$.

Finally, the `Top` function is a stack accessor which returns a `const` reference to the top item in the stack. The `Top` function is a `const` member function since it does not modify the stack. In particular, it does *not* remove the top item from the stack. The `Top` function first checks if the stack is empty. If the stack is empty, it throws a `domain_error` exception. Otherwise, it returns a reference to the top item, which is found at position `count - 1` in the array. Assuming stack underflow does not occur normally, the running time of the `Top` function is $O(1)$.

### The `Accept` Member Function

Program 6.5 defines the `Accept` member function for the `StackAsArray` class. As discussed in Chapter 5, the purpose of the `Accept` member function of a container is to accept a visitor, and cause it to visit one-by-one all of the contained objects.

In the array implementation of the stack, the elements contained in the container occupy positions $0, 1, \ldots,$ `count` $- 1$ of the array. The body of the `Accept` function is simply a loop which calls the `Visit` function for each object in the stack. The running time of the `Accept` function depends on the running time of the function `Visit`. Let $\mathcal{T}\langle\text{visit}()\rangle$ be the running time of the function `Visit`. In addition to the time for the function call, each iteration of the loop incurs a constant overhead. Consequently, the total running time for `Accept` is $n\mathcal{T}\langle\text{visit}()\rangle + O(n)$, where $n$ is the number of objects in the container. And if $\mathcal{T}\langle\text{visit}()\rangle = O(1)$, the total running time is $O(n)$.

---

**PROGRAM 6.5**
`StackAsArray` class `Accept` member function definition

---

```
1   void StackAsArray::Accept (Visitor& visitor) const
2   {
3       for (unsigned int i = 0;
4           i < count && !visitor.IsDone (); ++i)
5       {
6           visitor.Visit (*array [i]);
7       }
8   }
```

### Iterator

In addition to the **StackAsArray** class, Program 6.2 also defines the nested class **Iter**. Notice that the **StackAsArray::Iter** class is a *friend* of the **StackAsArray** class. The friend of a class has access to the private member variables and functions of that class. Consequently, the implementation of the iterator depends on the implementation of the container.

Recall from Chapter 5 that an iterator is meant to be used like this:

```
StackAsArray stack;
stack.Push (*new Int (3));
stack.Push (*new Int (1));
stack.Push (*new Int (4));
Iterator& i = stack.NewIterator ();
while (!i.IsDone ()) {
    cout << *i << endl;
    ++i;
}
delete &i;
```

This example declares the variable **stack**, pushes several **Int** objects onto the stack, and then uses an iterator to systematically print out all of the elements contained in the stack.

The **StackAsArray::Iter** class member functions are given in Program 6.6. Two member variables are defined—**stack** and **position**. The former is a **const** reference to a **StackAsArray**; the latter, an unsigned integer. The **StackAsArray:: Iter** constructor takes as its lone argument a **const** reference to a **StackAsArray** object and it makes the **stack** member variable refer to that object. Then, it calls the **Reset** member function which sets the **position** member variable to zero. The effect of all this is to associate the iterator with the given stack instance and to make it refer to the first element (i.e., the one at the bottom) of the associated stack. Clearly, the running time of the **StackAsArray::Iter** constructor is $O(1)$.

The **IsDone** member function is called in the loop termination test of the **while** loop given above. The purpose of the **IsDone** member function is to determine when all of the contained objects have been exhausted. In Program 6.6 this occurs when the variable **position** is equal to the **count** variable of the associated stack. The running time of **IsDone** is $O(1)$.

The dereferencing operator, **operator\***, is called in the body of the **for** loop to access the object to which the iterator refers. It returns a reference to the appropriate **Object** in the stack, provided that the list has not been exhausted, i.e., provided that the value of the **position** variable in the range between 0 and **count** $- 1$. Otherwise, it returns a reference to the **NullObject** instance when the position is invalid.

Finally, the increment operator, **operator++**, is used to cause the iterator to advance its position to the next contained object. In this case, advancing the position simply means adding one. This operator does nothing if the position is initially invalid. In either case, the running time is simply $O(1)$.

## PROGRAM 6.6
StackAsArray::Iter class member function definitions

```
1   StackAsArray::Iter::Iter (StackAsArray const& _stack) :
2       stack (_stack)
3       { Reset (); }
4
5   bool StackAsArray::Iter::IsDone () const
6       { return position >= stack.count; }
7
8   Object& StackAsArray::Iter::operator * () const
9   {
10      if (position < stack.count)
11          return *stack.array [position];
12      else
13          return NullObject::Instance ();
14  }
15
16  void StackAsArray::Iter::operator ++ ()
17  {
18      if (position < stack.count)
19          ++position;
20  }
21
22  void StackAsArray::Iter::Reset ()
23      { position = 0; }
```

## PROGRAM 6.7
StackAsLinkedList class definition

```
1   class StackAsLinkedList : public Stack
2   {
3       LinkedList<Object*> list;
4
5       class Iter;
6   public:
7       StackAsLinkedList ();
8       // ...
9       friend class Iter;
10  };
11
12  class StackAsLinkedList::Iter : public Iterator
13  {
14      StackAsLinkedList const& stack;
15      ListElement<Object*> const* position;
16  public:
17      Iter (StackAsLinkedList const&);
18      // ...
19  };
```

### 6.1.2 Linked List Implementation

In this section we will examine a pointer-based implementation of stacks that makes use of the `LinkedList<T>` data structure developed in Chapter 4. Program 6.7 gives the declaration of the concrete object class `StackAsLinkedList` and its associated iterator, `StackAsLinkedList::Iter`. As in the preceding section, the function prototypes for the interface inherited from the `Container` base class have been elided for the sake of brevity. Of course, implementations must be provided for all of the inherited member functions which are declared pure in the base class.

#### Member Variables

The implementation of the `StackAsLinkedList` class makes use of one member variable—`list`. The variable `list` is an instance of the `LinkedList<T>` class template with `T=Object*`. Thus, `list` is a linked list of pointers to `Object`s. This list will be used to keep track of the elements in the stack. Since we have decided to implement containers using indirect storage, the linked list contains *pointers* to the objects in the stack.

#### Constructor and Destructor

The definitions of the constructor and destructor functions for `StackAsLinkedList` objects are given in Program 6.8. In the case of the linked list implementation, it is

---

**PROGRAM 6.8**
`StackAsLinkedList` class constructor, destructor, and `Purge` member function definitions

```
1   StackAsLinkedList::StackAsLinkedList () :
2       list ()
3       {}
4
5   void StackAsLinkedList::Purge ()
6   {
7       if (IsOwner ())
8       {
9           ListElement<Object*> const* ptr;
10
11          for (ptr = list.Head (); ptr != 0; ptr = ptr->Next ())
12              delete ptr->Datum ();
13      }
14      list.Purge ();
15      count = 0;
16  }
17
18  StackAsLinkedList::~StackAsLinkedList ()
19      { Purge (); }
```

---

not necessary to preallocate storage. When using a linked list, the storage is allocated dynamically and incrementally on the basis of demand.

The constructor simply initializes the `list` variable using the default constructor for the `LinkedList<T>` class. The `LinkedList<T>` constructor runs in constant time. Thus, the running time of the `StackAsLinkedList` constructor is $O(1)$.

The `StackAsLinkedList` destructor simply calls the `Purge` member function. The `Purge` function deletes the contained objects if it owns them. Hence, the `Purge` function goes through the elements of the linked list and follows the pointers to delete the objects one-by-one. In general, because of the polymorphic implementation of `Object`s, we cannot know the running time to delete an object. However, if we assume that the destructors for all the objects run in constant time, the total running time for the `Purge` function is $O(n)$, where $n = $ `count`, that is, $n$ is the number of elements in the stack.

### Push, Pop, and Top Member Functions

The `Push`, `Pop`, and `Top`, member functions of the `StackAsLinkedList` class are defined in Program 6.9.

---

**PROGRAM 6.9**
`StackAsLinkedList` class `Push`, `Pop`, and `Top` member function definitions

---

```
1   void StackAsLinkedList::Push (Object& object)
2   {
3       list.Prepend (&object);
4       ++count;
5   }
6
7   Object& StackAsLinkedList::Pop ()
8   {
9       if (count == 0)
10          throw domain_error ("stack is empty");
11      Object& result = *list.First ();
12      list.Extract (&result);
13      --count;
14      return result;
15  }
16
17  Object& StackAsLinkedList::Top () const
18  {
19      if (count == 0)
20          throw domain_error ("stack is empty");
21      return *list.First ();
22  }
```

---

The implementation of **Push** is trivial. It takes as its lone argument a reference to the **Object** to be pushed onto the stack and simply prepends a pointer to that object to the linked list **list**. Then, one is added to the **count** variable. The running time of the **Push** function is constant, since the **Prepend** function has a constant running time, and updating the **count** only takes $O(1)$ time.

The **Pop** function is implemented using two of the **LinkedList<T>** member functions—**First** and **Extract**. The **First** function is used to obtain the first item in the linked list. The function **First** runs in constant time. The **Extract** function is then called to remove the first item from the linked list. In the worst case, **Extract** requires $O(n)$ time to delete an item from a linked list of length $n$. But the worst-case time arises only when it is the *last* element of the list which is to be deleted. In the case of the **Pop** function, it is the *first* element which is deleted. This can be done in constant time. Assuming that the exception which is raised when **Pop** is called on an empty list does not occur, the running time for **Pop** is $O(1)$.

There is a subtle point in this implementation: Since it is not possible for two different variables to occupy the same memory address,[1] all of the pointers in the linked list will be unique provided no object is pushed onto the stack more than once. This ensures that the datum deleted from the linked list by the **Extract** function is precisely the one returned by the **First** function.

The only way that an object can be pushed safely onto the stack more than once is if the stack does not own its contained objects. If the stack owns its objects, then when the stack is deleted its destructor first deletes all the contained objects. As a result, if an object is pushed onto the stack twice, that object's destructor would be called twice. Such a program is not valid since deleting an object which has already been deleted is an error.

The definition of the **Top** function is quite simple. It simply returns a reference to the first object in the linked list. Provided the linked list is not empty, the running time of **Top** is $O(1)$. If the linked list is empty, the **Top** function throws a **domain_error** exception.

### The **Accept** Member Function

The **Accept** member function of the **StackAsLinkedList** class is defined in Program 6.10. The **Accept** member function takes a visitor and calls its **Visit** function one-by-one for all of the objects on the stack.

The implementation of the **Accept** function for the **StackAsLinkedList** class mirrors that of the **StackAsArray** class shown in Program 6.5. In this case, the linked list is traversed from front to back, i.e., from the top of the stack to the bottom. As each element of the linked list is encountered, the **Visit** function is called. If $\mathcal{T}\langle\text{visit()}\rangle$ is the running time of the function **Visit**, the total running time for **Accept** is $n\mathcal{T}\langle\text{visit()}\rangle + O(n)$, where $n =$ **count** is the number of objects in the container. If we assume that $\mathcal{T}\langle\text{visit()}\rangle = O(1)$, the total running time is $O(n)$.

---

[1]Actually, it is possible for two variables to occupy the same memory location if a **union** is used. While there are legitimate uses for unions (see Chapter 13), it is reasonable to assume here that all objects have unique addresses.

**PROGRAM 6.10**
StackAsLinkedList class Accept member function definition

```
1   void StackAsLinkedList::Accept (Visitor& visitor) const
2   {
3       ListElement<Object*> const* ptr;
4
5       for (ptr = list.Head ();
6           ptr != 0 && !visitor.IsDone (); ptr = ptr->Next ())
7       {
8           visitor.Visit (*ptr->Datum ());
9       }
10  }
```

**PROGRAM 6.11**
StackAsLinkedList::Iter class member function definitions

```
1   StackAsLinkedList::Iter::Iter (
2       StackAsLinkedList const& _stack) :
3       stack (_stack)
4       { Reset (); }
5
6   bool StackAsLinkedList::Iter::IsDone () const
7       { return position == 0; }
8
9   Object& StackAsLinkedList::Iter::operator * () const
10  {
11      if (position != 0)
12          return *position->Datum ();
13      else
14          return NullObject::Instance ();
15  }
16
17  void StackAsLinkedList::Iter::operator ++ ()
18  {
19      if (position != 0)
20          position = position->Next ();
21  }
22
23  void StackAsLinkedList::Iter::Reset ()
24      { position = stack.list.Head (); }
```

**Iterator**

The `StackAsLinkedList::Iter` class member functions are defined in Program 6.11. Since the `StackAsLinkedList::Iter` class is declared as a friend of the `StackAsLinkedList` class, the member functions of the former can access the private member variables of the latter. Consequently, the implementation of the iterator depends on the implementation of the container.

`StackAsLinkedList::Iter` objects have two member variables, `stack` and `position`. The former is a reference to a `StackAsLinkedList` instance. The latter is declared as a `ListElement<Object*> const*`, i.e, a pointer to a `const` element of a linked list of pointers to `Object`s.

The `StackAsLinkedList::Iter` constructor simply calls the `Reset` member function. The `Reset` function makes `position` point at the first element of the linked list which represents the stack by calling the `Head` function of the `LinkedList<T>` class. Clearly the running time of the constructor is $O(1)$.

The `IsDone` member function simply tests for the null pointer. If the `position` variable is zero, `IsDone` returns `true`. Again, the running time is clearly $O(1)$.

The dereferencing operator, `operator*`, does what its name says! It returns a `const` reference to the object obtained by dereferencing the object pointer contained in the list element to which the `position` variable points, which takes $O(1)$ time. Note that if `pointer` is zero, a reference to the `NullObject` instance is returned.

Finally, the increment operator, `operator++`, advances the `position` pointer to the next element of the linked list. This is done by calling the `Next` function of the `ListElement<T>` class. This too is accomplished in constant time.

Because the interface of the `StackAsLinkedList` class is exactly the same as that of the `StackAsArray` class, `StackAsLinkedList` objects can be used in exactly the same way as their array-based counterparts:

```
StackAsLinkedList stack;
stack.Push (*new Int (3));
stack.Push (*new Int (1));
stack.Push (*new Int (4));
Iterator& i = stack.NewIterator ();
while (!i.IsDone ()) {
    cout << *i << endl;
    ++i;
}
delete &i;
```

This program fragment declares the variable `stack`, pushes several values onto the stack, and then uses an iterator to systematically print out all of the elements contained in the stack.

## 6.1.3   Applications

Consider the following expression

$$(5 + 9) \times 2 + 6 \times 5 \tag{6.1}$$

In order to determine the value of this expression, we first compute the sum $5 + 9$ and then multiply that by 2. Then we compute the product $6 \times 5$ and add it to the previous result to get the final answer. Notice that the order in which the operations are to be done is crucial. Clearly if the operations are not done in the correct order, the wrong result is computed.

The expression above is written using the usual mathematical notation. This notation is called *infix* notation. What distinguishes this notation is the way that expressions involving binary operators are written. A *binary operator* is an operator which has exactly two operands, such as $+$ and $\times$. In infix notation, binary operators appear *in between* their operands.

Another characteristic of *infix* notation is that the order of operations is determined by *operator precedence*. For example, the $\times$ (multiplication) operator has higher precedence than does the $+$ (addition) operator. When an evaluation order is desired that is different from that provided by the precedence, *parentheses*, "(" and ")", are used to override precedence rules. That is, an expression in parentheses is evaluated first.

As an alternative to infix, the Polish logician Jan Lukasiewicz introduced notations which require neither parentheses nor operator precedence rules. The first of these, the so-called *Polish notation*, places the binary operators before their operands; i.e., for Equation 6.1 we would write

$$+ \times + 5\, 9\, 2 \times 6\, 5$$

This is also called *prefix* notation, because the operators are written in front of their operands.

While prefix notation is completely unambiguous in the absence of parentheses, it is not very easy to read. A minor syntactic variation on prefix is to write the operands as a comma-separated list enclosed in parentheses as follows:

$$+(\times(+(5, 9), 2), \times(6, 5))$$

While this notation seems somewhat foreign, in fact it is precisely the notation that is used for function calls in C++:

```
operator+ (operator* (operator+ (5,9) ,2), operator* (6,5));
```

The second form of Lukasiewicz notation is the so-called *Reverse-Polish notation* (*RPN*). Equation 6.1 is written as follows in RPN:

$$5\, 9\, + 2 \times 6\, 5 \times + \tag{6.2}$$

This notation is also called *postfix* notation for the obvious reason—the operators are written *after* their operands.

Postfix notation, like prefix notation, does not make use of operator precedence nor does it require the use of parentheses. For example, the expression $1 + 2 \times 3$, in which

**FIGURE 6.3**
Evaluating the RPN expression in Equation 6.2 using a stack.

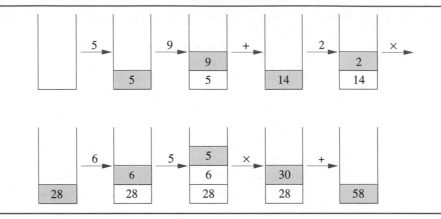

the multiplication is done first, is written $1\ 2\ 3 \times +$; whereas the expression $(1 + 2) \times 3$ is written $1\ 2 + 3 \times$.

### Evaluating Postfix Expressions

One of the most useful characteristics of a postfix expression is that the value of such an expression can be computed easily with the aid of a stack of values. The components of a postfix expression are processed from left to right as follows:

1.  If the next component of the expression is an operand, the value of the component is pushed onto the stack.
2.  If the next component of the expression is an operator, then its operands are in the stack. The required number of operands are popped from the stack; the specified operation is performed; and the result is pushed back onto the stack.

After all the components of the expression have been processed in this fashion, the stack will contain a single result which is the final value of the expression. Figure 6.3 illustrates the use of a stack to evaluate the RPN expression given in Equation 6.2.

### Implementation

Program 6.12 gives the implementation of a simple RPN calculator. The purpose of this example is to illustrate the use of the **Stack** class. The program shown accepts very simplified RPN expressions: The expression may contain only single-digit integers, the addition operator, **+**, and the multiplication operator, **\***. In addition, the operator **=** pops the top value off the stack and prints it on the standard output stream, **cout**. Furthermore, the calculator does its computation entirely with integers.

Notice that the **RPNCalculator** function is passed a reference to a **Stack** object. Consequently, the function manipulates the stack entirely through the abstract interface. The calculator does not depend on the stack implementation used! For example, if we

**PROGRAM 6.12**
Stack Application—A single-digit, RPN calculator

```
void RPNCalculator (Stack& stack)
{
    char c;
    while (cin >> c, !cin.eof ())
    {
        if (std::isdigit (c))
            stack.Push (*new Int (c - '0'));
        else if (c == '+')
        {
            Int& arg2 = dynamic_cast<Int&> (stack.Pop ());
            Int& arg1 = dynamic_cast<Int&> (stack.Pop ());
            stack.Push (*new Int (arg1 + arg2));
            delete &arg1;
            delete &arg2;
        }
        else if (c == '*')
        {
            Int& arg2 = dynamic_cast<Int&> (stack.Pop ());
            Int& arg1 = dynamic_cast<Int&> (stack.Pop ());
            stack.Push (*new Int (arg1 * arg2));
            delete &arg1;
            delete &arg2;
        }
        else if (c == '=')
        {
            Int& arg = dynamic_cast<Int&> (stack.Pop ());
            cout << arg << endl;
            delete &arg;
        }
    }
}
```

wish to use a stack implemented using an array, we would declare a **StackAsArray** variable and invoke the calculator as follows:

```
StackAsArray s (10);
RPNCalculator (s);
```

On the other hand, if we decided to use the pointer-based stack implementation, we would write

```
StackAsLinkedList s;
RPNCalculator (s);
```

The running time of the **RPNCalculator** function depends on the number of symbols, operators, and operands in the expression being evaluated. If there are *n* symbols, the body of the **for** loop is executed *n* times. It should be fairly obvious that the amount of work done per symbol is constant, regardless of the type of symbol encountered. This is the case for both the **StackAsArray** and the **StackAsLinkedList** stack implementations. Therefore, the total running time needed to evaluate an expression comprised of *n* symbols is $O(n)$.

## 6.2   Queues

In the preceding section we saw that a stack comprises a pile of objects that can be accessed only at one end—the top. In this section we examine a similar data structure called a *single-ended queue*. Whereas in a stack we add and remove elements at the same end of the pile, in a single-ended queue we add elements at one end and remove them from the other. Since it is always the first item to be put into the queue that is the first item to be removed, a queue is a *first-in, first-out* (FIFO) data structure. Figure 6.4 illustrates the basic queue operations.

Program 6.13 gives the **Queue** abstract class definition. The **Queue** class is derived from the **Container** class. The **Queue** class interface comprises all the functions inherited from the base classes plus the three functions, **Head**, **Enqueue**, and **Dequeue**.

As we did with stacks, we will examine two queue implementations—an array-based one and a pointer-based one. The array-based implementation uses the **Array<T>** class and the pointer-based implementation, the **LinkedList<T>** class, both of which are defined in Chapter 4.

### 6.2.1   Array Implementation

Program 6.14 declares the **QueueAsArray** class. The **QueueAsArray** class is a concrete class that provides an array-based queue implementation. As such, it must provide

**FIGURE 6.4**
Basic queue operations.

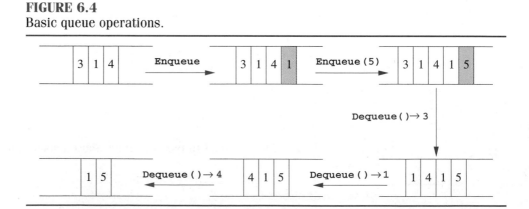

**PROGRAM 6.13**
Queue class definition

```
1  class Queue : public virtual Container
2  {
3  public:
4      virtual Object& Head () const = 0;
5      virtual void Enqueue (Object&) = 0;
6      virtual Object& Dequeue () = 0;
7  };
```

**PROGRAM 6.14**
QueueAsArray class definition

```
1  class QueueAsArray : public virtual Queue
2  {
3  protected:
4      Array<Object*> array;
5      unsigned int head;
6      unsigned int tail;
7  public:
8      QueueAsArray (unsigned int);
9      ~QueueAsArray ();
10     // ...
11 };
```

an implementation for all of the inherited pure virtual functions—the function proto-types have been elided for the sake of brevity.

## Member Variables

QueueAsArray objects comprise three member variables—array, head, and tail. In keeping with the decision to use indirect storage in the implementation of containers, the variable array is declared as an array of pointers to Objects.

The pointers to the objects contained in the queue will be held in a contiguous range of array elements as shown in Figure 6.5(a). The variables head and tail denote the left and right ends, respectively, of this range. In general, the region of contiguous elements will not necessarily occupy the left-most array positions. As elements are deleted at the head, the position of the left end will change. Similarly, as elements are added at the tail, the position of the right end will change. In some circumstances, the contiguous region of elements will wrap around the ends of the array as shown in Figure 6.5(b).

**FIGURE 6.5**
Array implementation of a queue.

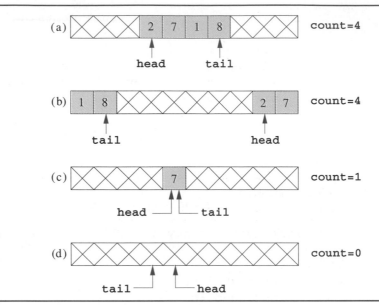

As shown in Figure 6.5, the left-most element is **array[head]**, and the right-most element is **array[tail]**. When the queue contains only one element, **head** = **tail** as shown in Figure 6.5(c).

Finally, Figure 6.5(b) shows that if the queue is empty, the **head** position will actually be to the right of the **tail** position. However, this is also the situation which arises when the queue is completely full! The problem is essentially this: Given an array of length $n$, then $0 \leq \mathbf{head} < n$ and $0 \leq \mathbf{tail} < n$. Therefore, the difference between the **head** and **tail** satisfies $0 \leq (\mathbf{head} - \mathbf{tail}) \bmod n < n$. Since there are only $n$ distinct differences, there can be only $n$ distinct queue lengths, $0, 1, \ldots, n-1$. It is not possible to distinguish the queue which is empty from the queue which has $n$ elements solely on the basis of the **head** and **tail** member variables.

There are two options for dealing with this problem: The first is to limit the number of elements in the queue to be at most $n-1$. The second is to use another member variable, **count**, to keep track explicitly of the actual number of elements in the queue rather than to infer the number from the **head** and **tail** variables. The second approach has been adopted for the implementation below.

### Constructor and Destructor

The definitions of the **QueueAsArray** class constructor and destructor are given in Program 6.15. The constructor takes a single parameter, **size**, which specifies the maximum number of items that can be stored in the queue. The constructor initializes the member variables as follows: The variable **array** is initialized to an array of

**PROGRAM 6.15**
QueueAsArray class constructor, destructor, and Purge member function
definitions

```
1    QueueAsArray::QueueAsArray (unsigned int size) :
2        array (size),
3        head (0),
4        tail (size - 1U)
5        {}
6
7    void QueueAsArray::Purge ()
8    {
9        if (IsOwner ())
10       {
11           for (unsigned int i = 0; i < count; ++i)
12           {
13               delete array [head];
14               if (++head == array.Length ())
15                   head = 0;
16           }
17       }
18       count = 0;
19   }
20
21   QueueAsArray::~QueueAsArray ()
22       { Purge (); }
```

length size, and the remaining variables, head and tail, are initialized to represent
the empty queue. Therefore, the total running time for the QueueAsArray constructor
is $O(1)$.

The QueueAsArray destructor simply calls the Purge member function. The
Purge function is responsible for deleting the contained objects if the queue (as a
container) is the owner of those objects. If the queue owns the contained objects, the
Purge function deletes them all one-by-one, starting from at the head and moving
toward the tail. Because we cannot know the types of the objects contained, we cannot
know the running time required to delete each of them. However, if we assume that
the destructors for all the objects each run in constant time, the total running time for
the QueueAsArray class Purge function is $O(n)$, where $n =$ count, i.e., $n$ is the
number of items in the queue.

**Head, Enqueue, and Dequeue Member Functions**
Program 6.16 defines the Head, Enqueue, and Dequeue member functions of the
QueueAsArray class.

The **Head** member function simply returns a reference to the object found at the head of the queue, having first checked to see that the queue is not empty. If the queue is empty, it throws a **domain_error** exception. Under normal circumstances, we expect that the queue will not be empty. Therefore, the normal running time of this function is $O(1)$.

The **Enqueue** function takes a single argument which is a reference to an object to be added to the tail of the queue. The **Enqueue** function first checks that the queue is not full—a **domain_error** exception is thrown when the queue is full. Next, the position at which to insert the new element is determined by increasing the member variable **tail** by one modulo the length of the array. Finally, a pointer to the object to be enqueued is put into the array at the correct position and the **count** is adjusted

---

**PROGRAM 6.16**
QueueAsArray class **Head**, **Enqueue**, and **Dequeue** member function definitions

```
1   Object& QueueAsArray::Head () const
2   {
3       if (count == 0)
4           throw domain_error ("queue is empty");
5       return *array [head];
6   }
7
8   void QueueAsArray::Enqueue (Object& object)
9   {
10      if (count == array.Length ())
11          throw domain_error ("queue is full");
12      if (++tail == array.Length ())
13          tail = 0;
14      array [tail] = &object;
15      ++count;
16  }
17
18  Object& QueueAsArray::Dequeue ()
19  {
20      if (count == 0)
21          throw domain_error ("queue is empty");
22      Object& result = *array [head];
23      if (++head == array.Length ())
24          head = 0;
25      --count;
26      return result;
27  }
```

---

accordingly. Under normal circumstances (i.e., when the exception is not thrown), the running time of **Enqueue** is $O(1)$.

The **Dequeue** function removes an object from the head of the queue and returns a reference to that object. First, it checks that the queue is not empty and throws an exception when it is. If the queue is not empty, the function sets aside a reference to the object at the head in the local variable **result**; it increases the **head** member variable by one modulo the length of the array; adjusts the **count** accordingly; and returns **result**. All this can be done in a constant amount of time so the running time of **Dequeue** is a constant.

## 6.2.2 Linked-List Implementation

This section presents a queue implementation which makes use of the singly-linked list data structure, **LinkedList<T>**, which is defined in Chapter 4. Program 6.17 declares the **QueueAsLinkedList** object class.

### Member Variables
Just like the **StackAsLinkedList** class, the implementation of the **QueueAs-LinkedList** class requires only one member variable—**list**. The variable **list** is a linked list of pointers to **Object**s. It is used to keep track of the elements in the queue.

### Constructor and Destructor
Program 6.18 defines the **QueueAsLinkedList** constructor and destructor functions. In the case of the linked-list implementation, it is not necessary to preallocate storage. The constructor simply initializes the **list** object as an empty list. The running time of the constructor is $O(1)$.

The **QueueAsLinkedList** destructor simply calls the **Purge** member function. The **Purge** function deletes the contained objects one-by-one by traversing the linked list. Assuming that the running time of the destructor for each the contained objects is

---

**PROGRAM 6.17**
QueueAsLinkedList class definition

```
1   class QueueAsLinkedList : public virtual Queue
2   {
3   protected:
4       LinkedList<Object*> list;
5   public:
6       QueueAsLinkedList ();
7       ~QueueAsLinkedList ();
8       // ...
9   };
```

---

**PROGRAM 6.18**
QueueAsLinkedList class constructor, destructor, and Purge member function definitions

```
1   QueueAsLinkedList::QueueAsLinkedList () :
2       list ()
3       {}
4
5   void QueueAsLinkedList::Purge ()
6   {
7       if (IsOwner ())
8       {
9           ListElement<Object*> const* ptr;
10
11          for (ptr = list.Head (); ptr != 0; ptr = ptr->Next ())
12              delete ptr->Datum ();
13      }
14      list.Purge ();
15      count = 0;
16  }
17
18  QueueAsLinkedList::~QueueAsLinkedList ()
19      { Purge (); }
```

---

a constant, the total running time for the **QueueAsLinkedList** destructor is $O(n)$, where $n =$ **count** is the number of items in the queue.

### Head, Enqueue, and Dequeue Member Functions

The **Head**, **Enqueue**, and **Dequeue** member functions of the **QueueAsLinkedList** class are given in Program 6.19.

The **Head** member function returns a **const** reference to the object at the head of the queue. The head of the queue is in the first element of the linked list. In Chapter 4 we saw that the running time of **LinkedList<T>::First** is a constant, Therefore, the normal running time for the **Head** function is $O(1)$.

The **Enqueue** function takes a single argument—a reference to the object to be added to the tail of the queue. The function simply calls the **LinkedList<T>:: Append** function. Since the running time for **Append** is $O(1)$, the running time of **Enqueue** is also $O(1)$.

The **Dequeue** function removes an object from the head of the queue and returns a reference to that object. First, it verifies that the queue is not empty and throws an exception when it is. If the queue is not empty, **Dequeue** saves a reference to the first item in the linked list in the local variable **result**. Then the item of the linked list is removed from the list. When using the **LinkedList<T>** class from Chapter 4, the time required to delete the first item from a list is $O(1)$ regardless of the number of items in the list. As a result, the running time of **Dequeue** is also $O(1)$.

**PROGRAM 6.19**
QueueAsLinkedList class Enqueue, Head, and Dequeue member function definitions

```
1   Object& QueueAsLinkedList::Head () const
2   {
3       if (count == 0)
4           throw domain_error ("queue is empty");
5       return *list.First ();
6   }
7
8   void QueueAsLinkedList::Enqueue (Object& object)
9   {
10      list.Append (&object);
11      ++count;
12  }
13
14  Object& QueueAsLinkedList::Dequeue ()
15  {
16      if (count == 0)
17          throw domain_error ("queue is empty");
18      Object& result = *list.First ();
19      list.Extract (&result);
20      --count;
21      return result;
22  }
```

**FIGURE 6.6**
A tree.

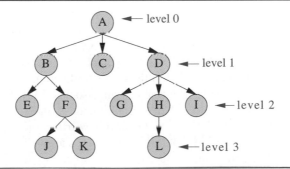

### 6.2.3 Applications

The FIFO nature of queues makes them useful in certain algorithms. For example, we will see in Chapter 16 that a queue is an essential data structure for many different graph algorithms. In this section we illustrate the use of a queue in the *breadth-first traversal* of a tree.

Figure 6.6 shows an example of a tree. A tree is comprised of *nodes* (indicated by the circles) and *edges* (shown as arrows between nodes). We say that the edges point from the *parent* node to a *child* node. The *degree* of a node is equal to the number of children of that node. For example, node A in Figure 6.6 has degree 3 and its children are nodes B, C, and D. A child and all of its descendents are called a *subtree*.

One way to represent such a tree is to use a collection of linked structures. Consider the following class definition which is an abridged version of the **NaryTree** class described in Chapter 9.

```
class NaryTree : public Object
{
    Object* key;
    unsigned int const degree;
    Array<NaryTree*> subtree;
public:
    Object& Key () const;
    unsigned int Degree () const;
    NaryTree& Subtree (unsigned int) const;
};
```

Each **NaryTree** object represents one node in a tree. The member variable **degree** keeps track of the degree of the node, and the variable **subtree** is an array of pointers to the children of the node. The **key** field points to an object which represents the contents of the node. For example, in Figure 6.6, each node carries a one-character label. The **key** field is intended to be used to represent that label. The member functions **Key**, **Degree**, and **Subtree** provide read-only access to the corresponding private member variables.

One of the essential operations on a tree is a *tree traversal*. A traversal *visits* one-by-one all the nodes in a given tree. To *visit a node* means to perform some computation using the information contained in that node—e.g., print the key. The standard tree traversals are discussed in Chapter 9. In this section we consider a traversal which is based on the levels of the nodes in the tree.

Each node in a tree has an associated level which arises from the position of that node in the tree. For example, node A in Figure 6.6 is at level 0; nodes B, C, and D are at level 1, etc. A *breadth-first traversal* visits the nodes of a tree in the order of their levels. At each level, the nodes are visited from left to right. For this reason, it is sometimes also called a *level-order traversal*. The breadth-first traversal of the tree in Figure 6.6 visits the nodes from A to L in alphabetical order.

One way to implement a breadth-first traversal of a tree is to make use of a queue as follows: To begin the traversal, the root node of the tree is enqueued. Then, we repeat the following steps until the queue is empty:

1. Dequeue and visit the first node in the queue.
2. Enqueue its children in order from left to right.

Figure 6.7 illustrates the breadth-first traversal algorithm by showing the contents of the queue immediately prior to each iteration.

### Implementation
Program 6.20 defines the function **BreadthFirstTraversal**. This function takes as its lone argument a reference to an **NaryTree** which is the root of the tree to be traversed. The algorithm makes use of the **QueueAsLinkedList** data structure, which was defined in the preceding section, to hold the appropriate tree nodes.

---

**FIGURE 6.7**
Queue contents during the breadth-first traversal of the tree in Figure 6.6.

---

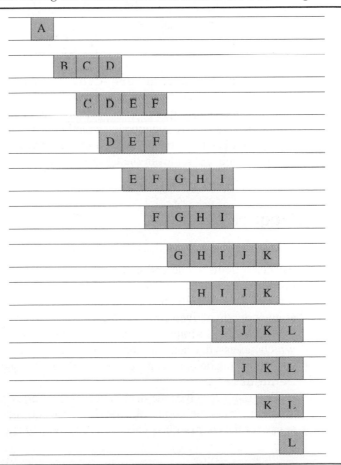

---

**PROGRAM 6.20**

Queue application—breadth-first tree traversal

---

```
1   void BreadthFirstTraversal (NaryTree& tree)
2   {
3       Queue& queue = *new QueueAsLinkedList ();
4       queue.Enqueue (tree);
5       while (!queue.IsEmpty ())
6       {
7           NaryTree& t =
8               dynamic_cast<NaryTree&> (queue.Dequeue ());
9           cout << t.Key () << endl;
10          for (unsigned int i = 0; i < t.Degree (); ++i)
11          {
12              NaryTree& subTree = t.Subtree (i);
13              queue.Enqueue (subTree);
14          }
15      }
16      delete &queue;
17  }
```

---

The running time of the **BreadthFirstTraversal** algorithm depends on the number of nodes in the tree which is being traversed. Each node of the tree is enqueued exactly once—this requires a constant amount of work. Furthermore, in each iteration of the loop, each node is dequeued exactly once—again a constant amount of work. As a result, the running time of the **BreadthFirstTraversal** algorithm is $O(n)$ where $n$ is the number of nodes in the traversed tree.

## 6.3 Deques

In the preceding section we saw that a queue comprises a pile of objects into which we insert items at one end and from which we remove items at the other end. In this section we examine an extension of the queue which provides a means to insert and remove items at both ends of the pile. This data structure is a *deque*. The word *deque* is an acronym derived from *double-ended queue*.[2]

Figure 6.8 illustrates the basic deque operations. A deque provides three operations which access the head of the queue, **Head**, **EnqueueHead**, and **DequeueHead**, and three operations to access the tail of the queue, **Tail**, **EnqueueTail**, and **DequeueTail**.

Program 6.21 gives the declaration of the **Deque** abstract class. Because a deque is an extension of the notion of a single-ended queue to a double-ended queue, it makes sense for the **Deque** class to be derived from the **Queue** class.

---

[2]The word *deque* is usually pronounced like "deck" and sometimes like "deek."

**FIGURE 6.8**
Basic deque operations.

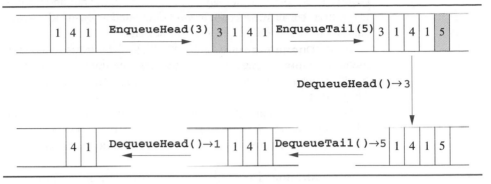

**PROGRAM 6.21**
Deque class definition

```
1   class Deque : public virtual Queue
2   {
3   public:
4       virtual Object& Head () const = 0;
5       virtual Object& Tail () const = 0;
6       virtual void Enqueue (Object&);
7       virtual void EnqueueHead (Object&) = 0;
8       virtual void EnqueueTail (Object&) = 0;
9       virtual Object& Dequeue ();
10      virtual Object& DequeueHead () = 0;
11      virtual Object& DequeueTail () = 0;
12  };
```

**PROGRAM 6.22**
Deque class Enqueue and Dequeue member function definitions

```
1   void Deque::Enqueue (Object& object)
2       { EnqueueTail (object); }
3
4   Object& Deque::Dequeue ()
5       { return DequeueHead (); }
```

Notice that the `Deque` class interface includes the `Enqueue` and `Dequeue` operations inherited from the `Queue` base class. In the base class only one enqueue is required because items are always enqueued at the tail and only one dequeue operation is required because items are always dequeued at the head. However, in a deque, items can be enqueued and dequeued at either end.

In order to ensure consistent semantics, the `Deque` class provides the default behaviors for the `Enqueue` and `Dequeue` functions as shown in Program 6.22. Viz., the `Enqueue` function simply calls `EnqueueTail` and the `Dequeue` function calls `DequeueHead`.

Why have we chosen to derive the `Deque` class from the `Queue` class and not the other way around? When we have two abstractions, one of which is essentially a subset of the other, there are two possible implementation approaches:

**Specialization** The more general abstraction is the base class, and the restricted abstraction is the derived class. For example, when using specialization we would derive the class `Queue` from the class `Deque` thus:

```
class Queue : public Deque { ... };
```

The `Queue` class interface should restrict access to only those base class member functions that are appropriate.

**Generalization** The more restricted abstraction is the base class from which the more general abstraction is derived. For example, when using generalization we would derive the class `Deque` from the class `Queue` thus:

```
class Deque : public Queue { ... };
```

The `Deque` class inherits and generalizes the interface of the `Queue` class.

Often when using generalization, it turns out that the inherited member functions need to be overridden because their functionality needs to be enhanced in some way. In those cases, specialization may be the preferred approach, since only one implementation needs to be written. The more general implementation serves the needs of both the general base class and the specialized derived class.

On the other hand, making the base class more general and the derived class more specialized means that sometimes we have more functionality at our disposal than we really need. If we only have single-ended queues, we don't want the overhead associated with double-ended queue operations. For this reason, we have chosen the generalization approach.

## 6.3.1 Array Implementation

Program 6.23 defines an array implementation of a deque. The `DequeAsArray` class is defined using multiple inheritance: It is derived from both the `Deque` abstract base

---

**PROGRAM 6.23**
**DesqueAsArray** class definition

```
1  class DequeAsArray : public Deque, public QueueAsArray
2  {
3  public:
4      DequeAsArray (unsigned int);
5      // ...
6  };
```

---

**PROGRAM 6.24**
**DequeAsArray** class **Head**, **EnqueueHead**, and **DequeueHead** member function definitions

```
1  Object& DequeAsArray::Head () const
2      { return QueueAsArray::Head (); }
3
4  void DequeAsArray::EnqueueTail (Object& object)
5      { QueueAsArray::Enqueue (object); }
6
7  Object& DequeAsArray::DequeueHead ()
8      { return QueueAsArray::Dequeue (); }
```

---

class and the **QueueAsArray** array-based implementation of a queue. The **Deque** class provides the interface; the **QueueAsArray**, the implementation.

The **QueueAsArray** implementation provides almost all of the required functionality. For example, Program 6.24 shows that the **Head**, **EnqueueTail**, and **DequeueHead** operations of the **DequeAsArray** class are implemented by calling the appropriate **QueueAsArray** class operations.

### **Tail**, **EnqueueHead**, and **DequeueTail** Member Functions

Program 6.25 defines the **Tail**, **EnqueueHead**, and **DequeueTail** member functions of the **DequeAsArray** class.

The **Tail** member function simply returns a reference to the object found at the tail of the deque, having first checked to see that the deque is not empty. If the deque is empty, it throws a **domain_error** exception. Under normal circumstances, we expect that the deque will not be empty. Therefore, the normal running time of this function is $O(1)$.

The **EnqueueHead** function takes a single argument which is a reference to an object to be added to the head of the deque. The **EnqueueHead** function first checks that the deque is not full—a **domain_error** exception is thrown when the deque is

**PROGRAM 6.25**

DequeAsArray class Tail, EnqueueTail, and DequeueTail member function definitions

```cpp
1  Object& DequeAsArray::Tail () const
2  {
3      if (count == 0)
4          throw domain_error ("deque is empty");
5      return *array [tail];
6  }
7
8  void DequeAsArray::EnqueueHead (Object& object)
9  {
10     if (count == array.Length ())
11         throw domain_error ("deque is full");
12     if (head-- == 0)
13         head = array.Length () - 1U;
14     array [head] = &object;
15     ++count;
16 }
17
18
19 Object& DequeAsArray::DequeueTail ()
20 {
21     if (count == 0)
22         throw domain_error ("deque is empty");
23     Object& result = *array [tail];
24     if (tail-- == 0)
25         tail = array.Length () - 1U;
26     --count;
27     return result;
28 }
```

full. Next, the position at which to insert the new element is determined by decreasing the member variable **head** by one modulo the length of the array. Finally, a pointer to the object to be enqueued is put into the array at the correct position and the **count** is adjusted accordingly. Under normal circumstances (i.e., when the exception is not thrown), the running time of **EnqueueHead** is $O(1)$.

The **DequeueTail** function removes an object from the tail of the deque and returns a reference to that object. First, it checks that the deque is not empty and throws an exception when it is. If the deque is not empty, the function sets aside a reference to the object at the tail in the local variable **result**; it decreases the **tail** member variable by one modulo the length of the array; adjusts the **count** accordingly; and returns **result**. All this can be done in a constant amount of time so the running time of **DequeueTail** is a constant.

---

**PROGRAM 6.26**
`DequeAsLinkedList` class definition

---

```
1  class DequeAsLinkedList : public Deque, public QueueAsLinkedList
2  {
3  public:
4      DequeAsLinkedList ();
5      // ...
6  };
```

---

## 6.3.2 Linked-List Implementation

Program 6.26 defines a linked-list implementation of a deque. The **DequeAsLinked-List** class is defined using multiple inheritance: It is derived from both the **Deque** abstract base class and the **QueueAsLinkedList** linked-list implementation of a queue. The **Deque** class provides the interface; the **QueueAsLinkedList**, the implementation.

The **QueueAsLinkedList** implementation provides almost all of the required functionality. For example, Program 6.27 shows that the **Head**, **EnqueueTail**, and **DequeueHead** operations of the **DequeAsLinkedList** class are implemented by calling the appropriate **QueueAsLinkedList** class operations.

**Tail, EnqueueHead, and DequeueTail Member Functions**
Program 6.28 defines the **Tail**, **EnqueueHead**, and **DequeueTail** member functions of the **DequeAsArray** class.

The **Tail** member function returns a **const** reference to the object at the tail of the deque. The tail of the deque is in the last element of the linked list. In Chapter 4 we saw that the running time of **LinkedList<T>::Last** is a constant, Therefore, the normal running time for the **Tail** function is $O(1)$.

---

**PROGRAM 6.27**
`DequeAsLinkedList` class `Head`, `EnqueueHead`, and `DequeueHead` member function definitions

---

```
1  Object& DequeAsLinkedList::Head () const
2      { return QueueAsLinkedList::Head (); }
3
4  void DequeAsLinkedList::EnqueueTail (Object& object)
5      { QueueAsLinkedList::Enqueue (object); }
6
7  Object& DequeAsLinkedList::DequeueHead ()
8      { return QueueAsLinkedList::Dequeue (); }
```

---

---

**PROGRAM 6.28**
`DequeAsLinkedList` class `Tail`, `EnqueueTail`, and `DequeueTail` member
function definitions

---

```
1   Object& DequeAsLinkedList::Tail () const
2   {
3       if (count == 0)
4           throw domain_error ("deque is empty");
5       return *list.Last ();
6   }
7
8   void DequeAsLinkedList::EnqueueHead (Object& object)
9   {
10      list.Prepend (&object);
11      ++count;
12  }
13
14  Object& DequeAsLinkedList::DequeueTail ()
15  {
16      if (count == 0)
17          throw domain_error ("deque is empty");
18      Object& result = *list.Last ();
19      list.Extract (&result);
20      --count;
21      return result;
22  }
```

---

The `EnqueueHead` function takes a single argument—a reference to the object to be added to the head of the deque. The function simply calls the `LinkedList<T>::Prepend` function. Since the running time for `Prepend` is $O(1)$, the running time of `EnqueueHead` is also $O(1)$.

The `DequeueTail` function removes an object from the tail of the deque and returns a reference to that object. First, it verifies that the deque is not empty and throws an exception when it is. If the deque is not empty, `DequeueTail` saves a reference to the last item in the linked list in the local variable `result`. Then the item of the linked list is removed from the list. When using the `LinkedList<T>` class from Chapter 4, the time required to delete the last item from a list is $O(n)$, where $n =$ `count` is the number of items in the list. As a result, the running time of `DequeueTail` is $O(n)$.

### 6.3.3 Doubly-Linked and Circular Lists

In the preceding section we saw that the running time of `DequeueHead` is $O(1)$, but that the running time of `DequeueTail` is $O(n)$, for the pointer based implementation of a deque. This is because the linked list data structure used, `LinkedList<T>` is a *singly-linked list*. Each element in a singly-linked list contains a single pointer—a pointer to the successor (next) element of the list. As a result, deleting the head of the linked list is easy: The new head is the successor of the old head.

However, deleting the tail of a linked list is not so easy: The new tail is the predecessor of the original tail. Since there is no pointer from the original tail to its predecessor, the predecessor must be found by traversing the linked list from the head. This traversal gives rise to the $O(n)$ running time.

In a *doubly-linked list,* each list element contains two pointers—one to its successor and one to its predecessor. There are many different variations of doubly-linked lists: Figure 6.9 illustrates four of them.

Figure 6.9(*a*) shows the simplest case: Two pointers, say *head* and *tail,* are used to keep track of the list elements. One of them points to the first element of the list, the other points to the last. The first element of the list has no predecessor, therefore that pointer is null. Similarly, the last element has no successor and the corresponding

**FIGURE 6.9**
Doubly-linked and circular list variations.

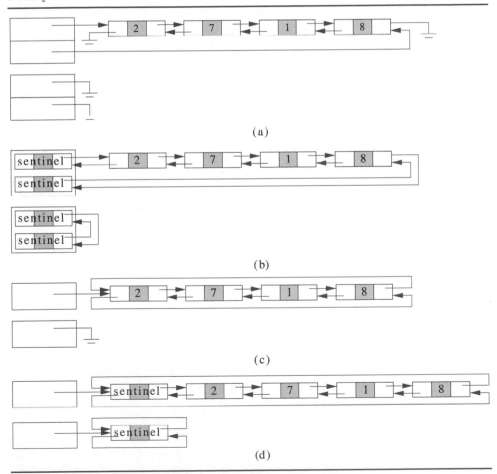

pointer is also null. In effect, we have two overlapping singly-linked lists which go in opposite directions. Figure 6.9 also shows the representation of an empty list. In this case the head and tail pointers are both null.

Figure 6.9(*b*) shows a case which uses sentinels. In this variation *two* sentinels are used because there are in effect two overlapping linked lists that go in opposite directions—one for each singly-linked list. Recall that the use of a sentinel is motivated by the fact that the code for insertion and deletion is often simpler to write because there are fewer special cases to consider. Figure 6.9(*b*) shows that in the empty list the two sentinels point to each other.

A *circular, doubly-linked list* is shown in Figure 6.9(*c*). A circular list is formed by making use of pointers which would otherwise be null: The last element of the list is made the predecessor of the first element; the first element, the successor of the last. The upshot is that we no longer need both a head and tail pointer to keep track of the list. Even if only a single pointer is used, both the first and the last list elements can be found in constant time.

Finally, Figure 6.9(*d*) shows a circular, doubly-linked list which has a single sentinel. This variation is similar to the preceding one in that both the first and the last list elements can be found in constant time. This variation has the advantage that no special cases are required when dealing with an empty list. Figure 6.9 shows that the empty list is represented by a list with exactly one element—the sentinel. In the case of the empty list, the sentinel is both its own successor and predecessor. Since the sentinel is always present, and since it always has both a successor and a predecessor, the code for adding elements to the empty list is identical to that for adding elements to a non-empty list.

## Exercises

**6.1.** The array-based stack implementation shown in Programs 6.2, 6.3, 6.4, and 6.5 uses a fixed length array. As a result, it is possible for the stack to become full. However, the `Array<T>` class defined in Chapter 4 provides a `SetLength` member function which can be used to change the length of the array.

  **a.** Rewrite the `Push` routine so that it doubles the length of the array when the array is full.

  **b.** Rewrite the `Pop` routine so that it halves the length of the array when the array is less than half full.

  **c.** Show that the *average* time for both push and pop operations is $O(1)$. **Hint:** Consider the running time required to push $n = 2^k$ items onto an empty stack, where $k \geq 0$.

**6.2** Consider a sequence $S$ of push and pop operations performed on a stack that is initially empty. The sequence $S$ is a valid sequence of operations if at no point is a pop operation attempted on an empty stack and if the stack is empty at the end of the sequence. Design a set of rules for generating a valid sequence.

**6.3** Devise an implementation of the `Queue` abstract data type *using two stacks*. Give algorithms for the `Enqueue` and `Dequeue` operations, and derive tight big-oh expressions for the running times of your implementation.

**6.4** Write each of the following *infix* expressions in *postfix* notation:

**a.** $a + b \times c \div d$

**b.** $a + b \times (c \div d)$

**c.** $(a + b) \times c \div d$

**d.** $(a + b) \times (c \div d)$

**e.** $(a + b \times c) \div d$

**f.** $(c \div d) \times (a + b)$

**6.5** Write each of the following *postfix* expressions in *infix* notation:

**a.** $w \, x \, y \div z \times -$

**b.** $w \, x \, y \, z \times \div -$

**c.** $w \, x - y \div z \times$

**d.** $w \, x - y \, z \times \div$

**e.** $w \, x \, y \div - z \times$

**f.** $y \, z \times w \, x - \div$

**6.6** Devise an algorithm which translates a *postfix* expression to a *prefix* expression. **Hint:** Use a stack of strings.

**6.7** The array-based queue implementation shown in Programs 6.14, 6.15, and 6.16 uses a fixed length array. As a result, it is possible for the queue to become full.

**a.** Rewrite the **Enqueue** routine so that it doubles the length of the array when the array is full.

**b.** Rewrite the **Dequeue** routine so that it halves the length of the array when the array is less than half full.

**c.** Show that the *average* time for both enqueue and dequeue operations is $O(1)$.

**6.8** Stacks and queues can be viewed as special cases of deques. Show how all the operations on stacks and queues can be mapped to operations on a deque. Discuss the merits of using a deque to implement a stack or a queue.

**6.9** Suppose we add a new operation to the stack ADT called **FindMinimum** that returns a reference to the smallest element in the stack. Show that it is possible to provide an implementation for **FindMinimum** that has a worst-case running time of $O(1)$.

**6.10** The *breadth-first traversal* routine shown in Program 6.20 visits the nodes of a tree in the order of their levels in the tree. Modify the algorithm so that the nodes are visited in reverse. **Hint:** Use a stack.

## Programming Projects

**6.1** Enhance the functionality of the RPN calculator given in Program 6.12 in the following ways:

   **a.** Use double-precision, floating-point arithmetic. That is, use the **Double** class defined in Program 5.8.

   **b.** Provide the complete repertoire of basic operators: $+$, $-$, $\times$, and $\div$.

   **c.** Add an exponentiation operator and a unary negation operator.

   **d.** Add a *clear* function that empties the operand stack and a *print* function that prints out the contents of the operand stack.

**6.2** Modify Program 6.12 so that it accepts expressions written in *prefix* (Polish) notation. **Hint:** See Exercise 6.6.

**6.3** Write a program to convert a *postfix* expression into an *infix* expression using a stack. One way to do this is to modify the RPN calculator program given in Program 6.12 to use a stack of infix expressions. The expressions can be represented as instances of the **String** class defined in Program 5.8. A binary operator should pop two strings from the stack and then push a string which is formed by concatenating the operator and its operands in the correct order. For example, suppose the operator is '`*`' and the two strings popped from the stack are "`(b+c)`" and "`a`". Then the result that gets pushed onto the stack is the string "`a*(b+c)`".

**6.4** Devise a scheme using a stack to convert an *infix* expression to a *postfix* expression. **Hint:** In a postfix expression operators appear *after* their operands, whereas in an infix expression they appear *between* their operands. Process the symbols in the prefix expression one-by-one. Output operands immediately, but save the operators in a stack until they are needed. Pay special attention to the precedence of the operators.

**6.5** Modify your solution to Project 6.4 so that it immediately evaluates the infix expression. That is, create an **InfixCalculator** routine in the style of Program 6.12.

**6.6** Consider a string of characters, $S$, comprised only of the characters (, ), [, ], {, and }. We say that $S$ is balanced if it has one of the following forms:

   • $S = $ "", i.e., $S$ is the string of length zero
   • $S = $ "$(T)$"
   • $S = $ "$[T]$"
   • $S = $ "$\{T\}$"
   • $S = $ "$TU$"

where both $T$ and $U$ are balanced strings, In other words, for every left parenthesis, bracket, or brace, there is a corresponding right parenthesis, bracket, or brace. For example, "`{()[()]}`" is balanced, but "`([)]`" is not. Write a program that uses a stack of characters to test whether a given string is balanced. (Use the **Char** class defined in Program 5.8.)

**6.7** Design and implement a **MultipleStack** class which provides $m \geq 1$ stacks in a single container. The declaration of the class should look something like this:

```
class MultipleStack : public Container
{
    // ...
public:
    MultipleStack (unsigned int);
    void Push (Object&, unsigned int);
    Object& Pop (unsigned int);
    // ...
};
```

- The constructor takes a single integer argument that specifies the number of stacks in the container.
- The **Push** function takes two arguments. The first gives the object to be pushed and the second specifies the stack on which to push it.
- The **Pop** function takes a single integer argument which specifies the stack to pop.

Choose one of the following implementation approaches:

a.  Keep all the stack elements in a single array.

b.  Use an array of **Stack** objects.

c.  Use a linked list of **Stack** objects.

**6.8**  Design and implement a class called **DequeAsDoublyLinkedList** that provides a deque implemented as a doubly-linked list. Select one of the approaches shown in Figure 6.9.

**6.9**  In Section 6.3, the **Deque** class is derived from the **Queue** class. This is the design paradigm known as *generalization*. The alternative paradigm is *specialization* in which the **Queue** class is derived from the **Deque** class. Redesign the **Deque** and **Queue** components of the class hierarchy using specialization.

**6.10**  Devise an approach for evaluating an arithmetic expression using a *queue* (rather than a stack). **Hint:** Transform the expression into a tree, as shown in Figure 6.10 and then do a *breadth-first traversal* of the tree *in reverse* (see Exercise 6.10). For example, the expression $(a + b) \times (c - d)$ becomes $d\,c\,b\,a - + \times$. Evaluate the resulting sequence from left to right using a queue in the same way that a postfix expression is evaluated using a stack.

---

**FIGURE 6.10**
Expression tree for $(a + b) \times (c - d)$.

---

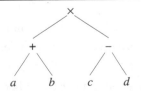

# 7 | Ordered Lists and Sorted Lists

The most simple, yet one of the most versatile containers is the *list*. In this chapter we consider lists as *abstract data types*. A list is a series of items. In general, we can insert and remove items from a list and we can visit all the items in a list in the order in which they appear.

In this chapter we consider two kinds of lists—ordered lists and sorted lists. In an *ordered list* the order of the items is significant. Consider a list of the titles of the chapters in this book. The order of the items in the list corresponds to the order in which they appear in the book. However, since the chapter titles are not sorted alphabetically, we cannot consider the list to be sorted. Since it is possible to change the order of the chapters in book, we must be able to do the same with the items of the list. As a result, we may insert an item into an ordered list at any position.

On the other hand, a *sorted list* is one in which the order of the items is defined by some collating sequence. For example, the index of this book is a sorted list. The items in the index are sorted alphabetically. When an item is inserted into a sorted list, it must be inserted at the correct position.

The list abstractions can be implemented in many ways. In this chapter we examine implementations based on the *array* and the *linked list* foundational data structures presented in Chapter 4 (see Figure 7.1).

## 7.1 Ordered Lists

The most basic of the searchable containers is an ordered list. In Chapter 5 we defined a searchable container as a container which supports the following additional operations:

**Insert** used to put objects into a the container;

**Withdraw** used to remove objects from the container;

**Find** used to locate objects in the container; and,

**IsMember** used to test whether a given object instance is in the container.

**FIGURE 7.1**
Object class hierarchy.

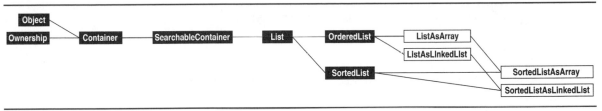

An ordered list is a container which holds a *sequence* of objects. Each object has a unique *position* in the sequence. In addition to the basic repertoire of operations supported by all searchable containers, ordered lists provide the following operations:

`FindPosition` used to find the position of an object in the ordered list;

`operator []` used to access the object at a given position in the ordered list;

`Withdraw(Position&)` used to remove the object at a given position from the ordered list.

`InsertAfter` used to insert an object into the ordered list *after* the object at a given position; and

`InsertBefore` used to insert an object into the ordered list *before* the object at a given position.

Program 7.1 declares two abstract classes—`List` and `OrderedList`. The `List` class is derived from the `SearchableContainer` class which is in turn derived from the `Container` class. Consequently, the `List` class interface comprises all of the member functions inherited from these base classes plus four additional member functions, `FindPosition`, two versions of `operator[]` and `Withdraw`. As befits the definition of an abstract class, all of these functions are pure virtual member functions of the `List` class.

The `OrderedList` class extends the `List` class by adding two more member functions—`InsertAfter` and `InsertBefore`. The two functions provided by the `OrderedList` class have been separated out from the `List` class interface because the `List` class is used as the base class from which other types of lists are derived.

Program 7.1 also defines the abstract class `Position`. The `Position` class abstracts the notion of the position of an item in a list. Since this abstraction is almost identical to that of an iterator, the `Position` class is derived from the `Iterator` abstract class. No additional member functions are defined.

As we did in the previous chapter with stacks, deques and queues, we will examine two ordered list implementations—an array-based one and a pointer-based one. Section 7.1.1 presents an implementation based on the `Array<T>` class; Section 7.1.2, a pointer-based implementation based on the `LinkedList<T>` class.

---

**PROGRAM 7.1**
List and Ordered class definitions

```
1  class Position : public Iterator
2  {
3  };
4
5  class List : public virtual SearchableContainer
6  {
7  public:
8      virtual Object& operator [] (unsigned int) const = 0;
9      virtual Object& operator [] (Position const&) const = 0;
10     virtual Position& FindPosition (Object const&) const = 0;
11     virtual void Withdraw (Position const&) = 0;
12 };
13
14 class OrderedList : public virtual List
15 {
16 public:
17     virtual void InsertAfter (Position const&, Object&) = 0;
18     virtual void InsertBefore (Position const&, Object&) = 0;
19 };
```

---

### 7.1.1 Array Implementation

This section presents an array-based implementation of ordered lists. Program 7.2 declares the **ListAsArray** class. The **ListAsArray** class is a concrete class and as such must provide implementations for all of the interface member functions which have been declared as pure virtual functions in the base classes from which the **ListAsArray** class is derived. The prototypes have been omitted from Program 7.2 since they have all been given earlier.

**Member Variables**
The **ListAsArray** class comprises one member variable, **array**, which is an array of pointers to **Object**s. The **array** variable is used to hold the items in the ordered list. Specifically, the items in the list are stored in array positions 0, 1, ..., **count** − 1. In an ordered list the position of an item is significant. The item at position 0 is the first item in the list; the item at position **count** − 1, the last.

An item at position $i + 1$ is the *successor* of the one at position $i$. That is, the one at $i + 1$ *follows* or comes *after* the one at $i$. Similarly, an item at position $i$ is the *predecessor* of the one at position $i + 1$; the one at position $i$ is said to *precede* or to come *before* the one at $i + 1$.

**Inserting and Accessing Items in a List**
Program 7.3 gives the definitions of the constructor and **Insert** member functions of the **ListAsArray** class. The constructor takes a single argument which specifies

---

**PROGRAM 7.2**
`ListAsArray` class definition

---

```
1   class ListAsArray : public virtual OrderedList
2   {
3   protected:
4       Array<Object*> array;
5
6       class Pos;
7   public:
8       ListAsArray (unsigned int);
9       // ...
10      friend class Pos;
11  };
```

---

the length of array to use in the representation of the ordered list. Thus if we use an array-based implementation, we need to know when a list is declared what will be the maximum number of items in that list. The constructor initializes the **array** variable as an array with the specified length. The running time of the constructor is clearly $O(1)$.

The **Insert** member function is part of the interface of all searchable containers. That is, it is a pure virtual function declared in the **SearchableContainer** class.

---

**PROGRAM 7.3**
`ListAsArray` class constructor, `Insert` member function, and subscripting operator definitions

---

```
1   ListAsArray::ListAsArray (unsigned int size) :
2       array (size)
3       {}
4
5   void ListAsArray::Insert (Object& object)
6   {
7       if (count == array.Length ())
8           throw domain_error ("list is full");
9       array [count] = &object;
10      ++count;
11  }
12
13  Object& ListAsArray::operator [] (unsigned int offset) const
14  {
15      if (offset >= count)
16          throw out_of_range ("invalid offset");
17      return *array [offset];
18  }
```

---

Its purpose is to put an object into the container. The obvious question which arises is, where should the inserted item be placed in the ordered list? The simple answer is, at the end.

In Program 7.3 we see that the **Insert** function simply adds the new item to the end of the list, provided there is still room in the array. Normally, the array will not be full, so the running time of this function is $O(1)$.

Program 7.3 also gives the definition of the subscripting operator, **operator[]**, which takes a subscript of type **unsigned int**. This function simply returns a reference to the object in the ordered list at the specified position. In this case, because the type **unsigned int** is used, the position is specified using a non-negative, integer-valued subscript expression. The implementation of this function is trivial—it simply makes use of the subscript operator provided by the **Array<T>** class. Assuming the specified position is valid, the running time of this function is $O(1)$.

### Finding Items in a List

Program 7.4 defines two **ListAsArray** class accessor functions which search for an object in the ordered list. The **IsMember** function tests whether a particular object instance is in the ordered list. The **Find** function locates in the list an object which *matches* its argument.

The **IsMember** function is a Boolean-valued function which takes as its lone argument a **const** reference to an **Object**. This function compares one-by-one the pointers contained in **array** with the *address* of the argument. Thus, this function tests whether *a particular object instance* is contained in the ordered list. In the worst case, the object sought is not in the list. In this case, the running time of the function is $O(n)$, where $n =$ **count** is the number of items in the ordered list.

The **Find** function also does a search of the ordered list. It also takes a single argument which is a **const** reference to an **Object**. However, find does not compare

---

**PROGRAM 7.4**
**ListAsArray** class **IsMember** and **Find** member function definitions

```
1   bool ListAsArray::IsMember (Object const& object) const
2   {
3       for (unsigned int i = 0; i < count; ++i)
4           if (array [i] == &object)
5               return true;
6       return false;
7   }
8
9   Object& ListAsArray::Find (Object const& object) const
10  {
11      for (unsigned int i = 0; i < count; ++i)
12          if (*array [i] == object)
13              return *array [i];
14      return NullObject::Instance ();
15  }
```

addresses. Instead, it uses **operator==** to compare the items. Thus, the **Find** function searches the list for an object which compares equal to its argument. The **Find** function returns a reference to the object found. If no match is found, it returns a reference to the **NullObject** instance. The running time of this function depends on the time required for the comparison operator, $\mathcal{T}\langle \text{op==(T\&, T\&)} \rangle$. In the worst case, the object sought is not in the list. In this case the running time is $n \times \mathcal{T}\langle \text{op==(T\&, T\&)} \rangle + O(n)$. For simplicity, we will assume that the comparison takes a constant amount of time. Hence, the running time of the function is also $O(n)$, where $n = $ **count** is the number of items in the list.

It is important to understand the subtle distinction between the search done by the **IsMember** function and that done by **Find**. The **IsMember** function searches for a specific object instance while **Find** simply looks for a matching object. Consider the following:

```
Object& object1 = *new Int (57);
Object& object2 = *new Int (57);
ListAsArray list (1);
list.Insert (object1);
```

This code fragment creates two **Int** class object instances, both of which have the value 57. Only the first object, **object1**, is inserted into the ordered list **list**. Consequently, the function call

```
list.IsMember (object1)
```

returns **true**; whereas the function call

```
list.IsMember (object2)
```

returns **false**.

On the other hand, if a search is done using the **Find** function like this;

```
Object& object3 = list.Find (object2);
```

the search will be successful! After the call, **object3** refers to **object1**.

### Removing Items from a List

Objects are removed from a searchable container using the **Withdraw** function. Program 7.5 defines the **Withdraw** function for the **ListAsArray** class. This function takes a single argument which is a reference to the object to be removed from the container. It is the specific object instance which is removed from the container, not simply one which matches (i.e., compares equal to) the argument.

The **Withdraw** function first needs to find the position of the item to be removed from the list. This part is identical to the main loop of the **IsMember** function. An exception is thrown if the list is empty, or if the object to be removed is not in the list. The number of iterations needed to find an object depends on its position. If the object to be removed is found at position $i$, then the search phase takes $O(i)$ time.

Removing an object from position $i$ of an ordered list which is stored in an array requires that all of the objects at positions $i + 1$, $i + 2$, ..., **count**$-1$, be moved one

---

**PROGRAM 7.5**
ListAsArray class Withdraw member function definition

---

```
1   void ListAsArray::Withdraw (Object& object)
2   {
3       if (count == 0)
4           throw domain_error ("list is empty");
5       unsigned int i = 0;
6       while (i < count && array [i] != &object)
7           ++i;
8       if (i == count)
9           throw invalid_argument ("object not found");
10
11      for ( ; i < count - 1U; ++i)
12          array [i] = array [i + 1];
13      --count;
14  }
```

---

position to the left. Altogether, $\text{count} - 1 - i$ objects need to be moved. Hence, this phase takes $O(\text{count} - i)$ time.

The running time of the **Withdraw** function is the sum of the running times of the two phases, $O(i) + O(\text{count} - i)$. Hence, the total running time is $O(n)$, where $n = \text{count}$ is the number of items in the ordered list.

Care must be taken when using the **Withdraw** function. Consider the following:

```
Object& object1 = *new Int (57);
Object& object2 = *new Int (57);
ListAsArray list (1);
list.Insert (object1);
```

To remove **object1** from the ordered list, we may write

```
list.Withdraw (object1);
```

However, the call

```
list.Withdraw (object2);
```

will fail because **object2** is not actually in the list. If for some reason we have lost track of **object1**, we can always write:

```
list.Withdraw (list.Find (object2));
```

which first locates the object in the ordered list (**object1**) which matches **object2** and then deletes that object.

### Positions of Items in a List

As shown in Program 7.1, the abstract class **Position** is derived from the class **Iterator**. Recall from Chapter 5 that an iterator is used to visit systematically one-by-one all of the items in a container. An essential characteristic of an iterator is that at any instant, it *refers* to exactly one item in the container. To refer to an item in the container, it must keep track of the position of the item. Therefore, we may view an iterator as a kind of abstract position in an ordered list.

Program 7.6 gives the declaration of the **ListAsArray::Pos** class which is a **Position** (and therefore an **Iterator**) associated with the **ListAsArray** ordered list class. **ListAsArray::Pos** objects contain two member variables—**list** and **offset**. The former is a reference to an ordered list; the latter records an offset in the corresponding array.

### Finding the Position of an Item and Accessing by Position

Program 7.7 defines two more member functions of the **ListAsArray** class, **Find Position** and **operator[]**. The **FindPosition** member function takes as its lone argument a **const** reference to an **Object**. The purpose of this function is to search the ordered list for an item which matches the object, and to return its position. The result is a reference to a **Position**. Since the **Position** class is an abstract base class, there can be no object instances of that class. However, there can be object instances of a concrete class derived from the **Position** class, such as the **ListAsArray::Pos** class. Therefore, the **FindPosition** function allocates a new instance of the **ListAsArray::Pos** class and returns a reference to that instance.

The search algorithm used in **FindPosition** is identical to that used in the **Find** routine (Program 7.4). The **FindPosition** makes use of **operator==** to locate a contained object which is equal to the search target. Notice that if no match is found, the **offset** is set to the value **count**, which is one position to the right of the last item in the ordered list. The running time of **FindPosition** is identical to that of **Find**: $n \times \mathcal{T}\langle \text{op==(T\&, T\&)} \rangle + O(n)$, where $n = \text{count}$.

The subscripting operator, **operator[]**, defined in Program 7.7 takes a **const** reference to a **Position** and returns a reference to the item in the ordered list at the given position. The **Position** argument is dynamically cast to a **ListAsArray::Pos**.

---

**PROGRAM 7.6**
**ListAsArray::Pos** class definition

```
1   class ListAsArray::Pos : public Position
2   {
3   protected:
4       ListAsArray const& list;
5       unsigned int offset;
6   public:
7       // ...
8       friend class ListAsArray;
9       friend class SortedListAsArray;
10  };
```

---

**PROGRAM 7.7**
ListAsArray class FindPosition member function and subscripting operator definitions

```
1   Position& ListAsArray::FindPosition (Object const& object) const
2   {
3       unsigned int i = 0;
4       while (i < count && *array [i] != object)
5           ++i;
6       return *new Pos (*this, i);
7   }
8
9   Object& ListAsArray::operator [] (Position const& arg) const
10  {
11      Pos const& position = dynamic_cast<Pos const&> (arg);
12
13      if (&position.list != this || position.offset >= count)
14          throw invalid_argument ("invalid position");
15      return *array [position.offset];
16  }
```

---

Remember that in C++, run-time checks are made to ensure that the cast is safe. After a simple validity check, the offset recorded in the position is used to index into the array variable, to obtain the desired result. If the offset is equal to count, the position is invalid. In this case, a reference to the NullObject instance is returned. The running time of this operator is clearly $O(1)$.

### Inserting an Item at an Arbitrary Position

Two member functions for inserting an item at an arbitrary position in an ordered list are declared in Program 7.1—InsertBefore and InsertAfter. Both of these take two arguments: a const reference to a Position and a reference to an Object. The effects of these two functions are illustrated in Figure 7.2.

Figure 7.2 shows that in both cases a number of items to the right of the insertion point need to be moved over to make room for the item that is being inserted into the ordered list. In the case of InsertBefore, items to the right *including the item at the point of insertion* are moved; for InsertAfter, only items to the right of the point of insertion are moved, and the new item is inserted in the array location following the insertion point.

Program 7.8 gives the implementation of the InsertAfter member function for the ListAsArray class. The code for the InsertBefore function is identical except for one line as explained below.

The InsertAfter function takes two arguments—a const reference to a Position and a reference to an Object. As was done in the FindPosition function, the first argument is dynamically cast to a ListAsArray::Pos. Next, some simple tests are done to ensure that the position is valid, and that there is room left in the array to do the insertion.

On line 11 the array index where the new item will ultimately be stored is computed. For InsertAfter the index is offset+1 as shown in Program 7.8. In the case of

**FIGURE 7.2**
Inserting an item in an ordered list implemented as an array.

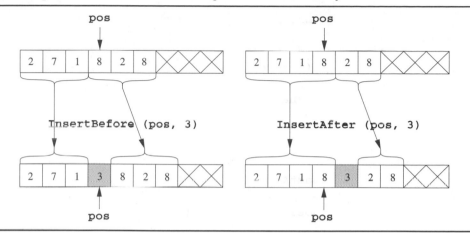

**InsertBefore**, the value required is simply **offset**. The loop on lines 13–14 moves items over and then a pointer **object** is saved on line 15.

If we assume that no exceptions are thrown, the running time of **InsertAfter** is dominated by the loop which moves list items. In the worst case, all the items in the array need to be moved. Thus, the running time of both the **InsertAfter** and **InsertBefore** functions is $O(n)$, where $n = $ **count**.

**PROGRAM 7.8**
**ListAsArray** class **InsertAfter** member function definition

```
1   void ListAsArray::InsertAfter (
2       Position const& arg, Object& object)
3   {
4       Pos const& position = dynamic_cast<Pos const&> (arg);
5
6       if (count == array.Length ())
7           throw domain_error ("list is full");
8       if (&position.list != this || position.offset >= count)
9           throw invalid_argument ("invalid position");
10
11      unsigned int const insertPosition = position.offset + 1;
12
13      for (unsigned int i = count; i > insertPosition; --i)
14          array [i] = array [i - 1U];
15      array [insertPosition] = &object;
16      ++count;
17  }
```

**FIGURE 7.3**
Withdrawing an item from an ordered list implemented as an array.

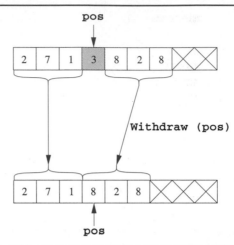

### Removing Arbitrary Items by Position

The final member function of the **ListAsArray** class that we will consider is the **Withdraw** function, which takes a **const** reference to a **Position**. The desired effect of this function is to remove from the ordered list the item at the specified position.

Figure 7.3 shows the way to delete an item from an ordered list which is implemented with an array. All of the items remaining in the list to the right of the deleted item need to be shifted to the left in the array by one position.

Program 7.9 gives the implementation of the **Withdraw** member function. As has been the pattern in all of the member functions which take a **const** reference to a **Position**, that argument is first dynamically cast to a **ListAsArray::Pos**. After

**PROGRAM 7.9**
**ListAsArray** class **Withdraw** member function definition

```
1   void ListAsArray::Withdraw (Position const& arg)
2   {
3       Pos const& position = dynamic_cast<Pos const&> (arg);
4
5       if (count == 0)
6           throw domain_error ("list is empty");
7       if (&position.list != this || position.offset >= count)
8           throw invalid_argument ("invalid position");
9       for (unsigned int i = position.offset; i < count-1U; ++i)
10          array [i] = array [i + 1];
11      --count;
12  }
```

checking the validity of the position, all of the items following the item to be withdrawn are moved one position to the left in the array.

The running time of the **Withdraw** function depends on the position in the array of the item being deleted and on the number of items in the ordered lists. In the worst case, the item to be deleted is in the first position. In this case, the work required to move the remaining items left is $O(n)$, where $n =$ **count**.

## 7.1.2 Linked List Implementation

This section presents a pointer-based implementation of ordered lists. Program 7.10 declares the **ListAsLinkedList** class.[1] Like its array-based counterpart **ListAs Array**, the **ListAsLinkedList** class is a concrete class derived from the abstract base class **List**. The sets of member functions comprising the public interfaces of the **ListAsArray** and **ListAsLinkedList** classes are identical.

### Member Variables
Objects of the **ListAsLinkedList** class contain one member variable, **linked List**, which is a linked list of pointers to **Objects**. The **linkedList** is used to hold the items in the ordered list. Since a linked list is used, there is no notion of an inherent limit on the number of items which can be placed in the ordered list. Items can be inserted until the available memory is exhausted.

### Inserting and Accessing Items in a List
Program 7.11 gives the implementation of the **Insert** member function of the **ListAsLinkedList** class. This function takes a reference to an **Object** which

---

**PROGRAM 7.10**
ListAsLinkedList class definition

```
1    class ListAsLinkedList : public virtual OrderedList
2    {
3    protected:
4        LinkedList<Object*> linkedList;
5
6        class Pos;
7    public:
8        ListAsLinkedList ();
9        //...
10       friend class Pos;
11   };
```

---

[1] I will admit that the name **ListAsLinkedList** is somewhat confusing. However, it is a whole word shorter than **OrderedListAsLinkedList** and that much easier to type!

---

**PROGRAM 7.11**
`ListAsLinkedList` class constructor, `Insert` member function and subscripting operator definitions

---

```
1   ListAsLinkedList::ListAsLinkedList () :
2       linkedList ()
3       {}
4
5   void ListAsLinkedList::Insert (Object& object)
6   {
7       linkedList.Append (&object);
8       ++count;
9   }
10
11  Object& ListAsLinkedList::operator [] (unsigned int offset) const
12  {
13      if (offset >= count)
14          throw out_of_range ("invalid offset");
15
16      unsigned int i = 0;
17      ListElement<Object*> const* ptr =
18          linkedList.Head ();
19      while (i < offset && ptr != 0)
20      {
21          ptr = ptr->Next ();
22          ++i;
23      }
24      if (ptr == 0)
25          throw logic_error ("should never happen");
26      return *ptr->Datum ();
27  }
```

---

is to be added to the ordered list. As in the case of the **ArrayAsLinkedList** class, the object is added at the end of the ordered list. This is done simply by calling the **Append** function from the **LinkedList<T>** class.

The running time of the **Insert** function is determined by that of **Append**. In Chapter 4 this was shown to be $O(1)$. The only other work done by the **Insert** function is to add one to the **count** variable. Consequently, the total running time for **Insert** is $O(1)$.

Program 7.11 also defines a subscripting operator, **operator[]**, which takes an argument of type **unsigned int**. This operator is used to access elements of the ordered list by their position in the list. In this case, the position is specified by a nonnegative, integer-valued subscript expression. Since there is no way to access directly the $k$th element of linked list, the implementation of this function comprises a loop which traverses the list to find the $k$th item. The function returns a reference to the $k$th item, provided $k <$ count. Otherwise, $k$ is not a valid subscript value and the function throws an exception.

The running time of this operator [] depends on the number of items in the list and on the value of the subscript expression. In the worst case, the item sought is at the end of the ordered list. Therefore, the worst-case running time of this algorithm, assuming the subscript expression is valid, is $O(n)$, where $n =$ count.

### Finding Items in a List

Program 7.12 defines the **IsMember** and **Find** member functions of the **ListAsLinkedList** class. The implementations of these functions are almost identical. However, they differ in two key aspects—the comparison used and the return value.

The **IsMember** function tests whether a particular object instance is contained in the ordered list. It returns a Boolean value indicating whether the object is present. The running time of this function is clearly $O(n)$, where $n =$ count, the number of items in the ordered list.

The **Find** member function locates an object which matches a given object. The match is determined by using operator==. **Find** returns a reference to the matching object if one is found. Otherwise, it returns a reference to the **NullObject** instance. The running time for this function is $n \times \mathcal{T} \langle \text{op==(T\&, T\&)} \rangle + O(n)$, where $\mathcal{T} \langle \text{op==(T\&, T\&)} \rangle$ is the time required to do the comparison, and $n =$ count is the number of items in the ordered list. This simplifies to $O(n)$ when the comparison can be done in constant time.

---

**PROGRAM 7.12**
ListAsLinkedList class **IsMember** and **Find** member function definitions

```
1   bool ListAsLinkedList::IsMember (Object const& object) const
2   {
3       ListElement<Object*> const* ptr;
4
5       for (ptr = linkedList.Head (); ptr != 0; ptr = ptr->Next ())
6           if (ptr->Datum () == &object)
7               return true;
8       return false;
9   }
10
11  Object& ListAsLinkedList::Find (Object const& object) const
12  {
13      ListElement<Object*> const* ptr;
14
15      for (ptr = linkedList.Head (); ptr != 0; ptr = ptr->Next ())
16          if (*ptr->Datum () == object)
17              return *ptr->Datum ();
18      return NullObject::Instance ();
19  }
```

---

---

**PROGRAM 7.13**
`ListAsLinkedList` class `Withdraw` member function definition

```
1  void ListAsLinkedList::Withdraw (Object& object)
2  {
3      if (count == 0)
4          throw domain_error ("list is empty");
5      linkedList.Extract (&object);
6      --count;
7  }
```

---

### Removing Items from a List

The `Withdraw` member function is used to remove a specific object instance from an ordered list. The implementation of the `Withdraw` member function for the `ListAsLinkedList` class is given in Program 7.13.

The implementation of `Withdraw` is straightforward: It simply calls the `Extract` function provided by the `LinkedList<T>` class to remove the specified object from the `linkedList` member variable. The running time of the `Withdraw` function is dominated by that of `Extract` which was shown in Chapter 4 to be $O(n)$, where $n$ is the number of items in the linked list.

### Positions of Items in a List

Program 7.14 gives the definition of a the `ListAsLinkedList::Pos` class, the purpose of which is to record the position of an item in an ordered list implemented as a linked list.

The `ListAsLinkedList::Pos` class has two member variables—`list` and `element`. The first is a reference to the ordered list which contains the item of interest; the second is a pointer to the linked-list element in which the item appears. Notice that the implementation of the `ListAsLinkedList::Pos` class is fundamentally different from the array version, `ListAsArray::Pos`. In the array version, the position was specified by an offset, i.e, by an *ordinal number* that shows the position of the item in the ordered sequence. In the linked-list version, the position is specified by

---

**PROGRAM 7.14**
`ListAsLinkedList::Pos` class definition

```
1  class ListAsLinkedList::Pos : public Position
2  {
3      ListAsLinkedList const& list;
4      ListElement<Object*> const* element;
5  public:
6      //...
7      friend class ListAsLinkedList;
8  };
```

---

a pointer to the element of the linked list in which the item is stored. Regardless of the implementation, both kinds of position provide exactly the same functionality—their public interfaces are identical.

### Finding the Position of an Item and Accessing by Position

The **FindPosition** member function of the **ListAsLinkedList** class is used to determine the position of an item in an ordered list implemented as a linked list. Its result is a reference to a **Position**. Such a position can be used with the subscripting operator, **operator[]** to access the item in the ordered list found at the given position. The **FindPosition** and **operator[]** member functions are defined in Program 7.15.

The **FindPosition** function takes as its lone argument a **const** reference to an **Object** that is the target of the search. The search algorithm used by **FindPosition** is identical to that of **Find**, which is given in Program 7.12. Consequently, the running time is the same:

$$n \times \mathcal{T}\langle_{\text{op==(T\&, T\&)}}\rangle + O(n)$$

where $\mathcal{T}\langle_{\text{op==(T\&, T\&)}}\rangle$ is the time required to match to **Object**s, and $n = $ **count** is the number of items in the ordered list.

The subscripting operator, **operator[]**, which takes as its subscript expression a reference to a **Position**, is also defined in Program 7.15. This routine assumes that the position it is passed is an instance of a **ListAsLinkedList::Pos**. It simply

---

**PROGRAM 7.15**
**ListAsLinkedList** class **FindPosition** member function and subscripting operator definitions

```
1   Position& ListAsLinkedList::FindPosition (
2       Object const& object) const
3   {
4       ListElement<Object*> const* ptr =
5           linkedList.Head ();
6       while (ptr != 0 && *ptr->Datum () != object)
7           ptr = ptr->Next ();
8       return *new Pos (*this, ptr);
9   }
10
11  Object& ListAsLinkedList::operator [] (
12      Position const& arg) const
13  {
14      Pos const& position = dynamic_cast<Pos const&> (arg);
15
16      if (&position.list != this || position.element == 0)
17          throw invalid_argument ("invalid position");
18      return *position.element->Datum ();
19  }
```

---

dereferences the `element` pointer contained in the `ListAsLinkedList::Pos` argument to obtain the required item in the ordered list. Assuming no exceptions are thrown, the running time is clearly $O(1)$.

### Inserting an Item at an Arbitrary Position

Once having determined the position of an item in an ordered list, we can make use of that position to insert items into the middle of the list. Two functions are specifically provided for this purpose—`InsertAfter` and `InsertBefore`. Both of these take the same set of arguments: A `const` reference to a `Position` which specifies the point at which the insertion is to be made, and a reference to the object to be inserted.

Program 7.16 gives the implementation for the `InsertAfter` member function of the `ListAsLinkedList` class. After casting the arguments to the appropriate types and performing some validity checks, this function simply calls the `InsertAfter` function provided by the `LinkedList<T>` class. Assuming no exceptions are thrown, the running time for this function is $O(1)$.

The implementation of `InsertBefore` is not shown—its similarity with `Insert After` should be obvious. Since it must call the `InsertBefore` routine provided by the `LinkedList<T>` class, we expect the worst case running time to be $O(n)$, where $n = $ `count`.

### Removing Arbitrary Items by Position

The final `ListAsLinkedList` member function to be considered is the version of `Withdraw` that takes as its lone argument a reference to a `Position`. The function removes an arbitrary item from an ordered list, where the position of that item is specified by an instance of `ListAsLinkedList::Pos`. The code for the `Withdraw` function is given in Program 7.17.

The `Withdraw` function first converts its `Position` argument to the appropriate type—a `ListAsLinkedList::Pos`. It then performs validity checks on that position, checking that the position refers to this list, and that the position is valid. The item at the specified position in the list is removed from the linked list by calling the `Extract` function provided by `LinkedList<T>`.

---

**PROGRAM 7.16**
`ListAsLinkedList` class `InsertAfter` member function definition

---

```
1   void ListAsLinkedList::InsertAfter (
2       Position const& arg, Object& object)
3   {
4       Pos const& position = dynamic_cast<Pos const&> arg;
5
6       if (&position.list != this || position.element == 0)
7           throw invalid_argument ("invalid position");
8       linkedList.InsertAfter (position.element, &object);
9       ++count;
10  }
```

---

**PROGRAM 7.17**
ListAsLinkedList class Withdraw member function definition

```
1   void ListAsLinkedList::Withdraw (Position const& arg)
2   {
3       Pos const& position = dynamic_cast<Pos const&> (arg);
4
5       if (count == 0)
6           throw domain_error ("list is empty");
7       if (&position.list != this || position.element == 0)
8           throw invalid_argument ("invalid position");
9
10      linkedList.Extract (position.element->Datum ());
11      --count;
12  }
```

The running time of the **Withdraw** member function of the **ListAsLinkedList** class depends on the running time of the **Extract** of the **LinkedList\<T>** class. The latter was shown to be $O(n)$ where $n$ is the number of items in the linked list. Consequently, the total running time is $O(n)$.

### 7.1.3  Performance Comparison: ListAsArray versus ListAsLinkedList

The running times calculated for the various member functions of the two ordered list implementations, **ListAsArray** and **ListAsLinkedList**, are summarized below in Table 7.1. With the exception of two member functions, the running times of the two implementations are asymptotically identical.

**TABLE 7.1**
Running Times of Operations on Ordered Lists

| Member Function | Ordered List Implementation | | |
| --- | --- | --- | --- |
| | ListAsArray | | ListAsLinkedList |
| Insert | $O(1)$ | | $O(1)$ |
| IsMember | $O(n)$ | | $O(n)$ |
| Find | $O(n)$ | | $O(n)$ |
| Withdraw(Object&) | $O(n)$ | | $O(n)$ |
| FindPosition | $O(n)$ | | $O(n)$ |
| operator[](Position&) | $O(1)$ | | $O(1)$ |
| operator[](unsigned int) | $O(1)$ | $\neq$ | $O(n)$ |
| Withdraw(Position&) | $O(n)$ | | $O(n)$ |
| InsertAfter | $O(n)$ | $\neq$ | $O(1)$ |
| InsertBefore | $O(n)$ | | $O(n)$ |

The two differences are the subscripting operator which takes an integer offset, `operator[] (unsigned int)`, and the `InsertAfter` function. The subscripting operation can be done constant time when using an array, but it requires $O(n)$ in a linked list. Conversely, `InsertAfter` requires $O(n)$ time when using an array, but can be done in constant time in the singly-linked list.

Table 7.1 does not tell the whole story. The other important difference between the two implementations is the amount of space required. Consider first the array implementation, `ListAsArray`. An array object is comprised of two member variables—`array` and `count`. The former has type `Array<Object*>`, and the latter is an `unsigned int`. The storage required for an `Array<T>` was computed in Chapter 4. Using that result, the storage needed for an `ListAsArray` which can hold *at most M* object pointers is given by:

$$\texttt{sizeof(count)} + \texttt{sizeof(array)} =$$
$$3\,\texttt{sizeof(unsigned int)} + \texttt{sizeof(Object**)} + M\,\texttt{sizeof(Object*)}$$

Notice that since we have implemented the ordered list container using indirect storage, we have calculated the space used by the pointers to the contained objects. However, since we cannot know the types of the contained objects, we cannot calculate the space required by those objects.

A similar calculation can also be done for the `ListAsLinkedList` class. In this case, we assume that the actual number of contained objects is $n$. The total storage required is given by:

$$\texttt{sizeof(count)} + \texttt{sizeof(linkedList)} =$$
$$\texttt{sizeof(unsigned int)} + n\,\texttt{sizeof(Object*)}$$
$$+ (n+2)\texttt{sizeof(ListElement<Object*>)}$$

If we assume that integers and pointers require four bytes each, the storage requirement for the `ListAsArray` class becomes $16 + 4M$ bytes; and for the `ListAsList` class, it becomes $12 + 8n$ bytes. That is, the storage needed for the array implementation is $O(M)$, where $M$ is the maximum length of the ordered list; whereas, the storage needed for the linked list implementation is $O(n)$, where $n$ is the actual number of items in the ordered list. Equating the two expressions, we get that the break-even point occurs at $n = (M + 1)/2$. That is, if $n < (M + 1)/2$, the array version uses more memory space; and for $n > (M + 1)/2$, the linked list version uses more memory space.

It is not just the amount of memory space used that should be considered when choosing an ordered list implementation. We must also consider the implications of the existence of the limit $M$. The array implementation requires a priori knowledge about the maximum number of items to be put in the ordered list. The total amount of storage then remains constant during the course of execution. On the other hand, the linked list version has no predetermined maximum length. It is only constrained by the total amount of memory available to the program. Furthermore, the amount of memory used by the linked list version varies during the course of execution. We do not have to commit a large chunk of memory for the duration of the program.

### 7.1.4 Applications

The applications of lists and ordered lists are myriad. In this section we will consider only one—the use of an ordered list to represent a polynomial. In general, an $n$th-order polynomial in $x$, for non-negative integer $n$, has the form

$$\sum_{i=0}^{n} a_i x^i = a_0 + a_1 x + a_2 x^2 + \cdots + a_n x^n$$

where $a_n \neq 0$. The term $a_i$ is the *coefficient* of the $i$th power of $x$. We shall assume that the coefficients are real numbers. That is, $\forall i : 0 \leq i \leq n, a_i \in \mathbb{R}$.

An alternative representation for such a polynomial consists of a sequence of ordered pairs:

$$\{(a_0, 0), (a_1, 1), (a_2, 2), \ldots, (a_n, n), \}.$$

Each ordered pair, $(a_i, i)$, corresponds to the term $a_i x^i$ of the polynomial. That is, the ordered pair is comprised of the coefficient of the $i$th term together with the subscript of that term, $i$. For example, the polynomial $31 + 41x + 59x^2$ can be represented by the sequence $\{(31, 0), (41, 1), (59, 2)\}$.

Consider now the 100th-order polynomial $x^{100} + 1$. Clearly, there are only two nonzero coefficients: $a_{100} = 1$ and $a_0 = 1$. The advantage of using the sequence of ordered pairs to represent such a polynomial is that we can omit from the sequence those pairs that have a zero coefficient. We represent the polynomial $x^{100} + 1$ by the sequence $\{(1, 100), (1, 0)\}$

Now that we have a way to represent polynomials, we can consider various operations on them. For example, consider the polynomial

$$p(x) = \sum_{i=0}^{n} a_i x^i.$$

We can compute its *derivative* with respect to $x$ by *differentiating* each of the terms to get

$$p'(x) = \sum_{i=0}^{n-1} a_i' x^i,$$

where $a_i' = (i+1)a_{i+1}$. In terms of the corresponding sequences, if $p(x)$ is represented by the sequence

$$\{(a_0, 0), (a_1, 1), (a_2, 2), \ldots, (a_i, i), \ldots, (a_n, n)\},$$

then its derivative is the sequence

$$\{(a_1, 0), (2a_2, 1), (3a_3, 2), \ldots, (a_i, i-1), \ldots, (na_n, n-1)\}.$$

This result suggests a very simple algorithm to differentiate a polynomial which is represented by a sequence of ordered pairs:

1. Drop the ordered pair that has a zero exponent.

2. For every other ordered pair, multiply the coefficient by the exponent, and then subtract one from the exponent.

Since the representation of an $n$th-order polynomial has at most $n + 1$ ordered pairs, and since a constant amount of work is necessary for each ordered pair, this is inherently an $\Omega(n)$ algorithm.

Of course, the worst-case running time of the polynomial differentiation will depend on the way that the sequence of ordered pairs is implemented. We will now consider an implementation that makes use of the **ListAsLinkedList** pointer-based implementation of ordered lists. To begin with, we need a class to represent the terms of the polynomial. Program 7.18 gives the definition of the **Term** class and several of its member functions.

Each **Term** instance has two member variables, **coefficient** and **exponent**, which correspond to the elements of the ordered pair as discussed above. The former is a **double** and the latter, an **unsigned int**.

The **Term** class is derived from the **Object** class because instances of the **Term** class will be put into a container. Program 7.18 gives the definitions of three member functions: a constructor, **CompareTo**, and **Differentiate**. The constructor simply takes a pair of arguments and initializes the corresponding member variables accordingly.

The **CompareTo** function is used to compare two **Term** instances. Consider two terms, $ax^i$ and $bx^j$. We define the relation $<$ on terms of a polynomial as follows:

$$ax^i < bx^j \iff (i < j) \lor (i = j \land a < b)$$

Note that the relation $<$ does not depend on the value of the variable $x$.

Finally, the **Differentiate** function does what its name says: It differentiates a term with respect to $x$. Given a term such as $(a_0, 0)$, it computes the result $(0, 0)$; and given a term such as $(a_i, i)$ where $i > 0$, it computes the result $(ia_i, i - 1)$.

We now consider the representation of a polynomial using an ordered list. Program 6.19 gives the definition of the class **Polynomial** which is derived in this case from the **ListAsLinkedList** class. In this example, the pointer-based implementation of lists is used.

Program 7.19 defines the member function **Differentiate** which has the effect of changing the polynomial to its derivative with respect to $x$. To compute this derivative, it is necessary to call the **Differentiate** member function of the **Term** class for each term in the polynomial. Since the polynomial is implemented as a container, there is an **Accept** member function which can be used to perform a given operation on all of the objects in that container. In this case, we define a visitor, **DifferentiatingVisitor**, which assumes its argument is an instance of the **Term** class and differentiates it.

**PROGRAM 7.18**
Term class definition

```
1   class Term : public Object
2   {
3       double coefficient;
4       unsigned int exponent;
5   public:
6       Term (double, unsigned int);
7       //...
8       int CompareTo (Object const&) const;
9       void Differentiate ();
10  };
11
12  Term::Term (double _coefficient, unsigned int _exponent) :
13      coefficient (_coefficient),
14      exponent (_exponent)
15      {}
16
17  int Term::CompareTo (Object const& object) const
18  {
19      Term const& term = dynamic_cast<Term const&> (object);
20      if (exponent == term.exponent)
21          return ::Compare (coefficient, term.coefficient);
22      else
23          return exponent - term.exponent;
24  }
25
26  void Term::Differentiate ()
27  {
28      if (exponent > 0)
29      {
30          coefficient *= exponent;
31          exponent -= 1;
32      }
33      else
34          coefficient = 0;
35  }
```

After the terms in the polynomial have been differentiated, it is necessary to check for the term $(0, 0)$ which arises from differentiating $(a_0, 0)$. The **Find** member function is used to locate the term, and if one is found the **Withdraw** function is used to remove it.

The analysis of the running time of the **Polynomial::Differentiate** function is straightforward. The running time of **Term::Differentiate** is clearly

---

**PROGRAM 7.19**
Polynomial class definition

```
1   class Polynomial : public ListAsLinkedList
2   {
3   public:
4       void Differentiate ();
5   };
6
7   class DifferentiatingVisitor : public Visitor
8   {
9   public:
10      void Visit (Object& object)
11      {
12          Term& term = dynamic_cast<Term&> (object);
13          term.Differentiate ();
14      }
15  };
16
17  void Polynomial::Differentiate ()
18  {
19      DifferentiatingVisitor visitor;
20      Accept (visitor);
21      Object& zeroTerm = Find (Term (0, 0));
22      if (!zeroTerm.IsNull ())
23      {
24          Withdraw (zeroTerm);
25          delete &zeroTerm;
26      }
27  }
```

---

$O(1)$. So too is the running time of the function the **Visit** member function of the **DifferentiatingVisitor**. The latter function is called once for each contained object. In the worst case, given an $n$th-order polynomial, there are $n + 1$ terms. Therefore, the time required to differentiate the terms is $O(n)$. Locating the zero term is $O(n)$ in the worst case, and so too is deleting it. Therefore, the total running time required to differentiate a $n$th-order polynomial is $O(n)$.

## 7.2 Sorted Lists

The next type of searchable container that we consider is a *sorted list*. A sorted list is like an ordered list: It is a searchable container that holds a sequence of objects. However, the position of an item in a sorted list is not arbitrary. The items in the sequence appear in order, say, from the smallest to the largest. Of course, for such an ordering to exist, the relation used to sort the items must be a *total order.*[2]

In addition to the basic repertoire of operations supported by all searchable containers, sorted lists provide the following operations:

**FindPosition**, used to find the position of an object in the sorted list;

**operator []**, used to access the object at a given position in the sorted list; and

**Withdraw**, used to remove the object at a given position from the sorted list.

These operations have similar semantics to the like-named ones for ordered lists. Conspicuous by their absence are the operations **InsertAfter** and **InsertBefore** which are provided by the **Ordered List** class. These operations are not provided for sorted lists because they allow arbitrary insertions, but arbitrary insertions do not necessarily result in sorted lists.

Program 7.20 gives the declaration of the class which is used to represent sorted lists: **SortedList**. Like its unsorted counterpart, the class **SortedList** is derived from the class **List** which is in turn derived from **SearchableContainer**. No new member functions are added to the inherited interface.

Sorted lists are very similar to ordered lists. As a result, we can make use of the code for ordered lists when implementing sorted lists. Specifically, we will consider an array-based implementation of sorted lists that is derived from the **ListAsArray** class defined in Section 7.1.1, and a pointer-based implementation of sorted lists that is derived from the **ListAsLinkedList** class given in Section 7.1.2.

### 7.2.1 Array Implementation

The **SortedListAsArray** class is declared in Program 7.21. Notice the use of multiple inheritance: The **SortedListAsArray** class is derived from both the **SortedList** class and the **ListAsArray** class. The **SortedList** base class is

---

**PROGRAM 7.20**
SortedList class definition

```
1   class SortedList : public virtual List
2   {
3   };
```

---

[2]A *total order* is a relation, say $<$, defined on a set of elements, say $\mathbb{Z}$, with the following properties:

1. For all pairs of elements $(i, j) \in \mathbb{Z} \times \mathbb{Z}$, such that $i \neq j$, exactly one of either $i < j$ or $j < i$ holds. (All elements are commensurate.)
2. For all triples $(i, j, k) \in \mathbb{Z} \times \mathbb{Z} \times \mathbb{Z}, i < j \wedge j < k \iff i < k$. (The relation $\leq$ is transitive.)

(See also Definition 15.1.)

---

**PROGRAM 7.21**
SortedListAsArray class definition

```
1  class SortedListAsArray :
2      public virtual SortedList, public virtual ListAsArray
3  {
4      unsigned int FindOffset (Object const&) const;
5  public:
6      SortedListAsArray (unsigned int);
7      //...
8  };
```

---

an abstract class. It provides the sorted list *interface*. The **ListAsArray** base class is a concrete class from which the sorted list class *inherits* much of its functionality.

There are no additional member variables required to implement the **SortedList-AsArray** class. That is, the member variables provided by the base class **List-AsArray** are sufficient. However, there is an additional private member function declared called **FindOffset**. As explained below, **FindOffset** is used by other member functions to locate an item in the sorted list.

### Inserting Items in a Sorted List

When inserting an item into a sorted list we have as a precondition that the list is already sorted. Furthermore, once the item is inserted, we have the postcondition that the list must still be sorted. Therefore, all the items initially in the list that are larger than the item to be inserted need to be moved to the right by one position as shown in Figure 7.4.

Program 7.22 defines the **Insert** member function for the **SortedListAsArray** class. This function takes as its lone argument a reference to the **Object** to be inserted in the list. Recall that the **Insert** function provided by the **ListAsLinkedList** class simply adds items at the end of the array. While this is both efficient and easy to implement, it is not suitable for the **SortedListAsArray** class since the items in the array must be end up in order.

---

**FIGURE 7.4**
Inserting an item into a sorted list implemented as an array.

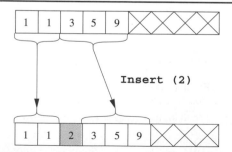

---

**PROGRAM 7.22**
`SortedListAsArray` class `Insert` member function definition

---

```
1    void SortedListAsArray::Insert (Object& object)
2    {
3        if (count == array.Length ())
4            throw domain_error ("list is full");
5        unsigned int i = count;
6        while (i > 0 && *array [i - 1U] > object)
7        {
8            array [i] = array [i - 1U];
9            --i;
10       }
11       array [i] = &object;
12       ++count;
13   }
```

---

The `Insert` function given in Program 7.22 first checks that there is still room in the array for one more item. Then, to insert the item into the list, all the items in the list that are larger than the one to be inserted are moved to the right. This is accomplished by the loop on lines 5–10. Finally, a pointer to the item to be inserted is recorded in the appropriate array position on line 11.

In the worst case, the item to be inserted is smaller than all the items already in the sorted list. In this case, all $n =$ count items must be moved one position to the right. Therefore, the running time of the `Insert` routine is $O(n)$.

### Locating Items in an Array—Binary Search

Given a sorted array of items, an efficient way to locate a given item is to use a *binary search*. The `FindOffset` member function of the `SortedListAsArray` class defined in Program 7.23 uses a binary search to locate an item in the array which matches a given item.

The binary search algorithm makes use of a *search interval* to determine the position of an item in the sorted list. The search interval is a range of array indices in which the item being sought is expected to be found. The initial search interval is $0 \ldots$ count $-1$. The interval is iteratively narrowed by comparing the item sought with the item found in the array at the middle of the search interval. If the middle item matches the item sought, then we are done. Otherwise, if the item sought is less than the middle item, then we can discard the middle item and the right half of the interval; if the item sought is greater than the middle item, we can discard the middle item and the left half of the interval. At each step, the size of the search interval is approximately halved. The algorithm terminates either when the item sought is found, or if the size of the search interval becomes zero.

In the worst case, the item sought is not in the sorted list. Specifically, the worst case occurs when the item sought is smaller than any item in the list because this case requires two comparisons in each iteration of the binary search loop. In the worst case, $\lceil \log n \rceil + 2$ iterations are required. Therefore, the running time of the `FindOffset`

---

**PROGRAM 7.23**
SortedListAsArray class FindOffset member function definition

---

```
1  unsigned int SortedListAsArray::FindOffset (
2      Object const& object) const
3  {
4      int left = 0;
5      int right = count - 1;
6
7      while (left <= right)
8      {
9          int const middle = (left + right) / 2;
10
11          if (object > *array [middle])
12              left = middle + 1;
13          else if (object < *array [middle])
14              right = middle - 1;
15          else
16              return middle;
17      }
18      return count;
19  }
```

---

function is $2(\lceil \log n \rceil + 2) \times \mathcal{T}\langle \text{op<(T\&, T\&)} \rangle + O(\log n)$, where $\mathcal{T}\langle \text{op<(T\&, T\&)} \rangle$ represents the running time required to compare to **Object** instances. If we assume that $\mathcal{T}\langle \text{op<(T\&, T\&)} \rangle = O(1)$, then the total running time is simply $O(\log n)$, where $n = $ **count**.

### Finding Items in a Sorted List

Program 7.24 defines the two public member functions of the **SortedListAsArray** class used to locate items in a sorted list. Both of these functions make use of the **FindOffset** member function described above.

The **Find** member function takes a **const** reference to an **Object** and returns a reference to the object contained in the sorted list which matches (i.e., compares equal to) its argument. It calls **FindOffset** to determine by doing a binary search the array index at which the matching object is found. **Find** returns a reference to the matching object, if one is found; otherwise, it returns a reference to the **NullObject** instance. The total running time of **Find** is dominated by **FindOffset**. Therefore, the running time is $O(\log n)$.

The **FindPosition** member function also takes a **const** reference an **Object**, but it returns a reference to a **Position** instead. **FindPosition** determines the position in the array of an object which matches its second argument.

The implementation of **FindPosition** is trivial: It calls **FindOffset** to determine the position at which the matching object is found and returns this position. The total running time of **FindPosition** is dominated by **FindOffset**. Therefore like **Find**, the running time of **FindPosition** is $O(\log n)$.

---

**PROGRAM 7.24**
SortedListAsArray class Find and FindPosition member function definitions

```
1   Object& SortedListAsArray::Find (Object const& object) const
2   {
3       unsigned int const offset = FindOffset (object);
4
5       if (offset < count)
6           return *array [offset];
7       else
8           return NullObject::Instance ();
9   }
10
11  Position& SortedListAsArray::FindPosition (
12      Object const& object) const
13  {
14      Pos& result = *new Pos (*this);
15      result.offset = FindOffset (object);
16      return result;
17  }
```

---

### Removing Items from a List

The purpose of the Withdraw function is to remove an item from the sorted list. Program 7.25 defines the Withdraw function which takes a reference to an Object.

The Withdraw function makes use of FindOffset to determine the array index of the item to be removed. Removing an object from position $i$ of an ordered list which is stored in an array requires that all of the objects at positions $i + 1, i + 2, \ldots,$ count$-1$

---

**PROGRAM 7.25**
SortedListAsArray class Withdraw member function definition

```
1    void SortedListAsArray::Withdraw (Object& object)
2    {
3        if (count == 0)
4            throw domain_error ("list is empty");
5
6        unsigned int const offset = FindOffset (object);
7
8        if (offset == count)
9            throw invalid_argument ("object not found");
10
11       for (unsigned int i = offset; i < count - 1U; ++i)
12           array [i] = array [i + 1];
13       --count;
14   }
```

---

be moved one position to the left. The worst case is when $i = 0$. In this case, $\text{count}-1$ items need to be moved to the left.

Although the `Withdraw` function is able to make use of `FindOffset` to locate the position of the item to be removed in $O(\log n)$ time, the total running time is dominated by the left shift, which is $O(n)$ in the worst case. Therefore, the running time of `Withdraw` is $O(n)$.

## 7.2.2   Linked List Implementation

This section presents a pointer-based implementation of sorted lists that is derived from the `ListAsLinkedList` class given in Section 7.1.2. The `SortedListAsLinkedList` class is declared in Program 7.26. The class definition makes use of multiple inheritance: The `SortedListAsLinkedList` class is derived from both the `SortedList` class and the `ListAsLinkedList` class. The former provides the sorted list interface; the latter provides almost all of the implementation.

There are no additional member variables or member functions defined in the `SortedListAsLinkedList` class. The inherited member variables are sufficient to implement a sorted list. In fact, the functionality inherited from the `ListAsLinkedList` class is almost sufficient—the only member function of which the functionality must change is the `Insert` operation.

### Inserting Items in a Sorted List

Program 7.27 gives the implementation of the `Insert` member function of the `SortedListAsLinkedList` class. This function takes a single argument: a reference to an `Object` to be inserted into the sorted list. The algorithm used for the insertion is as follows: First, the existing sorted, linked list is traversed in order to find the linked list element which is greater than or equal to the object to be inserted into the list. The traversal is done using two pointers—`prevPtr` and `ptr`. During the traversal, the latter keeps track of the current element and the former keeps track of the previous element.

By keeping track of the previous element, it is possible to efficiently insert the new item into the sorted list by calling the `InsertAfter` member function of the `LinkedList<T>` class. In Chapter 4, the `InsertAfter` function was shown to be $O(1)$.

---

**PROGRAM 7.26**
`SortedListAsLinkedList` class definition

```
1   class SortedListAsLinkedList :
2       public virtual SortedList, public virtual ListAsLinkedList
3   {
4   public:
5       SortedListAsLinkedList ();
6       //...
7   };
```

---

**PROGRAM 7.27**
SortedListAsLinkedList class Insert member function definition

```
1   void SortedListAsLinkedList::Insert (Object& object)
2   {
3       ListElement<Object*> const* prevPtr = 0;
4       ListElement<Object*> const* ptr =
5           linkedList.Head ();
6       while (ptr != 0 && *ptr->Datum () < object)
7       {
8           prevPtr = ptr;
9           ptr = ptr->Next ();
10      }
11      if (prevPtr == 0)
12          linkedList.Prepend (&object);
13      else
14          linkedList.InsertAfter (prevPtr, &object);
15      ++count;
16  }
```

---

In the event that the item to be inserted is smaller than the first item in the sorted list, then rather than using the **InsertAfter** function, the **Prepend** function is used. The **Prepend** function was also shown to be $O(1)$.

In the worst case, the object to be inserted into the linked list is larger than all of the objects already present in the list. In this case, the entire list needs to be traversed before doing the insertion. Consequently, the total running time for the **Insert** operation of the **SortedListAsLinkedList** class is $O(n)$, where $n =$ count.

### Other Operations on Sorted Lists

Unfortunately, it is not possible to do a binary search in a linked list. As a result, it is not possible to exploit the sortedness of the list in the implementation of any of the other required operations on sorted lists. The functions inherited from the **ListAsLinkedList** provide all of the needed functionality.

### 7.2.3 Performance Comparison: SortedListAsArray versus SortedListAsList

The running times calculated for the various member functions of the two sorted list implementations, **SortedListAsArray** and **SortedListAsLinkedList**, are summarized in Table 7.2. With the exception of two member functions, the running times of the two implementations are asymptotically identical.

Neither the **SortedListAsArray** nor **SortedListAsLinkedList** implementations required any additional member variables beyond those inherited from their respective base classes, **ListAsArray** and **ListAsLinkedList**. Consequently, the

**TABLE 7.2**
Running Times of Operations on Sorted Lists

| Member function | Sorted List Implementation | | |
|---|---|---|---|
| | `SortedListAsArray` | | `SortedListAsLinkedList` |
| `Insert` | $O(n)$ | | $O(n)$ |
| `IsMember` | $O(n)$ | | $O(n)$ |
| `Find` | $O(\log n)$ | $\neq$ | $O(n)$ |
| `FindPosition` | $O(\log n)$ | $\neq$ | $O(n)$ |
| `Withdraw` | $O(n)$ | | $O(n)$ |

space requirements analysis of the sorted list implementations is identical to that of the ordered list implementations given in Section 7.1.3.

## 7.2.4 Applications

In Section 7.1.4 we saw that an $n$th-order polynomial,

$$\sum_{i=0}^{n} a_i x^i = a_0 + a_1 x + a_2 x^2 + \cdots + a_n x^n$$

where $a_n \neq 0$, can be represented by a sequence of ordered pairs, thus

$$\{(a_0, 0), (a_1, 1), (a_2, 2), \ldots, (a_n, n), \}.$$

We also saw that it is possible to make use of an *ordered list* to represent such a sequence and that given such a representation, we can write an algorithm to perform differentiation.

As it turns out, the order of the terms in the sequence does not affect the differentiation algorithm. The correct result is always obtained and the running time is unaffected regardless of the order of the terms in the sequence.

Unfortunately, there are operations on polynomials whose running time depends on the order of the terms. For example, consider the addition of two polynomials:

$$(a_0 + a_1 x + a_2 x^2) + (b_3 x^3 + b_2 x^2 + b_1 x) = (a_0) + (a_1 + b_1)x + (a_2 + b_2)x^2 + (b_3)x^3$$

To perform the addition all the terms involving $x$ raised to the same power need to be grouped together.

If the terms of the polynomials are in an arbitrary order, then the grouping together of the corresponding terms is time consuming. On the other hand, if the terms are ordered, say, from smallest to largest exponent, then the summation can be done more efficiently. A single pass through the polynomials will suffice. It makes sense to represent each of the polynomials as a *sorted list* of terms using, say, the `SortedListAsLinkedList` class.

**PROGRAM 7.28**
Term class definition

```
1   class Term : public Object
2   {
3       double coefficient;
4       unsigned int exponent;
5   public:
6       //...
7       unsigned int Coefficient () const;
8       unsigned int Exponent () const;
9       friend Term operator + (Term const&, Term const&);
10  };
11
12  unsigned int Term::Coefficient () const
13      { return coefficient; }
14
15  unsigned int Term::Exponent () const
16      { return exponent; }
17
18  Term operator + (Term const& arg1, Term const& arg2)
19  {
20      if (arg1.exponent != arg2.exponent)
21          throw domain_error ("unequal exponents");
22      return Term (arg1.coefficient + arg2.coefficient,
23          arg1.exponent);
24  }
```

### Implementation

To begin with, we need to represent the terms of the polynomial. Program 7.28 repeats the definition of the **Term** class given in Section 7.1.4. The reason for repeating the definition here is that some changes are needed to support the the implementation of polynomial addition.

Three additional functions are declared in Program 7.28. The first two, **Coefficient** and **Exponent**, are simple accessor functions which provide read-only access to the corresponding member variables of a **Term** instance. Clearly, the running time of each of these functions is $O(1)$.

The third function overloads the addition operator, **operator+**, in such a way as to make it possible to add two **Terms** together. The result of the addition is another **Term**. The working assumption is that the terms to be added have identical exponents. If the exponents are allowed to differ, the result of of the addition is a polynomial which cannot be represented using a single term! To add terms with like exponents, we simply need to add their respective coefficients. Therefore, the running time of the **Term** addition operator is $O(1)$.

We now turn to the polynomial itself. Program 7.29 declares the **Polynomial** class. We have chosen in this implementation to use the pointer-based sorted list

---

**PROGRAM 7.29**
`Polynomial` class definition

---

```
1   class Polynomial : public SortedListAsLinkedList
2   {
3   public:
4       //...
5       friend Polynomial operator + (
6           Polynomial const&, Polynomial const&);
7   };
```

---

implementation to represent the sequence of terms. Therefore, the `Polynomial` class is derived from the `SortedListAsLinkedList` class.

Only one additional function is declared in Program 7.29. Specifically, the addition operator, `operator+`, has been overloaded to make it possible to add two `Polynomials` to obtain a third. Program 7.30 gives the implementation for this operator.

### Analysis

The proof of the correctness of Program 7.30 is left as an exercise for the reader (Exercise 7.12). We discuss here the running time analysis of the algorithm, as there are some subtle points to remember which lead to a result that may be surprising.

Consider the addition of a polynomial $p(x)$ with its arithmetic complement $-p(x)$. Suppose $p(x)$ has $n$ terms. Clearly $-p(x)$ also has $n$ terms. The sum of the polynomials is the zero polynomial. An important characteristic of the zero polynomial is that it *has no terms*! In this case, exactly $n$ iterations of the main loop are done (lines 7–29). Furthermore, zero iterations of the second and the third loops are required (lines 30–35 and 36–41). Since the result has no terms, there will be no calls to the `Insert` function. Therefore, the amount of work done in each iteration is a constant. Consequently, the best-case running time is $O(n)$.

Consider now the addition of two polynomials, $p(x)$ and $q(x)$, having $l$ and $m$ terms, respectively. Furthermore, suppose that the largest exponent in $p(x)$ is less than the smallest exponent in $q(x)$. Consequently, there is no power of $x$ which the two polynomials have in common. In this case, since $p(x)$ has the lower-order terms, exactly $l$ iterations of the main loop (lines 7–29) are done. In each of these iterations, exactly one new term is inserted into the result by calling the `Insert` function. Since all of the terms of $p(x)$ will be exhausted when the main loop is finished, there will be no iterations of the second loop (lines 30–35). However, there will be exactly $m$ iterations of the third loop (lines 36–41) in each of which one new term is inserted into the result by calling the `Insert` function.

Altogether, $l + m$ calls to the `Insert` will be made. It was shown earlier that the running time for the insert function is $O(k)$, where $k$ is the number of items in the sorted list. Consequently, the total running time for the $l + m$ insertions is

$$\sum_{k=0}^{l+m-1} O(k) = O((l + m)^2).$$

**Polynomial** addition operator definition

```
1   Polynomial operator + (
2       Polynomial const& arg1, Polynomial const& arg2)
3   {
4       Polynomial result;
5       Iterator& pos1 = arg1.NewIterator ();
6       Iterator& pos2 = arg2.NewIterator ();
7       while (!pos1.IsDone () && !pos2.IsDone ())
8       {
9           Term const& term1 = dynamic_cast<Term const&> (*pos1);
10          Term const& term2 = dynamic_cast<Term const&> (*pos2);
11          if (term1.Exponent () < term2.Exponent ())
12          {
13              result.Insert (*new Term (term1));
14              ++pos1;
15          }
16          else if (term1.Exponent () > term2.Exponent ())
17          {
18              result.Insert (*new Term (term2));
19              ++pos2;
20          }
21          else
22          {
23              Term sum = term1 + term2;
24              if (sum.Coefficient () != 0)
25                  result.Insert (*new Term (sum));
26              ++pos1;
27              ++pos2;
28          }
29      }
30      while (!pos1.IsDone ())
31      {
32          Term const& term1 = dynamic_cast<Term const&> (*pos1);
33          result.Insert (*new Term (term1));
34          ++pos1;
35      }
36      while (!pos2.IsDone ())
37      {
38          Term const& term2 = dynamic_cast<Term const&> (*pos2);
39          result.Insert (*new Term (term2));
40          ++pos2;
41      }
42      delete &pos1;
43      delete &pos2;
44      return result;
45  }
```

Consequently, the worst-case running time for the polynomial addition given in Program 7.30 is $O(n^2)$, where $n = l + m$. This is somewhat disappointing. The implementation is not optimal because it fails to take account of the order in which the terms of the result are computed. That is, the `Insert` function repeatedly searches the sorted list for the correct position at which to insert the next term. But we know that correct position is at the end! By replacing all of the calls in Program 7.30 to the `Insert` function by

```
result.linkedList.Append (...);
```

the total running time can be reduced to $O(n)$ from $O(n^2)$!

# Exercises

**7.1**  Devise an algorithm to reverse the contents of an ordered list. Determine the running time of your algorithm.

**7.2**  Devise an algorithm to append the contents of one ordered list to the end of another. Assume that both lists are represented using arrays. What is the running time of your algorithm?

**7.3**  Repeat Exercise 7.2, but this time assume that both lists are represented using linked lists. What is the running time of your algorithm?

**7.4**  Devise an algorithm to merge the contents of two sorted lists. Assume that both lists are represented using arrays. What is the running time of your algorithm?

**7.5**  Repeat Exercise 7.4, but this time assume that both lists are represented using linked lists. What is the running time of your algorithm?

**7.6**  The `Withdraw` function can be used to remove items from a list one at a time. Suppose we want to provide an additional a member function, `WithdrawAll`, that takes one argument and withdraws all the items in a list that *match* the given argument.

We can provide an abstract implementation of the `WithdrawAll` function in the `List` class like this:

```
void List::WithdrawAll (Object const& arg)
{
    for (;;)
    {
        Object& object = Find (arg);
        if (object.IsNull ())
            break;
        Withdraw (object);
    }
}
```

Determine the worst-case running time of this routine for each of the following cases:

**a.** an array-based implementation of an ordered list,

**b.** a linked-list implementation of an ordered list,

**c.** an array-based implementation of a sorted list, and

**d.** a linked-list implementation of a sorted list.

**7.7** Devise an $O(n)$ algorithm, to remove from an ordered list all the items that match a given item. Assume the list is represented using an array.

**7.8** Repeat Exercise 7.7, but this time assume the ordered list is represented using a linked list.

**7.9** Consider an implementation of the **OrderedList** class that uses a doubly-linked list such as the one shown in Figure 6.9(*a*). Compare the running times of the operations for this implementation with those given in Table 7.1.

**7.10** Derive an expression for the amount of space used to represent an ordered list of *n* elements using a doubly-linked list such as the one shown in Figure 6.9(*a*). Compare this with the space used by the array-based implementation. Assume that integers and pointers each occupy 4 bytes.

**7.11** Consider an implementation of the **SortedList** class that uses a doubly-linked list such as the one shown in Figure 6.9(*a*). Compare the running times of the operations for this implementation with those given in Table 7.2.

**7.12** Verify that Program 7.30 correctly computes the sum of two polynomials.

**7.13** Write an algorithm to multiply a polynomial by a scalar. **Hint:** Use a visitor.

## Programming Projects

**7.1** Write a visitor to solve each of the following problems:

**a.** Find the smallest element of a list.

**b.** Find the largest element of a list.

**c.** Compute the sum of all the elements of a list.

**d.** Compute the product of all the elements of a list.

**7.2** Design and implement a class called **OrderedAsDoublyLinkedList** which represents an ordered list using a doubly-linked list. Select one of the approaches shown in Figure 6.9.

**7.3** Consider the **Polynomial** class given in Program 7.19. Implement a function that computes the value of a polynomial, say $p(x)$, for a given value of *x*. **Hint:** Use a visitor that visits all the terms in the polynomial and accumulates the result.

**7.4**  Devise and implement an algorithm to multiply two polynomials. **Hint:** Consider the identity

$$\left(\sum_{i=0}^{n} a_i x^i\right) \times \left(\sum_{j=0}^{m} b_j x^j\right) = \sum_{i=0}^{n} a_i x^i \left(\sum_{j=0}^{m} b_j x^j\right)$$

Write a routine to multiply a **Polynomial** by a **Term** and use the polynomial addition operator defined in Program 7.30.

**7.5**  Devise and implement an algorithm to compute the $k$th power of a polynomial, where $k$ is a positive integer. What is the running time of your algorithm?

**7.6**  For some calculations it is necessary to have very large integers, i.e., integers with an arbitrarily large number of digits. We can represent such integers using lists. Design and implement a class for representing arbitrarily large integers. Your implementation should include operations to add, subtract, and multiply such integers, and to compute the $k$th power of such an integer, where $k$ is a *small* positive integer. **Hint:** Base your design on the **Polynomial** class given in Program 7.19.

# 8 | Hashing, Hash Tables, and Scatter Tables

A very common paradigm in data processing involves storing information in a table and then later retrieving the information stored there. For example, consider a database of driver's license records. The database contains one record for each driver's license issued. Given a driver's license number, we can look up the information associated with that number.

Similar operations are done by the C++ compiler. The compiler uses a *symbol table* to keep track of the user-defined symbols in a C++ program. As it compiles a program, the compiler inserts an entry in the symbol table every time a new symbol is declared. In addition, every time a symbol is used, the compiler looks up the attributes associated with that symbol to see that it is being used correctly and to guide the generation of the executable code.

Typically the database comprises a collection of key-and-value pairs. Information is retrieved from the database by searching for a given key. In the case of the driver's license database, the key is the driver's license number; in the case of the symbol table, the key is the name of the symbol.

In general, an application may perform a large number of insertion and/or look-up operations. Occasionally it is also necessary to remove items from the database. Because a large number of operations will be done, we want to do them as quickly as possible.

## 8.1 Hashing—The Basic Idea

In this chapter we examine data structures which are designed specifically with the objective of providing efficient insertion and find operations. In order to meet the design objective, certain concessions are needed. Specifically, we do not require that there be any specific ordering of the items in the container. In addition, while we still require the ability to remove items from the container, it is not our primary objective to make removal as efficient as the insertion and find operations.

Ideally we would build a data structure for which both the insertion and find operations are $O(1)$ in the worst case. However, this kind of performance can only be achieved with complete a priori knowledge. We need to know beforehand specifically

**201**

which items are to be inserted into the container. Unfortunately, we do not have this information in the general case. So, if we cannot guarantee $O(1)$ performance in the *worst case,* then we make it our design objective to achieve $O(1)$ performance *in the average case.*

The constant time performance objective immediately leads us to the following conclusion: Our implementation must be based in some way on an array rather than a linked list. This is because we can access the $k$th element of an array in constant time, whereas the same operation in a linked list takes $O(k)$ time.

In the previous chapter, we consider two searchable containers—the *ordered list* and the *sorted list.* In the case of an ordered list, the cost of an insertion is $O(1)$ and the cost of the find operation is $O(n)$. For a sorted list the cost of insertion is $O(n)$ and the cost of the find operation is $O(\log n)$ for the array implementation.

Clearly, neither the ordered list nor the sorted list meets our performance objectives. The essential problem is that a search, either linear or binary, is always necessary. In the ordered list, the find operation uses a linear search to locate the item. In the sorted list, a binary search can be used to locate the item because the data is sorted. However, in order to keep the data sorted, insertion becomes $O(n)$.

In order to meet the performance objective of constant time insert and find operations, we need a way to do them *without performing a search.* That is, given an item $x$, we need to be able to determine directly from $x$ the array position where it is to be stored.

**Example** We wish to implement a searchable container which will be used to contain character strings from the set of strings $K$,

$$K = \{\texttt{"ett"}, \texttt{"två"},^1 \texttt{"tre"}, \texttt{"fyra"}, \texttt{"fem"}, \texttt{"sex"},^2$$
$$\texttt{"sju"}, \texttt{"åtta"}, \texttt{"nio"}, \texttt{"tio"}, \texttt{"elva"}, \texttt{"tolv"}\}.$$

Suppose we define a function $h : K \mapsto \mathbb{Z}$ as given by the following table:

| $x$ | $h(x)$ | $x$ | $h(x)$ | $x$ | $h(x)$ |
|-----|--------|-----|--------|-----|--------|
| `"ett"` | 1 | `"fem"` | 5 | `"nio"` | 9 |
| `"två"` | 2 | `"sex"` | 6 | `"tio"` | 10 |
| `"tre"` | 3 | `"sju"` | 7 | `"elva"` | 11 |
| `"fyra"` | 4 | `"åtta"` | 8 | `"tolv"` | 12 |

Then, we can implement a searchable container using an array of length $n = 12$. To insert item $x$, we simply store it a position $h(x) - 1$ of the array. Similarly, to locate item $x$, we simply check to see if it is found at position $h(x) - 1$. If the function $h(\cdot)$ can be evaluated in constant time, then both the insert and the find operations are $O(1)$.

---

[1] This is the Swedish word for the number 2. Since there is no å in the ASCII character set, for the purposes of the discussion in this chapter we will use the ASCII code for a in its place. However, the Swedish national variant of the ISO 646 character set uses the code corresponding to the ASCII character "}".

[2] I have been advised that a book without sex will never be a best seller. "Sex" is the Swedish word for the number 6.

We expect that any reasonable implementation of the function $h(\cdot)$ will run in constant time, since the size of the set of strings, $K$, is a constant! This example illustrates how we can achieve $O(1)$ performance in the worst case when we have complete, a priori knowledge.

### 8.1.1 Keys and Hash Functions

We are designing a container which will be used to hold some number of items of a given set $K$. In this context, we call the elements of the set $K$ *keys*. The general approach is to store the keys in an array. The position of a key in the array is given by a function $h(\cdot)$, called a *hash function*, which determines the position of a given key directly from that key.

In the general case, we expect the size of the set of keys, $|K|$, to be relatively large or even unbounded. For example, if the keys are 32-bit integers, then $|K| = 2^{32}$. Similarly, if the keys are arbitrary character strings of arbitrary length, then $|K|$ is unbounded.

On the other hand, we also expect the actual number of items stored in the container to be significantly less than $|K|$. That is, if $n$ is the number of items actually stored in the container, then $n \ll |K|$. Therefore, it seems prudent to use an array of size $M$, where $M$ is as least as great as the maximum number of items to be stored in the container.

Consequently, what we need is a function $h : K \mapsto \{0, 1, \ldots, M - 1\}$. This function maps the set of values to be stored in the container to subscripts in an array of length $M$. This function is called a *hash function*.

In general, since $|K| \geq M$, the mapping defined by hash function will be a *many-to-one mapping;* that is, there will exist many pairs of distinct keys $x$ and $y$, such that $x \neq y$, for which $h(x) = h(y)$. This situation is called a *collision*. Several approaches for dealing with collisions are explored in the following sections.

What are the characteristics of a good hash function?

- A good hash function avoids collisions.
- A good hash function tends to spread keys evenly in the array.
- A good hash function is easy to compute.

#### Avoiding Collisions

Ideally, given a set of $n \leq M$ distinct keys, $\{k_1, k_2, \ldots, k_n\}$, the set of hash values $\{h(k_1), h(k_2), \ldots, h(k_n)\}$ contains no duplicates. In practice, unless we know something about the keys chosen, we cannot guarantee that there will not be collisions. However, in certain applications we have some specific knowledge about the keys that we can exploit to reduce the likelihood of a collision. For example, if the keys in our application are telephone numbers, and we know that the telephone numbers are all likely to be from the same geographic area, then it makes little sense to consider the area codes in the hash function—the area codes are likely to be all the same.

#### Spreading Keys Evenly

Let $p_i$ be the probability that the hash function $h(\cdot) = i$. A hash function which spreads keys evenly has the property that for $0 \leq i < M$, $p_i = 1/M$. In other words, the hash values computed by the function $h(\cdot)$ are *uniformly distributed*. Unfortunately, in order to say something about the distribution of the hash values, we need to know something about the distribution of the keys.

In the absence of any information to the contrary, we assume that the keys are equiprobable. Let $K_i$ be the set of keys that map to the value $i$, that is, $K_i = \{k \in K : h(k) = i\}$. If this is the case, the requirement to spread the keys uniformly implies that $|K_i| = |K|/M$. An equal number of keys should map into each array position.

### Ease of Computation

This does not necessarily mean that it is easy for someone to compute the hash function, nor does it mean that it is easy to write the algorithm to compute the function; it means that the running time of the hash function should be $O(1)$.

## 8.2   Hashing Methods

In this section we discuss several hashing methods. In the following discussion, we assume that we are dealing with integer-valued keys, i.e., $K = \mathbb{Z}$. Furthermore, we assume that the value of the hash function falls between 0 and $M - 1$.

### 8.2.1   Division Method

Perhaps the simplest of all the methods of hashing an integer $x$ is to divide $x$ by $M$ and then to use the remainder modulo $M$. This is called the *division method of hashing*. In this case, the hash function is

$$h(x) = x \bmod M.$$

Generally, this approach is quite good for just about any value of $M$. However, in certain situations some extra care is needed in the selection of a suitable value for $M$. For example, it is often convenient to make $M$ an even number. But this means that $h(x)$ is even if $x$ is even; and $h(x)$ is odd if $x$ is odd. If all possible keys are equiprobable, then this is not a problem. However if, say, even keys are more likely than odd keys, the function $h(x) = x \bmod M$ will not spread the hashed values of those keys evenly.

Similarly, it is often tempting to let $M$ be a power of two; for example, $M = 2^k$ for some integer $k > 1$. In this case, the hash function $h(x) = x \bmod 2^k$ simply extracts the bottom $k$ bits of the binary representation of $x$. While this hash function is quite easy to compute, it is not a desirable function because it does not depend on all the bits in the binary representation of $x$.

For these reasons $M$ is often chosen to be a prime number. For example, suppose there is a bias in the way the keys are created that makes it more likely for a key to be a multiple of some small constant, say 2 or 3. Then making $M$ a prime increases the likelihood that those keys are spread out evenly. Also, if $M$ is a prime number, the division of $x$ by that prime number depends on all the bits of $x$, not just the bottom $k$ bits, for some small constant $k$.

The division method is extremely simple to implement. The following C++ code illustrates how to do it:

```
unsigned int const M = 1031; // a prime

unsigned int h (unsigned int x)
    { return x % M; }
```

In this case, `M` is a constant. However, an advantage of the division method is that `M` need not be a compile-time constant—its value can be determined at run time. In any event, the running time of this implementation is clearly a constant.

A potential disadvantage of the division method is due to the property that consecutive keys map to consecutive hash values:

$$h(i) = i$$
$$h(i + 1) = i + 1 \bmod M$$
$$h(i + 2) = i + 2 \bmod M$$
$$\vdots$$

Although this ensures that consecutive keys do not collide, it does mean that consecutive array locations will be occupied. We will see that in certain implementations this can lead to degradation in performance. In the following sections we consider hashing methods that tend to scatter consecutive keys.

## 8.2.2  Middle Square Method

In this section we consider a hashing method which avoids the use of division. Since integer division is usually slower than integer multiplication, by avoiding division we can potentially improve the running time of the hashing algorithm. We can avoid division by making use of the fact that a computer does finite-precision integer arithmetic. For example, all arithmetic is done modulo $W$ where $W = 2^w$ is a power of two such that $w$ is the *word size* of the computer.

The *middle-square hashing method* works as follows. First, we assume that $M$ is a power of 2, say $M = 2^k$ for some $k \geq 1$. Then, to hash an integer $x$, we use the following hash function:

$$h(x) = \left\lfloor \frac{M}{W} (x^2 \bmod W) \right\rfloor .$$

Notice that since $M$ and $W$ are both powers of 2, the ratio $W/M = 2^{w-k}$ is also a power of 2. Therefore, in order to multiply the term $(x^2 \bmod W)$ by $M/W$ we simply shift it to the right by $w - k$ bits! In effect, we are extracting $k$ bits from the middle of the square of the key—hence the name of the method.

The following code fragment illustrates the middle-square method of hashing:

```
unsigned int const k = 10; // M==1024
unsigned int const w = bitsizeof (unsigned int);

unsigned int h (unsigned int x)
    { return (x * x) >> (w - k); }
```

Since **x** is an **unsigned int**, the product **x * x** is also an **unsigned int**. If 32-bit integers are used, the product is also a 32-bit integer. The final result is obtained by shifting the product $w - k$ bits to the right, where $w$ is the number of bits in an integer.[3] By definition, the right shift inserts zeroes on the left. Therefore, the result always falls between 0 and $M - 1$.

The middle-square method does a pretty good job when the integer-valued keys are equiprobable. The middle-square method also has the characteristic that it scatters consecutive keys nicely. However, since the middle-square method only considers a subset of the bits in the middle of $x^2$, keys which have a large number of leading zeroes will collide. For example, consider the following set of keys:

$$\{x \in \mathbb{Z}^+ : x < \sqrt{W/M}\}.$$

This set contains all keys $x$ such that $x < 2^{(w-k)/2}$. For all of these keys $h(x) = 0$.

A similar line of reasoning applies for keys which have a large number of trailing zeroes. Let $W$ be an even power of 2. Consider the set of keys

$$\{x \in \mathbb{Z}^+ : x = n\sqrt{W}, \quad n \in \mathbb{Z}+\}.$$

The least significant $w/2$ bits of the keys in this set are all zero. Therefore, the least significant $w$ bits of $x^2$ are also zero and as a result $h(x) = 0$ for all such keys!

### 8.2.3 Multiplication Method

A very simple variation on the middle-square method that alleviates its deficiencies is the *multiplication hashing method*. Instead of multiplying the key $x$ by itself, we multiply the key by a carefully chosen constant $a$, and then extract the middle $k$ bits from the result. In this case, the hashing function is

$$h(x) = \left\lfloor \frac{M}{W}\left(ax \bmod W\right) \right\rfloor.$$

What is a suitable choice for the constant $a$? If we want to avoid the problems that the middle-square method encounters with keys having a large number of lead-

---

[3] The function **bitsizeof** can be implemented as the C++ preprocessor macro

```
#define bitsizeof(T) (8*sizeof(T))
```

which determines the number of bits required to represent the type **T** assuming eight-bit bytes.

ing or trailing zeroes, then we should choose an $a$ that has neither leading nor trailing zeroes.

Furthermore, if we choose an $a$ that is *relatively prime*[4] to $W$, then there exists another number $a'$ such that $aa' = 1 \bmod W$. In other words, $a'$ is the *inverse* of $a$ modulo $W$, since the product of $a$ and its inverse is 1. Such a number has the nice property that if we take a key $x$, and multiply it by $a$ to get $ax$, we can recover the original key by multiplying the product again by $a'$, since $axa' = aa'x = 1x$.

There are many possible constants which have the desired properties. One possibility which is suited for 32-bit arithmetic (i.e., $W = 2^{32}$) is $a = 2\,654\,435\,769$. The binary representation of $a$ is

$$10\,011\,110\,001\,101\,110\,111\,100\,110\,111\,001.$$

This number has neither many leading nor trailing zeroes. Also, this value of $a$ and $W = 2^{32}$ are relatively prime and the inverse of $a$ modulo $W$ is $a' = 340\,573\,321$.

The following code fragment illustrates the multiplication method of hashing:

```
unsigned int const k = 10; // M==1024
unsigned int const w = bitsizeof (unsigned int);
unsigned int const a = 2654435769U;

unsigned int h (unsigned int x)
    { return (x * a) >> (w - k); }
```

Note, this implementation assumes that `sizeof(unsigned int)` = 4 *bytes*. That is, the natural word size of the machine is 32 bits. The code is a simple modification of the middle-square version. Nevertheless, the running time remains $O(1)$.

## 8.2.4 Fibonacci Hashing

The final variation of hashing to be considered here is called the *Fibonacci hashing method*. In fact, Fibonacci hashing is exactly the multiplication hashing method discussed in the preceding section using a very special value for $a$. The value we choose is closely related to the number called the golden ratio.

The *golden ratio* is defined as follows: Given two positive numbers $x$ and $y$, the ratio $\phi = x/y$ is the golden ratio if the ratio of $x$ to $y$ is the same as that of $x + y$ to $x$. The value of the golden ratio can be determined as follows:

$$\frac{x}{y} = \frac{x + y}{x} \Rightarrow 0 = x^2 - xy - y^2$$

$$\Rightarrow 0 = \phi^2 - \phi - 1$$

$$\Rightarrow \phi = \frac{1 + \sqrt{5}}{2}.$$

---

[4]Two numbers $x$ and $y$ are *relatively prime* if there is no number other than 1 that divides both $x$ and $y$ evenly.

There is an intimate relationship between the golden ratio and the Fibonacci numbers. In Section 3.4.3 it was shown that the $n$th Fibonacci number is given by

$$F_n = \frac{1}{\sqrt{5}}(\phi^n - \hat{\phi}^n),$$

where $\phi = (1 + \sqrt{5})/2$ and $\hat{\phi} = (1 - \sqrt{5})/2!$

In the context of Fibonacci hashing, we are interested not in $\phi$, but in the reciprocal, $\phi^{-1}$, which can be calculated as follows:

$$\begin{aligned}
\phi^{-1} &= \frac{2}{1 + \sqrt{5}} \\
&= \left(\frac{2}{1 + \sqrt{5}}\right)\left(\frac{\sqrt{5} - 1}{\sqrt{5} - 1}\right) \\
&= \frac{\sqrt{5} - 1}{2} \\
&\approx 0.618\,033\,887.
\end{aligned}$$

The Fibonacci hashing method is essentially the multiplication hashing method in which the constant $a$ is chosen as the integer that is relatively prime to $W$, which is closest to $\phi^{-1}W$. The following table gives suitable values of $a$ for various word sizes.

| $W$ | $a$ |
|---|---|
| $2^{16}$ | 40 503 |
| $2^{32}$ | 2 654 435 769 |
| $2^{64}$ | 11 400 714 819 323 198 485 |

Why is $a = \phi^{-1}W$ special? It has to do with what happens to consecutive keys when they are hashed using the multiplicative method. As shown in Figure 8.1, consecutive keys are spread out quite nicely. In fact, when we use $a = \phi^{-1}W$ to hash consecutive keys, the hash value for each subsequent key falls between the two widest spaced hash values already computed. Furthermore, it is a property of the golden ratio, $\phi$, that each subsequent hash value divides the interval into which it falls according to the golden ratio!

## 8.3   Hash Function Implementations

The preceding section presents methods of hashing integer-valued keys. In reality, we cannot expect that the keys will always be integers. Depending on the application, the

**FIGURE 8.1**
Fibonacci hashing.

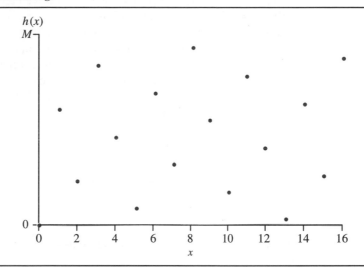

keys might be letters, character strings, pointers, or even more complex data structures such as **Associations** or **Containers**.

In general given a set of keys, $K$, and a positive constant, $M$, a hash function is a function of the form

$$h : K \mapsto \{0, 1, \ldots, M - 1\}.$$

In practice it is convenient to implement the hash function $h$ as the composition of two functions $f$ and $g$. The function $f$ maps keys into integers:

$$f : K \mapsto \mathbb{Z}^+,$$

where $\mathbb{Z}^+$ is the set of non-negative integers. The function $g$ maps non-negative integers into $\{0, 1, \ldots, M - 1\}$:

$$g : \mathbb{Z}^+ \mapsto \{0, 1, \ldots, M - 1\}.$$

Given appropriate functions $f$ and $g$, the hash function $h$ is simply defined as the composition of those functions

$$h = g \circ f.$$

That is, the hash value of a key $x$ is given by $g(f(x))$.

By decomposing the function $h$ in this way, we can separate the problem into two parts: The first involves finding a suitable mapping from the set of keys $K$ to the non-negative integers. The second involves mapping non-negative integers into the interval

$[0, M - 1]$. Ideally, the two problems would be unrelated. That is, the choice of the function $f$ would not depend on the choice of $g$ and vice versa. Unfortunately, this is not always the case. However, if we are careful, we can design the functions in such a way that $h = g \circ f$ is a good hash function.

The hashing methods discussed in the preceding section deal with integer-valued keys. But this is precisely the domain of the function $g$. Consequently, we have already examined several different alternatives for the function $g$. On the other hand, the choice of a suitable function for $f$ depends on the characteristics of its domain.

In the following sections, we consider various different domains (sets of keys) and develop suitable hash functions for each of them. Each domain considered corresponds to some type or class **T**. For each type **T**, we present the definition of the function **Hash** declared according to the following prototype:

```
typedef unsigned int HashValue;

HashValue Hash (T);
```

Notice we have chosen to represent the range of hash values using the type **unsigned int**.

### 8.3.1  Integral Keys

Out of all the C++ built-in data types, the *integral types* are the simplest to hash into integers. The integral data types are **char** and **wchar_t**, **int** of all sizes, and enumerations. Since the underlying representation of such data types can be viewed as an integer, the hash function $f$ is trivial. The only wrinkle involves dealing with negative values. Thus, a suitable function $f$ for an integral data type is the absolute value function

$$f(x) = |x|.$$

Program 8.1 shows how to do this for plain **char** and **int** data types. Clearly, the running time of both of the functions defined in Program 8.1 is $O(1)$.

---

**PROGRAM 8.1**
Integral **Hash** function definitions

---

```
1   typedef unsigned int HashValue;
2
3   HashValue Hash (char c)
4       { return abs (c); }
5
6   HashValue Hash (int i)
7       { return abs (i); }
```

---

## 8.3.2 Floating-Point Keys

Dealing with floating-point numbers involves only a little more work. In C++ the floating-point data types are **float**, **double**, and **long double**. Typically, the size of a **float** is 4 bytes, the size of a **double** is 8 bytes, and the size of a **long double** is 12 or 16 bytes.

We seek a function $f$ which maps a floating-point value into a non-negative integer. One possibility is to simply reinterpret the bit pattern used to represent the floating point number as an integer. However, this is only possible when the size of the floating-point type does not exceed the size of **unsigned int**. This condition is typically only satisfied by the **float** type.[5]

Another characteristic of floating-point numbers that must be dealt with is the extremely wide range of values which can be represented. For example, when using IEEE floating-point, the smallest double precision quantity that can be represented is $\approx 4.94 \times 10^{-324}$, and the largest is $\approx 1.80 \times 10^{308}$. Somehow we need to map values in this large domain into the range of an **unsigned int**.

Every nonzero floating-point quantity $x$ can be written uniquely as

$$x = m \times 2^e,$$

where $0.5 \leq |m| < 1$. The quantity $m$ is called the *mantissa* or *significant* and $e$ is called the *exponent*. This suggests the following definition for the function $f$:

$$f(x) = \begin{cases} 0 & x = 0, \\ \lfloor (2|m| - 1)W \rfloor & x = m \times 2^e, \end{cases} \tag{8.1}$$

where $W = 2^w$ such that $w$ is the word size of the machine.

This hashing method is best understood by considering the conditions under which a collision occurs between two distinct floating-point numbers $x$ and $y$. Let $m_x$ and $m_y$ be the mantissas of $x$ and $y$, respectively. The collision occurs when $f(x) = f(y)$.

$$
\begin{aligned}
f(x) = f(y) &\Rightarrow f(x) - f(y) = 0 \\
&\Rightarrow \lfloor (2|m_x| - 1)W \rfloor - \lfloor (2|m_y| - 1)W \rfloor = 0 \\
&\Rightarrow \left| (2|m_x| - 1)W - (2|m_y| - 1)W \right| \leq 1 \\
&\Rightarrow \left| |m_x| - |m_y| \right| \leq \frac{1}{2W}.
\end{aligned}
$$

Thus, $x$ and $y$ collide if the magnitudes of their mantissas differ by less than $1/2W$. Notice too that the exponents are not considered at all. Therefore, if $x$ and $y$ collide, then so too do $x$ and $y \times 2^k$ for all permissible values of $k$.

Program 8.2 gives an implementation for the hash function defined in Equation 8.1. This implementation makes use of the function **frexp** which extracts from a **double**

---

[5]Typically, on a 32-bit computer **sizeof(float)** = **sizeof(unsigned int)**.

---

**PROGRAM 8.2**
Floating-point `Hash` function definition

---

```
1  HashValue Hash (double d)
2  {
3      if (d == 0)
4          return 0;
5      else
6      {
7          int exponent;
8          double mantissa = std::frexp (d, &exponent);
9          return (2 * fabs (mantissa) - 1) * ~0U;
10     }
11 }
```

---

value its mantissa $m$ and exponent $e$ by doing efficient bit manipulations. Clearly the running time of the **Hash** function given in Program 8.2 is $O(1)$.

### 8.3.3 Character String Keys

Strings of characters are not a built-in C++ type. However, the standard C++ library provides the class called **string** which provides support for character string variables. A character string is simply a *null-terminated sequence* of characters. A null-terminated sequence of characters is comprised of zero or more non-null characters followed by the null character. Since such a sequence may be arbitrarily long, we have the problem again of mapping an unbounded domain into the finite range of **unsigned int**.

We can view a character string, $s$, as a sequence of $n$ characters,

$$\{s_0, s_1, \ldots, s_{n-1}\},$$

where $n$ is the length of the string *not counting the null terminator.* One very simple way to hash such a string would be to simply sum the numeric values associated with each character:

$$f(s) = \sum_{i=0}^{n-1} s_i. \tag{8.2}$$

As it turns out, this is not a particularly good way to hash character strings. Given that a **char** is universally 1 byte, $0 \leq s_i \leq B - 1$ where $B = 2^8$, for all $0 \leq i < n$. As a result, $0 \leq f(s) < (B - 1)n$. For example, given a string of length $n = 5$, the value of $f(s)$ falls between zero and 1275. In fact, the situation is even worse; the ASCII character set only uses seven bits. If the string is comprised of only ASCII characters, the result falls in the range between zero and 635.

Essentially the problem with a function $f$ which produces a result in a relatively small interval is the situation which arises when that function is composed with the function $g(x) = x \bmod M$. If the size of the range of the function $f$ is less than $M$, then

$h = g \circ f$ does not spread its values uniformly on the interval $[0, M - 1]$. For example, if $M = 1031$ only the first 635 values (62% of the range) are used!

Alternatively, suppose we have a priori knowledge that character strings are limited to length $n = 4$. Then, we can construct an integer by concatenating the binary representations of each of the characters. That is, given $s = \{s_0, s_1, s_2, s_3\}$, we can construct an integer with the function

$$f(s) = s_0 B^3 + s_1 B^2 + s_2 B + s_0. \tag{8.3}$$

Since $B = 2^8$ is a power of 2, this function is easy to write in C++:

```
HashValue Hash (string const& s)
    { return s[0] << 24 | s[1] << 16 | s[2] << 8 | s [3]; }
```

While this function certainly has a larger range, it still has two problems. First, it does not take into account the fact that the characters are usually ASCII values, and therefore do not require all 8 bits. However, the more significant deficiency of this function is that it cannot deal strings of arbitrary length.

Equation 8.3 can be generalized to deal with strings of arbitrary length as follows:

$$f(s) = \sum_{i=0}^{n-1} B^{n-i-1} s_i.$$

This function produces a unique integer for every possible string. Unfortunately, the range of $f(s)$ is unbounded. A simple modification of this algorithm suffices to bound the range

$$f(s) = \left( \sum_{i=0}^{n-1} B^{n-i-1} s_i \right) \bmod W, \tag{8.4}$$

where $W = 2^w$ such that $w$ is the word size of the machine. Unfortunately, since $W$ and $B$ are both powers of 2, the value computed by this hash function depends only on the last $W/B$ characters in the character string. For example, for $W = 2^{32}$ and $B = 2^8$, this result depends only on the last four characters in the string—all character strings having exactly the same last four characters collide!

We can improve matters somewhat by exploiting some of the characteristics of the ASCII code. For example, if we assume that the character string only contains 7-bit ASCII characters, then we may use $B = 2^7$ in Equation 8.4. However, this results in only a very slight improvement—for $W = 2^{32}$, the result now depends on the last four characters plus 4 bits of the fifth-last character.

Writing the code to compute Equation 8.4 is actually quite straightforward if we realize that $f(s)$ can be viewed as a polynomial in $B$, the coefficients of which are $s_0$, $s_1, \ldots, s_n$. Therefore, we can use *Horner's rule* (see Section 2.1.4) to compute $f(s)$ as follows:

```
HashValue result = 0;
for (unsigned int i = 0; s [i] != 0; ++i)
    result = result * B + s [i];
```

This implementation can be simplified even further if we make use of the fact that $B = 2^b$, where $b = 7$. Since $B$ is a power of two, in order to multiply the variable `result` by $B$ all we need to do is to shift it left by $b$ bits. Furthermore, having just shifted `result` left by $b$ bits, we know that the least significant $b$ bits of the result are zero. And since `s[i]` is a character which has no more than $b = 7$ bits, we can replace the addition operation with an *exclusive or* operation.

```
HashValue result = 0;
for (unsigned int i = 0; s [i] != 0; ++i)
    result = result << b ^ s [i];
```

Of the 128 characters in the 7-bit ASCII character set, only 97 characters are printing characters including the space, tab, and newline characters (see Appendix C). The remaining characters are control characters which, depending on the application, rarely occur in strings. Furthermore, if we assume that letters and digits are the most common characters in strings, then only 62 of the 128 ASCII codes are used frequently. Notice, the letters (both uppercase and lowercase) all fall between $0101_8$ and $0172_8$. All the information is in the least significant 6 bits. Similarly, the digits fall between $060_8$ and $071$—these differ in the least significant 4 bits. These observations suggest that using $B = 2^6$ should work well. That is, for $W = 2^{32}$, the hash value depends on the last five characters plus 2 bits of the sixth-last character.

We have developed a hashing scheme which works quite well given strings which differ in the trailing letters. For example, the strings `"temp1"`, `"temp2"`, and `"temp3"` all produce different hash values. However, in certain applications the strings differ in the leading letters. For example, the two *Internet domain names* `"ece.uwaterloo.ca"` and `"cs.uwaterloo.ca"` collide when using Equation 8.4. Essentially, the effect of the characters that differ is lost because the corresponding bits have been shifted out of the hash value.

This suggests a final modification, which is shown in Program 8.3. Instead of losing the $b = 6$ most significant bits when the variable `result` is shifted left, we retain those bits and *exclusive or* them back into the shifted `result` variable. Using this approach, the two strings `"ece.uwaterloo.ca"` and `"cs.uwaterloo.ca"` produce different hash values.

---

**PROGRAM 8.3**
Character string `Hash` function definition

---

```
1   unsigned int const shift = 6;
2   HashValue const mask = ~0U << (bitsizeof (HashValue) - shift);
3
4   HashValue Hash (string const& s)
5   {
6       HashValue result = 0;
7       for (unsigned int i = 0; s [i] != 0; ++i)
8           result = (result & mask) ^ (result << shift) ^ s [i];
9       return result;
10  }
```

---

**TABLE 8.1**
Sample Character String Keys and
the Hash Values Obtained
Using Program 8.3

| $x$ | Hash($x$) (octal) |
|---|---|
| "ett" | 01446564 |
| "två" | 01656741 |
| "tre" | 01656345 |
| "fyra" | 0147706341 |
| "fem" | 01474455 |
| "sex" | 01624470 |
| "sju" | 01625365 |
| "åtta" | 0140656541 |
| "nio" | 01575057 |
| "tio" | 01655057 |
| "elva" | 044556741 |
| "tolv" | 065565566 |

Table 8.1 lists a number of different character strings together with the hash values obtained using Program 8.3. For example, to hash the string **"fyra"**, the following computation is performed (all numbers in octal):

$$
\begin{array}{r}
\begin{array}{ccccccccc}
1 & 4 & 6 & & & & & & \text{f} \\
\oplus & & 1 & 7 & 1 & & & & \text{y} \\
\oplus & & & 1 & 6 & 2 & & & \text{r} \\
\oplus & & & & 1 & 4 & 1 & & \text{a} \\
\hline
1 & 4 & 7 & 7 & 0 & 6 & 3 & 4 & 1 \\
\end{array}
\end{array}
$$

## 8.3.4 Hashing Objects

In this section we consider hashing in the context of the object hierarchy defined in Chapter 5. The abstract base class called **Object**, which was defined in Section 5.2.2, has a **const** virtual member function called **Hash** which was declared as follows:

```
class Object
{
    ...
    virtual HashValue Hash () const = 0;
    ...
};
```

The idea is that every object instance of a class which is derived from the class **Object** has an associated member function called **Hash** which hashes that object to produce an integer **HashValue**. For example, given a reference to an object, **Object& obj**, the following computation

```
HashValue x = obj.Hash ();
```

---

**PROGRAM 8.4**
Wrapper<T> class Hash member function definition

```
1  template <class T>
2  HashValue Wrapper<T>::Hash () const
3      { return ::Hash (datum); }
```

---

sets the variable **x** to the value returned by the **Hash** function associated with the object to which **obj** refers.

A **Wrapper** class template was declared in Section 5.2.4 which is used to wrap instances of the C++ built-in data types within an **Object** abstract interface. Using the **Wrapper** template, the four classes **Char**, **Int**, **Double**, and **String** were declared as follows:

```
typedef Wrapper<char> Char;
typedef Wrapper<int> Int;
typedef Wrapper<double> Double;
typedef Wrapper<string> String;
```

Since these classes are meant to be concrete classes, they must provide implementations for all of the member functions including the **Hash** function.

Program 8.4 gives the definition of the **Hash** member function of the **Wrapper<T>** class. The implementation simply calls the appropriate hashing function from those given in Programs 8.1, 8.2, and 8.3. For example, the **Wrapper<int>::Hash** function calls **Hash(int)** and the **Wrapper<string>::Hash** function calls **Hash (string)**.

### 8.3.5 Hashing Containers

The **Container** class, which was defined in Section 5.2.5, abstracts the notion of an object which contains other objects. The **Container** class is derived from the **Object** class; therefore, it has a member function called **Hash**. What is a suitable hash function for a container?

Given a container $c$ which contains $n$ objects, $o_1, o_1, \ldots, o_n$, we can define the hash function $f(c)$ as follows:

$$f(c) = \left( \sum_{i=1}^{n} h(o_i) \right) \bmod W. \tag{8.5}$$

That is, to hash a container, simply compute the sum of the hash values of the contained objects.

Program 8.5 shows the implementation of the **Container::Hash** function. This function makes use of the **Accept** function to cause a special visitor, **Hashing-Visitor**, to visit all of the objects contained in the container. When the **Hashing-Visitor** visits an object, it calls that object's **Hash** function and accumulates the result.

**PROGRAM 8.5**
`Container` class `Hash` member function definition

```
1   class HashingVisitor : public Visitor
2   {
3       HashValue value;
4   public:
5       HashingVisitor (HashValue _value) : value (_value)
6           {}
7       void Visit (Object& object)
8           { value += object.Hash (); }
9       HashValue Value () const
10          { return value; }
11  };
12
13  HashValue Container::Hash () const
14  {
15      HashingVisitor visitor (::Hash (typeid (*this).name ()));
16      Accept (visitor);
17      return visitor.Value ();
18  }
```

Since the `Accept` function is a pure virtual member function of the `Container` class, all concrete classes derived from the `Container` class will provide an appropriate implementation for `Accept`. Note that it is not necessary for any derived class to redefine the behavior of the `Hash` member function—the behavior inherited from the `Container` class is completely generic and should suffice for all concrete container classes.

There is a slight problem with Equation 8.5. Different container types that happen to contain identical objects produce exactly the same hash value. For example, an empty stack and an empty list both produce the same hash value. We have avoided this situation in Program 8.5 by adding to the sum the value obtained from hashing the name of the container itself.

### 8.3.6 Using Associations

Hashing provides a way to determine the position of a given object directly from that object itself. Given an object $x$ we determine its position by evaluating the appropriate hash function, $h(x)$. We find the location of object $x$ in exactly the same way. But of what use is this ability to find an object if, in order to compute the hash function $h(x)$, we must be able to access the object $x$ in the first place?

In practice, when using hashing we are dealing with *keyed data*. Mathematically, keyed data consists of ordered pairs

$$A = \{(k, v) : k \in K, v \in V\},$$

---

**PROGRAM 8.6**

Association class Hash member function definition

---

```
1   HashValue Association::Hash () const
2       { return key->Hash (); }
```

---

where $K$ is a set of keys, and $V$ is a set of values. The idea is that we will access elements of the set $A$ using the key. That is, the hash function for elements of the set $A$ is given by

$$f_A((k, v)) = f_K(k),$$

where $f_K$ is the hash function associated with the set $K$.

For example, suppose we wish to use hashing to implement a database which contains driver's license records. Each record contains information about a driver, such as her name, address, and perhaps a summary of traffic violations. Furthermore, each record has a unique driver's license number. The driver's license number is the key and the other information is the value associated with that key.

In Section 5.2.11 the class **Association** was declared, and it comprises two objects, a key and a value:

```
class Association : public Object, public Ownership
{
 Object* key;
 Object* value;
 ...
};
```

Given this declaration, the definition of the hash function for **Association**s is trivial. As shown in Program 8.6. it simply calls the **Hash** member function of the object to which the **key** member variable points.


## 8.4  Hash Tables

A *hash table* is a searchable container. As such, its interface provides functions for putting an object into the container, finding an object in the container, and removing an object from the container. Program 8.7 declares the **HashTable** class, and Program 8.8 gives the definition of the **HashTable** constructor and the member function **H**.

The **HashTable** constructor takes a single argument and initializes the member variable **length** accordingly. The **HashTable::H** member function corresponds to the composition $h = g \circ f$ discussed in Section 8.3. The member function **H** takes as its sole argument a **const** reference to an object. That object is hashed and the result of the hash modulo **length** is returned by **H**.

---

**PROGRAM 8.7**
`HashTable` class definition

---

```
1   class HashTable : public virtual SearchableContainer
2   {
3   protected:
4       unsigned int length;
5   public:
6       HashTable (unsigned int);
7       virtual unsigned int H (Object const&) const;
8   };
```

---

---

**PROGRAM 8.8**
`HashTable` class constructor and `H` member function definitions

---

```
1   HashTable::HashTable (unsigned int _length) :
2       length (_length)
3       {}
4
5   unsigned int HashTable::H (Object const& object) const
6       { return object.Hash () % length; }
```

---

In this chapter we consider three ways to implement a hash table (see Figure 8.2). In all cases, the underlying implementation makes use of an array. The position of an object in the array is determined by hashing the object. The main problem to be resolved is how to deal with collisions—two different objects cannot occupy the same array position at the same time. In the following section, we consider an approach which solves the problem of collisions by keeping objects that collide in a linked list.

---

**FIGURE 8.2**
Object class hierarchy.

---

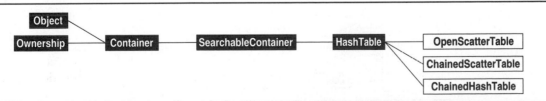

### 8.4.1 Separate Chaining

Figure 8.3 shows a hash table that uses *separate chaining* to resolve collisions. The hash table is implemented as an array of linked lists. To insert an item into the table, it is appended to one of the linked lists. The linked list to which it is appended is determined by hashing that item.

Figure 8.3 illustrates an example in which there are $M = 16$ linked lists. The 12 character strings `"ett"–"tolv"` have been inserted into the table using the hashed values and in the order given in Table 8.1. Notice that in this example since $M = 16$, the linked list is selected by the least significant 4 bits of the hashed value given in Table 8.1. In effect, it is only the last letter of a string that determines the linked list in which that string appears.

### Implementation

Program 8.9 declares the class **ChainedHashTable** which is derived from the **HashTable** class. This **ChainedHashTable** class definition introduces one member variable called **array**. It is declared as an array of linked lists of pointers to **Object**s.

### Constructor and Destructor

The constructor and destructor for the **ChainedHashTable** class are defined in Program 8.10. The constructor takes a single argument of type **unsigned int**

---

**FIGURE 8.3**
Hash table using separate chaining.

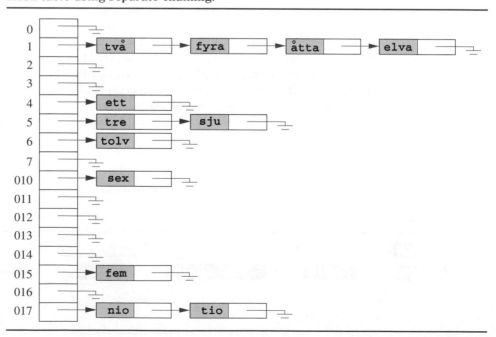

---

**PROGRAM 8.9**
`ChainedHashTable` class definition

```
1   class ChainedHashTable : public HashTable
2   {
3       Array<LinkedList<Object*> > array;
4   public:
5       ChainedHashTable (unsigned int);
6       // ...
7   };
```

---

**PROGRAM 8.10**
`ChainedHashTable` class constructor, destructor, and `Purge` member function definitions

```
1   ChainedHashTable::ChainedHashTable (unsigned int _length) :
2       HashTable (_length),
3       array (_length)
4       {}
5
6   void ChainedHashTable::Purge ()
7   {
8       for (unsigned int i = 0; i < length; ++i)
9       {
10          if (IsOwner ())
11          {
12              LinkedList<Object*>::Element const* ptr;
13
14              for (ptr = array [i].Head ();
15                      ptr != 0; ptr = ptr->Next ())
16                  delete ptr->Datum ();
17          }
18          array [i].Purge ();
19      }
20      count = 0;
21  }
22
23  ChainedHashTable::~ChainedHashTable ()
24      { Purge (); }
```

which specifies the size of hash table desired. The constructor simply initializes the **HashTable** base class and the **array** member variable accordingly. Initializing the **array** variable involves constructing the required number of empty linked lists. Consequently, the running time for the **ChainedHashTable** constructor is $O(M)$ where $M$ is the size of the hash table.

The **ChainedHashTable** destructor simply calls the **Purge** member function. Since the **ChainedHashTable** is a container, the **Purge** function must delete any contained objects if it is the owner of those objects. Therefore, the **Purge** function is required to traverse each of the linked lists in the array.

To determine the running time of the **Purge** function, we will assume that there are $n$ contained objects and the length of the array is $M$. Furthermore, let $n_i$ be the number of items in the $i$th linked list for $i = 0, 1, \ldots, M - 1$. Note that $\sum_{i=0}^{M-1} n_i = n$. The running time of the inner loop for the $i$th iteration of the outer loop is $n_i \mathcal{T} \langle \text{T::~T()} \rangle + O(n_i) + O(1)$. The constant overhead arises from the loop termination test which must be done at least once. The total running time of the destructor is given by

$$\sum_{i=0}^{M-1} (n_i \mathcal{T} \langle \text{T::~T()} \rangle + O(n_i) + O(1)) = n \mathcal{T} \langle \text{T::~T()} \rangle + O(n) + O(M).$$

If we assume that $\mathcal{T} \langle \text{T::~T()} \rangle = O(1)$, the running time simplifies to $O(M + n)$.

### Inserting and Removing Items

Program 8.11 gives the code for inserting and removing items from a **ChainedHash-Table**.

The implementations of the **Insert** and **Withdraw** functions are remarkably simple. For example, the **Insert** function first calls the hash function **H** to compute an array index which is used to select one of the linked lists. The **Append** member function provided by the **LinkedList<T>** class is used to add a pointer to the object to the selected linked list. The total running time for the **Insert** operation is $\mathcal{T} \langle \text{T::Hash()} \rangle +$

---

**PROGRAM 8.11**
ChainedHashTable class **Insert** and **Withdraw** member function definitions

```
1   void ChainedHashTable::Insert (Object& object)
2   {
3       array [H (object)].Append (&object);
4       ++count;
5   }
6
7   void ChainedHashTable::Withdraw (Object& object)
8   {
9       array [H (object)].Extract (&object);
10      --count;
11  }
```

$O(1)$, where $\mathcal{T}\langle\text{T::Hash()}\rangle$ is the running time of the **Object::Hash** function. Notice that if the hash function runs in constant time, then so too does hash table insertion operation!

The **Withdraw** function is almost identical to the **Insert** function. Instead of calling **Append**, it calls the linked list **Extract** function to remove the specified object from the appropriate linked list. The running time of **Withdraw** is determined by the time of the **Extract** operation. In Chapter 4 this was shown to be $O(n)$ where $n$ is the number of items in the linked list. In the worst case, all of the items in the **ChainedHashTable** have collided with each other and ended up in the same list. That is, in the worst case if there are $n$ items in the container, all $n$ of them are in a single linked list. In this case, the running time of the **Withdraw** operation is $\mathcal{T}\langle\text{T::Hash()}\rangle + O(n)$.

### Finding an Item

The definition of the **Find** member function of the **ChainedHashTable** class is given in Program 8.12 The **Find** function takes as its single argument a reference to an **Object**. The purpose of the **Find** operation is to return a reference to an object which is equal to the specified object.

The **Find** function simply hashes its argument to select the linked list in which it should be found. Then, it traverses the linked list to locate the target object. As for the **Withdraw** operation, the worst-case running time of the **Find** function occurs when all the objects in the container have collided, and the item that is being sought does not appear in the linked list. In this case, the running time of the find operation is $n\mathcal{T}\langle_{\text{==(T\&,T\&)}}\rangle + \mathcal{T}\langle\text{T::Hash()}\rangle + O(n)$.

## 8.4.2 Average Case Analysis

The previous section has shown that in the worst case, the running time to insert an object into a separately chained hash table is $O(1)$, and the time to find or delete an

---

**PROGRAM 8.12**
**ChainedHashTable** class **Find** member function definition

```
1   Object& ChainedHashTable::Find (Object const& object) const
2   {
3       ListElement<Object*> const* ptr;
4
5       for (ptr = array [H (object)].Head ();
6           ptr != 0; ptr = ptr->Next ())
7       {
8           if (object == *ptr->Datum ())
9               return *ptr->Datum ();
10      }
11      return NullObject::Instance ();
12  }
```

object is $O(n)$. But these bounds are no better than the same operations on plain lists! Why have we gone to all the trouble inventing hash tables?

The answer lies not in the worst-case performance, but in the average expected performance. Suppose we have a hash table of size $M$. Let there be exactly $n$ items in the hash table. We call the quantity $\lambda = n/M$ the *load factor*. The load factor is simply the ratio of the number of items in the hash table to the array length.

Let $n_i$ be the number of items in the $i$th linked list, for $i = 0, 1, \ldots, M - 1$. The average length of a linked list is

$$\frac{1}{M} \sum_{i=0}^{M-1} n_i = \frac{n}{M}$$
$$= \lambda.$$

The average length of a linked list is exactly the load factor!

If we are given the load factor $\lambda$, we can determine the *average* running times for the various operations. The average running time of **Insert** is the same as its worst-case time, $O(1)$—this result does not depend on $\lambda$. On the other hand, the average running time for **Withdraw** does depend on $\lambda$. It is $\mathcal{T}\langle \texttt{T::Hash()} \rangle + O(1) + O(\lambda)$ since the time required to delete an item from a linked list of length $\lambda$ is $O(\lambda)$.

To determine the average running time for the **Find** operation, we need to make an assumption about whether the item that is being sought is in the table. If the item is not found in the table, the search is said to be *unsuccessful*. The average running time for an unsuccessful search is

$$\mathcal{T}\langle \texttt{T::Hash()} \rangle + \lambda\mathcal{T}\langle \texttt{op==(T\&,T\&)} \rangle + O(1) + O(\lambda).$$

On the other hand, if the search target is in the table, the search is said to be *successful*. The average number of comparisons needed to find an arbitrary item in a linked list of length $\lambda$ is

$$\frac{1}{\lambda} \sum_{i=1}^{\lambda} i = \frac{\lambda + 1}{2}.$$

Thus, the average running time for a successful search is

$$\mathcal{T}\langle \texttt{T::Hash()} \rangle + ((\lambda + 1)/2)\mathcal{T}\langle \texttt{op==(T\&,T\&)} \rangle + O(1) + O(\lambda).$$

So, while any one search operation can be as bad as $O(n)$, if we do a large number of random searches, we expect that the average running time will be $O(\lambda)$. In fact, if we have a sufficiently good hash function and a reasonable set of objects in the container, we can expect that those objects are distributed throughout the table. Therefore, any one search operation will not be very much worse than the average case.

Finally, if we know how many objects will be inserted into the hash table a priori, then we can choose a table size $M$ which is larger than the maximum number of items expected. By doing this, we can ensure that $\lambda = n/M \leq 1$, that is, a linked list contains no more than one item on average. In this case, the average time for **Withdraw** is $\mathcal{T}\langle\text{T::Hash()}\rangle + O(1)$ and for **Find** it is $\mathcal{T}\langle\text{T::Hash()}\rangle + \mathcal{T}\langle\text{(op--T\&,T\&)}\rangle + O(1)$.

## 8.5 Scatter Tables

The separately chained hash table described in the preceding section is essentially a pointer-based implementation. We have seen both pointer-based and array-based implementations for all of the data structures considered so far, and hash tables are no exception. Array-based hash tables are called *scatter tables.*

The essential idea behind a scatter table is that all of the information is stored within a fixed size array. Hashing is used to identify the position where an item should be stored. When a collision occurs, the colliding item is stored somewhere else in the array.

One of the motivations for using scatter tables can be seen by considering again the pointer-based hash table shown in Figure 8.3. Since most of the linked lists are empty, much of the array is unused. At the same time, for each item that is added to the table, dynamic memory is consumed. Why not simply store the data in the unused array positions?

### 8.5.1 Chained Scatter Table

Figure 8.4 illustrates a *chained scatter table.* The elements of a chained scatter table are ordered pairs. Each array element contains a key and a pointer. All keys are stored in the table itself. Consequently, there is a fixed limit on the number of items that can be stored in a scatter table.

Since the pointers point to other elements in the array, they are implemented as integer-valued array subscripts rather than as address-valued pointer variables. Since valid array subscripts start from the value zero, the *null* pointer must be represented not as zero, but by an integer value that is outside the array bounds.

To find an item in a chained scatter table, we begin by hashing that item to determine the location from which to begin the search. For example, to find the string **"åtta"**, which hashes to the value $0140656541_8$, we begin the search in array location $1_8$. The item at that location is **"två"**, which does not match. So we follow the pointer in location $1_8$ to location $2_8$. The item there, **"fyra"**, does not match either. We follow the pointer again, this time to location $3_8$ where we ultimately find the string we are looking for.

Comparing Figure 8.3 and 8.4, we see that the chained scatter table has embedded within it the linked lists which appear to be the same as those in the separately chained hash table. However, the lists are not exactly identical. When using the chained scatter table, it is possible for lists to *coalesce.*

For example, when using separate chaining, the keys **"tre"** and **"sju"** appear in a separate list from the key **"tolv"**. This is because both **"tre"** and **"sju"** hash to

**FIGURE 8.4**
Chained scatter table.

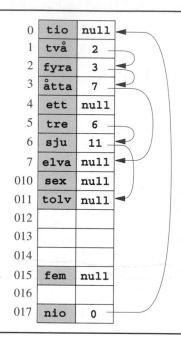

**PROGRAM 8.13**
**ChainedScatterTable** class definition

```
1   class ChainedScatterTable : public HashTable
2   {
3       class Entry
4       {
5       public:
6           enum { null = ~0U };
7           Object* object;
8           unsigned int next;
9
10          Entry ();
11      };
12
13      Array<Entry> array;
14  public:
15      ChainedScatterTable (unsigned int);
16      // ...
17  };
```

position $5_8$, whereas `"tolv"` hashes to position $6_8$. The same keys appear together in a single list starting at position $5_8$ in the chained scatter table. The two lists have *coalesced*.

### Implementation

The declaration of the class `ChainedScatterTable` is given in Program 8.13. The scatter table is implemented as an array of elements of the nested type `Entry`. Each `Entry` instance has two member variables—`object` and `next`. The former is a pointer to a contained object. The latter indicates the position in the array of the next element of a chain. The value of the enumerated constant `null` will be used instead of zero to mark the end of a chain. The value zero is not used to mark the end of a chain because zero is a valid array subscript.

The `ChainedScatterTable` class contains a single member variable—`array`. It is declared as an array of `ChainedScatterTable::Entry` objects.

### Constructors and Destructor

Program 8.14 gives the definition of the default constructor for the `ChainedScatterTable::Entry` class. It shall always be the case that an unused entry will have its `object` pointer set to zero and its `next` field set to `null`. By default, all entries are initially unused. Therefore, the default constructor simply initializes the two member variables accordingly.

The `ChainedScatterTable` constructor takes a single **unsigned int** argument which specifies the size of scatter table desired. The constructor simply initializes the `HashTable` base class and the `array` member variable as appropriate. Initializing the `array` variable involves setting all of the entries to the unused state. Consequently, the running time for the `ChainedScatterTable` constructor is $O(M)$ where $M$ is the size of the scatter table.

The `ChainedScatterTable` destructor calls the `Purge` member function. The `Purge` function must delete any contained objects if the scatter table is the owner of those objects. The `Purge` function traverses the array looking for occupied entries and deletes objects as they are found. Suppose that there are $n$ contained objects and the length of the array is $M$. Clearly, $n$ cannot be greater than $M$ since all objects are stored in the array. The running time of the `Purge` function is $n\mathcal{T}\langle\text{T::~T()}\rangle + O(M)$, and if we assume that $\mathcal{T}\langle\text{T::~T()}\rangle = O(1)$, the running time simplifies to $O(M)$.

### Inserting and Finding an Item

Program 8.15 gives the code for the `Insert` and `Find` member functions of the `ChainedScatterTable` class. To insert an item into a chained scatter table we need to find an unused array location in which to put the item. We first hash the item to determine the "natural" location for that item. If the natural location is unused, we store the item there and we are done.

However, if the natural position for an item is occupied, then a collision has occurred and an alternate location in which to store that item must be found. When a collision occurs it must be the case that there is a chain emanating from the natural position for the item. The insertion algorithm given always adds items at the end of the chain. Therefore, after a collision has been detected, the end of the chain is found (lines 8–9).

---

**PROGRAM 8.14**
`ChainedScatterTable::Entry` class constructor and `ChainedScatterTable` class constructor, destructor and `Purge` member function definitions

```
1    ChainedScatterTable::Entry::Entry () :
2        object (0),
3        next (null)
4        {}
5
6    ChainedScatterTable::ChainedScatterTable (unsigned int _length) :
7        HashTable (_length),
8        array (_length)
9        {}
10
11   void ChainedScatterTable::Purge ()
12   {
13       for (unsigned int i = 0; i < length; ++i)
14       {
15           if (array [i].object != 0)
16           {
17               if (IsOwner ())
18                   delete array [i] .object;
19               array [i] = Entry ();
20           }
21       }
22       count = 0;
23   }
24
25   ChainedScatterTable::~ChainedScatterTable ()
26       { Purge (); }
```

---

After the end of the chain is found, an unused array position in which to store the item must be found. This is done by a simple, linear search starting from the array position immediately following the end of the chain (lines 11–13). Once an unused position is found, it is linked to the end of the chain (line 14), and the item is stored in the unused position (lines 16–17).

The worst-case running time for insertion occurs when the scatter table has only one unused entry, that is, when the number of items in the table is $n = M - 1$, where $M$ is the table size. In the worst case, all of the used array elements are linked into a single chain of length $M - 1$ and the item to be inserted hashes to the head of the chain. In this case, it takes $O(M)$ to find the end of the chain. In the worst case, the end of the chain immediately follows the unused array position. Consequently, the linear search for the unused position is also $O(M)$. Once an unused position has been found,

**PROGRAM 8.15**
ChainedScatterTable class Insert and Find member function definitions

```
1   void ChainedScatterTable::Insert (Object& object)
2   {
3       if (count == length)
4           throw domain_error ("scatter table is full");
5       unsigned int probe = H (object);
6       if (array [probe].object != 0)
7       {
8           while (array [probe].next != Entry::null)
9               probe = array [probe].next;
10          unsigned int const tail = probe;
11          probe = (probe + 1) % length;
12          while (array [probe].object != 0)
13              probe = (probe + 1) % length;
14          array [tail].next = probe;
15      }
16      array [probe].object = &object;
17      array [probe].next = Entry::null;
18      ++count;
19  }
20
21  Object& ChainedScatterTable::Find (Object const& object) const
22  {
23      for (unsigned int probe = H (object);
24          probe != Entry::null; probe = array [probe].next)
25      {
26          if (object == *array [probe].object)
27              return *array [probe].object;
28      }
29      return NullObject::Instance ();
30  }
```

the actual insertion can be done in constant time. Therefore, the running time of the insertion operation is $\mathcal{T}\langle\text{T::Hash()}\rangle + O(M)$ in the worst case.

Program 8.15 also gives the code for the **Find** member function which is used to locate a given object in the scatter table. The algorithm is straightforward. The item is hashed to find its natural location in the table. If the item is not found in the natural location but a chain emanates from that location, the chain is followed to determine if that item appears anywhere in the chain.

The worst-case running time occurs when the item for which we are looking is not in the table, the table is completely full, and all of the entries are linked together into a single linked list. In this case, the running time of the **Find** algorithm is $\mathcal{T}\langle\text{T::Hash()}\rangle + M\mathcal{T}\langle\text{op==(T\&,T\&)}\rangle + O(M)$.

## Removing Items

Removing items from a chained scatter table is more complicated than putting them into the table. The goal when removing an item is to have the scatter table end up exactly as it would have appeared had that item never been inserted in the first place. Therefore, when an item is removed from the middle of a chain, items which follow it in the chain have to be moved up to fill in the hole. However, the moving-up operation is complicated by the fact that several chains may have coalesced.

Program 8.16 gives an implementation of the **Withdraw** member function of the **ChainedScatterTable** class. The algorithm begins by checking that the table is not empty (lines 3–4). To remove an item, we first have to find it. This is what the loop on lines 5–7 does. If the item to be deleted is not in the table, when this loop terminates, the variable **i** has the value **null** and an exception is thrown (lines 8–9). Otherwise, the item at position **i** in the table needs to be removed.

The purpose of the loop on lines 10–32 is to fill in the hole in the chain which results when the item at position **i** is removed by moving up items which follow it in the chain. What we need to do is to find the next item which follows the item at **i** that is safe to move into position **i**. The loop on lines 13–27 searches the rest of the chain following the item at **i** to find an item which can be safely moved.

Figure 8.5 illustrates the basic idea. The figures shows a chained scatter table of length ten that contains integer-valued keys. There is a single chain as shown in the figure. However, notice that the values in the chain are not all equal modulo 10. In fact, this chain must have resulted from the coalescing of three chains—one which begins in position 1, one which begins in position 2, and one which begins in position 5.

Suppose we wish to remove item 11 in position 2, which is indicated by the box in Figure 8.5(*a*). To delete it, we must follow the chain to find the next item that can be moved safely up to position 2. Item 02 follows 11 and can be moved safely up to position 2 because that is the location to which it hashes. Moving item 02 up moves the hole down the list to position 3 [Figure 8.5(*b*)]. Again we follow the chain to find that item 21 can be moved safely up giving rise to the situation in Figure 8.5(*c*).

Now we have a case where an item cannot be moved. Item 05 is the next candidate to be moved. However, it is in position 5 which is the position to which it hashes. If we were to move it up, then it would no longer be in the chain which emanates from position 5. In effect, the item would no longer be accessible! Therefore, it cannot be moved safely. Instead, we must move item 31 ahead of item 5 as shown in Figure 8.5(*d*). Eventually, the hole propagates to the end of the chain, where it can be deleted easily [Figure 8.5(*e*)].

The loop on lines 13–27 of Program 8.16 finds the position **j** of an item which can be safely moved to position **i**. The algorithm makes use of the following fact: An item can be safely moved up *only if it does not hash to a position which appears in the linked list between* **i** *and* **j**. This is what the code on lines 16–24 tests.

When execution reaches line 28, either we have found an item which can be safely moved or there does not exist such an item. If an item is found, it is moved up (lines 30–31) and we repeat the whole process again. On the other hand, if there are no more items to be moved up, then the process is finished and the main loop (lines 10–32) terminates.

The statements on lines 33–34 do the actual deed of removing the data from the position **i**, which by now is at the end of the chain. The final task to be done is to

**PROGRAM 8.16**
ChainedScatterTable class Withdraw member function definition

```
1   void ChainedScatterTable::Withdraw (Object& object)
2   {
3       if (count == 0)
4           throw domain_error ("scatter table is empty");
5       unsigned int i = H (object);
6       while (i != Entry::null && array [i].object != &object)
7           i = array [i].next;
8       if (i == Entry::null)
9           throw invalid_argument ("object not found");
10      for (;;)
11      {
12          unsigned int j;
13          for (j = array [i].next;
14                  j != Entry::null; j = array [j].next)
15          {
16              unsigned int const h = H (*array [j].object);
17              bool contained = false;
18              for (unsigned int k = array [i].next;
19                      k != array [j].next && !contained;
20                      k = array [k].next)
21              {
22                  if (k == h)
23                      contained = true;
24              }
25              if (!contained)
26                  break;
27          }
28          if (j == Entry::null)
29              break;
30          array [i].object = array [j].object;
31          i = j;
32      }
33      array [i].object = 0;
34      array [i].next = Entry::null;
35      for (unsigned int j = (i + length - 1U) % length;
36              j != i; j = (j + length - 1U) % length)
37      {
38          if (array [j].next == i)
39          {
40              array [j].next = Entry::null;
41              break;
42          }
43      }
44      --count;
45  }
```

**FIGURE 8.5**
Removing items from a chained scatter table.

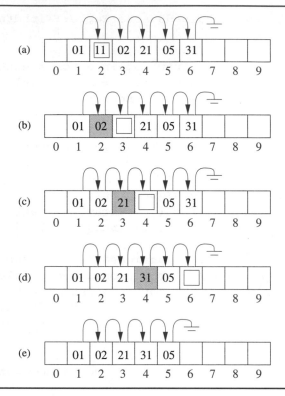

remove the pointer to position `i`, since there is no longer any data at that position. That is the job of the loop on lines 35–43.

### Worst-Case Running Time

Computing a tight bound on the worst-case running time of Program 8.16 is tricky. Assuming the item to be removed is actually in the table, then the time required to find the item (lines 3–9) is

$$\mathcal{T}\langle \text{T::Hash()}\rangle + M\mathcal{T}\langle \text{op==(T\&,T\&)}\rangle + O(M)$$

in the worst case.

The worst-case running time of the main loop occurs when the table is full, when there is only one chain, and when no items can be safely moved up in the chain. In this case, the running time of the main loop (lines 10–32) is

$$\left(\frac{(M-1)M}{2}\right)\mathcal{T}\langle \text{T::Hash()}\rangle + O(M^2).$$

Finally, the worst-case running time of the last loop (lines 35–43) is $O(M)$.

Therefore, the worst-case running time of the `Withdraw` function for chained scatter tables is

$$\left(1 + \frac{(M-1)M}{2}\right)\mathcal{T}\langle\text{T::Hash()}\rangle + M\mathcal{T}\langle\text{op==(T\&,T\&)}\rangle + O(M^2).$$

Clearly we don't want to be removing items from a chained scatter table very often!

### 8.5.2 Average Case Analysis

The previous section has shown that the worst-case running time to insert or to find an object in a chained scatter table is $O(M)$. The average case analysis of chained scatter tables is complicated by the fact that lists coalesce. However, if we assume that chains never coalesce, then the chains which appear in a chained scatter table for a given set of items are identical to those which appear in a separately chained hash table for the same set of items.

Unfortunately we cannot assume that lists do not coalesce—they do! We therefore expect that the average list will be longer than $\lambda$ and that the running times are correspondingly slower. Knuth has shown that the average number of probes in an unsuccessful search is

$$U(\lambda) \approx 1 + \frac{1}{4}(e^{2\lambda} - 1 - 2\lambda),$$

and the average number of probes in a successful search is approximately

$$S(\lambda) \approx 1 + \frac{1}{8\lambda}(e^{2\lambda} - 1 - 2\lambda) + \frac{\lambda}{4},$$

where $\lambda$ is the load factor[23]. The precise functional form of $U(\lambda)$ and $S(\lambda)$ is not so important here. What is important is that when $\lambda = 1$, i.e., when the table is full, $U(1) \approx 2.1$ and $S(1) \approx 1.8$. Regardless of the size of the table, an unsuccessful search requires just over two probes on average, and a successful search requires just under two probes on average!

Consequently, the average running time for insertion is

$$\mathcal{T}\langle\text{T::Hash()}\rangle + O(U(\lambda)) = \mathcal{T}\langle\text{T::Hash()}\rangle + O(1),$$

since the insertion is always done in first empty position found. Similarly, the running time for an unsuccessful search is

$$\mathcal{T}\langle\text{T::Hash()}\rangle + U(\lambda)\mathcal{T}\langle\text{op==(T\&,T\&)}\rangle + O(U(\lambda)),$$

and for a successful search it is

$$\mathcal{T}\langle\text{T::Hash()}\rangle + S(\lambda)\mathcal{T}\langle\text{op = =(T\&,T\&)}\rangle + O(S(\lambda)).$$

## 8.6  Scatter Table Using Open Addressing

An alternative method of dealing with collisions which entirely does away with the need for links and chaining is called *open addressing*. The basic idea is to define a *probe sequence* for every key which, when followed, always leads to the key in question.

The probe sequence is essentially a sequence of functions

$$\{h_0, h_1, \ldots, h_{M-1}\},$$

where $h_i$ is a hash function, $h_i : K \mapsto \{0, 1, \ldots, M - 1\}$. To insert item $x$ into the scatter table, we examine array locations $h_0(x)$, $h_1(x)$, $\ldots$, until we find an empty cell. Similarly, to find item $x$ in the scatter table we examine the same sequence of locations in the same order.

The most common probe sequences are of the form

$$h_i(x) = (h(x) + c(i)) \bmod M,$$

where $i = 0, 1, \ldots, M - 1$. The function $h(x)$ is the same hash function that we have seen before. That is, the function $h$ maps keys into integers in the range from zero to $M - 1$.

The function $c(i)$ represents the collision resolution strategy. It is required to have the following two properties:

**Property 1** $c(0) = 0$. This ensures that the first probe in the sequence is

$$h_0(x) = (h(x) + 0) \bmod M = h(x).$$

**Property 2** The set of values

$$\{c(0) \bmod M, c(1) \bmod M, c(2) \bmod M, \ldots, c(M - 1) \bmod M\}$$

must contain every integer between 0 and $M - 1$. This second property ensures that the probe sequence eventually probes *every possible array position*.

### 8.6.1  Linear Probing

The simplest collision resolution strategy in open addressing is called *linear probing*. In linear probing, the function $c(i)$ is a linear function in $i$. That is, it is of the form

$$c(i) = \alpha i + \beta.$$

Property 1 requires that $c(0) = 0$. Therefore, $\beta$ must be zero.

In order for $c(i) = \alpha i$ to satisfy Property 2, $\alpha$ and $M$ must be relatively prime. If we know the $M$ will always be a prime number, then any $\alpha$ will do. On the other hand, if we cannot be certain that $M$ is prime, then $\alpha$ must be 1. Therefore, the linear probing sequence that is usually used is

$$h_i = (h(x) + i) \bmod M,$$

for $i = 0, 1, 2, \ldots, M - 1$.

Figure 8.6 illustrates an example of a scatter table using open addressing together with linear probing. For example, consider the string `"åtta"`. This string hashes to array position $1_8$. The corresponding linear probing sequence begins at position $1_8$ and goes on to positions $2_8$, $3_8$, .... In this case, the search for the string `"åtta"` succeeds after three probes.

To insert an item $x$ into the scatter table, an empty cell is found by following the same probe sequence that would be used in a search for item $x$. Thus, linear probing finds an empty cell by doing a linear search beginning from array position $h(x)$.

An unfortunate characteristic of linear probing arises from the fact that as the table fills, clusters of consecutive cells form and the time required for a search increases with the size of the cluster. Furthermore, when we attempt to insert an item in the table at a position which is already occupied, that item is ultimately inserted at the end of the cluster—thereby increasing its length. This by itself is not inherently a bad thing. After all, when using the chained approach, every insertion increases the length of some chain by one. However, whenever an insertion is made between two clusters that are separated

**FIGURE 8.6**

Scatter table using open addressing and linear probing.

| | | |
|---|---|---|
| 0 | tio | occupied |
| 1 | två | occupied |
| 2 | fyra | occupied |
| 3 | åtta | occupied |
| 4 | ett | occupied |
| 5 | tre | occupied |
| 6 | sju | occupied |
| 7 | elva | occupied |
| 010 | sex | occupied |
| 011 | tolv | occupied |
| 012 | | empty |
| 013 | | empty |
| 014 | | empty |
| 015 | fem | occupied |
| 016 | | empty |
| 017 | nio | occupied |

by one unoccupied position, the two clusters become one, thereby potentially increasing the cluster length by an amount much greater than 1—a bad thing! This phenomenon is called *primary clustering*.

## 8.6.2   Quadratic Probing

An alternative to linear probing that addresses the primary clustering problem is called *quadratic probing*. In quadratic probing, the function $c(i)$ is a quadratic function in $i$.[6] The general quadratic has the form

$$c(i) = \alpha i^2 + \beta i + \gamma.$$

However, quadratic probing is usually done using $c(i) = i^2$.

Clearly, $c(i) = i^2$ satisfies property 1. What is not so clear is whether it satisfies property 2. In fact, in general it does not. The following theorem gives the conditions under which quadratic probing works:

**Theorem 8.1**
*When quadratic probing is used in a table of size M, where M is a prime number, the first $\lfloor M/2 \rfloor$ probes are distinct.*

**Proof (By contradiction).**    Let us assume that the theorem is false. Then there exist two distinct values $i$ and $j$ such that $0 \leq i < j < \lfloor M/2 \rfloor$, that probe exactly the same position.
Thus,

$$
\begin{aligned}
h_i(x) = h_j(x) &\Rightarrow h(x) + c(i) = h(x) + c(j) \pmod{M} \\
&\Rightarrow h(x) + i^2 = h(x) + j^2 \pmod{M} \\
&\Rightarrow i^2 = j^2 \pmod{M} \\
&\Rightarrow i^2 - j^2 = 0 \pmod{M} \\
&\Rightarrow (i - j)(i + j) = 0 \pmod{M}
\end{aligned}
$$

Since $M$ is a prime number, the only way that the product $(i - j)(i + j)$ can be zero modulo $M$ is for either $i - j$ to be zero or $i + j$ to be zero modulo $M$. Since $i$ and $j$ are distinct, $i - j \neq 0$. Furthermore, since both $i$ and $j$ are less than $\lfloor M/2 \rfloor$, the sum $i + j$ is less than $M$. Consequently, the sum cannot be zero. We have successfully argued an absurdity—if the theorem is false, one of two quantities must be zero, neither of which can possibly be zero. Therefore, the original assumption is not correct and the theorem is true.

---

[6]What else would it be?

Applying Theorem 8.1 we get that quadratic probing works as long as the table size is prime and there are fewer than $n = M/2$ items in the table. In terms of the load factor $\lambda = n/M$, this occurs when $\lambda < \frac{1}{2}$.

Quadratic probing eliminates the primary clustering phenomenon of linear probing because instead of doing a linear search, it does a quadratic search:

$$h_0(x) = (h(x) + 0 \bmod M)$$
$$h_1(x) = (h(x) + 1 \bmod M)$$
$$h_2(x) = (h(x) + 4 \bmod M)$$
$$h_3(x) = (h(x) + 9 \bmod M)$$

$$\vdots$$

### 8.6.3 Double Hashing

While quadratic probing does indeed eliminate the primary clustering problem, it places a restriction on the number of items that can be put in the table—the table must be less than half full. *Double Hashing* is yet another method of generating a probing sequence. It requires two distinct hash functions,

$$h : K \mapsto \{0, 1, \ldots, M - 1\},$$
$$h' : K \mapsto \{1, 2, \ldots, M - 1\}.$$

The probing sequence is then computed as follows:

$$h_i(x) = (h(x) + ih'(x)) \bmod M.$$

Since the collision resolution function is $c(i) = ih'(x)$, the probe sequence depends on the key as follows: If $h'(x) = 1$, then the probing sequence for the key $x$ is the same as linear probing. If $h'(x) = 2$, the probing sequence examines every other array position. This works as long as $M$ is not even.

Clearly since $c(0) = 0$, the double hashing method satisfies property 1. Furthermore, property 2 is satisfied as long as $h'(x)$ and $M$ are relatively prime. Since $h'(x)$ can take on any value between 1 and $M - 1$, $M$ must be a prime number.

But what is a suitable choice for the function $h'$? Recall that $h$ is defined as the composition of two functions, $h = g \circ f$, where $g(x) = x \bmod M$. We can define $h'$ as the composition $g' \circ f$, where

$$g'(x) = 1 + (x \bmod (M - 1)), \tag{8.6}$$

Double hashing reduces the occurrence of primary clustering since it only does a linear search if $h'(x)$ hashes to the value 1. For a good hash function, this should only happen with probability $1/(M - 1)$. However, for double hashing to work at all, the size of the scatter table, $M$, must be a prime number. Table 8.2 summarizes the characteristics of the various open addressing probing sequences.

**TABLE 8.2**
Characteristics of the Open Addressing Probing Sequences

| Probing Sequence | Primary Clustering | Capacity Limit | Size Restriction |
| --- | --- | --- | --- |
| Linear probing | yes | none | none |
| Quadratic probing | no | $\lambda < \frac{1}{2}$ | $M$ must be prime |
| Double hashing | no | none | $M$ must be prime |

### 8.6.4 Implementation

This section describes an implementation of a scatter table using open addressing with linear probing. Program 8.17 declares the **OpenScatterTable** class. The scatter table is implemented as an array of elements of the nested type **Entry**. Each **Entry** instance has two member variables—**object** and **state**. The former is a pointer to an **Object** class instance. The latter is an element of the enumeration **State**.

Each entry can be in one of three states—**empty**, **occupied**, or **deleted**. Initially, all entries are empty. When an object pointer is recorded in an entry, the state of

---

**PROGRAM 8.17**
OpenScatterTable class definition

```
1   class OpenScatterTable : public HashTable
2   {
3       class Entry
4       {
5       public:
6           enum State { empty, occupied, deleted };
7           State state;
8           Object* object;
9
10          Entry ();
11      };
12
13      Array<Entry> array;
14
15      unsigned int C (unsigned int) const;
16      unsigned int FindMatch (Object const&) const;
17      unsigned int FindInstance (Object const&) const;
18      unsigned int FindUnoccupied (Object const&) const;
19  public:
20      OpenScatterTable (unsigned int);
21      // ...
22  };
```

that entry is changed to `occupied`. The purpose of the third state, `deleted`, will be discussed in conjunction with the `Withdraw` function below.

In addition to the lone member variable `array`, the `OpenScatterTable` class definition contains a number of private member function declarations—`C`, `FindUnoccupied`, `FindMatch`, and `FindInstance`. The member function `C` embodies the *collision resolution strategy* which in this case is linear probing. The other three member functions encapsulate functionality which is useful in the implementation of the various scatter table operations.

### Constructors and Destructor

Program 8.18 gives the definition of the default constructor for the `OpenScatterTable::Entry` class. It shall always be the case that an unoccupied entry will have its `object` pointer set to zero and the default state of all entries is initially `empty`. The default constructor initializes the two corresponding member variables accordingly.

---

**PROGRAM 8.18**
`OpenScatterTable` class constructor and destructor and `OpenScatterTable::Entry` class constructor definitions

---

```
1   OpenScatterTable::Entry::Entry () :
2       state (empty),
3       object (0)
4       {}
5
6   OpenScatterTable::OpenScatterTable (unsigned int _length) :
7       HashTable (_length),
8       array (_length)
9       {}
10
11  void OpenScatterTable::Purge ()
12  {
13      for (unsigned int i = 0; i < length; ++i)
14      {
15          if (array [i].state == Entry::occupied)
16          {
17              if (IsOwner ())
18                  delete array [i].object;
19              array [i] = Entry ();
20          }
21      }
22      count = 0;
23  }
24
25  OpenScatterTable::~OpenScatterTable ()
26      { Purge (); }
```

---

The `OpenScatterTable` constructor takes a single argument of type **unsigned int** which specifies the size of scatter table desired. The constructor initializes the `HashTable` base class and the `array` member variable as required. Initializing the `array` variable requires setting all of the entries to the **empty** state. Consequently, the running time for the `OpenScatterTable` constructor is $O(M)$ where $M$ is the size of the scatter table.

The `OpenScatterTable` destructor calls the `Purge` member function. The `Purge` function must delete any contained objects if the scatter table is the owner of those objects. The `Purge` function traverses the array looking for occupied entries and deletes objects as they are found. If there are $n$ contained objects and the length of the array is $M$, then the running time of the `Purge` function is $n\mathcal{T}\langle \texttt{T::~T()} \rangle + O(M)$. Since $n \leq M$, if we assume that $\mathcal{T}\langle \texttt{T::~T()} \rangle = O(1)$ the running time becomes $O(M)$.

### Inserting Items

The procedure for inserting an item into a scatter table using open addressing is actually quite simple—find an unoccupied array location and then put the item in that location.

---

**PROGRAM 8.19**
`OpenScatterTable` class C, `FindUnoccupied`, and `Insert` member function definitions

```
1   unsigned int OpenScatterTable::C (unsigned int i) const
2       { return i; }
3
4   unsigned int OpenScatterTable::FindUnoccupied (
5       Object const& object) const
6   {
7       unsigned int const hash = H (object);
8       for (unsigned int i = 0; i < count + 1; ++i)
9       {
10          unsigned int const probe = (hash + C (i)) % length;
11          if (array [probe].state != Entry::occupied)
12              return probe;
13      }
14      return length;
15  }
16
17  void OpenScatterTable::Insert (Object& object)
18  {
19      if (count == length)
20          throw domain_error ("scatter table is full");
21      unsigned int const offset = FindUnoccupied (object);
22      array [offset].state = Entry::occupied;
23      array [offset].object = &object;
24      ++count;
25  }
```

To find an unoccupied array element, the array is probed according to a probing sequence. In this case, the probing sequence is linear probing. Program 8.19 defines the routines needed to insert an item into the scatter table.

The function C defines the probing sequence. As it turns out, the implementation required for a linear probing sequence is trivial. The function C is the identity function.

The purpose of the private member function **FindUnoccupied** is to locate an unoccupied array position. The **FindUnoccupied** routine probes the array according to the probing sequence determined by the C function. At most $n + 1$ probes are made, where $n = $ **count** is the number of items in the scatter table. When using linear probing it is always possible to find an unoccupied cell in this many probes as long as the table is not full. Notice also that we do not search for an **empty** cell. Instead, the search terminates when a cell is found, the state of which is not **occupied**, i.e., **empty** or **deleted**. The reason for this subtlety has to do with the way items may be removed from the table. The **FindUnoccupied** routine returns a value between 0 and $M - 1$, where $M = $ **length** is the length of the scatter table, if an unoccupied location is found. Otherwise, it returns $M$ to indicate that an unoccupied cell was not found.

The **Insert** routine takes a reference to an **Object** and puts that object into the scatter table. It does so by calling **FindUnoccupied** to determine the location of an unoccupied entry in which to put the object. The state of the unoccupied entry is set to **occupied** and a pointer to the object is saved in the entry.

The running time of the **Insert** routine is determined by that of **FindUnoccupied**. The worst-case running time of **FindUnoccupied** is $O(n)$, where $n$ is the number of items in the scatter table. Therefore, the running time of **Insert** is $\mathcal{T}\langle \text{T::Hash()} \rangle + O(n)$.

### Finding Items

The **Find** and **FindMatch** member functions of the **OpenScatterTable** class are defined in Program 8.20. The **FindMatch** function takes a **const** reference to an object and searches the scatter table for an object which matches the given one.

**FindMatch** follows the same probing sequence used by the **Insert** function. Therefore, if there is a matching object in the scatter table, **FindMatch** will make exactly the same number of probes to locate the object as were made to put the object into the table in the first place. The **FindMatch** routine makes at most $M$ probes, where $M = $ **length** is the size of the scatter table. However, note that the loop immediately terminates should it encounter an **empty** location. This is because if the target has not been found by the time an empty cell is encountered, then the target is not in the table. Notice also that the comparison is only attempted for entries which are marked **occupied**. Any locations marked **deleted** are not examined during the search but they do not terminate the search either.

The running time of the **Find** routine is determined by that of **FindMatch**. In the worst case **FindMatch** makes $n$ comparisons, where $n$ is the number of items in the table. Therefore, the running time of **Find** is $\mathcal{T}\langle \text{T::Hash()} \rangle + n\mathcal{T}\langle \text{op==(T\&,T\&)} \rangle + O(M)$.

### Removing Items

Removing items from a scatter table using open addressing has to be done with some care. The naïve approach would be to locate the item to be removed and then change the state of its location to **empty**. However, that approach does not work! Remember that

---

**PROGRAM 8.20**
OpenScatterTable class FindMatch and Find member function definitions

```
1    unsigned int OpenScatterTable::FindMatch (
2        Object const& object) const
3    {
4        unsigned int const hash = H (object);
5        for (unsigned int i = 0; i < length; ++i)
6        {
7            unsigned int const probe = (hash + C (i)) % length;
8            if (array [probe].state == Entry::empty)
9                break;
10           if (array [probe].state == Entry::occupied
11               && object == *array [probe].object)
12               return probe;
13       }
14       return length;
15   }
16
17   Object& OpenScatterTable::Find (Object const& object) const
18   {
19       unsigned int const offset = FindMatch (object);
20       if (offset < length)
21           return *array [offset].object;
22       else
23           return NullObject::Instance ();
24   }
```

---

the FindMatch routine which is used to locate an item stops its search when it encounters an empty cell. Therefore, if we change the state of a cell in the middle of a cluster to empty, all subsequent searches in that cluster will stop at the empty cell. As a result, subsequent searches for an object may fail even when the target is still in the table!

One way to deal with this is to make use of the third state, deleted. Instead of marking a location empty, we mark it deleted when an item is deleted. Remember that that the FindMatch routine was written in such a way that it continues past deleted cells in its search. Also, the FindUnoccupied routine was written to stop its search when it encounters either an empty or a deleted location. Consequently, the positions marked deleted are available for reuse when insertion is done.

Program 8.21 gives the implementation of the Withdraw. The Withdraw function takes a reference to an Object and removes it from the scatter table. It does so by first locating the specific object instance using FindInstance and then marking the location deleted. The implementation of FindInstance has been elided. It is simply a trivial variation of the FindMatch routine.

The running time of the Withdraw routine is determined by that of FindInstance. In the worst case FindInstance has to examine every array position. Therefore, the running time of Withdraw is $\mathcal{T}\langle\texttt{T::Hash()}\rangle + O(M)$.

**PROGRAM 8.21**
OpenScatterTable class Withdraw member function definition

```
1  void OpenScatterTable::Withdraw (Object& object)
2  {
3      if (count == 0)
4          throw domain_error ("scatter table is empty");
5      unsigned int const offset = FindInstance (object);
6      if (offset == length)
7          throw invalid_argument ("object not found");
8      array [offset].state = Entry::deleted;
9      array [offset].object = 0;
10     --count;
11 }
```

There is a very serious problem with the technique of marking locations as **deleted**. After a large number of insertions and deletions have been done, it is very likely that there will be no cells left that are marked **empty**. This is because, nowhere in any of the routines (except **Purge**) is a cell ever marked **empty**! This has the very unfortunate consequence that an unsuccessful search, i.e., a search for an object which is not in the scatter table, is $\Omega(M)$. Recall that **FindMatch** examines at most $M$ array locations and only stops its search early when an **empty** location is encountered. Since there are no more empty locations, the search must examine all $M$ locations.

If we are using the scatter table in an application in which we know a priori that no items will be removed, or perhaps only a very small number of items will be removed, then the **Withdraw** routine given in Program 8.20 will suffice. However, if the application is such that a significant number of withdrawals will be made, a better implementation is required.

Ideally, when removing an item the scatter table ends up exactly as it would have appeared had that item never been inserted in the first place. Note that exactly the same constraint is met by the **Withdraw** function for the **ChainedScatterTable** class given in Program 8.16. It turns out that a variation of that algorithm can be used to implement the **Withdraw** function for the **OpenScatterTable** class as shown in Program 8.22.

The algorithm begins by checking that the scatter table is not empty. Then it calls **FindInstance** to determine the position i of the item to be removed. If the item to be removed is not in the scatter table **FindInstance** returns **length** and an exception is thrown. Otherwise, **FindInstance** falls between 0 and **length** − 1, which indicates that the item was found.

In the general case, the item to be deleted falls in the middle of a cluster. Deleting it would create a hole in the middle of the cluster. What we need to do is to find another item further down in the cluster which can be moved up to fill in the hole that would be created when the item at position i is deleted. The purpose of the loop on lines 11–19 is to find the position j of an item which can be moved safely into position i. Note the implementation here implicitly assumes that a linear probing sequence is used—the C function is not called explicitly. An item at position j can be moved safely to position i

**PROGRAM 8.22**
OpenScatterTable class alternate Withdraw member function definition

```
1   void OpenScatterTable::Withdraw (Object& object)
2   {
3       if (count == 0)
4           throw domain_error ("scatter table is empty");
5       unsigned int i = FindInstance (object);
6       if (i == length)
7           throw invalid_argument ("object not found");
8       for (;;)
9       {
10          unsigned int j;
11          for (j = (i + 1) % length;
12              array [j].state == Entry::occupied;
13              j = (j + 1) % length)
14          {
15              unsigned int const h = H (*array [j].object);
16              if ((h <= i && i < j) || (i < j && j < h) ||
17                  (j < h && h <= i))
18                  break;
19          }
20          if (array [j].state == Entry::empty)
21              break;
22          array [i] = array [j];
23          i = j;
24      }
25      array [i].state = Entry::empty;
26      array [i].object = 0;
27      --count;
28  }
```

only if the hash value of the item at position j is not cyclically contained in the interval between i and j.

If an item is found at some position j that can be moved safely, then that item is moved to position i on line 22. The effect of moving the item at position j to position i is to move the hole from position i to position j (line 23). Therefore, another iteration of the main loop (lines 8–24) is needed to fill in the relocated hole in the cluster.

If no item can be found to fill in the hole, then it is safe to split the cluster in two. Eventually, either because no item can be found to fill in the hole or because the hole has moved to the end of the cluster, there is nothing more to do other than to delete the hole. Thus, on lines 25–26 the entry at position i is set to **empty** and the associated **object** pointer is set to zero. Notice that the third state **deleted** is not required in this implementation of **Withdraw**.

If we use the **Withdraw** implementation of Program 8.22, the scatter table entries will only ever be in one of two states—**occupied** or **empty**. Consequently, we can improve the bound on the worst case for the search from $\mathcal{T}\langle \texttt{T::Hash()}\rangle +$ $n\mathcal{T}\langle \texttt{op==(T\&,T\&)}\rangle + O(M)$ to $\mathcal{T}\langle \texttt{T::Hash()}\rangle + n\mathcal{T}\langle \texttt{op==(T\&,T\&)}\rangle + O(n)$, where $n$ is the number of items in the scatter table.

Determining the running time of Program 8.22 is a little tricky. Assuming the item to be deleted is actually in the table, the running time to find the position of that item (lines 3–7) is $\mathcal{T}\langle \texttt{T::Hash()}\rangle + O(n)$, where $n = \texttt{count}$ is the number of items actually in the scatter table. In the worst case, the scatter table is comprised of a single cluster of $n$ items, and we are deleting the first item of the cluster. In this case, the main loop on lines 8–24 makes one pass through the entire cluster, in the worst case moving the hole to the end of the cluster one position at a time. Thus, the running time of the main loop is $(n - 1)\mathcal{T}\langle \texttt{T::Hash()}\rangle + O(n)$. The remaining lines require a constant amount of additional time. Altogether, the running time for the **Withdraw** function is $n\mathcal{T}\langle \texttt{T::Hash()}\rangle + O(n)$ in the worst case.

### 8.6.5 Average Case Analysis

The average case analysis of open addressing is easy if we ignore the primary clustering phenomenon. Given a scatter table of size $M$ that contains $n$ items, we assume that each of the $\binom{M}{n}$ combinations of $n$ occupied and $(m - n)$ empty scatter table entries is equally likely. This is the *uniform hashing model*.

In this model we assume that the entries will either be occupied or empty, i.e., the **deleted** state is not used. Suppose a search for an empty cell requires exactly $i$ probes. Then the first $i - 1$ positions probed must have been occupied and the $i$th position probed was empty. Consider the $i$ cells which were probed. The number of combinations in which $i - 1$ of the probed cells are occupied and one is empty are $\binom{M-i}{n-i+1}$. Therefore, the probability that exactly $i$ probes are required is

$$P_i = \frac{\binom{M-i}{n-i+1}}{\binom{M}{n}}. \tag{8.7}$$

The average number of probes required to find an empty cell in a table which has $n$ occupied cells is $U(n)$ where

$$U(n) = \sum_{i=1}^{M} iP_i. \tag{8.8}$$

Using Equation 8.7 into Equation 8.8 and simplifying the result gives

$$U(n) = \frac{M+1}{M-n+1} \tag{8.9}$$

$$= \frac{1 + \frac{1}{M}}{1 - \lambda + \frac{1}{M}}, \qquad \text{where } \lambda = n/M$$

$$\approx \frac{1}{1-\lambda} \tag{8.10}$$

This result is actually quite intuitive. The load factor, $\lambda$, is the fraction of occupied entries. Therefore, $1 - \lambda$ entries are empty so we would expect to have to probe $1/(1 - \lambda)$ entries before finding an empty one! For example, if the load factor is 0.75, a quarter of the entries are empty. Therefore, we expect to have to probe four entries before finding an empty one.

To calculate the average number of probes for a successful search we make the observation that when an item is initially inserted we need to find an empty cell in which to place it. For example, the number of probes to find the empty position into which the $i$th item is to be placed is $U(i)$. And this is exactly the number of probes it takes to find the $i$th item again! Therefore, the average number of probes required for a successful search in a table which has $n$ occupied cells is $S(n)$ where

$$S(n) = \frac{1}{n} \sum_{i=0}^{n-1} U(i). \tag{8.11}$$

Substituting Equation 8.9 in Equation 8.11 and simplifying gives

$$\begin{aligned}
S(n) &= \frac{1}{n} \sum_{i=0}^{n} \frac{M+1}{M-i+1} \\
&= \frac{M+1}{N} (H_{M+1} - H_{M-n+1}) \\
&\approx \frac{1}{\lambda} \ln \frac{1}{1-\lambda} \tag{8.12}
\end{aligned}$$

where $H_k$ is the $k$th *harmonic number* (see Section 2.1.8). Again, there is an easy intuitive derivation for this result. We can use a simple integral to calculate the mean number of probes for a successful search using the approximation $U(n) = 1/(1 - \lambda)$ as follows

$$\begin{aligned}
S(n) &= \frac{1}{n} \sum_{i=0}^{n} U(i) \\
&\approx \frac{1}{\lambda} \int_{0}^{\lambda} \frac{1}{1-x} dx \\
&\approx \frac{1}{\lambda} \ln \frac{1}{1-\lambda}.
\end{aligned}$$

Empirical evidence has shown that the formulas derived for the *uniform hashing model* characterize quite well the performance of scatter tables using open addressing with quadratic probing and double hashing. However, they do not capture the effect of primary clustering which occurs when linear probing is used. Knuth has shown that when primary clustering is taken into account, the number of probes required to locate an empty cell is

$$U(n) = \frac{1}{2} \left( 1 + \left( \frac{1}{1-\lambda} \right)^2 \right), \tag{8.13}$$

**FIGURE 8.7**
Number of probes versus load factor for uniform hashing and linear probing.

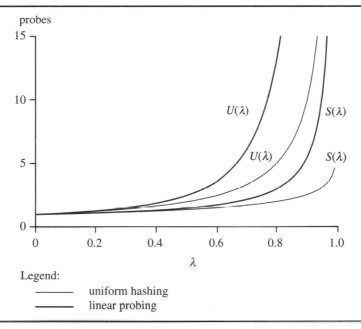

Legend:

——— uniform hashing
——— linear probing

and the number of probes required for a successful search is

$$S(n) = \frac{1}{2}\left(1 + \frac{1}{1-\lambda}\right). \tag{8.14}$$

The graph in Figure 8.7 compares the predictions of the uniform hashing model (Equation 8.10 and 8.12) with the formulas derived by Knuth (Equation 8.13 and 8.14). Clearly, while the results are qualitatively similar, the formulas are in agreement for small load factors and they diverge as the load factor increases.

## 8.7 Applications

Hash and scatter tables have many applications. The principal characteristic of such applications is that keyed information needs to be frequently accessed and the access pattern is either unknown or known to be random. For example, hash tables are often used to implement the *symbol table* of a programming language compiler. A symbol table is used to keep track of information associated with the symbols (variable and procedure names) used by a programmer. In this case, the keys are character strings and each key has associated with it some information about the symbol (e.g., type, address, value, lifetime, scope).

**PROGRAM 8.23**
Hash or scatter table application—counting words

```
1   class Counter : public Int
2   {
3   public:
4       Counter (int i) : Int (i)
5           {}
6       void operator ++ ()
7           { ++datum; }
8   };
9
10  void CountWords (HashTable& table)
11  {
12      std: string word;
13      while (cin >> word, !cin.eof ())
14      {
15          Object& obj =
16              table.Find (Association (*new String (word)));
17          if (obj.IsNull ())
18              table.Insert (*new Association (
19                  *new String (word), *new Counter (1)));
20          else
21          {
22              Association& assoc =
23                  dynamic_cast<Association&> (obj);
24              Counter& i =
25                  dynamic_cast<Counter&> (assoc.Value ());
26              ++i;
27          }
28      }
29      cout << table << endl;
30  }
```

This section presents a simple application of hash and scatter tables. Suppose we are required to count the number of occurrences of each distinct word contained in a text file. We can do this easily using a hash or scatter table. Program 8.23 gives the implementation.

The class **Counter** is derived from the class **Int** defined in Section 5.2.4. In addition to all the functionality inherited from the base class, the **Counter** class adds the member function **operator++** which increments the value by one.

The **CountWords** function does the actual work of counting the words in the input file. It takes as its lone argument a reference to a **HashTable**. Consequently, it can use any of the hash or scatter table implementations discussed in this chapter. The objects which are put into the hash table by **CountWords** are all instances of the class

**Association**. Each association has as its key a **String** class instance, and as its value a **Counter** class instance.

The **CountWords** function reads words from the standard input file, **cin**, one at a time. As each word is read, a **Find** operation is done on the hash table to determine if there is already an association for the given key. If none is found, a new association is created and inserted into the hash table. The given word is used as the key of the new association, and the value is a counter which is initialized to one. On the other hand, if there is already an association for the given word in the hash table, the corresponding counter is incremented. When it encounters the end of the input file, the **CountWords** function simply prints the hash table on the standard output file, **cout**.

The running time of the **CountWords** function depends on a number of factors, including the number of different keys, the frequency of occurrence of each key, and the distribution of the keys in the overall space of keys. Of course, the hash/scatter table implementation chosen has an effect as does the size of the table used. For a reasonable set of keys we expect the hash function to do a good job of spreading the keys uniformly in the table. Provided a sufficiently large table is used, the average search and insertion time is bounded by a constant. Under these ideal conditions the running time should be $O(n)$, where $n$ is the number of words in the input file.

## Exercises

**8.1** Suppose we know a priori that a given key is equally likely to be any integer between $a$ and $b$.

**a.** When is the *division method of hashing* a good choice?

**b.** When is the *middle square method of hashing* a good choice?

**8.2** Compute (by hand) the hash value obtained by Program 8.3 for the strings **"ece.uw.ca"** and **"cs.uw.ca"**. **Hint:** Refer to Appendix C.

**8.3** Canadian postal codes have the format **LDL␣DLD** where **L** is always a letter (**A–Z**), **D** is always a digit (**0–9**), and ␣ is always a single space; for example, the postal code for the University of Waterloo is **N2L␣3G1**. Devise a suitable hash function for Canadian postal codes.

**8.4** For each type of hash table listed below, show the hash table obtained when we insert the keys

```
{"un","deux","trois","quatre","cinq","six",
"sept","huit","neuf","dix","onze","douze"}.
```

in the order given into a table of size $M = 16$ that is initially empty. Use the following table of hash values:

| $x$ | Hash($x$) (octal) |
|---|---|
| "un" | 016456 |
| "deux" | 0145446470 |
| "trois" | 016563565063 |
| "quatre" | 010440656345 |
| "cinq" | 0142505761 |
| "six" | 01625070 |
| "sept" | 0162446164 |
| "huit" | 0151645064 |
| "neuf" | 0157446446 |
| "dix" | 01455070 |
| "onze" | 0156577345 |
| "douze" | 014556647345 |

a.  chained hash table,

b.  chained scatter table,

c.  open scatter table using *linear probing,*

d.  open scatter table using *quadratic probing,* and

e.  open scatter table using *double hashing.* (Use Equation 8.6 as the secondary hash function.)

**8.5**   For each table obtained in Exercise 8.4, show the result when the key **"deux"** is withdrawn.

**8.6**   For each table considered in Exercise 8.4 derive an expression for the total memory space used to represent a table of size $M$ that contains $n$ items.

**8.7**   Consider a chained hash table of size $M$ that contains $n$ items. The performance of the table decreases as the load factor $\lambda = n/M$ increases. In order to keep the load factor below 1, we propose to double the size of the array when $n = M$. However, in order to do so we must *rehash* all of the elements in the table. Explain why rehashing is necessary.

**8.8**   Give the sequence of $M$ keys that fills a *chained scatter table* of size $M$ in the *shortest* possible time. Find a tight, asymptotic bound on the minimum running time taken to fill the table.

**8.9**   Give the sequence of $M$ keys that fills a *chained scatter table* of size $M$ in the longest possible time. Find a tight, asymptotic bound on the minimum running time taken to fill the table.

**8.10**  Consider the chained hash table implementation shown in Program 8.9, 8.10, 8.11, and 8.12.

a.  Rewrite the **Insert** routine so that it doubles the length of the array when $\lambda = 1$.

b.  Rewrite the **Withdraw** routine so that it halves the length of the array when $\lambda = \frac{1}{2}$.

c.  Show that the *average* time for both insert and withdraw operations is still $O(1)$.

**8.11** Consider two sets of integers, $S = \{s_1, s_2, \ldots, s_m\}$ and $T = \{t_1, t_2, \ldots, t_n\}$.

    **a.** Devise an algorithm that uses a hash table to test whether $S$ is a subset of $T$. What is the average running time of your algorithm?

    **b.** Two sets are *equivalent* if and only if both $S \subseteq T$ and $T \subseteq S$. Show that we can test if two sets of integers are equivalent in $O(m + n)$ time (on average).

**8.12** (This question should be attempted *after* reading Chapter 10). Rather than use an array of linked lists, suppose we implement a hash table with an array of *binary search trees*.

    **a.** What are the worst-case running times for **Insert**, **Find**, and **Withdraw**.

    **b.** What are the average running times for **Insert**, **Find**, and **Withdraw**.

**8.13** (This question should be attempted *after* reading Section 14.5.1.) Consider a scatter table with open addressing. Devise a probe sequence of the form

$$h_i(x) = (h(x) + c(i)) \bmod M,$$

where $c(i)$ is a *full-period pseudo random number generator*. Why is such a sequence likely to be better than either linear probing or quadratic probing?

# Programming Projects

**8.1** Complete the implementation of the **ChainedHashTable** class declared in Program 8.9 by providing suitable definitions for the following member functions: **IsMember**, **CompareTo**, **Accept**, and **NewIterator**. Write a test program and test your implementation.

**8.2** Complete the implementation of the **ChainedScatterTable** class declared in Program 8.13 by providing suitable definitions for the following member functions: **IsFull**, **IsMember**, **CompareTo**, **Accept**, and **NewIterator**. Write a test program and test your implementation.

**8.3** Complete the implementation of the **ChainedScatterTable** class declared in Program 8.17 by providing suitable definitions for the following member functions: **IsFull**, **IsMember**, **FindInstance**, **CompareTo**, **Accept**, and **NewIterator**. Write a test program and test your implementation.

**8.4** The **Withdraw** routine defined in Program 8.10 has been written under the assumption that linear probing is used. Therefore, it does not call explicitly the collision resolution function **C**. Rewrite the **Withdraw** routine so that it works correctly regardless of the collision resolution strategy used.

**8.5** Consider an application that has the following profile: First, $n$ symbols (character strings) are read. As each symbol is read, it is assigned an ordinal number from 1 to $n$. Then, a large number of operations are performed. In each operation we are given either a symbol or a number and we need to determine its mate. Design, implement, and test a data structure that provides both mappings in $O(1)$ time.

**8.6** Spelling checkers are often implemented using hashing. However, the space required to store all the words in a complete dictionary is usually prohibitive. An alternative solution is to use a very large array of bits. The array is initialized as follows: First, all the bits are set to zero. Then for each word $w$ in the dictionary, we set bit $h(w)$ to one, where $h(\cdot)$ is a suitable hash function.

To check the spelling in a given document, we hash the words in the document one-by-one and examine the corresponding bit of the array. If the bit is a zero, the word does not appear in the dictionary and we conclude that it is misspelled. Note if the bit is a 1, the word may still be misspelled, but we cannot tell.

Design and implement a spelling checker. **Hint:** Use the `SetAsBitVector` class given in Chapter 12.

# 9 | Trees

In this chapter we consider one of the most important non-linear information structures—*trees*. A tree is often used to represent a *hierarchy*. This is because the relationships between the items in the hierarchy suggest the branches of a botanical tree.

For example, a tree-like *organization chart* is often used to represent the lines of responsibility in a business as shown in Figure 9.1. The president of the company is shown at the top of the tree, and the vice-presidents are indicated below her. Under the vice-presidents we find the managers and below the managers the rest of the clerks. Each clerk reports to a manager, each manager reports to a vice-president, and each vice-president reports to the president.

It just takes a little imagination to see the tree in Figure 9.1. Of course, the tree is upside-down. However, this is the usual way the data structure is drawn. The president is called the *root* of the tree, and the clerks are the *leaves*.

A tree is extremely useful for certain kinds of computations. For example, suppose we wish to determine the total salaries paid to employees by division or by department. The total of the salaries in division A can be found by computing the sum of the salaries paid in departments A1 and A2 plus the salary of the vice-president of division A. Similarly, the total of the salaries paid in department A1 is the sum of the salaries of the manager of department A1 and of the two clerks below her.

Clearly, in order to compute all the totals, it is necessary to consider the salary of every employee. Therefore, an implementation of this computation must *visit* all the employees in the tree. An algorithm that systematically *visits* all the items in a tree is called a *tree traversal*.

**FIGURE 9.1**
Representing a hierarchy using a tree.

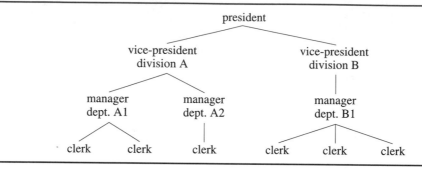

In this chapter we consider several different kinds of trees as well as several different tree traversal algorithms. In addition, we show how trees can be used to represent arithmetic expressions and how we can evaluate an arithmetic expression by doing a tree traversal.

## 9.1   Basics

The following is a mathematical definition of a tree:

**Definition 9.1 (Tree)**
*A tree T is a finite, non-empty set of nodes,*

$$T = \{r\} \cup T_1 \cup T_2 \cup \cdots \cup T_n,$$

*with the following properties:*

1. *A designated node of the set, r, is called the root of the tree.*
2. *The remaining nodes are partitioned into $n \geq 0$ subsets, $T_1, T_2, \ldots, T_n$, each of which is a tree.*

*For convenience, we shall use the notation $T = \{r, T_1, T_2, \ldots, T_n\}$ to denote the tree T.*

Notice that Definition 9.1 is *recursive*—a tree is defined in terms of itself! Fortunately, we do not have a problem with infinite recursion because every tree has a *finite* number of of nodes and because in the base case a tree has $n = 0$ subtrees.

It follows from Definition 9.1 that the minimal tree is a tree comprised of a single root node. For example, $T_a = \{A\}$ is such a tree. When there is more than one node, the remaining nodes are partitioned into subtrees. For example, $T_b = \{B, \{C\}\}$ is a tree which is comprised of the root node $B$ and the subtree $\{C\}$. Finally, the following is

**FIGURE 9.2**
Examples of trees.

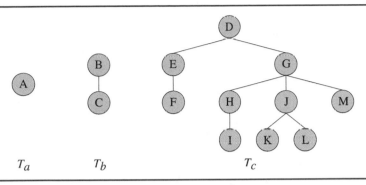

$T_a$       $T_b$       $T_c$

also a tree

$$T_c = \{D, \{E, \{F\}\}, \{G, \{H, \{I\}\}, \{J, \{K\}, \{L\}\}, \{M\}\}\}. \tag{9.1}$$

How do $T_a$, $T_b$, and $T_c$ resemble their arboreal namesake? The similarity becomes apparent when we consider the graphical representation of these trees shown in Figure 9.2. To draw such a pictorial representation of a tree, $T = \{r, T_1, T_2, \ldots, T_n\}$, the following recursive procedure is used: First, we draw the root node $r$. Then, we draw each of the subtrees, $T_1, T_2, \ldots, T_n$, beside each other below the root. Finally, lines are drawn from $r$ to the roots of each of the subtrees.

Of course, trees drawn in this fashion are upside-down. Nevertheless, this is the conventional way in which tree data structures are drawn. In fact, it is understood that when we speak of "up" and "down," we do so with respect to this pictorial representation. For example, when we move from a root to a subtree, we will say that we are moving *down* the tree.

The inverted pictorial representation of trees is probably due to the way that genealogical *lineal charts* are drawn. A *lineal chart* is a family tree that shows the descendants of some person. And it is from genealogy that much of the terminology associated with tree data structures is taken.

**Terminology**
Consider a tree $T = \{r, T_1, T_2, \ldots, T_n\}$, $n \geq 0$, as given by Definition 9.1.

- The *degree* of a node is the number of subtrees associated with that node. For example, the degree of tree $T$ is $n$.

- A node of degree zero has no subtrees. Such a node is called a *leaf.*

- Each root $r_i$ of subtree $T_i$ of tree $T$ is called a *child* of $r$. The term *grandchild* is defined in a similar manner.

- The root node $r$ of tree $T$ is the *parent* of all the roots $r_i$ of the subtrees $T_i$, $1 < i \leq n$. The term *grandparent* is defined in a similar manner.

- Two roots $r_i$ and $r_j$ of distinct subtrees $T_i$ and $T_j$ of tree $T$ are called *siblings.*

Clearly the terminology used for describing tree data structures is a curious mixture of the mathematical, the genealogical, and the botanical. There is still more terminology to be introduced, but in order to do that, we need the following definition:

### Definition 9.2 (Path and Path Length)
*Given a tree T containing the set of nodes R, a path in T is defined as a non-empty sequence of nodes*

$$P = \{r_1, r_2, \ldots, r_k\},$$

*where $r_i \in R$, for $1 \leq i \leq k$ such that the ith node in the sequence, $r_i$, is the parent of the $(i + 1)$th node in the sequence $r_{i+1}$. The length of path P is $k - 1$.*

For example, consider again the tree $T_c$ shown in Figure 9.2. This tree contains many different paths. In fact, if you count carefully, you should find that there are exactly 29 distinct paths in tree $T_c$. This includes the path of length zero, $\{D\}$; the path of length one, $\{E, F\}$; and the path of length three, $\{D, G, J, K\}$.

### More Terminology
Consider a tree $T$ containing the set of nodes $R$ as given by Definition 9.1.

- The *level* or *depth* of a node $r_i \in R$ in a tree $T$ is the length of the unique path in $T$ from its root $r$ to the node $r_i$. For example, the root of $T$ is at level zero and the roots of the subtrees of $T$ are at level one.

- The *height of a node* $r_i \in R$ in a tree $T$ is the length of the longest path from node $r_i$ to a leaf. Therefore, the leaves are all at height zero.

- The *height of a tree T* is the height of its root node $r$.

- Consider two nodes $r_i$ and $r_j$ in a tree $T$. The node $r_i$ is an *ancestor* of the node $r_j$ if there exists a path in $T$ from $r_i$ to $r_j$. Notice that $r_i$ and $r_j$ may be the same node. That is, a node is its own ancestor. However, the node $r_i$ is a *proper ancestor* if there exists a path $p$ in $T$ from $r_i$ to $r_j$ such that the length of the path $p$ is nonzero.

- Similarly, node $r_j$ is a *descendant* of the node $r_i$ if there exists a path in $T$ from $r_i$ to $r_j$. And since $r_i$ and $r_j$ may be the same node, a node is its own descendant. The node $r_j$ is a *proper descendant* if there exists a path $p$ in $T$ from $r_i$ to $r_j$ such that the length of the path $p$ is non-zero.

### Alternate Representations for Trees
Figure 9.3 shows an alternate representation of the tree $T_c$ defined in Equation 9.1. In this case, the tree is represented as a set of nested regions in the plane. In fact, what we have is a *Venn diagram* which corresponds to the view that a tree is a set of sets.

This hierarchical, set-within-a-set view of trees is also evoked by considering the nested structure of computer programs. For example, consider the following fragment of C++ code:

**FIGURE 9.3**
An alternate graphical representation for trees.

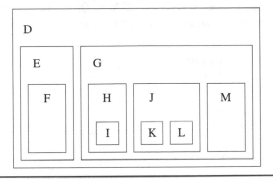

```
D: {
    E: {
        F: statement();
    }
    G: {
        H: {
            I: statement();
        }
        J: {
            K: statement();
            L: statement();
        }
        M: statement();
    }
}
```

The nesting structure of this program and the tree given in Equation 9.1 are *isomorphic*.[1] Therefore, it is not surprising that trees have an important rôle in the analysis and translation of computer programs.

## 9.2  *N*-ary Trees

In the preceding section we considered trees in which the nodes can have arbitrary degrees. In particular, the general case allows each of the nodes of a tree to have a different degree. In this section we consider a variation in which all of the nodes of the tree are required to have exactly the same degree.

---

[1]Isomorphic is a fancy word that means being of identical or similar form or shape or structure.

Unfortunately, simply adding to Definition 9.1 the requirement that all of the nodes of the tree have the same degree does not work. It is not possible to construct a tree which has a finite number of nodes all of which have the same degree $N$ in any case except the trivial case of $N = 0$. In order to make it work, we need to introduce the notion of an empty tree as follows.

### Definition 9.3 (*N*-ary Tree)
*An N-ary tree T is a finite set of nodes with one of the following properties:*

1. *Either the set is empty, $T = \varnothing$, or*
2. *The set consists of a root, R, and exactly N distinct N-ary trees. That is, the remaining nodes are partitioned into $N \geq 0$ subsets, $T_0, T_1, \ldots, T_{N-1}$, each of which is an N-ary tree such that $T = \{R, T_0, T_1, \ldots, T_{N-1}\}$.*

According to Definition 9.3, an $N$-ary tree is either the empty tree, $\varnothing$, or it is a non-empty set of nodes which consists of a root and exactly $N$ subtrees. Clearly, the empty set contains neither a root, nor any subtrees. Therefore, the degree of each node of an $N$-ary tree is either zero or $N$.

There is subtle, yet extremely important consequence of Definition 9.3 that often goes unrecognized. The empty tree, $T = \varnothing$, is a tree. That is, it is an object of the same type as a non-empty tree. Therefore, from the perspective of object-oriented program design, an empty tree must be an instance of some object class. It is inappropriate to use a null pointer to represent an empty tree, since a null pointer points to nothing at all!

The empty trees are called *external nodes* because they have no subtrees and therefore appear at the extremities of the tree. Conversely, the non-empty trees are called *internal nodes*.

Figure 9.4 shows the following *tertiary* ($N = 3$) trees:

$$T_a = \{A, \varnothing, \varnothing, \varnothing\},$$
$$T_b = \{B, \{C, \varnothing, \varnothing, \varnothing\}, \varnothing, \varnothing\},$$
$$T_c = \{D, \{E, \{F, \varnothing, \varnothing, \varnothing\}, \varnothing, \varnothing\},$$
$$\{G, \{H, \{I, \varnothing, \varnothing, \varnothing\}, \varnothing, \varnothing\}, \{J, \{K, \varnothing, \varnothing, \varnothing\}, \{L, \varnothing, \varnothing, \varnothing\}, \varnothing\},$$
$$\{M, \varnothing, \varnothing, \varnothing\}\}, \varnothing\}.$$

In the figure, square boxes denote the empty trees and circles denote non-empty nodes. Except for the empty trees, the tertiary trees shown in the figure contain the same sets of nodes as the corresponding trees shown in Figure 9.2.

Definition 9.1 and 9.3 both define trees in terms of sets. In mathematics, elements of a set are normally unordered. Therefore, we might conclude that the relative ordering of the subtrees is not important. However, most practical implementations of trees define an implicit ordering of the subtrees. Consequently, it is usual to assume that the subtrees are ordered. As a result, the two tertiary trees, $T_1 = \{x, \{y, \varnothing, \varnothing, \varnothing\}, \varnothing, \varnothing\}$ and $T_2 =$

**FIGURE 9.4**
Example of *N*-ary trees.

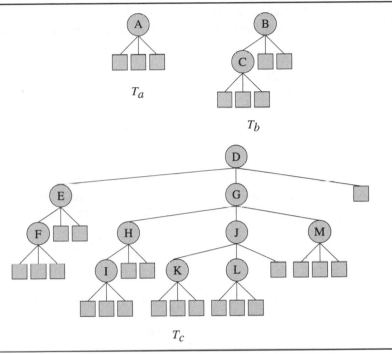

$T_a$

$T_b$

$T_c$

$\{x, \emptyset, \{y, \emptyset, \emptyset, \emptyset\}, \emptyset\}$, are considered to be distinct unequal trees. Trees in which the subtrees are ordered are called *ordered trees*. On the other hand, trees in which the order does not matter are called *oriented trees*. In this book, we shall assume that all trees are ordered unless otherwise specified.

Figure 9.4 suggests that every *N*-ary tree contains a significant number of external nodes. The following theorem tells us precisely how many external nodes we can expect.

**Theorem 9.1**
*An N-ary tree with $n \geq 0$ internal nodes contains $(N - 1)n + 1$ external nodes.*

**Proof** Let the number of external nodes be $l$. Since every node except the root (empty or not) has a parent, there must be $(n + l - 1)/N$ parents in the tree because every parent has $N$ children. Therefore, $n = (n + l - 1)/N$. Rearranging this gives $l = (N - 1)n + 1$.

Since the external nodes have no subtrees, it is tempting to consider them to be the leaves of the tree. However, in the context of *N*-ary trees, it is customary to define a *leaf node* as an internal node which has only external subtrees. According to this definition, the trees shown in Figure 9.4 have exactly the same sets of leaves as the corresponding general trees shown in Figure 9.2.

Furthermore, since height is defined with respect to the leaves, by having the leaves the same for both kinds of trees, the heights are also the same. The following theorem tells us something about the maximum size of a tree of a given height $h$.

**Theorem 9.2**

*Consider an N-ary tree T of height $h \geq 0$. The maximum number of internal nodes in T is given by*

$$\frac{N^{h+1} - 1}{N - 1}.$$

**Proof**   (By induction).

**Base Case**   Consider an $N$-ary tree of height zero. It consists of exactly one internal node and $N$ empty subtrees. Clearly the theorem holds for $h = 0$ since

$$\left.\frac{N^{h+1} - 1}{N - 1}\right|_{h=0} = 1.$$

**Inductive Hypothesis**   Suppose the theorem holds for $h = 0, 1, 2, \ldots, k$, for some $k \geq 0$. Consider a tree of height $k + 1$. Such a tree consists of a root and $N$ subtrees each of which contains at most $(N^{k+1} - 1)/(N - 1)$ nodes. Therefore, altogether the number of nodes is at most

$$N\left(\frac{N^{k+1} - 1}{N - 1}\right) + 1 = \frac{N^{k+2} - 1}{N - 1}. \tag{9.2}$$

That is, the theorem holds for $k + 1$. Therefore, by induction on $k$, the theorem is true for all values of $h$.

An interesting consequence of Theorem 9.1 and 9.2 is that the maximum number of external nodes in an $N$-ary tree of height $h$ is given by

$$(N - 1)\left(\frac{N^{h+1} - 1}{N - 1}\right) + 1 = N^h.$$

The final theorem of this section addresses the maximum number of *leaves* in an $N$-ary tree of height $h$.

**Theorem 9.3**

*Consider an N-ary tree T of height $h \geq 0$. The maximum number of leaf nodes in T is $N^h$.*

**Proof** (By induction).

**Base Case**    Consider an $N$-ary tree of height zero. It consists of exactly one internal node which has $N$ empty subtrees. Therefore, the one node is a leaf. Clearly the theorem holds for $h = 0$ since $N^0 = 1$.

**Inductive Hypothesis**    Suppose the theorem holds for $h = 0, 1, 2, \ldots, k$, for some $k \geq 0$. Consider a tree of height $k+1$. Such a tree consists of a root and $N$ subtrees each of which contains at most $N^k$ leaf nodes. Therefore, altogether the number of leaves is at most $N \times N^k = N^{k+1}$. That is, the theorem holds for $k + 1$. Therefore, by induction on $k$, the theorem is true for all values of $h$.

---

## 9.3  Binary Trees

In this section we consider an extremely important and useful category of tree structure—*binary trees*. A binary tree is an $N$-ary tree for which $N$ is 2. Since a binary tree is an $N$-ary tree, all of the results derived in the preceding section apply to binary trees. However, binary trees have some interesting characteristics that arise from the restriction that $N$ is 2. For example, there is an interesting relationship between binary trees and the binary number system. Binary trees are also very useful for the representation of mathematical expressions involving the binary operations, such as addition and multiplication

Binary trees are defined as follows:

**Definition 9.4 (Binary Tree)**
*A binary tree T is a finite set of nodes one of with the following properties:*

1. *Either the set is empty, $T = \varnothing$ or*
2. *The set consists of a root, r, and exactly two distinct binary trees $T_L$ and $T_R$,*
   $T = \{r, T_L, T_R\}$.

*The tree $T_L$ is called the left subtree of T, and the tree $T_R$ is called the right subtree of T.*

Binary trees are almost always considered to be *ordered trees*. Therefore, the two subtrees $T_L$ and $T_R$ are called the *left* and *right* subtrees, respectively. Consider the two binary trees shown in Figure 9.5. Both trees have a root with a single non-empty subtree. However, in one case it is the left subtree which is non-empty; in the other case it is the right subtree that is non-empty. Since the order of the subtrees matters, the two binary trees shown in Figure 9.5 are different.

We can determine some of the characteristics of binary trees from the theorems given in the preceding section by letting $N = 2$. For example, Theorem 9.1 tells us that a

**FIGURE 9.5**
Two distinct binary trees.

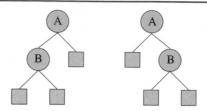

binary tree with $n \geq 0$ internal nodes contains $n + 1$ external nodes. This result is true regardless of the shape of the tree. Consequently, we expect that the storage overhead associated with the empty trees will be $O(n)$.

From Theorem 9.2 we learn that a binary tree of height $h \geq 0$ has at most $2^{h+1} - 1$ internal nodes. Conversely, the height of a binary tree with $n$ internal nodes is at least $\lceil \log_2 n + 1 \rceil - 1$. That is, the height of a binary tree with $n$ nodes is $\Omega(\log n)$.

Finally, according to Theorem 9.3, a binary tree of height $h \geq 0$ has at most $2^h$ leaves. Conversely, the height of a binary tree with $l$ leaves is at least $\lceil \log_2 l \rceil$. Thus, the height of a binary tree with $l$ leaves is $\Omega(\log l)$.

## 9.4 Tree Traversals

There are many different applications of trees. As a result, there are many different algorithms for manipulating them. However, many of the different tree algorithms have in common the characteristic that they systematically visit all the nodes in the tree. That is, the algorithm walks through the tree data structure and performs some computation at each node in the tree. This process of walking through the tree is called a *tree traversal*.

There are essentially two different methods in which to visit systematically all the nodes of a tree—*depth-first traversal* and *breadth-first traversal*. Certain depth-first traversal methods occur frequently enough that they are given names of their own: *preorder traversal, inorder traversal,* and *postorder traversal.*

The discussion that follows uses the tree in Figure 9.6 as an example. The tree shown in the figure is a general tree in the sense of Definition 9.1:

$$T = \{A, \{B, \{C\}\}, \{D, \{E, \{F\}, \{G\}\}, \{H, \{I\}\}\}\} \tag{9.3}$$

However, we can also consider the tree in Figure 9.6 to be an *N*-ary tree (specifically, a binary tree if we assume the existence of empty trees at the appropriate positions:

$$T = \{A, \{B, \varnothing, \{C, \varnothing, \varnothing\}\}, \{D, \{E, \{F, \varnothing, \varnothing\}, \{G, \varnothing, \varnothing\}\}, \{H, \{I, \varnothing, \varnothing\}, \varnothing\}\}\}$$

**FIGURE 9.6**
Sample tree.

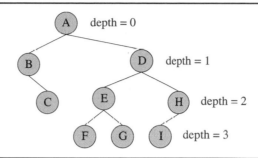

## Preorder Traversal

The first depth-first traversal method we consider is called *preorder traversal*. Preorder traversal is defined recursively as follows. To do a preorder traversal of a general tree:

1. Visit the root first; and then
2. Do a preorder traversal of each of the subtrees of the root one-by-one in the order given.

Preorder traversal gets its name from the fact that it visits the root first. In the case of a binary tree, the algorithm becomes:

1. Visit the root first; and then
2. traverse the left subtree; and then
3. traverse the right subtree.

For example, a preorder traversal of the tree shown in Figure 9.6 visits the nodes in the following order:

$$A, B, C, D, E, F, G, H, I.$$

Notice that the preorder traversal visits the nodes of the tree in precisely the same order in which they are written in Equation 9.3. A preorder traversal is often done when it is necessary to print a textual representation of a tree.

## Postorder Traversal

The second depth-first traversal method we consider is *postorder traversal*. In contrast with preorder traversal, which visits the root first, postorder traversal visits the root last. To do a postorder traversal of a general tree:

1. Do a postorder traversal of each of the subtrees of the root one-by-one in the order given; and then
2. visit the root.

To do a postorder traversal of a binary tree:

1. Traverse the left subtree, and then
2. traverse the right subtree, and then
3. visit the root.

A postorder traversal of the tree shown in Figure 9.6 visits the nodes in the following order:

$$C, B, F, G, E, I, H, D, A.$$

## Inorder Traversal

The third depth-first traversal method is *inorder traversal*. Inorder traversal only makes sense for binary trees. Whereas preorder traversal visits the root first and postorder traversal visits the root last, inorder traversal visits the root *in between* visiting the left and right subtrees:

1. Traverse the left subtree, and then
2. visit the root, and then
3. traverse the right subtree.

An inorder traversal of the tree shown in Figure 9.6 visits the nodes in the following order:

$$B, C, A, F, E, G, D, I, H.$$

## Breadth-First Traversal

Whereas the depth-first traversals are defined recursively, *breadth-first traversal* is best understood as a nonrecursive traversal. The breadth-first traversal of a tree visits the nodes in the order of their depth in the tree. Breadth-first traversal first visits all the nodes at depth zero (i.e., the root), then all the nodes at depth one, and so on. At each depth the nodes are visited from left to right.

A breadth-first traversal of the tree shown in Figure 9.6 visits the nodes in the following order:

$$A, B, D, C, E, H, F, G, I.$$

## 9.5 Expression Trees

Algebraic expressions such as

$$a/b + (c - d)e \qquad (9.4)$$

have an inherent tree-like structure. For example, Figure 9.7 is a representation of the expression in Equation 9.4. This kind of tree is called an *expression tree*.

The terminal nodes (leaves) of an expression tree are the variables or constants in the expression ($a$, $b$, $c$, $d$, and $e$). The non-terminal nodes of an expression tree are the operators ($+$, $-$, $\times$, and $\div$). Notice that the parentheses which appear in Equation 9.4 do not appear in the tree. Nevertheless, the tree representation has captured the intent of the parentheses since the subtraction is lower in the tree than the multiplication.

The common algebraic operators are either unary or binary. For example, addition, subtraction, multiplication, and division are all binary operations and negation is a unary operation. Therefore, the non-terminal nodes of the corresponding expression trees have either one or two non-empty subtrees. That is, expression trees are usually binary trees.

What can we do with an expression tree? Perhaps the simplest thing to do is to print the expression represented by the tree. Notice that an inorder traversal of the tree in Figure 9.7 visits the nodes in the order

$$a, \div, b, +, c, -, d, e.$$

Except for the missing parentheses, this is precisely the order in which the symbols appear in Equation 9.4!

This suggests that an inorder traversal should be used to print the expression. Consider an inorder traversal which, when it encounters a terminal node, it simply prints it out; and when it encounters a non-terminal node, does the following:

1. Print a left parenthesis; and then
2. traverse the left subtree; and then
3. print the root; and then

---

**FIGURE 9.7**
Tree representing the expression $a/b + (c - d)e$.

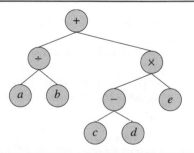

4. traverse the right subtree; and then

5. print a right parenthesis.

Applying this procedure to the tree given in Figure 9.7 we get

$$((a \div b) + ((c - d) \times e)), \tag{9.5}$$

which, despite the redundant parentheses, represents exactly the same expression as Equation 9.4.

## Infix Notation

The algebraic expression in Equation 9.5 is written in the usual way such mathematical expressions are written. The notation used is called *infix notation* because each operator appears *in between* its operands. As we have seen, there is a natural relationship between infix notation and inorder traversal.

Infix notation is only possible for binary operations such as addition, subtraction, multiplication, and division. Writing an operator in between its operands is possible only when it has exactly two operands. In Chapter 6 we saw two alternative notations for algebraic expressions—*prefix* and *postfix*.

## Prefix Notation

In prefix notation the operator is written before its operands. Therefore, in order to print the prefix expression from an expression tree, preorder traversal is done. That is, at every non-terminal node we do the following:

1. Print the root; and then

2. print a left parenthesis; and then

3. traverse the left subtree; and then

4. print a comma; and then

5. traverse the right subtree; and then

6. print a right parenthesis.

If we use this procedure to print the tree given in Figure 9.7 we get the prefix expression

$$+(\div(a, b), \times(-(c, d), e)). \tag{9.6}$$

While this notation may appear unfamiliar at first, consider the result obtained when we spell out the names of the operators:

```
plus (div (a,b), times (minus (c,d), e))
```

This is precisely the notation used in a typical programming language to invoke user-defined procedures **plus**, **minus**, **times**, and **div**.[2]

---

[2]Of course, in C++ we can overload the built-in operators. However, having done so we would write an infix expression rather than the prefix one.

### Postfix Notation

Since inorder traversal produces an infix expression and preorder traversal produces a prefix expression, it should not come as a surprise that postorder traversal produces a postfix expression. In a postfix expression, an operator always follows its operands. The beauty of postfix (and prefix) expressions is that parentheses are not necessary.

A simple postorder traversal of the tree in Figure 9.7 gives the postfix expression

$$a\ b \div c\ d - e \times +. \tag{9.7}$$

In Section 6.1.3 we saw that a postfix expression is easily evaluated using a stack. So, given an expression tree, we can evaluate the expression by doing a postorder traversal to create the postfix expression and then using the algorithm given in Section 6.1.3 to evaluate the expression.

In fact, it is not really necessary to first create the postfix expression before computing its value. The expression can be evaluated by making use of an *evaluation stack* during the course of the traversal as follows: When a terminal node is visited, its value is pushed onto the stack. When a non-terminal node is visited, two values are popped from the stack, the operation specified by the node is performed on those values, and the result is pushed back onto the evaluation stack. When the traversal terminates, there will be one result in the evaluation stack and that result is the value of the expression.

Finally, we can take this one step further. Instead of actually evaluating the expression, the code to compute the value of the expression is emitted. Again, a postorder traversal is done. However, now instead of performing the computation as each node is visited, the code needed to perform the evaluation is emitted. This is precisely what a compiler does when it compiles an expression such as Equation 9.5 for execution.

## 9.6  Implementing Trees

In this section we consider the implementation of trees including general trees, *N*-ary trees, and binary trees. The implementations presented have been developed in the context of the abstract data type framework presented in Chapter 5. That is, the various types of trees are viewed as classes of *containers* as shown in Figure 9.8.

---

**FIGURE 9.8**
Object class hierarchy.

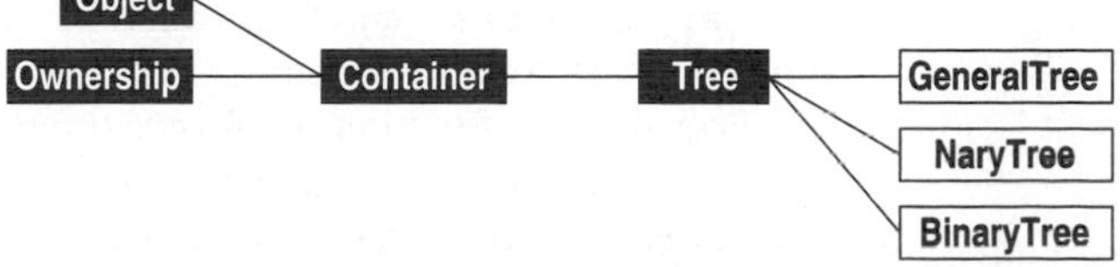

---

---

**PROGRAM 9.1**
**Tree** class definition

---

```
1   class Tree : public virtual Container
2   {
3       class Iter;
4   public:
5       virtual Object& Key () const = 0;
6       virtual Tree& Subtree (unsigned int) const = 0;
7       virtual bool IsEmpty () const = 0;
8       virtual bool IsLeaf () const = 0;
9       virtual unsigned int Degree () const = 0;
10      virtual int Height () const;
11      virtual void DepthFirstTraversal (PrePostVisitor&) const;
12      virtual void BreadthFirstTraversal (Visitor&) const;
13      void Accept (Visitor&) const;
14  }
```

---

Program 9.1 declares the **Tree** abstract class. The **Tree** class encapsulates those interface elements which are common to all of the tree implementations presented in this chapter. The **Tree** class combines the tree interface with the container interface given in Section 5.2.5.

The **Tree** class adds the following functions to the public interface inherited from the **Container** base class:

**Key** This accessor returns a reference to the object contained in the root node of a tree.

**Subtree** This accessor returns a reference to the *i*th subtree of the given tree.

**IsEmpty** This function is a Boolean-valued accessor which returns **true** if the root of the tree is an empty tree, i.e., an external node.

**IsLeaf** This function is a Boolean-valued accessor which returns **true** if the root of the tree is a leaf node.

**Degree** This accessor returns the degree of the root node of the tree. The result is an **unsigned int**. By definition, the degree of an external node is zero.

**Height** This accessor returns the height of the tree. The result is a (signed) **int**. By definition, the height of an empty tree is $-1$.

**DepthFirstTraversal** and **BreadthFirstTraversal** These functions are analogous to the **Accept** member function of the container class (see Section 5.2.5). Both of these functions perform a traversal. That is, all the nodes of the tree are visited systematically. The former takes a reference to a **PrePostVisitor**, and the latter takes a reference to a **Visitor**. When a node is visited, the appropriate functions of the visitor are applied to that node.

**PROGRAM 9.2**
`Tree` class traversal member function definitions

```
1   void Tree::DepthFirstTraversal (
2       PrePostVisitor& visitor) const
3   {
4       if (visitor.IsDone ())
5           return;
6       if (!IsEmpty ())
7       {
8           visitor.PreVisit (Key ());
9           for (unsigned int i = 0; i < Degree (); ++i)
10              Subtree (i).DepthFirstTraversal (visitor);
11          visitor.PostVisit (Key ());
12      }
13  }
```

The preceding member functions of the **Tree** class are all pure virtual functions. Therefore, the **Tree** class is an abstract base class from which specific concrete tree classes are derived.

## 9.6.1 Tree Traversals

The abstract **Tree** class provides default implementations for both the **DepthFirstTraversal** and **BreadthFirstTraversal** member functions. Both of these implementations call pure virtual member functions such as **Key** and **Subtree**. In effect, they are *abstract algorithms.* An abstract algorithm describes behavior in the absence of implementation!

### Depth-First Traversal

Program 9.2 gives the definition of the **DepthFirstTraversal** member function of the **Tree** class. The traversal routine takes one argument—a reference to an instance of the **PrePostVisitor** class defined in Program 9.3. A **PrePostVisitor** is a visitor with two additional member functions, **PreVisit** and **PostVisit**. During a depth-first traversal each function is called once for every node in the tree.

The depth-first traversal routine first calls the **PreVisit** function with the object in the root node. Then, it calls recursively the **DepthFirstTraversal** function for each subtree of the given node. After all the subtrees have been visited, the **PostVisit** function is called. Assuming that the **IsEmpty**, **Key**, and **Subtree** member functions all run in constant time, the total running time of the **DepthFirstTraversal** routine is

$$n(\mathcal{T}\langle \texttt{PreVisit()}\rangle + \mathcal{T}\langle \texttt{PostVisit()}\rangle) + O(n),$$

---

**PROGRAM 9.3**
PrePostVisitor, PreOrder, InOrder, and PostOrder class definitions

```
1   class PrePostVisitor : public Visitor
2   {
3   public:
4       virtual void PreVisit (Object&){}
5       virtual void Visit (Object&){}
6       virtual void PostVisit (Object&){}
7   };
8
9   class PreOrder : public PrePostVisitor
10  {
11      Visitor& visitor;
12  public:
13      PreOrder (Visitor& v) : visitor (v)
14          {}
15      void PreVisit (Object& object)
16          { visitor.Visit (object); }
17  };
18
19  class InOrder : public PrePostVisitor
20  {
21      Visitor& visitor;
22  public:
23      InOrder (Visitor& v) : visitor (v)
24          {}
25      void Visit (Object& object)
26          { visitor.Visit (object); }
27  };
28
29  class PostOrder : public PrePostVisitor
30  {
31      Visitor& visitor;
32  public:
33      PostOrder (Visitor& v) : visitor (v)
34          {}
35      void PostVisit (Object& object)
36          { visitor.Visit (object); }
37  };
```

---

where $n$ is the number of nodes in the tree, $\mathcal{T}\langle\texttt{PreVisit()}\rangle$ is the running time of `PreVisit`, and `PostVisit` is the running time of `PostVisit`.

### Preorder, Inorder, and Postorder Traversals

Preorder, inorder, and postorder traversals are special cases of the more general depth-first traversal described in the preceding section. Rather than implement each of these traversals directly, we make use of a design pattern, called *adapter,* which allows the single routine to provide all the needed functionality.

Suppose we have an instance of the `PuttingVisitor` class (see Section 5.2.6). As shown in Program 5.12, the `PuttingVisitor` class is derived from the abstract `Visitor` base class, and it provides a `Visit` routine that prints every object it visits. However, we cannot pass a `PuttingVisitor` instance to the `DepthFirstTraversal` routine shown in Program 9.2 because it expects a `PrePostVisitor` instance.

The problem is that the interface provided by the `PuttingVisitor` does not match the interface expected by the `DepthFirstTraversal` routine. The solution to this problem is to use an adapter. An *adapter* converts the interface provided by one class to the interface required by another. For example, if we want a preorder traversal, then the call to the `PreVisit` (made by `DepthFirstTraversal`) should be mapped to the `Visit` member function (provided by the `PuttingVisitor`). Similarly, a postorder traversal is obtained by mapping `PostVisit` to `Visit`.

Program 9.3 defines three adapter classes—`PreOrder`, `PostOrder`, and `InOrder`. All three classes are similar: They are all derived from the `Visitor` abstract base class; all have a single member variable that is a reference to a `Visitor` class instance; and all have a constructor that takes a `Visitor` reference and initializes the member variable.

Each class provides a different interface mapping. For example, the `PreVisit` member function of the `PreVisit` simply calls the `Visit` function on the `visitor` member variable. Notice that the adapter provides no functionality of its own—function calls to the `visitor` instance as required.

The following code fragment illustrates how these adapters are used:

```
PuttingVisitor v;
SomeTree t;
t.DepthFirstTraversal (PreOrder (v));
t.DepthFirstTraversal (InOrder (v));
t.DepthFirstTraversal (PostOrder (v));
```

### Breadth-First Traversal

Program 9.4 defines the `BreadthFirstTraversal` member function of the `Tree` class. As defined in Section 9.4 a breadth-first traversal of a tree visits the nodes in the order of their depth in the tree and at each level the nodes are visited from left to right.

We have already seen in Section 6.2.3 a nonrecursive breadth-first traversal algorithm for $N$-ary trees. This algorithm makes use of a queue as follows. Initially, the root node of the given tree is enqueued, provided it is not the empty tree. Then, the following steps are repeated until the queue is empty:

**PROGRAM 9.4**
Tree class `BreadthFirstTraversal` member function definition

```
1   void Tree::BreadthFirstTraversal (Visitor& visitor) const
2   {
3       Queue& queue = *new QueueAsLinkedList ();
4       queue.RescindOwnership ();
5
6       if (!IsEmpty ())
7           queue.Enqueue (const_cast<Tree&> (*this));
8       while (!queue.IsEmpty () && !visitor.IsDone())
9       {
10          Tree const& head =
11              dynamic_cast<Tree const &> (queue.Dequeue ());
12
13          visitor.Visit (head.Key ());
14          for (unsigned int i = 0; i < head.Degree (); ++i)
15          {
16              Tree& child = head.Subtree (i);
17              if (!child.IsEmpty ())
18                  queue.Enqueue (child);
19          }
20      }
21      delete &queue;
22  }
```

1.  Remove the node at the head of the queue and call it **head**.
2.  Visit the object contained in **head**.
3.  Enqueue in order each non-empty subtree of **head**.

Notice that empty trees are never put into the queue. Furthermore, it should be obvious that each node of the tree is enqueued exactly once. Therefore, it is also dequeued exactly once. Consequently, the running time for the breadth-first traversal is $n\mathcal{T}\langle \text{visit()} \rangle + O(n)$.

There are several aspects of the way in which the queue is used here that need to be explained. First, the queue will be used to contain trees which are subtrees of the given tree. Since the subtrees of a tree are owned by the tree, they cannot also be owned by the queue. Therefore, on line 4 of Program 9.4 the `RescindOwnership` function of the queue is called. This is really conservative programming, since the queue will normally be empty by the time its destructor is called so it will not have any contained objects to delete.

The `BreadthFirstTraversal` function is a **const** member function. Therefore, it must not modify the given tree. However, we need to push the tree onto the queue. And since the `Enqueue` function takes a non-**const Object** reference,

**PROGRAM 9.5**
**Tree** class **Accept** member function definition

```
1  void Tree::Accept (Visitor& visitor) const
2      { DepthFirstTraversal (PreOrder (visitor)); }
```

a **const_cast** is required on line 7 of Program 9.4 to cast away the **const**ness. This is not an unsafe cast in this context, because the queue is a local variable of the **BreadthFirstTraversal** routine, and because the routine does not modify anything which it later dequeues from the queue.

### Accept Member Function

The **Tree** class replaces the functionality provided by the single function **Accept** with two different kinds of traversal. Whereas the **Accept** function is allowed to visit the nodes of a tree in any order, the traversals visit the nodes in two different, but well-defined orders. Consequently, we have chosen to provide a default implementation of the **Accept** function which does a preorder traversal.

Program 9.5 shows the implementation of the **Accept** member function of the **Tree** class. This function uses the **PreOrder** adapter to pass on a given visitor to the **DepthFirstTraversal** routine.

## 9.6.2 Tree Iterators

According to the object hierarchy defined in Chapter 5, every class derived from the **Container** class must provide an associated **Iterator** class. This section describes the implementation of the **Tree::Iter** class which can be used to step through the contents of any tree instance.

For example, suppose we have declared a variable **tree** which is of type **BinaryTree**. Then we can view the **tree** instance as a container and print its contents as follows:

```
BinaryTree tree;
Iterator& i = tree.NewIterator;
while (!i.IsDone ()) {
    cout << *i << endl;
    ++i;
}
delete &i;
```

Every concrete class derived from the **Container** abstract base class must provide a **NewIterator** function. The purpose of this function is to create an instance of the appropriate type of **Iterator** and to associate that iterator with the corresponding container. The iterator can then be used to systematically visit the contents of the associated container.

---

**PROGRAM 9.6**
`Tree::Iter` class definition

---

```
1   class Tree::Iter : public Iterator
2   {
3       Tree const& tree;
4       Stack& stack;
5   public:
6       Iter (Tree const&);
7       ~Iter ();
8       void Reset ();
9       bool IsDone () const;
10      Object& operator * () const;
11      void operator ++ ();
12  };
```

---

We have already seen that when we systematically visit the nodes of a tree, we are doing a tree traversal. Therefore, the implementation of the iterator must also do a tree traversal. However, there is a catch. A recursive tree traversal routine such as **DepthFirstTraversal** keeps track of where it is *implicitly* using the processor stack. However, when we implement an iterator we must keep track of the state of the traversal *explicitly*. This section presents an iterator implementation which does a preorder traversal of the tree and keeps track of the current state of the traversal using a stack from Chapter 6.

Program 9.6 gives the declaration of the **Tree::Iter** class. The **NewIterator** member function of the abstract class **Tree** is implemented as follows:

```
Iterator& Tree::NewIterator () const
    { return *new Iter (*this); }
```

### Member Variables
A **Tree::Iter** contains two member variables—**tree** and **stack**. The former is a **const** reference to a **Tree**. Upon creation, an iterator is associated with a specific tree instance and that association remains until the iterator is destroyed. The second member variable is a reference to a **Stack** instance.

### Constructor and Reset Member Function
The code for the **Tree::Iter** constructor and **Reset** member functions is given in Program 9.7 The constructor is quite simple. It takes as its lone argument a reference to a **Tree** instance and initializes the two member variables as follows. First, **tree** is made to refer to the specified tree. Next a new instance of the **StackAsLinkedList** class is created. (The linked-list implementation of stacks is described in Section 6.1.2). This stack will be used to contain subtrees of the given tree. Since the subtrees of a tree are owned by that tree, they cannot also be owned by the stack. Therefore the

**PROGRAM 9.7**

Tree::Iter class constructor and Reset member function definitions

```
1   Tree::Iter::Iter (Tree const& _tree) :
2       tree (_tree),
3       stack (*new StackAsLinkedList ())
4   {
5       stack.RescindOwnership ();
6       Reset ();
7   }
8
9   Tree::Iter::~Iter ()
10      { delete &stack; }
11
12  void Tree::Iter::Reset ()
13  {
14      stack.Purge ();
15      if (!tree.IsEmpty ())
16          stack.Push (const_cast<Tree&> (tree));
17  }
```

RescindOwnership function of the stack is called. Finally the Reset function is called. The running time for the constructor is $O(1)$ assuming Reset takes a constant amount of time which indeed it does as we shall now see.

The Reset function is called whenever it is necessary to start a new preorder traversal. It begins by calling the Purge function to make sure that the stack is empty. Then, if the associated tree is not empty, that tree is pushed onto the stack. The running time of the Reset function depends on the number of items in the stack when it is called.

Of course, the stack is initially empty. Therefore, the first time Reset is called (by the constructor) it runs in constant time. However, if the Reset function is called only after a traversal is completed, the stack will always be empty when the function is called. Therefore, under these circumstances, the running time for the Reset function is $O(1)$.

## Operator Member Functions

Program 9.8 defines the three standard member functions for manipulating iterators, IsDone, operator*, and operator++. The purpose of IsDone is to return false as long as there are still more objects in the container which have not yet been visited. This is the case as long as there is something in the stack. Therefore, the implementation simply calls IsEmpty to test whether the stack is empty. Clearly, the running time for IsDone is $O(1)$.

The dereferencing operator, operator*, is used to access the object to which the iterator currently refers. In this case, the iterator refers to the object at the root of the tree which is at the top of the stack. Note, the stack will never contain an empty tree.

**PROGRAM 9.8**
`Tree::Iter` class constructor operator member function definitions

```
1   bool Tree::Iter::IsDone () const
2       { return stack.IsEmpty (); }
3
4   Object& Tree::Iter::operator * () const
5   {
6       if (!stack.IsEmpty ())
7       {
8           Tree const& top =
9               dynamic_cast<Tree const&> (stack.Top ());
10          return top.Key ();
11      }
12      else
13          return NullObject::Instance ();
14  }
15
16  void Tree::Iter::operator ++ ()
17  {
18      if (!stack.IsEmpty ())
19      {
20          Tree const& top =
21              dynamic_cast<Tree const&> (stack.Pop ());
22
23          for (int i = top.Degree () - 1; i >= 0; --i)
24          {
25              Tree& subtree = top.Subtree (i);
26              if (!subtree.IsEmpty ())
27                  stack.Push (subtree);
28          }
29      }
30  }
```

Therefore, if the stack is not empty, then there is a referent. The dereferencing operator obtains a reference to the tree at the top of the stack by calling **Top**, and then calls the **Key** member function to access the root of the tree. The running time for **operator\*** is $O(1)$. When the stack is empty, this function returns a reference to the **NullObject** instance.

Finally, the pre-increment operator, **operator++**, is used to advance the iterator to the next node in a preorder traversal. It does so by popping the top tree from the stack and then pushing its subtrees onto the stack provided that they are not empty. Notice the order is important here. In a preorder traversal, the first subtree of a node is traversed before the second subtree. Therefore, the second subtree should appear in the stack *below* the first subtree. That is why subtrees are pushed in reverse order. The running time for **operator++** is $O(1)$.

### 9.6.3 General Trees

This section outlines an implementation of general trees in the sense of Definition 9.1. The salient features of the definition are (1), that the nodes of a general tree have arbitrary degrees; and (2), that there is no such thing as an empty tree.

The recursive nature of Definition 9.1 has important implications when considering the implementation of such trees as containers. In effect, since a tree contains zero or more subtrees, when implemented as a container, we get a container which contains other containers! Fortunately, we have chosen by design to implement containers using *indirect containment*. Therefore, it is possible for a tree to contain other trees simply by keeping around pointers to those trees.

Figure 9.9 shows the approach we have chosen for implementing general trees. This figure shows how the general tree $T_c$ in Figure 9.2 can be stored in memory. The basic idea is that each node has associated with it a linked list of pointers to the subtrees of that node. A linked list is used because there is no a priori restriction on its length. This allows each node to have an arbitrary degree. Furthermore, since there are no empty trees, we need not worry about representing them. An important consequence of this is that the implementation never makes use of a zero-valued tree node pointer!

Program 9.9 declares the **GeneralTree** class which is used to represent general trees as specified by Definition 9.1. The class **GeneralTree** is derived from the base class **Tree** which is discussed in the preceding section.

---

**FIGURE 9.9**
Representing general trees using linked lists.

---

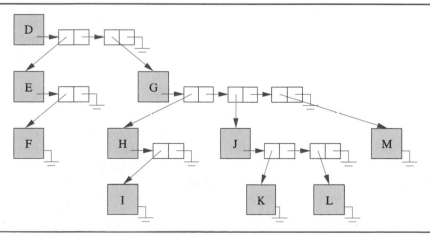

**PROGRAM 9.9**
GeneralTree class definition

```
1   class GeneralTree : public Tree
2   {
3   protected:
4       Object* key;
5       unsigned int degree;
6       LinkedList<GeneralTree*> list;
7   public:
8       GeneralTree (Object&);
9       ~GeneralTree ();
10
11      Object& Key () const;
12      GeneralTree& Subtree (unsigned int) const;
13      virtual void AttachSubtree (GeneralTree&);
14      virtual GeneralTree& DetachSubtree (GeneralTree&);
15      // ...
16  };
```

### Member Variables
The GeneralTree class definition comprises three member variables—key, degree, and list. The first, key, represents the root node of the tree. It is a pointer to an Object. The second, an unsigned integer degree, records the degree of the root node of the tree. The third, list, is a linked list of pointers to GeneralTree instances. It is declared by instantiating the LinkedList<T> template class for T=GeneralTree*. This list contains pointers to the subtrees of the given tree.

### Member Functions
Since the GeneralTree class is derived from the Tree base class, its interface comprises all of the public interfaces of the base classes. Furthermore, two member functions are added to the inherited interface—AttachSubtree and DetachSubtree.

Since the GeneralTree class is a concrete class derived from an abstract base class, it must provide implementations for all of the member functions declared as pure virtual functions in the base class. In the interest of brevity, the declarations of these functions have been elided from Program 9.9.

### Constructor, Destructor, and Purge Member Function
Program 9.10 defines the GeneralTree constructor, destructor, and the Purge member function. According to Definition 9.1, a general tree must contain at least one node—an empty tree is not allowed. Therefore, the constructor takes one argument, a reference to an Object instance. The constructor initializes the member variables as follows: The variable key is made to point at the object argument; the degree is set to zero; and, the linked list list is configured as an empty list. The running time of the constructor is clearly $O(1)$.

**PROGRAM 9.10**
`GeneralTree` class constructor, destructor, and `Purge` member function definitions

```
1   GeneralTree::GeneralTree (Object& _key):
2       key (&_key),
3       degree (0),
4       list ()
5       {}
6
7   void GeneralTree::Purge ()
8   {
9       ListElement<GeneralTree*> const* ptr;
10
11      if (IsOwner ())
12          delete key;
13      for (ptr = list.Head (); ptr != 0; ptr = ptr->Next ())
14          delete ptr->Datum ();
15      key = 0;
16      list.Purge ();
17  }
18
19  GeneralTree::~GeneralTree ()
20      { Purge (); }
```

The `Purge` member function is inherited from the `Container` class interface. The purpose of `Purge` is to delete all contained objects and to release the associated storage if the container is the owner of those objects. Each node in a `GeneralTree` is a container with two varieties of contained objects—the root object and the subtrees. The approach taken in this implementation stipulates that the ownership of the root object is determined in the usual way but that all the subtrees of a given tree always are owned by that tree.

The `GeneralTree` class destructor simply calls the `Purge` member function to do its work. The `Purge` function first deletes the root object if it is the owner of that object. Then, it traverses the linked lists, deleting each of the attached subtrees. Finally, it deletes the linked list itself. Given a tree comprised of $n$ nodes, the running time of the `Purge` function is $(2n - 1)\mathcal{J}\langle \text{T::~T()}\rangle + O(n)$ in the worst case. The factor $(2n - 1)$ is the sum of the number of contained objects deleted, $n$, and the number of trees deleted, $n - 1$.

### `Key` and `Subtree` Member Functions

Program 9.11 defines the various `GeneralTree` class member functions for manipulating general trees. The `Key` member function is a member variable accessor that simply returns a reference to the object contained by the root node of the tree. Clearly, its running time is $O(1)$.

The `Subtree` member function takes as its lone argument an `unsigned int, i`, which must be between 0 and `degree`−1, where `degree` is the degree of the root node

---

**PROGRAM 9.11**
GeneralTree class `Key`, `Subtree`, `AttachSubtree`, and `DetachSubtree`
member function definitions

---

```
1   Object& GeneralTree::Key () const
2       { return *key; }
3
4   GeneralTree& GeneralTree::Subtree (unsigned int i) const
5   {
6       if (i >= degree)
7           throw out_of_range ("invalid subtree index");
8
9       unsigned int j = 0;
10      ListElement<GeneralTree*> const* ptr =
11          list.Head ();
12      while (j < i && ptr != 0)
13      {
14          ++j;
15          ptr = ptr->Next ();
16      }
17      if (ptr == 0)
18          throw logic_error ("should never happen");
19      return *ptr->Datum ();
20  }
21
22  void GeneralTree::AttachSubtree (GeneralTree& t)
23  {
24      list.Append (&t);
25      ++degree;
26  }
27
28  GeneralTree& GeneralTree::DetachSubtree (GeneralTree& t)
29  {
30      list.Extract (&t);
31      --degree;
32      return t;
33  }
```

---

of the tree. It returns a reference to the ith subtree of the given tree. The **Subtree** routine simply takes i steps down the linked list and returns a reference to the appropriate subtree. Assuming that i is valid, the worst-case running time for **Subtree** is $O(d)$, where $d = $ **degree** is the degree of the root node of the tree.

### AttachSubtree and DetachSubtree Member Functions
Program 9.11 also defines two functions for manipulating the subtrees of a general tree. The purpose of the **AttachSubtree** member function is to add the specified

subtree to the root of a given tree. This function takes as its lone argument a reference to a **GeneralTree** instance which is to be attached. The **AttachSubtree** routine simply appends to the linked list a pointer to the tree to be attached and then adds one to the **degree** variable. The running time for **AttachSubtree** is $O(1)$.

Similarly, the **DetachSubtree** member function removes the specified subtree from the given tree. This function takes as its lone argument a reference to a **GeneralTree** instance which is to be removed. It removes the appropriate pointer from the linked list and then subtracts one from the **degree** variable. The running time for **DetachSubtree** is $O(d)$ in the worst case, where $d$ = **degree**.

### 9.6.4 *N*-ary Trees

We now turn to the implementation of *N*-ary trees as given by Definition 9.3. According to this definition, an *N*-ary tree is either an empty tree or it is a tree comprised of a root and exactly *N* subtrees. The implementation follows the design pattern established in the preceding section. Specifically, we view an *N*-ary tree as a container.

Figure 9.10 illustrates the way in which *N*-ary trees can be represented. The figure gives the representation of the tertiary ($N = 3$) tree

$$\{A, \{B, \varnothing, \varnothing, \varnothing\}, \varnothing, \varnothing\}.$$

The basic idea is that each node has associated with it an array of length *N* of pointers to the subtrees of that node. An array is used because we assume that the *arity* of the tree, *N*, is known a priori.

Notice that we explicitly represent the empty trees. That is, a separate data structure is allocated for the representation each empty tree. Of course, an empty tree contains neither root nor subtrees.

**FIGURE 9.10**
Representing *N*-ary trees using pointer arrays.

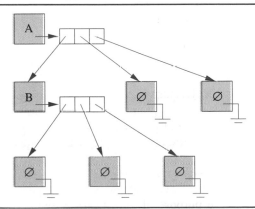

Program 9.12 declares the **NaryTree** class which represents *N*-ary trees as specified by Definition 9.3. The class **NaryTree** is derived from the base class **Tree** which, as discussed in the preceding section, combines the tree and container interfaces.

## Member Variables

The implementation of the **NaryTree** class is very similar to that of the **GeneralTree** class. The **NaryTree** class definition also comprises three member variables—**key**, **degree**, and **subtree**. The first, **key**, represents the root node of the tree. It is a pointer to an **Object**. The second, an unsigned integer constant **degree**, records the degree of the root node of the tree. The third, **subtree**, is an array of pointers to **NaryTree** instances. It is declared by instantiating the **Array<T>** template class for **T=GeneralTree\***. This array contains pointers to the subtrees of the given tree.

## Member Functions

Like the **GeneralTree**, the **NaryTree** class is derived from the **Tree** base class. Its interface comprises all of the public interfaces which are common to trees and containers. In addition to the inherited functions, the following four additional member functions are defined: **AttachKey**, **DetachKey**, **AttachSubtree**, and **DetachSubtree**.

## Constructors

The **NaryTree** class declares two constructors. Implementations for the two constructors are given in Program 9.13 The first constructor takes a single argument of type

---

**PROGRAM 9.12**
NaryTree class definition

---

```
1   class NaryTree : public Tree
2   {
3   protected:
4       Object* key;
5       unsigned int const degree;
6       Array<NaryTree*> subtree;
7   public:
8       NaryTree (unsigned int);
9       NaryTree (unsigned int, Object&);
10      ~NaryTree ();
11
12      Object& Key () const;
13      NaryTree& Subtree (unsigned int) const;
14      virtual void AttachKey (Object&);
15      virtual Object& DetachKey ();
16      virtual void AttachSubtree (unsigned int, NaryTree&);
17      virtual NaryTree& DetachSubtree (unsigned int);
18      // ...
19  };
```

---

**unsigned int** which specifies the degree of the tree. This constructor creates an empty tree. It does so by setting the **key** pointer to zero, and by setting the length of the **subtree** array to zero. The running time of this constructor is $O(1)$.

The second constructor takes two arguments. The first specifies the degree of the tree, and the second is a reference to an **Object** instance. This constructor creates a non-empty tree in which the specified object occupies the root node. According to Definition 9.3, every internal node in an $N$-ary tree must have exactly $N$ subtrees. Therefore, this constructor creates and attaches $N$ empty subtrees to the root node. The running time of this constructor is $O(N)$, since $N$ empty subtrees are created and constructed and the constructor for an empty $N$-ary tree takes $O(1)$ time.

### IsEmpty Member Function

The purpose of the **IsEmpty** accessor function is to determine whether a given $N$-ary tree is the empty tree. The implementation of this function is given in Program 9.14. In this implementation, the **key** pointer is zero if the tree is the empty tree. Therefore, **IsEmpty** returns **true** when the **key** member variable is zero. Clearly this is a constant time, $O(1)$, operation.

### Key, AttachKey, and DetachKey Member Functions

Program 9.14 also defines three functions for manipulating the root of an $N$-ary tree. The first, **Key**, is an accessor which returns a reference to the object contained in the root node of the tree. Clearly, this operation is not defined for the empty tree. If the tree is not empty, the running time of this routine is $O(1)$.

The purpose of **AttachKey** is to insert the specified object into a given $N$-ary tree at the root node. This operation is only defined for an empty tree. The **AttachKey** routine takes as its lone argument a reference to the object to be inserted in the root node and

---

**PROGRAM 9.13**
**NaryTree** class constructor definitions

```
1   NaryTree::NaryTree (unsigned int _degree) :
2       key (0),
3       degree (_degree),
4       subtree (0)
5       {}
6
7   NaryTree::NaryTree (unsigned int _degree, Object& _key):
8       key (&key),
9       degree (_degree),
10      subtree (_degree)
11  {
12      for (unsigned int i = 0; i < degree; ++i)
13          subtree [i] = new NaryTree (degree);
14  }
```

---

**PROGRAM 9.14**
`NaryTree` class member function definitions

---

```
1   book NaryTree::IsEmpty () const
2       { return key == 0; }
3
4   Object& NaryTree::Key () const
5   {
6       if (IsEmpty ())
7           throw domain_error ("invalid operation");
8       return *key;
9   }
10
11  void NaryTree::AttachKey (Object& object)
12  {
13      if (!IsEmpty ())
14          throw domain_error ("invalid operation");
15      key = &object;
16      subtree.SetLength (degree);
17      for (unsigned int i = 0; i < degree; ++i)
18          subtree [i] = new NaryTree (degree);
19  }
20
21  Object& NaryTree::DetachKey ()
22  {
23      if (!IsLeaf ())
24          throw domain_error ("invalid operation");
25      Object& result = *key;
26      key = 0;
27      for (unsigned int i = 0; i < degree; ++i)
28          delete subtree [i];
29      subtree.SetLength (0);
30      return result;
31  }
```

---

makes the **key** member variable point at the given object. Since the node is no longer empty, it must have exactly $N$ subtrees. Therefore, $N$ new empty subtrees are created and attached to the node. The running time is $O(N)$ since $N$ subtrees are created, and the running time of the constructor for an empty $N$-ary tree takes $O(1)$.

Finally, **DetachKey** is used to remove the object from the root of a tree. In order that the tree which remains still conforms to Definition 9.3, it is only permissible to remove the root from a leaf node. And upon removal, the leaf node becomes an empty tree. The implementation given in Program 9.14 throws an exception if an attempt is made to remove the root from a non-leaf node. Otherwise, the node is a leaf which means that its $N$ subtrees are all empty. When the root is detached, all the subtrees are deleted.

The running time of this routine is clearly $O(N)$ since there are $N$ empty subtrees to be deleted and the cost of deleting an empty $N$-ary tree is constant.

**`Subtree`, `AttachSubtree`, and `DetachSubtree` Member Functions**
Program 9.15 defines the three member functions for manipulating the subtrees of an $N$-ary tree. The `Subtree` member function takes as its lone argument an **unsigned int**, `i`, which must be between 0 and $N - 1$. It returns a reference to the `i`th subtree of the given tree. Note that this operation is only defined for a non-empty $N$-ary tree. Given that the tree is not empty, the running time is $O(1)$.

The `AttachSubtree` member function takes two arguments. The first is an unsigned integer `i` between 0 and $N - 1$. The second is a reference to a **NaryTree** instance. The purpose of this routine is to make the $N$-ary tree specified by the second argument become the `i`th subtree of the given tree. It is only possible to attach a subtree to a non-empty node, and it is only possible to attach a subtree in a place occupied by an empty subtree. If none of the exceptions are thrown, the running time of this function is simply $O(1)$.

---

**PROGRAM 9.15**
**NaryTree** class member function definitions

---

```
1   NaryTree& NaryTree::Subtree (unsigned int i) const
2   {
3       if (IsEmpty ())
4           throw domain_error ("Invalid operation");
5       return *subtree [i];
6   }
7
8   void NaryTree::AttachSubtree (unsigned int i, NaryTree& t)
9   {
10      if (IsEmpty ())
11          throw domain_error ("invalid operation");
12      if (!subtree [i]->IsEmpty ())
13          throw domain_error ("non-empty subtree present");
14      delete subtree [i];
15      subtree [i] = &t;
16  }
17
18  NaryTree& NaryTree::DetachSubtree (unsigned int i)
19  {
20      if (IsEmpty ()
21          throw domain_error ("invalid operation");
22      NaryTree& result = *subtree [i];
23      subtree [i] = new NaryTree (degree);
24      return result;
25  }
```

---

The **DetachSubtree** member function takes a single argument **i** which is an unsigned integer between 0 and $N - 1$. This routine removes the **i**th subtree from a given $N$-ary tree and returns a reference to that subtree. Of course, it is only possible to remove a subtree from a non-empty tree. Since every non-empty node must have $N$ subtrees, when a subtree is removed it is replaced by an empty tree. Clearly, the running time is $O(1)$ if we assume that no exceptions are thrown.

### 9.6.5  Binary Trees

This section presents an implementation of binary trees in the sense of Definition 9.4. A binary tree is essentially an $N$-ary tree where $N = 2$. Therefore, it is possible to implement binary trees using the **NaryTree** class presented in the preceding section. However, because the **NaryTree** class implementation is a general implementation which can accommodate any value of $N$, it is somewhat less efficient in both time and space than an implementation which is designed specifically for the case $N = 2$. Since binary trees occur quite frequently in practice, it is important to have a good implementation.

Another consequence of restricting $N$ to 2 is that we can talk of the left and right subtrees of a tree. Consequently the interface provided by a binary tree class is quite different from the general interface provided by an $N$-ary tree class.

Figure 9.11 shows how the binary tree given in Figure 9.6 is represented. The basic idea is that each node of the tree contains two pointers to the subtrees of that node. Just as we did for $N$-ary trees, we represent explicitly the empty trees. Since an empty tree

**FIGURE 9.11**
Representing binary trees.

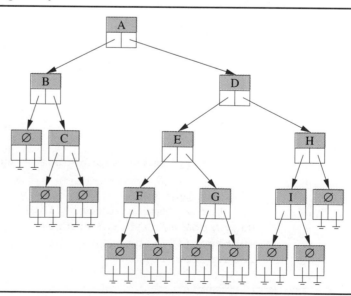

node contains neither root nor subtrees it is represented by a structure in which all the pointers have the value zero.

The **BinaryTree** class is declared in Program 9.16 It is derived from the same base class, **Tree**, as the classes **GeneralTree** and **NaryTree**. Therefore, it shares with those classes the common aspects of the tree and container interfaces. While the declarations of the three classes differ in the details, they all three follow a similar design pattern. Comparing Programs 9.9, 9.12, and 9.16, we see that in addition to the constructors and destructor, they all possess similar routines for accessing and manipulating the root and the subtrees of a tree.

### Member Variables

The **BinaryTree** class has three member variables—**key**, **left**, and **right**. All three of them are pointers. The first is a pointer to an **Object** instance, and the latter two are pointers to **BinaryTree** instances. All three pointers are zero if the node represents the empty tree. Otherwise, the tree must have a root and two subtrees. Consequently, all three pointers are nonzero in a non-empty node.

### Constructors

Program 9.17 defines the two **BinaryTree** class constructors. The default constructor, the constructor which takes no arguments, initializes the binary tree as an empty

---

**PROGRAM 9.16**
BinaryTree class definition

```
1   class BinaryTree : public virtual Tree
2   {
3   protected:
4       Object* key;
5       BinaryTree* left;
6       BinaryTree* right;
7   public:
8       BinaryTree ();
9       BinaryTree (Object&);
10      ~BinaryTree ();
11
12      Object& Key () const;
13      virtual void AttachKey (Object&);
14      virtual Object& DetachKey ();
15      virtual BinaryTree& Left () const;
16      virtual BinaryTree& Right () const;
17      virtual void AttachLeft (BinaryTree&);
18      virtual void AttachRight (BinaryTree&);
19      virtual BinaryTree& DetachLeft ();
20      virtual BinaryTree& DetachRight ();
21      // ...
22  };
```

---

**PROGRAM 9.17**
BinaryTree class constructor definitions

```
1   BinaryTree::BinaryTree () :
2       key (0),
3       left (0),
4       right (0)
5       {}
6
7   BinaryTree::BinaryTree (Object& _key) :
8       key (&_key),
9       left (new BinaryTree ()),
10      right (new BinaryTree ())
11      {}
```

---

tree. It simply sets all three member variables to zero. Clearly the running time of this constructor is $O(1)$.

The second constructor takes as its lone argument a reference to an **Object** class instance. The purpose of this constructor is to create a binary tree with the specified object as its root. Since every binary tree has exactly two subtrees, the constructor creates two empty subtrees and sets the **left** and **right** member variables to point at them. The running time of this constructor is also $O(1)$.

### Destructor and Purge Member Functions

The destructor for the **BinaryTree** class is defined in Program 9.18 It simply calls the **Purge** member function to do the job. The **Purge** member function is part of the **Container** class interface which all container instances must provide. The purpose of the **Purge** routine is to delete all the owned objects in the container and to return the container to its initial empty state.

Clearly the **Purge** function has nothing to do if the tree is already an empty tree. If the tree is not the empty tree, then the **Purge** function has some cleaning up to do. It begins by deleting the root only if the binary tree is the owner of the contained objects. Then, because a tree always owns its subtrees, the **Purge** routine deletes the left and right subtrees.

Suppose the binary tree contains $n$ non-empty nodes. Theorem 9.1 tells us that there are $n+1$ empty nodes. Altogether there are $2n+1 = O(n)$ nodes. Therefore, the running time of **Purge** is $n\mathcal{T}\langle \text{T::~T()}\rangle + O(n)$ in the worst case.

## 9.6.6   Binary Tree Traversals

Program 9.19 defines the **DepthFirstTraversal** member function of the **Binary-Tree** class. This routine supports all three tree traversal methods—preorder, inorder, and postorder. The implementation follows directly from the definitions given in Section 9.4. The traversal is implemented using recursion. That is, the function calls itself

**PROGRAM 9.18**
BinaryTree class Purge member function and destructor definitions

```
1   void BinaryTree::Purge ()
2   {
3       if (!IsEmpty ())
4       {
5           if (IsOwner ())
6               delete key;
7           delete left;
8           delete right;
9           key = 0;
10          left = 0;
11          right = 0;
12      }
13  }
14
15  BinaryTree::~BinaryTree ()
16      { Purge (): }
```

recursively to visit the subtrees of the given node. Note that the recursion terminates properly when an empty tree is encountered since the routine does nothing in that case.

The traversal routine takes as its lone argument a reference to a **PrePostVisitor**. As each node is "visited" during the course of the traversal, the **PreVisit**, **Visit**, and **PostVisit** member functions of the visitor are applied to the object contained in that node.

**PROGRAM 9.19**
BinaryTree class DepthFirstTraversal member function definition

```
1   void BinaryTree::DepthFirstTraversal (
2       PrePostVisitor& visitor) const
3   {
4       if (visitor.IsDone ())
5           return;
6       if (!IsEmpty ())
7       {
8           visitor.PreVisit (*key);
9           left->DepthFirstTraversal (visitor);
10          visitor.Visit (*key);
11          right->DepthFirstTraversal (visitor);
12          visitor.PostVisit (*key);
13      }
14  }
```

### 9.6.7   Comparing Trees

A problem which is relatively easy to solve is determining if two trees are equivalent. Two trees are *equivalent* if they both have the same topology and if the objects contained in corresponding nodes are equal. Clearly, two empty trees are equivalent. Consider two nonempty binary trees $T_A = \{R_A, T_{AL}, T_{AR}\}$ and $T_B = \{R_B, T_{BL}, T_{BR}\}$. Equivalence of trees is given by

$$T_A \equiv T_B \iff R_A = R_B \wedge T_{AL} \equiv T_{BL} \wedge T_{AR} \equiv T_{BR}.$$

A simple, recursive algorithm suffices to test the equivalence of trees.

Since the **BinaryTree** class is ultimately derived from the **Object** base class, we must provide a **CompareTo** member function to compare binary trees. Recall that the compare function is used to compare two objects, say **obj1** and **obj2** like this:

```
int result = obj1.CompareTo (obj2);
```

The **CompareTo** function returns a negative number if **obj1** < **obj2**; a positive number if **obj1** > **obj2**; and zero if **obj1** $\equiv$ **obj2**.

So what we need is to define a *total order* relation on binary trees. Fortunately, it is possible to define such a relation for binary trees provided that the objects contained in the nodes of the trees are drawn from a totally ordered set.

**Theorem 9.4**
*Consider two binary trees $T_A$ and $T_B$ and the relation $<$ given by*

$$
\begin{aligned}
T_A < T_B \iff & T_B \neq \emptyset \wedge (T_A = \emptyset \vee \\
& T_A \neq \emptyset \wedge (R_A < R_B \vee \\
& R_A = R_B \wedge (T_{AL} < T_{BL} \vee \\
& T_{AL} = T_{BL} \wedge T_{AR} < T_{BR})))
\end{aligned}
$$

*where $T_A$ is either $\emptyset$ or $T_A = \{R, T_{AL}, T_{AR}\}$ and $T_B$ is $T_B = \{R, T_{BL}, T_{BR}\}$. The relation $<$ is a total order.*

The proof of Theorem 9.4 is straightforward albeit tedious. Essentially we need to show the following:

- For any two distinct trees $T_A$ and $T_B$, such that $T_A \neq T_B$, either $T_A < T_B$ or $T_B < T_A$.
- For any three distinct trees $T_A$, $T_B$, and $T_C$, if $T_A < T_B$ and $T_B < T_C$ then $T_A < T_C$.

The details of the proof are left as an exercise for the reader (Exercise 9.10).

Program 9.20 gives an implementation of the **CompareTo** member function for the **BinaryTree** class. This implementation is based on the total order relation $<$ defined in Theorem 9.4. The `CompareTo` function takes as its lone argument a `const` reference to an `Object`. However, normally that object will be another `BinaryTree` instance. Therefore, the `dynamic_cast` on line 4 is normally successful.

The `CompareTo` function compares the two binary trees `*this` and `arg`. If they are both empty trees, `CompareTo` returns zero. If `*this` is empty and `arg` is not, `CompareTo` returns −1; if `arg` is empty and `*this` is not, it returns 1.

Otherwise, both trees are non-empty. In this case, `CompareTo` first compares their respective roots. If the roots are equal, then the left subtrees are compared. Then, if the roots and the left subtrees are equal, the right subtrees are compared.

Clearly the worst-case running occurs when comparing identical trees. Suppose there are exactly $n$ nodes in each tree. Then, the running time of the `CompareTo` function is $n\mathcal{T}\langle \mathtt{op==(T\&T\&)}\rangle + O(n)$, where $\mathcal{T}\langle \mathtt{op==(T\&T\&)}\rangle$ is the time needed to compare the objects contained in the nodes of the trees.

### 9.6.8 Applications

Section 6.1.3 shows how a stack can be used to compute the value of a postfix expression such as

$$a\, b \div c\, d - e \times +. \tag{9.8}$$

---

**PROGRAM 9.20**
`BinaryTree` class `CompareTo` member function definition

---

```
1   int BinaryTree::CompareTo (Object const& object) const
2   {
3       BinaryTree const& arg =
4           dynamic_cast<BinaryTree const&> (object);
5       if (IsEmpty ())
6           return arg.IsEmpty () ? 0 : -1;
7       else if (arg.IsEmpty ())
8           return 1;
9       else
10      {
11          int result = Key ().Compare (arg.Key ());
12          if (result == 0)
13              result = Left ().CompareTo (arg.Left ());
14          if (result == 0)
15              result = Right ().CompareTo (arg.Right ());
16          return result;
17      }
18  }
```

---

Suppose instead of evaluating the expression, we are interested in constructing the corresponding expression tree. Once we have an expression tree, we can use the methods described in Section 9.5 to print out the expression in prefix or infix notation. Thus, we have a means for translating expressions from one notation to another.

It turns out that an expression tree can be constructed from the postfix expression relatively easily. The algorithm to do this is a modified version of the algorithm for evaluating the expression. The symbols in the postfix expression are processed from left to right as follows:

1. If the next symbol in the expression is an operand, a tree comprised of a single node labeled with that operand is pushed onto the stack.

2. If the next symbol in the expression is a binary operator, the top two trees in the stack correspond to its operands. Two trees are popped from the stack and a new tree is created which has the operator as its root and the two trees corresponding to the operands as its subtrees. Then the new tree is pushed onto the stack.

After all the symbols of the expression have been processed in this fashion, the stack will contain a single tree which is the desired expression tree. Figure 9.12 illustrates the use of a stack to construct the expression tree from the postfix expression given in Equation 9.8.

### Implementation

Program 9.21 gives the implementation of a routine, **PostfixToInfix**, which translates a postfix expression to an infix expression using the method described above. This routine reads an expression from the standard input file one character at at time. The expression is assumed to be a syntactically valid postfix expression comprised of single-digit numbers, single-letter variables, and the binary operators +, -, *, and /.

Since only binary operators are allowed, the resulting expression tree is a binary tree. Consequently, the class **ExpressionTree** is derived from the class **BinaryTree**.

The main program loop, lines 13–26, reads characters from the input one at a time. If a letter or a digit is found, a new tree with the character as its root is created and pushed onto the stack (line 16). If an operator is found, a new tree is created with the operator as its root (line 19). Next, two trees are popped from the stack and attached to the new tree which is then pushed onto the stack (lines 20–24).

When the **PostfixToInfix** routine encounters the end-of-file, its main loop terminates. The resulting expression tree is popped from the stack, printed, and then deleted. To print the expression, the **PostfixToInfix** routine uses the **InfixVisitor** which is defined in Program 9.22.

The **InfixVisitor** is intended to be used in a depth-first traversal. At each nonterminal node of the expression tree, the depth-first traversal first calls **PreVisit**, which prints a left parenthesis. In between the traversals of the left and right subtrees, the **Visit** function is called, which prints the object contained within the node. Finally, after traversing the right subtree, **PostVisit** prints a right parenthesis. Given the input **ab/cd-e*+**, the program constructs the expression tree as shown in Figure 9.12, and then prints the infix expression

$$(((a)/(b))+(((c)-(d))*(e))).$$

**FIGURE 9.12**
Postfix to infix conversion using a stack of trees.

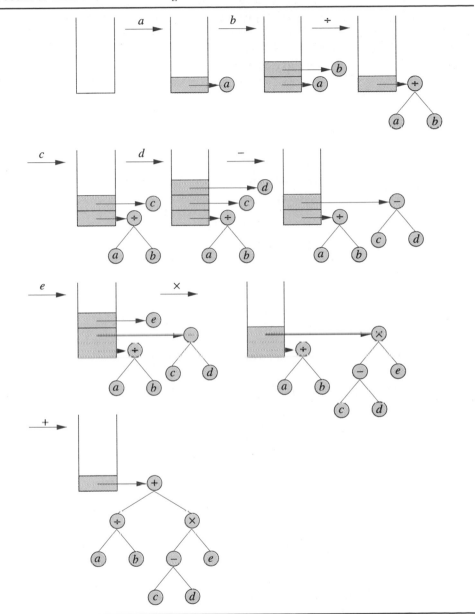

**PROGRAM 9.21**
Binary tree application—postfix to infix conversion

```
1   class ExpressionTree : public BinaryTree
2   {
3   public:
4       ExpressionTree (char c) :
5           BinaryTree (*new Char (c)) {}
6   };
7
8   void PostfixToInfix ()
9   {
10      char c;
11      Stack& stack = *new StackAsLinkedList ();
12
13      while (cin >> c, !cin.eof ())
14      {
15          if (std::isdigit (c) || std::isalpha (c))
16              stack.Push (*new ExpressionTree (c));
17          else if (c == '+' || c == '-' || c == '*' || c == '/')
18          {
19              ExpressionTree& result = *new ExpressionTree (c);
20              result.AttachRight (
21                  dynamic_cast<ExpressionTree&> (stack.Pop ()));
22              result.AttachLeft (
23                  dynamic_cast<ExpressionTree&> (stack.Pop ()));
24              stack.Push (result);
25          }
26      }
27      ExpressionTree& result =
28          dynamic_cast<ExpressionTree&> (stack.Pop ());
29      InfixVisitor visitor;
30      result.DepthFirstTraversal (visitor);
31      delete &result;
32      delete &stack;
33  }
```

The running time of the **PostfixToInfix** routine depends on the number of symbols in the input. The running time for one iteration of the main loop is $O(1)$. Therefore, the time required to construct the expression tree given $n$ input symbols is $O(n)$. The **DepthFirstTraversal** routine visits each node of the expression tree exactly once, and a constant amount of work is required to print a node. As a result, printing the infix expression is also $O(n)$ where $n$ is the number of input symbols.

The output expression contains all of the input symbols plus the parentheses added by the **PutInfix** routine. It can be shown that a valid postfix expression that contains $n$ symbols always has $(n-1)/2$ binary operators and $(n+1)/2$ operands (Exercise 9.9).

**PROGRAM 9.22**
Binary tree application—printing infix expressions

```
1   class InfixVisitor : public PrePostVisitor
2   {
3   public:
4       void PreVisit (Object&)
5           { cout << "("; }
6       void Visit (Object& object)
7           { cout << object; }
8       void PostVisit (Object&)
9           { cout << ")"; }
10  };
```

Hence, the expression tree contains $(n - 1)/2$ nonterminal nodes and since a pair of parentheses is added for each nonterminal node in the expression tree, the output string contains $2n - 1 = O(n)$ symbols altogether. Therefore, the overall running time needed to translate a postfix expression comprised of $n$ symbols to an infix expression is $O(n)$.

# Exercises

**9.1**  For each tree shown in Figure 9.13 show the order in which the nodes are visited during the following tree traversals:

**a.**  preorder traversal,

**b.**  inorder traversal (if defined),

**c.**  postorder traversal, and

**d.**  breadth-first traversal.

**9.2**  Write a visitor that prints the nodes of a general tree in the format of Equation 9.1.

**FIGURE 9.13**
Sample trees for Exercise 9.1.

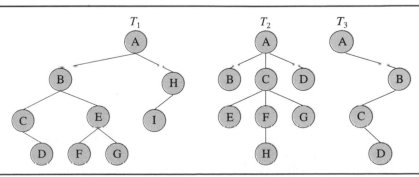

**9.3** Derive an expression for the total space needed to represent a tree of $n$ internal nodes using each of the following classes:

a.  `GeneralTree` defined in Program 9.9,

b.  `NaryTree` defined in Program 9.12, and

c.  `BinaryTree` defined in Program 9.16.

**9.4** A full node in a binary tree is a node with two non-empty subtrees. Let $l$ be the number of leaf nodes in a binary tree. Show that the number of full nodes is $l - 1$.

**9.5** The generic `DepthFirstTraversal` routine defined in Program 9.2 is a recursive function. Write a nonrecursive depth-first traversal routine that has exactly the same effect as the recursive version.

**9.6** Program 9.22 defines a visitor that prints using *infix* notation the expression represented by an expression tree. Write a visitor that prints the same expression in *prefix* notation with the following format:

$$+(/(a,b),*(-(c,d),e)) \ .$$

**9.7** Repeat Exercise 9.6, but this time write a visitor that the expression in *postfix* notation with the following format:

$$ab/cd-e*+ \ .$$

**9.8** The `InfixVisitor` defined in Program 9.22 prints many redundant parentheses because it does not take into consideration the precedence of the operators. Rewrite the visitor so that it prints

$$a/b+(c-d)*e \ .$$

rather than

$$(((a)/(b))+(((c)-(d))*(e))) \ .$$

**9.9** Consider postfix expressions involving only binary operators. Show that if such an expression contains $n$ symbols, it always has $(n-1)/2$ operators and $(n+1)/2$ operands.

**9.10** Prove Theorem 9.4.

**9.11** Generalize Theorem 9.4 so that it applies to $N$-ary trees.

**9.12** Consider two binary trees, $T_A = \{R_A, T_{AL}, T_{AR}\}$ and $T_B = \{R_B, T_{BL}, T_{BR}\}$, and the relation $\simeq$ given by

$$T_A \simeq T_B \iff \Big(T_A = \varnothing \wedge T_B = \varnothing\Big) \vee$$
$$\Big((T_A \neq \varnothing \wedge T_B \neq \varnothing) \wedge$$
$$((T_{AL} \simeq T_{BL} \wedge T_{AR} \simeq T_{BR}) \vee$$
$$(T_{AL} \simeq T_{BR} \wedge T_{AR} \simeq T_{BL}))\Big).$$

If $T_A \simeq T_B$, the trees are said to be *isomorphic*. Devise an algorithm to test whether two binary trees are isomorphic. What is the running time of your algorithm?

# Programming Projects

**9.1** Devise an algorithm to compute the height of a tree. Write an implementation of your algorithm as the **Height** member function of the abstract class **Tree** declared in Program 9.1.

**9.2** Devise an algorithm to count the number of internal nodes in a tree. Write an implementation of your algorithm as the **Count** member function of the abstract class **Tree** declared in Program 9.1.

**9.3** Devise an algorithm to count the number of leaves in a tree. Write an implementation of your algorithm as a member function of the abstract class **Tree** declared in Program 9.1.

**9.4** Devise an abstract (generic) algorithm to compare trees. (See Exercise 9.11). Write an implementation of your algorithm as the **CompareTo** member function of the abstract class **Tree** declared in Program 9.1.

**9.5** The **Tree::Iter** class defined in Programs 9.6, 9.7, and 9.8 does a *preorder* traversal of a tree.

  **a.** Write an iterator class that does a *postorder* traversal.

  **b.** Write an iterator class that does a *breadth-first* traversal.

  **c.** Write an iterator class that does an *inorder* traversal. (In this case, assume that the tree is a **BinaryTree**.)

**9.6** Complete the **GeneralTree** class declared in Program 9.9 by providing suitable definitions for the following member functions: **IsEmpty**, **IsLeaf**, **Degree**, and **CompareTo**. Write a test program and test your implementation.

**9.7** Complete the **NaryTree** class declared in Program 9.9 by providing suitable definitions for the following member functions: **~NaryTree** (destructor), **Purge**, **IsLeaf**, **Degree**, and **CompareTo**. Write a test program and test your implementation.

**9.8** Complete the **BinaryTree** class declared in Program 9.16 by providing suitable definitions for the following member functions: **IsEmpty**, **IsLeaf**, **Degree**, **Key**, **AttachKey**, **DetachKey**, **Left**, **AttachLeft**, **DetachLeft**, **Right**, **AttachRight**, **DetachRight**, and **Subtree**. Write a test program and test your implementation.

**9.9** Write a visitor that draws a picture of a tree on the screen.

**9.10** Design and implement an algorithm that constructs an expression tree from an *infix* expression such as

$$a/b+(c-d)*e \ .$$

**Hint**: See Project 6.4.

# 10 | Search Trees

In the preceding chapter we consider trees in which the relative positions of the nodes in the tree are unconstrained. In other words, a given item may appear anywhere in the tree. Clearly, this allows us complete flexibility in the kind of tree that we may construct. And depending on the application, this may be precisely what we need. However, if we lose track of an item, in order to find it again it may be necessary to do a complete traversal of the tree (in the worst case).

In this chapter we consider trees that are designed to support efficient search operations. In order to make it easier to search, we constrain the relative positions of the items in the tree. In addition, we show that by constraining the *shape* of the tree as well as the relative positions of the items in the tree, search operations can be made even more efficient.

## 10.1 Basics

A tree which supports efficient search, insertion, and withdrawal operations is called a *search tree*. In this context the tree is used to store a finite set of keys drawn from a totally ordered set of keys $K$. Each node of the tree contains one or more keys, and all the keys in the tree are unique, i.e., no duplicate keys are permitted.

What makes a tree into a search tree is that the keys do not appear in arbitrary nodes of the tree. Instead, there is a *data ordering criterion* which determines where a given key may appear in the tree in relation to the other keys in that tree. The following sections present two related types of search trees, $M$-way search trees and binary search trees.

### 10.1.1   $M$-Way Search Trees

**Definition 10.1 ($M$-way Search Tree)**
*An M-way search tree $T$ is a finite set of keys. Either the set is empty, $T = \emptyset$; or the set consists of $n$ M-way subtrees $T_0, T_1, \ldots, T_{n-1}$ and $n - 1$ keys, $k_1, k_2, \ldots, k_{n-1}$,*

$$T = \{T_0, k_1, T_1, k_2, T_2, \ldots, k_{n-1}, T_{n-1}\},$$

*where* $2 \le n \le M$, *such that the keys and nodes satisfy the following* data ordering properties:

1. *The keys in each node are distinct and ordered, i.e.,* $k_i < k_{i+1}$ *for* $1 \le i \le n - 1$.

2. *All the keys contained in subtree* $T_{i-1}$ *are less than* $k_i$, *i.e.,* $\forall k \in T_{i-1} : k < k_i$ *for* $1 \le i \le n - 1$. *The tree* $T_{i-1}$ *is called the* left subtree *with respect to the key* $k_i$.

3. *All the keys contained in subtree* $T_i$ *are greater than* $k_i$, *i.e.,* $\forall k \in T_i : k > k_i$ *for* $1 \le i \le n - 1$. *The tree* $T_{i+1}$ *is called the* right subtree *with respect to the key* $k_i$.

Figure 10.1 gives an example of an $M$-way search tree for $M = 4$. In this case, each of the non-empty nodes of the tree has between one and three keys and at most four subtrees. All the keys in the tree satisfy the data ordering properties. Specifically, the keys in each node are ordered and for each key in the tree, all the keys in the left subtree with respect to the given key are less than the given key, and all the keys in the right subtree with respect to the given key are larger than the given key. Finally, it is important to note that the topology of the tree is not determined by the particular set of keys it contains.

## 10.1.2   Binary Search Trees

Just as the binary tree is an important category of $N$-ary trees, the *binary search tree* is an important category of $M$-way search trees.

---

**FIGURE 10.1**
An $M$-way search tree.

---

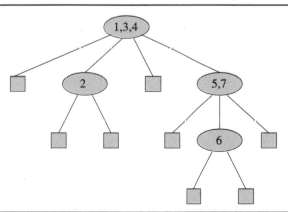

**FIGURE 10.2**
A binary search tree.

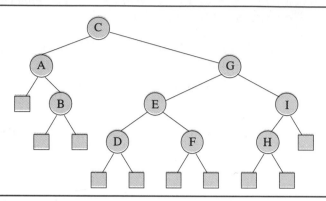

**Definition 10.2 (Binary Search Tree)**
*A binary search tree T is a finite set of keys. Either the set is empty, $T = \emptyset$, or the set consists of a root $r$ and exactly two binary search trees $T_L$ and $T_R$, $T = \{r, T_L, T_R\}$, such that the following properties are satisfied:*

1. *All the keys contained in left subtree, $T_L$, are less than $r$, i.e., $\forall k \in T_L : k < r$.*
2. *All the keys contained in the right subtree, $T_R$, are greater than $r$, i.e., $\forall k \in T_R : k > r$.*

Figure 10.2 shows an example of a binary search tree. In this case, since the nodes of the tree carry alphabetic rather than numeric keys, the ordering of the keys is alphabetic. That is, all the keys in the left subtree of a given node precede alphabetically the root of the that node, and all the keys in the right subtree of a given node follow alphabetically the root of that node. The empty trees are shown explicitly as boxes in Figure 10.2. However, in order to simplify the graphical representation, the empty trees are often omitted from the diagrams.

## 10.2 Searching a Search Tree

The main advantage of a search tree is that the data ordering criterion ensures that it is not necessary to do a complete tree traversal in order to locate a given item. Since search trees are defined recursively, it is easy to define a recursive search method.

### 10.2.1 Searching an *M*-way Tree

Consider the search for a particular item, say *x*, in an *M*-way search tree. The search always begins at the root. If the tree is empty, the search fails. Otherwise, the keys contained in the root node are examined to determine if the object of the search is present. If it is, the search terminates successfully. If it is not, there are three possibilities: Either the object of the search, $x$, is less than $k_1$, in which case subtree $T_0$ is searched; or $x$ is greater than $k_{n-1}$, in which case subtree $T_{n-1}$ is searched; or there exists an $i$ such that $1 \leq i < n - 1$ for which $k_i < x < k_{i+1}$, in which case subtree $T_i$ is searched.

Notice that when $x$ is not found in a given node, only one of the $n$ subtrees of that node is searched. Therefore, a complete tree traversal is not required. A successful search begins at the root and traces a downward path in the tree, which terminates at the node containing the object of the search. Clearly, the running time of a successful search is determined by the *depth* in the tree of object of the search.

When the object of the search is not in the search tree, the search method described above traces a downward path from the root which terminates when an empty subtree is encountered. In the worst case, the search path passes through the deepest leaf node. Therefore, the worst-case running time for an unsuccessful search is determined by the *height* of the search tree.

## 10.2.2 Searching a Binary Tree

The search method described above applies directly to binary search trees. As above, the search begins at the root node of the tree. If the object of the search, $x$, matches the root $r$, the search terminates successfully. If it does not, then if $x$ is less than $r$, the left subtree is searched; otherwise $x$ must be greater than $r$, in which case the right subtree is searched.

Figure 10.3 shows two binary search trees. The tree $T_a$ is an example of a particularly bad search tree because it is not really very tree-like at all. In fact, it is topologically isomorphic with a linear, linked list. In the worst case, a tree which contains $n$ items

---

**FIGURE 10.3**
Examples of search trees.

---

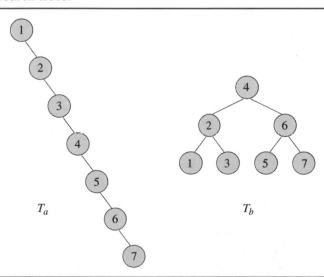

$T_a$

$T_b$

has height $O(n)$. Therefore, in the worst case an unsuccessful search must visit $O(n)$ internal nodes.

On the other hand, tree $T_b$ in Figure 10.3 is an example of a particularly good binary search tree. This tree is an instance of a *perfect binary tree*.

**Definition 10.3 (Perfect Binary Tree)**
*A perfect binary tree of height $h \geq 0$ is a binary tree $T = \{r, T_L, T_R\}$ with the following properties:*

1. *If $h = 0$, then $T_L = \varnothing$ and $T_R = \varnothing$.*
2. *Otherwise, $h > 0$, in which case both $T_L$ and $T_R$ are both perfect binary trees of height $h - 1$.*

It is fairly easy to show that a perfect binary tree of height $h$ has exactly $2^{h+1} - 1$ internal nodes. Conversely, the height of a perfect binary tree with $n$ internal nodes is $\log_2(n + 1) - 1$. If we have a search tree that has the shape of a perfect binary tree, then every unsuccessful search visits exactly $h + 1$ internal nodes. Thus, the worst case for an unsuccessful search in a perfect tree is $O(\log n)$.

## 10.3   Average Case Analysis

### 10.3.1   Successful Search

When a search is successful, exactly $d + 1$ internal nodes are visited, where $d$ is the depth in the tree of object of the search. For example, if the object of the search is at the root which has depth zero, the search visits just one node—the root itself. Similarly, if the object of the search is at depth one, two nodes are visited, and so on. We shall assume that it is equally likely for the object of the search to appear in any node of the search tree. In that case, the *average* number of nodes visited during a successful search is $\bar{d} + 1$, where $\bar{d}$ is the average of the depths of the nodes in a given tree. That is, given a binary search tree with $n > 0$ nodes,

$$\bar{d} = \frac{1}{n} \sum_{i=1}^{n} d_i,$$

where $d_i$ is the depth of the $i$th node of the tree.

The quantity $\sum_{i=1}^{n} d_i$ is called the *internal path length*. The internal path length of a tree is simply the sum of the depths (levels) of all the internal nodes in the tree. Clearly, the average depth of an internal node is equal to the internal path length divided by $n$, the number of nodes in the tree.

Unfortunately, for any given number of nodes $n$, there are many different possible search trees. Furthermore, the internal path lengths of the various possibilities are not equal. Therefore, to compute the average depth of a node in a tree with $n$ nodes, we must consider all possible trees with $n$ nodes. In the absence of any contrary information, we shall assume that all trees having $n$ nodes are equiprobable and then compute the average depth of a node in the average tree containing $n$ nodes.

Let $I(n)$ be the average internal path length of a tree containing $n$ nodes. Consider first the case of $n = 1$. Clearly, there is only one binary tree that contains one node—the tree of height zero. Therefore, $I(1) = 0$.

Now consider an arbitrary tree, $T_n(l)$, having $n \geq 1$ internal nodes altogether, $l$ of which are found in its left subtree, where $0 \leq l < n$. Such a tree consists of a root, the left subtree with $l$ internal nodes, and and a right subtree with $n - l - 1$ internal nodes. The average internal path length for such a tree is the sum of the average internal path length of the left subtree, $I(l)$, plus that of the right subtree, $I(n - l - 1)$, plus $n - 1$ because the nodes in the two subtrees are one level lower in $T_n(l)$.

In order to determine the average internal path length for a tree with $n$ nodes, we must compute the average of the internal path lengths of the trees $T_n(l)$ averaged over all possible sizes, $l$, of the (left) subtree, $0 \leq l < n$.

To do this we consider an ordered set of $n$ distinct keys, $k_0 < k_1 < \cdots < k_{n-1}$. If we select the $l$th key, $k_l$, to be the root of a binary search tree, then there are $l$ keys, $k_0, k_1, \ldots, k_{l-1}$, in its left subtree and $n - l - 1$ keys, $k_{l+1}, k_{l+2}, \ldots, k_{n-1}$ in its right subtree.

If we assume that it is equally likely for any of the $n$ keys to be selected as the root, then all the subtree sizes in the range $0 \leq l < n$ are equally likely. Therefore, the average internal path length for a tree with $n \geq 1$ nodes is

$$I(n) = \frac{1}{n} \sum_{i=0}^{n-1} \Big( I(i) + I(n - i - 1) + n - 1 \Big), \quad n > 1$$

$$= \frac{2}{n} \sum_{i=0}^{n-1} I(i) + n - 1.$$

Thus, in order to determine $I(n)$ we need to solve the recurrence

$$I(n) = \begin{cases} 0 & n = 1, \\ \dfrac{2}{n} \sum_{i=0}^{n-1} I(i) + n - 1 & n > 1. \end{cases} \tag{10.1}$$

To solve this recurrence we consider the case $n > 1$ and then multiply Equation 10.1 by $n$ to get

$$nI(n) = 2 \sum_{i=0}^{n-1} I(i) + n^2 - n. \tag{10.2}$$

Since this equation is valid for any $n > 1$, by substituting $n - 1$ for $n$ we can also write

$$(n - 1)I(n - 1) = 2 \sum_{i=0}^{n-2} I(i) + n^2 - 3n + 2, \tag{10.3}$$

which is valid for $n > 2$. Subtracting Equation 10.3 from Equation 10.2 gives

$$nI(n) - (n - 1)I(n - 1) = 2I(n - 1) + 2n - 2,$$

which can be rewritten as

$$I(n) = \frac{(n + 1)I(n - 1) + 2n - 2}{n}. \tag{10.4}$$

Thus, we have shown that the solution to the recurrence in Equation 10.1 is the same as the solution of the recurrence

$$I(n) = \begin{cases} 0 & n = 1, \\ 1 & n = 2, \\ ((n + 1)I(n - 1) + 2n - 2)/n & n > 2. \end{cases} \tag{10.5}$$

### 10.3.2   Solving the Recurrence—Telescoping

This section presents a technique for solving recurrence relations such as Equation 10.5 called *telescoping*. The basic idea is this: We rewrite the recurrence formula so that a similar functional form appears on both sides of the equal sign. For example, in this case, we consider $n > 2$ and divide both sides of Equation 10.5 by $n + 1$ to get

$$\frac{I(n)}{n + 1} = \frac{I(n - 1)}{n} + \frac{2}{n} - \frac{4}{n(n + 1)}.$$

Since this equation is valid for any $n > 2$, we can write the following series of equations:

$$\frac{I(n)}{n + 1} = \frac{I(n - 1)}{n} + \frac{2}{n} - \frac{4}{n(n + 1)}, \quad n > 2 \tag{10.6}$$

$$\frac{I(n - 1)}{n} = \frac{I(n - 2)}{n - 1} + \frac{2}{n - 1} - \frac{4}{(n - 1)n}, \quad n - 1 > 2$$

$$\frac{I(n - 2)}{n - 1} = \frac{I(n - 3)}{n - 2} + \frac{2}{n - 2} - \frac{4}{(n - 2)(n - 1)}, \quad n - 2 > 2$$

$$\vdots$$

$$\frac{I(n - k)}{n - k + 1} = \frac{I(n - k - 1)}{n - k} + \frac{2}{n - k} - \frac{4}{(n - k)(n - k + 1)}, \quad n - k > 2$$

$$\vdots$$

$$\frac{I(3)}{4} = \frac{I(2)}{3} + \frac{2}{3} - \frac{4}{3 \cdot 4} \tag{10.7}$$

Each subsequent equation in this series is obtained by substituting $n - 1$ for $n$ in the preceding equation. In principle, we repeat this substitution until we get an expression on the right-hand side involving the base case. In this example, we stop at $n - k - 1 = 2$.

Because Equation 10.6 has a similar functional form on both sides of the equal sign, when we add Equation 10.6 through Equation 10.7 together, most of the terms cancel leaving

$$
\begin{aligned}
\frac{I(n)}{n+1} &= \frac{I(2)}{3} + 2\sum_{i=3}^{n}\frac{1}{i} - 4\sum_{i=3}^{n}\frac{1}{i(i+1)}, \quad n > 2 \\
&= 2\sum_{i=1}^{n}\frac{1}{i} - 4\sum_{i=1}^{n}\frac{1}{i(i+1)} \\
&= 2H_n - 4n/(n+1),
\end{aligned}
$$

where $H_n$ is the $n$th *harmonic number.* In Section 2.1.8 it is shown that $H_n \approx \ln n + \gamma$, where $\gamma \approx 0.577\,215$ is called *Euler's constant.* Thus, we get that the average internal path length of the average binary search tree with $n$ internal nodes is

$$
\begin{aligned}
I(n) &= 2(n+1)H_n - 4n \\
&\approx 2(n+1)(\ln n + \gamma) - 4n.
\end{aligned}
$$

Finally, we get to the point: The average depth of a node in the average binary search tree with $n$ nodes is

$$
\begin{aligned}
\bar{d} &= I(n)/n \\
&= 2\left(\frac{n+1}{n}\right)H_n - 4 \\
&\approx 2\left(\frac{n+1}{n}\right)(\ln n + \gamma) - 4 \\
&= O(\log n).
\end{aligned}
$$

### 10.3.3 Unsuccessful Search

All successful searches terminate when the object of the search is found. Therefore, all successful searches terminate at an internal node. In contrast, all unsuccessful searches terminate at an external node. In terms of the binary tree shown in Figure 10.2, a successful search terminates in one of the nodes which is drawn as a circle and an unsuccessful search terminates in one of the boxes.

The preceding analysis shows that the average number of nodes visited during a successful search depends on the *internal path length,* which is simply the sum of the depths of all the internal nodes. Similarly, the average number of nodes visited during an unsuccessful search depends on the *external path length,* which is the sum of the depths of all the external nodes. Fortunately, there is a simple relationship between the internal path length and the external path length of a binary tree.

### Theorem 10.1

*Consider a binary tree T with n internal nodes and an internal path length of I. The external path length of T is given by*

$$E = I + 2n.$$

In other words, Theorem 10.1 says that the *difference* between the internal path length and the external path length of a binary tree with $n$ internal nodes is $E - I = 2n$.

**Proof**    (By induction).

**Base Case**    Consider a binary tree with one internal node and internal path length of zero. Such a tree has exactly two empty subtrees immediately below the root and its external path length is two. Therefore, the theorem holds for $n = 1$.

**Inductive Hypothesis**    Assume that the theorem holds for $n = 1, 2, 3, \ldots, k$ for some $k \geq 1$. Consider an arbitrary tree, $T_k$, that has $k$ internal nodes. According to Theorem 9.1, $T_k$ has $k + 1$ external nodes. Let $I_k$ and $E_k$ be the internal and external path length of $T_k$, respectively, According to the inductive hypothesis, $E_k - I_k = 2k$.

Consider what happens when we create a new tree $T_{k+1}$ by removing an external node from $T_k$ and replacing it with an internal node that has two empty subtrees. Clearly, the resulting tree has $k + 1$ internal nodes. Furthermore, suppose the external node we remove is at depth $d$. Then the internal path length of $T_{k+1}$ is $I_{k+1} = I_k + d$ and the external path length of $T_{k+1}$ is $E_{k+1} = E_k - d + 2(d + 1) = E_k + d + 2$.

The difference between the internal path length and the external path length of $T_{k+1}$ is

$$\begin{aligned}
E_{k+1} - I_{k+1} &= (E_k + d + 2) - (I_k + d) \\
&= E_k - I_k + 2 \\
&= 2(k + 1).
\end{aligned}$$

Therefore, by induction on $k$, the difference between the internal path length and the external path length of a binary tree with $n$ internal nodes is $2n$ for all $n \geq 1$.

---

Since the difference between the internal and external path lengths of any tree with $n$ internal nodes is $2n$, then we can say the same thing about the *average* internal and external path lengths averaged over all search trees. Therefore, $E(n)$, the average external path length of a binary search tree, is given by

$$\begin{aligned}
E(n) &= I(n) + 2n \\
&= 2(n + 1)H_n - 2n \\
&\approx 2(n + 1)(\ln n + \gamma) - 2n.
\end{aligned}$$

A binary search tree with internal $n$ nodes has $n+1$ external nodes. Thus, the average depth of an external node of a binary search tree with $n$ internal nodes, $\bar{e}$, is given by

$$
\begin{aligned}
\bar{e} &= E(n)/(n + 1) \\
&= 2H_n - 2n/(n + 1) \\
&\approx 2(\ln n + \gamma) - 2n/(n + 1) \\
&= O(\log n).
\end{aligned}
$$

These very nice results are the raison d'être for binary search trees. What they say is that the average number of nodes visited during either a successful or an unsuccessful search in the average binary search tree having $n$ nodes is $O(\log n)$. We must remember, however, that these results are premised on the assumption that all possible search trees of $n$ nodes are equiprobable. It is important to be aware that in practice this may not always be the case.

## 10.3.4 Traversing a Search Tree

In Section 9.4, the inorder traversal of a binary tree is defined as follows:

1. Traverse the left subtree, and then
2. visit the root, and then
3. traverse the right subtree.

It should not come as a surprise that when an *inorder traversal* of a binary search tree is done, the nodes of the tree are visited *in order*!

In an inorder traversal the root of the tree is visited after the entire left subtree has been traversed, and in a binary search tree everything in the left subtree is less than the root. Therefore, the root is visited only after all the keys less than the root have been visited.

Similarly, in an inorder traversal the root is visited before the right subtree is traversed and everything in the right subtree is greater than the root. Hence, the root is visited before all the keys greater than the root are visited. Therefore, by induction, the keys in the search tree are visited in order.

Inorder traversal is not defined for arbitrary $N$-ary trees—it is only defined for the case of $N = 2$. Essentially this is because the nodes of $N$-ary trees contain only a single key. On the other hand, if a node of an $M$-way search tree has $n$ subtrees, then it must contain $n - 1$ keys, such that $2 < n \le M$. Therefore, we can define *inorder traversal of an M-way tree* as follows:

To traverse a node of an $M$-way tree having $n$ subtrees,

1. Traverse $T_0$; and then
2. visit $k_1$; and then
3. traverse $T_1$; and then
4. visit $k_2$; and then

**5.** traverse $T_2$; and then

$$\vdots$$

**2n − 2.** visit $k_{n-1}$; and then

**2n − 1.** traverse $T_{n-1}$.

## 10.4 Implementing Search Trees

Since search trees are designed to support efficient searching, it is only appropriate that they be implemented as classes derived from the **SearchableContainer** abstract base class. Recall from Section 5.2.12 that the searchable container interface includes the member functions **Find**, **IsMember**, **Insert**, and **Withdraw**. In addition, because search tree are trees, it makes sense that they be derived from the **Tree** abstract base class as shown in Figure 10.4.

Program 10.1 declares the **SearchTree** abstract base class. The **SearchTree** is derived from the classes **Tree** and **SearchableContainer**. The **Tree** class encapsulates those interface elements which are common to trees and search trees. The common member functions include **Key**, **Subtree**, **IsEmpty**, **IsLeaf**, **Height**, and **Degree**, as well as all of the various traversal routines (see Section 9.6).

In addition, two more member functions are defined—**FindMin** and **FindMax**. These functions are accessors. The function **FindMin** returns a reference to the object contained in the search tree having the smallest key. Similarly, the function **FindMax** returns a reference to the contained object having the largest key.

### 10.4.1 Binary Search Trees

The class **BST** declared in Program 10.2 represents binary search trees. Since binary trees and binary search trees are topologically similar, the **BST** class is derived from the **BinaryTree** class given in Section 9.6.5. In addition, because it represents search trees, the **BST** class is also derived from the **SearchTree** class.

As shown in Program 10.2, the **BST** class inherits much of its functionality from the **BinaryTree** base class. However, several functions are overridden, including **AttachKey**, **DetachKey**, **Left**, and **Right**. In addition a new function, **Balance**,

---

**FIGURE 10.4**
Object class hierarchy.

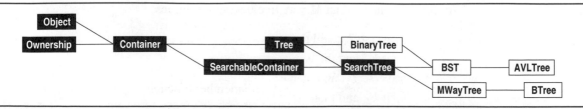

---

**PROGRAM 10.1**
SearchTree class definition

---

```
1   class SearchTree :
2       public virtual Tree, public virtual SearchableContainer
3   {
4   public:
5       virtual Object& FindMin () const = 0;
6       virtual Object& FindMax () const = 0;
7   };
```

---

---

**PROGRAM 10.2**
BST class definition

---

```
1    class BST : public BinaryTree, public SearchTree
2    {
3    protected:
4        virtual void AttachKey (Object&);
5        virtual Object& DetachKey ();
6        virtual void Balance ();
7    public:
8        BST& Left () const;
9        BST& Right () const;
10       // ...
11   };
```

---

has been added to the **protected** interface. The purpose of this function is to support the **AVL** class discussed in Section 10.5.

## Member Variables

The **BST** class inherits the three member variables **key**, **left**, and **right** for the **BinaryTree** class. All three of them are pointers. The first is a pointer to an **Object** instance, and the latter two are pointers to **BinaryTree** instances. All three pointers are zero if the node represents the empty tree. Otherwise, the tree must have a root and two subtrees. Therefore, all three pointers are nonzero in an internal node.

Program 10.3 defines the two member functions **Left** and **Right** which return the left and right subtrees, respectively, of a given binary search tree. Since the implementation extends the **BinaryTree** class, the **left** and **right** member variables are declared as pointers to **BinaryTree**s. However, in a binary search tree, the subtrees will be instances of the **BST** class. Therefore, these functions make use of the **dynamic_cast** operator to return a reference of the correct type.

## Find Member Function

Program 10.4 gives the code for the **Find** member function of the **BST** class. The **Find** function takes as its lone argument a **const** reference to an **Object** instance. The

---

**PROGRAM 10.3**
BST class `Left` and `Right` member function definitions

---

```
1   BST& BST::Left () const
2       { return dynamic_cast<BST&> (BinaryTree::Left ()); }
3
4   BST& BST::Right () const
5       { return dynamic_cast<BST&> (BinaryTree::Right ()); }
```

---

purpose of the routine is to search the tree for an object which matches the argument. If a match is found, **Find** returns a reference to the matching object. Otherwise, **Find** returns `NullObject::Instance()`.

The recursive **Find** member function starts its search at the root and descends one level in the tree for each recursive call. At each level at most one object comparison is made (line 5). The worst-case running time for a search is

$$n\mathcal{T}\langle \texttt{T::Compare(T\&,T\&)}\rangle + O(n),$$

where $\mathcal{T}\langle \texttt{T::Compare(T\&,T\&)}\rangle$ is the time to compare two objects and $n$ is the number of internal nodes in the tree. The same asymptotic running time applies for both successful and unsuccessful searches.

The average running time for a successful search is $(\bar{d} + 1)\mathcal{T}\langle \texttt{T::Compare(T\&,T\&)}\rangle + O(\bar{d})$, where $\bar{d} = 2(n + 1)H_n/n - 4$ is the average depth of an internal node in a binary search tree. If $\mathcal{T}\langle \texttt{T::Compare(T\&,T\&)}\rangle = O(1)$, the average time of a successful search is $O(\log n)$.

The average running time for an unsuccessful search is $\bar{e}\mathcal{T}\langle \texttt{T::Compare(T\&,T\&)}\rangle + O(\bar{e})$, where $\bar{e} = 2H_n - 4n/(n + 1)$ is the average depth of an external node in a binary search tree. If $\mathcal{T}\langle \texttt{T::Compare(T\&,T\&)}\rangle = O(1)$, the average time of an unsuccessful search is $O(\log n)$.

### FindMin Member Function

Program 10.4 also shows a recursive implementation of the **FindMin** member function of the **BST** class. It follows directly from the data ordering property of search trees that to find the node containing the smallest key in the tree, we start at the root and follow the chain of left subtrees until we get to the node that has an empty left subtree. The key in that node is the smallest in the tree. Notice that no object comparisons are necessary to identify the smallest key in the tree.

The running time analysis of the **FindMin** routine follows directly from that of the **Find** function. The worst-case running time of **FindMin** is $O(n)$ and the average running time is $O(\log n)$, where $n$ is the number of internal nodes in the tree.

## 10.4.2   Inserting Items in a Binary Search Tree

The simplest way to insert an item into a binary search tree is to pretend that the item is already in the tree and then follow the path taken by the **Find** routine to determine

---

**PROGRAM 10.4**
BST class `Find` and `FindMin` member function definitions

```
1   Object& BST::Find (Object const& object) const
2   {
3       if (IsEmpty ())
4           return NullObject::Instance ();
5       int const diff = object.Compare (*key);
6       if (diff == 0)
7           return *key;
8       else if (diff < 0)
9           return Left ().Find (object);
10      else
11          return Right ().Find (object);
12  }
13
14  Object& BST::FindMin () const
15  {
16      if (IsEmpty ())
17          return NullObject::Instance ();
18      else if (Left ().IsEmpty ())
19          return *key;
20      else
21          return Left ().FindMin();
22  }
```

---

where the item would be. Assuming that the item is not already in the tree, the search will be unsuccessful and will terminate an external, empty node. That is precisely where the item to be inserted is placed!

### `Insert` and `AttachKey` Member Functions

The `Insert` member function of the `BST` class is defined in Program 10.6. This function takes as its lone argument a reference to the object instance which is to be inserted into the binary search tree. It is assumed in this implementation that duplicate keys are not permitted. That is, all of the keys contained in the tree are unique.

The `Insert` routine behaves like the `Find` routine until it arrives at an external, empty node. Once the empty node has been found, it is transformed into an internal node by calling the `AttachKey` function. `AttachKey` works as follows: A pointer to the object being inserted is saved in the `key` member variable, and two new empty binary trees are attached to the node.

Notice that after the insertion is done, the function `Balance` is called. However, as shown in Program 10.5, the `BST::Balance` function does nothing. Section 10.5 describes the class `AVLTree` which is derived from the `BST` class and which inherits the `Insert` function but overrides the `Balance` operation.

---

**PROGRAM 10.5**
BST class `Insert`, `AttachKey`, and `Balance` member function definitions

```
1    void BST::Insert (Object& object)
2    {
3        if (IsEmpty ())
4            AttachKey (object);
5        else
6        {
7            int const diff = object.Compare (*key);
8            if (diff == 0)
9                throw invalid_argument ("duplicate key");
10           if (diff < 0)
11               Left ().Insert (object);
12           else
13               Right ().Insert (object);
14       }
15       Balance ();
16   }
17
18   void BST::AttachKey (Object& object)
19   {
20       if (!IsEmpty ())
21           throw domain_error ("invalid operation");
22       key = &object;
23       left = new BST ();
24       right = new BST ();
25   }
26
27   void BST::Balance ()
28       {}
```

---

The asymptotic running time of the **Insert** member function is the same as that of **Find** for an unsuccessful search. That is, in the worst case the running time is $n\mathcal{T}\langle\text{T::Compare(T\&,T\&)}\rangle + O(n)$ and the average case running time is

$$\bar{e}\mathcal{T}\langle\text{T::Compare(T\&,T\&)}\rangle + O(\bar{e}),$$

where $\bar{e} = 2H_n - 2n/(n + 1)$ is the average depth of an external node in a binary search tree with $n$ internal nodes. When $\mathcal{T}\langle\text{T::Compare(T\&,T\&)}\rangle = O(1)$, the worst-case running time is $O(n)$, and the average case is $O(\log n)$.

## 10.4.3 Removing Items from a Binary Search Tree

When removing an item from a search tree, it is imperative that the tree which remains satisfies the data ordering criterion. If the item to be removed is in a leaf node, then it is fairly easy to remove that item from the tree since doing so does not disturb the relative order of any of the other items in the tree.

For example, consider the binary search tree shown in Figure 10.5(a). Suppose we wish to remove the node labeled 4. Since node 4 is a leaf, its subtrees are empty. When we remove it from the tree, the tree remains a valid search tree, as shown in Figure 10.5(b).

To remove a non-leaf node, we move it down in the tree until it becomes a leaf node since a leaf node is easily deleted. To move a node down we swap it with another node which is further down in the tree. For example, consider the search tree shown in Figure 10.6(a). Node 1 is not a leaf since it has an empty left subtree but a non-empty right subtree. To remove node 1, we swap it with the smallest key in its right subtree, which in this case is node 2, Figure 10.6(b). Since node 1 is now a leaf, it is easily deleted. Notice that the resulting tree remains a valid search tree, as shown in Figure 10.6(c).

To move a non-leaf node down in the tree, we either swap it with the smallest key in the right subtree or with the largest one in the left subtree. At least one such swap is always possible, since the node is a non-leaf and therefore at least one of its subtrees is

**FIGURE 10.5**
Removing a leaf node from a binary search tree.

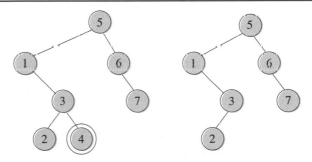

**FIGURE 10.6**
Removing a non-leaf node from a binary search tree.

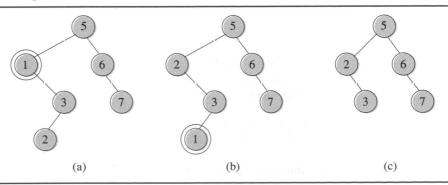

(a)                    (b)                    (c)

**PROGRAM 10.6**
BST class `Withdraw` and `DetachKey` member function definitions

```
1   void BST::Withdraw (Object& object)
2   {
3       if (IsEmpty ())
4           throw invalid_argument ("object not found");
5       int const diff = object.Compare (*key);
6       if (diff == 0)
7       {
8           if (!Left ().IsEmpty ())
9           {
10              Object& max = Left ().FindMax ();
11              key = &max;
12              Left ().Withdraw (max);
13          }
14            else if (!Right ().IsEmpty ())
15          {
16              Object& min = Right ().FindMin ();
17              key = &min;
18              Right ().Withdraw (min);
19          }
20          else
21              DetachKey ();
22      }
23      else if (diff < 0)
24          Left ().Withdraw (object);
25      else
26          Right ().Withdraw (object);
27      Balance ();
28  }
29
30  Object& BST::DetachKey ()
31  {
32      if (!IsLeaf ())
33          throw domain_error ("invalid operation");
34      Object& result = *key;
35      delete left;
36      delete right;
37      key = 0;
38      left = 0;
39      right = 0;
40      return result;
41  }
```

non-empty. If after the swap, the node to be deleted is not a leaf, then we push it further down the tree with yet another swap. Eventually, the node must reach the bottom of the tree where it can be deleted.

### `Withdraw` and `DetachKey` Member Functions

Program 10.6 gives the code for the `Withdraw` and `DetachKey` member functions of the `BST` class. The `Withdraw` function takes as its lone argument a reference to the `Object` instance to be removed from the tree. The algorithm first determines the location of the object to be removed and then removes it according to the method described above.

## 10.5 AVL Search Trees

The problem with binary search trees is that while the average running times for search, insertion, and withdrawal operations are all $O(\log n)$, any one operation is still $O(n)$ in the worst case. This is so because we cannot say anything in general about the shape of the tree.

For example, consider the two binary search trees shown Figure 10.3. Both trees contain the same set of keys. The tree $T_a$ is obtained by starting with an empty tree and inserting the keys in the following order

$$1, 2, 3, 4, 5, 6, 7.$$

The tree $T_b$ is obtained by starting with an empty tree and inserting the keys in this order

$$4, 2, 6, 1, 3, 5, 7.$$

Clearly, $T_b$ is a better tree search tree than $T_a$. In fact, since $T_b$ is a *perfect binary tree*, its height is $\log_2(n + 1) - 1$. Therefore, all three operations, search, insertion, and withdrawal, have the same worst case asymptotic running time, $O(\log n)$.

The reason that $T_b$ is better than $T_a$ is that it is the more *balanced* tree. If we could ensure that the search trees we construct are balanced then the worst-case running time of search, insertion, and withdrawal could be made logarithmic rather than linear. But under what conditions is a tree *balanced*?

If we say that a binary tree is balanced if the left and right subtrees of every node have the same height, then the only trees which are balanced are the perfect binary trees. A perfect binary tree of height $h$ has exactly $2^{h+1} - 1$ internal nodes. Therefore, it is only possible to create perfect trees with $n$ nodes for $n = 1, 3, 7, 15, 31, 63, \ldots$. Clearly, this is an unsuitable balance condition because it is not possible to create a balanced tree for every $n$.

What are the characteristics of a good *balance condition*?

1. A good balance condition ensures that the height of a tree with $n$ nodes is $O(\log n)$.

2. A good balance condition can be maintained efficiently. That is, <u>the additional work necessary to balance the tree</u> when an item is inserted or deleted is <u>$O(1)$.</u>

Adelson-Velskii and Landis[1] were the first to propose the following balance condition and show that it has the desired characteristics.

### Definition 10.4 (AVL Balance Condition)
*An empty binary tree is* AVL balanced. *A non-empty binary tree, $T = \{r, T_L, T_R\}$, is* AVL balanced *if both $T_L$ and $T_R$ are AVL balanced and*

$$|h_L - h_R| \leq 1,$$

*where $h_L$ is the height of $T_L$ and $h_R$ is the height of $T_R$.*

Clearly, all perfect binary trees are AVL balanced. What is not so clear is that heights of all trees that satisfy the AVL balance condition are logarithmic in the number of internal nodes.

### Theorem 10.2
*The height, h, of an AVL balanced tree with n internal nodes satisfies*

$$\log_2(n + 1) < h \leq 1.440 \log(n + 2) - 0.328.$$

**Proof**    The lower bound follows directly from Theorem 9.2. It is in fact true for all binary trees regardless of whether they are AVL balanced.

To determine the upper bound, we turn the problem around and ask the question, what is the minimum number of internal nodes in an AVL balanced tree of height $h$?

Let $T_h$ represent an AVL balanced tree of height $h$ which has the smallest possible number of internal nodes, say $N_h$. Clearly, $T_h$ must have at least one subtree of height $h - 1$, and that subtree must be $T_{h-1}$. To remain AVL balanced, the other subtree can have height $h - 1$ or $h - 2$. Since we want the smallest number of internal nodes, it must be $T_{h-2}$. Therefore, the number of internal nodes in $T_h$ is $N_h = N_{h-1} + N_{h-2} + 1$, where $h \geq 2$.

Clearly, $T_0$ contains a single internal node, so $N_0 = 1$. Similarly, $T_1$ contains exactly two nodes, so $N_1 = 2$. Thus, $N_h$ is given by the recurrence

$$N_h = \begin{cases} 1 & h = 0, \\ 2 & h = 1, \\ N_{h-1} + N_{h-2} + 1 & h \geq 2. \end{cases} \tag{10.8}$$

The remarkable thing about Equation 10.8 is its similarity with the definition of *Fibonacci numbers* (Equation 3.4). In fact, it can easily be shown by induction that

$$N_h \geq F_{h+2} - 1$$

---

[1]Russian mathematicians G. M. Adel'son-Vel'skiǐ and E. M. Landis published this result in 1962.

for all $h \geq 0$, where $F_k$ is the $k$th Fibonacci number.

**Base Cases**

$$N_0 = 1, \quad F_2 = 1 \Rightarrow \quad N_0 \geq F_2 - 1,$$
$$N_1 = 2, \quad F_3 = 2 \Rightarrow \quad N_1 \geq F_3 - 1.$$

**Inductive Hypothesis**  Assume that $N_h \geq F_{h+2} - 1$ for $h = 0, 1, 2, \ldots, k$. Then

$$
\begin{aligned}
N_{h+1} &= N_h + N_{h-1} + 1 \\
&\geq F_{h+2} - 1 + F_{h+1} - 1 + 1 \\
&\geq F_{h+3} - 1 \\
&\geq F_{(h+1)+2} - 1.
\end{aligned}
$$

Therefore, by induction on $k$, $N_h \geq F_{h+2} - 1$, for all $h \geq 0$.

According to Theorem 3.9, the Fibonacci numbers are given by

$$F_n = \frac{1}{\sqrt{5}}(\phi^n - \hat{\phi}^n),$$

where $\phi = (1 + \sqrt{5})/2$ and $\hat{\phi} = (1 - \sqrt{5})/2$. Furthermore, since $\hat{\phi} \approx -0.618$, $|\hat{\phi}^n/\sqrt{5}| < 1$.

Therefore,

$$
\begin{aligned}
N_h \geq F_{h+2} - 1 &\Rightarrow N_h \geq \phi^{h+2}/\sqrt{5} - 2 \\
&\Rightarrow \sqrt{5}(N_h + 2) \geq \phi^{h+2} \\
&\Rightarrow \log_\phi(\sqrt{5}(N_h + 2)) \geq h + 2 \\
&\Rightarrow h \leq \log_\phi(N_h + 2) + \log_\phi \sqrt{5} - 2 \\
&\Rightarrow h \leq 1.440 \log_2(N_h + 2) - 0.328
\end{aligned}
$$

This completes the proof of the upper bound.

---

So, we have shown that the AVL balance condition satisfies the first criterion of a good balance condition—the height of an AVL balanced tree with $n$ internal nodes is $\Theta(\log n)$. What remains to be shown is that the balance condition can be efficiently maintained. To see that it can, we need to look at an implementation.

## 10.5.1 Implementing AVL Trees

Having already implemented a binary search tree class, **BST**, we can make use of much of the existing code to implement an AVL tree class. Program 10.7 gives the declaration of the **AVLTree** class which is derived from the class **BST**. The **AVLTree** class inherits

---

**PROGRAM 10.7**
AVLTree class definition

```
1   class AVLTree : public BST
2   {
3   protected:
4       int height;
5
6       int BalanceFactor () const;
7       void AdjustHeight ();
8       void LLRotation ();
9       void LRRotation ();
10      void RRRotation ();
11      void RLRotation ();
12      void AttachKey (Object&);
13      Object& DetachKey ();
14      void Balance ();
15  public:
16      AVLTree ();
17
18      int Height () const;
19      AVLTree& Left () const;
20      AVLTree& Right () const;
21  };
```

---

most of its functionality from the binary tree class. In particular, it uses the inherited **Insert** and **Withdraw** functions! In addition, the inherited **Balance**, **AttachKey**, and **DetachKey** member functions are overridden and a number of new member functions are declared.

Program 10.7 indicates that the **Height** member function is redefined for the **AVLTree** class. This turns out to be necessary because we need to be able to determine quickly, i.e., in $O(1)$ time, that the AVL balance condition is satisfied at a given node in the tree. In general, the running time required to compute the height of a tree containing $n$ nodes is $O(n)$. Therefore, to determine whether the AVL balance condition is satisfied at a given node, it is necessary to traverse completely the subtrees of the given node. But this cannot be done in constant time.

To make it possible to verify the AVL balance condition in constant time, the member variable **height** has been added. Thus, every node in an **AVLTree** keeps track of its own height. In this way it is possible for the **Height** member function to run in constant time—all it needs to do is to return the value of the **height** member variable. And this makes it possible to test whether the AVL balanced condition is satisfied at a given node in constant time.

### Constructor

The default constructor for the **AVLTree** class is shown in Program 10.8. The default constructor creates an empty AVL tree. It does this by calling the default constructor

---

**PROGRAM 10.8**
`AVLTree` class constructor, `Height`, `AdjustHeight`, and `BalanceFactor`
member function definitions

---

```
1   AVLTree::AVLTree () :
2       BST (),
3       height (-1)
4       {}
5
6   int AVLTree::Height () const
7       { return height; }
8
9   void AVLTree::AdjustHeight ()
10  {
11      if (IsEmpty ())
12          height = -1;
13      else
14          height = Max (left->Height (), right->Height ()) + 1;
15  }
16
17  int AVLTree::BalanceFactor () const
18  {
19      if (IsEmpty ())
20          return 0;
21      else
22          return left->Height () - right->Height ();
23  }
```

---

of the `BST` class. The `height` field is set to the value $-1$, which is consistent with the
empty tree. Notice that according to Definition 10.4, the empty tree is AVL balanced.
Therefore, the result is a valid AVL tree. Clearly, the running time of the constructor is
$O(1)$.

### Height, AdjustHeight, and BalanceFactor Member Functions

The `Height` member function is implemented as an `AVLTree` member variable accessor that simply returns the value of the `height` member variable. Clearly the running
time of this function is constant.

The purpose of `AdjustHeight` is to recompute the height of a node and to update
the `height` member variable. This routine must be called whenever the height of one
of the subtrees changes in order to ensure that the `height` variable is always up to
date. The `AdjustHeight` routine determines the height of a node by adding one to
the height of the highest subtree. Since the running time of the `Height` function is
constant, so too is the running time of `AdjustHeight`.

The `BalanceFactor` member function simply returns the difference between the
heights of the left and right subtrees of a given AVL tree. By Definition 10.4, the empty
node is AVL balanced. Therefore, the `BalanceFactor` returns zero for an empty tree.

Again, since the running time of the `Height` function is constant, the running time of `BalanceFactor` is also constant.

## 10.5.2 Inserting Items into an AVL Tree

Inserting an item into an AVL tree is a two-part process. First, the item is inserted into the tree using the usual method for insertion in binary search trees. After the item has been inserted, it is necessary to check that the resulting tree is still AVL balanced and to balance the tree when it is not.

Just as in a regular binary search tree, items are inserted into AVL trees by attaching them to the leaves. To find the correct leaf we pretend that the item is already in the tree and follow the path taken by the `Find` routine to determine where the item should go. Assuming that the item is not already in the tree, the search is unsuccessful and terminates an an external, empty node. The item to be inserted is placed in that external node.

Inserting an item in a given external node affects potentially the heights of all of the nodes along the *access path*, i.e., the path from the root to that node. Of course, when an item is inserted in a tree, the height of the tree may increase by 1. Therefore, to ensure that the resulting tree is still AVL balanced, the heights of all the nodes along the access path must be recomputed and the AVL balance condition must be checked.

Sometimes increasing the height of a subtree does not violate the AVL balance condition. For example, consider an AVL tree $T = \{r, T_L, T_R\}$. Let $h_L$ and $h_R$ be the heights of $T_L$ and $T_R$, respectively. Since $T$ is an AVL tree, then $|h_L - h_R| \leq 1$. Now, suppose that $h_L = h_R + 1$. Then, if we insert an item into $T_R$, its height may increase by 1 to $h'_R = h_R + 1$. The resulting tree is still AVL balanced since $h_L - h'_R = 0$. In fact, this particular insertion actually makes the tree more balanced! Similarly if $h_L = h_R$ initially, an insertion in either subtree will not result in a violation of the balance condition at the root of $T$.

On the other hand, if $h_L = h_R + 1$ and the insertion of an item into the left subtree $T_L$ increases the height of that tree to $h'_L = h_L + 1$, the AVL balance condition is no longer satisfied because $h'_L - h_R = 2$. Therefore it is necessary to change the structure of the tree to bring it back into balance.

### Balancing AVL Trees
When an AVL tree becomes unbalanced, it is possible to bring it back into balance by performing an operation called a *rotation*. It turns out that there are only four cases to consider and each case has its own rotation.

### Single Rotations
Figure 10.7(a) shows an AVL balanced tree. For example, the balance factor for node $A$ is zero, since its left and right subtrees have the same height; and the balance factor of node $B$ is $+1$, since its left subtree has height $h + 1$ and its right subtree has height $h$.

Suppose we insert an item into $A_L$, the left subtree of $A$. The height of $A_L$ can either increase or remain the same. In this case we assume that it increases. Then, as

**FIGURE 10.7**
Balancing an AVL tree with a single (LL) rotation.

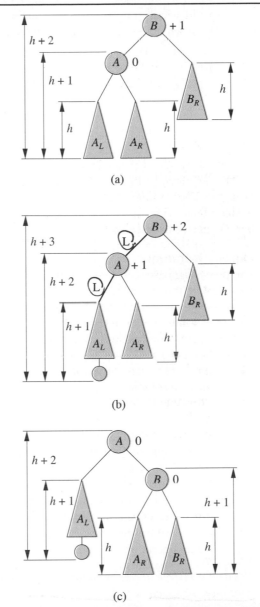

(a)

(b)

(c)

shown in Figure 10.7(b), the resulting tree is no longer AVL balanced. Notice where the imbalance has been manifested— node $A$ is balanced but node $B$ is not.

Balance can be restored by reorganizing the two nodes $A$ and $B$, and the three subtrees, $A_L$, $A_R$, and $B_R$, as shown in Figure 10.7(c). This is called an _LL rotation_, because the first two edges in the insertion path from node $B$ both go to the left.

There are three important properties of the LL rotation:

1. The rotation does not destroy the data ordering property so the result is still a valid search tree. Subtree $A_L$ remains to the left of node $A$, subtree $A_R$ remains between nodes $A$ and $B$, and subtree $B_R$ remains to the right of node $B$.

2. After the rotation both $A$ and $B$ are AVL balanced. Both nodes $A$ and $B$ end up with zero balance factors.

3. After the rotation, the tree has the same height it had originally. Inserting the item did not increase the overall height of the tree!

Notice, the LL rotation was called for because the root became unbalanced with a positive balance factor (i.e., its left subtree was too high) and the left subtree of the root also had a positive balance factor.

Not surprisingly, the left-right mirror image of the LL rotation is called an *RR rotation*. An RR rotation is called for when the root becomes unbalanced with a negative balance factor (i.e., its right subtree is too high) and the right subtree of the root also has a negative balance factor.

### Double Rotations

The preceding cases have dealt with access paths LL and RR. Clearly two more cases remain to be implemented. Consider the case where the root becomes unbalanced with a positive balance factor but the left subtree of the root has a negative balance factor. This situation is shown in Figure 10.8(*b*).

The tree can be restored by performing an RR rotation at node $A$, followed by an LL rotation at node $C$. The tree which results is shown in Figure 10.8(*c*). The LL and RR rotations are called *single rotations*. The combination of the two single rotations is called a *double rotation* and is given the name *LR rotation* because the first two edges in the insertion path from node $C$ both go left and then right.

Obviously, the left-right mirror image of the LR rotation is called an *RL rotation*. An RL rotation is called for when the root becomes unbalanced with a negative balance factor but the right subtree of the root has a positive balance factor. Double rotations have the same properties as the single rotations: The resulting tree is AVL-balanced and its height is the same as that of the initial tree.

Clearly the four rotations, LL, RR, LR, and RL, cover all the ways in which any one node can become unbalanced. But how many rotations are required to balance a tree when an insertion is done? The following theorem addresses this question:

### Theorem 10.3

*When an AVL tree becomes unbalanced after an insertion, exactly one single or double rotation is required to balance the tree.*

**Proof** When an item, $x$, is inserted into an AVL tree, $T$, that item is placed in an external node of the tree. The only nodes in $T$ whose heights may be affected by the insertion of $x$ are those nodes which lie on the access path from the root of $T$ to $x$. Therefore, the only nodes at which an imbalance can appear are those along the access path. Furthermore, when a node is inserted into a tree, either the height of the tree remains the same or the height of the tree increases by 1.

**FIGURE 10.8**
Balancing an AVL tree with a double (LR) rotation.

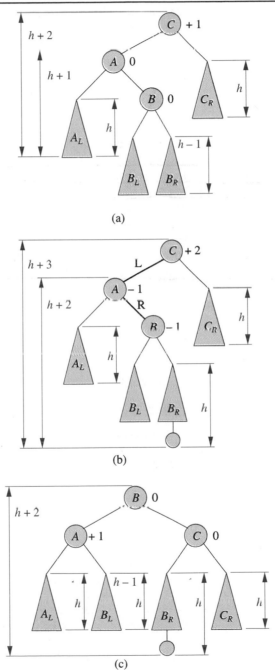

(a)

(b)

(c)

Consider some node $c$ along the access path from the root of $T$ to $x$. When $x$ is inserted, the height of $c$ either increases by 1, or remains the same. If the height of $c$ does not change, then no rotation is necessary at $c$ or at any node above $c$ in the access path.

If the height of $c$ increases then there are two possibilities: Either $c$ remains balanced or an imbalance appears at $c$. If $c$ remains balanced, then no rotation is necessary at $c$. However, a rotation may be needed somewhere above $c$ along the access path.

On the other hand, if $c$ becomes unbalanced, then a single or a double rotation must be performed at $c$. After the rotation is done, the height of $c$ is the same as it was before the insertion. Therefore, no further rotation is needed above $c$ in the access path.

Theorem 10.3 suggests the following method for balancing an AVL tree after an insertion: Begin at the node containing the item which was just inserted and move back along the access path toward the root. For each node determine its height and check the balance condition. If the height of the current node does not increase, then the tree is AVL balanced and no further nodes need be considered. If the node has become unbalanced, a rotation is needed to balance it. After the rotation, the height of the node remains unchanged, the tree is AVL balanced, and no further nodes need be considered. Otherwise, the height of the node increases by 1, but no rotation is needed and we proceed to the next node on the access path.

### Implementation

Program 10.9 gives the code for the **LLRotation** procedure of the **AVLTree** class. This code implements the LL rotation shown in Figure 10.7. The purpose of the

**PROGRAM 10.9**
AVLTree class **LLRotation** member function definition

```
1   void AVLTree::LLRotation ()
2   {
3       if (IsEmpty ())
4           throw domain_error ("invalid rotation");
5       BinaryTree* const tmp = right;
6       right = left;
7       left = Right ().left;
8       Right ().left = Right ().right;
9       Right ().right = tmp;
10
11      Object* const tmpObj = key;
12      key = Right ().key;
13      Right ().key = tmpObj;
14
15      Right ().AdjustHeight ();
16      AdjustHeight ();
17  }
```

**PROGRAM 10.10**
`AVLTree` class `LRRotation` member function definition

```
1   void AVLTree::LRRotation ()
2   {
3       if (IsEmpty ())
4           throw domain_error ("invalid rotation");
5       Left ().RRRotation ();
6       LLRotation ();
7   }
```

`LLRotation` member function is to perform an LL rotation at the root of a given AVL tree instance.

The rotation is simply a sequence of pointer manipulations followed by two height adjustments. Notice the rotation is done in such a way that the the given `AVLTree` instance remains the root of the tree. This is done so that if the tree has a parent, it is not necessary to modify the contents of the parent.

The `AVLTree` class also requires an `RRRotation` member function to implement an RR rotation. The implementation of that function follows directly from Program 10.9. Clearly, the running time for the single rotations is $O(1)$.

Program 10.10 gives the implementation for the `LRRotation` member function of the `AVLTree` class. This double rotation is trivially implemented as a sequence of two single rotations. As above, the routine for the complementary rotation is easily derived from the given code. The running time for each of the double rotation functions is also $O(1)$.

When an imbalance is detected, it is necessary to correct the imbalance by doing the appropriate rotation. The code given in Program 10.11 takes care of this. The `Balance` routine tests for an imbalance by calling the `BalanceFactor` function. The balance test itself takes constant time. If the node is balanced, only a constant-time height adjustment is needed.

Otherwise, the `Balance` routine of the `AVLTree` class determines which of the four cases has occurred and invokes the appropriate rotation to correct the imbalance. To determine which case has occurred, the `Balance` routine calls the `BalanceFactor` function two more times. Therefore, the time for selecting the case is constant. In all, only one rotation is done to correct the imbalance. Therefore, the running time of this routine is $O(1)$.

The `Insert` routine for AVL trees is inherited from the `BST` class (see Program 10.5). The very last thing that routine does is call the `Balance` function which has been overridden. As a result the `Insert` routine adjusts the heights of the nodes along the insertion path and does a rotation when an imbalance is detected. Since the height of an AVL tree is guaranteed to be $O(\log n)$, the time for insertion is simply $O(\log n)$.

### 10.5.3   Removing Items from an AVL Tree

The procedure for removing items from an AVL tree is inherited from the `BST` class in the same way as AVL insertion. (See Program 10.6.) All the differences are

**PROGRAM 10.11**
AVLTree class Balance member function definition

```
1   void AVLTree::Balance ()
2   {
3       AdjustHeight ();
4       if (abs (BalanceFactor ()) > 1)
5       {
6           if (BalanceFactor () > 0)
7           {
8               if (Left ().BalanceFactor () > 0)
9                   LLRotation ();
10              else
11                  LRRotation ();
12          }
13          else
14          {
15              if (Right ().BalanceFactor () < 0)
16                  RRRotation ();
17              else
18                  RLRotation ();
19          }
20      }
21  }
```

**PROGRAM 10.12**
AVLTree class AttachKey and DetachKey member function definitions

```
1   void AVLTree::AttachKey (Object& object)
2   {
3       if (!IsEmpty ())
4           throw domain_error ("invalid operation");
5       key = &object;
6       left = new AVLTree ();
7       right = new AVLTree ();
8       height = 0;
9   }
10
11  Object& AVLTree::DetachKey ()
12  {
13      height = -1;
14      return BST::DetachKey ();
15  }
```

encapsulated in the `DetachKey` and `Balance` functions. The `Balance` function is discussed above. The `DetachKey` function is defined in Program 10.12.

# 10.6 *M*-Way Search Trees

As defined in Section 10.1.1, an internal node of an *M*-way search tree contains $n$ subtrees and $n-1$ keys, where $2 \leq n \leq M$, for some fixed value of $M \geq 2$. The preceding sections give implementations for the special case in which the fixed value of $M = 2$ is assumed (binary search trees). In this section, we consider the implementation of *M*-way search trees for *arbitrary,* larger values of $M \gg 2$.

Why are we interested in larger values of *M*? Suppose we have a very large data set—so large that we cannot get it all into the main memory of the computer at the same time. In this situation we implement the search tree in secondary storage, i.e., on disk. The unique characteristics of disk-based storage *vis-à-vis* memory-based storage make it necessary to use larger values of *M* in order to implement search trees efficiently.

The typical disk access time is 1–10 ms, whereas the typical main memory access time is 10–100 ns. Thus, main memory accesses are between 10 000 and 1 000 000 times faster than typical disk accesses. Therefore to maximize performance, it is imperative that the total number of disk accesses be minimized.

In addition, disks are block-oriented devices. Data are transfered between main memory and disk in large blocks. The typical block sizes are between 512 bytes and 4096 bytes. Consequently, it makes sense to organize the data structure to take advantage of the ability to transfer entire blocks of data efficiently.

By choosing a suitably large value for *M*, we can arrange that one node of an *M*-way search tree occupies an entire disk block. If every internal node in the *M*-way search tree has exactly *M* children, we can use Theorem 9.2 to determine the height of the tree:

$$h \geq \lceil \log_M((M-1)n + 1) \rceil - 1, \tag{10.9}$$

where $n$ is the number of internal nodes in the search tree. A node in an *M*-way search tree that has *M* children contains exactly $M - 1$ keys. Therefore, altogether there are $K = (M-1)n$ keys and Equation 10.9 becomes $h \geq \lceil \log_M(K + 1) \rceil - 1$. Ideally the search tree is well balanced and the inequality becomes an equality.

For example, consider a search tree which contains $K = 2\,097\,151$ keys. Suppose the size of a disk block is such that we can fit a node of size $M = 128$ in it. Since each node contains at most 127 keys, at least 16 513 nodes are required. In the best case, the height of the *M*-way search tree is only 2 and at most three disk accesses are required to retrieve any key! This is a significant improvement over a binary tree, the height of which is at least 20.

## 10.6.1 Implementing *M*-Way Search Trees

In order to illustrate the basic ideas, this section describes an implementation of *M*-way search trees in main memory. According to Definition 10.1, each internal node of an

**FIGURE 10.9**
Representing a node of an *M*-way search tree.

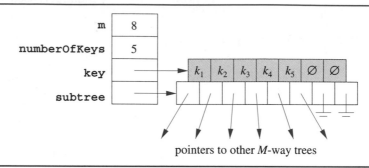

pointers to other *M*-way trees

*M*-way search tree has *n* subtrees, where *n* is at least 2 and at most *M*. Furthermore, if a node has *n* subtrees, it must contain $n - 1$ keys.

Figure 10.9 shows how we can implement a single node of an *M*-way search tree. The idea is that we use two arrays in each node—the first holds the keys and the second contains pointers to the subtrees. Since there are at most $M - 1$ keys and *M* subtrees, the first array is one element shorter than the second array.

## Implementation

Program 10.13 declares the class **MWayTree**. An **MWayTree** is derived from the class **SearchTree** which is in turn derived from **Tree** and **SearchableContainer**.

**PROGRAM 10.13**
**MWayTree** class definition

```
1   class MWayTree : public SearchTree
2   {
3   protected:
4       unsigned int const m;
5       unsigned int numberOfKeys;
6       Array<Object*> key;
7       Array<MWayTree*> subtree;
8
9       unsigned int FindIndex (Object const&) const;
10  public:
11      MWayTree (unsigned int);
12      ~MWayTree ();
13
14      Object& Key (unsigned int) const;
15      MWayTree& Subtree (unsigned int) const;
16      //...
17  };
```

The four member variables, **m, numberOfKeys, key**, and **subtree**, correspond to the components of a node shown in Figure 10.9.

The first member variable, **m**, is a constant. It is used to record the degree of the node which cannot change after the node is created (i.e., $|m| \equiv M$). The second member variable, **numberOfKeys**, keeps track of the number of keys contained in the node. Recall, a node which has $n$ subtrees contains $n - 1$ keys. Therefore, **numberOfKeys** $\equiv$ $n - 1$. We have chosen to keep track of the number of keys of a node rather than the number of subtrees because it simplifies the coding of the algorithms by eliminating some of the special cases which arise if we keep track of $n$ explicitly.

The third member variable, **key**, is an array of pointers to **Object** class instances. It is used to contain pointers to the keys contained in the node. The fourth and final member variable, **subtree**, is an array of pointers to the **MWayTree** instances which are the subtrees of the given node.

### Member Functions

Program 10.13 also declares the constructor, the destructor, and the two member functions **Key** and **Subtree**. The constructor takes a single **unsigned int** argument, say $M$, and initializes the fields of the object as follows: The constant member variable **m** is set to $M$; the member variable **numberOfKeys** is set to zero; the **key** array is initialized to length $M - 1$ and base 1; and, the **subtree** array is initialized to length $M$.

The member functions **Key** and **Subtree** are member variable accessors which are used to access the components of an **MWayTree**. The first, **Key**, takes an **unsigned int** argument between 1 and $M - 1$ and returns a reference to the specified element of the key array. Similarly, the **Subtree** function takes an **unsigned int** argument between 0 and $M - 1$ and returns a reference to the specified subtree.

### Inorder Traversal

Whereas inorder traversal of an *N*-ary tree is *not* defined for $N > 2$, inorder traversal *is* defined for an *M*-way search tree: By definition, the inorder traversal of a search tree visits all the keys contained in the search tree *in order*.

Program 10.14 is an implementation of the algorithm for depth-first traversal of an *M*-way search tree given in Section 10.3.4. The algorithm recursively traverses the subtrees of a given node in order. After traversing $T_{i-1}$ but before traversing $T_i$, the visitor's **PostVisit** function is called for key $k_{i-1}$; its **Visit** function is called for key $k_i$; and its **PreVisit** function is called for key $k_{i+1}$.

It is clear that the amount of work done at each node during the course of a depth-first traversal is proportional to the number of keys contained in that node. Therefore, the total running time for the depth-first traversal is $K(\mathcal{T}\langle\text{PreVisit}()\rangle + \mathcal{T}\langle\text{Visit}()\rangle + \mathcal{T}\langle\text{PostVisit}()\rangle) + O(K)$, where $K$ is the number of keys contained in the search tree.

## 10.6.2  Finding Items in an *M*-Way Search Tree

Two algorithms for finding items in an *M*-way search tree are described in this section. The first is a naïve implementation using linear search. The second version improves upon the first by using a binary search.

**PROGRAM 10.14**
MWayTree class DepthFirstTraversal member function definition

```
1   void MWayTree::DepthFirstTraversal (
2       PrePostVisitor& visitor) const
3   {
4       if (!IsEmpty ())
5       {
6           for (int i = 0; i <= numberOfKeys + 1; ++i)
7           {
8               if (i >=2)
9                   visitor.PostVisit (*key [i - 1]);
10              if (i >=1 && i <= numberOfKeys)
11                  visitor.Visit (*key [i]);
12              if (i <= numberOfKeys - 1)
13                  visitor.PreVisit (*key [i + 1]);
14              if (i <= count)
15                  subtree [i]->DepthFirstTraversal (visitor);
16          }
17      }
18  }
```

**PROGRAM 10.15**
MWayTree class Find member function definition (linear search)

```
1   Object& MWayTree::Find (Object const& object) const
2   {
3       if (IsEmpty ())
4           return NullObject::Instance ();
5       unsigned int i = numberOfKeys;
6       while (i > 0)
7       {
8           int const diff = object.Compare (*key [i]);
9           if (diff == 0)
10              return *key [i];
11          if (diff > 0)
12              break;
13          --i;
14      }
15      return subtree [i]->Find (object);
16  }
```

## Linear Search

Program 10.15 gives the naïve version of the **Find** member function of the **MWayTree** class. The **Find** member function takes a **const** reference to an **Object** instance and locates the item in the search tree which matches the given instance.

Consider the execution of the **Find** function for a node $T$ of a an $M$-way search tree. Suppose the object of the search is $x$. Clearly, the search fails when $T = \varnothing$ (lines 3–4). In this case, a reference to the **NullObject** instance is returned. Suppose $T = \{T_0, k_1, T_1, k_2, T_2, \ldots, k_{n-1}, T_{n-1}\}$. The linear search on lines 5–14 considers the keys $k_{n-1}, k_{n-2}, k_{n-3}, \ldots, k_1$, in that order. If a match is found, a reference to the matching object is returned immediately (lines 9–10).

Otherwise, when the main loop terminates there are three possibilities: $i = 0$ and $x < k_{i+1}$; $1 \leq i \leq n - 2$ and $k_i < x < k_{i+1}$; or $i = n - 1$ and $k_i < x$. In all three cases, the appropriate subtree in which to continue the search is $T_i$ (line 15).

Clearly the running time of Program 10.15 is determined by the main loop. In the worst case, the loop is executed $M - 1$ times. Therefore, at each node in the search path at most $M - 1$ object comparisons are done.

Consider an unsuccessful search in an $M$-way search tree. The running time of the **Find** function is

$$(M - 1)(h + 1)\mathcal{T}\langle \texttt{T::Compare(T\&,T\&)}\rangle + O(Mh)$$

in the worst case, where $h$ is the height of the tree and $\mathcal{T}\langle \texttt{T::Compare(T\&,T\&)}\rangle$ is the time required to compare two objects. Clearly, the time for a successful search has the same asymptotic bound. If the tree is balanced and $\mathcal{T}\langle \texttt{T::Compare(T\&,T\&)}\rangle = O(1)$, then the running time of Program 10.15 is $O(M \log_M K)$, where $K$ is the number of keys in the tree.

## Binary Search

We can improve the performance of the $M$-way search tree search algorithm by recognizing that since the keys are kept in a sorted array, we can do a binary search rather than a linear search. Program 10.16 gives an alternate implementation for the **Find** member function of the **MWayTree** class. This routine makes use of the private member function **FindIndex** which does the actual binary search.

The **FindIndex** member function takes as its lone argument a **const** reference to an **Object** instance, say $x$, and returns an **unsigned int** in the range between 0 and $n - 1$, where $n$ is the number of subtrees of the given node. The result is the largest integer $i$, if it exists, such that $x \geq k_i$ where $k_i$ is the $i$th key. Otherwise, it returns the value 0.

**FindIndex** determines its result by doing a binary search. In the worst case, $\lceil \log_2(M - 1) \rceil + 1$ iterations of the main loop (lines 9–16) are required to determine the correct index. One object comparison is done before the loop (line 5), and one comparison is done in each loop iteration (line 12). Therefore, the running time of the **FindIndex** function is

$$(\lceil \log_2(M - 1) \rceil + 2)\mathcal{T}\langle \texttt{T::Compare(T\&,T\&)}\rangle + O(\log_2 M).$$

If $\mathcal{T}\langle \texttt{T::Compare(T\&,T\&)}\rangle = O(1)$, this simplifies to $O(\log M)$.

**PROGRAM 10.16**
MWayTree class FindIndex and Find member function definitions (binary search)

```
1   unsigned int MWayTree::FindIndex (Object const& object) const
2   {
3       if (IsEmpty ())
4           throw domain_error ("invalid operation");
5       if (object < *key [1])
6           return 0;
7       unsigned int left = 1;
8       unsigned int right = numberOfKeys;
9       while (left < right)
10      {
11          int const middle = (left + right + 1) / 2;
12          if (object >= *key [middle])
13              left = middle;
14          else
15              right = middle - 1U;
16      }
17      return left;
18  }
19
20  Object& MWayTree::Find (Object const& object) const
21  {
22      if (IsEmpty ())
23          return NullObject::Instance ();
24      unsigned int const index = FindIndex (object);
25      if (index != 0 && object == *key [index])
26          return *key [index];
27      else
28          return subtree [index]->Find (object);
29  }
```

The **Find** member function of the **MWayTree** class does the actual search. It calls **FindIndex** to determine largest integer $i$, if it exists, such that $x \geq k_i$ where $k_i$ is the $i$th key (line 24). If it turns out that $x = k_i$, then the search is done (lines 25–26). Otherwise, **Find** calls itself recursively to search subtree $T_i$ (line 28).

Consider a search in an $M$-way search tree. The running time of the second version of **Find** is

$$(h + 1)(\lceil \log_2(M - 1) \rceil + 2)\mathcal{T}\langle \text{T::Compare(T\&, T\&)} \rangle + O(h \log M),$$

where $h$ is the height of the tree and regardless of whether the search is successful. If the tree is balanced and $\mathcal{T}\langle \text{T::Compare(T\&, T\&)} \rangle = O(1)$, then the running time of Program 10.16 is simply $O((\log_2 M)(\log_M K))$, where $K$ is the number of keys in the tree.

### 10.6.3 Inserting Items into an *M*-Way Search Tree

The routine for inserting items in an *M*-way search tree follows directly from the algorithm for insertion in a binary search tree given in Section 10.4.2. The added wrinkle in an *M*-way tree is that an internal node may contain between 1 and $M - 1$ keys, whereas an internal node in a binary tree must contain exactly one key.

Program 10.17 gives the implementation of the **Insert** member function of the **MWayTree** class. This function takes as its lone argument a reference to the **Object** instance to be inserted into the search tree.

The general procedure for insertion is to search for the item to be inserted and then to insert it at the point where the search terminates. If the search terminates at an external

---

**PROGRAM 10.17**
**MWayTree** class **Insert** member function definition

```
 1   void MWayTree::Insert (Object& object)
 2   {
 3       if (IsEmpty ())
 4       {
 5           subtree [0] = new MWayTree (m);
 6           key [1] = &object;
 7           subtree [1] = new MWayTree (m);
 8           numberOfKeys = 1;
 9       }
10       else
11       {
12           unsigned int const index = FindIndex (object);
13           if (index != 0 && object == *key [index])
14               throw invalid_argument ("duplicate key");
15           if (numberOfKeys < m - 1U)
16           {
17               for(unsigned int i = numberOfKeys; i > index; --i)
18               {
19                   key [i + 1] = key [i];
20                   subtree [i + 1] = subtree [i];
21               }
22               key [index + 1] = &object;
23               subtree [index + 1] = new MWayTree (m);
24               ++numberOfKeys;
25           }
26           else
27               subtree [index]->Insert (object);
28       }
29   }
```

---

node, that node is transformed to an internal node of the form $\{\varnothing, x, \varnothing\}$, where $x$ is the key just inserted (lines 5–8).

   If the search terminates at an internal node, we insert the new item into the sorted list of keys at the appropriate offset. Inserting the key $x$ in the array of keys moves all the keys larger than $x$ and the associated subtrees to the right one position (lines 17–22). The hole in the list of subtrees is filled with an empty tree (line 23).

---

**PROGRAM 10.18**
`MWayTree` class `Withdraw` member function definition

---

```
1   void MWayTree::Withdraw (Object& object)
2   {
3       if (IsEmpty ())
4           throw invalid_argument ("object not found");
5       unsigned int const index = FindIndex (object);
6       if (index != 0 && object == *key [index])
7       {
8           if (!subtree [index - 1U]->IsEmpty ())
9           {
10              Object& max = subtree [index - 1U]->FindMax ();
11              key [index] = &max;
12              subtree [index - 1U]->Withdraw (max);
13          }
14          else if (!subtree [index]->IsEmpty ())
15          {
16              Object& min = subtree [index]->FindMin ();
17              key [index] = &min;
18              subtree [index]->Withdraw (min);
19          }
20          else
21          {
22              --numberOfKeys;
23              delete subtree [index];
24              for(unsigned int i = index; i <= numberOfKeys; ++i)
25              {
26                  key [i] = key [i + 1];
27                  subtree [i] = subtree [i + 1];
28              }
29              if (numberOfKeys == 0)
30                  delete subtree [0];
31          }
32      }
33      else
34          subtree [index]->Withdraw (object);
35  }
```

---

The preceding section gives the running time for a search in an $M$-way search tree as

$$(h + 1)(\lceil \log_2(M - 1) \rceil + 2)\mathcal{T}\langle \texttt{T::Compare(T\&,T\&)} \rangle + O(h \log M),$$

where $h$ is the height of the tree. The additional time required to insert the item into the node once the correct node has been located is $O(M)$. Therefore, the total running time for the **Insert** algorithm given in Program 10.17 is

$$(h + 1)(\lceil \log_2(M - 1) \rceil + 2)\mathcal{T}\langle \texttt{T::Compare(T\&,T\&)} \rangle + O(h \log M) + O(M).$$

### 10.6.4 Removing Items from an $M$-Way Search Tree

The procedure for removing items from an $M$-way search tree follows directly from the algorithm for removing items from a binary search tree given in Section 10.4.3. The basic idea is that the item to be deleted is pushed down the tree from its initial position to a node from which it can be easily deleted. Clearly, items are easily deleted from leaf nodes. In addition, consider an internal node of an $M$-way search tree of the form

$$T = \{T_0, k_1, T_1, \ldots, T_{i-1}, k_i, T_i, \ldots, k_{n-1}, T_{n-1}\}.$$

If both $T_{i-1}$ and $T_i$ are empty trees, then the key $k_i$ can be deleted from $T$ by removing both $k_i$ and $T_i$, say. If $T_{i-1}$ is non-empty, $k_i$ can be pushed down the tree by swapping it with the largest key in $T_{i-1}$; if $T_i$ is non-empty, $k_i$ can be pushed down the tree by swapping it with the smallest key in $T_i$.

Program 10.18 gives the code for the **Withdraw** function of the **MWayTree** class. The general form of the algorithm follows that of the **Withdraw** routine for the **BST** class (Program 10.6).

## 10.7 B-Trees

Just as AVL trees are balanced binary search trees, *B-trees* are balanced *M*-way search trees.[2] By imposing a *balance condition,* the shape of an AVL tree is constrained in a way which guarantees that the search, insertion, and withdrawal operations are all $O(\log n)$, where $n$ is the number of items in the tree. The shapes of B-Trees are constrained for the same reasons and with the same effect.

### Definition 10.5 (B-Tree)
*A B-Tree of order $M$ is either the empty tree or it is an $M$-way search tree $T$ with the following properties:*

---

[2]Obviously since B-Trees are *M*-way trees, the "B" in *B-Tree* does not stand for *binary.* B-Trees were invented by R. Bayer and E. McCright in 1972, so the "B" either stands for *balanced* or *Bayer*—take your pick.

1. *The root of T has at least two subtrees and at most M subtrees.*

2. *All internal nodes of T (other than its root) have between $\lceil M/2 \rceil$ and M subtrees.*

3. *All external nodes of T are at the same level.*

A B-tree of order 1 is clearly impossible. Hence, B-trees of order $M$ are really only defined for $M \geq 2$. However, in practice we expect that $M$ is large for the same reasons that motivate $M$-way search trees—large databases in secondary storage.

Figure 10.10 gives an example of a B-tree of order $M = 3$. By Definition 10.5, the root of a B-tree of order three has either two or three subtrees and the internal nodes also have either two or three subtrees. Furthermore, all the external nodes, which are shown as small boxes in Figure 10.10, are at the same level.

It turns out that the balance conditions imposed by Definition 10.5 are good in the same sense as the AVL balance conditions. That is, the balance condition guarantees that the height of B-trees is logarithmic in the number of keys in the tree and the time required for insertion and deletion operations remains proportional to the height of the tree even when balancing is required.

### Theorem 10.4

*The minimum number of keys in a B-tree of order $M \geq 2$ and height $h \geq 0$ is $n_h = 2\lceil M/2 \rceil^h - 1$.*

**Proof**    Clearly, a B-tree of height zero contains at least one node. Consider a B-tree order $M$ and height $h > 0$. By Definition 10.5, each internal node (except the root) has at least $\lceil M/2 \rceil$ subtrees. This implies that the minimum number of keys contained in an internal node is $\lceil M/2 \rceil - 1$. The minimum number of keys at level zero is 1; at level one, $2(\lceil M/2 \rceil - 1)$; at level two, $2\lceil M/2 \rceil(\lceil M/2 \rceil - 1)$; at level three, $2\lceil M/2 \rceil^2(\lceil M/2 \rceil - 1)$; and so on.

---

**FIGURE 10.10**
A B-tree of order 3.

---

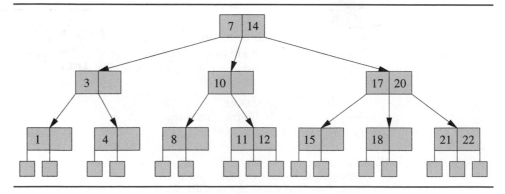

Therefore, the minimum number of keys in a B-tree of height $h > 0$ is given by the summation

$$n_h = 1 + 2(\lceil M/2 \rceil - 1) \sum_{i=0}^{h-1} \lceil M/2 \rceil^i$$

$$= 1 + 2(\lceil M/2 \rceil - 1)\left(\frac{\lceil M/2 \rceil^h - 1}{\lceil M/2 \rceil - 1}\right)$$

$$= 2\lceil M/2 \rceil^h - 1.$$

A corollary of Theorem 10.4 is that the height, $h$, of a B-tree containing $n$ keys is given by

$$h \le \log_{\lceil M/2 \rceil}((n + 1)/2).$$

Thus, we have shown that a B-tree satisfies the first criterion of a good balance condition—the height of B-tree with $n$ internal nodes is $O(\log n)$. What remains to be shown is that the balance condition can be efficiently maintained during insertion and withdrawal operations. To see that it can, we need to look at an implementation.

### 10.7.1 Implementing B-Trees

Having already implemented the $M$-way search tree class, **MWayTree**, we can make use of much the existing code to implement a B-tree class. Program 10.19 gives the

**PROGRAM 10.19**
**BTree** class definition

```
1   class BTree : public MWayTree
2   {
3       BTree* parent;
4
5       void InsertPair (Object&, BTree&);
6       void AttachKey (unsigned int, Object&);
7       void AttachSubtree (unsigned int, MWayTree&);
8       Object& InsertKey (unsigned int, Object&);
9       BTree& InsertSubtree (unsigned int, BTree&);
10      void AttachLeftHalfOf (BTree const&);
11      void AttachRightHalfOf (BTree const&, Object&, BTree&);
12  public:
13      BTree (unsigned int);
14      BTree (unsigned int, BTree&);
15
16      void Insert (Object&);
17      void Withdraw (Object&);
18  };
```

declaration of the **BTree** class which is derived from the class **MWayTree**. With the exception of the two functions which modify the tree, **Insert** and **Withdraw**, the **AVLTree** class inherits all its public functionality from the $M$-way tree class. Of course, the **Insert** and **Withdraw** member functions need to be redefined in order to ensure that every time the tree is modified the tree which results is a B-tree.

### Member Variables

To simplify the implementation of the algorithms, the member variable **parent** has been added. The **parent** member variable is a pointer to the **BTree** node which is the parent of the given node. Whereas the array of pointers to the children of a node, i.e., the **subtree** member variable of the **MWayTree** class, allows an algorithm to move down the tree; the **parent** member variable admits movement up the tree. Since the root of a tree has no parent, the **parent** member variable of the root node contains the null pointer.

### Constructors

Two constructors are declared in Program 10.19 The first takes a single **unsigned int** argument $M$ and creates an empty B-tree of order $M$. The second constructor takes two arguments, an **unsigned int** and a pointer to a **BTree**. The integer argument specifies the order, $M$, of the tree to be constructed. The second argument specifies the parent of the node.

### Private Member Functions

In addition to the public member functions, seven private member functions are declared in Program 10.19. These are used to implement the **Insert** and **Withdraw** member functions and are explained below.

## 10.7.2 Inserting Items into a B-Tree

The algorithm for insertion into a B-Tree begins as do all the other search tree insertion algorithms: To insert item $x$, we begin at the root and conduct a search for it. Assuming the item is not already in the tree, the unsuccessful search will terminate at a leaf node. This is the point in the tree at which the $x$ is inserted.

If the leaf node has fewer than $M - 1$ keys in it, we simply insert the item in the leaf node and we are done. For example, consider a leaf node with $n < M$ subtrees and $n - 1$ keys of the form

$$T = \{T_0, k_1, T_1, k_2, T_2, \ldots, k_{n-1}, T_{n-1}\}.$$

For every new key inserted in the node, a new subtree is required too. In this case because $T$ is a leaf, all its subtrees are empty trees. Therefore, when we insert item $x$, we really insert the pair of items $(x, \varnothing)$. Suppose the key to be inserted falls between $k_i$ and $k_{i+1}$, i.e., $k_i < x < k_{i+1}$. When we insert the pair $(x, \varnothing)$ into $T$ we get the new leaf $T'$ given by

$$T' = \{T_0, k_1, T_1, k_2, T_2, \ldots, k_i, T_i, x, \varnothing, k_{i+1}, T_{i+1}, \ldots, k_{n-1}, T_{n-1}\}.$$

What happens when the leaf is full? That is, suppose we wish to insert the pair, $(x, \emptyset)$, into a node $T$ which already has $M - 1$ keys. Inserting the pair in its correct position gives a result of the form

$$T' = \{T_0, k_1, T_1, k_2, T_2, \ldots, k_M, T_M\}.$$

However, this is not a valid node in a B-tree of order $M$ because it has $M + 1$ subtrees and $M$ keys. The solution is to split node $T'$ in half as follows:

$$T'_L = \{T_0, k_1, T_1, \ldots, k_{\lceil M/2 \rceil - 1}, T_{\lceil M/2 \rceil - 1}\}$$

$$T'_R = \{T_{\lceil M/2 \rceil}, k_{\lceil M/2 \rceil + 1}, T_{\lceil M/2 \rceil + 1}, \ldots, k_M, T_M\}$$

Note, $T'_L$ is a valid B-tree node because it contains $\lceil M/2 \rceil$ subtrees and $\lceil M/2 \rceil - 1$ keys. Similarly, $T'_R$ is a valid B-tree node because it contains $\lceil (M + 1)/2 \rceil$ subtrees and $\lceil (M + 1)/2 \rceil - 1$ keys. Note that there is still a key left over, namely $k_{\lceil M/2 \rceil}$.

There are now two cases to consider—either $T$ is the root or it is not. Suppose $T$ is not the root. Where we once had the single node $T$, we now have the two nodes, $T'_L$ and $T'_R$, and the left-over key, $k_{\lceil M/2 \rceil}$. This situation is resolved as follows: First, $T'_L$ replaces $T$ in the parent of $T$. Next, we take the pair $(k_{\lceil M/2 \rceil}, T'_R)$ and recursively insert it in the parent of $T$.

Figure 10.11 illustrates this case for a B-tree of order three. Inserting the key 6 in the tree causes the leaf node to overflow. The leaf is split in two. The left half contains key 5; and the right, key 7; and key 6 is left over. The two halves are reattached to the parent in the appropriate place with the left-over key between them.

If the parent node fills up, then it too is split and the two new nodes are inserted in the grandparent. This process may continue all the way up the tree to the root. What do we do when the root fills up? When the root fills, it is also split. However, since there is no parent into which to insert the two new children, a new root is inserted above the old root. The new root will contain exactly two subtrees and one key, as allowed by Definition 10.5.

Figure 10.12 illustrates this case for a B-tree of order 3. Inserting the key 3 in the tree causes the leaf node to overflow. Splitting the leaf and reattaching it causes the parent to overflow. Similarly, splitting the parent and reattaching it causes the grandparent to overflow but the grandparent is the root. The root is split, and a new root is added above it.

Notice that the height of the B-tree only increases when the root node splits. Furthermore, when the root node splits, the two halves are both attached under the new root. Therefore, the external nodes all remain at the same depth, as required by Definition 10.5.

## Implementation

Insertion in a B-tree is a two-pass process. The first pass moves down the tree from the root in order to locate the leaf in which the insertion is to begin. This part of the algorithm is quite similar to the **Find** routine given in Program 10.16. The second pass moves from the bottom of the tree back up to the root, splitting nodes and inserting them further up the tree as needed. Program 10.20 gives the code for the first (downward)

**FIGURE 10.11**
Inserting items into a B-tree (insert 6).

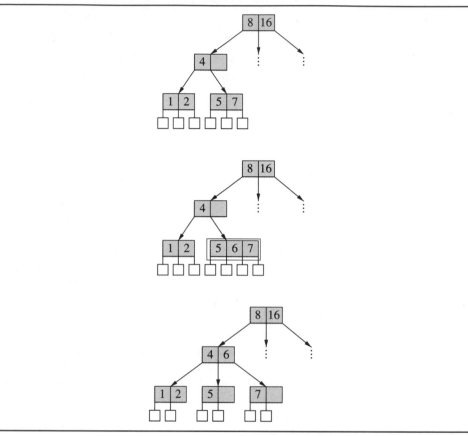

pass (member function **Insert**) and the Program 10.21 gives the code for the second (upward) pass (member function **InsertPair**).

In the implementation shown, the downward pass starts at the root node and descends the tree until it arrives at an external node. If the external node has no parent, it must be the root and, therefore, the tree is empty. In this case, the root becomes an internal node containing a single key and two empty subtrees (lines 7–10). Otherwise, we have arrived at an external node in a non-empty tree and the second pass begins by calling **InsertPair** to insert the pair $(x, \varnothing)$ in the parent.

The upward pass of the insertion algorithm is done by the recursive **InsertPair** routine shown in Program 10.21. The **InsertPair** routine takes two arguments. The first, **object**, is a pointer to an **Object** instance and the second, **child**, is a pointer to a **BTree** instance. It is assumed that all the keys in **child** are strictly greater than **object**.

The **InsertPair** routine calls **FindIndex** to determine the position in the array of keys at which **object** should be inserted (line 3). It then calls **InsertKey** to insert the given key at the specified position in the array of keys (line 4). In the event that the

**FIGURE 10.12**
Inserting items into a B-tree (insert 3).

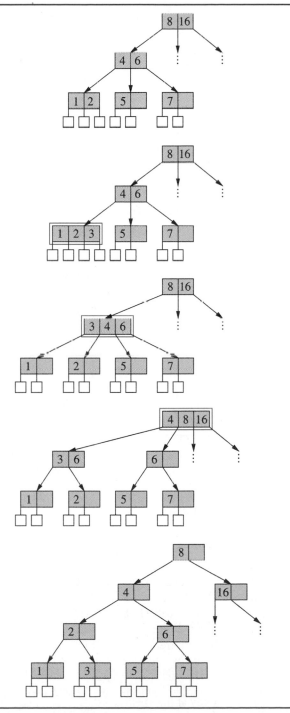

---

**PROGRAM 10.20**
BTree class Insert member function definition

---

```
1   void BTree::Insert (Object& object)
2   {
3       if (IsEmpty ())
4       {
5           if (parent == 0)
6           {
7               AttachSubtree (0, *new BTree (m, *this));
8               AttachKey (1, object);
9               AttachSubtree (1, *new BTree (m, *this));
10              numberOfKeys = 1;
11          }
12          else
13              parent->InsertPair (object, *new BTree (m, *parent));
14      }
15      else
16      {
17          unsigned int const index = FindIndex (object);
18          if (index != 0 && object == *key [index])
19              throw invalid_argument ("duplicate key");
20          subtree [index]->Insert (object);
21      }
22  }
```

---

array of keys is already full, i.e., when it contains $M - 1$ items, the **InsertKey** function returns the key which falls off the right end of the array. This is assigned to **extraKey**.

The **InsertSubtree** function does a similar insertion (line 5). That is, it inserts the **child** B-tree at the specified position. If the array of subtrees is full, which occurs if it already contains $M$ subtrees, the **InsertSubtree** function returns the tree which falls off the right end of the array. This is assigned to **extraTree**.

If the **numberOfKeys** is equal to $M$, the node has overflowed and it is necessary to balance the B-tree. On the other hand, if the **numberOfKeys** is less than $M$, there is nothing more to do (line 7).

If the node overflows and it is the root, then two new B-trees, **left** and **right** are created (lines 11–12). The first $\lceil M/2 \rceil - 1$ keys and $\lceil M/2 \rceil$ subtrees of the given node are moved to the **left** tree by the **AttachLeftHalfOf** function (line 13); and the last $\lceil (M + 1)/2 \rceil - 1$ keys and $\lceil (M + 1)/2 \rceil$ subtrees of the given node are moved to the **right** tree by the **AttachRightHalfOf** function (line 14). The left-over key is the one in the middle of the array, i.e., $k_{\lceil M/2 \rceil}$. Finally, the root node is modified so that it contains the two new subtrees and the single left-over key (lines 15–18).

If the node overflows and it is not the root, then one new B-tree is created, **right** (line 23). The last $\lceil (M + 1)/2 \rceil - 1$ keys and $\lceil (M + 1)/2 \rceil$ subtrees of the given node are moved to the **left** tree by the **AttachRightHalfOf** function (line 24); and the first $\lceil M/2 \rceil - 1$ keys and $\lceil M/2 \rceil$ subtrees of the given node remain attached to the given

**PROGRAM 10.21**
BTree class InsertPair member function definition

```
1   void BTree::InsertPair (Object& object, BTree& child)
2   {
3       unsigned int const index = FindIndex (object);
4       BTree& extraTree = InsertSubtree (index + 1, child);
5       Object& extraKey = InsertKey (index + 1, object);
6
7       if (++numberOfKeys == m)
8       {
9           if (parent == 0)
10          {
11              BTree& left = *new BTree (m, *this);
12              BTree& right = *new BTree (m, *this);
13              left.AttachLeftHalfOf (*this);
14              right.AttachRightHalfOf (*this, extraKey, extraTree);
15              AttachSubtree (0, left);
16              AttachKey (1, *key [(m + 1)/2]);
17              AttachSubtree (1, right);
18              numberOfKeys = 1;
19          }
20          else
21          {
22              numberOfKeys = (m + 1)/2 - 1;
23              BTree& right = *new BTree (m, *parent);
24              right.AttachRightHalfOf (*this, extraKey, extraTree);
25              parent->InsertPair (*key [(m + 1)/2], right);
26          }
27      }
28  }
```

node. Finally, the InsertPair routine calls itself recursively to insert the left-over key, $k_{\lceil M/2 \rceil}$, and the new B-tree, right, into the parent of the given node (line 25). It should now be clear why the parent member variable is needed.

### Running Time Analysis

The running time of the downward pass of the insertion algorithm is identical to that of an unsuccessful search (assuming the item to be inserted is not already in the tree). That is, for a B-tree of height $h$, the worst-case running time of the downward pass is

$$(h + 1)(\lceil \log_2(M - 1) \rceil + 2)\mathcal{T}\langle \text{T::Compare(T\&,T\&)} \rangle + O(h \log M).$$

The second pass of the insertion algorithm does the insertion and balances the tree if necessary. In the worst case, all of the nodes in the insertion path up to the root need to be balanced. Each time the InsertPair routine is invoked, it calls FindIndex which has running time $(\lceil \log_2(M-1) \rceil + 2)\mathcal{T}\langle \texttt{T::Compare(T\&,T\&)} \rangle + O(\log M)$ in the worst case. The additional time required to balance a node is $O(M)$. Therefore, the worst-case running time of the upward pass is

$$(h+1)(\lceil \log_2(M-1) \rceil + 2)\mathcal{T}\langle \texttt{T::Compare(T\&,T\&)} \rangle + O(hM).$$

Therefore, the total running time for insertion is

$$2(h+1)(\lceil \log_2(M-1) \rceil + 2)\mathcal{T}\langle \texttt{T::Compare(T\&,T\&)} \rangle + O(hM).$$

According to Theorem 10.4, the height of a B-tree is $h \leq \log_{\lceil M/2 \rceil}((n+1)/2)$, where $n$ is the number of keys in the B-tree. If we assume that two keys can be compared in constant time, i.e., $\mathcal{T}\langle \texttt{T::Compare(T\&,T\&)} \rangle = O(1)$, then the running time for insertion in a B-tree is simply $O(M \log n)$.

### 10.7.3 Removing Items from a B-Tree

The procedure for removing items from a B-tree is similar to the algorithm for removing item from an AVL tree. That is, once the item to be removed has been found, it is pushed down the tree to a leaf node where it can be easily deleted. When an item is deleted from a node it is possible that the number of keys remaining is less than $\lceil M/2 \rceil - 1$. In this case, balancing is necessary.

The procedure of balancing after deletion is like the balancing after insertion in that it progresses from the leaf node up the tree toward the root. Given a node $T$ which has $\lceil M/2 \rceil - 2$ keys, there are four cases to consider.

In the first case, $T$ is the root. If no keys remain, $T$ becomes the empty tree. Otherwise, no balancing is needed because the root is permitted to have as few as two subtrees and one key. For the remaining cases $T$ is not the root.

In the second case $T$ has $\lceil M/2 \rceil - 2$ keys and it also has a sibling immediately on the left with at least $\lceil M/2 \rceil$ keys. The tree can be balanced by doing an LL rotation, as shown in Figure 10.13. Notice that after the rotation, both siblings have at least $\lceil M/2 \rceil - 1$ keys. Furthermore, the heights of the siblings remain unchanged. Therefore, the resulting tree is a valid B-tree.

The third case is the left-right mirror of the second case. That is, $T$ has $\lceil M/2 \rceil - 2$ keys and it also has a sibling immediately on the right with a least $\lceil M/2 \rceil$ keys. In this case, the tree can be balanced by doing an RR rotation.

In the fourth and final case, $T$ has $\lceil M/2 \rceil - 2$ keys, and its immediate sibling(s) have $\lceil M/2 \rceil - 1$ keys. In this case, the sibling(s) cannot give up a key in a rotation because they already have the minimum number of keys. The solution is to *merge* $T$ with one of its siblings, as shown in Figure 10.14.

The merged node contains $\lceil M/2 \rceil - 2$ keys from $T$, $\lceil M/2 \rceil - 1$ keys from the sibling, and one key from the parent (the key $x$ in Figure 10.14). The resulting node contains $2\lceil M/2 \rceil - 2$ keys altogether, which is $M - 2$ if $M$ is even and $M - 1$ if $M$ is odd. Either way, the resulting node contains no more than $M - 1$ keys and is a valid B-tree node. Notice that in this case a key has been removed from the parent of $T$. Therefore, it may be necessary to balance the parent. Balancing the parent may necessitate balancing the grandparent, and so on, up the tree to the root.

**FIGURE 10.13**
LL rotation in a B-tree.

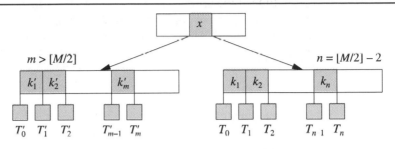

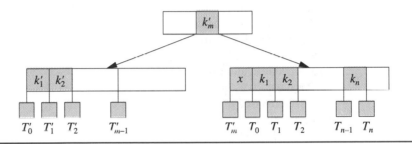

**FIGURE 10.14**
Merging nodes in a B-tree.

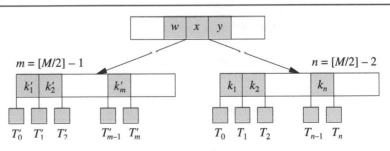

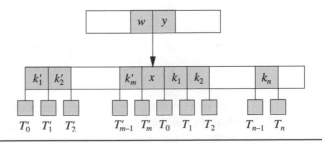

## 10.8  Applications

There are many applications for search trees. The principal characteristic of such applications is that a database of keyed information needs to be frequently accessed and the access pattern is either unknown or known to be random. For example, *dictionaries* are often implemented using search trees. A dictionary is essentially a container that contains ordered key/value pairs. The keys are words in a source language and, depending on the application, the values may be the definitions of the words or the translation of the word in a target language.

This section presents a simple application of search trees. Suppose we are required to translate the words in an input file one-by-one from some source language to another target language. In this example, the translation is done one word at a time. That is, no natural language syntactic or semantic processing is done.

In order to implement the translator we assume that there exists a text file, say **"dict.txt"** which contains pairs of words. The first element of the pair is a word in the source language, and the second element is a word in the target language. To translate a text, we first read the words and the associated translations and build a search tree. The translation is created one word at a time by looking up each word in the text.

Program 10.22 gives an implementation of the translator. Two functions are given, **ReadDictionary** and **TranslateText**. The first function takes a reference to a **SearchTree** instance which is used to hold the pairs of words. Notice, this implementation works with all the search tree types described in this chapter (e.g., **BST**, **AVLTree**, **MWayTree**, and **BTree**).

The **ReadDictionary** reads pairs of strings from the file **"dict.txt"** (lines 6–7). The **Association** class defined in Section 5.2.11 is used to contain the key/value pairs. A new instance is created for each key/value pair which is then inserted into the search tree (lines 8–9). The process of building the search tree terminates when the end-of-file is encountered.

The **TranslateText** function takes as its lone argument a reference to a search tree which is assumed to contain the set of key/value pairs read in by the **ReadDictionary** function. The **TranslateText** function reads words one at a time from the standard input, **cin**, and writes the translation of each word on the standard output, **cout**. Each word is looked up as it is read (lines 18–19). If no key matches the given word, the word is printed followed by a question mark (lines 20–21). Otherwise, the value associated with the matching key is printed (lines 24–26).

## Exercises

**10.1**  For each of the following key sequences determine the binary search tree obtained when the keys are inserted one-by-one in the order given into an initially empty tree:

**a.**  1, 2, 3, 4, 5, 6, 7.

**b.**  4, 2, 1, 3, 6, 5, 7.

**c.**  1, 6, 7, 2, 4, 3, 5.

**PROGRAM 10.22**
Application of search trees—word translation

```
1   void ReadDictionary (SearchTree& dictionary)
2   {
3       std::string key;
4       std::string value;
5
6       ifstream file ("dict.txt");
7       while (file >> key >> value, !file.eof ())
8           dictionary.Insert (*new Association (
9               *new String (key), *new String (value)));
10  }
11
12  void TranslateText (SearchTree& dictionary)
13  {
14      std::string word;
15
16      while (cin >> word, !cin.eof ())
17      {
18          Object& obj = dictionary.Find (
19              Association (*new String (word)));
20          if (obj.IsNull ())
21              cout << word << "?" << endl;
22          else
23          {
24              Association& assoc = dynamic_cast<Association&> (obj);
25              cout << assoc.Value () << endl;
26          }
27      }
28  }
```

**10.2**   For each of the binary search trees obtained in Exercise 10.1 determine the tree obtained when the root is withdrawn.

**10.3**   Repeat Exercise 10.1 and 10.2 for AVL trees.

**10.4**   Derive an expression for the total space needed to represent a tree of $n$ internal nodes using each of the following classes:

   **a.**   BST defined in Program 10.2,

   **b.**   AVLTree defined in Program 10.7,

   **c.**   MWayTree defined in Program 10.13, and

   **d.**   BTree defined in Program 10.19.

   **Hint**: For the MWayTree and BTree assume that the tree contains are $k$ keys, where $k \geq n$.

**10.5**   To delete a non-leaf node from a binary search tree, we swap it either with the smallest key in its right subtree or with the largest key in its left subtree and then recursively delete it from the subtree. In a tree of $n$ nodes, what is the maximum number of swaps needed to delete a key?

**10.6** Devise an algorithm to compute the internal path length of a tree. What is the running time of your algorithm?

**10.7** Devise an algorithm to compute the external path length of a tree. What is the running time of your algorithm?

**10.8** Suppose that you are given a sorted sequence of $n$ keys, $k_0 \le k_1 \le \cdots \le k_{n-1}$, to be inserted into a binary search tree.

   **a.** What is the minimum height of a binary tree that contains $n$ nodes?

   **b.** Devise an algorithm to insert the given keys into a binary search tree so that the height of the resulting tree is minimized.

   **c.** What is the running time of your algorithm?

**10.9** Devise an algorithm to construct an AVL tree of a given height $h$ that contains the minimum number of nodes. The tree should contain the keys $1, 2, 3, \ldots, N_h$, where $N_h$ is given by Equation 10.8.

**10.10** Consider what happens when we insert the keys $1, 2, 3, \ldots, 2^{h+1} - 1$ one-by-one in the order given into an initially empty AVL tree for $h \ge 0$. Prove that the result is always a perfect tree of height $h$.

**10.11** The `Find` routine defined in Program 10.4 is recursive. Write a nonrecursive routine to find a given item in a binary search tree.

**10.12** Repeat Exercise 10.11 for the `FindMin` function defined in Program 10.4.

**10.13** Devise an algorithm to select the $k$th key in a binary search tree. For example, given a tree with $n$ nodes, $k = 0$ selects the smallest key, $k = n - 1$ selects the largest key, and $k = \lceil n/2 \rceil - 1$ selects the median key.

**10.14** Devise an algorithm to test whether a given binary search tree is AVL balanced. What is the running time of your algorithm?

**10.15** Devise an algorithm that takes two values, $a$ and $b$, such that $a \le b$, and which visits all the keys $x$ in a binary search tree such that $a \le x \le b$. The running time of your algorithm should be $O(N + \log n)$, where $N$ is the number of keys visited and $n$ is the number of keys in the tree.

**10.16** Devise an algorithm to merge the contents of two binary search trees into one. What is the running time of your algorithm?

**10.17** (This question should be attempted *after* reading Chapter 11). Prove that a *complete binary tree* (Definition 11.2) is AVL balanced.

**10.18** Do Exercise 8.12.

**10.19** For each of the following key sequences determine the three-way search tree obtained when the keys are inserted one-by-one in the order given into an initially empty tree:

   **a.** 0, 1, 2, 3, 4, 5, 6, 7, 8, 9.

   **b.** 3, 1, 4, 5, 9, 2, 6, 8, 7, 0.

   **c.** 2, 7, 1, 8, 4, 5, 9, 0, 3, 6.

**10.20** Repeat Exercise 10.19 for B-trees of order 3.

# Programming Projects

**10.1** Complete the implementation of the **BST** class declared in Program 10.2 by providing suitable definitions for the following member functions: **IsMember** and **FindMax**. You must also have a complete implementation of the base class **BinaryTree**. (See Project 9.8.) Write a test program and test your implementation.

**10.2** Complete the implementation of the **AVLTree** class declared in Program 10.7 by providing suitable definitions for the following member functions: **Left**, **Right**, **RRRotation** and **RLRotation**. You must also have a complete implementation of the base class **BST**. (See Project 10.1.) Write a test program and test your implementation.

**10.3** Complete the implementation of the **MWayTree** class declared in Program 10.13 by providing suitable definitions for the following member functions: **MWayTree** (constructor), **~MWayTree** (destructor), **Purge**, **Count**, **IsEmpty**, **IsLeaf**, **Degree**, **Key**, **Subtree**, **IsMember**, **FindMin**, **FindMax**, **BreadthFirstTraversal**, and **NewIterator**. Write a test program and test your implementation.

**10.4** Complete the implementation of the **BTree** class declared in Program 10.19 by providing suitable definitions for the following member functions: **BTree**, **InsertKey**, **InsertSubtree**, **AttachKey**, **AttachSubtree**, **AttachLeftHalfOf**, **AttachRightHalfOf**, and **Withdraw**. You must also have a complete implementation of the base class **MWayTree**. (See Project 10.3.) Write a test program and test your implementation.

**10.5** The binary search tree **Withdraw** routine shown in Program 10.6 is biased in the following way: If the key to be deleted is in a non-leaf node with two non-empty subtrees, the key is swapped with the maximum key in the left subtree and then recursively deleted from the left subtree. Following a long series of insertions and deletions, the search tree will tend to have more nodes in the right subtrees and fewer nodes in the left subtrees. Devise and conduct an experiment that demonstrates this phenomenon.

**10.6** Consider the implementation of AVL trees. In order to check the AVL balance condition in constant time, we record in each node the height of that node. An alternative to keeping track of the height information explicitly is to record in each node the *difference* in the heights of its two subtrees. In an AVL-balanced tree, this difference is either $-1, 0$ or $+1$. Replace the **height** member variable of the AVL class defined in Program 10.7 with one called **diff** and rewrite the various member functions accordingly.

**10.7** The *M*-way tree implementation given in Section 10.6.1 is an *internal* data structure—it is assumed that all the nodes reside in the main memory. However, the motivation for using an *M*-way tree is that it is an efficient way to organize an *external* data structure—one that is stored on disk. Design, implement, and test an external *M*-way tree implementation.

# 11 | Heaps and Priority Queues

In this chapter we consider priority queues. A priority queue is essentially a list of items in which each item has associated with it a *priority*. In general, different items may have different priorities and we speak of one item having a higher priority than another. Given such a list we can determine which is the highest (or the lowest) priority item in the list. Items are inserted into a priority queue in any arbitrary order. However, items are withdrawn from a priority queue in order of their priorities starting with the highest priority item first.

For example, consider the software which manages a printer. In general, it is possible for users to submit documents for printing much more quickly than it is possible to print them. A simple solution is to place the documents in a *FIFO* queue (Chapter 6). In a sense this is fair, because the documents are printed on a first-come, first-served basis.

However, a user who has submitted a short document for printing will experience a long delay when much longer documents are already in the queue. An alternative solution is to use a priority queue in which the shorter a document, the higher its priority. By printing the shortest documents first, we reduce the level of frustration experienced by the users. In fact, it can be shown that printing documents in order of their length minimizes the average time a user waits for her document.

Priority queues are often used in the implementation of algorithms. Typically the problem to be solved consists of a number of subtasks and the solution strategy involves prioritizing the subtasks and then performing those subtasks in the order of their priorities. For example, in Chapter 14 we show how a priority queue can improve the performance of backtracking algorithms; in Chapter 15 we will see how a priority queue can be used in sorting; and in Chapter 16 several graph algorithms that use a priority queue are discussed.

## 11.1 Basics

A priority queue is a container which provides the following three operations:

`Enqueue` used to put objects into the container;

`FindMin` returns a reference to the smallest object in the container; and

`DequeueMin` removes the smallest object from the container.

A priority queue is used to store a finite set of keys drawn from a totally ordered set of keys $K$. As distinct from search trees, duplicate keys *are* allowed in priority queues.

Program 11. gives the declaration of the `PriorityQueue` abstract class. The `PriorityQueue` class is derived from the `Container` class. In addition to the inherited functions, the public interface of the `PriorityQueue` class comprises the three functions listed above.

Program 11.1 also declares one additional class—`MergeablePriorityQueue`. A *mergeable priority queue* is one which provides the ability to merge efficiently two priority queues into one. Of course it is always possible to merge two priority queues by dequeuing the elements of one queue and enqueuing them in the other. However, the mergeable priority queue implementations we will consider allow more efficient merging than this.

It is possible to implement the required functionality using data structures that we have already considered. For example, a priority queue can be implemented simply as a list. If an *unsorted list* is used, enqueuing can be accomplished in constant time. However, finding the minimum and removing the minimum each require $O(n)$ time where $n$ is the number of items in the queue. On the other hand, if a *sorted list* is used,

---

**PROGRAM 11.1**
`PriorityQueue` and `MergeablePriorityQueue` class definitions

```
1  class PriorityQueue : public virtual Container
2  {
3  public:
4      virtual void Enqueue (Object&) = 0;
5      virtual Object& FindMin () const = 0;
6      virtual Object& DequeueMin () = 0;
7  };
8
9  class MergeablePriorityQueue : public virtual PriorityQueue
10 {
11 public:
12     virtual void Merge (MergeablePriorityQueue&) = 0;
13 };
```

finding the minimum and removing it is easy—both operations can be done in constant time. However, enqueuing an item in a sorted list requires $O(n)$ time.

Another possibility is to use a search tree. For example, if an *AVL tree* is used to implement a priority queue, then all three operations can be done in $O(\log n)$ time. However, search trees provide more functionality than we need. Viz., search trees support finding the largest item with **FindMax**, deletion of arbitrary objects with **Withdraw**, and the ability to visit in order all the contained objects via **DepthFirstTraversal**. All these operations can be done as efficiently as the priority queue operations. Because search trees support more functions than we really need for priority queues, it is reasonable to suspect that there are more efficient ways to implement priority queues. And indeed there are!

Three different priority queue implementation are described in this chapter. They are **BinaryHeap**, **LeftistHeap**, and **BinomialQueue** (see Figure 11.1). All the implementations have one thing in common—they are all based on a special kind of tree called a *min heap* or simply a *heap*.

### Definition 11.1 ((Min) Heap)
*A (Min) Heap is a tree,*

$$T = \{R, T_0, T_1, T_2, \ldots, T_{n-1}\},$$

*with the following properties:*

1. *Every subtree of T is a heap; and,*
2. *The root of T is less than or equal to the root of every subtree of T. That is,* $\forall i, 0 \le i < n : R \le R_i$, *where* $R_i$ *is the root of* $T_i$.

According to Definition 11.1, the key in each node of a heap is less than or equal to the roots of all the subtrees of that node. Therefore, by induction, the key in each node is less than or equal to all the keys contained in the subtrees of that node. Note, however, that the definition says nothing about the relative ordering of the keys in the subtrees of a given node. For example, in a binary heap either the left or the right subtree of a given node may have the larger key.

---

**FIGURE 11.1**
Object class hierarchy.

---

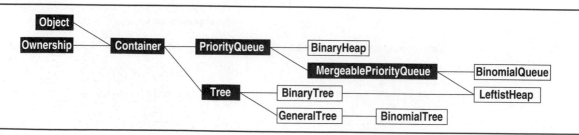

## 11.2  Binary Heaps

A binary heap is a heap-ordered binary tree which has a very special shape called a
*complete tree*. As a result of its special shape, a binary heap can be implemented using
an array as the underlying foundational data structure. Thus, the implementation is
based on array subscript calculations rather than pointer manipulations. And since an
array is used, the storage overhead associated with the pointers contained in the nodes
of the trees is eliminated.

### 11.2.1  Complete Trees

The preceding chapter introduces the idea of a *perfect tree* (see Definition 10.3). Complete trees and perfect trees are closely related, yet quite distinct. As pointed out in the
preceding chapter, a perfect binary tree of height $h$ has exactly $n = 2^{h+1} - 1$ internal
nodes. Since, the only permissible values of $n$ are

$$0, 1, 3, 7, 15, 31, \ldots, 2^{h+1} - 1, \ldots,$$

there is no *perfect* binary tree which contains, say 2, 4, 5, or 6 nodes.

However, we want a data structure that can hold an arbitrary number of objects so
we cannot use a perfect binary tree. Instead, we use a *complete binary tree*, which is
defined as follows:

**Definition 11.2 (Complete Binary Tree)**
*A complete binary tree of height $h \geq 0$, is a binary tree $\{R, T_L, T_R\}$ with the following
properties.*

1.  *If $h = 0$, $T_L = 0$ and $T_R = 0$.*
2.  *For $h > 0$ there are two possibilities:*
    (a)  *$T_L$ is a perfect binary tree of height $h - 1$ and $T_R$ is a complete binary tree
         of height $h - 1$; or*
    (b)  *$T_L$ is a complete binary tree of height $h - 1$ and $T_R$ is a perfect binary tree
         of height $h - 2$.*

Figure 11.2 shows an example of a complete binary tree of height 4. Notice that
the left subtree of node 1 is a complete binary tree of height 3; and the right subtree
is a perfect binary tree of height 2. This corresponds to case 2(b) of Definition 11.2.
Similarly, the left subtree of node 2 is a perfect binary tree of height 2; and the right
subtree is a complete binary tree of height 2. This corresponds to case 2(a) of Definition 11.2.

Is there a complete binary tree with exactly $n$ nodes for every integer $n > 0$? The following theorem addresses this question indirectly by defining the relationship between
the height of a complete tree and the number of nodes it contains.

**FIGURE 11.2**
A complete binary tree.

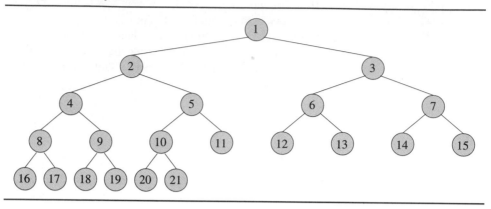

**Theorem 11.1**

*A complete binary tree of height $h \geq 0$ contains at least $2^h$ and at most $2^{h+1} - 1$ nodes.*

**Proof**  First, we prove the lower bound by induction. Let $m_h$ be the *minimum* number of nodes in a complete binary tree of height $h$. To prove the lower bound, we must show that $m_h = 2^h$.

**Base Case**  There is exactly one node in a tree of height zero. Therefore, $m_0 = 1 = 2^0$.

**Inductive Hypothesis**  Assume that $m_h = 2^h$ for $h = 0, 1, 2, \ldots, k$, for some $k \geq 0$. Consider the complete binary tree of height $k + 1$ which has the smallest number of nodes. Its left subtree is a complete tree of height $k$ having the smallest number of nodes and its right subtree is a perfect tree of height $k - 1$.

From the inductive hypothesis, there are $2^k$ nodes in the left subtree and there are exactly $2^{(k-1)+1} - 1$ nodes in the perfect right subtree. Thus,

$$m_{k+1} = 1 + 2^k + 2^{(k-1)+1} - 1$$
$$= 2^{k+1}.$$

Therefore, by induction $m_h = 2^h$ for all $h \geq 0$, which proves the lower bound.

Next, we prove the upper bound by induction. Let $M_h$ be the *maximum* number of nodes in a complete binary tree of height $h$. To prove the upper bound we must show that $M_h = 2^{h+1} - 1$.

**Base Case**  There is exactly one node in a tree of height zero. Therefore, $M_0 = 1 = 2^1 - 1$.

**Inductive Hypothesis**    Assume that $M_h = 2^{h+1} - 1$ for $h = 0, 1, 2, \ldots, k$, for some $k \geq 0$. Consider the complete binary tree of height $k + 1$ which has the largest number of nodes. Its left subtree is a perfect tree of height $k$, and its right subtree is a complete tree of height $k$ having the largest number of nodes.

There are exactly $2^{k+1} - 1$ nodes in the perfect left subtree. From the inductive hypothesis, there are $2^{k+1} - 1$ nodes in the right subtree. Thus,

$$M_{k+1} = 1 + 2^{k+1} - 1 + 2^{k+1} - 1$$
$$= 2^{(k+1)+1} - 1.$$

Therefore, by induction $M_h = 2^{h+1} - 1$ for all $h \geq 0$, which proves the upper bound.

---

It follows from Theorem 11.1 that there exists exactly one complete binary tree that contains exactly $n$ internal nodes for every integer $n \geq 0$. It also follows from Theorem 11.1 that the height of a complete binary tree containing $n$ internal nodes is $h = \lfloor \log_2 n \rfloor$.

Why are we interested in complete trees? As it turns out, complete trees have some useful characteristics. For example, in the preceding chapter we saw that the internal path length of a tree, i.e., the sum of the depths of all the internal nodes, determines the average time for various operations. A complete binary tree has the nice property of having the smallest possible internal path length:

### Theorem 11.2
*The internal path length of a binary tree with $n$ nodes is at least as big as the internal path length of a complete binary tree with $n$ nodes.*

**Proof**    Consider a binary tree with $n$ nodes that has the smallest possible internal path length. Clearly, there can only be one node at depth zero—the root. Similarly, at most two nodes can be at depth 1; at most four nodes can be at depth 2; and so on. Therefore, the internal path length of a tree with $n$ nodes is always at least as large as the sum of the first $n$ terms in the series

$$\underbrace{0}_{1}, \underbrace{1, 1}_{2}, \underbrace{2, 2, 2, 2}_{4}, \underbrace{3, 3, 3, 3, 3, 3, 3, 3}_{8}, 4, \ldots$$

But this summation is precisely the internal path length of a complete binary tree!

---

Since the depth of the average node in a tree is obtained by dividing the internal path length of the tree by $n$, Theorem 11.2 tells us that complete trees are the best possible in the sense that the average depth of a node in a complete tree is the smallest possible. But how small is small? That is, does the average depth grow logarithmically with $n$? The following theorem addresses this question.

## Theorem 11.3

*The* internal path length *of a complete binary tree with n nodes is*

$$\sum_{i=1}^{n} \lfloor \log_2 i \rfloor = (n + 1)\lfloor \log_2(n + 1) \rfloor - 2^{\lfloor \log_2(n+1) \rfloor + 1} + 2.$$

**Proof**  The proof of Theorem 11.3 is left as an exercise for the reader (Exercise 11.6).

---

From Theorem 11.3 we may conclude that the internal path length of a complete tree is $O(n \log n)$. Consequently, the depth of the average node in a complete tree is $O(\log n)$.

### Complete *N*-ary Trees

Definition 11.2 can be easily extended to trees with arbitrary fixed degree $N \geq 2$.

### Definition 11.3 (Complete *N*-ary Tree)

*A complete N-ary tree of height $h \geq 0$ is an N-ary tree $\{R, T_0, T_1, T_2, \ldots, T_{N-1}\}$ with the following properties.*

**1.**  *If $h = 0$, $T_i = \varnothing$ for all $i$, $0 \leq i < N$.*

**2.**  *For $h > 0$ there exists a $j$, $0 \leq j < N$ such that*

   **(a)**  *$T_i$ is a perfect binary tree of height $h - 1$ for all $i : 0 \leq i < j$;*

   **(b)**  *$T_j$ is a complete binary tree of height $h - 1$; and,*

   **(c)**  *$T_i$ is a perfect binary tree of height $h - 2$ for all $i : j < i < N$.*

Note that while it is expressed in somewhat different terms, the definition of a complete *N*-ary tree is consistent with the definition of a binary tree for $N = 2$. Figure 11.3 shows an example of a complete ternary ($N = 3$) tree.

Informally, a complete tree is a tree in which all the levels are full except for the bottom level and the bottom level is filled from left to right. For example, in Figure 11.3, the first three levels are full. The fourth level which comprises nodes 14–21 is partially full and has been filled from left to right.

The main advantage of using complete binary trees is that they can be easily stored in an array. Specifically, consider the nodes of a complete tree numbered consecutively in *level-order* as they are in Figure 11.2 and 11.3. There is a simple formula that relates the number of a node with the number of its parent and the numbers of its children.

Consider the case of a complete binary tree. The root node is node 1 and its children are nodes 2 and 3. In general, the children of node $i$ are $2i$ and $2i + 1$. Conversely, the parent of node $i$ is $\lfloor i/2 \rfloor$. Figure 11.4 illustrates this idea by showing how the complete binary tree shown in Figure 11.2 is mapped into an array. When using this approach, the pointers are no longer explicitly recorded.

A remarkable characteristic of complete trees is that filling the bottom level from left to right corresponds to adding elements at the end of the array! Thus, a complete tree containing $n$ nodes occupies the first $n$ consecutive array positions.

**FIGURE 11.3**
A complete ternary tree.

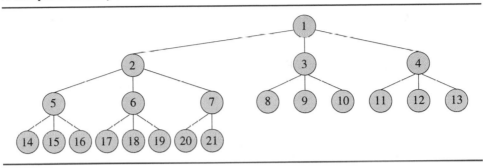

**FIGURE 11.4**
Array representation of a complete binary tree.

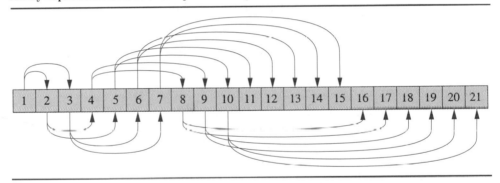

The array subscript calculations given above can be easily generalized to complete $N$-ary trees. Assuming that the root occupies position 1 of the array, its $N$ children occupy positions $2, 3, \ldots, N + 1$. In general, the children of node $i$ occupy positions

$$N(i - 1) + 2, N(i - 1) + 3, N(i - 1) + 4, \ldots, Ni + 1,$$

and the parent of node $i$ is found at

$$\lceil (i - 1)/N \rceil.$$

## 11.2.2 Implementation

A binary heap is a heap-ordered complete binary tree which is implemented using an array. In a heap the smallest key is found at the root and since the root is always found in the first position of the array, finding the smallest key is a trivial operation in a binary heap.

---

**PROGRAM 11.2**
BinaryHeap class definition

```
1   class BinaryHeap : public PriorityQueue
2   {
3       Array<Object*> array;
4   public:
5       BinaryHeap (unsigned int);
6       ~BinaryHeap ();
7       // ...
8   };
```

---

Program 11.2 declares the class **BinaryHeap**. The **BinaryHeap** class is derived from the **PriorityQueue** abstract base class. Since **BinaryHeap** is a concrete class, it provides implementations for all of the member functions declared as pure virtual functions in the base class. In the interest of brevity, the declarations of these functions have been elided from Program 11.2.

### Member Variables

The **BinaryHeap** class has a rather simple implementation. In particular, it requires only a single member variable, **array**, which is declared as an array of pointers to **Object** class instances. This array is used to hold pointers to the objects which are contained in the binary tree. When there are $n$ items in the heap, the pointers to those items occupy the first $n$ array positions.

### Constructor, Destructor, and Purge Member Functions

Program 11.3 defines the **BinaryHeap** class constructor. The constructor takes a single argument of type **unsigned int** which specifies the maximum capacity of the binary heap. The argument passed on to the constructor for the **array** member variable. Notice too that the array is initialized so that its positions are numbered starting from subscript 1 rather than the default of zero.

The purpose of the **Purge** member function of the **BinaryHeap** class is to delete from the priority queue all contained and owned objects. Pointers to the contained objects are found in the first $n$ = **count** array positions. Clearly the worst-case running time for the **Purge** function is

$$n\mathcal{T}\langle \texttt{T::~T()}\rangle + O(n)$$

where $\mathcal{T}\langle \texttt{T::~T()}\rangle$ is the worst-case time required to delete an object instance.

The implementation of the destructor for the **BinaryHeap** class is trivial as it simply calls **Purge** to do its work. Consequently, the destructor has the same running time as above.

**PROGRAM 11.3**
BinaryHeap class constructor, destructor, and Purge member function definitions

```
1   BinaryHeap::BinaryHeap (unsigned int length) :
2       array (length, 1)
3       {}
4
5   void BinaryHeap::Purge ()
6   {
7       if (IsOwner ())
8       {
9           for (unsigned int i = 1; i < count + 1; ++i)
10          delete array [i];
11      }
12      count = 0;
13  }
14
15  BinaryHeap::~BinaryHeap ()
16      { Purge (); }
```

### 11.2.3 Putting Items into a Binary Heap

There are two requirements which must be satisfied when an item is inserted in a binary heap. First, the resulting tree must have the correct shape. Second, the tree must remain heap-ordered. Figure 11.5 illustrates the way in which this is done.

Since the resulting tree must be a complete tree, there is only one place in the tree where a node can be added. That is, since the bottom level must be filled from left to right, the node must be added at the next available position in the bottom level of the tree, as shown in Figure 11.5(*a*).

In this example, the new item to be inserted has the key 2. Note that we cannot simply drop the new item into the next position in the complete tree because the resulting tree is no longer heap ordered. Instead, the hole in the heap is moved toward the root by moving items down in the heap as shown in Figure 11.5(*b*) and (*c*). The process of moving items down terminates either when we reach the root of the tree, or when the hole has been moved up to a position in which when the new item is inserted the result is a heap.

Program 11.4 gives the code for inserting an item in a binary heap. The **Enqueue** member function of the **BinaryHeap** class takes as its lone argument a reference to the item to be inserted in the heap. If the priority queue is full an exception is thrown. Otherwise, the item is inserted as described above.

The implementation of the algorithm is actually remarkably simple. Lines 6–11 move the hole in the heap up by moving items down. When the loop terminates, the new item can be inserted at position *i*. Therefore, the loop terminates either at the root,

**FIGURE 11.5**
Inserting an item into a binary heap.

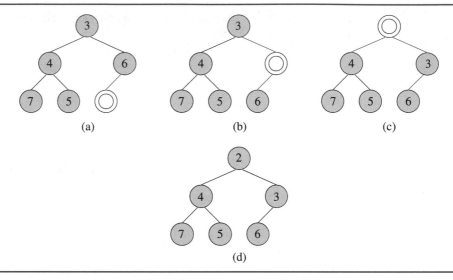

(a)          (b)          (c)

(d)

**PROGRAM 11.4**
**BinaryHeap** class **Enqueue** member function definition

```
1   void BinaryHeap::Enqueue (Object& object)
2   {
3       if (count == array.Length ())
4           throw domain_error ("priority queue is full");
5       ++count;
6       unsigned int i = count;
7       while (i > 1 && *array [i / 2] > object)
8       {
9           array [i] = array [i / 2];
10          i /= 2;
11      }
12      array [i] = &object;
13  }
```

$i = 1$, or when the key in the parent of $i$, which is found at position $\lfloor i/2 \rfloor$, is smaller than the item to be inserted.

Notice too that a good optimizing compiler will recognize that the subscript calculations involve only division by 2. Therefore, the divisions can be replaced by bitwise right shifts which usually run much more quickly.

Since the depth of a complete binary tree with $n$ nodes is $\lfloor \log_2 n \rfloor$, the worst-case running time for the **Enqueue** operation is

$$\lfloor \log_2 n \rfloor \mathcal{T} \langle \texttt{T::Compare(T\&,T\&)} \rangle + O(\log n),$$

where $\mathcal{T} \langle \texttt{T::Compare(T\&,T\&)} \rangle$ is the time required to compare to objects. If

$$\mathcal{T} \langle \texttt{T::Compare(T\&,T\&)} \rangle = O(1),$$

the **Enqueue** operation is simply $O(\log n)$ in the worst case.

### 11.2.4 Removing Items from a Binary Heap

The **DequeueMin** function removes from a priority queue the item having the smallest key. In order to remove the smallest item, it needs first to be located. Therefore, the **DequeueMin** operation is closely related to **FindMin**.

The smallest item is always at the root of a min heap. Therefore, the **FindMin** operation is trivial. Program 11.5 gives the code for the **FindMin** member function of the **BinaryHeap** class. Assuming that no exception is thrown, the running time of **FindMin** is clearly $O(1)$.

Since the bottom row of a complete tree is filled from left to right as items are added, it follows that the bottom row must be emptied from right to left as items are removed. So, we have a problem: The datum to be removed from the heap by **DequeueMin** is in the root, but the node to be removed from the heap is in the bottom row.

Figure 11.6(*a*) illustrates the problem. The **DequeueMin** operation removes the key 2 from the heap, but it is the node containing key 6 that must be removed from the tree to make it into a complete tree again. When key 2 is removed from the root, a hole is created in the tree as shown in Figure 11.6(*b*).

The trick is to move the hole down in the tree to a point where the leftover key, in this case the key 6, can be reinserted into the tree. To move a hole down in the tree, we consider the children of the empty node and move up the smallest key. Moving up the smallest key ensures that the result will be a min heap.

---

**PROGRAM 11.5**
**BinaryHeap** class **FindMin** member function definition

```
1   Object& BinaryHeap::FindMin () const
2   {
3       if (count == 0)
4           throw domain_error ("priority queue is empty");
5       return *array [1];
6   }
```

---

**FIGURE 11.6**
Removing an item from a binary heap.

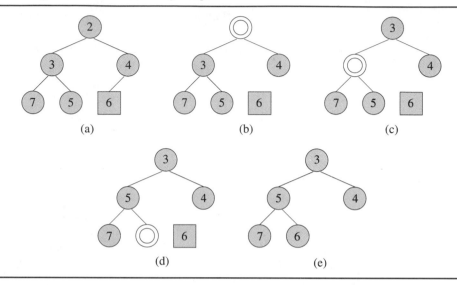

(a)          (b)          (c)

(d)          (e)

The process of moving up continues until either the hole has been pushed down to a leaf node, or until the hole has been pushed to a point where the leftover key can be inserted into the heap. In the example shown in Figure 11.6(*b*)–(*c*), the hole is pushed from the root node to a leaf node where the key 6 is ultimately placed as shown in Figure 11.6(*d*).

Program 11.6 gives the code for the **DequeueMin** function of the **BinaryHeap** class. This function implements the deletion algorithm described above. The main loop (lines 9–19) moves the hole in the tree down by moving the child with the smallest key up until either a leaf node is reached or until the hole has been moved down to a point, where the last element of the array can be reinserted.

In the worst case, the hole must be pushed from the root to a leaf node. Each iteration of the loop makes at most two object comparisons and moves the hole down one level. Therefore, the running time of the **DequeueMin** operation is

$$2\lfloor \log_2 n \rfloor \mathcal{T}\langle \texttt{T::Compare(T\&,T\&)}\rangle + O(\log n),$$

where $n = $ **count** is the number of items in the heap and the $\mathcal{T}\langle \texttt{T::Compare(T\&,T\&)}\rangle$ is the time required to compare two object instances. If

$$\mathcal{T}\langle \texttt{T::Compare(T\&,T\&)}\rangle = O(1),$$

the **DequeueMin** operation is simply $O(\log n)$ in the worst case.

## 11.3  Leftist Heaps

A leftist heap is a heap-ordered binary tree which has a very special shape called a *leftist tree*. One of the nice properties of leftist heaps is that it is possible to merge two

**PROGRAM 11.6**
BinaryHeap class DequeueMin member function definition

```
 1  Object& BinaryHeap::DequeueMin ()
 2  {
 3      if (count == 0)
 4          throw domain_error ("priority queue is empty");
 5      Object& result = *array [1];
 6      Object& last = *array [count];
 7      --count;
 8      unsigned int i = 1;
 9      while (2 * i < count + 1)
10      {
11          unsigned int child = 2 * i;
12          if (child + 1 < count + 1
13              && *array [child + 1] < *array [child])
14              child += 1;
15          if (last <= *array [child])
16              break;
17          array [i] = array [child];
18          i = child;
19      }
20      array [i] = &last;
21      return result;
22  }
```

leftist heaps efficiently. As a result, leftist heaps are suited for the implementation of mergeable priority queues.

## 11.3.1  Leftist Trees

A *leftist tree* is a tree which tends to "lean" to the left. The tendency to lean to the left is defined in terms of the shortest path from the root to an external node. In a leftist tree, the shortest path to an external node is always found on the right.

Every node in a binary tree has associated with it a quantity called its *null path length* which is defined as follows:

### Definition 11.4 (Null Path and Null Path Length)
*Consider an arbitrary node x in some binary tree T. The* null path *of node x is the shortest path in T from x to an external node of T.*
*The* null path length *of node x is the length of its null path.*

Sometimes it is convenient to talk about the null path length of an entire tree rather than of a node:

### Definition 11.5 (Null Path Length of a Tree)
*The* null path length *of an empty tree is zero, and the null path length of a non-empty binary tree* $T = \{R, T_L, T_R\}$ *is the null path length of its root R.*

When a new node or subtree is attached to a given tree, it is usually attached in place of an external node. Since the null path length of a tree is the length of the shortest path from the root of the tree to an external node, the null path length gives a lower bound on the cost of insertion. For example, the running time for insertion in a binary search tree, Program 10.4, is at least

$$d\mathcal{T}\langle \texttt{T::Compare(T\&,T\&)}\rangle + \Omega(d)$$

where $d$ is the null path length of the tree.

A *leftist tree* is a tree in which the shortest path to an external node is always on the right. This informal idea is defined more precisely in terms of the null path lengths as follows:

### Definition 11.6 (Leftist Tree)
*A* leftist tree *is a binary tree T with the following properties:*

1. *Either $T = \emptyset$; or*
2. *$T = \{R, T_L, T_R\}$, where both $T_L$ and $T_R$ are leftist trees which have null path lengths $d_L$ and $d_R$, respectively, such that*

$$d_L \geq d_R.$$

Figure 11.7 shows an example of a leftist heap. A leftist heap is simply a heap-ordered leftist tree. The external depth of the node is shown to the right of each node in Figure 11.7. The figure clearly shows that it is not necessarily the case in a leftist tree that the number of nodes to the left of a given node is greater than the number to the right. However, it is always the case that the null path length on the left is greater than or equal to the null path length on the right for every node in the tree.

The reason for our interest in leftist trees is illustrated by the following theorems.

### Theorem 11.4
*Consider a leftist tree T which contains n internal nodes. The path leading from the root of T downwards to the right-most external node contains at most $\lfloor\log_2(n+1)\rfloor$ nodes.*

**Proof**    Assume that $T$ has null path length $d$. Then $T$ must contain at least $2^d$ leaves. Otherwise, there would be a shorter path than $d$ from the root of $T$ to an external node.

A binary tree with exactly $l$ leaves has exactly $l - 1$ non-leaf internal nodes. Since $T$ has at least $2^d$ leaves, it must contain at least $n \geq 2^{d+1} - 1$ internal nodes altogether. Therefore, $d \leq \log_2(n + 1) - 1$.

Since $T$ is a leftist tree, the shortest path to an external node must be the path on the right. Thus, the length of the path to the rightmost external is at most $\lfloor\log_2(n + 1)\rfloor$.

**FIGURE 11.7**
A leftist heap.

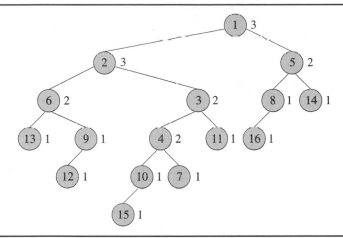

There is an interesting dichotomy between AVL balanced trees and leftist trees. The shape of an AVL tree satisfies the AVL balance condition which stipulates that the difference in the heights of the left and right subtrees of every node may differ by at most one. The effect of AVL balancing is to ensure that the height of the tree is $O(\log n)$.

On the other hand, leftist trees have an "imbalance condition" which requires the null path length of the left subtree to be greater than or equal to that of the right subtree. The effect of the condition is to ensure that the length of the right path in a leftist tree is $O(\log n)$. Therefore, by devising algorithms for manipulating leftist heaps which only follow the right path of the heap, we can achieve running times which are logarithmic in the number of nodes.

The dichotomy also extends to the structure of the algorithms. For example, an imbalance sometimes results from an insertion in an AVL tree. The imbalance is rectified by doing rotations. Similarly, an insertion into a leftist tree may result in a violation of the "imbalance condition." That is, the null path length of the right subtree of a node may become greater than that of the left subtree. Fortunately, it is possible to restore the proper condition simply by swapping the left and right subtrees of that node.

## 11.3.2 Implementation

This section presents a pointer-based implementation of leftist heaps. Program 11.7 gives the declaration of the **LeftistHeap** class. The **LeftistHeap** class is derived from both the **MergeablePriorityQueue** abstract class and the **BinaryTree** concrete class.

**Member Variables**
Since a leftist heap is a heap-ordered binary tree, it inherits from the **BinaryTree** base class the three member variables: **key**, **left**, and **right**. The **key** is a pointer to the object contained in the given node, and the **left** and **right** member variables point to

---

**PROGRAM 11.7**
`LeftistHeap` class definition

---

```
1  class LeftistHeap :
2      public BinaryTree, public MergeablePriorityQueue
3  {
4      unsigned int nullPathLength;
5
6      void SwapContents (LeftistHeap&);
7  public:
8      LeftistHeap ();
9      LeftistHeap (Object&);
10
11     LeftistHeap& Left () const;
12     LeftistHeap& Right () const;
13     void Merge (MergeablePriorityQueue&);
14     // ...
15 };
```

---

the left and right subtrees of the given node, respectively. In addition, the member variable **nullPathLength** records the null path length of the given node. By recording the null path length in the node, it is possible to check the leftist heap balance condition in constant time.

**SwapContents Member Function**
In addition to the inherited public interface, the **LeftistHeap** class definition includes the private member function **SwapContents**. This routine is used to implement the various operations on leftist heaps. The **SwapContents** routine takes a reference to another leftist heap node. The effect of the routine is to exchange the contents of "**this**" node with those of the given node. The implementation of **SwapContents** is trivial and the running time required is obviously $O(1)$.

## 11.3.3  Merging Leftist Heaps

In order to merge two leftist heaps, say **h1** and **h2**, declared as follows,

```
LeftistHeap h1;
LeftistHeap h2;
```

we invoke the **Merge** operation like this:

```
h1.Merge (h2);
```

The effect of the **Merge** routine is to take all the nodes from **h2** and to attach them to **h1**, thus leaving **h2** as the empty heap.

In order to achieve a logarithmic running time, it is important for the `Merge` routine to do all its work on the right sides of `h1` and `h2`. It turns out that the algorithm for merging leftist heaps is actually quite simple.

To begin with, if `h1` is the empty heap, then we can simply swap the contents of `h1` and `h2`. Otherwise, let us assume that the root of `h2` is larger than the root of `h1`. Then we can merge the two heaps by recursively merging `h2` with the *right* subheap of `h1`. After doing so, it may turn out that the right subheap of `h1` now has a larger null path length than the left subheap. This we rectify by swapping the left and right subheaps so that the result is again leftist. On the other hand, if `h2` initially has the smaller root, we simply exchange the rôles of `h1` and `h2` and proceed as above.

Figure 11.8 illustrates the merge operation. In this example, we wish to merge the two trees $T_1$ and $T_2$ shown in Figure 11.8(*a*). Since $T_2$ has the larger root, it is recursively merged with the right subtree of $T_1$. The result of that merge replaces the right subtree of $T_1$, as shown in Figure 11.8(*b*). Since the null path length of the right subtree is now greater than the left, the subtrees of $T_1$ are swapped giving the leftist heap shown in Figure 11.8(*c*).

Program 11.8 gives the code for the `Merge` member function of the `LeftistHeap` class. Clearly, the `Merge` routine only visits nodes on the right-most paths of the trees being merged. Suppose we are merging two trees, say $T_1$ and $T_2$, with null path lengths $d_1$ and $d_2$, respectively. Then the running time of the `Merge` routine is

$$(d_1 - 1 + d_2 - 1)\mathcal{T}\langle\texttt{T::Compare(T\&,T\&)}\rangle + O(d_1 + d_2)$$

where $\mathcal{T}\langle\texttt{T::Compare(T\&,T\&)}\rangle$ is the time required to compare two keys. If we assume that the time to compare two keys is a constant, then we get $O(\log n_1 + \log n_2)$, where $n_1$ and $n_2$ are the number of internal nodes in trees $T_1$ and $T_2$, respectively.

## 11.3.4  Putting Items into a Leftist Heap

The `Enqueue` member function of the `LeftistHeap` class is used to put items into the heap. `Enqueue` is easily implemented using the `Merge` operation. That is, to enqueue an item in a given heap, we simply create a new heap containing the one item to be enqueued and merge it with the given heap. The algorithm to do this is shown in Program 11.9.

The expression for the running time for the `Insert` operation follows directly from that of the `Merge` operation. That is, the time required for the `Insert` operation in the worst case is

$$(d - 1)\mathcal{T}\langle\texttt{T::Compare(T\&,T\&)}\rangle + O(d),$$

where $d$ is the null path length of the heap into which the item is inserted. If we assume that two keys can be compared in constant time, the running time for `Insert` becomes simply $O(\log n)$, where $n$ is the number of nodes in the tree into which the item is inserted.

**FIGURE 11.8**
Merging leftist heaps.

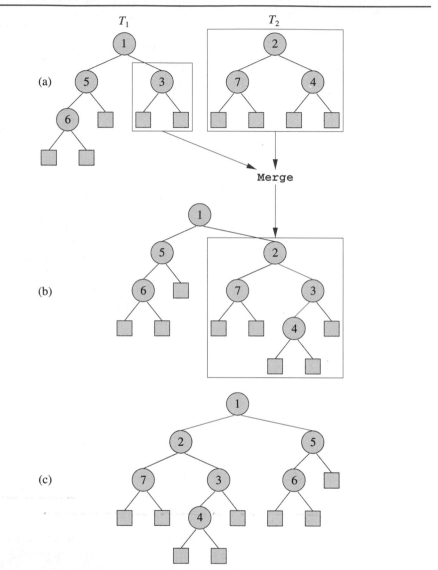

## 11.3.5 Removing Items from a Leftist Heap

The **FindMin** member function locates the item with the smallest key in a given priority queue and the **DequeueMin** member function removes it from the queue. Since the smallest item in a heap is found at the root, the **FindMin** operation is easy to implement. Program 11.10 shows how it can be done. Clearly, the running time of the **FindMin** operation is $O(1)$.

**PROGRAM 11.8**
LeftistHeap class Merge member function definition

```
1   void LeftistHeap::Merge (MergeablePriorityQueue& queue)
2   {
3       LeftistHeap& arg = dynamic_cast<LeftistHeap&> (queue);
4       if (IsEmpty ())
5           SwapContents (arg);
6       else if (!arg.IsEmpty ())
7       {
8           if (*key > *arg.key)
9               SwapContents (arg);
10          Right ().Merge (arg);
11          if (Left ().nullPathLength < Right ().nullPathLength)
12              Swap (left, right);
13          nullPathLength = 1 + Min (Left ().nullPathLength,
14              Right ().nullPathLength);
15      }
16  }
```

**PROGRAM 11.9**
LeftistHeap class Enqueue member function definition

```
1   void LeftistHeap::Enqueue (Object& object)
2   {
3       LeftistHeap heap (object);
4       Merge (heap);
5   }
```

**PROGRAM 11.10**
LeftistHeap class FindMin member function definitions

```
1   Object& LeftistHeap::FindMin () const
2   {
3       if (IsEmpty ())
4           throw domain_error ("priority queue is empty");
5       return *key;
6   }
```

Since the smallest item in a heap is at the root, the DequeueMin operation must delete the root node. Since a leftist heap is a binary heap, the root has at most two children. In general when the root is deleted, we are left with two non-empty leftist heaps. Since we already have an efficient way to merge leftist heaps, the solution is to simply merge the two children of the root to obtain a single heap again! Program 11.11 shows how the DequeueMin operation of the LeftistHeap class can be implemented.

**PROGRAM 11.11**
LeftistHeap class DequeueMin member function definition

```
1   Object& LeftistHeap::DequeueMin ()
2   {
3       if (IsEmpty ())
4           throw domain_error ("priority queue is empty");
5       Object& result = *key;
6       LeftistHeap& oldLeft = Left ();
7       LeftistHeap& oldRight = Right ();
8       key = 0;
9       left = 0;
10      right = 0;
11      SwapContents (oldLeft);
12      delete &oldLeft;
13      Merge (oldRight);
14      delete &oldRight;
15      return result;
16  }
```

The running time of Program 11.11 is determined by the time required to merge the two children of the root (line 13) since the rest of the work in **DequeueMin** can be done in constant time. Consider the running time to delete the root of a leftist heap $T$ with $n$ internal nodes. The running time to merge the left and right subtrees of $T$

$$(d_L - 1 + d_R - 1)\mathcal{T}\langle\texttt{T::Compare(T\&,T\&)}\rangle + O(d_L + d_R),$$

where $d_L$ and $d_R$ are the null path lengths of the left and right subtrees $T$, respectively. In the worst case, $d_R = 0$ and $d_L = \lfloor\log_2 n\rfloor$. If we assume that $\mathcal{T}\langle\texttt{T::Compare(T\&,T\&)}\rangle = O(1)$, the running time for **DequeueMin** is $O(\log n)$.

## 11.4 Binomial Queues

A binomial queue is a priority queue that is implemented not as a single tree but as a collection of heap-ordered trees. A collection of trees is called a *forest*. Each of the trees in a binomial queue has a very special shape called a *binomial tree*. Binomial trees are general trees. That is, the maximum degree of a node is not fixed.

The remarkable characteristic of binomial queues is that the merge operation is similar in structure to binary addition. That is, the collection of binomial trees that make up the binomial queue is like the set of bits that make up the binary representation of a non-negative integer. Furthermore, the merging of two binomial queues is done by adding the binomial trees that make up that queue in the same way that the bits are combined when adding two binary numbers.

### 11.4.1 Binomial Trees

A binomial tree is a general tree with a very special shape:

**Definition 11.7 (Binomial Tree)**
*The binomial tree of order $k \geq 0$ with root R is the tree $B_k$ defined as follows:*

1.  *If $k = 0$, $B_k = B_0 = \{R\}$. That is, the binomial tree of order zero consists of a single node, R.*
2.  *If $k > 0$, $B_k = \{R, B_0, B_1, \ldots, B_{k-1}\}$. That is, the binomial tree of order $k > 0$ comprises the root R, and k binomial subtrees, $B_0, B_1, \ldots, B_{k-1}$.*

Figure 11.9 shows the first five binomial trees, $B_0$–$B_4$. It follows directly from Definition 11.7 that the root of $B_k$, the binomial tree of order $k$, has degree $k$. Since $k$ may be arbitrarily large, so too can the degree of the root. Furthermore, the root of a binomial tree has the largest fanout of any of the nodes in that tree.

The number of nodes in a binomial tree of order $k$ is a function of $k$.

### Theorem 11.5
*The binomial tree of order k, $B_k$, contains $2^k$ nodes.*

**Proof** (By induction). Let $n_k$ be the number of nodes in $B_k$, a binomial tree of order $k$.

**Base Case** By definition, $B_0$ consists of a single node. Therefore, $n_0 = 1 = 2^0$.

**Inductive Hypothesis** Assume that $n_k = 2^k$ for $k = 0, 1, 2, \ldots, l$, for some $l \geq 0$. Consider the binomial tree of order $l + 1$:

$$B_{l+1} = \{R, B_0, B_1, B_2, \ldots, B_l\}.$$

Therefore, the number of nodes in $B_{l+1}$ is given by

$$n_{l+1} = 1 + \sum_{i=0}^{l} n_i$$

$$= 1 + \sum_{i=0}^{l} 2^i$$

$$= 1 + \frac{2^{l+1} - 1}{2 - 1}$$

$$= 2^{l+1}.$$

Therefore, by induction on $l$, $n_k = 2^k$ for all $k \geq 0$.

**FIGURE 11.9**
Binomial trees $B_0$, $B_1$, ..., $B_4$.

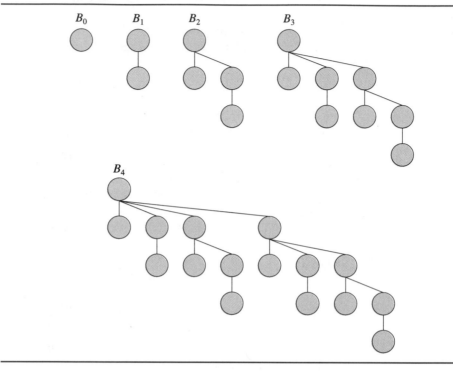

It follows from Theorem 11.5 that binomial trees only come in sizes that are a power of 2. That is, $n_k \in \{1, 2, 4, 8, 16, \ldots\}$. Furthermore, for a given power of 2, there is exactly one shape of binomial tree.

### Theorem 11.6
*The height of $B_k$, the binomial tree of order k, is k.*

**Proof** (By induction). Let $h_k$ be the height of $B_k$, a binomial tree of order $k$.

**Base Case** By definition, $B_0$ consists of a single node. Therefore, $h_0 = 0$.

**Inductive Hypothesis** Assume that $h_k = k$ for $k = 0, 1, 2, \ldots, l$, for some $l \geq 0$. Consider the binomial tree of order $l + 1$:

$$B_{l+1} = \{R, B_0, B_1, B_2, \ldots, B_l\}.$$

Therefore, the height $B_{l+1}$ is given by

$$
\begin{aligned}
h_{l+1} &= 1 + \max_{0 \le i \le l} h_i \\
&= 1 + \max_{0 \le i \le l} i \\
&= l + 1.
\end{aligned}
$$

Therefore, by induction on $l$, $h_k = k$ for all $k \ge 0$.

---

Theorem 11.6 tells us that the height of a binomial tree of order $k$ is $k$, and Theorem 11.5 tells us that the number of nodes is $n_k = 2^k$. Therefore, the height of $B_k$ is exactly $O(\log n)$.

Figure 11.10 shows that there are two ways to think about the construction of binomial trees. The first way follows directly from the Definition 11.7. That is, binomial $B_k$ consists of a root node to which the $k$ binomial trees $B_0$, $B_1$, ..., $B_{k-1}$ are attached, as shown in Figure 11.10(a).

Alternatively, we can think of $B_k$ as being comprised of two binomial trees of order $k - 1$. For example, Figure 11.10(b) shows that $B_4$ is made up of two instances of $B_3$. In general, suppose we have two trees of order $k - 1$, say $B_{k-1}^1$ and $B_{k-1}^2$, where $B_{k-1}^1 = \{R^1, B_0^1, B_1^1, B_2^1, \ldots, B_{k-2}^1\}$. Then we can construct a binomial tree of order $k$ by combining the trees to get

$$
B_k = \{R^1, B_0^1, B_1^1, B_2^1, \ldots, B_{k-2}^1, B_{k-1}^2\}.
$$

Why do we call $B_k$ a *binomial* tree? We do so because the number of nodes at a given depth in the tree is determined by the *binomial coefficient*. And the binomial coefficient derives its name from the *binomial theorem*. And the binomial theorem tells us how to compute the $n$th power of a *binomial*. And a binomial is an expression which consists of two terms, such as $x + y$. That is why it is called a binomial tree!

### Theorem 11.7 (Binomial Theorem)
*The $n$th power of the binomial $x + y$ for $n \ge 0$ is given by*

$$
(x + y)^n = \sum_{i=0}^{n} \binom{n}{i} x^i y^{n-i},
$$

*where $\binom{n}{i} = \frac{n!}{i!(n-i)!}$ is called the* binomial coefficient.

**Proof**   The proof of the binomial theorem is left as an exercise for the reader (Exercise 11.15).[1]

---

[1] Isaac Newton discovered the binomial theorem in 1676 but did not publish a proof. Leonhard Euler attempted a proof in 1774. Karl Friedrich Gauss produced the first correct proof in 1812.

**FIGURE 11.10**
Two views of binomial tree $B_4$.

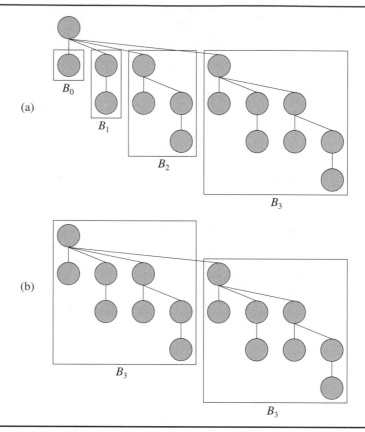

The following theorem gives the expression for the number of nodes at a given depth in a binomial tree.

### Theorem 11.8

*The number of nodes at level l in $B_k$, the binomial tree of order k, where $0 \leq l \leq k$, is given by the* binomial coefficient $\binom{k}{l}$.

**Proof**    (By induction). Let $n_k(l)$ be the number of nodes at level $l$ in $B_k$, a binomial tree of order $k$.

**Base Case**    Since $B_0$ contains a single node, there is only one level in the tree, $l = 0$, and exactly one node at that level. Therefore, $n_0(0) = 1 = \binom{0}{0}$.

**Inductive Hypothesis**    Assume that $n_k(l) = \binom{k}{l}$ for $k = 0, 1, 2, \ldots, h$, for some $h \geq 0$. The binomial tree of order $h + 1$ is composed of two binomial trees of height $h$, one attached under the root of the other. Hence, the number of nodes at level $l$ in $B_{h+1}$ is equal to the number of nodes at level $l$ in $B_h$ plus the number of nodes at level $l-1$ in $B_h$:

$$
\begin{aligned}
n_{h+1}(l) &= n_h(l) + n_h(l-1) \\
&= \binom{h}{l} + \binom{h}{l-1} \\
&= \frac{h!}{(h-l)!l!} + \frac{h!}{(h-(l-1))!(l-1)!} \\
&= \frac{h!(h+1-l)}{(h+1-l)(h-l)!l!} + \frac{h!l}{(h+1-l)!l(l-1)!} \\
&= \frac{h!(h+1-l) + h!l}{(h+1-l)!l!} \\
&= \frac{(h+1)!}{(h+1-l)!l!} \\
&= \binom{h+1}{l}
\end{aligned}
$$

Therefore, by induction on $h$, $n_k(l) = \binom{k}{l}$.

---

## 11.4.2 Binomial Queues

If binomial trees only come in sizes that are powers of 2, how do we implement a container which holds an arbitrary number of items $n$ using binomial trees? The answer is related to the binary representation of the number $n$. Every non-negative integer $n$ can be expressed in binary form as

$$
n = \sum_{i=0}^{\lfloor \log_2 n \rfloor} b_i 2^i,
\tag{11.1}
$$

where $b_i \in \{0, 1\}$ is the $i$th *binary digit* or *bit* in the representation of $n$. For example, $n = 27$ is expressed as the binary number $11011_2$ because $27 = 16 + 8 + 2 + 1$.

To make a container which holds exactly $n$ items, we use a collection of binomial trees. A collection of trees is called a *forest*. The forest contains binomial tree $B_i$ if the $i$th bit in the binary representation of $n$ is a 1. That is, the forest $F_n$ which contains exactly $n$ items is given by

$$
F_n = \{B_i : b_i = 1\},
$$

where $b_i$ is determined from Equation 11.1. For example, the forest which contains 27 items is $F_{27} = \{B_4, B_3, B_1, B_0\}$.

The analogy between $F_n$ and the binary representation of $n$ carries over to the merge operation. Suppose we have two forests, say $F_n$ and $F_m$. Since $F_n$ contains $n$ items and

$F_m$ contains $m$ items, the combination of the two contains $n + m$ items. Therefore, the resulting forest is $F_{n+m}$.

For example, consider $n = 27$ and $m = 10$. In this case, we need to merge $F_{27} = \{B_4, B_3, B_1, B_0\}$ with $F_{10} = \{B_3, B_1\}$. Recall that two binomial trees of order $k$ can be combined to obtain a binomial tree of order $k + 1$; for example, $B_1 + B_1 = B_2$. But this is just like adding binary digits! In binary notation, the sum $27 + 10$ is calculated like this:

$$
\begin{array}{r}
1\ \ 1\ \ 0\ \ 1\ \ 1 \\
+\qquad 1\ \ 0\ \ 1\ \ 0 \\
\hline
1\ \ 0\ \ 0\ \ 1\ \ 0\ \ 1
\end{array}
$$

The merging of $F_{27}$ and $F_{20}$ is done in the same way:

$$
\begin{array}{ccccccc}
 & B_4 & B_3 & \varnothing & B_1 & B_0 & F_{27} \\
+ & & B_3 & \varnothing & B_1 & \varnothing & F_{10} \\
\hline
B_5 & \varnothing & \varnothing & B_2 & \varnothing & B_0 & F_{37}
\end{array}
$$

Therefore, the result is $F_{37} = \{B_5, B_2, B_0\}$.

### 11.4.3   Implementation

**Heap-Ordered Binomial Trees**

Since binomial trees are simply general trees with a special shape, we can make use of the **GeneralTree** class presented in Section 9.6.3 to implement the **BinomialTree** class. As shown in Program 11.12, the **BinomialTree** class is derived from the **GeneralTree** class from which it inherits almost all its functionality. In addition to the constructor, only two more member functions are declared—**SwapContents** and **Add**.

No new member variables are declared in the **BinomialTree** class. Remember that the implementation of the **GeneralTree** class uses a linked list to contain the pointers to the subtrees, since the degree of a node in a general tree may be arbitrarily large. Also, the **GeneralTree** class already keeps track of the degree of a node in its member variable **degree**. Since the degree of the root node of a binomial tree of order $k$ is $k$, it is not necessary to keep track of the order explicitly. The **degree** variable serves this purpose nicely.

The purpose of the **SwapContents** member function is evident from its name— it simply exchanges the contents of two nodes of a binomial tree. It is relatively easy to implement an algorithm to swap the contents of a node of a binomial tree. It is not difficult to ensure that the running time of **SwapContents** is $O(1)$, regardless of the degrees of the nodes whose contents are swapped.

The **Add** member function is used to combine two binomial trees of the same order, say $k$, into a single binomial tree of order $k + 1$. Each of the two trees to be combined is

**PROGRAM 11.12**
BinomialTree class definition

```
1  class BinomialTree : public GeneralTree
2  {
3      void SwapContents (BinomialTree&);
4  public:
5      BinomialTree (Object&);
6
7      void Add (BinomialTree&);
8      BinomialTree& Subtree (unsigned int) const;
9  };
```

heap-ordered. Since the smallest key is at the root of a heap-ordered tree, we know that the root of the result must be the smaller root of the two trees which are to be combined. Therefore, to combine the two trees, we simply attach the tree with the larger root under the root of the tree with the smaller root. For example, Figure 11.11 illustrates how two heap-ordered binomial trees of order two are combined into a single heap-ordered tree of order three.

The implementation of the Add function is given in Program 11.13. The Add function takes a reference to a BinomialTree and attaches the specified tree to this node. This is only permissible when both trees have the same order.

In order to ensure that the resulting binomial tree is heap ordered, the roots of the trees are compared. If necessary, the contents of the nodes are exchanged using SwapContents (lines 5–6) before the subtree is attached (line 7). Clearly the running time of the Add member function is

$$\mathcal{T}\langle \text{T::Compare(T\&,T\&)} \rangle + O(1).$$

That is, exactly one comparison and a constant amount of additional work is needed to combine two binomial trees.

**PROGRAM 11.13**
BinomialTree class Add member function definition

```
1  void BinomialTree::Add (BinomialTree& tree)
2  {
3      if (degree != tree.degree)
4          throw invalid_argument ("incompatible degrees");
5      if (*key > *tree.key)
6          SwapContents (tree);
7      AttachSubtree (tree);
8  }
```

**FIGURE 11.11**
Adding binomial trees.

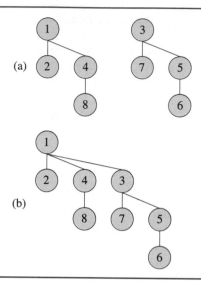

(a)

(b)

## Binomial Queues

A binomial queue is a mergeable priority queue implemented as a forest of binomial trees. In this section we present a pointer-based implementation of the forest. That is, the forest is represented using a linked list of pointers to binomial trees.

Program 11.14 defines the **BinomialQueue** class. The **BinomialQueue** is derived from the **MergeablePriorityQueue** abstract base class.

## Member Variables

The **BinomialQueue** class definition contains the single-member variable **list**, which is declared as a linked list of pointers to **BinomialTree** instances. The binomial trees contained in the linked list are stored in increasing order. That is, the binomial tree at the head of the list will have the smallest order, and the binomial tree at the tail will have the largest order.

**AddTree and** RemoveTree   The private member functions **AddTree** and **Remove-Tree** of the **BinomialQueue** class facilitate the implementation of the various priority queue operations. These functions are defined in Program 11.15. The **AddTree** function takes a reference to a **BinomialTree** and appends a pointer to that tree to **list**. **AddTree** also adjusts the **count** in order to keep track of the number of items in the priority queue. It is assumed that the order of the tree which is added is larger than all the others in the list and, therefore, that it belongs at the end of the list. The running time of **AddTree** is clearly $O(1)$.

The **RemoveTree** function takes a reference to a binomial tree and removes it from the **list**. It is assumed that the specified tree is actually in the list. **RemoveTree** also adjusts the **count** as required. The running time of **RemoveTree** depends on the

---

**PROGRAM 11.14**
`BinomialQueue` class definition.

```
1   class BinomialQueue : public MergeablePriorityQueue
2   {
3       LinkedList<BinomialTree*> list;
4
5       BinomialTree& FindMinTree () const;
6       void AddTree (BinomialTree&);
7       void RemoveTree (BinomialTree&);
8
9       static BinomialTree* Sum (
10          BinomialTree*, BinomialTree*, BinomialTree*);
11      static BinomialTree* Carry (
12          BinomialTree*, BinomialTree*, BinomialTree*);
13  public:
14      BinomialQueue ();
15      ~BinomialQueue ();
16      //...
17  };
```

---

**PROGRAM 11.15**
`BinomialQueue` class `AddTree` and `RemoveTree` member function definitions

```
1   void BinomialQueue::AddTree (BinomialTree& tree)
2   {
3       list.Append (&tree);
4       count += tree.Count ();
5   }
6
7   void BinomialQueue::RemoveTree (BinomialTree& tree)
8   {
9       list.Extract (&tree);
10      count -= tree.Count ();
11  }
```

---

position of the tree in the list. A binomial queue which contains exactly $n$ items altogether has at most $\lceil \log_2(n + 1) \rceil$ binomial trees. Therefore, the running time of ʀᴇᴍᴏᴠᴇTree is $O(\log n)$ in the worst case.

**`FindMinTree` and `FindMin` Member Functions**    A binomial queue that contains $n$ items consists of at most $\lceil \log_2(n + 1) \rceil$ binomial trees. Each of these binomial trees is heap ordered. In particular, the smallest key in each binomial tree is at the root of that tree. So, we know that the smallest key in the queue is found at the root of one of the binomial trees, but we do not know which tree it is.

---

**PROGRAM 11.16**

BinomialQueue class FindMinTree and FindMin member function definitions

---

```
1   BinomialTree& BinomialQueue::FindMinTree () const
2   {
3       ListElement<BinomialTree*> const* ptr;
4
5       BinomialTree* minTree = 0;
6       for (ptr = list.Head (); ptr != 0; ptr = ptr->Next ())
7       {
8           BinomialTree* tree = ptr->Datum ();
9           if (minTree == 0 || tree->Key () < minTree->Key ())
10              minTree = tree;
11      }
12      return *minTree;
13  }
14
15  Object& BinomialQueue::FindMin () const
16  {
17      if (count == 0)
18          throw domain_error ("priority queue is empty");
19      return FindMinTree ().Key ();
20  }
```

---

The private member function **FindMinTree** is used to determine which of the binomial trees in the queue has the smallest root. As shown in Program 11.16, the **FindMinTree** simply traverses the entire linked list to find the tree with the smallest key at its root. Since there are at most $\lceil \log_2(n+1) \rceil$ binomial trees, the worst-case running time of **FindMinTree** is

$$(\lceil \log_2(n+1) \rceil - 1)\mathcal{T}\langle \texttt{T::Compare(T\&,T\&)} \rangle + O(\log n).$$

Program 11.16 also defines the public **FindMin** function which returns the smallest key in the priority queue. The **FindMin** function uses **FindMinTree** to locate the tree with the smallest key at its root and returns a reference to that key. Clearly, the asymptotic running time of **FindMin** is the same as that of **FindMinTree**.

## 11.4.4 Merging Binomial Queues

Merging two binomial queues is like doing binary addition. For example, consider the addition of $F_{27}$ and $F_{10}$:

$$
\begin{array}{ccccccc}
 & B_4 & B_3 & \varnothing & B_1 & B_0 & F_{27} \\
+ & & B_3 & \varnothing & B_1 & \varnothing & F_{10} \\
\hline
 & B_5 & \varnothing & \varnothing & B_2 & \varnothing & B_0 & F_{37}
\end{array}
$$

The usual algorithm for addition begins with the least significant "bit." Since $F_{27}$ contains a $B_0$ tree and $F_{10}$ does not, the result is simply the $B_0$ tree from $F_{27}$.

In the next step, we add the $B_1$ from $F_{27}$ and the $B_1$ from $F_{10}$. Combining the two $B_1$s we get a $B_2$ which we *carry* to the next column. Since there are no $B_1$s left, the result does not contain any. The addition continues in a similar manner until all the columns have been added up.

Program 11.17 gives an implementation of this addition algorithm. The **Merge** member function of the **BinomialQueue** class takes a reference to a **BinomialQueue** and adds its subtrees to **this** binomial queue.

**PROGRAM 11.17**
BinomialQueue class Merge member function definition

```
1   void BinomialQueue::Merge (MergeablePriorityQueue& queue)
2   {
3       BinomialQueue& arg = dynamic cast<BinomialQueue&> (queue);
4       LinkedList<BinomialTree*> oldList = list;
5       list.Purge ();
6       count = 0;
7       LinkedElement<BinomialTree*> const* p =
8           oldList.Head ();
9       LinkedElement<BinomialTree*> const* q =
10          arg.list.Head();
11      BinomialTree* carry = 0;
12      for (unsigned int i = 0; p || q || carry; ++i)
13      {
14          BinomialTree* a = 0;
15          if (p && p->Datum ()->Degree () == i)
16              { a = p->Datum (); p = p->Next (); }
17          BinomialTree* b = 0;
18          if (q && q->Datum ()->Degree () == i)
19              { b = q->Datum (); q = q->Next (); }
20          BinomialTree* sum = Sum (a, b, carry);
21          if (sum)
22              AddTree (*sum);
23          carry = Carry (a, b, carry);
24      }
25      arg.list.Purge ();
26      arg.count = 0;
27  }
```

---

**PROGRAM 11.18**
BinomialQueue class `Sum` and `Carry` member function definitions

---

```
1   BinomialTree* BinomialQueue::Sum (
2       BinomialTree* a, BinomialTree* b, BinomialTree* c)
3   {
4       if (a && !b && !c)
5           return a;
6       else if (!a && b && !c)
7           return b;
8       else if (!a && !b && c)
9           return c;
10      else if (a && b && c)
11          return c;
12      else
13          return 0;
14  }
15
16  BinomialTree* BinomialQueue::Carry (
17      BinomialTree* a, BinomialTree* b, BinomialTree* c)
18  {
19      if (a && b && !c)
20          { a->Add (*b); return a; }
21      else if (a && !b && c)
22          { a->Add (*c); return a; }
23      else if (!a && b && c)
24          { b->Add (*c); return b; }
25      else if (a && b && c)
26          { a->Add (*b); return a; }
27      else
28          return 0;
29  }
```

---

Each iteration of the main loop of the algorithm (lines 12–24) computes the $i$th "bit" of the result—the $i$th bit is a binomial tree of order $i$. At most, three terms need to be considered: the carry from the preceding iteration and two $B_i$s, one from each of the queues that are being merged.

Two functions, **Sum** and **Carry**, compute the result required in each iteration. Program 11.18 defines both **Sum** and **Carry**. Notice that the **Sum** function simply selects and returns one of its arguments. Therefore, the running time for **Sum** is clearly $O(1)$.

In the worst case, the **Carry** function calls the **Add** function to combine two **BinomialTree**s into one. Therefore, the worst-case running time for **Carry** is

$$\mathcal{T}\langle \text{T::Compare(T\&,T\&)}\rangle + O(1).$$

Suppose the **Merge** routine of Program 11.17 is used to combine a binomial queue with $n$ items with another that contains $m$ items. Since the resulting priority queue contains $n + m$ items, there are at most $\lceil \log_2(n + m + 1) \rceil$ binomial trees in the result. Thus, the running time for the **Merge** operation is

$$\lceil \log_2(n + m + 1) \rceil \mathcal{T} \langle \text{T::Compare(T\&,T\&)} \rangle + O(\log(n + m)).$$

### 11.4.5 Putting Items into a Binomial Queue

With the **Merge** routine at our disposal, the **Enqueue** operation is easy to implement. To enqueue an item in a given binomial queue, we create another binomial queue that contains just the one item to be enqueued and merge that queue with the original one.

Program 11.19 shows how easily this can be done. Creating the empty queue (line 3) takes a constant amount of time. Creating the binomial tree $B_0$ with the one object at its root (line 4) can also be done in constant time. Finally, the time required to merge the two queues is

$$\lceil \log_2(n + 2) \rceil \mathcal{T} \langle \text{T::Compare(T\&,T\&)} \rangle + O(\log n),$$

where $n$ is the number of items originally in the queue.

### 11.4.6 Removing an Item from a Binomial Queue

A binomial queue is a forest of heap-ordered binomial trees. Therefore, to dequeue the smallest item from the queue, we must withdraw the root of one of the binomial trees. But what do we do with the rest of the tree once its root has been removed?

The solution lies in realizing that the collection of subtrees of the root of a binomial tree is a forest! For example, consider the binomial tree of order $k$,

$$B_k = \{R, B_0, B_1, B_2, \ldots, B_{k-1}\}.$$

Taken all together, its subtrees form the binomial queue $F_{2^k-1}$:

$$F_{2^k-1} = \{B_0, B_1, B_2, \ldots, B_{k-1}\}.$$

---

**PROGRAM 11.19**
**BinomialQueue** class **Enqueue** member function definition

```
1   void BinomialQueue::Enqueue (Object& object)
2   {
3       BinomialQueue queue;
4       queue.AddTree (*new BinomialTree (object));
5       Merge (queue);
6   }
```

---

---

**PROGRAM 11.20**
BinomialQueue class DequeueMin member function definition

---

```
1   Object& BinomialQueue::DequeueMin ()
2   {
3       if (count == 0)
4           throw domain_error ("priority queue is empty");
5
6       BinomialTree& minTree = FindMinTree ();
7       RemoveTree (minTree);
8
9       BinomialQueue queue;
10      while (minTree.Degree () > 0)
11      {
12          BinomialTree& child = minTree.Subtree (0);
13
14          minTree.DetachSubtree (child);
15          queue.AddTree (child);
16      }
17      Merge (queue);
18
19      Object& result = minTree.Key ();
20      minTree.RescindOwnership ();
21      delete &minTree;
22
23      return result;
24  }
```

---

Therefore, to delete the smallest item from a binomial queue, we first identify the binomial tree with the smallest root and remove that tree from the queue. Then, we consider all the subtrees of the root of that tree as a binomial queue and merge that queue back into the original one. Program 11.20 shows how this can be coded.

The DequeueMin function begins by calling FindMinTree to find the tree with the smallest root and then removing that tree using RemoveTree (lines 6–7). The time required to find the appropriate tree and to remove it is

$$(\lceil \log_2(n + 1) \rceil - 1)\mathcal{T}\langle \texttt{T::Compare(T\&,T\&)}\rangle + O(\log n),$$

where $n$ is the number of items in the queue.

A new binomial queue is created on line 9. All the children of the root of the minimum tree are detached from the tree and added to the new binomial queue (lines 10–15). In the worst case, the minimum tree is the one with the highest order. That is, $B_{\lfloor \log_2 n \rfloor}$, and the root of that tree has $\lfloor \log_2 n \rfloor$ children. Therefore, the running time of the loop on lines 10–15 is $O(\log n)$.

The new queue is then merged with the original one (line 16). Since the resulting queue contains $n - 1$ keys, the running time for the **Merge** operation in this case is

$$\lceil \log_2 n \rceil \mathcal{T} \langle \texttt{T::Compare(T\&,T\&)} \rangle + O(\log n).$$

The remaining operations (lines 19–21) are just housekeeping which can be done in constant time.

# 11.5 Applications

## 11.5.1 Discrete Event Simulation

One of the most important applications of priority queues is in *discrete event simulation*. Simulation is a tool which is used to study the behavior of complex systems. The first step in simulation is *modeling*. We construct a mathematical model of the system we wish to study. Then we write a computer program to evaluate the model. In a sense the behavior of the computer program mimics the system we are studying.

The systems studied using *discrete event simulation* have the following characteristics: The system has a *state* which evolves or changes with time. Changes in state occur at distinct points in simulation time. A state change moves the system from one state to another instantaneously. State changes are called *events*.

For example, suppose we wish to study the service received by customers in a bank. Suppose a single teller is serving customers. If the teller is not busy when a customer arrives at the bank, that customer is immediately served. On the other hand, if the teller is busy when another customer arrives, that customer joins a queue and waits to be served.

We can model this system as a discrete event process, as shown in Figure 11.12. The state of the system is characterized by the state of the server (the teller), which is either busy or idle, and by the number of customers in the queue. The events which cause state changes are the arrival of a customer and the departure of a customer.

If the server is idle when a customer arrives, the server immediately begins to serve the customer and therefore changes its state to busy. If the server is busy when a customer arrives, that customer joins the queue.

**FIGURE 11.12**
A simple queueing system.

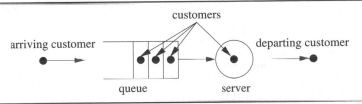

When the server finishes serving the customer, that customer departs. If the queue is not empty, the server immediately commences serving the next customer. Otherwise, the server becomes idle.

How do we keep track of which event to simulate next? Each event (arrival or departure) occurs at a discrete point in *simulation time*. In order to ensure that the simulation program is correct, it must compute the events in order. This is called the *causality constraint*—events cannot change the past.

In our model, when the server begins to serve a customer we can compute the departure time of that customer. So, when a customer arrives at the server we *schedule* an event in the future which corresponds to the departure of that customer. In order to ensure that events are processed in order, we keep them in a priority queue in which the time of the event is its priority. Since we always process the pending event with the smallest time next and since an event can schedule new events only in the future, the causality constraint will not be violated.

## 11.5.2 Implementation

This section presents the simulation of a system comprised of a single queue and server as shown in Figure 11.12. Program 11.21 declares the class **Event** which represents the events. There are two parts to an event, a **Type** (either **arrival** or **departure**), and a **Time** (a **double**).

---

**PROGRAM 11.21**
**Event** class definition

---

```
1   typedef double time;
2
3   class Event : public Association
4   {
5   public:
6       enum type
7       {
8           arrival, departure
9       };
10      typedef Wrapper<type> Type;
11      typedef Wrapper<time> Time;
12
13      Event (type typ, time tim) :
14          Association (*new Time (tim), *new Type (typ)) {}
15      Time& Key () const
16          { return dynamic_cast<Time&> (Association::Key ()); }
17      Type& Value () const
18          { return dynamic_cast<Type&> (Association::Value()); }
19  };
```

---

Since events will be put into a priority queue, the **Event** class is derived from the **Association** class which is defined in Section 5.2.11. An association is an ordered pair comprised of a key and a value. In the case of the **Event** class, the key is the time of the event and the value is the type of the event. Therefore, the events in a priority queue are prioritized by their times.

Program 11.22 defines the function which implements the discrete event simulation. This function takes two arguments. The first, **eventList**, is a reference to a priority queue. This priority queue is used to hold the events during the course of the simulation. The second parameter, **timeLimit**, specifies the total amount of time to be simulated.

The state of the system being simulated is represented by the two variables **serverBusy** and **numberInQueue**. The first is a Boolean value which indicates whether the server is busy. The second keeps track of the number of customers in the queue.

In addition to the state variables, there are two instances of the class **ExponentialRV**. The class **ExponentialRV** is a random number generator defined in Section 14.5.1. This class provides a member function called **Sample** which is used to sample the random number generator; that is, every time **Sample** is called, a different (random) result is returned. The random values are exponentially distributed around a mean value which is specified in the constructor. For example, in this case both **serviceTime** and **interArrivalTime** produce random distributions with the mean value of 100 (lines 5–6).

It is assumed that the **eventList** priority queue is initially empty. The simulation begins by enqueuing a customer arrival at time zero (line 8). The **while** loop (lines 9–46) constitutes the main simulation loop. This loop continues as long as the **eventList** is not empty, i.e., as long as there is an event to be simulated.

Each iteration of the simulation loop begins by dequeuing the next event in the event list (lines 11–12). If the time of that event exceeds **timeLimit**, the event is discarded, the **eventList** is purged, and the simulation is terminated. Otherwise, the simulation proceeds.

The simulation of an event depends on the type of that event. The **switch** statement (line 20) invokes the appropriate code for the given event. If the event is a customer arrival and the server is not busy, **serverBusy** is set to **true** and the **serviceTime** random number generator is sampled to determine the amount of time required to service the customer. A customer departure is scheduled at the appropriate time in the future (lines 25–27). On the other hand, if the server is already busy when the customer arrives, we add one to the **numberInQueue** variable (line 30).

Another customer arrival is scheduled after every customer arrival. The **interArrivalTime** random number generator is sampled, and the arrival is scheduled at the appropriate time in the future (lines 31–32).

If the event is a customer departure and the queue is empty, the server becomes idle (lines 35–36). When a customer departs and there are still customers in the queue, the next customer in the queue is served. Therefore, **numberInQueue** is decreased by 1 and the **serviceTime** random number generator is sampled to determine the amount of time required to service the next customer. A customer departure is scheduled at the appropriate time in the future (lines 39–41).

Clearly the execution of the **Simulation** routine given in Program 11.22 mimics the modeled system. Of course, the program given produces no output. For it to be of

```
1    void Simulation (PriorityQueue& eventList, time timeLimit)
2    {
3        bool serverBusy = false;
4        unsigned int numberInQueue = 0;
5        ExponentialRV serviceTime (100.);
6        ExponentialRV interArrivalTime (100.);
7
8        eventList.Enqueue (*new Event (Event::arrival, 0));
9        while (!eventList.IsEmpty ())
10       {
11           Event& event =
12               dynamic_cast<Event&> (eventList.DequeueMin ());
13           Event::Time& t = event.Key ();
14           if (t > timeLimit)
15           {
16               delete &event;
17               eventList.Purge ();
18               break;
19           }
20           switch (event.Value ())
21           {
22           case Event::arrival:
23               if (!serverBusy)
24               {
25                   serverBusy = true;
26                   eventList.Enqueue (*new Event (Event::departure,
27                       t + serviceTime.Sample ()));
28               }
29               else
30                   ++numberInQueue;
31               eventList.Enqueue (*new Event (Event::arrival,
32                   t + interArrivalTime.Sample ()));
33               break;
34           case Event::departure:
35               if (numberInQueue == 0)
36                   serverBusy = false;
37               else
38               {
39                   --numberInQueue;
40                   eventList.Enqueue (*new Event (Event::departure,
41                       t + serviceTime.Sample ()));
42               }
43               break;
44           }
45           delete &event;
46       }
47   }
```

any practical value, the simulation program should be instrumented to allow the user to study its behavior. For example, the user may be interested in knowing statistics, such as the average queue length and the average waiting time that a customer waits for service. And such instrumentation can be easily incorporated into the given framework.

## Exercises

**11.1** For each of the following key sequences determine the binary heap obtained when the keys are inserted one-by-one in the order given into an initially empty heap:

   **a.** 0, 1, 2, 3, 4, 5, 6, 7, 8, 9.

   **b.** 3, 1, 4, 1, 5, 9, 2, 6, 5, 4.

   **c.** 2, 7, 1, 8, 2, 8, 1, 8, 2, 8.

**11.2** For each of the binary heaps obtained in Exercise 11.1 determine the heap obtained after three consecutive **DequeueMin** operations.

**11.3** Repeat Exercise 11.1 and 11.2 for a leftist heap.

**11.4** Show the result obtained by inserting the keys $1, 2, 3, \ldots, 2^h$ one-by-one in the order given into an initially empty binomial queue.

**11.5** A *full* binary tree is a tree in which each node is either a leaf or it is a *full node* (see Exercise 9.4). Consider a *complete* binary tree with $n$ nodes.

   **a.** For what values of $n$ is a complete binary tree a *full* binary tree?

   **b.** For what values of $n$ is a complete binary a *perfect* binary tree?

**11.6** Prove by induction Theorem 11.3.

**11.7** Devise an algorithm to determine whether a given binary tree is a heap. What is the running time of your algorithm?

**11.8** Devise an algorithm to find the *largest* item in a binary *min* heap. **Hint:** First, show that the largest item must be in one of the leaves. What is the running time of your algorithm?

**11.9** Suppose we are given an arbitrary array of $n$ keys to be inserted into a binary heap all at once. Devise an $O(n)$ algorithm to do this. **Hint:** See Section 15.5.2.

**11.10** Devise an algorithm to determine whether a given binary tree is a leftist tree. What is the running time of your algorithm?

**11.11** Prove that a complete binary tree is a leftist tree.

**11.12** Suppose we are given an arbitrary array of $n$ keys to be inserted into a leftist heap all at once. Devise an $O(n)$ algorithm to do this. **Hint:** See Exercise 11.9 and 11.11.

**11.13** Consider a complete binary tree with its nodes numbered as shown in Figure 11.2. Let $K$ be the number of a node in the tree. The binary representation of $K$ is

$$K = \sum_{i=0}^{k} b_i 2^i,$$

where $k = \lfloor \log_2 K \rfloor$.

**a.** Show that path from the root to a given node $K$ passes through the following nodes:

$$b_k$$
$$b_k b_{k-1}$$
$$b_k b_{k-1} b_{k-2}$$
$$\vdots$$
$$b_k b_{k-2} b_{k-2} \ldots b_2 b_1$$
$$b_k b_{k-1} b_{k-2} \ldots b_2 b_1 b_0.$$

**b.** Consider a complete binary tree with $n$ nodes. The nodes on the path from the root to the $n$th are *special*. Show that every non-special node is the root of a perfect tree.

**11.14** The **Enqueue** algorithm for the **BinaryHeap** class does $O(\log n)$ object comparisons in the worst case. In effect, this algorithm does a linear search from a leaf to the root to find the point at which to insert a new key. Devise an algorithm that uses a binary search instead. Show that the number of comparisons required becomes $O(\log \log n)$. **Hint:** See Exercise 11.13.

**11.15** Prove Theorem 11.7.

**11.16** Do Exercise 10.17.

## Programming Projects

**11.1** Design and implement a sorting algorithm using one of the priority queue implementations described in this chapter.

**11.2** Complete the **BinaryHeap** class declared in Program 11.2 by providing suitable definitions for the following member functions: **CompareTo**, **IsFull**, **Accept**, and **NewIterator**. Write a test program and test your implementation.

**11.3** Complete the **LeftistHeap** class declared in Program 11.17 by providing suitable definitions for the following member functions: **LeftistHeap** (two constructors), **Left**, **Right**, and **SwapContents**. You must also have a complete implementation of the base class **BinaryTree**. (See Project 9.8.) Write a test program and test your implementation.

**11.4** Complete the implementation of the **BinomialTree** class declared in Program 11.12 by providing suitable definitions for the following member functions: **BinomialTree** (constructor), **Count**, **Subtree**, and **SwapContents**.

You must also have a complete implementation of the base class `GeneralTree`. (See Project 9.6.) Write a test program and test your implementation.

**11.5**   Complete the implementation of the `BinomialQueue` class declared in Program 11.14 by providing suitable definitions for the following member functions: `BinomialQueue` (constructor), `~BinomialQueue` (destructor), `Purge`, `CompareTo`, `Accept`, and `NewIterator`. You must also have a complete implementation of the `BinomialTree` class. (See Project 11.4.) Write a test program and test your implementation.

**11.6**   The binary heap described in this chapter uses an array as the underlying foundational data structure. Alternatively we may base an implementation on the `BinaryTree` class described in Chapter 9. Implement a concrete priority queue class using multiple inheritance to inherit the functionality from the `BinaryTree` class (Program 9.16) and the interface from the `PriorityQueue` class (Program 11.1).

**11.7**   Implement a concrete priority queue class using the binary search tree class from Chapter 10. Specifically, use multiple inheritance to inherit the functionality from the `BST` class (Program 10.2) and the interface from the `PriorityQueue` class (Program 11.1). You will require a complete implementation of the base class `BST`. (See Project 10.1.) Write a test program and test your implementation.

**11.8**   Devise and implement an algorithm to multiply two polynomials:

$$\left( \sum_{i=0}^{n} a_i x^i \right) \times \left( \sum_{j=0}^{m} b_j x^j \right).$$

Generate the terms of the result in order by putting intermediate product terms into a priority queue. That is, use the priority queue to group terms with the same exponent. **Hint:** See also Project 7.4.

# 12 | Sets, Multisets, and Partitions

In mathematics a *set* is a collection of elements, especially a collection having some feature or features in common. The set may have a finite number of elements, e.g., the set of prime numbers less than 100; or it may have an infinite number of elements, e.g., the set of right triangles. The *elements* of a set may be anything at all—from simple integers to arbitrarily complex objects. However, all the elements of a set are distinct—a set may contain only one instance of a given element.

For example, $\{\}$, $\{a\}$, $\{a, b, c, d\}$, and $\{d, e\}$ are all sets the elements of which are drawn from $U = \{a, b, c, d, e\}$. The set of all possible elements, $U$, is called the *universal set*. Note also that the elements comprising a given set are not ordered. Thus, $\{a, b, c\}$ and $\{b, c, a\}$ are the same set.

There are many possible operations on sets. In this chapter we consider the most common operations for *combining sets*—union, intersection, difference:

**union** The *union* (or *conjunction*) of sets $S$ and $T$, written $S \cup T$, is the set comprised of all the elements of $S$ together with all the element of $T$. Since a set cannot contain duplicates, if the same item is an element of both $S$ and $T$, only one instance of that item appears in $S \cup T$. If $S = \{a, b, c, d\}$ and $T = \{d, e\}$, then $S \cup T = \{a, b, c, d, e\}$.

**intersection** The *intersection* (or *disjunction*) of sets $S$ and $T$ is written $S \cap T$. The elements of $S \cap T$ are those items which are elements of *both* $S$ and $T$. If $S = \{a, b, c, d\}$ and $T = \{d, e\}$, then $S \cap T = \{d\}$.

**difference** The *difference* (or *subtraction*) of sets $S$ and $T$, written $S - T$, contains those elements of $S$ which are *not also* elements of $T$. That is, the result $S - T$ is obtained by taking the set $S$ and removing from it those elements which are also found in $T$. If $S = \{a, b, c, d\}$ and $T = \{d, e\}$, then $S - T = \{a, b, c\}$.

Figure 12.1 illustrates the basic set operations using a *Venn diagram*. A Venn diagram represents the membership of sets by regions of the plane. In Figure 12.1 the two sets $S$ and $T$ divide the plane into the four regions labeled *I–IV*. The following table illustrates the basic set operations by enumerating the regions that comprise each set.

| Set | Region(s) of Figure 12.1 |
|-----|--------------------------|
| $U$ | $I, II, III, IV$ |
| $S$ | $I, II$ |
| $S'$ | $III, IV$ |
| $T$ | $II, III$ |
| $S \cup T$ | $I, II, III$ |
| $S \cap T$ | $II$ |
| $S - T$ | $I$ |
| $T - S$ | $III$ |

## 12.1 Basics

In this chapter we consider sets, the elements of which are integers. By using integers as the universe rather than arbitrary objects, certain optimizations are possible. For example, we can use a bit-vector of length $N$ to represent a set whose universe is $\{0, 1, \ldots, N - 1\}$. Of course, using integers as the universe does not preclude the use of more complex objects, provided there is a one-to-one mapping between those objects and the elements of the universal set.

A crucial requirement of any set representation scheme is that it supports the common set operations including *union*, *intersection*, and set *difference*. We also need to compare sets and, specifically, to determine whether a given set is a subset of another.

### 12.1.1 Implementing Sets

As discussed above, this chapter addresses the implementation of sets of integers (see Figure 12.2). A set is a collection of elements. Naturally, we want to insert and withdraw objects from the collection and to test whether a given object is a member of the collection. Therefore, we consider sets as being derived from the **SearchableContainer** class defined in Chapter 5.

---

**FIGURE 12.1**
Venn diagram illustrating the basic set operations.

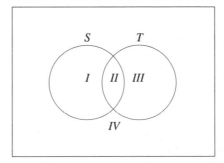

**FIGURE 12.2**
Object class hierarchy.

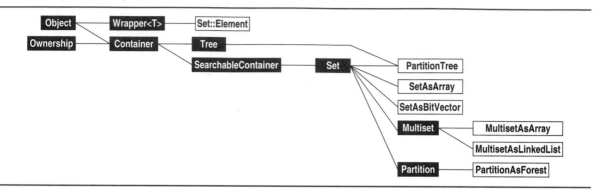

In general, a searchable container can hold arbitrary objects. However, in this chapter we will assume that the elements of a set are integers. Furthermore, all the searchable container implementations which we have seen so far have been based on two assumptions: (1) the container *owns* the objects it contains; and (2) that indirect storage is used, i.e., a pointer to the contained object is actually held by the container. Since we deal with integers and not with arbitrary objects, the set implementations in this chapter invalidate both assumptions.

Program 12.1 defines the abstract class **Set**. The **Set** class is derived from **SearchableContainer**, which is defined in Section 5.2.5. The definition does not declare any new member functions—the interface inherited from the base class is sufficient. In addition, a new type called **Set::Element** is defined.

The items *contained* in a set are unsigned integers. However, the member functions of the base class interface such as **Insert**, **IsMember**, and **Withdraw**, expect their arguments to be derived from the class **Object**. Therefore, the **Wrapper** template (defined in Section 5.2.4) is used to define the type **Set::Element** as the encapsulation of an **unsigned int**. We assume that the only **Object** instances which are passed to a set are instances of the class **Set::Element**.

**PROGRAM 12.1**
**Set** class definition

```
1   class Set : public virtual SearchableContainer
2   {
3   protected:
4       unsigned int universeSize;
5
6   public:
7       Set (unsigned int n) : universeSize (n) {}
8
9       typedef Wrapper<unsigned int> Element;
10  };
```

The default constructor for the **Set** class is also given in Program 12.1. It takes a single argument, $N =$ **universeSize**, which specifies that the universal set shall be $\{0, 1, \ldots, N - 1\}$.

## 12.2 Array and Bit-Vector Sets

In this section we consider finite sets over a finite universe. Specifically, the universe we consider is $\{0, 1, \ldots, N - 1\}$, the set of integers in the range from zero to $N - 1$, for some fixed and relatively small value of $N$.

Let $U = \{0, 1, \ldots, N - 1\}$ be the universe. Every set which we wish to represent is a subset of $U$. The set of all subsets of $U$ is called the *power set* of $U$ and is written $2^U$. Thus, the sets which we wish to represent are the *elements* of $2^U$. The number of elements in the set $U$, written $|U|$, is $N$. Similarly, $|2^U| = 2^{|U|} = 2^N$. This observation should be obvious: For each element of the universal set $U$ there are only two possibilities: Either it is or it is not a member of the given set.

This suggests a relatively straightforward representation of the elements of $2^U$—an array of Boolean values, one for each element of the universal set. By using array subscripts in $U$, we can represent the set implicitly, that is, $i$ is a member of the set if the $i$th array element is true.

Program 12.2 declares the class **SetAsArray**. This class uses an array of length $N =$ **numberOfItems** to represent the elements of $2^U$ where $U = \{0, 1, \ldots, N - 1\}$. A **SetAsArray** is a **Set**. Therefore, it supports the basic operations of searchable containers including **Insert**, **IsMember**, and **Withdraw**.

---

**PROGRAM 12.2**
**SetAsArray** class definition

---

```
 1  class SetAsArray : public Set
 2  {
 3      Array<bool> array;
 4  public:
 5      SetAsArray (unsigned int);
 6      // ...
 7      friend SetAsArray operator + (
 8          SetAsArray const&, SetAsArray const&);
 9      friend SetAsArray operator - (
10          SetAsArray const&, SetAsArray const&);
11      friend SetAsArray operator * (
12          SetAsArray const&, SetAsArray const&);
13      friend bool operator == (
14          SetAsArray const&, SetAsArray const&);
15      friend bool operator <= (
16          SetAsArray const&, SetAsArray const&);
17  };
```

---

In addition, Program 12.2 overloads the operators +, *, -, ==, and <=. The first three operators correspond to set union, set intersection, and set difference (respectively). The last two are used to compare two sets and to determine whether one set is a subset of another.

## Basic Operations

Program 12.3 defines the constructor for the **SetAsArray** class as well as the three basic operations—**Insert**, **IsMember**, and **Withdraw**. The constructor takes a single argument $N$ = **numberOfItems**, which defines the universe and, consequently, the size of the array of Boolean values. The constructor creates the empty set by initializing all the element of the Boolean array to **false**. Clearly, the running time of the constructor is $O(N)$.

The **Insert** function is used to put an item into the set. The function takes a reference to an **Object** instance which is assumed to be a **Set::Element**. A dynamic cast is used to ensure that the object to be inserted is of the correct type and to extract the integer value from that object. Then the corresponding element of **array** is set to **true**

---

**PROGRAM 12.3**
**SetAsArray** class constructor, **Insert**, **Withdraw**, and **IsMember** member function definitions

```
1   SetAsArray::SetAsArray (unsigned int n) :
2       Set (n),
3       array (n)
4   {
5       for (unsigned int item = 0; item < universeSize; ++item)
6           array [item] = false;
7   }
8
9   void SetAsArray::Insert (Object& object)
10  {
11      unsigned int const item = dynamic_cast<Element&> (object);
12      array [item] = true;
13  }
14
15  bool SetAsArray::IsMember (Object const& object) const
16  {
17      unsigned int const item =
18          dynamic_cast<Element const&> (object);
19      return array [item];
20  }
21
22  void SetAsArray::Withdraw (Object& object)
23  {
24      unsigned int const item = dynamic_cast<Element&> (object);
25      array [item] = false;
26  }
```

to indicate that the specified object has been added to the set. Note that the set does not keep track of the actual object instance that was inserted. Therefore, the set cannot own contained objects. Instead, objects that are inserted are represented *implicitly* by array indices. The running time of the **Insert** operation is $O(1)$.

The **IsMember** function is used to test whether a given item is an element of the set. The semantics are somewhat subtle. Since a set does not actually keep track of the specific object instances that are inserted, the membership test is based on the *value* of the argument. Again, a dynamic cast is used to ensure that the argument is of the correct type and to extract the integer value from that object. The function simply returns the value of the appropriate element of the **array**. The running time of the **IsMember** operation is $O(1)$.

The **Withdraw** member function is used to take an item out of a set. The withdrawal operation is the opposite of insertion. Instead of setting the appropriate array element to **true**, it is set to **false**. The running time of the **Withdraw** is identical to that of **Insert**, viz., is $O(1)$.

### Union, Intersection, and Difference

Program 12.4 overloads the three operators, **operator+**, **operator\***, and **operator-**, to provide the union, intersection, and difference operations for **SetAs Array** instances. Operators **+**, **\***, and **-** correspond to $\cup$, $\cap$ and $-$, respectively.

The set union operator takes two references to **SetAsArray** instances, **s** and **t**, and computes a result of type **SetAsArray**. The implementation given requires that the **s** and **t** sets be compatible. Two sets are deemed to be compatible if they have the same universe. The result also has the same universe. Consequently, the Boolean array in all three sets has the same length, $N$. The set union routine creates a result array of the required size and then computes the elements of the array as required. The $i$th element of the result is **true** if either the $i$th element of **s** or the $i$th element of **t** is **true**. Thus, set union is implemented using the Boolean *or* operator, | |.

The set intersection operator is almost identical to set union, except that the elements of the result are computed using the Boolean *and* operator. The set difference operator is also very similar. In this case, an item is an element of the result only if it is a member of **s** and not a member of **t**.

Because all three routines are almost identical, their running times are essentially the same. That is, the running time of the set union, intersection, and difference operations is $O(N)$, where $N = $ **numberOfItems**.

### Comparing Sets

There is a special family of operators for comparing sets. Consider two sets, say $S$ and $T$. We say that $S$ is a *subset* of $T$, written $S \subseteq T$, if every element of $S$ is also an element of $T$. If there is at least one element of $T$ that is not also an element of $S$, we say that $S$ is a *proper subset* of $T$, written $S \subset T$. We can also reverse the order in which the expressions are written to get $T \supset S$ or $T \supseteq S$, which indicates that $T$ is a (proper) *superset* of $S$.

The set comparison operators follow the rule that if $S \subseteq T$ and $T \subseteq S$ then $S \equiv T$, which is analogous to a similar property of numbers: $x \leq y \wedge y \leq x \iff x = y$. However, set comparison is unlike numeric comparison in that there exist sets $S$ and $T$

---

**PROGRAM 12.4**
`SetAsArray` class union, intersection, and difference operator definitions

---

```
1   SetAsArray operator + (SetAsArray const& s, SetAsArray const& t)
2   {
3       if (s.universeSize != t.universeSize)
4           throw invalid_argument ("mismatched sets");
5       SetAsArray result (s.universeSize);
6       for (unsigned int i = 0; i < s.universeSize; ++i)
7           result.array [i] = s.array [i] || t.array [i];
8       return result;
9   }
10
11  SetAsArray operator * (SetAsArray const& s, SetAsArray const& t)
12  {
13      if (s.universeSize != t.universeSize)
14          throw invalid_argument ("mismatched sets");
15      SetAsArray result (s.universeSize);
16      for (unsigned int i = 0; i < s.universeSize; ++i)
17          result.array [i] = s.array [i] && t.array [i];
18      return result;
19  }
20
21  SetAsArray operator - (SetAsArray const& s, SetAsArray const& t)
22  {
23      if (s.universeSize != t.universeSize)
24          throw invalid_argument ("mismatched sets");
25      SetAsArray result (s.universeSize);
26      for (unsigned int i = 0; i < s.universeSize; ++i)
27          result.array [i] = s.array [i] && !t.array [i];
28      return result;
29  }
```

---

for which neither $S \subseteq T$ nor $T \subseteq S$! For example, clearly this is the case for $S = \{1, 2\}$ and $T = \{2, 3\}$. Mathematically, the relation $\subseteq$ is called a *partial order* because there exist some pairs of sets for which neither $S \subseteq T$ nor $T \subseteq S$ holds; whereas the relation $\leq$ (among integers, say) is a total order.

Program 12.5 overloads the operators `==` and `<=` for `SetAsArray` operands. The former tests its operands for equality, and the latter determines whether the relation $\subseteq$ holds between its operands. Both operators return a Boolean result. The worst-case running time of each of these operations is clearly $O(N)$.

A complete repertoire of comparison operators would also include definitions for `<`, `>`, `>=`, and `!=`. These operations follow directly from the implementation shown in Program 12.5 (Exercise 12.2).

**PROGRAM 12.5**
`SetAsArray` class comparison operator definitions

```
1  bool operator == (SetAsArray const& s, SetAsArray const& t)
2  {
3      if (s.universeSize != t.universeSize)
4          throw invalid_argument ("mismatched sets");
5      for (unsigned int item = 0; item < s.universeSize; ++item)
6          if (s.array [item] != t.array [item])
7              return false;
8      return true;
9  }
10
11  bool operator <= (SetAsArray const& s, SetAsArray const& t)
12  {
13      if (s.universeSize != t.universeSize)
14          throw invalid_argument ("mismatched sets");
15      for (unsigned int item = 0; item < s.universeSize; ++item)
16          if (s.array [item] && !t.array [item])
17              return false;
18      return true;
19  }
```

### 12.2.1   Bit-Vector Sets

In the typical C++ implementation, a **bool** occupies between 1 and 4 bytes. However, since there are only the two values, **true** and **false**, a single bit is sufficient to hold a Boolean value. Therefore, we can realize a significant reduction in the memory space required to represent a set if we use an array of bits. Furthermore, by using bitwise operations to implement the basic set operations such as union and intersection, we can achieve a commensurate reduction in execution time. Unfortunately, these improvements are not free—the operations **Insert**, **IsMember**, and **Withdraw**, all slow down by a constant factor.

Since C++ does not directly support arrays of bits, we must simulate an array of bits using an array of machine words. Program 12.6 illustrates how this can be done. The class **SetAsBitVector** represents the elements of a set using the bits in an array of unsigned integers (i.e., type **Word**). The enumerated constant **wordBits** is defined as the number of bits in a single **Word**.

#### Basic Operations

Program 12.7 defines the constructor for the **SetAsBitVector** class as well as the three basic operations—**Insert**, **IsMember**, and **Withdraw**. The constructor takes a single argument $N =$ **numberOfItems**, which specifies the universe and, consequently, the number of bits needed in the bit array. The constructor creates a vector of **Word**s of length $\lceil N/w \rceil$, where $w =$ **wordBits** is the number of bits in a word,

**PROGRAM 12.6**
`SetAsBitVector` class definition

```
1   class SetAsBitVector : public Set
2   {
3       typedef unsigned int Word;
4       enum { wordBits = bitsizeof (Word) };
5
6       Array<Word> vector;
7   public:
8       SetAsBitVector (unsigned int);
9       //...
10  };
```

**PROGRAM 12.7**
`SetAsBitVector` class constructor, `Insert`, `Withdraw`, and `IsMember`
member function definitions

```
1   SetAsBitVector::SetAsBitVector (unsigned int n) :
2       Set (n),
3       vector ((n + wordBits - 1U) / wordBits)
4   {
5       for (unsigned int i = 0; i < vector.Length (); ++i)
6           vector [i] = 0;
7   }
8
9   void SetAsBitVector::Insert (Object& object)
10  {
11      unsigned int const item = dynamic_cast<Element&> (object);
12      vector [item / wordBits] |= 1 << item % wordBits;
13  }
14
15  void SetAsBitVector::Withdraw (Object& object)
16  {
17      unsigned int const item = dynamic_cast<Element&> (object);
18      vector [item / wordBits] &= ~(1 << item % wordBits);
19  }
20
21  bool SetAsBitVector::IsMember (Object const& object) const
22  {
23      unsigned int const item =
24          dynamic_cast<Element const&> (object);
25      return vector [item / wordBits] & (1 << item % wordBits);
26  }
```

and sets the elements of the vector to zero. The running time of the constructor is $O(\lceil N/w \rceil) = O(N)$.

To insert an item into the set, we need to change the appropriate bit in the array of bits to one. The $i$th bit of the bit array is bit $i$ mod $w$ of word $\lfloor i/w \rfloor$. Thus, the **Insert** function is implemented using a *bitwise or* operation to change the $i$th bit to 1, as shown in Program 12.7. Even though it is slightly more complicated than the corresponding operation for the **SetAsArray** class, the running time for this operation is still $O(1)$. Since $w = $ **wordBits** is a power of 2, it is possible to replace the division and modulo operations, **/** and **%**, with shifts and masks like this:

```
vector [item >> shift] |= 1 << (item & mask);
```

for a suitable definition of the constants **shift** and **mask**. Depending on the compiler and machine architecture, doing so may improve the performance of the **Insert** operation by a constant factor. Of course, its asymptotic performance is still $O(1)$.

To withdraw an item from the set, we need to clear the appropriate bit in the array of bits and to test if an item is a member of the set, we test the corresponding bit. The **IsMember** and **Withdraw** routines in Program 12.7 show how this can be done. Like **Insert**, both these routines have constant worst-case running times.

### Union, Intersection, and Difference

The implementations of the union, intersection, and difference operators (**+**, **\***, and **-**, respectively) for operands of type **SetAsBitVector** are shown in Program 12.8. The code is quite similar to that for the **SetAsArray** class given in Program 12.4.

Instead of using the Boolean operators **&&**, **||**, and **!**, we have used the bitwise operators **&**, **|**, and **~**. By using the bitwise operators, $w = $ **wordBits** bits of the result are computed in each iteration of the loop. Therefore, the number of iterations required is $\lceil N/w \rceil$ instead of $N$. The worst-case running time of each of these operations is $O(\lceil N/w \rceil) = O(N)$.

Notice that the asymptotic performance of these **SetAsBitVector** class operations is the same as the asymptotic performance of the **SetAsArray** class operations; that is, both of them are $O(N)$. Nevertheless, the **SetAsBitVector** class operations are faster. In fact, the bit-vector approach is asymptotically faster than the the array approach by the factor $w$.

## 12.3  Multisets

A *multiset* is a set in which an item may appear more than once. That is, whereas duplicates are not permitted in a regular set, they are permitted in a multiset. Multisets are also known simply as *bags*.

Sets and multisets are in other respects quite similar: Both support operations to insert and withdraw items; both provide a means to test the membership of a given item; and both support the basic set operations of union, intersection, and difference. As a result, the **Set** abstract class and the **Multiset** abstract class share a common interface, as shown in Program 12.9.

**PROGRAM 12.8**
SetAsBitVector class union, intersection, and difference operator definitions

```
1   SetAsBitVector operator + (
2       SetAsBitVector const& s, SetAsBitVector const& t)
3   {
4       if (s.universeSize != t.universeSize)
5           throw invalid_argument ("mismatched sets");
6       SetAsBitVector result (s.universeSize);
7       for (unsigned int i = 0; i < s.vector.Length (); ++i)
8           result.vector [i] = s.vector [i] | t.vector [i];
9       return result;
10  }
11
12  SetAsBitVector operator * (
13      SetAsBitVector const& s, SetAsBitVector const& t)
14  {
15      if (s.universeSize != t.universeSize)
16          throw invalid_argument ("mismatched sets");
17      SetAsBitVector result (s.universeSize);
18      for (unsigned int i = 0; i < s.vector.Length (); ++i)
19          result.vector [i] = s.vector [i] & t.vector [i];
20      return result;
21  }
22
23  SetAsBitVector operator - (
24      SetAsBitVector const& s, SetAsBitVector const& t)
25  {
26      if (s.universeSize != t.universeSize)
27          throw invalid_argument ("mismatched sets");
28      SetAsBitVector result (s.universeSize);
29      for (unsigned int i = 0; i < s.vector.Length (); ++i)
30          result.vector [i] = s.vector [i] & ~t.vector [i];
31      return result;
32  }
```

**PROGRAM 12.9**
Multiset class definition

```
1   class Multiset : public Set
2   {
3   public:
4       Multiset (unsigned int n) : Set (n) {}
5   };
```

### 12.3.1 Array Implementation

A regular set may contain either zero or one instance of a particular item. As shown in the preceding section, if the number of possible items is not excessive we may use an array of Boolean variables to keep track of the number of instances of a particular item in a regular set. The natural extension of this idea for a multiset is to keep a separate count of the number of instances of each item in the multiset.

Program 12.10 declares the class **MultisetAsArray**. The multiset is implemented using an array of $N$ = **numberOfItems** counters. Each counter is an **unsigned int** in this case.

#### Basic Operations

Program 12.11 defines the constructor for the **MultisetAsArray** class as well as the three basic operations—**Insert**, **IsMember**, and **Withdraw**. The constructor takes a single argument, $N$ = **numberOfItems**, and initializes an array of length $N$ counters all to zero. The running time of the constructor is $O(N)$.

To insert an item, we simply increase the appropriate counter; to delete an item, we decrease the counter; and to test whether an item is in the set, we test whether the corresponding counter is greater than zero. In all cases the operation can be done in constant time.

#### Union, Intersection, and Difference

Because multisets permit duplicates but sets do not, the definitions of union, intersection, and difference are slightly modified for multisets. The *union* of multisets $S$ and $T$, written $S \cup T$, is the multiset comprised of all the elements of $S$ together with all the element of $T$. Since a multiset may contain duplicates, it does not matter if the same element appears in $S$ and $T$.

The subtle difference between union of sets and union of multisets gives rise to an interesting and useful property. If $S$ and $T$ are regular sets,

$$\max(|S|, |T|) \leq |S \cup T| \leq |S| + |T|.$$

On the other hand, if $S$ and $T$ are *multisets*,

$$|S \cup T| = |S| + |T|.$$

---

**PROGRAM 12.10**
**MultisetAsArray** class definition

---

```
1   class MultisetAsArray : public Multiset
2   {
3       Array<unsigned int> array;
4   public:
5       MultisetAsArray (unsigned int);
6       //...
7   };
```

**PROGRAM 12.11**
MultisetAsArray class constructor, Insert, Withdraw, and IsMember member function definitions

```
1   MultisetAsArray::MultisetAsArray (unsigned int n) :
2       Multiset (n),
3       array (n)
4   {
5       for (unsigned int item = 0; item < universeSize; ++item)
6           array [item] = 0;
7   }
8
9   void MultisetAsArray::Insert (Object& object)
10  {
11      unsigned int const item = dynamic_cast<Element&> (object);
12      ++array [item];
13  }
14
15  void MultisetAsArray::Withdraw (Object& object)
16  {
17      unsigned int const item = dynamic_cast<Element&> (object);
18      if (array [item] > 0)
19          --array [item];
20  }
21
22  bool MultisetAsArray::IsMember (Object const& object) const
23  {
24      unsigned int const item =
25          dynamic_cast<Element const&> (object);
26      return array [item] > 0;
27  }
```

The *intersection* of sets $S$ and $T$ is written $S \cap T$. The elements of $S \cap T$ are those items which are elements of *both* $S$ and $T$. If a given element appears more than once in $S$ or $T$ (or both), the intersection contains $m$ copies of that element, where $m$ is the smaller of the number of times the element appears in $S$ or $T$. For example, if $S = \{0, 1, 1, 2, 2, 2\}$ and $T = \{1, 2, 2, 3\}$, the intersection is $S \cap T = \{1, 2, 2\}$.

The *difference* of sets $S$ and $T$, written $S - T$, contains those elements of $S$ which are *not also* elements of $T$. That is, the result $S - T$ is obtained by taking the set $S$ and removing from it those elements which are also found in $T$.

Program 12.12 gives the implementations of the union, intersection, and difference operators (+, *, and -, respectively) for operands of type MultisetAsArray. This code is quite similar to that of the SetAsArray class (Program 12.4) and the SetAsBitVector class (Program 12.7). The worst-case running time of each of these operations is $O(N)$.

**PROGRAM 12.12**
MultisetAsArray class union, intersection, and difference operator definitions

```
1  MultisetAsArray operator + (
2      MultisetAsArray const& s, MultisetAsArray const& t)
3  {
4      if (s.universeSize != t.universeSize)
5          throw invalid_argument ("mismatched sets");
6      MultisetAsArray result (s.universeSize);
7      for (unsigned int i = 0; i < s.universeSize; ++i)
8          result.array [i] = s.array [i] + t.array [i];
9      return result;
10 }
11
12 MultisetAsArray operator * (
13     MultisetAsArray const& s, MultisetAsArray const& t)
14 {
15     if (s.universeSize != t.universeSize)
16         throw invalid_argument ("mismatched sets");
17     MultisetAsArray result (s.universeSize);
18     for (unsigned int i = 0; i < s.universeSize; ++i)
19         result.array [i] = Min (s.array [i], t.array [i]);
20     return result;
21 }
22
23 MultisetAsArray operator - (
24     MultisetAsArray const& s, MultisetAsArray const& t)
25 {
26     if (s.universeSize != t.universeSize)
27         throw invalid_argument ("mismatched sets");
28     MultisetAsArray result (s.universeSize);
29     for (unsigned int i = 0; i < s.universeSize; ++i)
30         if (t.array [i] <= s.array [i])
31             result.array [i] = s.array [i] - t.array [i];
32     return result;
33 }
```

Instead of using the Boolean operators &&, ||, and !, we have used + (integer addition), Min and - (integer subtraction). The following table summarizes the operators used in the various set and multiset implementations.

| | Class | | |
| operation | SetAsArray | SetAsBitVector | MultisetAsArray |
| --- | --- | --- | --- |
| union | \|\| | \| | + |
| intersection | && | & | Min |
| difference | && and ! | & and - | <= and - |

## 12.3.2 Linked-List Implementation

The array implementation of multisets is really only practical if the number of items in the universe, $N = |U|$, is not too large. If $N$ is large, then it is impractical, or at least extremely inefficient, to use an array of $N$ counters to represent the multiset. This is especially so if the number of elements in the multisets is significantly less than $N$.

If we use a linked list of elements to represent a multiset $S$, the space required is proportional to the size of the multiset, $|S|$. When the size of the multiset is significantly less than the size of the universe, $|S| \ll |U|$, it is more efficient in terms of both time and space to use a linked list.

Program 12.13 gives the declaration of the **MultisetAsLinkedList** class. The **MultisetAsLinkedList** class is a concrete class derived from the abstract base class **Multiset**. In this case a linked list of **unsigned int**s is used to record the contents of the multiset.

How should the elements of the multiset be stored in the list? Perhaps the simplest way is to store the elements in the list in no particular order. Doing so makes the **Insert** operation efficient—it can be done in constant time. Furthermore, the **IsMember** and **Withdraw** operations both take $O(n)$ time, where $n$ is the number of items in the multiset, *regardless of the order of the items in the linked list*.

Consider now the union, intersection, and difference of two multisets, say $S$ and $T$. If the linked list is unordered, the worst-case running time for the union operation is $O(m + n)$, where $m = |S|$ and $n = |T|$. Unfortunately, intersection and difference are both $O(mn)$.

If, on the other hand, we use an *ordered* linked list, union, intersection, and difference can all be done in $O(m + n)$ time. The trade-off is that the insertion becomes an $O(n)$ operation rather than a $O(1)$. The **MultisetAsLinkedList** implementation presented in this section records the elements of the multiset in an *ordered* linked list.

### Union

The union operation for **MultisetAsLinkedList** class requires the merging of two ordered, linked lists, as shown in Program 12.14. We have assumed that the smallest element contained in a multiset is found at the head of the linked list and the largest is at the tail.

---

**PROGRAM 12.13**
**MultisetAsLinkedList** class definition

---

```
1   class MultisetAsLinkedList : public Multiset
2   {
3       LinkedList<unsigned int> list;
4   public:
5       MultisetAsLinkedList (unsigned int);
6       //...
7   };
```

---

**PROGRAM 12.14**
`MultisetAsLinkedList` class union operator definition

```
1   MultisetAsLinkedList operator + (
2       MultisetAsLinkedList const& s, MultisetAsLinkedList const& t)
3   {
4       if (s.universeSize != t.universeSize)
5           throw invalid_argument ("mismatched sets");
6       MultisetAsLinkedList result (s.universeSize);
7       ListElement<unsigned int> const* p = s.list.Head ();
8       ListElement<unsigned int> const* q = t.list.Head ();
9       while (p && q)
10      {
11          if (p->Datum () <= q->Datum ())
12          {
13              result.list.Append (p->Datum ());
14              p = p->Next ();
15          }
16          else
17          {
18              result.list.Append (q->Datum ());
19              q = q->Next ();
20          }
21      }
22      for ( ; p; p = p->Next ())
23          result.list.Append (p->Datum ());
24      for ( ; q; q = q->Next ())
25          result.list.Append (q->Datum ());
26      return result;
27  }
```

The union operator takes two multisets and computes a third multiset, the `result`, as follows. The main loop of the program (lines 9–21) traverses the linked lists of the two operands. In each iteration it appends the smallest remaining element to the result. Once one of the lists has been exhausted, the remaining elements in the other list are simply appended to the result (lines 22–25). The total running time for the union operation, `operator+`, is $O(m + n)$, where $m = |s|$ and $n = |t|$ and `s` and `t` are the two operand multisets.

### Intersection

The implementation of the intersection operator for the `MultisetAsLinkedList` class is similar to that of union. However, instead of merging two ordered, linked lists to construct a third, we compare the elements of two lists and append an item to the third

---

**PROGRAM 12.15**
MultisetAsLinkedList class intersection operator definition

---

```
1  MultisetAsLinkedList operator * (
2      MultisetAsLinkedList const& s, MultisetAsLinkedList const& t)
3  {
4      if (s.universeSize != t.universeSize)
5          throw invalid_argument ("mismatched sets");
6      MultisetAsLinkedList result (s.universeSize);
7      ListElement<unsigned int> const* p = s.list.Head ();
8      ListElement<unsigned int> const* q = t.list.Head ();
9      while (p && q)
10     {
11         int const diff = p->Datum () - q->Datum ();
12         if (diff == 0)
13             result.list.Append (p->Datum ());
14         if (diff <= 0)
15             p = p->Next ();
16         if (diff >= 0)
17             q = q->Next ();
18     }
19     return result;
20 }
```

---

only when it appears in both of the input lists. The intersection operator, **operator\***, is shown in Program 12.15.

The main loop of the program traverses the linked lists of both input operands at once using two pointers (lines 9–18). If the next element in each list is the same, that element is appended to the result and both pointers are advanced. Otherwise, only one of the pointers is advanced—the one pointing to the smaller element.

The number of iterations of the main loop actually done depends on the contents of the respective linked lists. The best case occurs when both lists are identical. In this case, the number of iterations is $m$, where $m = |\mathbf{s}| = |\mathbf{t}|$. In the worst-case, the number of iterations done is $m + n$. Therefore, the running time of the intersection operation, **operator\***, is $O(m + n)$.

## 12.4 Partitions

Consider the finite universal set $U = \{0, 1, \ldots, N - 1\}$. A *partition* of $U$ is a finite set of sets $P = \{S_1, S_2, \ldots, S_p\}$ with the following properties:

1. The sets $S_1, S_2, \ldots, S_p$ are pairwise *disjoint*, that is,

$$\forall i, j, 1 \le i < j \le p : S_i \cap S_j = \emptyset.$$

2. The sets $S_1, S_2, \ldots, S_p$ *span* the universe $U$, that is,

$$\bigcup_{i=1}^{p} S_i = S_1 \cup S_2 \cup \cdots \cup S_p$$
$$= U.$$

For example, consider the universe $U = \{1, 2, 3\}$. There are exactly five partitions of $U$:

$$P_0 = \{\{1\}, \{2\}, \{3\}\},$$
$$P_1 = \{\{1\}, \{2, 3\}\},$$
$$P_2 = \{\{2\}, \{1, 3\}\},$$
$$P_3 = \{\{3\}, \{1, 2\}\}, \text{ and}$$
$$P_4 = \{\{1, 2, 3\}\}.$$

In general, given a universe $U$ of size $n > 0$, i.e., $|U| = n$, there are $\sum_{m=0}^{n} \left\{ {n \atop m} \right\}$ partitions of $U$, where $\left\{ {n \atop m} \right\}$ is the *Stirling number of the second kind* which denotes the number of ways to partition a set of $n$ elements into $m$ nonempty disjoint subsets.[1]

Applications which use partitions typically start with an initial partition and refine that partition either by joining, or by splitting elements of the partition according to some application-specific criterion. The result of such a computation is the partition obtained when no more elements can be split or joined.

In this chapter we consider only applications that begin with the initial partition of $U$ in which each item in $U$ is in a separate element of the partition. Thus, the initial partition consists of $|U|$ sets, each of size 1 (like $P_0$ above). Furthermore, we restrict the applications in that we only allow elements of a partition to be joined—we do not allow elements to split.

The two operations to be performed on partitions are:

**Find** Given an item in the universe, say $i \in U$, find the element of the partition that contains $i$; that is, find $S_j \in P$ such that $i \in S_j$.

**Join** Given two distinct elements of a partition $P$, say $S_i \in P$ and $S_j \in P$ such that $i \ne j$, create a new partition $P'$ by removing the two elements $S_i$ and $S_j$ from $P$ and replacing them with a single element $S_i \cup S_j$.

---

[1] *Stirling numbers of the second kind* are given by the formula

$$\left\{ {n \atop m} \right\} = \begin{cases} 1 & n = 1, \\ 1 & n = m, \\ m\left\{ {n-1 \atop m} \right\} + \left\{ {n-1 \atop m-1} \right\} & \text{otherwise,} \end{cases}$$

where $n > 0$ and $1 \le m \le n$.

---

**PROGRAM 12.16**
`Partition` class definition

---

```
1  class Partition : public Set
2  {
3  public:
4      Partition (unsigned int n) : Set (n) {}
5
6      virtual Set& Find (Object const&) const = 0;
7      virtual void Join (Set&, Set&) = 0;
8  };
```

---

For example, consider the partition $P = \{S_1, S_2, S_3\} = \{\{1\}, \{2, 3\}, \{4\}\}$. The result of the operation *find*(3) is the set $S_2 = \{2, 3\}$ because 3 is a member of $S_2$. Furthermore, when we *join* sets $S_1$ and $S_3$, we get the partition $P' = \{\{1, 4\}, \{2, 3\}\}$.

### Representing Partitions

Program 12.16 declares the abstract class `Partition`. Since a partition is a set of sets, it makes sense to use a class derived from the abstract base class `Set` defined in Section 12.1.1. The two member functions, `Find` and `Join`, correspond to the partition operations described above.

The elements of a partition are also sets. Consequently, the objects contained in a `Partition` are also derived from the `Set` class. The `Find` member function of the `Partition` class expects as its argument a reference to a `Set::Element` and returns a reference to the `Set` which contains the specified element.

The `Join` member function takes two arguments, both of them references to `Set` instances. The two arguments are expected to be distinct elements of the partition. The effect of the `Join` operation is to remove the specified sets from the partition and replace them with a `Set` which represents the *union* of the two.

## 12.4.1  Implementing a Partition using a Forest

A partition is a set of sets. Consequently, there are two related issues to consider when developing an approach for representing partitions:

1.  How are the individual elements or parts of the partition represented?
2.  How are the elements of a partition combined into the whole?

This section presents an approach in which each element of a partition is a tree. Therefore, the whole partition is a *forest*.

For example, Figure 12.3 shows how the partition

$$P = \{S_1, S_2, S_3, S_4\}$$
$$= \{\{0, 4\}, \{2, 6, 8\}, \{10\}, \{1, 3, 5, 7, 9, 11\}\}$$

can be represented using a forest. Notice that each element of the universal set $U = \{0, 1, \ldots, 11\}$ appears in exactly one node of exactly one tree.

The trees in Figure 12.3 have some very interesting characteristics. The first characteristic concerns the shapes of the trees: The nodes of the trees have arbitrary degrees. The second characteristic concerns the positions of the keys: There are no constraints on the positions of the keys in a tree. The final characteristic has to do with the way the tree is represented: Instead of pointers to its children, each node of a tree contains only one pointer—a pointer to its parent!

Since there is no particular order to the nodes in the trees, it is necessary to keep track of the position of each node explicitly. Figure 12.4 shows how this can be done using an array of pointers. (This figure shows the same partition as in Figure 12.3.) The array contains a pointer for each element of the universal set $U$. Specifically, the $i$th array element contains a pointer to the node that contains item $i$. Having found the desired node, we can follow the chain of parent pointers to find the root of the corresponding tree.

---

**FIGURE 12.3**
Representing a partition as a forest.

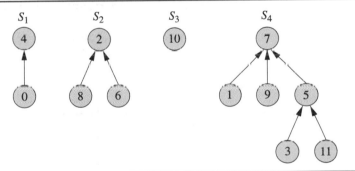

---

**FIGURE 12.4**
Finding the elements of a partition.

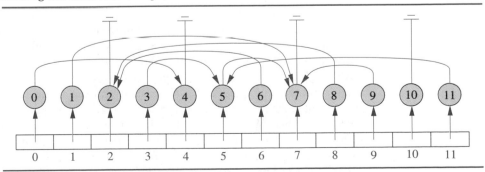

---

**PROGRAM 12.17**
PartitionTree and PartitionAsForest class definitions

```
1   class PartitionTree : public Set, public Tree
2   {
3       unsigned int const item;
4       PartitionTree* parent;
5       unsigned int rank;
6
7       PartitionTree (unsigned int, unsigned int);
8       //...
9       friend class PartitionAsForest;
10  };
11
12  class PartitionAsForest : public Partition
13  {
14      Array<PartitionTree*> array;
15
16      void CheckArguments (
17          PartitionTree const&, PartitionTree const&);
18  public:
19      PartitionAsForest (unsigned int);
20      ~PartitionAsForest ();
21      //...
22  };
23
```

---

### Implementation

Program 12.17 declares two classes—**PartitionTree** and **PartitionAsForest**. The former is used to represent the individual elements or parts of a partition, and the latter encapsulates all of the parts that make up a given partition.

The **PartitionTree** class is derived from the abstract base classes **Set** and **Tree**. Since we are representing the parts of a partition using trees, it makes sense that we derive them from the **Tree** class. On the other hand, since a partition is a set of sets, we must also derive the parts of a partition from the **Set** class. In particular, this is necessary because of the way that the **Find** and **Join** member functions are defined.

The **PartitionTree** class has three member variables—**parent**, **item**, and **rank**. Each instance of this class represents one node of a tree. The **parent** member variable points to the parent of a given node and the **item** member variable records the element of the universal set that the given node represents. The remaining variable, **rank**, is optional. While it is not required in order to provide the basic functionality, as shown below, the **rank** variable can be used in the implementation of the **Join** operation to improve the performance of subsequent **Find** operations.

The **PartitionAsForest** class represents a complete partition. Since a partition is a set of sets, it is a container. And since it supports a *find* operation, the class **PartitionAsForest** is derived from the abstract base class **Searchable-Container**. The **PartitionAsForest** class contains a single member variable, **array**, which is an array of pointers to **PartitionTree** instances. The $i$th element of the array always points to the tree node that contains element $i$ of the universe.

### Constructors and Destructor

Program 12.18 gives the code for the **PartitionTree** constructor. The constructor creates a tree comprised of a single node. It takes an argument which specifies the element of the universal set that the node is to represent. The **parent** field is set to zero to indicate that the node has no parent. Consequently, the node is a root node. Finally, the **rank** field is initialized to zero. The running time of the constructor is $O(1)$.

Program 12.18 also shows the constructor and destructor for the **PartitionAs-Forest** class. The constructor takes a single argument $N$ which specifies that the universe shall be $U = \{0, 1, \ldots, N - 1\}$. It creates an initial partition of the universe consisting of $N$ parts. Each part contains one element of the universal set and, therefore, comprises a one-node tree. The **PartitionAsForest** is a container, and the **PartitionTree** instances that the constructor creates are the contained objects.

The destructor is responsible for deleting the objects in the container; that is, it deletes all the **PartitionTree** instances that were created in the constructor. Both the constructor and destructor run in $O(N)$ time, where $N$ is the number of elements in the universe.

---

**PROGRAM 12.18**
**PartitionTree** and **PartitionAsForest** class constructor and destructor definitions

```
1   PartitionTree::PartitionTree (unsigned int i, unsigned int n) :
2       Set (n),
3       item (i),
4       parent (0),
5       rank (0)
6       { count = 1; }
7
8   PartitionAsForest::PartitionAsForest (unsigned int n) :
9       Partition (n),
10      array (n)
11  {
12      for (unsigned int item = 0; item < universeSize; ++item)
13          array [item] = new PartitionTree (item, universeSize);
14      count = n;
15  }
16
17  PartitionAsForest::~PartitionAsForest ()
18  {
19      for (unsigned int item = 0; item < universeSize; ++item)
20          delete array [item];
21  }
```

---

**PROGRAM 12.19**
PartitionAsForest class Find member function definition

---

```
1   Set& PartitionAsForest::Find (Object const& object) const
2   {
3       unsigned int const item =
4           dynamic_cast<Set::Element const&> (object);
5       PartitionTree* ptr = array [item];
6       while (ptr->parent != 0)
7           ptr = ptr->parent;
8       return *ptr;
9   }
```

---

### Find and Join Member Functions

Two elements of the universe are in the same part of the partition if and only if they share the same root node. Since every tree has a unique root, it makes sense to use the root node as the "handle" for that tree. Therefore, the *find* operation takes an element of the universal set and returns the root node of the tree that contains that element. And because of the way in which the trees are represented, we can follow the chain of parent pointers to find the root node.

Program 12.19 gives the code for the **Find** member function of the **PartitionAsForest** class. The **Find** function takes as its lone argument a reference to an **Object** instance and returns a reference to a **Set**. The argument is expected to be actually a **Set::Element** that specifies the item of the universe that is the object of the search.

The **Find** operation begins at the node **array[item]** and follows the chain of parent pointers to find the root node of the tree that contains the specified item. The result of the function is a reference to the root node.

The running time of the **Find** operation is $O(d)$, where $d$ is the depth in the tree of the node from which the search begins. If we don't do anything special to prevent it, the worst case running time is $O(N)$, where $N$ is the size of the universe. The best performance is achieved when every non-root node points to the root node. In this case, the running time is $O(1)$.

Another advantage of having a pointer to the parent in each node is that the *join* operation can be implemented easily and efficiently. For example, suppose we wish to *join* the two sets $S_1$ and $S_2$ shown in Figure 12.5. While there are many possible representations for $S_1 \cup S_2$, it turns out that there are two simple alternatives which can be obtained in constant time. These are shown in Figure 12.4. In the first alternative, the root of $S_2$ is made a child of the root of $S_1$. This can be done in constant time simply by making the parent pointer of the root of $S_2$ point to the root of $S_1$. The second alternative is essentially the same as the first, except that the rôles of $S_1$ and $S_2$ are exchanged.

Program 12.20 gives the simplest possible implementation for the **Join** operation. The **Join** member function of the **PartitionAsForest** class takes two arguments—both of them references to **Set**s. Both arguments are required to be references to distinct **PartitionTree** instances which are contained in the given partition. Furthermore, both of them are required to be root nodes. Therefore, the sets that the

**FIGURE 12.5**
Alternatives for joining elements of a partition.

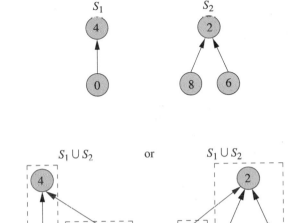

---

**PROGRAM 12.20**
`PartitionAsForest` class simple `Join` member function definition

```
1   void PartitionAsForest::CheckArguments (
2       PartitionTree const& s, PartitionTree const& t)
3   {
4       if (!IsMember (s) || s.parent != 0 ||
5           !IsMember (t) || t.parent != 0 || s == t)
6           throw invalid_argument ("incompatible sets");
7   }
8
9   void PartitionAsForest::Join (Set& s, Set& t)
10  {
11      PartitionTree& p = dynamic_cast<PartitionTree&> (s);
12      PartitionTree& q = dynamic_cast<PartitionTree&> (t);
13      CheckArguments (p, q);
14      q.parent = &p;
15      --count;
16  }
```

arguments represent are *disjoint*. The member function **CheckArguments** makes sure that the arguments satisfy these conditions.

The **Join** operation is trivial and executes in constant time: It simply makes one node the parent of the other. In this case, we have arbitrarily chosen that the node specified by the first argument shall always become the parent.

### 12.4.2   Collapsing Find

Unfortunately, using the **Join** algorithm given in Program 12.20 can result in particularly bad trees. For example, Figure 12.6 shows the worst possible tree that can be obtained. Such a tree is bad because its height is $O(N)$. In such a tree both the worst-case and the average-case running time for the **Find** operation is $O(N)$.

There is an interesting trick we can play that can improve matters significantly. Recall that the **Find** operation starts from a given node and locates the root of the tree containing that node. If, having found the root, we replace the parent pointer of the given node with a pointer to the root, the next time we do a **Find** it will be more efficient.

In fact, we can go one step further and replace the parent pointer of every node along the search path to the root. This is called a *collapsing find* operation. Doing so does not change the asymptotic complexity of the **Find** operation. However, a subsequent **Find** operation which begins at any point along the search path to the root will run in constant time!

Program 12.21 gives the code for a collapsing version of the **Find** operation. The **Find** function first determines the root node as before. Then, a second pass is made up the chain from the initial node to the root, during which the parent pointer of each node is made to point at the root. Clearly, this version of **Find** is slower than the one given

---

**FIGURE 12.6**
A degenerate tree.

---

**PROGRAM 12.21**
`PartitionAsForest` class collapsing `Find` member function definition

```
1   Set& PartitionAsForest::Find (Object const& object) const
2   {
3       unsigned int const item =
4           dynamic_cast<Set::Element const&> (object);
5       PartitionTree* root = array [item];
6       while (root->parent != 0)
7           root = root->parent;
8       PartitionTree* ptr = array [item];
9       while (ptr->parent != 0)
10      {
11          PartitionTree* const tmp = ptr->parent;
12          ptr->parent = root;
13          ptr = tmp;
14      }
15      return *root;
16  }
```

in Program 12.19 because it makes two passes up the chain rather than one. However, the running of this version of **Find** is still $O(d)$, where $d$ is the depth of the node from which the search begins.

Figure 12.7 illustrates the effect of a collapsing find operation. After the find, all the nodes along the search path are attached directly to the root; that is, they have had their depths decreased to one. As a side effect, any node which is in the subtree of a node along the search path may have its depth decreased by the collapsing find operation. The depth of a node is never increased by the find operation. Eventually, if we do enough collapsing find operations, it is possible to obtain a tree of height 1 in which all the non-root nodes point directly at the root.

**FIGURE 12.7**
Example of collapsing find.

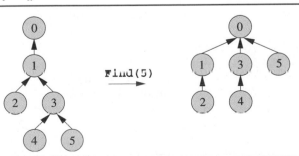

### 12.4.3 Union by Size

While using collapsing find does mitigate the negative effects of poor trees, a better approach is to avoid creating bad trees in the first place. As shown in Figure 12.5, when we join to trees we have a choice—Which node should we choose to be the root of the new tree? A simple, but effective choice is to attach the smaller tree under the root of the larger one. In this case, the smaller tree is the one which has fewer nodes. This is the *union-by-size* join algorithm. Program 12.22 shows how this can be done.

The implementation uses the **count** field of the **Container** class, from which **PartitionTree** is derived, to keep track of the number of items contained in the tree. (Since each node contains one item from the universal set, the number of items contained in a tree is equal to the number of nodes in that tree.) The algorithm simply selects the tree with the largest number of nodes to become the root of the result and attaches the root of the smaller tree under that of the larger one. Clearly, the running time of the union-by-size version of **Join** is $O(1)$.

The following theorem shows that when using the union-by-size join operation, the heights of the resulting trees grow logarithmically.

### Theorem 12.1
*Consider an initial partition P of the universe $U = \{0, 1, \ldots, N - 1\}$ comprised of N sets of size 1. Let S be an element of the partition obtained from P after some sequence of* union-by-size *join operations, such that $|S| = n$ for some $n \geq 1$. Let T be the tree*

---

**PROGRAM 12.22**
**PartitionAsForest** class union-by-size **Join** member function definition

```
1   void PartitionAsForest::Join (Set& s, Set& t)
2   {
3       PartitionTree& p = dynamic_cast<PartitionTree&> (s);
4       PartitionTree& q = dynamic_cast<PartitionTree&> (t);
5       CheckArguments (p, q);
6       if (p.count > q.count)
7       {
8           q.parent = &p;
9           p.count += q.count;
10      }
11      else
12      {
13          p.parent = &q;
14          q.count += p.count;
15      }
16      --count;
17  }
```

*representing the set S. The height of tree T satisfies the inequality*

$$h \leq \lfloor \log_2 n \rfloor.$$

**Proof**    (By induction.)

**Base Case**    Since a tree comprised of a single node has height zero, the theorem clearly holds for $n = 1$.

**Inductive Hypothesis**    Suppose the theorem holds for trees containing $n$ nodes for $n = 1, 2, \ldots, k$ for some $k \geq 1$. Consider a union-by-size join operation that produces a tree containing $k + 1$ nodes. Such a tree is obtained by joining a tree $T_l$ having $l \leq k$ nodes with another tree $T_m$ that has $m \leq k$ nodes, such that $l + m = k + 1$.

Without loss of generality, suppose $1 \leq l \leq (k + 1)/2$. As a result, $l$ is less than or equal to $m$. Therefore, the union-by-size algorithm will attach $T_l$ under the root of $T_m$. Let $h_l$ and $h_m$ be the heights of $T_l$ and $T_r$, respectively. The height of the resulting tree is $\max(h_l + 1, h_m)$. According to the inductive hypothesis, the height of $T_m$ is given by

$$\begin{aligned}
h_m &\leq \lfloor \log_2 m \rfloor \\
&\leq \lfloor \log_2(k + 1 - l) \rfloor \\
&\leq \lfloor \log_2(k + 1) \rfloor.
\end{aligned}$$

Similarly, the quantity $h_l + 1$ is bounded by

$$\begin{aligned}
h_l + 1 &\leq \lfloor \log_2 l \rfloor + 1 \\
&\leq \lfloor \log_2((k + 1)/2) \rfloor + 1 \\
&\leq \lfloor \log_2(k + 1) \rfloor.
\end{aligned}$$

Therefore, the height of the tree containing $k + 1$ nodes is no greater than $\max(h_l + 1, h_m) = \lfloor \log_2(k + 1) \rfloor$. By induction on $k$, the theorem holds for all values of $n \geq 1$.

---

Note that Theorem 12.1 and its proof do not require that we use the collapsing find algorithm of Section 12.4.2. That is, the height of a tree containing $n$ nodes is guaranteed to be $O(\log n)$ when the simple find is used. Of course, there is nothing precluding the use of the collapsing find in conjunction with the union-by-size join routine; and doing so only makes things better.

## 12.4.4   Union by Height or Rank

The union-by-size join algorithm described above controls the heights of the trees indirectly by basing the join algorithm on the sizes of the trees. If we explicitly keep track of the height of a node in the node itself, we can accomplish the same thing.

Program 12.23 gives an implementation of the **Join** routine that always attaches the shorter tree under the root of the taller one. This routine assumes that the **rank** field is

---

**PROGRAM 12.23**
`PartitionAsForest` class union-by-rank `Join` member function definition

```
1   void PartitionAsForest::Join (Set& s, Set& t)
2   {
3       PartitionTree& p = dynamic_cast<PartitionTree&> (s);
4       PartitionTree& q = dynamic_cast<PartitionTree&> (t);
5       CheckArguments (p, q);
6       if (p.rank > q.rank)
7           q.parent = &p;
8       else
9       {
10          p.parent = &q;
11          if (p.rank == q.rank)
12              q.rank += 1;
13      }
14      --count;
15  }
```

---

used to keep track of the height of a node. (The reason for calling it **rank** rather than **height** will become evident shortly.)

The only time that the height of node increases is when joining two trees that have the same height. In this case, the height of the root increases by exactly 1. If the two trees being joined have different heights, attaching the shorter tree under the root of the taller one has no effect on the height of the root.

Unfortunately, there is a slight complication if we combine union-by-height with the collapsing find. Since the collapsing find works by moving nodes closer to the root, it affects potentially the height of any node moved. It is not at all clear how to recompute efficiently the heights that have changed. The solution is not to do it at all!

If we don't recompute the heights during the collapsing find operations, then the heights will no longer be exact. Nevertheless, the quantities remain useful estimates of the heights of nodes. We call the estimated height of a node its *rank* and the join algorithm which uses rank instead of height is called *union by rank*.

Fortunately, Theorem 12.1 applies equally well when union-by-rank is used. That is, the height of tree which contains $n$ nodes is $O(\log n)$. Thus, the worst-case running time for the **Find** operation grows logarithmically with $n$. And as before, collapsing find only makes things better.

## 12.5  Applications

One of the most important applications of partitions involves the processing of equivalence relations. Equivalence relations arise in many interesting contexts. For example, two nodes in an electric circuit are electrically equivalent if there is a conducting path (a wire) connecting the two nodes. In effect, the wires establish an electrical equivalence relation over the nodes of a circuit.

A similar relation arises among the user-defined data types in a C++ program. Consider the following C++ code fragment:

```
class A;
typedef A B;
typedef A C;
typedef B D;
```

The four data types A, B, C, and D are equivalent in the sense that values of one type can be assigned directly to variables of another (without requiring a type conversion). In effect, the **typedef** declarations establish a type equivalence relation over the user-defined data types in a C++ program.

### Definition 12.1 (Equivalence Relation)

*An* equivalence relation *over a universal set U is a relation $\equiv$ with the following properties:*

1. *The relation $\equiv$ is* reflexive, *that is, for every $x \in U$, $x \equiv x$.*
2. *The relation $\equiv$ is* symmetric, *that is, for every pair $x \in U$ and $y \in U$, if $x \equiv y$ then $y \equiv x$.*
3. *The relation $\equiv$ is* transitive, *that is, for every triple $x \in U$, $y \in U$ and $z \in U$, if $x \equiv y$ and $y \equiv z$ then $x \equiv z$.*

An important characteristic of an equivalence relation is that it partitions the elements of the universal set $U$ into a set of *equivalence classes*. That is, $U$ is partitioned into $P = \{S_1, S_2, \ldots, S_p\}$, such that for every pair $x \in U$ and $y \in U$, $x \equiv y$ if and only if $x$ and $y$ are in the same element of the partition. That is,

$$x \equiv y \iff \exists i, 1 \le i \le p : x \in S_i \wedge y \in S_i.$$

For example, consider the universe $U = \{0, 1, \ldots, 9\}$ and the equivalence relation $\equiv$ defined over $U$ defines as follows:

$$0 \equiv 0, 1 \equiv 1, 1 \equiv 2, 2 \equiv 2, 3 \equiv 3, 3 \equiv 4, 3 \equiv 5, 4 \equiv 4, 4 \equiv 5, 5 \equiv 5,$$
$$6 \equiv 6, 6 \equiv 7, 6 \equiv 8, 6 \equiv 9, 7 \equiv 7, 7 \equiv 8, 7 \equiv 9, 8 \equiv 8, 8 \equiv 9, 9 \equiv 9. \quad (12.1)$$

This relation results in the following partition of $U$:

$$\{\{0\}, \{1, 2\}, \{3, 4, 5\}, \{6, 7, 8, 9\}\}.$$

The list of equivalences in Equation 12.1 contains many redundancies. Since we know that the relation $\equiv$ is reflexive, symmetric, and transitive, it is possible to infer

**PROGRAM 12.24**
Application of disjoint sets—finding equivalence classes

```
1   void EquivalenceClasses ()
2   {
3       unsigned int n;
4       cin >> n;
5       Partition& p = *new PartitionAsForest (n);
6
7       unsigned int i;
8       unsigned int j;
9       while (cin >> i >> j, !cin.eof ())
10      {
11          Set& s = p.Find (Set::Element (i)));
12          Set& t = p.Find (Set::Element (j)));
13          if (s != t)
14              p.Join (s, t);
15          else
16              cout << "redundant pair: "
17                  << i << ", " << j << endl;
18      }
19      cout << p << endl;
20      delete &p;
21  }
```

the complete relation from the following list

$$1 \equiv 2, 3 \equiv 4, 3 \equiv 5, 6 \equiv 7, 6 \equiv 8, 6 \equiv 9.$$

The problem of finding the set of equivalence classes from a list of equivalence pairs is easily solved using a partition. Program 12.24 shows how it can be done using the **PartitionAsForest** class defined in Section 12.4.1.

The algorithm first gets a positive integer, **n**, from the input and creates a partition, **p**, of the universe $U = \{0, 1 \dots, n - 1\}$ (lines 3–5). As explained in Section 12.4.1, the initial partition comprises **n** disjoint sets of size 1. That is, each element of the universal set is in a separate element of the partition.

Each iteration of the main loop processes one equivalence pair (lines 9–18). An equivalence pair consists of two numbers, **i** and **j**, such that $i \in U$ and $j \in U$. The *find* operation is used to determine the sets **s** and **t** in partition **p** that contain elements **i** and **j**, respectively, (lines 11–12).

If **s** and **t** are not the same set, then the disjoint sets are united using the *join* operation (lines 13–14). Otherwise, **i** and **j** are already in the same set and the equivalence pair is redundant (lines 15–17). After all the pairs have been processed, the final partition is printed (line 19).

# Exercises

**12.1** For each of the following implementations, derive an expression for the total memory space required to represent a set which contains of $n$ elements drawn from the universe $U = \{0, 1, \ldots, N - 1\}$.

**a.** `SetAsArray` (Program 12.2),

**b.** `SetAsBitVector` (Program 12.6),

**c.** `MultisetAsArray` (Program 12.10), and

**d.** `MultisetAsLinkedList` (Program 12.13).

**12.2** In addition to = and $\subseteq$, a complete repertoire of set operators includes $\subset, \supset, \supseteq$, and $\neq$. For each of the set implementations listed in Exercise 12.1 show how to implement the remaining operators.

**12.3** The *symmetric difference* of two sets $S$ and $T$, written $S \triangle T$ is given by

$$S \triangle T = (S \cup T) - (S \cap T).$$

For each of the set implementations listed in Exercise 12.1 devise an algorithm to compute symmetric difference. What is the running time of your algorithm?

**12.4** The *complement* of a set $S$ over universe $U$, written $S'$ is given by

$$S' = U - S.$$

Devise an algorithm to compute the complement of a set represented as a bit vector. What is the running time of your algorithm?

**12.5** Devise an algorithm to sort a list of integers using a multiset. What is the running time of your algorithm? **Hint**: See Section 15.8.1.

**12.6** Consider a multiset implemented using linked lists. When the multiset contains duplicate items, each of those items occupies a separate list element. An alternative is to use a linked list of ordered pairs of the form $(i, n_i)$ where $i$ is an element of the universal set $U$ and $n_i$ is a non-negative integer that counts the number of instances of the element $i$ in the multiset.

Derive an expression for the total memory space required to represent a multiset which contains of $n$ instances of $m$ distinct element drawn from the universe $U = \{0, 1, \ldots, N - 1\}$.

**12.7** Consider a multiset implemented as described in Exercise 12.6. Devise algorithms for set union, intersection, and difference. What are the running times of your algorithms?

**12.8** Consider the initial partition $P = \{\{0\}, \{1\}, \{2\}, \ldots, \{9\}\}$. For each of the methods of computing the union listed below show the result of the following sequence *join* operations: *join*(0, 1), *join*(2, 3), *join*(2, 4), *join*(2, 5), *join*(6, 7), *join*(8, 9), *join*(6, 8), *join*(0, 6), *join*(0, 2).

    **a.**  simple union,

    **b.**  union by size,

    **c.**  union by height, and

    **d.**  union by rank.

**12.9**  For each final partition obtained in Exercise 12.8, show the result of performing a *collapsing find* operation for item 9.

**12.10**  Consider the initial partition $P$ of the universe $U = \{0, 1, \ldots, N-1\}$ comprised of $N$ sets[19].

    **a.**  Show that $N-1$ join operations can be performed before the number of elements in the partition is reduced to one.

    **b.**  Show that if $n$ join operations are done ($0 \leq n < N$), the size of the largest element of the partition is at most $n+1$.

    **c.**  A *singleton* is an element of a partition that contains only one element of the universal set. Show that when $n$ join operations are done ($0 \leq n < N$), at least $\max\{N-2n, 0\}$ singletons are left.

    **d.**  Show that if less than $\lceil N/2 \rceil$ join operations are done, at least one singleton is left.

## Programming Projects

**12.1**  Complete the **SetAsArray** class declared in Program 12.2 by providing suitable definitions for the following member functions: **~SetAsArray** (destructor), **Purge**, **IsEmpty**, **IsFull**, **Count**, **Accept**, and **NewIterator**. Write a test program and test your implementation.

**12.2**  Complete the **SetAsBitVector** class declared in Program 12.6 by providing suitable definitions for the following member functions: **~SetAsBitVector** (destructor), **Purge**, **IsEmpty**, **IsFull**, **Count**, **Accept**, and **NewIterator**. Write a test program and test your implementation.

**12.3**  Rewrite the **Insert**, **Withdraw**, and **IsMember** member functions of the **SetAsBitVector** implementation so that they use bitwise shift and mask operations rather than division and modulo operations. Compare the running times of the modified routines with the original ones and explain your observations.

**12.4**  Complete the **MultisetAsArray** class declared in Program 12.10 by providing suitable definitions for the following member functions: **~MultisetAsArray** (destructor), **Purge**, **Count**, **Accept**, and **NewIterator**. Write a test program and test your implementation.

**12.5**  Complete the **MultisetAsLinkedList** class declared in Program 12.13 by providing suitable definitions for the following member functions: **~SetAsArray** (destructor), **Purge**, **IsEmpty**, **IsFull**, **Count**, **CompareTo**, **Accept**, and **NewIterator**. Write a test program and test your implementation.

**12.6** Design and implement a multiset class in which the contents of the set are represented by a linked list of ordered pairs of the form $(i, n_i)$, where $i$ is an element of the universal set $U$ and $n_i$ is a non-negative integer that counts the number of instances of the element $i$ in the multiset. (See Exercises 12.6 and 12.7.)

**12.7** Write a program to compute the number of ways in which a set of $n$ elements can be partitioned; that is, compute $\sum_{m=0}^{n} \left\{ {n \atop m} \right\}$, where

$$\left\{ {n \atop m} \right\} = \begin{cases} 1 & n = 1, \\ 1 & n = m, \\ m\left\{ {n-1 \atop m} \right\} + \left\{ {n-1 \atop m-1} \right\} & \text{otherwise.} \end{cases}$$

**Hint**: See Section 14.4.2.

# 13 | Dynamic Storage Allocation: The Other Kind of Heap

In the preceding chapters when analyzing an algorithm involving dynamically allocated storage, we assume that the time taken to acquire or to release storage is bounded by a constant. Specifically, Axiom 2.6 Chapter 2 states that the running time of operator **new** is a constant, $\tau_{\text{new}}$, and that the running time of operator **delete** is also a constant, $\tau_{\text{delete}}$.

But is this really so? To answer this question, we consider in this chapter the dynamic management of a pool of memory. In particular, we consider several different implementations for the operators **new** and **delete** and we show that the assumptions of constant running times are not always valid.

## 13.1 Basics

A memory pool is a region of contiguous memory locations that is subdivided into non-overlapping areas which are then allocated to the user. For example, Figure 13.1 shows the *memory map* of a 128KB pool of memory. The gray bars denote the blocks of memory that are currently in use; the blank areas are unreserved and available for use.

A memory pool supports the following two operations:

**Acquire** The *acquire* operation locates in the pool a region of contiguous, unused memory locations of a specified size and returns a pointer to that region. The region is marked *reserved*, which indicates that the memory locations contained therein are in use.

Should there be insufficient memory to satisfy the request, the acquire operation fails—the typical implementation throws an exception.

**FIGURE 13.1**

Memory map of a storage pool.

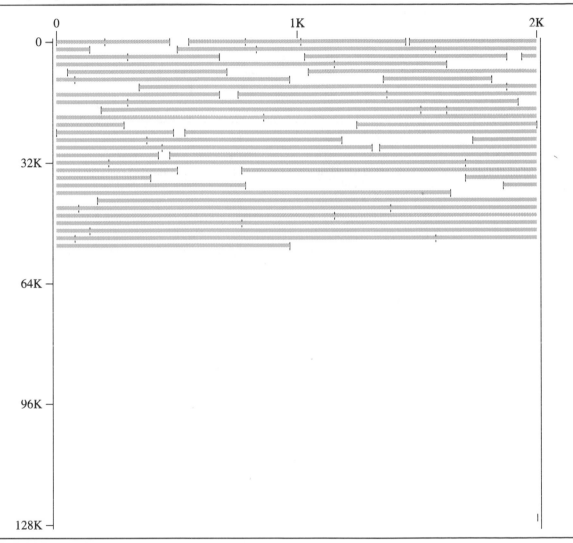

**Release**  The *release* operation returns a region of reserved memory locations to the pool. After a region is returned to the pool, it is no longer reserved and can be allocated in a subsequent *acquire* operation.

It is an error to attempt to release a region which is not reserved. The behavior of the pool under these circumstances is typically undefined.

Program 13.1 gives the definition of the **StoragePool** abstract class. This class serves as the base class from which concrete memory pool implementations are derived.

---

**PROGRAM 13.1**
StoragePool class definition

---

```
1   class StoragePool
2   {
3   public:
4       virtual ~StoragePool ();
5       virtual void* Acquire (size_t) = 0;
6       virtual void Release (void*) = 0;
7   };
```

---

In addition to the virtual destructor, two pure virtual member functions, **Acquire** and **Release**, are defined.

The **Acquire** function takes a single argument of type **size_t**, and its return value is a pointer to **void**. The purpose of this function is to acquire a region of memory locations, the size of which is specified by the argument (in bytes). A pointer to the region is returned. We shall assume that if for any reason the request cannot be satisfied, an exception of type **bad_alloc** is thrown.

The **Release** function takes as its lone argument a pointer to **void**. This pointer is assumed to be a pointer previously returned by the **Acquire** function; that is, it is a pointer to a region of reserved memory locations. The purpose of this function is to return the storage to the memory pool.

### 13.1.1   C++ Magic

Program 13.1 defines the abstract interface, **StoragePool**. That is, given an instance **p** of a concrete class derived from **StoragePool**, say **SomePool**, we can call the member functions like this:

```
SomePool p;
void* ptr = p.Acquire (100);
// ...
p.Release (ptr);
```

This code sequence first acquires and subsequently releases a 100-byte area of memory.

What is the relationship between the **StoragePool** class and the operators **new** and **delete**? In a C++ program, the **new** operator is typically used in a statement of the form

```
T* tptr = new T;
```

where **T** is the name of a type. The **new** operator creates a new instance of type **T** and returns a pointer to that instance. This operation involves three distinct steps:

1. Sufficient storage to hold an instance of type **T** (i.e., **sizeof(T)** bytes) is acquired; and then,
2. The constructor for **T** is called to initialize the the object instance; and then,
3. A pointer to the object is returned.

The C++ compiler accomplishes the first step by calling the function **operator new**, the prototype of which is:

```
void* operator new (size_t);
```

that is, the function **operator new** takes an argument that specifies and returns a pointer to that storage.

Similarly, the statement **delete tptr** releases the object to which **tptr** points and returns it to the pool of available storage. This operation involves two distinct steps:

1. The destructor for object in question is called to finalize the object instance; and then,
2. The memory locations once occupied by the object are released.

The C++ compiler accomplishes the second step by calling the function **operator delete**, the prototype of which is

```
void operator delete (void*);
```

The programmer can take over the management of dynamic storage by overloading (or redefining) the functions **operator new** and **operator delete**. For example, given an instance **p** of a concrete class derived from **StoragePool**, say **SomePool**, we can overload the functions like this:

```
SomePool p;

void* operator new (size_t bytes)
    { return p.Acquire (bytes); }

void operator delete (void* vptr)
    { p.Release (vptr); }
```

In this case, the storage pool is represented by a statically allocated global variable **p**. All dynamic storage is acquired from and released back to the storage pool **p**.[1]

---

[1] Actually, the programmer must be careful when doing this kind of thing. Because C++ cannot guarantee the order in which globals declared in separate files are constructed, in some circumstances it may be possible for **operator new** and **operator delete** to be called before the storage pool **p** has been initialized by its constructor. The solution to this is to use a technique such as *double construction*[33]. Such trickery is beyond the scope of this text. *Caveat emptor.*

### Working with Multiple Storage Pools

C++ provides the means for the programmer to control the placement of dynamically allocated storage. The *placement syntax* provides additional arguments to the **new** operator like this:

```
T* tptr = new ( argument list...) T;
```

The extra arguments in the *argument list* are passed to a suitably overloaded version of **operator new**.

For example, suppose that we provide an **operator new** function with the following definition:

```
void* operator new (size_t bytes, StoragePool& p)
   { return p.Acquire (bytes); }
```

That is, we have declared a version of **operator new** that takes two arguments. The first specifies the number of bytes to be allocated, and the second is a reference to an instance of a storage pool from which the storage is to be acquired. We can then write the following statement:

```
SomePool p, q;
T* tptr1 = new (p) T;
T* tptr2 = new (q) T;
```

Two distinct storage pools are declared—**p** and **q**. The first instance of **T** is allocated in the pool **p**, whereas the second instance is allocated in the pool **q**.

Unfortunately, but not without good cause, it is not possible to overload **operator delete** in an analogous fashion. There is no explicit way to return storage to a specific pool using **operator delete**. That is, the only way to release storage is by using **operator delete** like this:

```
delete tptr1;
delete tptr2;
```

What we would like to happen is for the first **delete** to invoke the **Release** member function of the pool **p**, and for the second **delete** to invoke the **Release** function of the pool **q**.

One way to achieve this is to keep track explicitly of the pool from which the memory was acquired in each block of dynamically allocated storage. We can accomplish this by attaching to each block a *tag* which contains a pointer to a pool to which it belongs. Program 13.2 shows how this can be done.

The **Tag struct** encapsulates the tag which is attached to each block of dynamically allocated storage. In this implementation, the tag appears in memory immediately *before* the memory address returns to the caller. This means that when *N* bytes of storage are required, **sizeof(Tag)** + *N* bytes are actually allocated. The tag occupies the first **sizeof(Tag)** bytes. However, it is a pointer to the remaining *N* bytes that is returned to the user.

**PROGRAM 13.2**
Overloading `operator new` and `operator delete`

```
1   struct Tag
2   {
3       StoragePool* pool;
4   };
5
6   void* operator new (size_t bytes, StoragePool& p)
7   {
8       Tag* const tag = reinterpret_cast<Tag*> (
9           p.Acquire (bytes + sizeof (Tag)));
10      tag->pool = &p;
11      return tag + 1;
12  }
13
14  void* operator new (size_t bytes)
15  {
16      Tag* const tag = reinterpret_cast<Tag*> (
17          std::malloc (bytes + sizeof (Tag));
18      tag->pool = 0;
19      return tag + 1;
20  }
21
22  void operator delete (void* arg)
23  {
24      Tag* const tag = reinterpret_cast<Tag*> (arg) - 1U;
25      if (tag->pool)
26          tag->pool->Release (tag);
27      else
28          std::free (tag);
29  }
```

Two versions of `operator new` are defined in Program 13.2. The first version makes use of the placement syntax described above to allow the user to specify the storage pool from which to allocate storage. This version saves a pointer to the pool from which the storage is allocated in the adjacent tag (lines 6–12). Notice that the function returns `tag + 1` which is the address of the memory location that immediately follows the tag.

The second version of `operator new` is the version that gets invoked when the user does not use the placement syntax to specify the memory pool from which to acquire the storage. In this case, since no storage pool is specified, the standard C library routine `malloc` is called. And since no pool has been specified, the adjacent tag field is set to zero (lines 14–20).

Since every block of dynamically allocated storage will have been tagged, the `delete` operator can determine the pool to which the storage is to be returned from the tag field. As shown in Program 13.2, `operator delete` obtains a pointer to a `StoragePool` from the tag and calls the `Release` member function of that pool if the pointer is nonzero. If the pointer is zero, the `malloc` routine was used to acquire the storage. Therefore, the C library routine `free` is called to release the storage (lines 22–29).

Given that we have defined the operations as shown in Program 13.2 and that we have at our disposal a concrete storage pool class, say `SomePool`, we can safely write the following program fragment:

```
SomePool p, q;
T* tptr0 = new T;
T* tptr1 = new (p) T;
T* tptr2 = new (q) T;
// ...
delete tptr0;
delete tptr1;
delete tptr2;
```

Each of the three instances of class `T` is allocated in a different memory pool. Nevertheless, each object is properly returned to the pool from which it came by the `delete` operation!

### 13.1.2   The Heap

A storage pool in which regions of memory are dynamically allocated is often called *a heap*. For example, in C++ the space for a variable is allocated essentially in one of three possible places: Global variables are allocated in the space of *initialized static variables*; the local variables of a procedure are allocated in the procedure's *activation record*, which is typically found in the *processor stack*; and dynamically allocated variables are allocated in *the heap*. In this context the term *heap* is taken to mean the storage pool for dynamically allocated variables.

In Chapter 11 we consider *heaps* and *heap-ordered trees* in the context of priority queue implementations. Unfortunately, the only thing that the heaps of Chapter 11 and the heap considered here have in common is the name. While it may be possible to use a heap (in the sense of Definition 11.1) to manage a dynamic storage pool, typical implementations do not. In this context the technical meaning of the term *heap* is closer to its dictionary definition—"a pile of many things."[9]

## 13.2   Singly-Linked Free Storage

The objective in the implementation of a storage pool is to make the running times for `Acquire` and `Release` operations as small as possible. Ideally, both operations run in constant time. In this section, we present a storage pool implementation that uses a singly-linked list to keep track of the unused areas of memory. The consequence of using this approach is that the running times are not ideal.

There are several requirements that the implementation of a storage pool must satisfy: It must keep track somehow of the blocks of memory that have been allocated as well as the areas of memory that remain unallocated.

For example, in order to implement the **Acquire** operation, we must have the means to locate an unused area of memory of sufficient size in order to satisfy the request. The approach taken in this section is to use a singly-linked list to keep track of the free areas in the pool.

In addition to keeping track of the free areas, it is necessary to keep track of the size of each block that is allocated. This is necessary because the **Release** operation takes only a pointer to the block of memory to be released; that is, the size of the block is *not* provided as an argument to the **Release** function.

Where should we keep track of this extra information? It turns out that the usual approach is to keep the necessary information *in the storage pool itself*. An area that has not been allocated to a user is available for use by the pool itself. Specifically, the nodes of the linked list of free areas themselves occupy the free areas.

We implement the storage pool as an array of **Block**s. The structure of a **Block** is shown in Figure 13.2. A sequence of consecutive, contiguous blocks in the array constitutes an *area*. Only the first block in each area is used to keep track of the entire area.

An area which has been allocated is said to be *reserved*. The first word of the first block in the area is used to keep track of the length of the area (in blocks). The remaining memory locations in the area are given up to the user.

An area which has not been allocated is said to be *free*. The first word of the first block in the area is used to keep track of the length of the area (in blocks). All of the free areas are linked together in a singly-linked list, known as the *free list*. The second word of the first block in the area contains a pointer to the next free area in the free list. For reasons explained below, we keep the free list sorted by the address of areas contained therein.

**FIGURE 13.2**
**SinglyLinkedPool::Block** structure layout.

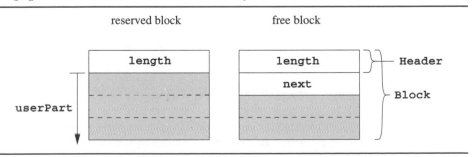

### 13.2.1 Implementation

Program 13.3 gives the declaration of the concrete storage pool class **SinglyLinked-Pool**. This class is derived from the abstract base class **StoragePool**. The public interface of the class comprises a constructor, the destructor, and the two member functions **Acquire** and **Release**.

The two nested **struct** definitions, **Header** and **Block**, correspond to the structure layout shown in Figure 13.2. Specifically, the **Header** structure contains information which appears in the first block of an area, *regardless of whether it is reserved or free*. The **Block** structure contains a **union**. In C++, the elements of a union occupy the same space. That is, if the block is *reserved*, the **userPart** of the block has been allocated to the user. On the other hand, if the block is **free**, the **next** field is used to point to the next element of the free list.

---

**PROGRAM 13.3**
SinglyLinkedPool class definition

---

```
1   class SinglyLinkedPool : public StoragePool
2   {
3   public:
4       struct Header
5       {
6           unsigned int length;
7       };
8       struct Block : public Header
9       {
10          enum { size = 16 };
11          union
12          {
13              Block* next;
14              char userPart [size - sizeof (Header)];
15          };
16      };
17  private:
18      unsigned int numberOfBlocks;
19      Block* pool;
20      Block& sentinel;
21  public:
22      SinglyLinkedPool (size_t);
23      ~SinglyLinkedPool ();
24
25      void* Acquire (size_t);
26      void Release (void*);
27  };
```

Notice how the size of the **Block** structure is controlled. In this case, the size is set to 16 bytes. Recall that an *area* is a set of contiguous blocks. Therefore, the size of an area is a multiple of 16 bytes. The selection of a block size of 16 represents a trade-off. If the block size is too large, then space is wasted when a user requests an amount of storage that is not a multiple of 16. On the other hand, if the block size is too small, then it is possible for the memory pool to become excessively *fragmented*. For example, it is possible for the free list to contain many small areas. The choice of 16 is somewhat arbitrary. However, values between 8 and 16 are typical. In this implementation the size of a block (in bytes) is required to be at least

$$\texttt{sizeof(Header)+sizeof(Block*)}$$

because we must be able to link a one-block area into the free list. On a 32-bit machine the minimum block size is typically 8 bytes.

### Constructor and Destructor

Program 13.4 defines both the constructor and the destructor for the **SinglyLinked-Pool** class. The constructor takes a single argument of type **size_t** which specifies the desired size of the storage pool in bytes. Initially, the entire storage pool is empty. Therefore, the entire pool constitutes a single area and the free list contains a single entry.

The three member variables of the **SinglyLinkedPool** class are defined in Program 13.3. The **numberOfBlocks** variable records the total number of blocks in the storage pool that are available to be allocated. The **pool** variable points to the array of blocks that make up the storage pool. Finally, the **sentinel** variable refers to an extra block that is used as the *sentinel* for the free list.

---

**PROGRAM 13.4**
**SinglyLinkedPool** class constructor and destructor definitions

---

```
1   SinglyLinkedPool::SinglyLinkedPool (size_t n) :
2       numberOfBlocks ((n + sizeof (Block) - 1U) / sizeof (Block)),
3       pool (new Block [numberOfBlocks + 1]),
4       sentinel (pool [numberOfBlocks])
5   {
6       Block& head = pool [0];
7       head.length = numberOfBlocks;
8       head.next = 0;
9
10      sentinel.length = 0;
11      sentinel.next = &head;
12  }
13
14  SinglyLinkedPool::~SinglyLinkedPool ()
15      { delete [] pool; }
```

---

The constructor initializes the member variables as follows: The **numberOfBlocks** is set to $\lceil N/$**sizeof(Block)**$\rceil$, where $N$ is the desired size of the storage pool in bytes. The **pool** member variable is set to point at an array of **Block**s of length **numberOfBlocks**+1. The array is itself dynamically allocated using **operator new**!

The extra block allocated at the end of the array is used as the sentinel for the free list. Therefore, the **sentinel** member variable is initialized in the constructor as a reference to the last array element. A sentinel is used because it simplifies the linked-list manipulations by eliminating some of the conditional tests that would otherwise be needed.

Initially, the entire pool constitutes a single unallocated area. The entire area is represented by the first block in the pool, **pool[0]**. Therefore, the length field of the first block is set to **numberOfBlocks** and the block is linked into the free list by attaching it to the sentinel. Except for the call to **operator new** to acquire the pool in the first place, the worst-case running time of the constructor is $O(1)$.

The destructor is quite simple. It simply releases the storage pool that was dynamically allocated in the constructor. Notice that it is not necessary that all storage acquired from the pool be released before the destructor is invoked. For example, the programmer may have deliberately chosen not to release the storage or she may have unintentionally forgotten to release the storage (called a *memory leak*). In any event, after the pool has been finalized, it is a serious error to attempt to dereference a pointer to an area in that pool.

## Acquiring an Area

The **Acquire** function is used to reserve an area in the pool. The code for the **Acquire** member function of the **SinglyLinkedPool** class is given in Program 13.5. The **Acquire** function takes a single argument that specifies the size of the memory area to be allocated (in bytes). The function returns a pointer to the allocated area of the pool.

The function begins by calculating the number of blocks required using the formula

$$\texttt{blocks} = \lceil \texttt{(bytes+sizeof(Header))/sizeof(Block)} \rceil.$$

That is, enough storage is set aside to hold the requested number of bytes *plus* a **Header** (lines 3–5).

The **Acquire** function then traverses the linked list of free areas to find a free area that is large enough to satisfy the request (lines 7–13). This is the *first-fit allocation strategy*: It always allocates storage in the first free area that is large enough to satisfy the request.

An alternative to the first-fit strategy is the *best-fit allocation strategy*. In the best-fit strategy, the **Acquire** function allocates storage from the free area the size of which matches most closely the requested size. Under certain circumstances, the best-fit strategy may prevent excessive fragmentation of the storage pool. However, the best-fit strategy requires that the entire free list be traversed. Since we are interested in the fastest possible execution time, the first-fit strategy is used here.

**PROGRAM 13.5**
SinglyLinkedPool class Acquire member function definition

```
1    void* SinglyLinkedPool::Acquire (size_t bytes)
2    {
3        unsigned int const blocks =
4            (bytes + sizeof (Header) + sizeof (Block) - 1U) /
5                sizeof (Block);
6
7        Block* prevPtr = &sentinel;
8        Block* ptr = prevPtr->next;
9        while (ptr != 0 && ptr->length < blocks)
10       {
11           prevPtr = ptr;
12           ptr = ptr->next;
13       }
14       if (ptr == 0)
15           throw bad_alloc ("out of memory");
16       if (ptr->length > blocks)
17       {
18           Block& newBlock = ptr [blocks];
19           newBlock.length = ptr->length - blocks;
20           newBlock.next = ptr->next;
21           ptr->length = blocks;
22           ptr->next = &newBlock;
23       }
24       prevPtr->next = ptr->next;
25       return ptr->userPart;
26   }
```

If the search for a free area is unsuccessful, a **bad_alloc** exception is thrown (lines 14–15). Otherwise, the variable **ptr** points to the free area in which the allocation takes place and the variable **prevPtr** points to its predecessor in the singly-linked list. If the free area is exactly the correct size, it is simply unlinked from the free list (line 24) and a pointer to the **userPart** of the area is returned (line 25).

On the other hand, if the free area is larger than needed, the area is split into two areas. The size of the first area is set to the number of blocks requested, and the size of the second area is equal to the number of blocks that remain. The second area is then inserted into the free list (lines 16–23). Notice that the area which is unlinked from the free list (line 24) is always equal in size to the required number of blocks.

The running time of the **Acquire** function is determined by the number of iterations of the loop on lines 9–13. All of the remaining statements in the function require a constant amount of time in the worst case. The number of iterations of the loop is determined by three factors: the length of the free list, the size of the area requested, and the position in the free list of an area that is large enough to satisfy the request.

If we make no assumptions about the distribution of the sizes requested and of the pattern of **Acquire** and **Release** operations, we cannot say very much about the running time. In the worst case, if there are $n$ blocks in the storage pool, the running time of the **Acquire** function is $O(n)$.

On the other hand, if we know a priori that all the requests are for the same amount of memory, then we can expect the running time of the **Acquire** function to be $O(1)$ in the worst case. This is because every single block in the free list is guaranteed to be large enough to satisfy any request. And since we are using the first-fit strategy, the request is satisfied by allocating storage in the first area in the free list.

---

**PROGRAM 13.6**
SinglyLinkedPool class **Release** member function definition

---

```
1   void SinglyLinkedPool::Release (void* arg)
2   {
3       Block& block = *reinterpret_cast<Block*> (
4           reinterpret_cast<Header*> (arg) - 1U);
5
6       if (&block < pool || &block >= pool + numberOfBlocks)
7           throw invalid_argument ("invalid block");
8
9       Block* prevPtr = &sentinel;
10      Block* ptr = prevPtr->next;
11      while (ptr != 0 && ptr < &block)
12      {
13          prevPtr = ptr;
14          ptr = ptr->next;
15      }
16      if (ptr != 0 && &block + block.length == ptr)
17      {
18          block.length += ptr->length;
19          block.next = ptr->next;
20      }
21      else
22          block.next = ptr;
23      if (prevPtr + prevPtr->length == &block)
24      {
25          prevPtr->length += block.length;
26          prevPtr->next = block.next;
27      }
28      else
29          prevPtr->next = &block;
30  }
```

---

### Releasing an Area

It seems that releasing an area to the free list should be quite simple and fast. For example, to release an area we might simply insert it at the head of the free list. This could be done in constant time.

However, there is a problem with this: The **Acquire** function occasionally splits free areas. And if we never coalesce adjacent free areas, the free list will eventually contain a large number of small areas that are each individually too small to satisfy a given request, even though there is sufficient contiguous memory available.

Therefore, the **Release** function needs to check when an area is freed whether the adjacent areas are already free. However, the problem is this: How do we know the location of the adjacent areas? The solution we have adopted is to keep the list of free areas sorted by the starting addresses of the areas.

This means that in order to free an area, it must be inserted in the appropriate place in the linked list. And at the point where the appropriate place to do the insertion has been determined, we can check to see if the area to be freed needs to be merged with an adjacent free area.

Program 13.6 gives the code for the **Release** function of the **SinglyLinkedPool** class. This function takes as its lone argument the address of the **userPart** of an area that was previously obtained from the **Acquire** function. The **Release** function begins by determining the block which corresponds to the given area and checking that this block is indeed a part of the memory pool (lines 3–7).

The loop on lines 9-15 traverses the linked list of free areas, and when it terminates, the following is true: The pointer **prevPtr** either points to the sentinel or it points at a free area the address of which is less than that of the area to be released. The pointer **ptr** is either zero or it points to a free area the address of which is greater than that of the area to be released. And **prevPtr** and **ptr** always point to adjacent elements of the linked list. Figure 13.3 illustrates this situation.

The area immediately preceding the area to be freed can itself be either reserved or free. Similarly, the area immediately following the area to be freed may be reserved or free. Figure 13.3 shows two of the four possible situations that can arise. Specifically, in Figure 13.3($a$) both adjacent areas are reserved and in Figure 13.3($b$) both adjacent areas are free.

If the area to be freed immediately precedes a free area, the two areas are combined (lines 16–20). Otherwise, the area is inserted into the free list *in front of* the area pointed to by **ptr** (line 22).

Similarly, if the area to be freed immediately follows a free area, the two areas are combined (lines 23–27). Otherwise, it is inserted into the free list *following* the area pointed to by **prevPtr** (line 29).

Unfortunately, since the free list is kept sorted, the running time of the **Release** function is determined by the number of iterations required to find the position in the list at which to do the insertion. In the worst case, this is $O(n)$ where $n$ is the number blocks in the storage pool. In practice, the free list is significantly shorter than $n$, and the running time varies accordingly.

The combination of keeping the free list sorted by address, and the first-fit allocation strategy sometimes leads to a degradation in the performance because the smaller free areas tend to appear near the head of the free list, whereas the larger areas are found

**FIGURE 13.3**
Using a singly-linked, sorted free list.

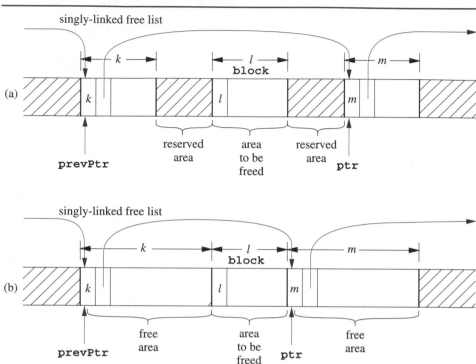

near the tail of the free list. This is because storage is always allocated in the first area that is large enough and if that area is too large, it is split in two and the leftover area is inserted into the free list. Eventually, many of the areas near the head of the free list are too small to satisfy most requests. Nevertheless, it is necessary to visit those areas every time the free list is traversed.

The use of a minimum block size alleviates partially this bias. That is, the minimum block size sets the lower bound beyond which areas are not split. For example, in the implementation given the block size is 16 bytes. As a result, any request for storage up to 12 bytes can be satisfied in constant time because the first area in the free list is guaranteed to be at least one block in length.

## 13.3  Doubly-Linked Free Storage

The singly-linked free list used in the preceding section is kept sorted in order to facilitate the coalescing of adjacent free areas. The only way to determine whether a particular area is free is to see if it appears in the free list. Since we need to examine *adjacent* areas to determine whether they can be combined, the free list is kept sorted. That way, adjacent areas appear next to one another in the free list.

Unfortunately since the free list must be kept sorted, every time an area is released it must be inserted into the list at the correct position. This means that the running time of the **Release** operation is $O(n)$ in the worst case, where $n$ is the number of blocks in the storage pool.

The essence of the problem is that we cannot tell by looking at an area whether it is reserved or free. So, the solution must be to record the allocation status of the area *in the area itself*.

A secondary problem with the use of a singly-linked free list is that, given a pointer to an area, we cannot extract that area from the free list without traversing the list. This is because in order to extract an element from a linked list, we need to know the predecessor of that element. And in a singly-linked list we must search from the head of the list to find the predecessor. The solution is, of course, to use a *doubly-linked* free list.

Finally, we shall play an interesting algorithmic trick: In order to coalesce adjacent free areas, we need to traverse the free list. However, since we must traverse the free list in the **Acquire** operation, in order to find a free area of a suitable size, we shall do the coalescing in the **Acquire** operation and not in the **Release** operation. While this does increase slightly the running time for **Acquire**, it means that **Release** can run in constant time.

Figure 13.4 shows a memory map of a storage pool managed using a doubly-linked list. The reserved areas in Figure 13.4 are exactly the same as those shown in Figure 13.1. The figure clearly indicates that there are adjacent uncoalesced free areas in the free list. What the figure cannot show is that the areas in the free list are not sorted.

As before, we implement the storage pool as an array of **Block**s. The structure of a **Block** is shown in Figure 13.5. A sequence of consecutive, contiguous blocks in the array constitutes an *area*. Only the first block in each area is used to keep track of the entire area.

Notice that we now encode two pieces of information in the block header: A single bit is used to indicate whether the area is reserved or free, and the remaining bits are used to record the length of the area (in blocks). By packing this information in a single word, we have not increased the space overhead associated with reserved areas.

Free areas are linked in a *doubly-linked free list*. Two pointers are required to accomplish this—**prev** and **next**. The effect of the extra pointer is to increase the minimum block size. However, since the pointers occupy space in the pool which would otherwise be unused, we do not require any additional space.

## 13.3.1  Implementation

Program 13.7 declares the class **DoublyLinkedPool**. It is a concrete class derived from the abstract base class **StoragePool**. The public interface of the class comprises a constructor, the destructor, and the two member functions **Acquire** and **Release**. In addition, two private member functions, **Unlink** and **InsertAfter** are declared. These comprise the common linked-list manipulations.

**FIGURE 13.4**
Memory map of a doubly-linked storage pool.

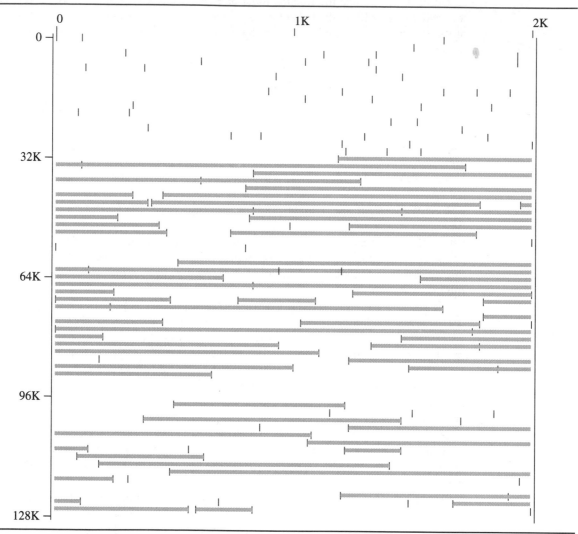

The nested structures **Header** and **Block** are used to implement the layout shown in Figure 13.5. The **Header** structure contains information which appears in the first block of an area, *regardless of whether it is reserved or free*. In this case, the header comprises two members, **status** and **length**, packed into a single word of memory. The first member is a 1-bit field of type **Status**. **Status** is an enumeration of the values **reserved** and **free**. The second field in the header, **length**, records the length in blocks of the associated area.

The **Block** structure contains a **union**. The union overlays an instance of the structure **Links**, which is used to hold pointers to the next and previous elements of the free

**FIGURE 13.5**
`DoublyLinkedPool::Block` structure layout.

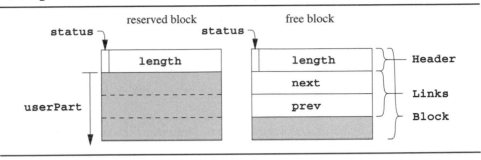

list when the block is free, with the **userPart** of the block which is the space given to the user when the block is reserved.

In this implementation the size of a block (in bytes) is required to be at least

$$\texttt{sizeof(Header)} + 2 \times \texttt{sizeof(Block*)}.$$

On a 32-bit machine the minimum block size is typically 12 bytes. In the implementation shown in Program 13.7, the size of the **Block** structure is set to 16 bytes.

### Constructor and Destructor

The constructor and the destructor of the **DoublyLinkedPool** class are defined in Program 13.8. The constructor takes as its lone argument an integer which specifies the size of the storage pool in bytes. The constructor is responsible for allocating the memory for the storage pool and for creating the initial free list. Since the storage pool starts out empty, the free list contains initially just a single entry that treats the entire pool as one large, free area.

The constructor must initialize the three member variables, **numberOfBlocks**, **pool**, and **sentinel**, which are declared in Program 13.7. The number of blocks is set to $\lceil N/\texttt{sizeof(Block)} \rceil$, where $N$ is the desired size of the storage pool (in bytes). An array of **Block**s of length **numberOfBlocks**+1 is dynamically allocated using **operator new**, and the member variable **pool** is set to point at the array.

The last block in the array is used as the sentinel for the doubly-linked free list. The member variable **sentinel** is initialized as a reference to the last block in the array. Since the sentinel block is never to be allocated, it is marked **reserved**. The **next** and **prev** pointers of the sentinel both are initialized to point at the sentinel itself. Thus, the free list is initially empty.

The entire pool is initially a single unallocated area. We represent the area by the first block in the pool, **pool[0]**. The block is marked **free**, and the length field is set to **numberOfBlocks**. Then, the block is inserted into the doubly-linked free list by calling the private member function **InsertAfter**. The **InsertAfter** function can do the insertion in constant time. The implementation is left as an project for the reader (Project 13.2). Except for the call to **operator new** to allocate space for the pool in the first place, the worst-case running time of the constructor is $O(1)$.

**PROGRAM 13.7**
DoublyLinkedPool class definition

```
1   class DoublyLinkedPool : public StoragePool
2   {
3   public:
4       enum Status { free, reserved };
5       struct Header
6       {
7           Status status : 1;
8           unsigned int length : bitsizeof (unsigned int) - 1U;
9       };
10      struct Block : public Header
11      {
12          enum { size = 16 };
13          struct Links
14          {
15              Block* next;
16              Block* prev;
17          };
18          union
19          {
20              Links link;
21              char userPart [size - sizeof (Header)];
22          };
23      };
24  private:
25      unsigned int numberOfBlocks;
26      Block* pool;
27      Block& sentinel;
28
29      static void Unlink (Block&);
30      static void InsertAfter (Block&, Block&);
31  public:
32      DoublyLinkedPool (size_t);
33      ~DoublyLinkedPool ();
34
35      void* Acquire (size_t);
36      void Release (void*);
37  };
```

### Releasing an Area

Program 13.9 gives the code for the **Release** member function of the **Doubly-LinkedPool** class. This function takes as its lone argument a pointer to the user part of the memory area to be released.

**PROGRAM 13.8**
DoublyLinkedPool class constructor and destructor definitions

```
1   DoublyLinkedPool::DoublyLinkedPool (size_t n) :
2       numberOfBlocks ((n + sizeof (Block) - 1U) / sizeof (Block)),
3       pool (new Block [numberOfBlocks + 1]),
4       sentinel (pool [numberOfBlocks])
5   {
6       sentinel.status = reserved;
7       sentinel.link.next = &sentinel;
8       sentinel.link.prev = &sentinel;
9
10      Block& head = pool [0];
11      head.status = free;
12      head.length = numberOfBlocks;
13      InsertAfter (sentinel, head);
14  }
15
16  DoublyLinkedPool::~DoublyLinkedPool ()
17      { delete [] pool; }
```

**PROGRAM 13.9**
DoublyLinkedPool class Release member function definition

```
1    void DoublyLinkedPool::Release (void* arg)
2    {
3        Block& block = *reinterpret_cast<Block*> (
4            reinterpret_cast<Header*> (arg) - 1U);
5
6        if (&block < pool || &block >= pool + numberOfBlocks)
7            throw invalid_argument ("invalid block");
8
9        block.status = free;
10       InsertAfter (sentinel, block);
11   }
```

The implementation shown is both simple and fast. The **Release** function makes no attempt to combine adjacent free areas. And since the free list is not sorted, it simply inserts the area to be freed at the front of the free list. This is done by inserting the area into the free list immediately *after* the sentinel. The private member function **InsertAfter** is called to accomplish this.

Because the free list is a doubly-linked list, the insertion can be done in constant time. Therefore, the worst-case running time of the **Release** function is $O(1)$.

### Acquiring an Area

The `Acquire` function of the `DoublyLinkedPool` class is defined in Program 13.10. This function takes a single integer-valued argument that specifies the size (in bytes) of the area to be allocated. `Acquire` returns a pointer to the storage if there is sufficient space left in the pool to accommodate the request. Otherwise, a `bad_alloc` exception is thrown.

---

**PROGRAM 13.10**

`DoublyLinkedPool` class `Acquire` member function definition

```
1   void* DoublyLinkedPool::Acquire (size_t bytes)
2   {
3       unsigned int const blocks =
4           (bytes + sizeof (Header) + sizeof (Block) - 1U) /
5               sizeof (Block);
6
7       Block* ptr;
8       for (ptr = sentinel.link.next; ptr != &sentinel;
9           ptr = ptr->link.next)
10      {
11          for (;;)
12          {
13              Block& successor = ptr [ptr->length];
14              if (successor.status == reserved)
15                  break;
16              Unlink (successor);
17              ptr->length += successor.length;
18          }
19          if (ptr->length >= blocks)
20              break;
21      }
22      if (ptr == &sentinel)
23          throw bad_alloc ("out of memory");
24      if (ptr->length > blocks)
26      {
27          Block& newBlock = ptr [blocks];
28          newBlock.status = free;
29          newBlock.length = ptr->length - blocks;
30          ptr->length = blocks;
31          InsertAfter (sentinel, newBlock);
32      }
33      Unlink (*ptr);
34      ptr->status = reserved;
35      return ptr->userPart;
36  }
```

---

In order to find a suitable area in which to allocate space, the **Acquire** function must traverse the free list. In this case, we choose again to use the *first-fit allocation strategy*; that is, storage is allocated in the first area that is large enough.

Recall that the **Release** function given in the preceding section does not combine adjacent free areas. Therefore, it is the responsibility of the **Acquire** function to do this. The algorithmic trick is this: Adjacent free areas are recombined while the free list is traversed in search of a free area large enough to accommodate the allocation request!

The **Acquire** function begins by computing the number of blocks required using the formula

$$\lceil (\texttt{bytes + sizeof(Header))/sizeof(Block)} \rceil.$$

That is, we need enough space for the requested number of bytes *plus* a **Header** (lines 3–5).

Then the **Acquire** function traverses the free list in search of an area that is large enough (lines 7–21). As each area in the free list is visited, the area that immediately follows the given area in memory is examined to see if it too is free, and, therefore, if it should be combined with the given area. Since the size of an area is recorded in its header, we can easily find the area which follows it in memory, as shown in Figure 13.6. And since the *status* of an area (**free** or **reserved**) is recorded in the area itself, we can determine whether the following area is free.

If the area which follows a given area is indeed free, then it must be in the free list! And because the free list is doubly-linked, we can easily extract that area from the free list in constant time. This is the purpose of the **Unlink** function on line 16.

When combining a given area with the area that follows it in memory, we obtain an area the size of which is equal to the sum of the sizes of the areas that were combined (line 17). After the combining, it is possible that the area that follows the new larger area is also free. Therefore, we need to repeat the combining process again. This is what

**FIGURE 13.6**
Using a doubly-linked (unsorted) free list.

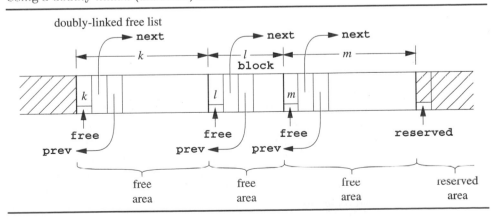

the loop on lines 11–18 does—it keeps combining adjacent free areas until the area that follows is a **reserved** area (lines 14–15).

The search for a free area to satisfy the **Acquire** request terminates at the first area that is large enough (lines 19–20). Notice that if the entire free list is traversed, all the adjacent areas that can be merged will have been merged. If the free list is traversed and an area is not found that is large enough to satisfy the request, then the request cannot be satisfied because there is insufficient contiguous memory to do so. In this case a **bad_alloc** exception is thrown (lines 22–23).

When the free area is larger than needed, it is split in two. The size of the first area is set to the number of blocks requested and the size of the second area is equal to the number of blocks that remain. The second area is then inserted into the free list by calling the **InsertAfter** member function (lines 24–31).

In all cases, by the time execution reaches line 32, the free area is exactly the correct size. The area is unlinked from the free list and marked **reserved** (lines 32–33). Finally, a pointer to the **userPart** of the area is returned (line 34).

At first glance it might seem that the nested **for** loops (lines 8 and 11) would result in a worst-case running time of $O(n^2)$ where $n$ is the number of blocks in the storage pool. However, the outer loop traverses the free list while every complete iteration of the inner loop removes one element from the free list. As a result, the worst-case running time for the nested loops is actually only $O(n)$.

The nice thing about this approach is that the asymptotic running time of the **Acquire** function would be $O(n)$ even if it did not combine adjacent free areas. In particular, this asymptotic bound is the same as for the singly-linked storage pool. On the other hand, the running time of the **Release** function is $O(1)$ for the doubly-linked pool which is certainly better than the $O(n)$ worst-case running time of the singly-linked pool. Finally, since the free list is not kept sorted, there is not the same tendency for the short areas to accumulate at the head of the free list as there is in the singly-linked pool.

## 13.4 Buddy System for Storage Management

The preceding sections describe two storage pool implementations that both use a linear list to keep track of the free areas. When the singly-linked list is used, the linear list is kept sorted by address; when the doubly-linked list is used, the order of the areas in the list is essentially random.

Each time an area is to be reserved, the free lists are searched in order to find an area that is sufficiently large to satisfy the request. Since there is no direct relationship between the size of an area and its position in the free list, the search has worst-case running time that is $O(l)$, where $l$ is the length of the free list. And in the worst case $l$ is $O(n)$, where $n$ is the number of blocks in the storage pool.

In this section we present a storage pool implementation, called a *buddy system,* that uses more than one free list. All of the areas in a given free list have the same size, and there is a separate free list for each available size of area. As a result a suitable free area can be found quickly.

Given a storage pool of size $N$ bytes, we would require $N$ free lists altogether if we were to place no restriction on the allowable size of an area. This is clearly infeasible. Instead we require that $N$ is a power of 2, i.e., $N = 2^m$ for some positive integer $m$. Furthermore, the size of each area in the pool must also be a power of 2. As a result, we only need $m + 1$ free lists, since the allowed sizes of an area (in bytes) are

$$2^0, 2^1, 2^2, \ldots, 2^m.$$

The key feature of a buddy system is that when a request is made for an area of size $2^k$ for some $k$ less than $m$, we first look in the corresponding free list for an area with the correct size. Notice that if there are no areas of size $2^k$ left, we can obtain one by splitting an area of size $2^{k+1}$ in two. And if there are no areas of size $2^{k+1}$ left, we can obtain one of those by splitting an area of size $2^{k+2}$ in two, and so on.

The two areas obtained when a larger area is split in two are called *buddies*. Whenever an area is freed, we check to see if its buddy is also free. If an area of size $2^k$ and its buddy are both free, they can be combined into a single area of size $2^{k+1}$.

Of course, the user does not always need an amount of storage that is exactly a power of 2. In those situations where it is not, we shall allocate an amount of memory that is the smallest power of 2 no less than the amount requested.

Figure 13.7 shows a memory map of a storage pool managed using the buddy system. The reserved areas in Figure 13.7 are exactly the same as those shown in Figure 13.1. Figure 13.7 shows an important characteristic of the buddy pool: An area of size $2^k$ bytes is always aligned on a $2^k$ byte boundary. For example, all 1KB areas are aligned on 1KB boundaries; that is, they begin at 0KB, 1KB, 2KB, $\ldots$

Let $b$ be the offset from the start of the pool (in bytes) of an area of size $2^k$. Then for $b$ to be aligned on a $2^k$ byte boundary means that $b = 0 (\mathrm{mod}\, 2^k)$. In other words, the binary representation of the number $b$ has the form

$$b_{m-1} b_{m-2} b_{m-3} \cdots b_{k+1} \underbrace{0000 \cdots 0}_{k \text{ zeroes}},$$

where $b_i \in \{0, 1\}$ is the $i$th bit in the representation of $b$.

If we take the block of size $2^k$ at offset $b$ and split it into two blocks of size $2^{k-1}$, the offsets of the two blocks which result are

$$b_{m-1} b_{m-2} b_{m-3} \cdots b_{k+1} \quad 0 \underbrace{000 \cdots 0}_{k-1 \text{ zeroes}}, \quad \text{and}$$

$$b_{m-1} b_{m-2} b_{m-3} \cdots b_{k+1} \quad 1 \underbrace{000 \cdots 0}_{k-1 \text{ zeroes}}.$$

That is, the offsets of the buddies of size $2^k$ differ in only the $k$th bit position. This gives us a very simple way to determine the position of the buddy of a given area. That is, given the offset of a buddy of size $2^k$ is $b$, the offset of the buddy is given by

$$Buddy_k(b) = \begin{cases} b + 2^k & \text{if } b = 0 \pmod{2^{k+1}}, \\ b - 2^k & \text{if } b = 2^k \pmod{2^{k+1}}. \end{cases} \tag{13.1}$$

**FIGURE 13.7**
Memory map of a buddy system storage pool.

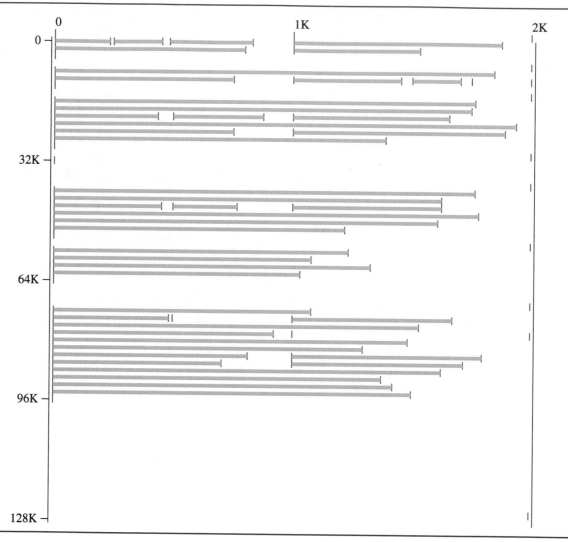

Fortunately, it is quite simple to compute Equation 13.1 since all we need to do is toggle the $k$th bit of the binary representation $b$. This can be done using the *bitwise exclusive-or operation* as the following function definition shows:

```
unsigned int Buddy (unsigned int b, unsigned int k)
     { return b ^ (1 << (k - 1U)); }
```

As before, we implement the storage pool as an array of **Block**s. The structure of a **Block** is shown in Figure 13.8. A sequence of contiguous blocks in the array constitutes

**FIGURE 13.8**
`BuddyPool::Block` structure layout.

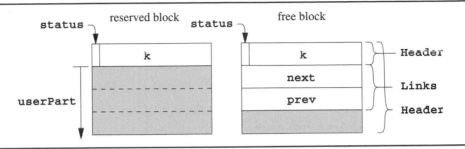

an area. This time the size (in bytes) of every area in the pool is an integer power of 2. The first block in each area is used to keep track the entire area.

The structure of the block is quite similar to that used in the implementation of the `DoublyLinkedPool` class. That is, the header is comprised of two parts: A single bit which indicates whether the area represented by the block is reserved or free and a field called **k** which specifies the size of the area; that is, the size of the block is $2^k$ bytes.

The free lists are implemented as doubly-linked lists. Therefore, a free block contains two pointers, **prev** and **next**, which point to the previous and next areas (respectively) in the free list.

## 13.4.1  Implementation

The class **BuddyPool** is declared in Program 13.11. **BuddyPool** is a concrete class derived from the abstract base class **StoragePool**. The public interface includes a constructor, a destructor, and the member functions **Acquire** and **Release**. Three additional private member functions, **Buddy**, **Unlink**, and **InsertAfter** are declared.

The nested structures **Header** and **Block** implement the layout given in Figure 13.8. The **Header** contains fields which are used in the representation of both **reserved** and **free** areas. A **Header** comprises the two members **status** and **k**. The former is a one-bit field of type **Status**. The latter encodes the length of the block as described above.

The **Block** structure contains a **union** that overlays an instance of the structure **Links** with the **userPart** of the block. If the block is a free block, the contents of the **Links** structure are used to link the associated area in the appropriate free list. If the block is reserved, the space in the **userPart** has been allocated to the user.

The minimum size of a block is the same as for the **DoublyLinkedPool** class, viz.,

$$\texttt{sizeof(Header)} + 2 \times \texttt{sizeof(Block*)},$$

**PROGRAM 13.11**
BuddyPool class definition

```
1   class BuddyPool : public StoragePool
2   {
3   public:
4       enum Status { free, reserved };
5       struct Header
6       {
7           Status status: 1;
8           unsigned int k : bitsizeof (unsigned int) - 1U;
9       };
10      struct Block : public Header
11      {
12          enum { size = 16 };
13          struct Links
14          {
15              Block* next;
16              Block* prev;
17          };
18          union
19          {
20              Links link;
21              char userPart [size - sizeof (Header)];
22          };
23      };
24  private:
25      unsigned int m;
26      unsigned int numberOfBlocks;
27      Block* pool;
28      Block* sentinel;
29
30      static void Unlink (Block&);
31      static void InsertAfter (Block&, Block&);
32      Block& Buddy (Block&) const;
33  public:
34      BuddyPool (size_t);
35      ~BuddyPool ();
36
37      void* Acquire (size_t);
38      void Release (void*);
39  };
```

which on a 32-bit machine is typically 12 bytes. In the **BuddyPool** implementation given in Program 13.11, the size of the **Block** structure is set to 16 bytes.

### Constructor and Destructor

Program 13.12 defines both the constructor and the destructor for the **BuddyPool** class. The constructor takes an integer which specifies the desired size of the storage pool in bytes. The constructor allocates the memory for the storage pool and initializes the free lists.

The **BuddyPool** class has four member variables, **m**, **numberOfBlocks**, **pool**, and **sentinel** that are initialized by the constructor as follows: The member variable m represents the size of the storage pool; that is, the size of the pool is $2^m$ bytes. The constructor computes the quantity $m = \lceil \log_2 n \rceil$, where $n$ is the size of storage pool requested by calling the function **Log2Ceil**[2].

---

**PROGRAM 13.12**
BuddyPool class constructor and destructor definitions

---

```
 1  BuddyPool::BuddyPool (size_t bytes) :
 2      m (Log2Ceil (bytes)),
 3      numberOfBlocks ((1 << m) / sizeof (Block)),
 4      pool (new Block [numberOfBlocks + m + 1]),
 5      sentinel (pool + numberOfBlocks)
 6  {
 7      for (unsigned int i = 0; i <= m; ++i)
 8      {
 9          sentinel [i].link.next = &sentinel [i];
10          sentinel [i].link.prev = &sentinel [i];
11      }
12
13      Block& head = pool [0];
14      head.status = free;
15      head.k = m;
16      InsertAfter (sentinel [m], head);
17  }
18
19  BuddyPool::~BuddyPool ()
20      { delete [] pool; }
```

---

---

[2]We assume that there exists the function

```
unsigned int Log2Ceil (unsigned int n);
```

which computes $\lceil \log_2 n \rceil$. It is possible to compute this function in constant time using simple bit manipulations. Most computers have instructions that make the implementation trivial.

The number of blocks required for the storage pool is $2^m/$`sizeof(Block)`. The member variable `numberOfBlocks` is set to this value. An array that contains `numberOfBlocks`+m+1 blocks is dynamically allocated using `operator new`, and the member variable `pool` is set to point at the array.

Since there are $m + 1$ free lists, the last $m + 1$ blocks are used as the sentinels for the free lists. The member variable `sentinel` points at the block whose offset in the array is `numberOfBlocks`. That way, we can access the $i$th sentinel by writing `sentinel[i]`. Each of the $m + 1$ free lists is initially empty. Therefore, the `next` and `prev` pointers in each sentinel are set to point at the given sentinel itself (lines 7–11).

The entire pool is initially an unallocated area of size $2^m$. The area is represented by the first block in the pool, `pool[0]`. This area is marked `free` and the `k` field is set to $m$. Finally, the block is inserted into the free list for blocks of size $2^m$ which is the list attached to `sentinel[m]`. The insertion is done using the private member function `InsertAfter`. Since all the free lists are doubly-linked lists, the `InsertAfter` can easily do its work in constant time.

Except for the call to `operator new` to allocate the array of `Block`s, the running time of the constructor is dominated by the loop which creates the free lists. As a result, the worst-case running time for the constructor is $O(m)$.

---

**PROGRAM 13.13**
`BuddyPool` class `Acquire` member function definition

---

```
1   void* BuddyPool::Acquire (size_t bytes)
2   {
3       unsigned int kPrime = Log2Ceil (bytes + sizeof (Header));
4
5       unsigned int i = kPrime;
6       while (i <= m && sentinel [i].link.next == &sentinel [i])
7           ++i;
8       if (i > m)
9           throw bad_alloc ("out of memory");
10
11      Block& block = *sentinel [i].link.next;
12      Unlink (block);
13      while (block.k > kPrime)
14      {
15          block.k -= 1;
16          Block& buddy = Buddy (block);
17          buddy.status = free;
18          buddy.k = block.k;
19          InsertAfter (sentinel [buddy.k], buddy);
20      }
21      block.status = reserved;
22      return block.userPart;
23  }
```

---

## Acquiring an Area

The **Acquire** member function of the **BuddyPool** class is defined in Program 13.13. This function takes an integer-valued argument which specifies the size of storage area required. The function returns a pointer to the region of memory that is allocated.

The size of the area actually allocated by **Acquire** is $2^{k'}$ bytes where $k'$ is given by

$$k' = \lceil \log_2(\texttt{bytes} + \texttt{sizeof(Header)}) \rceil,$$

where **bytes** is the number of bytes of storage requested by the user. That is, the area must be sufficiently large to hold both the user's data plus the **Header** used by the storage pool. Of course if $k' > m$, the request can never be satisfied.

The next step is to find the smallest free area the size of which is at least $2^{k'}$ bytes. Specifically, we find the smallest value of $i$, $k' \leq i \leq m$, such that the free list for areas of size $2^i$ is not empty (lines 5–7). If all free lists for areas of size $2^{k'}$ through $2^m$ are empty, the request cannot be satisfied and a **bad_alloc** exception is thrown (lines 8–9).

Having determined the value of $i$, we remove the first area from the free list of areas of size $2^i$ (lines 11–12). The private member function **Unlink** is called to remove the area from the doubly-linked free list. To remove a given element from a doubly-linked free list takes constant time.

If $i = k'$, the area has the correct size and we are done. Otherwise, $i > k'$ and the area is too large. If the area is too large, we can split it into two areas (buddies) of size $2^{i-1}$. One of the buddies is retained while the other is inserted into the appropriate free list. After the split, if $i - 1 = k'$, then we are done. Otherwise, the area is still too large and it can be split again (lines 13–20).

Eventually, the size of the area is exactly $2^{k'}$ bytes. The area is marked **reserved**, and a pointer to the **userPart** is returned (lines 21–22).

The running time of the **Acquire** function is $O(i - k' + 1)$. For example, when we request a block of size $2^{k'}$ and the free list for blocks of size $2^{k'}$ is not empty, then $i = k'$ and the running time is $O(1)$. On the other hand, suppose that we request an area of size $2^0$ but all the free lists are empty except for one entry in the free list of areas of size $2^m$. In this case $i = m$ and $k' = 0$. Therefore, the worst-case running time is $O(m) = O(\log N)$, where $N$ is the number of blocks in the storage pool.

## Releasing an Area

To release an area of size $2^k$, we first examine its buddy to see if it is reserved or free. If the area and its buddy are both free, the two free areas can be combined into a single area of size $2^{k+1}$. We then repeat the process to release the combined area of size $2^{k+1}$. Eventually we get an area whose buddy is reserved or, if $k = m$, the area does not have a buddy. When this occurs, we simply insert the area into the appropriate free list. Program 13.14 shows how this algorithm can be implemented.

The **Release** member function of the **BuddyPool** class takes a pointer to the user part of a reserved area, and it frees the area as described above. The **Release** function begins by determining the block which corresponds to the given area and checking that this block is indeed a part of the memory pool (lines 3–7). Then the block is marked **free** (line 9).

**PROGRAM 13.14**
BuddyPool class `Release` member function definition

```
1   void BuddyPool::Release (void* arg)
2   {
3       Block& block = *reinterpret_cast<Block*> (
4           reinterpret_cast<Header*> (arg) - 1U);
5
6       if (&block < pool || &block >= pool + numberOfBlocks)
7           throw invalid_argument ("invalid pointer");
8
9       block.status = free;
10      Block* ptr;
11      for (ptr = &block; ptr->k < m; ptr->k += 1)
12      {
13          Block& buddy = Buddy (*ptr);
14          if (buddy.status == reserved || buddy.k != ptr->k)
15              break;
16          Unlink (buddy);
17          if (&buddy < ptr)
18              ptr = &buddy;
19      }
20      InsertAfter (sentinel [ptr->k], *ptr);
21  }
```

Each iteration of the main loop (lines 11–19) determines whether the buddy of the area to be released is also free and combines the two areas as needed. The buddy of the area is determined by calling the private member function `Buddy` (line 13). This function takes as its lone argument a reference to the first block of the area whose buddy we seek. The `Buddy` function returns a reference to the first block of the buddy. (Since the size of the block, $k$, is found in the block itself, it is not necessary to pass it as a parameter to the `Buddy` function). If the buddy is found to be `reserved`, no more combinations are possible and the main loop terminates (lines 14–15).

If the area and its buddy are both free, the buddy is withdrawn from its free list using the private member function `Unlink` (line 16). Since the free lists are all doubly-linked lists, it is possible to withdraw the buddy from its free list in constant time. After combining the two areas of size $2^k$, the combined area has size $2^{k+1}$ and is represented by the buddy with the smaller address (lines 17–18). Eventually, when no more combining is possible, the main loop terminates and we insert the area into the appropriate free list (line 20). This insertion makes use of the private member function `InsertAfter` which runs in constant time.

The running time of the `Release` function depends on the number of iterations of the main loop. If the buddy of the area to be released is `reserved`, then the `Release` function runs in constant time. In the worst case, there is only one reserved area of size

$2^0$ in the storage pool. If we release this area, $m$ iterations of the main loop are required. Therefore, the worst-case running time for the **Release** function is $O(m) = O(\log N)$, where $N$ is the number of blocks in the storage pool.

In the preceding analysis (and in the implementation) we have assumed the smallest area has size $2^0$. However, since every area must contain a **Header**, the smallest area that will ever occur has size $2^{\lceil \log_2(\texttt{sizeof(Header)}) \rceil}$. For example, on a 32-bit machine the size of the header is likely to be four bytes. Since we cannot have an area of size $2^0$ or $2^1$, the corresponding free lists are never used.

It is also quite common to limit the maximum size of an area to a size $2^{m'}$ where $m' < m$. Consequently, since there are never any blocks of sizes between $2^{m'+1}$ and $2^m$, the corresponding free lists are never used. Limiting the maximum size of the free lists improves matters slightly, since the worst-case running times for both the **Acquire** and the **Release** functions become $O(m')$.

## 13.5 Applications

One of the problems with building storage pool implementations is that it is very difficult to predict how they will behave when subjected to the sequence of **Acquire** and **Release** operations generated by a particular application. Furthermore, an implementation that performs well when subjected to the access pattern of one application may perform very poorly when subjected to the access pattern of another. When things become too difficult to analyze, people often turn to simulation for the answer. In this section, we show how to test a storage pool implementation under a simulated load.

A simulated load is a sequence of **Acquire** and **Release** operations that is generated by a program whose behavior is supposed to mimic the behavior of a real application. A typical application periodically calls the **Acquire** function to allocate some memory for its use. The application holds on to this memory for some amount of time, and then it calls **Release** to return the memory to the storage pool.

We shall mimic this behavior with a time-stepped simulation. A time-stepped simulation is a program which has the following form:

```
for (time t = 0; t < timeLimit; ++t)
{
        Simulate the behavior of the application at time t.
}
```

At each point in time, the application performs the following steps:

1.  It releases all the storage areas that were previously scheduled to be freed at this time.

2.  It acquires a storage area of size $\alpha$ and schedules the release of that storage area $\beta$ time units from now.

**PROGRAM 13.15**
**Event** class definition

```
1   typedef unsigned int time;
2
3   class Event : public Association
4   {
5   public:
6       typedef Wrapper<time> Time;
7       typedef Wrapper<void*> VoidPtr;
8
9       Event (time t, void* ptr) :
10          Association (*new Time (t), *new VoidPtr (ptr)) {}
11      Time& Key () const
12          { return dynamic_cast<Time&> (Association::Key ()); }
13      VoidPtr& Value () const
14          { return dynamic_cast<VoidPtr&> (Association::Value()); }
15  };
```

In order to keep track of the storage areas to be released, a priority queue is used (Chapter 11). The elements of the priority queue record the address of the area to be freed and are keyed using the time at which the area is to be freed.

The values $\alpha$ and $\beta$ in step 2 are randomly generated. The random distributions are chosen to mimic the system behavior that we expect.

For example, we may specify that the size $\alpha$ (in bytes) is uniformly distributed in the interval [100, 2 000] and that the time $\beta$ is uniformly distributed in the interval [1, 100]. That is, at each time step, the application allocates between 100 and 2 000 bytes of storage which it releases after between 1 and 100 time steps.

### 13.5.1   Implementation

This section shows how to write the simulation described above. Program 13.15 declares the class **Event** which is used to keep track of the address of an area and the time at which it is to be freed. Therefore, there are two parts to an event, a **VoidPtr** and a **Time**.

Since events will be put into a priority queue, the **Event** class is derived from the **Association** class which is defined in Section 5.2.11. An association is an ordered pair comprised of a key and a value. In the case of the **Event** class, the key is the time of the event and the value is the address of the area to be freed. The events in a priority queue are prioritized by their times.

The simulation program is embodied in the function **StoragePoolTest** defined in Program 13.16. This function takes two arguments, a reference to the storage pool to be tested and an integer which specifies the number of simulation cycles to execute.

**PROGRAM 13.16**
Simulation procedure for exercising a storage pool

```
1   void StoragePoolTest (StoragePool& pool, time timeLimit)
2   {
3       UniformRV size (100, 2001);
4       UniformRV latency (1, 101);
5       PriorityQueue& queue = *new LeftistHeap ();
6
7       RandomNumberGenerator::SetSeed (1);
8       for (time t = 0; t < timeLimit; ++t)
9       {
10          while (!queue.IsEmpty ())
11          {
12              Event& event = dynamic_cast<Event&> (
13                  queue.FindMin ());
14              if (event.Key () > t)
15                  break;
16              queue.DequeueMin ();
17              pool.Release (event.Value ());
18              delete &event;
19          }
20          unsigned int const length = size.Sample ();
21          void* const address = pool.Acquire (length);
22          unsigned int const releaseTime = t + latency.Sample ();
23          queue.Enqueue (*new Event (releaseTime, address));
24      }
25      cout << pool << endl;
26      delete &queue;
27  }
```

The variables `size` and `latency` are `UniformRV`s. The class `UniformRV` is a random number generator defined in Section 14.5.1. This class provides a member function called `Sample` which is used to sample the random number generator. That is, every time `Sample` is called, a different (random) result is returned. The random values are uniformly distributed on the interval which is specified in the constructor (lines 3–4).

The `StoragePoolTest` routine uses a `LeftistHeap` priority queue (see Section 11.3) to keep track of scheduled events (line 5).

The body of the main loop directly implements the steps outlined above. First, any events scheduled for the current time step are withdrawn from the priority queue and the associated storage areas are released (lines 10–19).

Second, the random variable `size` is sampled to determine the size of area to allocate and the random variable `latency` is sampled to determine when the allocated area should be deleted. An area of the required size is acquired, and an event is scheduled in a priority queue that will cause the area to be freed after the appropriate amount of time has elapsed.

The **StoragePoolTest** function given in Program 13.16 was used by the author to create Figure 13.1, 13.4, and 13.7. Figure 13.1 shows the condition of a **SinglyLinkedPool** after 5000 simulation cycles. Figure 13.4 shows the condition of a **DoublyLinkedPool**, and Figure 13.7 shows the condition of a **BuddyPool** after exactly the same 5000 simulation cycles.

# Exercises

**13.1** Consider the memory map shown in Figure 13.1. The figure suggests that smaller areas (both free and reserved) are more likely to be found at lower address than at higher addresses.

   **a.** Explain why this phenomenon occurs and why it is undesirable.

   **b.** Propose a modification to the acquire algorithm that alleviates this effect.

**13.2** Consider a singly-linked storage pool. Several strategies are possible when searching a free list for an area of a given size:

**first fit**   Select the first area encountered that is large enough to satisfy the request.

**next fit**   This is similar to first fit, except that the free list is treated as a circular list. Each subsequent search begins from the position where the previous search ended.

**best fit**   Select the smallest area that is large enough to satisfy the request.

**worst fit**   Select the largest area as long as it is large enough to satisfy the request.

   **a.** Devise a scenario which illustrates that *next fit* can be better than *first fit*.

   **b.** Devise a scenario which illustrates that *best fit* can be better than *first fit*.

   **c.** Devise a scenario which illustrates that *first fit* can be better than *best fit*.

   **d.** Under what conditions (if any) does the *worst fit* scenario make sense?

**13.3** Show how Program 13.5 can be modified to implement the *next fit* storage allocation strategy described in Exercise 13.2. What is the running time of your algorithm?

**13.4** Show how Program 13.5 can be modified to implement the *best fit* storage allocation. What is the running time of your algorithm?

**13.5** Devise optimal algorithms for **acquire** and **release** given we know a priori that all the areas acquired from a storage pool will have the same size. What are the running times of your algorithms?

**13.6** Consider the memory maps shown in Figure 13.1 and Figure 13.4. When using the **SinglyLinkedPool** a large block of unused memory is located at one end of the pool whereas when using the `DoublyLinkedPool` the large free area is located at the other end. Explain why this is so.

**13.7** Show how Program 13.10 can be modified to implement the *best fit* storage allocation.

   **a.** What effect does using the best-fit strategy have on the length of the free list in this case?

   **b.** What is the running time of your algorithm?

**13.8** Consider the implementations of the `SinglyLinkedPool` and `Doubly-LinkedPool` classes. In both cases, the sentinel is located immediately following the last block of the storage pool. Explain how the implementations depend on this.

**13.9** Devise an algorithm that uses bit manipulation operations to compute

$$\lceil \log_2 n \rceil,$$

where $n$ is an integer such that $n \geq 1$.

**13.10** It is possible to implement a buddy pool the size of which is not a power of 2. What modifications to the algorithms are necessary in order to do this?

## Programming Projects

**13.1** Compare experimentally the first-fit, best-fit, next-fit, and worst-fit storage allocation schemes described in Exercise 13.2 by making suitable variations of the `SinglyLinkedPool` class declared in Program 13.3. **Hint:** Use a simulation program such as the one given in Program 13.16.

**13.2** Complete the `DoublyLinkedPool` class declared in Program 13.7 by providing suitable definitions for the following member functions: `Unlink` and `InsertAfter`. Write a test program and test your implementation.

**13.3** Complete the `BuddyPool` class declared in Program 13.11 by providing suitable definitions for the following member functions: `Unlink` and `Insert After`. Write a test program and test your implementation.

**13.4** All three storage pool implementations given in this chapter allocate the memory used for the pool dynamically by using `operator new` in the pool constructor. Show by implementing suitable constructors for each of the classes that it is possible to allocate the memory used by one storage pool *inside* another storage pool—for example, the code sequence

```
Pool& p = *new SinglyLinkedPool (8192);
Pool& q = *new (p) SinglyLinkedPool (1024, p);
```

creates two pools, p and q. Pool q is allocated in storage acquired from p.

**13.5** Design and implement a storage pool class that manages a region of memory that is contained entirely within the pool object itself. Because the size of a class must be determined at compile time, this means that the size of the pool is a fixed constant. Write a test program and test your implementation.

**13.6** Modify the `SinglyLinkedPool` class declared in Program 13.5 so that instead of allocating memory in the constructor, we pass to the constructor the address and size of a region to be managed. Write a test program and test your implementation.

**13.7** Find a C++ program that you have written which uses dynamically allocated storage. Replace the storage manager provided by your compiler and operating system by overloading operators **new** and **delete** to use one of the storage pool implementations presented in this chapter. Compare the performance of your program when using the different implementations.

**13.8** Most C++ programs allocate dynamically only a small number of different object types. Consequently, only a small number of distinct sizes of areas need to be acquired. Modify the simulation shown in Program 13.16 as follows: In each cycle acquire either 4 bytes or 32 bytes. Use a suitable random number generator (see Section 14.5.1) so that the smaller block is acquired 75% of the time. In addition, suppose that the number of cycles that a block is in use is an exponentially distributed random variable. Assume that the smaller blocks are held on average for 10 cycles and that the larger blocks are held on average for 100 cycles. Use the modified simulation program to compare the various storage pool implementations given in this chapter.

# 14 | Algorithmic Patterns and Problem Solvers

This chapter presents a number of different algorithmic patterns. Each pattern addresses a category of problems and describes a core solution strategy for that category. Given a problem to be solved, we may find that there are several possible solution strategies. We may also find that only one strategy applies or even that none of them do. A good programmer is proficient at examining the problem to be solved and identifying the appropriate algorithmic technique. The following algorithmic patterns are discussed in this chapter:

**direct solution strategies**  Brute force algorithms and greedy algorithms.

**backtracking strategies**  Simple backtracking and branch-and-bound algorithms.

**top-down solution strategies**  Divide-and-conquer algorithms.

**bottom-up solution strategies**  Dynamic programming.

**randomized strategies**  Monte Carlo algorithms and simulated annealing.

## 14.1  Brute-Force and Greedy Algorithms

In this section we consider two closely related algorithm types—brute-force and greedy. *Brute-force algorithms* are distinguished not by their structure or form, but by the way in which the problem to be solved is approached. A brute-force algorithm solves a problem in the most simple, direct, or obvious way. As a result, such an algorithm can end up doing far more work to solve a given problem than a more clever or sophisticated algorithm might do. On the other hand, a brute-force algorithm is often easier to implement than a more sophisticated one and, because of this simplicity, sometimes it can be more efficient.

Often a problem can be viewed as a sequence of decisions to be made. For example, consider the problem of finding the best way to place electronic components on a

**463**

circuit board. To solve this problem we must decide where on the board to place each component. Typically, a brute-force algorithm solves such a problem by exhaustively enumerating all the possibilities. That is, for every decision we consider each possible outcome.

A greedy algorithm is one that makes the sequence of decisions (in some order) such that once a given decision has been made, that decision is never reconsidered. For example, if we use a greedy algorithm to place the components on the circuit board, once a component has been assigned a position it is never again moved. Greedy algorithms can run significantly faster than brute force ones. Unfortunately, it is not always the case that a greedy strategy leads to the correct solution.

### 14.1.1 Example—Counting Change

Consider the problem a cashier solves every time she counts out some amount of currency. The cashier has at her disposal a collection of notes and coins of various denominations and is required to count out a specified sum using the smallest possible number of pieces.

The problem can be expressed mathematically as follows: Let there be $n$ pieces of money (notes or coins), $P = \{p_1, p_2, \ldots, p_n\}$, and let $d_i$ be the denomination of $p_i$. For example, if $p_i$ is a dime, then $d_i = 10$. To count out a given sum of money $A$ we find the smallest subset of $P$, say $S \subseteq P$, such that $\sum_{p_i \in S} d_i = A$.

One way to represent the subset $S$ is to use $n$ variables $X = \{x_1, x_2, \ldots, x_n\}$, such that

$$x_i = \begin{cases} 1 & p_i \in S, \\ 0 & p_i \notin S. \end{cases}$$

Given $\{d_1, d_2, \ldots, d_n\}$ our *objective* is to minimize

$$\sum_{i=1}^{n} x_i$$

subject to the constraint

$$\sum_{i=1}^{n} d_i x_i = A.$$

### Brute-Force Algorithm

Since each of the elements of $X = \{x_1, x_2, \ldots, x_n\}$ is either a zero or 1, there are $2^n$ possible values for $X$. A brute-force algorithm to solve this problem finds the best solution by enumerating all the possible values of $X$.

For each possible value of $X$ we check first if the constraint $\sum_{i=1}^{n} d_i x_i = A$ is satisfied. A value which satisfies the constraint is called a *feasible solution*. The solution to the problem is the feasible solution which minimizes $\sum_{i=1}^{n} x_i$ which is called the *objective function*.

Since there are $2^n$ possible values of $X$ the running time of a brute-force solution is $\Omega(2^n)$. The running time needed to determine whether a possible value is a feasible solution is $O(n)$, and the time required to evaluate the objective function is also $O(n)$. Therefore, the running time of the brute-force algorithm is $O(n2^n)$.

**Greedy Algorithm**

A cashier does not really consider all the possible ways in which to count out a given sum of money. Instead, she counts out the required amount beginning with the largest denomination and proceeding to the smallest denomination.

For example, suppose we have ten coins: five pennies, two nickels, two dimes, and a quarter. That is, $\{d_1, d_2, \ldots, d_{10}\} = \{1, 1, 1, 1, 1, 5, 5, 10, 10, 25\}$. To count out 32 cents, we start with a quarter, then add a nickel followed by two pennies. This is a greedy strategy because once a coin has been counted out, it is never taken back. Furthermore, the solution obtained is the correct solution because it uses the fewest number of coins.

If we assume that the pieces of money (notes and coins) are sorted by their denomination, the running time for the greedy algorithm is $O(n)$. This is significantly better than that of the brute-force algorithm given above.

Does this greedy algorithm always produce the correct answer? Unfortunately it does not. Consider what happens if we introduce a 15-cent coin. Suppose we are asked to count out 20 cents from the following set of coins: $\{1, 1, 1, 1, 1, 10, 10, 15\}$. The greedy algorithm selects 15 followed by five ones—six coins in total. Of course, the correct solution requires only two coins. The solution found by the greedy strategy is a feasible solution, but it does not minimize the objective function.

## 14.1.2 Example—0/1 Knapsack Problem

The *0/1 knapsack problem* is closely related to the change counting problem discussed in the preceding section: We are given a set of $n$ items from which we are to select some number of items to be carried in a knapsack. Each item has both a *weight* and a *profit*. The objective is to choose the set of items that fits in the knapsack and maximizes the profit.

Let $w_i$ be the weight of the $i$th item, $p_i$ be the profit accrued when the $i$th item is carried in the knapsack, and $C$ be the capacity of the knapsack. Let $x_i$ be a variable the value of which is either zero or 1. The variable $x_i$ has the value 1 when the $i$th item is carried in the knapsack.

Given $\{w_1, w_2, \ldots, w_n\}$ and $\{p_1, p_2, \ldots, p_n\}$, our *objective* is to maximize

$$\sum_{i=1}^{n} p_i x_i$$

subject to the constraint

$$\sum_{i=1}^{n} w_i x_i \leq C.$$

Clearly, we can solve this problem by exhaustively enumerating the feasible solutions and selecting the one with the highest profit. However, since there are $2^n$ possible solutions, the running time required for the brute-force solution becomes prohibitive as $n$ gets large.

An alternative is to use a greedy solution strategy which solves the problem by putting items into the knapsack one-by-one. This approach is greedy because once an item has been put into the knapsack, it is never removed.

How do we select the next item to be put into the knapsack? There are several possibilities:

**Greedy by profit** At each step select from the remaining items the one with the highest profit (provided the capacity of the knapsack is not exceeded). This approach tries to maximize the profit by choosing the most profitable items first.

**Greedy by weight** At each step select from the remaining items the one with the least weight (provided the capacity of the knapsack is not exceeded). This approach tries to maximize the profit by putting as many items into the knapsack as possible.

**Greedy by profit density** At each step select from the remaining items the one with the largest *profit density*, $p_i/w_i$ (provided the capacity of the knapsack is not exceeded). This approach tries to maximize the profit by choosing items with the largest profit per unit of weight.

While all three approaches generate feasible solutions, we cannot guarantee that any of them will always generate the optimal solution. In fact, it is even possible that none of them does! Table 14.1 gives an example where this is the case.

The bottom line about greedy algorithms is this: Before using a greedy algorithm you must make sure that it always gives the correct answer. Fortunately, in many cases this is true.

**TABLE 14.1**
0/1 Knapsack Problem Example ($C = 100$)

| $i$ | $w_i$ | $p_i$ | $p_i/w_i$ | Greedy by Profit | Greedy by Weight | Greedy by Density | Optimal Solution |
|---|---|---|---|---|---|---|---|
| 1 | 100 | 40 | 0.4 | 1 | 0 | 0 | 0 |
| 2 | 50 | 35 | 0.7 | 0 | 0 | 1 | 1 |
| 3 | 45 | 18 | 0.4 | 0 | 1 | 0 | 1 |
| 4 | 20 | 4 | 0.2 | 0 | 1 | 1 | 0 |
| 5 | 10 | 10 | 1.0 | 0 | 1 | 1 | 0 |
| 6 | 5 | 2 | 0.4 | 0 | 1 | 1 | 1 |
| | | Total weight | | 100 | 80 | 85 | 100 |
| | | Total profit | | 40 | 34 | 51 | 55 |

## 14.2 Backtracking Algorithms

In this section we consider *backtracking algorithms*. As in the preceding section, we view the problem to be solved as a sequence of decisions. A backtracking algorithm systematically considers all possible outcomes for each decision. In this sense, backtracking algorithms are like the brute-force algorithms discussed in the preceding section. However, backtracking algorithms are distinguished by the way in which the space of possible solutions is explored. Sometimes a backtracking algorithm can detect that an exhaustive search is unnecessary and, therefore, it can perform much better.

### 14.2.1 Example—Balancing Scales

Consider the set of *scales* shown in Figure 14.1. Suppose we are given a collection of $n$ weights, $\{w_1, w_2, \ldots, w_n\}$, and we are required to place *all* of the weights onto the scales so that they are balanced.

The problem can be expressed mathematically as follows: Let $x_i$ represent the pan in which weight $w_i$ is placed such that

$$x_i = \begin{cases} 0 & w_i \text{ is placed in the left pan,} \\ 1 & w_i \text{ is placed in the right pan.} \end{cases}$$

The scales are balanced when the sum of the weights in the left pan equals the sum of the weights in the right pan,

$$\sum_{i=1}^{n} w_i x_i = \sum_{i=1}^{n} w_i (1 - x_i).$$

Given an arbitrary set of $n$ weights, there is no guarantee that a solution to the problem exists. A solution always exists if, instead of balancing the scales, the goal is to minimize the difference between the total weights in the left and right pans. Thus, given $\{w_1, w_2, \ldots, w_n\}$, our *objective* is to *minimize $\delta$* where

$$\delta = \left| \sum_{i=1}^{n} w_i x_i - \sum_{i=1}^{n} w_i (1 - x_i) \right|$$

subject to the constraint that *all* the weights are placed on the scales.

Given a set of scales and collection of weights, we might solve the problem by trial and error: Place all the weights onto the pans one-by-one. If the scales balance, a solution has been found. If not, remove some number of the weights and place them back on the scales in some other combination. In effect, we search for a solution to the problem by first trying one solution and then backing up to try another.

Figure 14.2 shows the *solution space* for the scales balancing problem. In this case the solution space takes the form of a tree: Each node of the tree represents a *partial solution* to the problem. At the root (node A) no weights have been placed yet and

**FIGURE 14.1**
A set of scales.

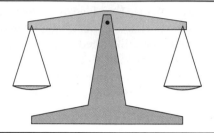

the scales are balanced. Let $\delta$ be the difference between the the sum of the weights currently placed in the left and right pans. Therefore, $\delta = 0$ at node A.

Node B represents the situation in which weight $w_1$ has been placed in the left pan. The difference between the pans is $\delta = -w_1$. Conversely, node C represents the situation in which the weight $w_1$ has been placed in the right pan. In this case $\delta = +w_1$. The complete solution tree has depth $n$ and $2^n$ leaves. Clearly, the solution is the leaf node having the smallest $|\delta|$ value.

In this case (as in many others) the solution space is a tree. In order to find the best solution a backtracking algorithm visits all the nodes in the solution space, that is, it does a tree *traversal*. Section 9.4 presents the two most important tree traversals—*depth-first* and *breadth-first*. Both kinds can be used to implement a backtracking algorithm.

## 14.2.2 Representing the Solution Space

This section presents an abstract base class for representing the nodes of a solution space. By defining an abstract interface, it is possible to hide the details of the specific

**FIGURE 14.2**
Solution space for the scales balancing problem.

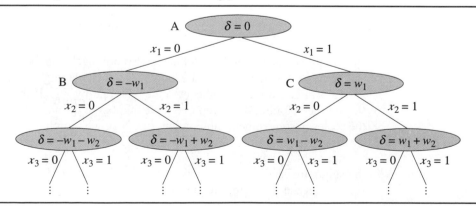

problem to be solved from the backtracking algorithm. In so doing, it is possible to implement completely generic backtracking problem solvers.

Although a backtracking algorithm behaves as if it is traversing a solution tree, it is important to realize that it is not necessary to have the entire solution tree constructed at once. Instead, the backtracking algorithm creates and destroys the nodes dynamically as it explores the solution space.

Program 14.1 defines the abstract class called `Solution`. The `Solution` class is intended to serve as the base class from which problem-specific classes are derived. Each `Solution` instance represents a single node in the solution space.

The `Solution` class is derived from the `Object` base class. Consequently, instances of the `Solution` class can be inserted in the various containers discussed in the preceding chapters. The `Solution` class adds the following functions to the inherited interface:

**IsFeasible** This function returns true if the solution instance is a feasible solution to the given problem. A solution is feasible if it satisfies the problem constraints.

**IsComplete** This function returns true if the solution instance represents a complete solution. A solution is complete when all possible decisions have been made.

**Objective** This function returns the value of the objective function for the given solution instance.

**Bound** This function returns a value that is a lower bound (if it exists) on the objective function for the given solution instance as well as all the solutions that can possibly be derived from that instance. This is a hook provided to facilitate the implementation of *branch-and-bound* backtracking, which is described in Section 14.2.4.

**Clone** This function is used to *clone* the given solution instance. It returns a reference to another, dynamically allocated solution that is identical to the given solution instance.

**PROGRAM 14.1**
`Solution` class definition

```
1   class Solution : public Object
2   {
3   public:
4       virtual bool IsFeasible () const = 0;
5       virtual bool IsComplete () const = 0;
6       virtual int Objective () const = 0;
7       virtual int Bound () const = 0;
8       virtual Solution& Clone () const = 0;
9       virtual Iterator& Successors () const = 0;
10  };
```

**Successors** This function returns an iterator that enumerates all of the successors (i.e., the children) of the given solution instance. It is assumed that this iterator creates the children of the given node *dynamically*.

### 14.2.3 Abstract Backtracking Solvers

The usual way to implement a backtracking algorithm is to write a function or procedure which traverses the solution space. This section presents an alternate, object-oriented approach that is based on the notion of an *abstract solver*.

Think of a solver as an abstract machine, the sole purpose of which is to search a given solution space for the best possible solution. A machine is an object. Therefore, it makes sense that we represent it as an instance of some class.

Program 14.2 declares the abstract class **Solver**. The public interface of this class consists of the single function **Solve**. This function takes as its lone argument a reference to a **Solution** instance that is the node in the solution space from which to begin the search. The **Solve** function returns a reference to the best solution found.

Program 14.2 also declares two protected member variables, **bestSolution** and **bestObjective**, and two protected member functions, **UpdateBest** and **DoSolve**. Since **DoSolve** is a pure virtual function, its implementation must be given in a derived class. Program 14.3 gives the implementations for **Solve** and **UpdateBest**.

The **Solve** function does not search the solution space itself. It is the **DoSolve** routine, which is provided by a derived class, that does the actual searching. The **Solve** routine merely sets things up for **DoSolve**. When **DoSolve** returns it is expected that the **bestSolution** variable will point to the best solution and that **bestObjective** will be the value of the objective function for the best solution. In this case, it is assumed that the goal is to *minimize* the objective function.

The **UpdateBest** function is meant to be called by the **DoSolve** routine as it explores the solution space. As each complete solution is encountered, the **UpdateBest** routine is called to keep track of the solution which minimizes the objective function.

---

**PROGRAM 14.2**
**Solver** class definition

```
1   class Solver
2   {
3   protected:
4       Solution* bestSolution;
5       int bestObjective;
6       void UpdateBest (Solution const&);
7       virtual void DoSolve (Solution const&) = 0;
8   public:
9       virtual Solution& Solve (Solution const&);
10  };
```

**PROGRAM 14.3**
Solver class Solve and UpdateBest member function definitions

```
1   Solution& Solver::Solve (Solution const& initial)
2   {
3       bestSolution = 0;
4       bestObjective = numeric_limits<int>::max ();
5       DoSolve (initial);
6       if (bestSolution == 0)
7           throw domain_error ("no feasible solution found");
8       return *bestSolution;
9   }
10
11  void Solver::UpdateBest (Solution const& solution)
12  {
13      if (solution.IsFeasible() &&
14          solution.Objective () < bestObjective)
15      {
16          delete bestSolution;
17          bestSolution = &(solution.Clone ());
18          bestObjective = solution.Objective ();
19      }
20  }
```

### Depth-First Solver

This section presents a backtracking solver that finds the best solution to a given problem by performing depth-first traversal of the solution space. Program 14.4 declares the concrete DepthFirstSolver class. This DepthFirstSolver class simply provides an implementation for the DoSolve routine.

The DoSolve routine for the DepthFirstSolver class is given in Program 14.5. Clearly, this routine simply does a complete, depth-first traversal of the solution space.[1] Note that the implementation does not depend on the characteristics of the problem

**PROGRAM 14.4**
DepthFirstSolver class definition

```
1   class DepthFirstSolver : public Solver
2   {
3       void DoSolve (Solution const&);
4   };
```

---

[1]The reader may find it instructive to compare Program 14.5 with Program 9.2 and Program 16.7.

**PROGRAM 14.5**
DepthFirstSolver class DoSolve member function definition

```
1   void DepthFirstSolver::DoSolve (Solution const& solution)
2   {
3       if (solution.IsComplete ())
4           UpdateBest (solution);
5       else
6       {
7           Iterator& i = solution.Successors ();
8           while (!i.IsDone ()) {
9               Solution& successor = dynamic_cast<Solution&> (*i);
10              DoSolve (successor);
11              delete &successor;
12              ++i;
13          }
14          delete &i;
15      }
16  }
```

being solved. In this sense the solver is a generic, *abstract solver* and can be used to solve any problem that has a tree-structured solution space!

Since the **DoSolve** routine in Program 14.5 visits all the nodes in the solution space, it is essentially a *brute-force* algorithm. And because the recursive routine backs up and then tries different alternatives, it is called a *backtracking* algorithm.

### Breadth-First Solver

If we can find the optimal solution by doing a depth-first traversal of the solution space, then we can find the solution with a breadth-first traversal too. As defined in Section 9.4, a breadth-first traversal of a tree visits the nodes in the order of their depth in the tree. That is, first the root is visited, then the children of the root are visited, then the grandchildren are visited, and so on.

As shown in Program 14.6, the **BreadthFirstSolver** class simply provides an implementation for the **DoSolve** member function.

**PROGRAM 14.6**
BreadthFirstSolver class definition

```
1   class BreadthFirstSolver : public Solver
2   {
3       void DoSolve (Solution const&);
4   };
```

---

**PROGRAM 14.7**
BreadthFirstSolver class DoSolve member function definition

---

```
1   void BreadthFirstSolver::DoSolve (Solution const& initial)
2   {
3       Queue& queue = *new QueueAsLinkedList ();
4       queue.Enqueue (initial.Clone ());
5       while (!queue.IsEmpty ())
6       {
7           Solution& solution =
8               dynamic_cast<Solution&> (queue.Dequeue ());
9           if (solution.IsComplete ())
10              UpdateBest (solution);
11          else
12          {
13              Iterator& i = solution.Successors ();
14              while (!i.IsDone ()) {
15                  Solution& succ = dynamic_cast<Solution&> (*i);
16                  queue.Enqueue (succ);
17                  ++i;
18              }
19              delete &i;
20          }
21          delete &solution;
22      }
23      delete &queue;
24  }
```

---

The body of the **DoSolve** routine is given in Program 14.7. This nonrecursive, breadth-first traversal algorithm uses a queue to keep track of nodes to be visited. The initial solution is enqueued first. Then the following steps are repeated until the queue is empty:

1. Dequeue the first solution in the queue.
2. If the solution is complete, call the **UpdateBest** routine to keep track of the solution which minimizes the objective function—
3. Otherwise, the solution is not complete. Enqueue all its successors.

Clearly, this algorithm does a complete traversal of the solution space.[2]

---

[2]The reader may find it instructive to compare Program 14.7 with Program 9.4 and Program 16.8.

### 14.2.4 Branch-and-Bound Solvers

The depth-first and breadth-first backtracking algorithms described in the preceding sections both naïvely traverse the entire solution space. However, sometimes we can determine that a given node in the solution space does not lead to the optimal solution—either because the given solution and all its successors are infeasible or because we have already found a solution that is guaranteed to be better than any successor of the given solution. In such cases, the given node and its successors need not be considered. In effect, we can *prune* the solution tree, thereby reducing the number of solutions to be considered.

For example, consider the scales balancing problem described in Section 14.2.1. Consider a partial solution $P_k$ in which we have placed $k$ weights onto the pans ($0 \leq k < n$) and, therefore, $n - k$ weights remain to be placed. The difference between the weights of the left and right pans is given by

$$\delta = \sum_{i=1}^{k} w_i x_i - \sum_{i=1}^{k} w_i(1 - x_i),$$

and the sum of the weights still to be placed is

$$r = \sum_{i=k+1}^{n} w_i.$$

Suppose that $|\delta| > r$, that is, the total weight remaining is less than the difference between the weights in the two pans. Then, the best possible solution that we can obtain without changing the positions of the weights that have already been placed is $\hat{\delta} = |\delta| - r$. The quantity $\hat{\delta}$ is a *lower bound* on the value of the objective function for all the solutions in the solution tree below the given partial solution $P_k$.

In general, during the traversal of the solution space we may have already found a complete, feasible solution for which the objective function is *less* than $\hat{\delta}$. In that case, there is no point in considering any of the solutions below $P_k$. That is, we can *prune* the subtree rooted at node $P_k$ from the solution tree. A backtracking algorithm that prunes the search space in this manner is called a *branch-and-bound* algorithm.

### Depth-First, Branch-and-Bound Solver

Only a relatively minor modification of the simple, depth-first solver shown in Program 14.5 is needed to transform it into a branch-and-bound solver. Program 14.8 gives the implementation of the **DoSolve** routine of the **DepthFirstBranchAndBoundSolver** class.[3]

The only difference between the simple, depth-first solver and the branch-and-bound version is the **if** statement on lines 11–12. As each node in the solution space is visited

---

[3]The declaration of the class itself has been omitted since it follows directly from Programs 14.2 and 14.4.

**PROGRAM 14.8**
DepthFirstBranchAndBoundSolver class DoSolve member function definition

```
1   void DepthFirstBranchAndBoundSolver::DoSolve (
2       Solution const& solution)
3   {
4       if (solution.IsComplete ())
5           UpdateBest (solution);
6       else
7       {
8           Iterator& i = solution.Successors ();
9           while (!i.IsDone ()) {
10              Solution& successor = dynamic_cast<Solution&> (*i);
11              if (successor.IsFeasible () &&
12                      successor.Bound () < bestObjective)
13                  DoSolve (successor);
14              delete &successor;
15              ++i;
16          }
17          delete &i;
18      }
19  }
```

two tests are done: First, the IsFeasible routine is called to check whether the given node represents a feasible solution. Next, the Bound routine is called to determine the lower bound on the best possible solution in the given subtree. The second test determines whether this bound is less than the value of the objective function of the best solution already found. The recursive call to explore the subtree is only made if both tests succeed. Otherwise, the subtree of the solution space is pruned.

The degree to which the solution space may be pruned depends strongly on the nature of the problem being solved. In the worst case, no subtrees are pruned and the branch-and-bound routine visits all the nodes in the solution space. The branch-and-bound technique is really just *heuristic*—sometimes it works and sometimes it does not.

It is important to understand the trade-off being made: The solution space is being pruned at the added expense of performing the tests as each node is visited. The technique is successful only if the savings which accrue from pruning exceed the additional execution time arising from the tests.

## 14.2.5 Example—0/1 Knapsack Problem Again

Consider again the 0/1 knapsack problem described in Section 14.1.2. We are given a set of $n$ items from which we are to select some number of items to be carried in a knapsack. The solution to the problem has the form $\{x_1, x_2, \ldots, x_n\}$, where $x_i$ is one if the $i$th item is placed in the knapsack and zero otherwise. Each item has both a *weight*,

$w_i$, and a *profit*, $p_i$. The goal is to maximize the total profit,

$$\sum_{i=1}^{n} p_i x_i,$$

subject to the knapsack capacity constraint

$$\sum_{i=1}^{n} w_i x_i \leq C.$$

A partial solution to the problem is one in which only the first $k$ items have been considered. That is, the solution has the form $S_k = \{x_1, x_2, \ldots, x_k\}$, where $1 \leq k < n$. The partial solution $S_k$ is feasible if and only if

$$\sum_{i=1}^{k} w_i x_i \leq C. \tag{14.1}$$

Clearly if $S_k$ is infeasible, then every possible complete solution containing $S_k$ is also infeasible.

If $S_k$ is feasible, the total profit of any solution containing $S_k$ is bounded by

$$\sum_{i=1}^{k} p_i x_i + \sum_{i=k+1}^{n} p_i. \tag{14.2}$$

That is, the bound is equal to the *actual* profit accrued from the $k$ items already considered, plus the sum of the profits of the remaining items.

Clearly, the 0/1 knapsack problem can be solved using a backtracking algorithm. Furthermore, by using Equations 14.1 and 14.2 a branch-and-bound solver can potentially prune the solution space, thereby arriving at the solution more quickly.

For example, consider the 0/1 knapsack problem with $n = 6$ items given in Table 14.1. There are $2^n = 64$ possible solutions and the solution space contains $2^{n+1} - 1 = 127$ nodes. The simple **DepthFirstSolver** given in Program 14.5 visits all 127 nodes and generates all 64 solutions because it does a complete traversal of the solution tree. The **BreadthFirstSolver** of Program 14.7 behaves similarly. On the other hand, the **DepthFirstBranchAndBoundSolver** shown in Program 14.8 visits only 67 nodes and generates only 27 complete solutions. In this case, the branch-and-bound technique prunes almost half the nodes from the solution space!

## 14.3  Top-Down Algorithms: Divide-and-Conquer

In this section we discuss a top-down algorithmic paradigm called *divide and conquer*. To solve a given problem, it is subdivided into one or more subproblems each of which is similar to the given problem. Each of the subproblems is solved independently. Finally, the solutions to the subproblems are combined in order to obtain the solution to the original problem.

Divide-and-conquer algorithms are often implemented using recursion. However, not all recursive functions are divide-and-conquer algorithms. Generally, the subproblems solved by a divide-and-conquer algorithm are *non-overlapping*.

### 14.3.1 Example—Binary Search

Consider the problem of finding the position of an item in a sorted list. That is, given the sorted sequence $S = \{a_1, a_2, \ldots, a_n\}$ and an item $x$, find $i$ (if it exists) such that $a_i = x$. The usual solution to this problem is *binary search*.

Binary search is a divide-and-conquer strategy. The sequence $S$ is split into two subsequences, $S_L = \{a_1, a_2, \ldots, a_{\lfloor n/2 \rfloor}\}$ and $S_R = \{a_{\lfloor n/2 \rfloor+1}, a_{\lfloor n/2 \rfloor+1} \ldots, a_n.\}$. The original problem is split into two subproblems: Find $x$ in $S_L$ or $S_R$. Of course, since the original list is sorted, we can quickly determine the list in which $x$ must appear. Therefore, we only need to solve one subproblem.

Program 14.9 defines the function **BinarySearch** which takes four arguments, **array**, **x**, **i**, and **n**. This routine looks for the position in the **array** at which item **x**

---

**PROGRAM 14.9**
Divide-and-conquer example—binary search

```
1   template <class T>
2   unsigned int BinarySearch (
3       Array<T> const& array, T const& target,
4       unsigned int i, unsigned int n)
5   {
6       if (n == 0)
7           throw invalid_argument ("empty array");
8       if (n == 1)
9       {
10          if (array [i] == target)
11              return i;
12          throw domain_error ("target not found");
13      }
14      else
15      {
16          unsigned int const j = i + n / 2;
17          if (array [j] <= target)
18              return BinarySearch (array, target, j, n - n / 2);
19          else
20              return BinarySearch (array, target, i, n / 2);
21      }
22  }
```

is found. Specifically, it considers the following elements of the array:

$$\texttt{array[i], array[i + 1], array[i + 2], \ldots, array[i + n - 1]}.$$

The running time of the algorithm is clearly a function of $n$, the number of elements to be searched. Although Program 14.9 works correctly for arbitrary values of $n$, it is much easier to determine the running time if we assume that $n$ is a power of 2. In this case, the running time is given by the recurrence

$$T(n) = \begin{cases} O(1) & n \leq 1, \\ T(n/2) + O(1) & n > 1. \end{cases} \tag{14.3}$$

Equation 14.3 is easily solved using repeated substitution:

$$\begin{aligned} T(n) &= T(n/2) + 1 \\ &= T(n/4) + 2 \\ &= T(n/8) + 3 \\ &\ \ \vdots \\ &= T(n/2^k) + k \end{aligned}$$

Setting $n/2^k = 1$ gives $T(n) = \log n + 1 = O(\log n)$.

### 14.3.2 Example—Computing Fibonacci Numbers

The Fibonacci numbers are given by the following recurrence

$$F_n = \begin{cases} 0 & n = 0, \\ 1 & n = 1, \\ F_{n-1} + F_{n-2} & n \geq 2. \end{cases} \tag{14.4}$$

Section 3.4.3 presents a recursive function to compute the Fibonacci numbers by implementing directly Equation 14.4. (See Program 3.4.) The running time of that program is shown to be $T(n) = \Omega((3/2)^n)$.

In this section we present a divide-and-conquer style of algorithm for computing Fibonacci numbers. We make use of the following identities

$$F_{2k-1} = (F_k)^2 + (F_{k-1})^2$$
$$F_{2k} = (F_k)^2 + 2F_k F_{k-1}$$

for $k \geq 1$. (See Exercise 3.6.) Thus, we can rewrite Equation 14.4 as

$$F_n = \begin{cases} 0 & n = 0, \\ 1 & n = 1, \\ (F_{\lceil n/2 \rceil})^2 + (F_{\lceil n/2 \rceil - 1})^2 & n \geq 2 \text{ and } n \text{ is odd}, \\ (F_{\lceil n/2 \rceil})^2 + 2F_{\lceil n/2 \rceil}F_{\lceil n/2 \rceil - 1} & n \geq 2 \text{ and } n \text{ is even}. \end{cases} \tag{14.5}$$

**PROGRAM 14.10**
Divide-and-conquer example—computing Fibonacci numbers

```
1   unsigned int Fibonacci (unsigned int n)
2   {
3       if (n == 0 || n == 1)
4           return n;
5       else
6       {
7           unsigned int const a = Fibonacci ((n + 1) / 2);
8           unsigned int const b = Fibonacci ((n + 1) / 2 - 1);
9           if (n % 2 == 0)
10              return a * (a + 2 * b);
11          else
12              return a * a + b * b;
13      }
14  }
```

Program 14.10 defines the function **Fibonacci** which implements directly Equation 14.5. Given $n > 1$ it computes $F_n$ by calling itself recursively to compute $F_{\lceil n/2 \rceil}$ and $F_{\lceil n/2 \rceil - 1}$ and then combines the two results as required.

To determine a bound on the running time of the **Fibonacci** routine in Program 14.10 we assume that $T(n)$ is a nondecreasing function, that is, $T(n) \geq T(n-1)$ for all $n \geq 1$. Therefore, $T(\lceil n/2 \rceil) \geq T(\lceil n/2 \rceil - 1)$. Although the program works correctly for all values of $n$, it is convenient to assume that $n$ is a power of 2. In this case, the running time of the routine is upper-bounded by $T(n)$ where

$$T(n) = \begin{cases} O(1) & n \leq 1, \\ 2T(n/2) + O(1) & n > 1. \end{cases} \tag{14.6}$$

Equation 14.6 is easily solved using repeated substitution:

$$\begin{aligned} T(n) &= 2T(n/2) + 1 \\ &= 4T(n/4) + 1 + 2 \\ &= 8T(n/8) + 1 + 2 + 4 \\ &\quad \vdots \\ &= 2^k T(n/2^k) + \sum_{i=0}^{k-1} 2^i \\ &\quad \vdots \\ &= nT(1) + n - 1 \quad (n = 2^k). \end{aligned}$$

Thus, $T(n) = 2n - 1 = O(n)$.

### 14.3.3 Example—Merge Sorting

Sorting algorithms and sorters are covered in detail in Chapter 15. In this section we consider a divide-and-conquer sorting algorithm—*merge sort*. Given an array of $n$ items in arbitrary order, the objective is to rearrange the elements of the array so that they are ordered from the smallest to the largest element.

The merge sort algorithm sorts a sequence of length $n > 1$ by splitting it into two subsequences—one of length $\lfloor n/2 \rfloor$, the other of length $\lceil n/2 \rceil$. Each subsequence is sorted and then the two sorted sequences are merged into one.

Program 14.11 defines the function `MergeSort` which takes three arguments, `array`, `i`, and `n`. The routine sorts the following $n$ elements:

$$\texttt{array[i]}, \ \texttt{array[i+1]}, \ \texttt{array[i+2]}, \ldots, \ \texttt{array[i+n-1]}.$$

The `MergeSort` routine calls itself as well as the `Merge` routine. The purpose of the `Merge` routine is to merge two sorted sequences, one of length $\lfloor n/2 \rfloor$, the other of length $\lceil n/2 \rceil$, into a single sorted sequence of length $n$. This can easily be done in $O(n)$ time. (See Program 15.17.)

The running time of the `MergeSort` routine depends on the number of items to be sorted, $n$. Although Program 14.11 works correctly for arbitrary values of $n$, it is much easier to determine the running time if we assume that $n$ is a power of 2. In this case, the running time is given by the recurrence

$$T(n) = \begin{cases} O(1) & n \le 1, \\ 2T(n/2) + O(n) & n > 1. \end{cases} \tag{14.7}$$

Equation 14.7 is easily solved using repeated substitution:

$$\begin{aligned} T(n) &= 2T(n/2) + n \\ &= 4T(n/4) + 2n \\ &= 8T(n/8) + 3n \\ &\quad\vdots \\ &= 2^k T(n/2^k) + kn \end{aligned}$$

Setting $n/2^k = 1$ gives $T(n) = n + n \log n = O(n \log n)$.

### 14.3.4 Running Time of Divide-and-Conquer Algorithms

A number of divide-and-conquer algorithms are presented in the preceding sections. Because these algorithms have a similar form, the recurrences which give the running times of the algorithms are also similar in form. Table 14.2 summarizes the running times of Programs 14.9, 14.10, and 14.11.

**TABLE 14.2**
Running Times of Divide-and-Conquer Algorithms

| Program | Recurrence | Solution |
|---|---|---|
| Program 14.9 | $T(n) = T(n/2) + O(1)$ | $O(\log n)$ |
| Program 14.10 | $T(n) = 2T(n/2) + O(1)$ | $O(n)$ |
| Program 14.11 | $T(n) = 2T(n/2) + O(n)$ | $O(n \log n)$ |

**PROGRAM 14.11**
Divide-and-conquer example—merge sorting

```
1   template <class T>
2   void MergeSort (Array<T>& array, unsigned int i, unsigned int n)
3   {
4       if (n > 1)
5       {
6           MergeSort (array, i, n / 2);
7           MergeSort (array, i + n / 2, n - n / 2);
8           Merge (array, i, n / 2, n - n / 2);
9       }
10  }
```

In this section we develop a general recurrence that characterizes the running times of many divide-and-conquer algorithms. Consider the form of a divide-and-conquer algorithm to solve a given problem. Let $n$ be a measure of the size of the problem. Since the divide-and-conquer paradigm is essentially recursive, there must be a base case. That is, there must be some value of $n$, say $n_0$, for which the solution to the problem is computed directly. We assume that the worst-case running time for the base case is bounded by a constant.

To solve an arbitrarily large problem using divide-and-conquer, the problem is *divided* into a number of smaller problems, each of which is solved independently. Let $a$ be the number of smaller problems to be solved ($a \in \mathbb{Z}$, $a \geq 1$). The size of each of these problems is some fraction of the original problem, typically either $\lceil n/b \rceil$ or $\lfloor n/b \rfloor$ ($b \in \mathbb{Z}$, $b \geq 1$).

The solution to the original problem is constructed from the solutions to the smaller problems. The running time required to do this depends on the problem to be solved. In this section we consider polynomial running times, that is, $O(n^k)$ for some integer $k \geq 0$.

For the assumptions stated above, the running time of a divide-and-conquer algorithm is given by

$$T(n) = \begin{cases} O(1) & n \leq n_0, \\ aT(\lceil n/b \rceil) + O(n^k) & n > n_0. \end{cases} \qquad (14.8)$$

In order to make it easier to find the solution to Equation 14.8, we drop the $O(\cdot)$s as well as the $\lceil \cdot \rceil$ from the recurrence. We can also assume (without loss of generality) that $n_0 = 1$. As a result, the recurrence becomes

$$T(n) = \begin{cases} 1 & n = 1, \\ aT(n/b) + n^k & n > 1. \end{cases}$$

Finally, we assume that $n$ is a power of $b$, that is, $n = b^m$ for some integer $m \geq 0$. Consequently, the recurrence formula becomes

$$T(b^m) = \begin{cases} 1 & m = 0, \\ T(b^m) = aT(b^{m-1}) + b^{mk} & m > 0. \end{cases} \tag{14.9}$$

We solve Equation 14.9 as follows. Divide both sizes of the recurrence by $a^m$ and then *telescope*:

$$\frac{T(b^m)}{a^m} = \frac{T(b^{m-1})}{a^{m-1}} + \left(\frac{b^k}{a}\right)^m \tag{14.10}$$

$$\frac{T(b^{m-1})}{a^{m-1}} = \frac{T(b^{m-2})}{a^{m-2}} + \left(\frac{b^k}{a}\right)^{m-1}$$

$$\frac{T(b^{m-2})}{a^{m-2}} = \frac{T(b^{m-3})}{a^{m-3}} + \left(\frac{b^k}{a}\right)^{m-2}$$

$$\vdots$$

$$\frac{T(b)}{a} = T(1) + \left(\frac{b^k}{a}\right). \tag{14.11}$$

Adding Equation 14.10 through Equation 14.11, substituting $T(1) = 1$ and multiplying both sides by $a^m$ gives

$$T(n) = a^m \sum_{i=0}^{m} \left(\frac{b^k}{a}\right)^i. \tag{14.12}$$

In order to evaluate the summation in Equation 14.11 we must consider three cases:

**Case 1** $(a > b^k)$ In this case, the term $b^k/a$ falls between zero and 1. Consider the *infinite* geometric series summation:

$$\sum_{i=0}^{\infty} \left(\frac{b^k}{a}\right)^i = \frac{a}{a - b^k} = C.$$

Since the infinite series summation approaches a finite constant $C$ and since each term in the series is positive, the *finite* series summation in Equation 14.11 is bounded from above by $C$:

$$\sum_{i=0}^{m} \left(\frac{b^k}{a}\right)^i \leq C.$$

Substituting this result into Equation 14.11 and making use of the fact that $n = b^m$, and therefore $m = \log_b n$, gives

$$\begin{aligned} T(n) &\leq Ca^m \\ &= O(a^m) \\ &= O(a^{\log_b n}) \\ &= O(a^{\log_a n \log_b a}) \\ &= O(n^{\log_b a}). \end{aligned}$$

**Case 2 ($a = b^k$)**   In this case the term $b^k/a$ is exactly 1. Therefore, the series summation in Equation 14.11 is simply

$$\sum_{i=0}^{m} \left(\frac{b^k}{a}\right)^i = m + 1.$$

Substituting this result into Equation 14.11 and making use of the fact that $n = b^m$ and $a = b^k$ gives

$$\begin{aligned} T(n) &= (m + 1)a^m \\ &= O(ma^m) \\ &= O(m(b^k)^m) \\ &= O((b^m)^k m) \\ &= O(n^k \log_b n). \end{aligned}$$

**Case 3 ($a < b^k$)**   In this case the term $b^k/a$ is greater than 1 and we make use of the general formula for a finite geometric series summation (see Section 2.2.4) to evaluate the summation

$$\sum_{i=0}^{m} \left(\frac{b^k}{a}\right)^i = \frac{(b^k/a)^{m+1} - 1}{b^k/a - 1}.$$

Substituting this result in Equation 14.11 and simplifying gives:

$$T(n) = a^m \left( \frac{(b^k/a)^{m+1} - 1}{b^k/a - 1} \right)$$

$$= a^m \left( \frac{(b^k/a)^m - a/b^k}{1 - a/b^k} \right)$$

$$= O(a^m (b^k/a)^m)$$

$$= O(b^{km})$$

$$= O(n^k).$$

**Summary**   For many divide-and-conquer algorithms the running time is given by the general recurrence shown in Equation 14.8. Solutions to the recurrence depend on the relative values of the constants $a$, $b$, and $k$. Specifically, the solutions satisfy the following bounds:

$$T(n) = \begin{cases} O(n^{\log_b a}) & a > b^k, \\ O(n^k \log_b n) & a = b^k, \\ O(n^k) & a < b^k. \end{cases} \tag{14.13}$$

Table 14.3 shows how to apply Equation 14.13 to find the running times of the divide-and-conquer algorithms described in the preceding sections. Comparing the solutions in Table 14.3 with those given in Table 14.2 shows that the results obtained using the general formula agree with the analyses done in the preceding sections.

### 14.3.5   Example—Matrix Multiplication

Consider the problem of computing the product of two matrices. That is, given two $n \times n$ matrices, $A$ and $B$, compute the $n \times n$ matrix $C = A \times B$, the elements of which are given by

$$c_{i,j} = \sum_{k=0}^{n-1} a_{i,k} b_{k,j}. \tag{14.14}$$

**TABLE 14.3**
Computing running times using Equation 14.13

| Program | Recurrence | $a$ | $b$ | $k$ | Case | Solution |
|---|---|---|---|---|---|---|
| Program 14.9 | $T(n) = T(n/2) + O(1)$ | 1 | 2 | 0 | $a = b^k$ | $O(n^0 \log_2 n)$ |
| Program 14.10 | $T(n) = 2T(n/2) + O(1)$ | 2 | 2 | 0 | $a > b^k$ | $O(n^{\log_2 2})$ |
| Program 14.11 | $T(n) = 2T(n/2) + O(n)$ | 2 | 2 | 1 | $a = b^k$ | $O(n^1 \log_2 n)$ |

Section 4.3.4 shows that the direct implementation of Equation 14.14 results in an $O(n^3)$ running time. In this section we show that the use of a divide-and-conquer strategy results in a slightly better asymptotic running time.

To implement a divide-and-conquer algorithm we must break the given problem into several subproblems that are similar to the original one. In this instance we view each of the $n \times n$ matrices as a $2 \times 2$ matrix, the elements of which are $(\frac{n}{2}) \times (\frac{n}{2})$ submatrices. Thus, the original matrix multiplication, $C = A \times B$, can be written as

$$\begin{bmatrix} C_{1,1} & C_{1,2} \\ C_{2,1} & C_{2,2} \end{bmatrix} = \begin{bmatrix} A_{1,1} & A_{1,2} \\ A_{2,1} & A_{2,2} \end{bmatrix} \times \begin{bmatrix} B_{1,1} & B_{1,2} \\ B_{2,1} & B_{2,2} \end{bmatrix},$$

where each $A_{i,j}$, $B_{i,j}$ and $C_{i,j}$ is an $(\frac{n}{2}) \times (\frac{n}{2})$ matrix.

From Equation 14.14 we get that the result submatrices can be computed as follows:

$$C_{1,1} = A_{1,1} \times B_{1,1} + A_{1,2} \times B_{2,1}$$
$$C_{1,2} = A_{1,1} \times B_{1,2} + A_{1,2} \times B_{2,2}$$
$$C_{2,1} = A_{2,1} \times B_{1,1} + A_{2,2} \times B_{2,1}$$
$$C_{2,2} = A_{2,1} \times B_{1,2} + A_{2,2} \times B_{2,2}.$$

Here the symbols $+$ and $\times$ are taken to mean addition and multiplication (respectively) of $(\frac{n}{2}) \times (\frac{n}{2})$ matrices.

In order to compute the original $n \times n$ matrix multiplication we must compute eight $(\frac{n}{2}) \times (\frac{n}{2})$ matrix products (*divide*) followed by four $(\frac{n}{2}) \times (\frac{n}{2})$ matrix sums (*conquer*). Since matrix addition is an $O(n^2)$ operation, the total running time for the multiplication operation is given by the recurrence

$$T(n) = \begin{cases} O(1) & n = 1, \\ 8T(n/2) + O(n^2) & n > 1. \end{cases} \tag{14.15}$$

Note that Equation 14.15 is an instance of the general recurrence given in Equation 14.8. In this case, $a = 8$, $b = 2$, and $k = 2$. We can obtain the solution directly from Equation 14.13. Since $a > b^k$, the total running time is $O(n^{\log_b a}) = O(n^{\log_2 8}) = O(n^3)$. But this is no better than the original, direct algorithm!

Fortunately, it turns out that one of the eight matrix multiplications is redundant. Consider the following series of seven $(\frac{n}{2}) \times (\frac{n}{2})$ matrices:

$$M_0 = (A_{1,1} + A_{2,2}) \times (B_{1,1} + B_{2,2})$$
$$M_1 = (A_{1,2} - A_{2,2}) \times (B_{2,1} + B_{2,2})$$
$$M_2 = (A_{1,1} - A_{2,1}) \times (B_{1,1} + B_{1,2})$$
$$M_3 = (A_{1,1} + A_{1,2}) \times B_{2,2}$$
$$M_4 = A_{1,1} \times (B_{1,2} - B_{2,2})$$
$$M_5 = A_{2,2} \times (B_{2,1} - B_{1,1})$$
$$M_6 = (A_{2,1} + A_{2,2}) \times B_{1,1}$$

Each equation above has only one multiplication. Ten additions and seven multiplications are required to compute $M_0$ through $M_6$. Given $M_0$ through $M_6$, we can compute the elements of the product matrix $C$ as follows:

$$
\begin{aligned}
C_{1,1} &= M_0 + M_1 - M_3 + M_5 \\
C_{1,2} &= M_3 + M_4 \\
C_{2,1} &= M_5 + M_6 \\
C_{2,2} &= M_0 - M_2 + M_4 - M_6
\end{aligned}
$$

Altogether this approach requires seven $(\frac{n}{2}) \times (\frac{n}{2})$ matrix multiplications and $18 (\frac{n}{2}) \times (\frac{n}{2})$ additions. Therefore, the worst-case running time is given by the following recurrence:

$$
T(n) = \begin{cases} O(1) & n = 1, \\ 7T(n/2) + O(n^2) & n > 1. \end{cases} \tag{14.16}
$$

As above, Equation 14.16 is an instance of the general recurrence given in Equation 14.8, and we obtain the solution directly from Equation 14.13. In this case, $a = 7$, $b = 2$, and $k = 2$. Therefore, $a > b^k$, and the total running time is

$$
O(n^{\log_b a}) = O(n^{\log_2 7}).
$$

Note $\log_2 7 \approx 2.807\,355$. Consequently, the running time of the divide-and-conquer matrix multiplication strategy is $O(n^{2.8})$ which is better (asymptotically) than the straightforward $O(n^3)$ approach.

# 14.4 Bottom-Up Algorithms: Dynamic Programming

In this section we consider a bottom-up algorithmic paradigm called *dynamic programming*. In order to solve a given problem, a series of subproblems is solved. The series of subproblems is devised carefully in such a way that each subsequent solution is obtained by combining the solutions to one or more of the subproblems that have already been solved. All intermediate solutions are kept in a table in order to prevent unnecessary duplication of effort.

## 14.4.1 Example—Generalized Fibonacci Numbers

Consider the problem of computing the *generalized Fibonacci numbers*. The generalized Fibonacci numbers of order $k \geq 2$ are given by

$$
F_n^{(k)} = \begin{cases} 0 & 0 \leq n < k - 1, \\ 1 & n = k - 1, \\ \sum_{i=1}^{k} F_{n-i}^{(k)} & n \geq k. \end{cases} \tag{14.17}
$$

Notice that the "normal" Fibonacci numbers considered in Section 3.4.3 are the same as the generalized Fibonacci numbers of order 2.

If we write a recursive function that implements directly Equation 14.17, we get an algorithm with exponential running time. For example, in Section 3.4.3 it is shown that the time to compute the second-order Fibonacci numbers is $T(n) = \Omega((3/2)^n)$.

The problem with the direct recursive implementation is that it does far more work than is needed because it solves the same subproblem many times. For example, to compute $F_{10}^{(2)}$ it is necessary to compute both $F_9^{(2)}$ and $F_8^{(2)}$. However, in computing $F_9^{(2)}$ it is also necessary to compute $F_8^{(2)}$, and so on.

An alternative to the top-down recursive implementation is to do the calculation from the bottom up. In order to do this we compute the series of sequences

$$
\begin{aligned}
S_0 &= \{F_0^{(k)}\} \\
S_1 &= \{F_0^{(k)}, F_1^{(k)}\} \\
&\;\;\vdots \\
S_n &= \{F_0^{(k)}, F_1^{(k)}, \ldots, F_n^{(k)}\}.
\end{aligned}
$$

Notice that we can compute $S_{i+1}$ from the information contained in $S_i$ simply by using Equation 14.17.

---

**PROGRAM 14.12**
Dynamic programming example—computing generalized Fibonacci numbers

```
1   unsigned int Fibonacci (unsigned int n, unsigned int k)
2   {
3       if (n < k - 1U)
4           return 0;
5       else if (n == k - 1U)
6           return 1;
7       else
8       {
9           Array<unsigned int> f (n + 1);
10          for (unsigned int i = 0; i < k - 1U; ++i)
11              f [i] = 0;
12          f [k - 1U] = 1;
13          for (unsigned int i = k; i <= n; ++i)
14          {
15              unsigned int sum = 0;
16              for (unsigned int j = 1; j <= k; ++j)
17                  sum += f [i - j];
18              f [i] = sum;
19          }
20          return f [n];
21      }
22  }
```

Program 14.12 defines the function **Fibonacci** which takes two integer arguments $n$ and $k$ and computes the $n$th Fibonacci number of order $k$ using the approach described above. This algorithm uses an array to represent the series of sequences $S_0, S_1, \ldots, S_n$. As each subsequent Fibonacci number is computed it is added to the end of the array.

The worst-case running time of the **Fibonacci** routine given in Program 14.12 is a function of both $n$ and $k$:

$$T(n, k) = \begin{cases} O(1) & 0 \le n < k, \\ O(kn) & n \ge k. \end{cases}$$

## 14.4.2   Example—Computing Binomial Coefficients

Consider the problem of computing the *binomial coefficient*

$$\binom{n}{m} = \frac{n!}{(n - m)!m!} \tag{14.18}$$

given non-negative integers $n$ and $m$ (see Theorem 11.7).

The problem with implementing directly Equation 14.18 is that the factorials grow quickly with increasing $n$ and $m$; for example, $13! = 6\,227\,020\,800 > 2^{32}$. Therefore, it is not possible to represent $n!$ for $n \ge 13$ using unsigned 32-bit integers. Nevertheless it is possible to represent the binomial coefficients $\binom{n}{m}$ up to $n = 34$ without overflowing, for example, $\binom{34}{17} = 2\,333\,606\,220 < 2^{32}$.

Consider the following *recursive* definition of the binomial coefficients:

$$\binom{n}{m} = \begin{cases} 1 & m = 0, \\ 1 & n = m, \\ \binom{n-1}{m} + \binom{n-1}{m-1} & \text{otherwise.} \end{cases} \tag{14.19}$$

This formulation does not require the computation of factorials. In fact, the only computation needed is addition.

If we implement Equation 14.19 directly as a recursive function, we get a routine whose running time is given by

$$T(n, m) = \begin{cases} O(1) & m = 0, \\ O(1) & n = m, \\ T(n - 1, m) + T(n - 1, m - 1) + O(1) & \text{otherwise.} \end{cases}$$

which is very similar to Equation 14.19. In fact, we can show that $T(n, m) = \Omega(\binom{n}{m})$ which (by Equation 14.18) is not a very good running time at all! Again the problem with the direct recursive implementation is that it does far more work than is needed because it solves the same subproblem many times.

An alternative to the top-down recursive implementation is to do the calculation from the bottom up. In order to do this we compute the series of sequences

$$S_0 = \left\{ \binom{0}{0} \right\}$$

$$S_1 = \left\{ \binom{1}{0}, \binom{1}{1} \right\}$$

$$S_2 = \left\{ \binom{2}{0}, \binom{2}{1}, \binom{2}{2} \right\}$$

$$\vdots$$

$$S_n = \left\{ \binom{n}{0}, \binom{n}{1}, \binom{n}{2}, \dots, \binom{n}{n} \right\}.$$

Notice that we can compute $S_{i+1}$ from the information contained in $S_i$ simply by using Equation 14.19. Table 14.4 shows the sequence in tabular form—the $i$th row of the table corresponds the sequence $S_i$. This tabular representation of the binomial coefficients is known as *Pascal's triangle*.[4]

Program 14.13 defines the function **Binom** which takes two integer arguments $n$ and $m$ and computes the binomial coefficient $\binom{n}{m}$ by computing Pascal's triangle. According to Equation 14.19, each subsequent row depends only on the preceding row—it is only necessary to keep track of one row of data. The implementation shown uses an array of length $n$ to represent a row of Pascal's triangle. Consequently, instead of a table of size $O(n^2)$, the algorithm gets by with $O(n)$ space. The implementation has been coded carefully so that the computation can be done in place. That is, the elements of $S_{i+1}$ are computed in reverse so that they can be written over the elements of $S_i$ that are no longer needed.

The worst-case running time of the **Binom** routine given in Program 14.13 is clearly $O(n^2)$.

**TABLE 14.4**
Pascal's Triangle

| $n$ | $\binom{n}{0}$ | $\binom{n}{1}$ | $\binom{n}{2}$ | $\binom{n}{3}$ | $\binom{n}{4}$ | $\binom{n}{5}$ | $\binom{n}{6}$ | $\binom{n}{7}$ |
|---|---|---|---|---|---|---|---|---|
| 0 | 1 | | | | | | | |
| 1 | 1 | 1 | | | | | | |
| 2 | 1 | 2 | 1 | | | | | |
| 3 | 1 | 3 | 3 | 1 | | | | |
| 4 | 1 | 4 | 16 | 4 | 1 | | | |
| 5 | 1 | 5 | 10 | 10 | 5 | 1 | | |
| 6 | 1 | 6 | 15 | 20 | 15 | 6 | 1 | |
| 7 | 1 | 7 | 21 | 35 | 35 | 21 | 7 | 1 |

---

[4]The table is named in honor of *Blaise Pascal*, who published a treatise on the subject in 1653.

---

**PROGRAM 14.13**
Dynamic programming example—computing binomial coefficients

---

```
1   unsigned int Binom (unsigned int n, unsigned int m)
2   {
3       Array<unsigned int> b (n + 1);
4       b [0] = 1;
5       for (unsigned int i = 1; i <= n; ++i)
6       {
7           b [i] = 1;
8           for (unsigned int j = i - 1U; j > 0; --j)
9               b [j] += b [j - 1U];
10      }
11      return b [m];
12  }
```

---

### 14.4.3 Application: Typesetting Problem

Consider the problem of typesetting a paragraph of justified text. A paragraph can be viewed as a sequence of $n > 0$ words, $\{w_1, w_2, \ldots, w_n\}$. The objective is to determine how to break the sequence into individual lines of text of the appropriate size. Each word is separated from the next by some amount of space. By stretching or compressing the space between the words, the left and right ends of consecutive lines of text are made to line up. A paragraph looks best when the amount of stretching or compressing is minimized.

We can formulate the problem as follows: Assume that we are given the lengths of the words $\{l_1, l_2, \ldots, l_n\}$, and that the desired length of a line is $D$. Let $W_{i,j}$ represent the sequence of words from $w_i$ to $w_j$ (inclusive), that is,

$$W_{i,j} = \{w_i, w_{i+1}, \ldots, w_j\},$$

for $1 \leq i \leq j \leq n$.

Let $L_{i,j}$ be the sum of the lengths of the words in the sequence $W_{i,j}$, that is,

$$L_{i,j} = \sum_{k=i}^{j} l_k.$$

The *natural length* for the sequence $W_{i,j}$ is the sum of the lengths of the words $L_{i,j}$ plus the normal amount of space between those words. Let $s$ be the normal size of the space between two words. Then the natural length of $W_{i,j}$ is $L_{i,j} + (j - i)s$. Note, we can also define $L_{i,j}$ *recursively* as follows:

$$L_{i,j} = \begin{cases} l_i & i = j, \\ L_{i,j-1} + l_j & i < j. \end{cases} \tag{14.20}$$

In general, when we typeset the sequence $W_{i,j}$ all on a single line, we need to stretch or compress the spaces between the words so that the length of the line is the desired length $D$. Therefore, the amount of stretching or compressing is given by the difference $D - (L_{i,j} + (j - i)s)$. However, if the sum of the lengths of the words, $L_{i,j}$, is longer than the desired line length $D$, it is not possible to typeset the sequence on a single line.

Let $P_{i,j}$ be the *penalty* associated with typesetting the sequence $L_{i,j}$ on a single line. Then,

$$P_{i,j} = \begin{cases} |D - L_{i,j} - (j - i)s| & D \geq L_{i,j}, \\ \infty & D < L_{i,j}. \end{cases} \qquad (14.21)$$

This definition of penalty is consistent with the stated objectives: The penalty increases as the difference between the natural length of the sequence and the desired length increases and the infinite penalty disallows lines that are too long.

Finally, we define the quantity $C_{i,j}$ for $1 \leq i \leq j \leq n$ as the minimum total penalty required to typeset the sequence $W_{i,j}$. In this case, the text may be all on one line or it may be split over more than one line. The quantity $C_{i,j}$ is given by

$$C_{i,j} = \begin{cases} P_{i,j} & i = j, \\ \min\left\{ P_{i,j}, \min_{i \leq k < j} (P_{i,k} + C_{k+1,j}) \right\} & \text{otherwise.} \end{cases} \qquad (14.22)$$

We obtain Equation 14.22 as follows: When $i = j$ there is only one word in the paragraph. The minimum total penalty associated with typesetting the paragraph in this case is just the penalty which results from putting the one word on a single line.

In the general case, there is more than one word in the sequence $W_{i,j}$. In order to determine the optimal way in which to typeset the paragraph we consider the cost of putting the first $k$ words of the sequence on the first line of the paragraph, $P_{i,k}$, plus the minimum total cost associated with typesetting the rest of the paragraph $C_{k+1,j}$. The value of $k$ which minimizes the total cost also specifies where the line break should occur.

## Example

Suppose we are given a sequence of $n = 5$ words, $W = \{w_1, w_2, w_3, w_4, w_5\}$ having lengths $\{10, 10, 10, 12, 50\}$, respectively, which are to be typeset in a paragraph of width $D - 60$. Assume that the normal width of an inter-word space is $s = 10$.

We begin by computing the lengths of all the subsequences of $W$ using Equation 14.20. The lengths of all $n(n - 1)/2$ subsequences of $W$ are tabulated in Table 14.5.

Given $L_{i,j}$, $D$ and $s$, it is a simple matter to apply Equation 14.21 to obtain the one-line penalties, $P_{i,j}$, which measure the amount of stretching or compressing needed to set all the words in a given subsequence on a single line. These are tabulated in Table 14.6.

Given the one-line penalties, $P_{i,j}$, we can use Equation 14.22 to find for each subsequence of $W$ the minimum total penalty, $C_{i,j}$, associated with forming a paragraph from the words in that subsequence. These are tabulated in Table 14.6.

**TABLE 14.5**
Typesetting Problem

| | | $L_{i,j}$ | | | | |
|---|---|---|---|---|---|---|
| $i$ | $l_i$ | $j = 1$ | 2 | 3 | 4 | 5 |
| 1 | 10 | 10 | 20 | 30 | 42 | 92 |
| 2 | 10 | | 10 | 20 | 32 | 82 |
| 3 | 10 | | | 10 | 22 | 72 |
| 4 | 12 | | | | 12 | 62 |
| 5 | 50 | | | | | 50 |

**TABLE 14.6**
Penalties

| | $P_{i,j}$ | | | | | $C_{i,j}$ | | | | |
|---|---|---|---|---|---|---|---|---|---|---|
| $i$ | $j = 1$ | 2 | 3 | 4 | 5 | $j = 1$ | 2 | 3 | 4 | 5 |
| 1 | 50 | 30 | 10 | 12 | $\infty$ | 50 | 30 | 10 | 12 | 22 |
| 2 | | 50 | 30 | 8 | $\infty$ | | 50 | 30 | 8 | 18 |
| 3 | | | 50 | 28 | $\infty$ | | | 50 | 28 | 38 |
| 4 | | | | 48 | $\infty$ | | | | 48 | 58 |
| 5 | | | | | 10 | | | | | 10 |

**FIGURE 14.3**
Typesetting a paragraph.

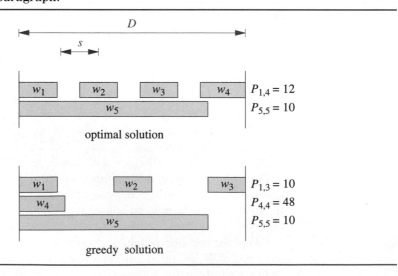

optimal solution

greedy solution

The $C_{1,5}$ entry in Table 14.6 gives the minimum total cost of typesetting the entire paragraph. The value 22 was obtained as follows:

$$
\begin{aligned}
C_{1,5} &= \min\{P_{1,1} + C_{2,5}, P_{1,2} + C_{3,5}, P_{1,3} + C_{4,5}, P_{1,4} + C_{5,5}, P_{1,5}\}\\
&= P_{1,4} + C_{5,5}\\
&= 12 + 10.
\end{aligned}
$$

This indicates that the optimal solution is to set words $w_1$, $w_2$, $w_3$, and $w_4$ on the first line of the paragraph and leave $w_5$ by itself on the last line of the paragraph. Figure 14.3 illustrates this result.

This formulation of the typesetting problem seems like overkill. Why not just type-set the lines of text one-by-one, minimizing the penalty for each line as we go? In other words why don't we just use a greedy strategy? Unfortunately, the obvious greedy solution strategy *does not work*!

For example, the greedy strategy begins by setting the first line of text. To do so it must decide how many words to put on that line. The obvious thing to do is select the value of $k$ for which $P_{1,k}$ is the smallest. From Table 14.6 we see that $P_{1,3} = 10$ has the smallest penalty. Therefore, the greedy approach puts three words on the first line, as shown in Figure 14.3.

Since the remaining two words do not both fit on a single line, they are set on separate lines. The total of the penalties for the paragraph typeset using the greedy algorithm is $P_{1,3} + P_{4,4} + P_{5,5} = 68$. Clearly, the solution is not optimal (nor is it very pleasing esthetically).

### Implementation

Program 14.14 defines the function **Typeset** which takes three arguments. The first, **l**, is an array of $n$ unsigned integers that gives the lengths of the words in the sequence to be typeset. The second, **D**, specifies the desired paragraph width and the third, **s**, specifies the normal inter-word space.

The routine first computes the lengths, $L_{i,j}$, of all possible subsequences (lines 5–11). This is done by using the dynamic programming paradigm to evaluate the recursive definition of $L_{i,j}$ given in Equation 14.20. The running time for this computation is clearly $O(n^2)$.

The next step computes the one-line penalties, $P_{i,j}$, as given by Equation 14.21 (lines 12–20). This calculation is straightforward, and its running time is also $O(n^2)$.

Finally, the minimum total costs, $C_{i,j}$, of typesetting each subsequence are determined for all possible subsequences (lines 21–26). Again we make use of the dynamic programming paradigm to evaluate the recursive definition of $C_{i,j}$ given in Equation 14.22. The running time for this computation is $O(n^3)$. As a result, the overall running time required to determine the best way to typeset a paragraph of $n$ words is $O(n^3)$.

## 14.5 Randomized Algorithms

In this section we discuss algorithms that behave randomly. By this we mean that there is an element of randomness in the way the algorithm solves a given problem. Of

**PROGRAM 14.14**
Dynamic programming example—typesetting a paragraph

```
1   void Typeset (Array<unsigned int> const& l,
2       unsigned int D, unsigned int s)
3   {
4       unsigned int const n = l.Length ();
5       Array2D<unsigned int> L (n, n);
6       for (unsigned int i = 0; i < n; ++i)
7       {
8           L [i][i] = l [i];
9           for (unsigned int j = i + 1; j < n; ++j)
10              L [i][j] = L [i][j - 1U] + l [j];
11      }
12      Array2D<unsigned int> P (n, n);
13      for (unsigned int i = 0; i < n; ++i)
14          for (unsigned int j = i; j < n; ++j)
15          {
16              if (L [i][j] < D)
17                  P [i][j] = abs (D - L [i][j] - (j - i) * s);
18              else
19                  P [i][j] = numeric_limits<unsigned int>::max ();
20          }
21      Array2D<unsigned int> C (n, n);
22      for (unsigned int j = 0; j < n; ++j)
23      {
24          C [j][j] = P [j][j];
25          for (int i = j - 1; i >= 0; --i)
26          {
27              unsigned int min = P [i][j];
28              for (unsigned int k = i; k < j; ++k)
29              {
30                  unsigned int const tmp = P [i][k] + C [k + 1][j];
31                  if (tmp < min)
32                      min = tmp;
33              }
34              C [i][j] = min;
35          }
36      }
37  }
```

course, if an algorithm is to be of any use, it must find a solution to the problem at hand, so it cannot really be completely random.

Randomized algorithms are said to be methods of last resort. This is because they are used often when no other feasible solution technique is known. For example, randomized methods are used to solve problems for which no closed-form, analytic solution is known. They are also used to solve problems for which the solution space is so large that an exhaustive search is infeasible.

To implement a randomized algorithm we require a source of randomness. The usual source of randomness is a random number generator. Therefore, before presenting randomized algorithms, we first consider the problem of computing random numbers.

## 14.5.1   Generating Random Numbers

In this section we consider the problem of generating a sequence of *random numbers* on a computer. Specifically, we desire an infinite sequence of statistically independent random numbers uniformly distributed between zero and 1. In practice, because the sequence is generated algorithmically using finite-precision arithmetic, it is neither infinite nor truly random. Instead, we say that an algorithm is "good enough" if the sequence it generates satisfies almost any statistical test of randomness. Such a sequence is said to be *pseudorandom*.

The most common algorithms for generating pseudorandom numbers are based on the *linear congruential* random number generator invented by Lehmer. Given a positive integer $m$ called the *modulus* and an initial *seed* value $X_0$ $(0 \leq X_0 < m)$, Lehmer's algorithm computes a sequence of integers between 0 and $m - 1$. The elements of the sequence are given by

$$X_{i+1} = (aX_i + c) \bmod m, \qquad (14.23)$$

where $a$ and $c$ are carefully chosen integers such that $2 \leq a < m$ and $0 \leq c < m$.

For example, the parameters $a = 13$, $c = 1$, $m = 16$, and $X_0 = 0$ produce the sequence

$$0, 1, 14, 7, 12, 13, 10, 3, 8, 9, 6, 15, 4, 5, 2, 11, 0, \ldots$$

The first $m$ elements of this sequence are distinct and appear to have been drawn at random from the set $\{0, 1, 2 \ldots, 15\}$. However, since $X_m = X_0$ the sequence is cyclic with *period m*.

Notice that the elements of the sequence alternate between odd and even integers. This follows directly from Equation 14.23 and the fact that $m = 16$ is a multiple of 2. Similar patterns arise when we consider the elements as binary numbers:

$$0000, 0001, 1110, 0111, 1100, 1101, 1010, 0011, 1000, \ldots$$

The least significant two bits are cyclic with period 4 and the least significant three bits are cyclic with period 8! (These patterns arise because $m = 16$ is also a multiple of 4 and 8). The existence of such patterns make the sequence *less random*. This suggests that the best choice for the modulus $m$ is a prime number.

Not all parameter values result in a period of $m$. For example, changing the multiplier $a$ to 11 produces the sequence

$$0, 1, 12, 5, 8, 9, 4, 13, 0, \ldots$$

the period of which is only $m/2$. In general because each subsequent element of the sequence is determined solely from its predecessor and because there are $m$ possible values, the longest possible period is $m$. Such a generator is called a *full period* generator.

In practice, the *increment c* is often set to zero. In this case, Equation 14.23 becomes

$$X_{i+1} = aX_i \bmod m. \tag{14.24}$$

This is called a *multiplicative linear congruential* random number generator. (For $c \neq 0$ it is called a *mixed linear congruential* generator).

In order to prevent the sequence generated by Equation 14.24 from collapsing to zero, the modulus $m$ must be prime and $X_0$ cannot be zero. For example, the parameters $a = 6$, $m = 13$, and $X_0 = 1$ produce the sequence

$$1, 6, 10, 8, 9, 2, 12, 7, 3, 5, 4, 11, 1, \ldots$$

Notice that the first 12 elements of the sequence are distinct. Since a multiplicative congruential generator can never produce a zero, the maximum possible period is $m - 1$. Therefore, this is a full period generator.

As the final step of the process, the elements of the sequence are *normalized* by division by the modulus:

$$U_i = X_i/m.$$

In so doing, we obtain a sequence of random numbers that fall between zero and 1. Specifically, a mixed congruential generator ($c \neq 0$) produces numbers in the interval $[0, 1)$, whereas a multiplicative congruential generator ($c = 0$) produces numbers in the interval $(0, 1)$.

### The Minimal Standard Random Number Generator

A great deal of research has gone into the question of finding an appropriate set of parameters to use in Lehmer's algorithm. A good generator has the following characteristics:

- It is a *full period* generator.
- The generated sequence passes statistical tests of *randomness*.
- The generator can be implemented efficiently using 32-bit integer arithmetic.

The choice of modulus depends on the arithmetic precision used to implement the algorithm. A signed 32-bit integer can represent values between $-2^{31}$ and $2^{31} - 1$.

Fortunately, the quantity $2^{31} - 1 = 2\,147\,483\,647$ is a prime number![5] Therefore, it is an excellent choice for the modulus $m$.

Because Equation 14.24 is slightly simpler than Equation 14.23, we choose to implement a multiplicative congruential generator ($c = 0$). The choice of a suitable multiplier is more difficult. However, a popular choice is $a = 16\,807$ because it satisfies all three criteria given above: It results in a full-period random number generator; the generated sequence passes a wide variety of statistical tests for randomness; and it is possible to compute Equation 14.24 using 32-bit arithmetic without overflow.

The algorithm is derived as follows: First, let $q = m$ div $a$ and $r = m$ mod $a$.[6] In this case, $q = 127\,773$, $r = 2\,836$, and $r < q$.

Next, we rewrite Equation 14.24 as follows:

$$
\begin{aligned}
X_{i+1} &= aX_i \bmod m \\
&= aX_i - m(aX_i \operatorname{div} m) \\
&= aX_i - m(X_i \operatorname{div} q) + m(X_i \operatorname{div} q - aX_i \operatorname{div} m).
\end{aligned}
$$

This somewhat complicated formula can be simplified if we let $\delta(X_i) = X_i \operatorname{div} q - aX_i \operatorname{div} m$:

$$
\begin{aligned}
X_{i+1} &= aX_i - m(X_i \operatorname{div} q) + m\delta(X_i) \\
&= a\big(q(X_i \operatorname{div} q) + X_i \bmod q\big) - m(X_i \operatorname{div} q) + m\delta(X_i) \\
&= a(X_i \bmod q) + (aq - m)(X_i \operatorname{div} q) + m\delta(X_i).
\end{aligned}
$$

Finally, we make use of the fact that $m = aq - r$ to get

$$
X_{i+1} = a(X_i \bmod q) - r(X_i \operatorname{div} q) + m\delta(X_i). \tag{14.25}
$$

Equation 14.25 has several nice properties: Both $a(X_i \bmod q)$ and $r(X_i \operatorname{div} q)$ are positive integers between 0 and $m - 1$. Therefore, the difference $(X_i \bmod q) - r(X_i \operatorname{div} q)$ can be represented using a signed 32-bit integer without overflow. Finally, $\delta(X_i)$ is either a zero or a 1. Specifically, it is zero when the sum of the first two terms in Equation 14.25 is positive and it is 1 when the sum is negative. As a result, it is not necessary to compute $\delta(X_i)$—a simple test suffices to determine whether the third term is 0 or $m$.

### Implementation
We now describe the implementation of a random number generator based on Equation 14.25. Program 14.15 defines the **RandomNumberGenerator** class. This class has only *static members*. Because there can only be one instance of a static data member, the implementation of the **RandomNumberGenerator** class follows the *singleton* design pattern.

---

[5] Prime numbers of the form $2^p - 1$ are known as *Mersenne primes*.
[6] For convenience, we use the notation $m$ div $a$ to denote $\lfloor m/a \rfloor$.

**PROGRAM 14.15**
RandomNumberGenerator class definition

```
1   class RandomNumberGenerator
2   {
3   private:
4       static long int seed;
5       static long int const a;
6       static long int const m;
7       static long int const q;
8       static long int const r;
9   public:
10      static void SetSeed (long int);
11      static double Next ();
12  };
```

**PROGRAM 14.16**
RandomNumberGenerator class SetSeed and Next member function definitions

```
1   long int RandomNumberGenerator::seed = 1L;
2   long int const RandomNumberGenerator::a = 16807L;
3   long int const RandomNumberGenerator::m = 2147483647L;
4   long int const RandomNumberGenerator::q = 127773L;
5   long int const RandomNumberGenerator::r = 2836L;
6
7   void RandomNumberGenerator::SetSeed (long int s)
8   {
9       if (s < 1 || s >= m)
10          throw invalid_argument ("invalid seed");
11      seed = s;
12  }
13
14  double RandomNumberGenerator::Next ()
15  {
16      seed = a * (seed % q) - r * (seed / q);
17      if (seed < 0)
18          seed += m;
19      return (double) seed / (double) m;
20  }
```

Program 14.16 gives the implementation of the **RandomNumberGenerator** class. The **SetSeed** function is used to specify the initial seed, $X_0$. The seed must fall between 0 and $m - 1$. If it does not, an exception is thrown.

The **Next** function generates the elements of the random sequence. Each subsequent call returns the next element of the sequence. The implementation follows directly from Equation 14.25. Notice that the return value is normalized. Therefore, the values computed by the **Next** function are uniformly distributed on the interval $(0, 1)$.

## 14.5.2 Random Variables

In this section we introduce the notion of an abstract *random variable*. In this context, a random variable is an object that behaves like a random number generator in that it produces a pseudorandom number sequence. The distribution of the values produced depends on the class of random variable used.

Program 14.17 declares several random variable classes. The abstract **RandomVariable** class defines the shared interface. A single, pure virtual member function is declared—**Sample**. Given an instance, say **rv**, of a concrete class derived from **RandomVariable**, repeated calls of the form

```
rv.Sample ();
```

are expected to return successive elements of a pseudorandom sequence.

Program 14.17 also declares three concrete random variable classes:

**SimpleRV** This class generates random numbers uniformly distributed in the interval $(0, 1)$. (It is merely a wrapper for the **RandomNumberGenerator** defined in the preceding section.)

**UniformRV** This class generates random numbers which are uniformly distributed in an arbitrary interval $(u, v)$, where $u < v$. The parameters $u$ and $v$ are specified in the constructor.

**ExponentialRV** This class generates exponentially distributed random numbers with a mean value of $\mu$. The mean value $\mu$ is specified in the constructor.

### Implementation

Program 14.18 gives the implementations for the three concrete random variable classes declared in Program 14.17.

The implementation of the **SimpleRV** class is trivial because the **RandomNumberGenerator** class generates the desired distribution of random numbers. Consequently, the **SimpleRV::Sample** function simply calls **RandomNumberGenerator::Next**.

The **UniformRV** class is also quite simple. Given that the **RandomNumberGenerator** class generates a sequence random numbers $U_i$ uniformly distributed on the interval $(0, 1)$, the linear transformation

$$V_i = u + (v - u)U_i$$

**PROGRAM 14.17**
RandomVariable, SimpleRV, UniformRV, and ExponentialRV class definitions

```
1   class RandomVariable
2   {
3   public:
4       virtual double Sample () = 0;
5   };
6
7   class SimpleRV : public RandomVariable
8   {
9   public:
10      double Sample ();
11  };
12
13  class UniformRV : public RandomVariable
14  {
15      double u;
16      double v;
17  public:
18      UniformRV (double _u, double _v) : u (_u), v (_v) {}
19      double Sample ();
20  };
21
22  class ExponentialRV : public RandomVariable
23  {
24      double mu;
25  public:
26      ExponentialRV (double _mu) : mu (_mu) {}
27      double Sample ();
28  };
```

**PROGRAM 14.18**
SimpleRV, UniformRV, and ExponentialRV member function definitions

```
1   double SimpleRV::Sample ()
2       { return RandomNumberGenerator::Next (); }
3
4   double UniformRV::Sample ()
5       { return u + (v - u) * RandomNumberGenerator::Next (); }
6
7   double ExponentialRV::Sample ()
8       { return -mu * std::log (RandomNumberGenerator::Next ()); }
```

suffices to produce a sequence of random numbers $V_i$ uniformly distributed on the interval $(u, v)$.

The `ExponentialRV` class generates a sequence of random numbers, $X_i$, *exponentially distributed* on the interval $(0, \infty)$ and having a mean value $\mu$. The numbers are said to be *exponentially distributed* because the probability that $X_i$ falls between 0 and $z$ is given by

$$P[0 < X_i < z] = \int_0^z p(x)dx,$$

where $p(x) = \frac{1}{\mu}e^{-x/\mu}$. The function $p(x)$ is called the *probability density function*. Thus,

$$P[0 < X_i < z] = \int_0^z \frac{1}{\mu}e^{-x/\mu}dx$$
$$= 1 - e^{-z/\mu}.$$

Notice that $P[0 < X_i < z]$ is a value between zero and 1. Therefore, given a random variable, $U_i$, uniformly distributed between zero and 1, we can obtain an exponentially distributed variable $X_i$ as follows:

$$U_i = 1 - e^{X_i/\mu} \Rightarrow X_i = -\mu \ln(U_i - 1)$$
$$= X_i = -\mu \ln(U_i'), \quad U_i' = U_i \quad 1 \tag{14.26}$$

Note, if $U_i$ is uniformly distributed on $(0, 1)$, then so too is $U_i'$. The implementation of the `ExponentialRV::Sample` function follows directly from Equation 14.26.

### 14.5.3 Monte Carlo Methods

In this section we consider a method for solving problems using random numbers. The method exploits the statistical properties of random numbers in order to ensure that the correct result is computed in the same way that a gambling casino sets the betting odds in order to ensure that the "house" will always make a profit. For this reason, the problem-solving technique is called a *Monte Carlo method*.

To solve a given problem using a Monte Carlo method we devise an experiment in such a way that the solution to the original problem can be obtained from the experimental results. The experiment typically consists of a series of random trials. A random number generator such as the one given in the preceding section is used to create the series of trials.

The accuracy of the final result usually depends on the number of trials conducted. That is, the accuracy usually increases with the number of trials. This trade-off between the accuracy of the result and the time taken to compute it is an extremely useful characteristic of Monte Carlo methods. If only an approximate solution is required, then a Monte Carlo method can be very fast.

**FIGURE 14.4**
Illustration of a Monte Carlo method for computing $\pi$.

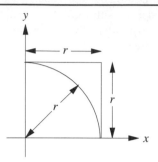

## Example—Computing $\pi$

This section presents a simple, Monte Carlo algorithm to compute the value of $\pi$ from a sequence of random numbers. Consider a square positioned in the *x-y* plane with its bottom left corner at the origin as shown in Figure 14.4. The area of the square is $r^2$, where *r* is the length of its sides. A quarter circle is inscribed within the square. Its radius is *r*, and its center is at the origin of *x-y* plane. The area of the quarter circle is $\pi r^2/4$.

Suppose we select a large number of points at random inside the square. Some fraction of these points will also lie inside the quarter circle. If the selected points are uniformly distributed, we expect the fraction of points in the quarter circle to be

$$ f = \frac{\pi r^2/4}{r^2} = \frac{\pi}{4}. $$

**PROGRAM 14.19**
Monte Carlo program to compute $\pi$

```
double Pi (unsigned int trials)
{
    unsigned int hits = 0;
    for (unsigned int i = 0; i < trials; ++i)
    {
        double const x = RandomNumberGenerator::Next ();
        double const y = RandomNumberGenerator::Next ();
        if (x * x + y * y < 1.0)
            ++hits;
    }
    return 4.0 * hits / trials;
}
```

Therefore, by measuring $f$, we can compute $\pi$. Program 14.19 shows how this can be done.

The `Pi` routine uses the `RandomNumberGenerator` defined to generate $(x, y)$ pairs uniformly distributed on the unit square ($r = 1$). Each point is tested to see if it falls inside the quarter circle. A given point is inside the circle when its distance from the origin, $\sqrt{x^2 + y^2}$, is less than $r$. In this case since $r = 1$, we simply test whether $x^2 + y^2 < 1$.

How well does Program 14.19 work? When 1,000 trials are conducted, 792 points are found to lie inside the circle. This gives the value of 3.168 for $\pi$, which is only 0.8% too large. When $10^8$ trials are conducted, 78 535 956 points are found to lie inside the circle. In this case, we get $\pi \approx 3.141\,438\,24$ which is within 0.005% of the correct value!

### 14.5.4 Simulated Annealing

Despite its name, *simulated annealing* has nothing to do either with simulation or annealing. Simulated annealing is a problem solving technique based loosely on the way in which a metal is annealed in order to increase its strength. When a heated metal is cooled very slowly, it freezes into a regular (minimum-energy) crystalline structure.

A simulated annealing algorithm searches for the optimum solution to a given problem in an analogous way. Specifically, it moves about randomly in the solution space looking for a solution that minimizes the value of some objective function. Because it is generated randomly, a given move may cause the objective function to increase, to decrease, or to remain unchanged.

A simulated annealing algorithm always accepts moves that *decrease* the value of the objective function. Moves that *increase* the value of the objective function are accepted with probability

$$p = e^{\Delta/T},$$

where $\Delta$ is the change in the value of the objective function and $T$ is a control parameter called the *temperature*. That is, a random number generator that generates numbers distributed uniformly on the interval $(0, 1)$ is sampled, and if the sample is less than $p$, the move is accepted.

By analogy with the physical process, the temperature $T$ is initially high; therefore, the probability of accepting a move that increases the objective function is initially high. The temperature is gradually decreased as the search progresses, that is, the system is *cooled* slowly. In the end, the probability of accepting a move that increases the objective function becomes vanishingly small. In general, the temperature is lowered in accordance with an *annealing schedule*.

The most commonly used annealing schedule is called *exponential cooling*. Exponential cooling begins at some initial temperature, $T_0$, and decreases the temperature in steps according to $T_{k+1} = \alpha T_k$, where $0 < \alpha < 1$. Typically, a fixed number of moves must be accepted at each temperature before proceeding to the next. The algorithm terminates either when the temperature reaches some final value, $T_f$, or when some other stopping criterion has been met.

The choice of suitable values for $\alpha$, $T_0$, and $T_f$ is highly problem dependent. However, empirical evidence suggests that a good value for $\alpha$ is 0.95 and that $T_0$ should be chosen so that the initial acceptance probability is 0.8. The search is terminated typically after some fixed, total number of solutions has been considered.

Finally, there is the question of selecting the initial solution from which to begin the search. A key requirement is that it be generated quickly. Therefore, the initial solution is generated typically at random. However, sometimes the initial solution can be generated by some other means such as with a greedy algorithm.

### Example—Balancing Scales

Consider again the *scales balancing problem* described in Section 14.2.1. That is, we are given a set of $n$ weights, $\{w_1, w_2, \ldots, w_n\}$, which are to be placed on a pair of scales in the way that minimizes the difference between the total weight in each pan. Feasible solutions to the problem all have the form $X = \{x_1, x_2, \ldots, x_n\}$, where

$$x_i = \begin{cases} 0 & w_i \text{ is placed in the left pan,} \\ 1 & w_i \text{ is placed in the right pan.} \end{cases}$$

To solve this problem using simulated annealing, we need a strategy for generating random moves. The move generator should make small, random changes to the current solution, and it must ensure that all possible solutions can be reached. A simple approach is to use the formula

$$X_{i+1} = X_i \oplus U$$

where $X_i$ is the initial solution, $X_{i+1}$ is a new solution, $U = \{u_1, u_2, \ldots, u_n\}$ is a sequence of zeroes and ones generated randomly, and $\oplus$ denotes element-wise addition modulo 2.

## Exercises

**14.1** Consider the greedy strategy for counting out change given in Section 14.1.1. Let $\{d_1, d_2, \ldots, d_n\}$ be the set of available denominations. For example, the set $\{1, 5, 10, 25, 100, 200\}$ represents the denominations of the commonly circulated Canadian coins. What condition(s) must the set of denominations satisfy to ensure the greedy algorithm always finds an optimal solution?

**14.2** Devise a greedy algorithm to solve optimally the scales balancing problem described in Section 14.2.1.

**a.** Does your algorithm always find the optimal solution?

**b.** What is the running time of your algorithm?

**14.3**  Consider the following 0/1-knapsack problem:

| $i$ | $w_i$ | $p_i$ |
|---|---|---|
| 1 | 10 | 10 |
| 2 | 6 | 6 |
| 3 | 3 | 4 |
| 4 | 8 | 9 |
| 5 | 1 | 3 |

$C = 18$

**a.**  Solve the problem using the greedy by profit, greedy by weight, and greedy by profit density strategies.

**b.**  What is the optimal solution?

**14.4**  Consider the breadth-first solver shown in Program 14.7. Suppose we replace the queue (line 3) with a *priority queue*.

**a.**  How should the solutions in the priority queue be prioritized?

**b.**  What possible benefit might there be from using a priority queue rather than a FIFO queue?

**14.5**  Repeat Exercise 14.4, but this time consider what happens if we replace the queue with a *LIFO stack*.

**14.6**  Repeat Exercises 14.4 and 14.5, but this time consider a *branch-and-bound* breadth-first solver.

**14.7**  (This question should be attempted *after* reading Chapter 16). For some problems the solution space is more naturally a graph rather than a tree.

**a.**  What problem arises if we use the `DepthFirstSolver` given in Program 14.5 to explore a search space that is not a tree.

**b.**  Modify the `DepthFirstSolver` so that it explores a solution space that is not a tree. **Hint**: See Program 16.7.

**c.**  What problem arises if we use the `BreadthFirstSolver` given in Program 14.7 to explore a search space that is not a tree.

**d.**  Modify the `BreadthFirstSolver` so that it explores a solution space that is not a tree. **Hint**: See Program 16.8.

**14.8**  Devise a backtracking algorithm to solve the *N-queens problem*: Given an $N \times N$ chess board, find a way to place $N$ queens on the board in such a way that no queen can take another.

**14.9**  Consider a binary search tree that contains $n$ keys, $k_1, k_2, \ldots, k_n$, at depths $d_1$, $d_2, \ldots, d_n$, respectively. Suppose the tree will be subjected to a large number of **Find** operations. Let $p_i$ be the probability that we access key $k_i$. Suppose we know *a priori* all the access probabilities. Then we can say that the *optimal* *binary search tree* is the tree which minimizes the quantity

$$\sum_{i=1}^{n} p_i(d_i + 1).$$

**a.** Devise a dynamic programming algorithm that, given the access probabilities, determines the optimal binary search tree.

**b.** What is the running time of your algorithm?

**Hint**: Let $C_{i,j}$ be the *cost* of the optimal binary search tree that contains the set of keys $\{k_i, k_{i+1}, k_{i+2}, \ldots, k_j\}$ where $i \leq j$. Show that

$$C_{i,j} = \begin{cases} p_i & i = j, \\ \min_{i \leq k \leq j}\{C_{i,k-1} + C_{k+1,j} + \sum_{l=i}^{j} p_l\} & i < j. \end{cases}$$

**14.10** Consider the typesetting problem discussed in Section 14.4.3. The objective is to determine how to break a given sequence of words into lines of text of the appropriate size. This was done either by stretching or compressing the space between the words. Explain why the greedy strategy always finds the optimal solution if we stretch but do not compress the space between words.

**14.11** Consider two complex numbers, $a + bi$ and $c + di$. Show that we can compute the product $(ac - bd) + (ad + bc)i$ with only three multiplications.

**14.12** Devise a divide-and-conquer strategy to find the root of a polynomial. For example, given a polynomial such as $p(x) = 2x^2 + 3x - 4$, and an interval $[u, v]$, such that $\exists r : u \leq r \leq v$ such that $\forall x : u \leq x \leq r, p(x) \leq 0$ and $\forall x : r \leq x \leq v, p(x) \geq 0$, find $r$.

**14.13** Devise an algorithm to compute a *normally distributed random variable*. A normal distribution is complete defined by its mean and standard deviation. The probability density function for a normal distribution is

$$p(x) = \frac{1}{\sigma\sqrt{2\pi}} \exp\left(-\frac{1}{2\sigma^2}(x - \mu)^2\right),$$

where $\mu$ is the mean and $\sigma$ is the standard deviation of the distribution. **Hint**: Consider the *central limit theorem*.

**14.14** Devise an algorithm to compute a *geometrically distributed random variable*. A geometrically distributed random variable is an integer in the interval $[1, \infty)$ given by the probability density function

$$P[X = i] = \theta(1 - \theta)^{i-1},$$

where $\theta^{-1}$ is the mean of the distribution. **Hint**: Use the fact $P[X = i] = P[i - 1 < Z \leq i]$, where $Z$ is an exponentially distributed random variable with mean $\mu = -1/\ln(1 - \theta)$.

**14.15** Do Exercise 8.13.

# Programming Projects

**14.1** Design and implement a class derived from the abstract **Solution** class defined in Program 14.1 which represents the nodes of the solution space of a *0/1-knapsack problem* described in Section 14.1.2.

Devise a suitable representation for the state of a node and then implement the following member functions **IsFeasible**, **IsComplete**, **Objective**, **Bound**, **Clone**, and **Successors**. Note, the **Successors** function requires an iterator which enumerates all the successors of a given node.

   **a.** Use your class with the **DepthFirstSolver** defined in Program 14.5 to solve the problem given in Table 14.1.

   **b.** Use your class with the **BreadthFirstSolver** defined in Program 14.7 to solve the problem given in Table 14.1.

   **c.** Use your class with the **DepthFirstBranchAndBoundSolver** defined in Program 14.8 to solve the problem given in Table 14.1.

**14.2** Do Project 14.1 for the *change counting problem* described in Section 14.1.1.

**14.3** Do Project 14.1 for the *scales balancing problem* described in Section 14.2.1.

**14.4** Do Project 14.1 for the *N-queens problem* described in Exercise 14.8.

**14.5** Design and implement a **GreedySolver** class, along the lines of the **DepthFirstSolver** and **BreadthFirstSolver** classes, that conducts a greedy search of the solution space. To do this you will have to add a member function to the abstract **Solution** class:

```
class GreedySolution : public Solution
{
    virtual Solution& GreedySuccessor () const = 0;
};
```

**14.6** Design and implement a **SimulatedAnnealingSolver** class, along the lines of the **DepthFirstSolver** and **BreadthFirstSolver** classes, that implements the simulated annealing strategy described in Section 14.5.4. To do this you will have to add a member function to the abstract **Solution** class:

```
class SimulatedAnnealingSolution : public Solution
{
    virtual Solution& RandomSuccessor () const = 0;
};
```

**14.7** Design and implement a dynamic programming algorithm to solve the change counting problem. Your algorithm should always find the optimal solution—even when the greedy algorithm fails.

**14.8** Consider the divide-and-conquer strategy for matrix multiplication described in Section 14.3.5.

a. Rewrite the implementation of the multiplication operator, **operator***, of the **Matrix<T>** class declared in Program 4.22.

b. Compare the running time of your implementation with the $O(n^3)$ algorithm given in Program 4.23.

14.9 Consider random number generator that generates random numbers uniformly distributed between zero and one. Such a generator produces a sequence of random numbers $x_1, x_2, x_2, \ldots$. A common test of randomness evaluates the correlation between consecutive pairs of numbers in the sequence. One way to do this is to plot on a graph the points

$$(x_1, x_2), (x_2, x_3), (x_3, x_4), \ldots.$$

a. Write a program to compute the first 1000 pairs of numbers generated using the **UniformRV** declared in Program 14.16 and 14.18.

b. What conclusions can you draw from your results?

# 15 | Sorting Algorithms and Sorters

## 15.1 Basics

Consider an arbitrary sequence $S = \{s_1, s_2, s_3, \ldots, s_n\}$ comprised of of $n \geq 0$ elements drawn from some universal set $U$. The goal of *sorting* is to rearrange the elements of $S$ to produce a new sequence, say $S'$, in which the elements of $S$ appear *in order.*

But what does it mean for the elements of $S'$ to be *in order?* We shall assume that there is a relation, $<$, defined over the universe $U$. The relation $<$ must be a *total order,* which is defined as follows.

**Definition 15.1**
*A total order is a relation, say $<$, defined on the elements of some universal set $U$ with the following properties:*

1. *For all pairs of elements $(i, j) \in U \times U$, exactly one of the following is true: $i < j$, $i = j$, or $j < i$.*
   *(All elements are commensurate.)*
2. *For all triples $(i, j, k) \in U \times U \times U$, $i < j \wedge j < k \iff i < k$.*
   *(The relation $<$ is transitive.)*

In order to *sort* the elements of the sequence $S$, we determine the *permutation* $P = \{p_1, p_2, p_3, \ldots, p_n\}$ of the elements of $S$ such that

$$s_{p_1} \leq s_{p_2} \leq s_{p_3} \leq \cdots \leq s_{p_n}.$$

In practice, we are not interested in the permutation $P$, per se. Instead, our objective is to compute the sorted sequence $S' = \{s'_1, s'_2, s'_3, \ldots, s'_n\}$ in which $s'_i = s_{p_i}$ for $1 \leq i \leq n$.

Sometimes the sequence to be sorted, $S$, contains duplicates. That is, $\exists i, j : 1 \leq i < j \leq n$ such that $s_i = s_j$. In general when a sequence that contains duplicates is sorted, there is no guarantee that the duplicated elements retain their relative positions, that is, $s_i$ could appear either before or after $s_j$ in the sorted sequence $S'$. If duplicates retain their relative positions in the sorted sequence the sort is said to be *stable*. In order for $s_i$ and $s_j$ to retain their relative order in the sorted sequence, we require that $s'_{p_i}$ precedes $s'_{p_j}$ in $S'$. Therefore, the sort is stable if $p_i < p_j$.

## 15.2 Sorting and Sorters

The traditional way to implement a sorting algorithm is to write a function or procedure that sorts an array of data. This chapter presents an alternate, object-oriented approach that is based on the notion of an *abstract sorter*.

Think of a sorter as an abstract machine, the sole purpose of which is to sort arrays of data. A machine is an object. Therefore, it makes sense that we represent it as an instance of some class. The machine sorts data. Therefore, the class will have a member function, say **Sort**, which sorts an array of data.

Program 15.1 declares the abstract class template **Sorter<T>**. The public interface of this class consists of the single function **Sort**. This function takes as its lone argument a reference to an **Array<T>** instance and it sorts the data contained therein. We use the **Array<T>** class defined in Section 4.1 to represent the data to be sorted because all array subscript operations are bounds-checked and because we can determine the length of the array by calling the **Length** member function of the **Array<T>** class.

Program 15.1 also declares the member variable **n**, the static member function **Swap**, and the pure virtual function **DoSort**. Since **DoSort** is a pure virtual function, an implementation must be given in a derived class. Program 15.2 gives the implementations for **Sort** and **Swap**.

The **Sort** function does not sort the data itself. It is the **DoSort** routine, which is provided by a derived class, that does the actual sorting. The **Sort** routine merely sets things up for **DoSort**.

---

**PROGRAM 15.1**
Sorter class definition

---

```
1   template <class T>
2   class Sorter
3   {
4   protected:
5       unsigned int n;
6
7       static void Swap (T&, T&);
8       virtual void DoSort (Array<T>&) = 0;
9   public:
10      void Sort (Array<T>&);
11  };
```

---

**PROGRAM 15.2**
Sorter<T> class Swap and Sort member function definitions

```
1    template <class T>
2    void Sorter<T>::Swap (T& x, T& y)
3    {
4        T const tmp = x;
5        x = y;
6        y = tmp;
7    }
8
9    template <class T>
10   void Sorter<T>::Sort (Array<T>& array)
11   {
12       n = array.Length ();
13       if (n > 0)
14       {
15           unsigned int const tmp = array.Base ();
16           array.SetBase (0);
17           DoSort (array);
18           array.SetBase (tmp);
19       }
20   }
```

The Sort function takes a reference to an Array<T> instance which allows arbitrary array subscript ranges. For example, the first element of an array a is the one at position a[a.Base()]. However, in most cases it is easier to write the sorting algorithm for a fixed lower bound of, say, zero, For this reason, the Sort function sets the array base to zero. Of course, the caller does not expect the array base to be changed. Therefore, the Sort routine restores the original array base before it returns.

The Swap function is used to implement most of the sorting algorithms presented in this chapter. The swap function takes two references to objects of some type T, and exchanges the contents of these two objects. The exchange is done as a sequence of three assignments. Therefore, if a T instance can be assigned in constant time, the Swap routine runs in constant time.[1]

### Sorter Class Hierarchy
This chapter describes nine different sorting algorithms. These are organized into the following five categories:

- insertion sorts
- exchange sorts

---

[1]In this chapter we assume that $\mathcal{T}_{\langle \text{T::T(T\&)} \rangle} = O(1)$ and that $\mathcal{T}_{\langle \text{T::Compare(T\&,T\&)} \rangle} = O(1)$.

- selection sorts
- merge sorts
- distribution sorts.

As shown in Figure 15.1, the sorter classes have been arranged in a class hierarchy that reflects this classification scheme.

Program 15.3 defines five abstract sorter class templates: `InsertionSorter<T>`, `ExchangeSorter<T>`, `SelectionSorter<T>`, `MergeSorter<T>`, and

**FIGURE 15.1**
Sorter class hierarchy.

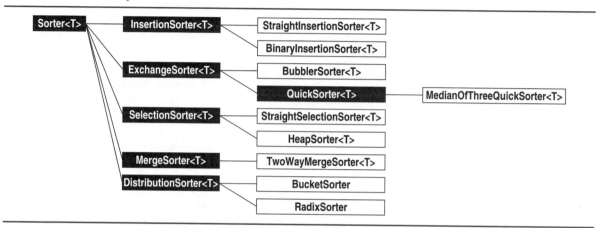

**PROGRAM 15.3**
Classes of sorters

```
1   template <class T>
2   class InsertionSorter : public Sorter<T> {};
3
4   template <class T>
5   class ExchangeSorter : public Sorter<T> {};
6
7   template <class T>
8   class SelectionSorter : public Sorter<T> {};
9
10  template <class T>
11  class MergeSorter : public Sorter<T> {};
12
13  template <class T>
14  class DistributionSorter : public Sorter<T> {};
```

`DistributionSorter<T>`. Notice that these classes are all trivial (i.e., empty) extensions of the `Sorter<T>` abstract base class.

## 15.3 Insertion Sorting

The first class of sorting algorithm that we consider comprises algorithms that *sort by insertion*. An algorithm that sorts by insertion takes the initial, unsorted sequence, $S = \{s_1, s_2, s_3, \dots, s_n\}$, and computes a series of *sorted* sequences $S_0', S_1', S_2', \dots, S_n'$, as follows:

1. The first sequence in the series, $S_0'$ is the empty sequence, that is, $S_0' = \{\}$.
2. Given a sequence $S_i'$ in the series, for $0 \leq i < n$, the next sequence in the series, $S_{i+1}'$, is obtained by inserting the $(i+1)$th element of the unsorted sequence $s_{i+1}$ into the correct position in $S_i'$.

Each sequence $S_i'$, $0 \leq i < n$, contains the first $i$ elements of the unsorted sequence $S$. Therefore, the final sequence in the series, $S_n'$, is the sorted sequence we seek, that is, $S' = S_n'$.

Figure 15.2 illustrates the insertion sorting algorithm. The figure shows the progression of the insertion sorting algorithm as it sorts an array of ten integers. The array is sorted *in place*. That is, the initial unsorted sequence, $S$, and the series of sorted sequences, $S_0', S_1', \dots$, occupy the same array.

In the $i$th step, the element at position $i$ in the array is inserted into the sorted sequence $S_i'$ which occupies array positions 0 to $(i-1)$. After this is done, array positions 0 to $i$ contain the $i+1$ elements of $S_{i+1}'$. Array positions $(i+1)$ to $(n-1)$ contain the remaining $n - i - 1$ elements of the unsorted sequence $S$.

As shown in Figure 15.2, the first step ($i = 0$) is trivial—inserting an element into the empty list involves no work. Altogether, $n - 1$ nontrivial insertions are required to sort a list of $n$ elements.

### 15.3.1 Straight Insertion Sort

The key step of any insertion sorting algorithm involves the insertion of an item into a sorted sequence. There are two aspects to an insertion—finding the correct position in the sequence at which to insert the new element and moving all the elements over to make room for the new one.

This section presents the *straight insertion sorting* algorithm. Straight insertion sorting uses a *linear search* to locate the position at which the next element is to be inserted.

#### Implementation
Program 15.4 defines the class template `StraightInsertionSorter<T>`. This class simply provides an implementation for the `DoSort` routine. `DoSort` takes one

**FIGURE 15.2**
Insertion sorting.

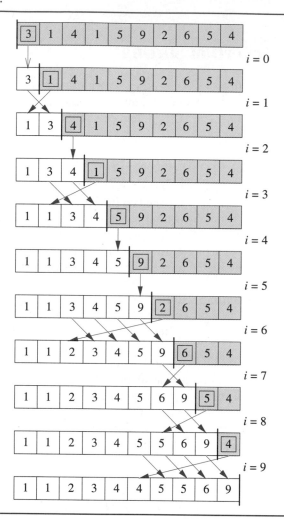

argument—a reference to an **Array<T>** instance. The array initially contains the data to be sorted. When the function returns, the contents of the array are sorted.

In order to determine the running time of the **DoSort** routine given in Program 15.4, we need to determine the number of iterations of the inner loop (lines 12–14). The number of iterations of the inner loop in the $i$th iteration of the outer loop depends on the positions of the values in the array. In the best case, the value in position $i$ of the array is larger than that in position $i - 1$ and zero iterations of the inner loop are done. In this case, the running time for insertion sort is $O(n)$. Notice that the best case performance occurs when we sort an array that is already sorted!

**PROGRAM 15.4**
`StraightInsertionSorter<T>` class `DoSort` member function definition

```
1   template <class T>
2   class StraightInsertionSorter : public InsertionSorter<T>
3   {
4   protected:
5       void DoSort (Array<T>&);
6   };
7
8   template <class T>
9   void StraightInsertionSorter<T>::DoSort (Array<T>& array)
10  {
11      for (unsigned int i = 1; i < n; ++i)
12          for (unsigned int j = i;
13              j > 0 && array [j - 1U] > array [j]; --j)
14              Swap (array [j], array [j - 1U]);
15  }
```

In the worst case, $i$ iterations of the inner loop are required in the $i$th iteration of the outer loop. This occurs when the value in position $i$ of the array is smaller than the values at positions 0 through $i - 1$. Therefore, the worst case arises when we sort an array in which the elements are initially sorted in reverse. In this case the running time for insertion sort is $O(n^2)$.

## 15.3.2 Average Running Time

The best-case running time of insertion sorting is $O(n)$ but the worst-case running time is $O(n^2)$. Therefore, we might suspect that the average running time falls somewhere in between. In order to determine it, we must define more precisely what we mean by the *average* running time. A simple definition of average running time is to say that it is the running time needed to sort the average sequence. But what is the average sequence?

The usual way to determine the average running time of a sorting algorithm is to consider only sequences that contain no duplicates. Since every sorted sequence of length $n$ is simply a permutation of an unsorted one, we can represent every such sequence by a permutation of the sequence $S = \{1, 2, 3, \ldots, n\}$. When computing the average running time, we assume that every permutation is equally likely. Therefore, the average running time of a sorting algorithm is the running time averaged over all permutations of the sequence $S$.

Consider a permutation $P = \{p_1, p_2, p_3, \ldots, p_n\}$ of the sequence $S$. An *inversion* in $P$ consists of two elements, say $p_i$ and $p_j$, such that $p_i > p_j$ but $i < j$. That is, an inversion in $P$ is a pair of elements that are in the wrong order. For example, the permutation $\{1, 4, 3, 2\}$ contains three inversions—(4, 3), (4, 2), and (3, 2). The following theorem tells us how many inversions we can expect in the average sequence:

**Theorem 15.1**

*The average number of inversions in a permutation of n distinct elements is n(n − 1)/4.*

**Proof** Let $S$ be an arbitrary sequence of $n$ distinct elements and let $S^R$ be the same sequence, but in reverse. For example, if $S = \{s_1, s_2, s_3, \ldots, s_n\}$, then $S^R = \{s_n, s_{n-1}, s_{n-2}, \ldots, s_1\}$.

Consider any pair of distinct elements in S, say $s_i$ and $s_j$ where $1 \leq i < j \leq n$. There are two distinct possibilities: (1) $s_i < s_j$, in which case $(s_j, s_i)$ is an inversion in $S^R$; or (2) $s_j < s_i$, in which case $(s_i, s_j)$ is an inversion in S. Therefore, every pair contributes exactly one inversion either to $S$ or to $S^R$.

The total number of pairs in S is $\binom{n}{2} = n(n - 1)/2$. Since every such pair contributes an inversion either to $S$ or to $S^R$, we expect *on average* that half of the inversions will appear in $S$. Therefore, the average number of inversions in a sequence of $n$ distinct elements is $n(n - 1)/4$.

---

What do inversions have to do with sorting? As a list is sorted, inversions are removed. In fact, since the inner loop of the insertion sort routine swaps *adjacent* array elements, inversions are removed *one at a time!* Since a swap takes constant time, and since the average number of inversions is $n(n - 1)/4$, the *average* running time for the insertion sort routine is $O(n^2)$.

## 15.3.3 Binary Insertion Sort

The straight insertion algorithm presented in the preceding section does a linear search to find the position in which to do the insertion. However, since the element is inserted into a sequence that is already sorted, we can use a binary search instead of a linear search. Whereas a linear search requires $O(n)$ comparisons in the worst case, a binary search only requires $O(\log n)$ comparisons. Therefore, if the cost of a comparison is significant, the binary search may be preferred.

Program 15.5 defines the **DoSort** routine of the **BinaryInsertionSorter<T>** class. The framework of this routine is essentially the same as that of the **Straight-InsertionSorter<T>** class.

Exactly $n - 1$ iterations of the outer loop are done (lines 11–26). In each iteration, a binary search is done to determine the position at which to do the insertion (lines 13–23). In the $i$th iteration of the outer loop, the binary search considers array positions 0 to $i$ (for $1 \leq i < n$). The running time for the binary search in the $i$th iteration is $O(\lfloor \log_2(i + 1) \rfloor) = O(\log i)$. Once the correct position is found, at most $i$ swaps are needed to insert the element in its place.

The worst-case running time of the binary insertion sort is dominated by the $i$ swaps needed to do the insertion. Therefore, the worst-case running time is $O(n^2)$. Furthermore, since the algorithm only swaps adjacent array elements, the average running time is also $O(n^2)$ (see Section 15.3.2). Asymptotically, the binary insertion sort is no better than straight insertion.

**PROGRAM 15.5**
BinaryInsertionSorter<T> class DoSort member function definition

```
1   template <class T>
2   class BinaryInsertionSorter : public InsertionSorter<T>
3   {
4   protected:
5       void DoSort (Array<T>&);
6   };
7
8   template <class T>
9   void BinaryInsertionSorter<T>::DoSort (Array<T>& array)
10  {
11      for (unsigned int i = 1; i < n; ++i)
12      {
13          T const& tmp = array [i];
14          unsigned int left = 0;
15          unsigned int right = i;
16          while (left < right)
17          {
18              unsigned int const middle = (left + right) / 2;
19              if (tmp >= array [middle])
10                  left = middle + 1;
21              else
22                  right = middle;
23          }
24          for (unsigned int j = i; j > left; --j)
25              Swap (array [j - 1U], array [j]);
26      }
27  }
```

However, the binary insertion sort does fewer array element comparisons than insertion sort. In the $i$th iteration of the outer loop, the binary search requires $\lfloor \log_2(i + 1) \rfloor$ comparisons, for $1 \leq i < n$. Therefore, the total number of comparisons is

$$\sum_{i=1}^{n-1} \lfloor \log_2(i + 1) \rfloor = \sum_{i=1}^{n} \lfloor \log_2 i \rfloor$$

$$= (n + 1) \lfloor \log_2(n + 1) \rfloor + 2^{\lfloor \log_2(n+1) \rfloor + 1} + 2$$

$$= O(n \log n).$$

(This result follows directly from Theorem 11.3.)

The number of comparisons required by the straight insertion sort is $O(n^2)$ in the worst case as well as on average. Therefore on average, the binary insertion sort uses

**TABLE 15.1**
Running Times for Insertion Sorting

| Algorithm | Running Time | | |
| --- | --- | --- | --- |
| | Best Case | Average Case | Worst Case |
| Straight insertion sort | $O(n)$ | $O(n^2)$ | $O(n^2)$ |
| Binary insertion sort | $O(n \log n)$ | $O(n^2)$ | $O(n^2)$ |

fewer comparisons than straight insertion sort. On the other hand, the previous section shows that in the best case the running time for straight insertion is $O(n)$. Since the binary insertion sort routine *always* does the binary search, its best-case running time is $O(n \log n)$. Table 15.1 summarizes the asymptotic running times for the two insertion sorts.

## 15.4   Exchange Sorting

The second class of sorting algorithm that we consider comprises algorithms that *sort by exchanging* pairs of items until the sequence is sorted. In general, an algorithm may exchange adjacent elements as well as widely separated ones.

In fact, since the insertion sorts considered in the preceding section accomplish the insertion by swapping adjacent elements, insertion sorting can be considered as a kind of exchange sort. The reason for creating a separate category for insertion sorts is that the essence of those algorithms is insertion into a sorted list. On the other hand, an exchange sort does not necessarily make use of such a sorted list.

### 15.4.1   Bubble Sort

The simplest and, perhaps, the best known of the exchange sorts is the *bubble sort*.[2] Figure 15.3 shows the operation of bubble sort.

To sort the sequence $S = \{s_0, s_1, s_2, \ldots, s_{n-1}\}$, bubble sort makes $n - 1$ passes through the data. In each pass, adjacent elements are compared and swapped if necessary. First, $s_0$ and $s_1$ are compared; next, $s_1$ and $s_2$; and so on.

Notice that after the first pass through the data, the largest element in the sequence has *bubbled up* into the last array position. In general, after $k$ passes through the data, the last $k$ elements of the array are correct and need not be considered any longer. In this regard the bubble sort differs from the insertion sort algorithms—the sorted subsequence of $k$ elements is never modified (by an insertion).

---

[2]Unfortunately, the fame of bubble sort exceeds by far its practical value.

**FIGURE 15.3**
Bubble sorting.

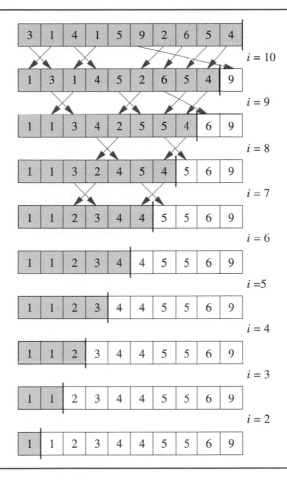

Figure 15.3 also shows that while $n - 1$ passes through the data are required to guarantee that the list is sorted in the end, it is possible for the list to become sorted much earlier! When no exchanges are made in a given pass, then the array is sorted and no additional passes are required. A minor algorithmic modification would be to count the exchanges made in a pass, and to terminate the sort when none are made.

Program 15.6 defines the **BubbleSorter<T>** class template. This class simply provides an implementation for the **DoSort** routine. The **DoSort** routine takes a reference to an **Array<T>** instance and sorts its elements in place. The implementation makes use of the **Swap** routine described in Section 15.3.1.

The outer loop (lines 11–14) is done for $i = n - 1, n - 2, n - 3, \ldots, 2$. That makes $n - 1$ iterations in total. During the $i$th iteration of the outer loop, exactly $i - 1$ iterations

---

**PROGRAM 15.6**
BubbleSorter<T> class DoSort member function definition

---

```
1   template <class T>
2   class BubbleSorter : public ExchangeSorter<T>
3   {
4   protected:
5       void DoSort (Array<T>&);
6   };
7
8   template <class T>
9   void BubbleSorter<T>::DoSort (Array<T>& array)
10  {
11      for (unsigned int i = n; i > 1; --i)
12          for (unsigned int j = 0; j < i - 1U; ++j)
13              if (array [j] > array [j + 1])
14                  Swap (array [j], array [j + 1]);
15  }
```

---

of the inner loop are done (lines 12–14). Therefore, the number of iterations of the inner loop, summed over all the passes of the outer loop, is

$$\sum_{i=2}^{n}(i - 1) = \sum_{i=1}^{n-1} i = \frac{n(n - 1)}{2}.$$

Consequently, the running time of bubble sort is $\Theta(n^2)$.

The body of the inner loop compares adjacent array elements and swaps them if necessary (lines 13–14). This takes at most a constant amount of time. Of course, the algorithm will run slightly faster when no swapping is needed. For example, this occurs if the array is already sorted to begin with. In the worst case, it is necessary to swap in every iteration of the inner loop. This occurs when the array is sorted initially in reverse order. Since only adjacent elements are swapped, bubble sort removes inversions one at time. Therefore, the average number of swaps required is $O(n^2)$. Nevertheless, the running time of bubble sort is always $\Theta(n^2)$.

## 15.4.2  Quicksort

The second exchange sort we consider is the *quicksort* algorithm. Quicksort is a *divide-and-conquer* style algorithm. A divide-and-conquer algorithm solves a given problem by splitting it into two or more smaller subproblems, recursively solving each of the subproblems, and then combining the solutions to the smaller problems to obtain a solution to the original one.

To sort the sequence $S = \{s_1, s_2, s_3, \ldots, s_n\}$, quicksort performs the following steps:

1. Select one of the elements of $S$. The selected element, $p$, is called the *pivot*.

2. Remove $p$ from $S$ and then partition the remaining elements of $S$ into two distinct sequences, $L$ and $G$, such that every element in $L$ is less than or equal to the pivot and every element in $G$ is greater than or equal to the pivot. In general, both $L$ and $G$ are *unsorted*.

3. Rearrange the elements of the sequence as follows:

$$S' = \{\underbrace{l_1, l_2, \ldots, l_{|L|}}_{L}, \underbrace{p}_{\text{pivot}}, \underbrace{g_1, g_2, \ldots, g_{|G|}}_{G}\}$$

Notice that the pivot is now in the position in which it belongs in the sorted sequence, since all the elements to the left of the pivot are less than or equal to the pivot and all the elements to the right are greater than or equal to it.

4. Recursively quicksort the unsorted sequences $L$ and $G$.

The first step of the algorithm is a crucial one. We have not specified how to select the pivot. Fortunately, the sorting algorithm works no matter which element is chosen as the pivot. However, the pivot selection directly affects the running time of the algorithm. If we choose poorly the running time will be poor.

Figure 15.4 illustrates the detailed operation of quicksort as it sorts the sequence $\{3, 1, 4, 1, 5, 9, 2, 6, 5, 4\}$. To begin the sort, we select a pivot. In this example, the value 4 in the last array position is chosen. Next, the remaining elements are partitioned into two sequences, one which contains values less than or equal to 4 ($L = \{3, 1, 2, 1\}$) and one which contains values greater than or equal to 4 ($G = \{5, 9, 4, 6, 5\}$). Notice that the partitioning is accomplished by exchanging elements. This is why quicksort is considered an exchange sort.

After the partitioning, the pivot is inserted between the two sequences. This is called *restoring* the pivot. To restore the pivot, we simply exchange it with the first element of $G$. Notice that the 4 is in its correct position in the sorted sequence and it is not considered any further.

Now the quicksort algorithm calls itself recursively, first to sort the sequence $L = \{3, 1, 2, 1\}$; second to sort the sequence $G = \{9, 4, 6, 5, 5\}$. The quicksort of $L$ selects 1 as the pivot, and creates the two subsequences $L' = \{1\}$ and $G' = \{2, 3\}$. Similarly, the quicksort of $G$ uses 5 as the pivot and creates the two subsequences $L'' = \{5, 4\}$ and $G'' = \{9, 6\}$.

At this point in the example the recursion has been stopped. It turns out that to keep the code simple, quicksort algorithms usually stop the recursion when the length of a subsequence falls below a critical value called the *cut-off*. In this example, the cut-off is two (i.e., a subsequence of two or fewer elements is not sorted). This means that when the algorithm terminates, the sequence is not yet sorted. However, as Figure 15.4 shows, the sequence is *almost* sorted. In fact, every element is guaranteed to be less than two positions away from its final resting place.

**FIGURE 15.4**
"Quick" sorting.

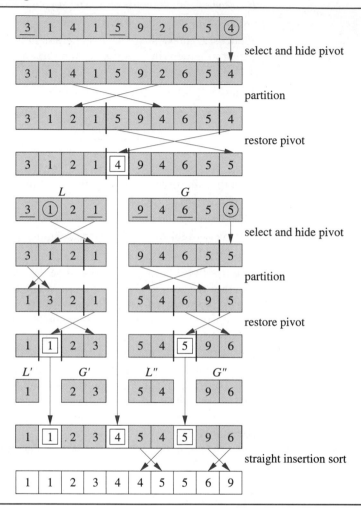

We can complete the sorting of the sequence by using a straight insertion sort. In Section 15.3.1 it is shown that straight insertion is quite good at sorting sequences that are almost sorted. In fact, if we know that every element of the sequence is at most $d$ positions from its final resting place, the running time of straight insertion is $O(dn)$ and since $d = 2$ is a constant, the running time is $O(n)$.

### Implementation
Program 15.7 declares the abstract **QuickSorter<T>** class template. The **Quick-Sorter** class declares two versions of the **DoSort** routine, as well as the pure virtual

---

**PROGRAM 15.7**
QuickSorter class definition

---

```
1  template <class T>
2  class QuickSorter : public ExchangeSorter<T>
3  {
4  protected:
5      static unsigned int const cutOff;
6
7      virtual unsigned int SelectPivot (
8          Array<T>&, unsigned int, unsigned int) = 0;
9      void DoSort (Array<T>&, unsigned int, unsigned int);
10      void DoSort (Array<T>&);
11  };
```

---

function SelectPivot. Since SelectPivot is a pure virtual function, its implementation is given in a derived class.

Program 15.8 defines the DoSort routine of the QuickSorter<T> class that takes three arguments—a reference to the array to be sorted, array, and two integers, left and right, which denote left and right ends, respectively, of the sequence of the array to be sorted. That is, this DoSort routine sorts

$$array[left],array[left+1], \ldots ,array[right].$$

As discussed above, the QuickSorter only sorts sequences whose length exceeds the *cut-off* value. Since the implementation shown only works correctly when the number of elements in the sequence to be sorted is three or more, the *cut-off* value of two is used (line 5).

The algorithm begins by calling the function SelectPivot which chooses one of the elements to be the pivot (line 7). The implementation of SelectPivot is discussed below. All that we require here is that the value $p$ returned by SelectPivot satisfies $left \leq p \leq right$. Having selected an element to be the pivot, we *hide* the pivot by swapping it with the right-most element of the sequence (line 8). The pivot is *hidden* in order to get it out of the way of the next step.

The next step partitions the remaining elements into two sequences—one comprised of values less than or equal to the pivot, the other comprised of values greater than or equal to the pivot. The partitioning is done using two array indices, i and j. The first, i, starts at the left end and moves to the right; the second, j, starts at the right end and moves to the left.

The variable i is increased as long as array[i] is less than the pivot (line 14). Then the variable j is decreased as long as array[j] is greater than the pivot (line 15). When i and j meet, the partitioning is done (line 16). Otherwise, i < j but array[i] $\geq$ pivot $\geq$ array[j]. This situation is remedied by swapping array[i] and array[j] (line 17).

**PROGRAM 15.8**

QuickSorter<T> class recursive DoSort member function definition

```
1   template <class T>
2   void QuickSorter<T>::DoSort (
3       Array<T>& array, unsigned int left, unsigned int right)
4   {
5       if (right - left + 1 > cutOff)
6       {
7           unsigned int const p = SelectPivot (array, left, right);
8           Swap (array [p], array [right]);
9           T& pivot = array [right];
10          unsigned int i = left;
11          unsigned int j = right - 1U;
12          for (;;)
13          {
14              while (i < j && array [i] < pivot) ++i;
15              while (i < j && array [j] > pivot) --j;
16              if (i >= j) break;
17              Swap (array [i++], array [j--]);
18          }
19          if (array [i] > pivot)
20              Swap (array [i], pivot);
21          if (left < i)
22              DoSort (array, left, i - 1U);
23          if (right > i)
24              DoSort (array, i + 1, right);
25      }
26  }
```

**PROGRAM 15.9**

QuickSorter<T> class main DoSort member function definition

```
1   template <class T>
2   void QuickSorter<T>::DoSort (Array<T>& array)
3   {
4       DoSort (array, 0, n - 1U);
5       StraightInsertionSorter<T> s;
6       s.Sort (array);
7   }
```

When the partitioning loop terminates, the pivot is still in **array[right]**; the value in **array[i]** is greater than or equal to the pivot; everything to the left is less than or equal to the pivot; and everything to the right is greater than or equal to the pivot. We can now put the pivot in its proper place by swapping it with **array[i]** (lines 19–20). This is called *restoring* the pivot. With the pivot in its final resting place, all we need to do is sort the subsequences on either side of the pivot (lines 21–24).

Program 15.9 defines the main **DoSort** routine of the **QuickSorter** class. The main **DoSort** acts as the front end to the recursive **DoSort** given in Program 15.8. This routine takes as its lone argument a reference to the array to be sorted. It calls the recursive **DoSort** routine with **left** set to zero and **right** set to $n - 1$, where $n$ is the length of the array to be sorted. Finally, it uses a **StraightInsertionSorter<T>** to finish sorting the list.

### 15.4.3 Running Time Analysis

The running time of the recursive **DoSort** routine (Program 15.8) is given by

$$T(n) = \begin{cases} O(1) & n \leq 2, \\ \mathcal{T}\langle \text{SelectPivot}(\cdot) \rangle + T(i) + T(n - i - 1) + O(n) & n > 2, \end{cases} \quad (15.1)$$

where $n$ is the number of elements in sequence to be sorted, $\mathcal{T}\langle \text{SelectPivot}(\cdot) \rangle$ is the running time of the **SelectPivot** function, and $i$ is the number of elements which end up to the left of the pivot, $0 \leq i \leq n - 1$.

The running time of **DoSort** is affected by the **SelectPivot** routine in two ways: First, the value of the pivot chosen affects the sizes of the subsequences. That is, the pivot determines the value $i$ in Equation 15.1. Second, the running time of the **SelectPivot** routine itself, $\mathcal{T}\langle \text{SelectPivot}(\cdot) \rangle$, must be taken into account. Fortunately, if $\mathcal{T}\langle \text{SelectPivot}(\cdot) \rangle = O(n)$, we can ignore its running time because there is already an $O(n)$ term in the expression.

In order to solve Equation 15.1, we assume that $\mathcal{T}\langle \text{SelectPivot}(\cdot) \rangle = O(n)$ and then drop the $O(\cdot)$s from the recurrence to get

$$T(n) = \begin{cases} 1 & n \leq 2, \\ T(i) + T(n - i - 1) + n & n > 2, \end{cases} \quad 0 \leq i \leq n - 1. \quad (15.2)$$

Clearly the solution depends on the value of $i$.

#### Worst-Case Running Time
In the worst case the $i$ in Equation 15.2 is always zero.[3] In this case, we solve the recurrence using repeated substitution like this:

---

[3]There is also the symmetrical case in which $i$ is always $n - 1$.

$$
\begin{aligned}
T(n) &= T(n-1) + n \\
&= T(n-2) + (n-1) + n \\
&= T(n-3) + (n-2) + (n-1) + n \\
&\;\;\vdots \\
&= T(n-k) + \sum_{j=n-k}^{n} j \\
&\;\;\vdots \\
&= T(2) + \sum_{j=2}^{n} j \\
&= n(n+1)/2 \\
&= O(n^2).
\end{aligned}
$$

The worst case occurs when the two subsequences are as unbalanced as they can be—one sequence has all the remaining elements and the other has none.

### Best-Case Running Time

In the best case, the partitioning step divides the remaining elements into two sequences with exactly the same number of elements. For example, suppose that $n = 2^m - 1$ for some integer $m > 0$. After removing the pivot $2^m - 2$ elements remain. If these are divided evenly, each sequence will have $2^{m-1} - 1$ elements. In this case Equation 15.2 gives

$$
\begin{aligned}
T(2^m - 1) &= 2T(2^{m-1} - 1) + 2^m - 1 \\
&= 2^2 T(2^{m-2} - 1) + 2 \cdot 2^m - 2 - 1 \\
&= 2^3 T(2^{m-3} - 1) + 3 \cdot 2^m - 3 - 2 - 1 \\
&\;\;\vdots \\
&= 2^k T(2^{m-k} - 1) + k2^m - \sum_{j=1}^{k} j \\
&= 2^{m-1} T(1) + (m-1)2^m - \sum_{j=1}^{m-1} j, \quad m - k = 1 \\
&= \left(2^m(2m - 1) - m(m-1)\right)/2 \\
&= \left[(n+1)(2\log_2(n+1) - 1) - (\log_2(n+1) - 1)\log_2(n+1)\right]/2 \\
&= O(n \log n).
\end{aligned}
$$

### 15.4.4 Average Running Time

To determine the average running time for the quicksort algorithm, we shall assume that each element of the sequence has an equal chance of being selected for the pivot. Therefore, if $i$ is the number of elements in a sequence of length $n$ less than the pivot, then $i$ is uniformly distributed in the interval $[0, n - 1]$. Consequently, the average value of $T(i) = \frac{1}{n} \sum_{j=0}^{n-1} T(j)$. Similarly, the average value of $T(n - i - 1) = \frac{1}{n} \sum_{j=0}^{n-1} T(n - j - 1)$. To determine the average running time, we rewrite Equation 15.2 as follows:

$$T(n) = \begin{cases} 1 & n \leq 2, \\ \frac{1}{n} \sum_{j=0}^{n-1} T(j) + \frac{1}{n} \sum_{j=0}^{n-1} T(n - j - 1) + n & n > 2 \end{cases}$$

$$= \begin{cases} 1 & n \leq 2, \\ \frac{2}{n} \sum_{j=0}^{n-1} T(j) + n & n > 2. \end{cases} \tag{15.3}$$

To solve this recurrence, we consider the case $n > 2$ and then multiply Equation 15.3 by $n$ to get

$$nT(n) = 2 \sum_{j=0}^{n-1} T(j) + n^2. \tag{15.4}$$

Since this equation is valid for any $n > 2$, by substituting $n - 1$ for $n$ we can also write

$$(n - 1)T(n - 1) = 2 \sum_{j=0}^{n-2} T(j) + n^2 - 2n + 1 \tag{15.5}$$

which is valid for $n > 3$. Subtracting Equation 15.5 from Equation 15.3 gives

$$nT(n) - (n - 1)T(n - 1) = 2T(n - 1) + 2n - 1$$

which can be rewritten as

$$\frac{T(n)}{n + 1} = \frac{T(n - 1)}{n} + \frac{2}{n + 1} - \frac{1}{n(n + 1)}. \tag{15.6}$$

Equation 15.6 can be solved by telescoping like this:

$$\frac{T(n)}{n + 1} = \frac{T(n - 1)}{n} + \frac{2}{n + 1} - \frac{1}{(n)(n + 1)} \tag{15.7}$$

$$\frac{T(n - 1)}{n} = \frac{T(n - 2)}{n - 1} + \frac{2}{n} - \frac{1}{(n - 1)(n)}$$

$$\frac{T(n - 1)}{n - 1} = \frac{T(n - 3)}{n - 2} + \frac{2}{n - 1} - \frac{1}{(n - 2)(n - 1)}$$

$$\vdots$$

$$\frac{T(n-k)}{n-k+1} = \frac{T(n-k-1)}{n-k} + \frac{2}{n-k+1} - \frac{1}{(n-k)(n-k+1)}$$

$$\vdots$$

$$\frac{T(3)}{4} = \frac{T(2)}{2} + \frac{2}{4} - \frac{1}{(3)(4)}. \tag{15.8}$$

Adding together Equation 15.7 through Equation 15.8 gives

$$\frac{T(n)}{n+1} = \frac{T(2)}{3} + 2\sum_{i=4}^{n+1} \frac{1}{i} - \sum_{i=3}^{n} \frac{1}{i(i+1)}$$

$$= 2\sum_{i=1}^{n+1} \frac{1}{i} - \sum_{i=1}^{n} \frac{1}{i(i+1)} - 2$$

$$= 2H_{n+1} + \frac{1}{n+1} - 3,$$

where $H_{n+1}$ is the $(n+1)$th *harmonic number*. Finally, multiplying through by $n+1$ gives

$$T(n) = 2(n+1)H_{n+1} - 3n - 2.$$

In Section 2.1.8 it is shown that $H_n \approx \ln n + \gamma$, where $\gamma \approx 0.577\,215$ is called *Euler's constant*. Thus, we get that the average running time of quicksort is

$$T(n) \approx 2(n+1)\Big(\ln(n+1) + \gamma\Big) - 3n - 3$$

$$= O(n \log n).$$

Table 15.2 summarizes the asymptotic running times for the quicksort routine and compares it to those of bubble sort. Notice that the best-case and average-case running times for the quicksort algorithm have the same asymptotic bound!

### 15.4.5   Selecting the Pivot

The analysis in the preceding section shows that selecting a good pivot is important. If we do a bad job of choosing the pivot, the running time of quicksort is $O(n^2)$. On the other hand, the average-case analysis shows that if every element of a sequence is equally likely to be chosen for the pivot, the running time is $O(n \log n)$. This suggests that we can expect to get good performance simply by selecting *a random pivot!*

If we expect to be sorting random input sequences, then we can achieve random pivot selection simply by always choosing, say, the first element of the sequence to be the pivot. Clearly this can be done in constant time. (Remember, the analysis requires that $\mathcal{T}\langle \texttt{selectPivot}(\cdot)\rangle = O(n)$.) As long as each element in the sequence is equally likely to appear in the first position, the average running time will be $O(n \log n)$.

**TABLE 15.2**
Running Times for Exchange Sorting

| Algorithm | Running Time | | |
| --- | --- | --- | --- |
| | Best Case | Average Case | Worst Case |
| Bubble Sort | $O(n^2)$ | $O(n^2)$ | $O(n^2)$ |
| Quicksort (random pivot selection) | $O(n \log n)$ | $O(n \log n)$ | $O(n^2)$ |

In practice it is often the case that the sequence to be sorted is almost sorted. In particular, consider what happens if the sequence to be sorted using quicksort is already sorted. If we always choose the first element as the pivot, then we are guaranteed to have the worst-case running time! This is also true if we always pick the last element of the sequence. And it is also true if the sequence is initially sorted in reverse.

Therefore, we need to be more careful when choosing the pivot. Ideally, the pivot divides the input sequence exactly in two. That is, the ideal pivot is the *median* element of the sequence. This suggests that the `SelectPivot` routine should find the median. To ensure that the running time analysis is valid, we need to find the median in $O(n)$ time.

How do you find the median? One way is to sort the sequence and then select the $\lceil n/2 \rceil$th element. But this is not possible, because we need to find the median to sort the sequence in the first place! While it is possible to find the median of a sequence of $n$ elements in $O(n)$ time, it is usually not necessary to do so. All that we really need to do is select a random element of the sequence while avoiding the problems described above.

A common way to do this is the *median-of-three pivot selection* technique. In this approach, we choose as the pivot the median of the element at the left end of the sequence, the element at the right end of the sequence, and the element in the middle of the sequence. Clearly, this does the *right thing* if the input sequence is initially sorted (either in forward or reverse order).

Program 15.10 declares the `MedianOfThreeQuickSorter<T>` class template. The `MedianOfThreeQuickSorter<T>` class is derived from the `QuickSorter<T>` abstract base class. It provides an implementation for the `SelectPivot` function based on median-of-three pivot selection. Notice that this algorithm does exactly three comparisons to select the pivot. As a result, its running time is $O(1)$. In practice this scheme performs sufficiently well that more complicated pivot selection approaches are unnecessary.

## 15.5 Selection Sorting

The third class of sorting algorithm that we consider comprises algorithms that sort *by selection*. Such algorithms construct the sorted sequence one element at a time by adding elements to the sorted sequence *in order*. At each step, the next element to be added to the sorted sequence is selected from the remaining elements.

---

**PROGRAM 15.10**
MedianOfThreeQuickSorter<T> class `SelectPivot` member function definition

---

```
1   template <class T>
2   class MedianOfThreeQuickSorter : public QuickSorter<T>
3   {
4   protected:
5       unsigned int SelectPivot (
6           Array<T>&, unsigned int, unsigned int);
7   };
8
9   template <class T>
10  unsigned int MedianOfThreeQuickSorter<T>::SelectPivot (
11      Array<T>& array, unsigned int left, unsigned int right)
12  {
13      unsigned int middle = (left + right) / 2;
14      if (array [left] > array [middle])
15          Swap (left, middle);
16      if (array [left] > array [right])
17          Swap (left, right);
18      if (array [middle] > array [right])
19          Swap (middle, right);
20      return middle;
21  }
```

---

Because the elements are added to the sorted sequence in order, they are always added at one end. This is what makes selection sorting different from insertion sorting. In insertion, sorting elements are added to the sorted sequence in an arbitrary order. Therefore, the position in the sorted sequence at which each subsequent element is inserted is arbitrary.

Both selection sorts described in this section sort the arrays *in place*. Consequently, the sorts are implemented by exchanging array elements. Nevertheless, selection differs from exchange sorting because at each step we *select* the next element of the sorted sequence from the remaining elements and then we move it into its final position in the array by exchanging it with whatever happens to be occupying that position.

### 15.5.1  Straight Selection Sorting

The simplest of the selection sorts is called *straight selection*. Figure 15.5 illustrates how straight selection works. In the version shown, the sorted list is constructed from the right (i.e., from the largest to the smallest element values).

At each step of the algorithm, a linear search of the unsorted elements is made in order to determine the position of the largest remaining element. That element is then moved into the correct position of the array by swapping it with the element which currently occupies that position.

**FIGURE 15.5**
Straight selection sorting.

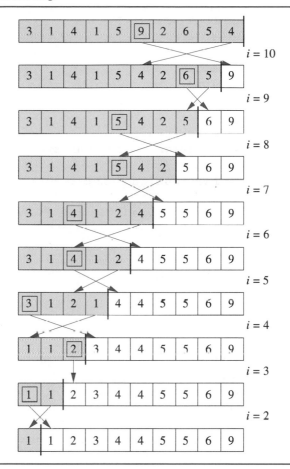

For example, in the first step shown in Figure 15.5, a linear search of the entire array reveals that 9 is the largest element. Since 9 is the largest element, it belongs in the last array position. To move it there, we swap it with the 4 that initially occupies that position. The second step of the algorithm identifies 6 as the largest remaining element and moves it next to the 9. Each subsequent step of the algorithm moves one element into its final position. Therefore, the algorithm is done after $n - 1$ such steps.

## Implementation

Program 15.11 defines the **StraightSelectionSorter<T>** class. This class is derived from the abstract **Sorter<T>** base class and it provides an implementation for **DoSort**. The **DoSort** routine follows directly from the algorithm discussed above. In each iteration of the main loop (lines 11–18), exactly one element is selected from the unsorted elements and moved into the correct position. A linear search of the unsorted elements is done in order to determine the position of the largest remaining element (lines 14–16). That element is then moved into the correct position (line 17).

---

**PROGRAM 15.11**
StraightSelectionSorter<T> class DoSort member function definition

---

```
1   template <class T>
2   class StraightSelectionSorter : public SelectionSorter<T>
3   {
4   protected:
5       void DoSort (Array<T>&);
6   };
7
8   template <class T>
9   void StraightSelectionSorter<T>::DoSort (Array<T>& array)
10  {
11      for (unsigned int i = n; i > 1; --i)
12      {
13          unsigned int max = 0;
14          for (unsigned int j = 1; j < i; ++j)
15              if (array [j] > array [max])
16                  max = j;
17          Swap (array [i - 1U], array [max]);
18      }
19  }
```

---

Altogether $n - 1$ iterations of the outer loop are needed to sort the array. Notice that exactly one swap is done in each iteration of the outer loop. Therefore, $n - 1$ data exchanges are needed to sort the list.

Furthermore, in the $i$th iteration of the outer loop, $i - 1$ iterations of the inner loop are required and each iteration of the inner loop does one data comparison. Therefore, $O(n^2)$ data comparisons are needed to sort the list.

The total running time of the straight selection DoSort routine is $O(n^2)$. Because the same number of comparisons and swaps are always done, this running time bound applies in all cases. That is, the best-case, average-case, and worst-case running times are all $O(n^2)$.

## 15.5.2   Sorting with a Heap

Selection sorting involves the repeated selection of the next element in the sorted sequence from the set of remaining elements. For example, the straight insertion sorting algorithm given in the preceding section builds the sorted sequence by repeatedly selecting the largest remaining element and prepending it to the sorted sequence developing at the right end of the array.

At each step the largest remaining element is withdrawn from the set of remaining elements. A linear search is done because the order of the remaining elements is arbitrary. However, if we consider the value of each element as its priority, we can view the set of remaining elements as a priority queue. In effect, a selection sort repeatedly dequeues the highest priority element from a priority queue.

Chapter 11 presents a number of priority queue implementations, including binary heaps, leftist heaps, and binomial queues. In this section we present a version of selection sorting that uses a *binary heap* to hold the elements that remain to be sorted. Therefore, it is called a *heapsort*. The principal advantage of using a binary heap is that it is easily implemented using an array and the entire sort can be done in place.

As explained in Section 11.2, a binary heap is a *complete binary tree* which is easily represented in an array. The $n$ nodes of the heap occupy positions 1 through $n$ of the array. The root is at position 1. In general, the children of the node at position $i$ of the array are found at positions $2i$ and $2i + 1$, and the parent is found at position $\lfloor i/2 \rfloor$.

The heapsort algorithm consists of two phases. In the first phase, the unsorted array is transformed into a heap. (This is called *heapifying* the array.) In this case, a *max-heap* rather than a min-heap is used. The data in a max-heap satisfies the following condition: For every node in the heap that has a parent, the item contained in the parent is greater than or equal to the item contained in the given node.

The second phase of heapsort builds the sorted list. The sorted list is built by repeatedly selecting the largest element, withdrawing it from the heap, and adding it to the sorted sequence. As each element is withdrawn from the heap, the remaining elements are heapified.

### Implementation

Program 15.12 defines the class template **HeapSorter<T>**. The **HeapSorter<T>** class is derived from the abstract **Sorter<T>** base class. Three protected member functions are defined—BuildHeap, PercolateDown, and DoSort. The DoSort routine comprises the body of the sorting algorithm. The **BuildHeap** and **Percolate-Down** routines are used by **DoSort** to build the heap and then to sort the array.

In the first phase of heapsort, the unsorted array is transformed into a max-heap. Throughout the process we view the array as a complete binary tree. Since the data in the array is initially unsorted, the tree is not initially heap ordered. We make the tree into a max-heap from the bottom up. That is, we start with the leaves and work toward the root. Figure 15.6 illustrates this process.

---

**PROGRAM 15.12**
HeapSorter<T> class definition

```
1   template <class T>
2   class HeapSorter : public SelectionSorter<T>
3   {
4   protected:
5       void BuildHeap (Array<T>&);
6       void PercolateDown (Array<T>&, unsigned int, unsigned int);
7       void DoSort (Array<T>&);
8   };
```

**FIGURE 15.6**
Combining heaps by percolating values.

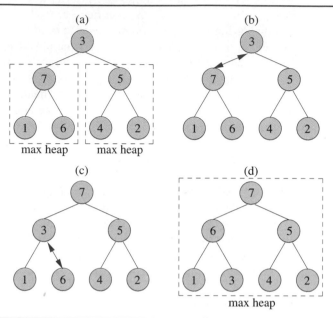

Figure 15.6(*a*) shows a complete tree that is not yet heap ordered—the root is smaller than both its children. However, the two subtrees of the root *are* heap ordered. Given that both of the subtrees of the root are already heap ordered, we can heapify the tree by *percolating* the value in the root down the tree.

To percolate a value down the tree, we swap it with its largest child. For example, in Figure 15.6(*b*) we swap 3 and 7. Swapping with the largest child ensures that after the swap the new root is greater than or equal to *both* its children.

Notice that after the swap the heap order is satisfied at the root, but not in the left subtree of the root. We continue percolating the 3 down by swapping it with 6 as shown in Figure 15.6(*c*). In general, we percolate a value down either until it arrives in a position in which the heap order is satisfied or until it arrives in a leaf. As shown in Figure 15.6(*d*), the tree obtained when the percolation is finished is a max-heap

The **PercolateDown** routine shown in Program 15.13 implements the algorithm described above. The **PercolateDown** routine takes three arguments: a reference to the array; the number of elements in the array to be considered, *n*; and the position, *i*, of the node to be percolated.

The purpose of the **PercolateDown** routine is to transform the subtree rooted at position *i* into a max-heap. It is assumed that the left and right subtrees of the node at position *i* are already max-heaps. Recall that the children of node *i* are found at positions $2i$ and $2i + 1$. **PercolateDown** percolates the value in position *i* down the tree by swapping elements until the value arrives in a leaf node or until both children of *i* contain a smaller value.

**PROGRAM 15.13**

HeapSorter<T> class PercolateDown member function definition

```
1   template <class T>
2   void HeapSorter<T>::PercolateDown (
3       Array<T>& array, unsigned int length, unsigned int i)
4   {
5       while (i <= length / 2)
6       {
7           unsigned int child = 2 * i;
8           if (child + 1 <= length
9                   && array [child + 1] > array [child])
10              child = child + 1;
11          if (array [i] >= array [child])
12              break;
13          Swap (array [i], array [child]);
14          i = child;
15      }
16  }
```

A constant amount of work is done in each iteration. Therefore, the running time of the **PercolateDown** routine is determined by the number of iterations of its main loop (lines 5–15). In fact, the number of iterations required in the worst case is equal to the height in the tree of node $i$.

Since the root of the tree has the greatest height, the worst case occurs for $i = 1$. In Chapter 11 it is shown that the height of a complete binary tree is $\lfloor \log_2 n \rfloor$. Therefore, the worst-case running time of the **PercolateDown** routine is $O(\log n)$.

### 15.5.3 Building the Heap

The **BuildHeap** routine shown in Program 15.14 transforms an unsorted array into a max-heap. It does so by calling the **PercolateDown** routine for $i = \lfloor n/2 \rfloor, \lfloor n/2 \rfloor - 1, \lfloor n/2 \rfloor - 2, \ldots, 1$.

Why does **BuildHeap** start percolating at $\lfloor n/2 \rfloor$? A complete binary tree with $n$ nodes has exactly $\lceil n/2 \rceil$ leaves. Therefore, the last node in the array which has a child

**PROGRAM 15.14**

HeapSorter<T> class BuildHeap member function definition

```
1   template <class T>
2   void HeapSorter<T>::BuildHeap (Array<T>& array)
3   {
4       for (unsigned int i = n / 2; i > 0; --i)
5           PercolateDown (array, n, i);
6   }
```

**FIGURE 15.7**
Building a heap.

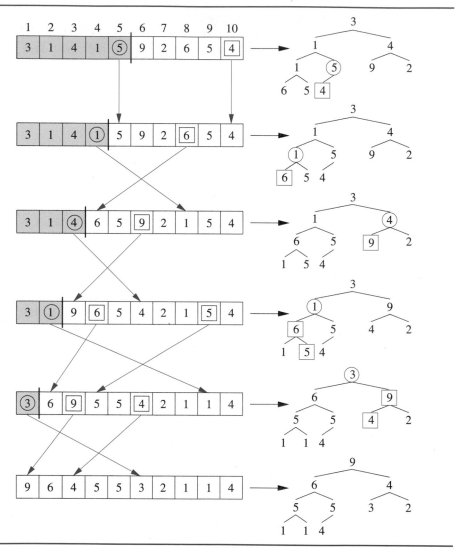

is in position $\lfloor n/2 \rfloor$. Consequently, the **BuildHeap** routine starts doing percolate down operations from that point.

The **BuildHeap** visits the array elements in reverse order. In effect the algorithm starts at the deepest node that has a child and works toward the root of the tree. Each array position visited is the root of a subtree. As each such subtree is visited, it is transformed into a max-heap. Figure 15.7 illustrates how the **BuildHeap** routine heapifies an array that is initially unsorted.

### Running Time Analysis

The `BuildHeap` routine does exactly $\lfloor n/2 \rfloor$ `PercolateDown` operations. As discussed above, the running time for `PercolateDown` is $O(h_i)$, where $h_i$ is the height in the tree of the node at array position $i$. The highest node in the tree is the root, and its height is $O(\log n)$. If we make the simplifying assumption that the running time for `PercolateDown` is $O(\log n)$ for every value of $i$, we get that the total running time for `BuildHeap` is $O(n \log n)$.

However, $n \log n$ is not a tight bound. The maximum number of iterations of the `PercolateDown` loop done during the entire process of building the heap is equal to the sum of the heights of all of the nodes in the tree! The following theorem shows that this is $O(n)$.

### Theorem 15.2

*Consider a* perfect *binary tree $T$ of height $h$ having $n = 2^{h+1} - 1$ nodes. The sum of the heights of the nodes in $T$ is $2^{h+1} - 1 - (h + 1) = n - \log_2(n + 1)$.*

**Proof**  A perfect binary tree has one node at height $h$, two nodes at height $h - 1$, four nodes at height $h - 2$, and so on. In general, there are $2^i$ nodes at height $h - i$. Therefore, the sum of the heights of the nodes is $\sum_{i=0}^{h}(h - i)2^i$.

The summation can be solved as follows: First, we make the simple variable substitution $i = j - 1$:

$$\sum_{i=0}^{h}(h - i)2^i = \sum_{j-1=0}^{h} (h - (j - 1))2^{j-1}$$

$$= \frac{1}{2} \sum_{j=1}^{h+1}(h - j + 1)2^j$$

$$= \frac{1}{2} \sum_{j=0}^{h}(h - j + 1)2^j - (h + 1)/2 \qquad (15.9)$$

$$- \frac{1}{2} \sum_{j=0}^{h}(h - j)2^j + \sum_{j=0}^{h} 2^j - (h + 1)/2$$

$$= \frac{1}{2} \sum_{j=0}^{h}(h - j)2^j + (2^{h+1} - 1 - h + 1)/2$$

Note that the summation which appears on the right-hand side is identical to that on the left. Rearranging Equation 15.9 and simplifying gives

$$\sum_{i=0}^{h}(h - i)2^i = 2^{h+1} - 1 - h + 1$$

$$= n - \log_2(n + 1).$$

It follows directly from Theorem 15.2 that the sum of the heights of a perfect binary tree is $O(n)$. But a heap is not a *perfect* tree—it is a *complete* tree. Nevertheless, it is easy to show that the same bound applies to a complete tree. The proof is left as an exercise for the reader (Exercise 15.15). Therefore, the running time for the **BuildHeap** routine is $O(n)$, were $n$ is the length of the array to be heapified.

### The Sorting Phase

Once the max-heap has been built, heapsort proceeds to the selection sorting phase. In this phase the sorted sequence is obtained by repeatedly withdrawing the largest element from the max-heap. Figure 15.8 illustrates how this is done.

The largest element of the heap is always found at the root, and the root of a complete tree is always in array position 1. Suppose the heap occupies array positions 1 through $k$. When an element is withdrawn from the heap, its length decreases by 1, that is, after the withdrawal the heap occupies array positions 1 through $k - 1$. Thus, array position $k$ is

**FIGURE 15.8**
Heap sorting.

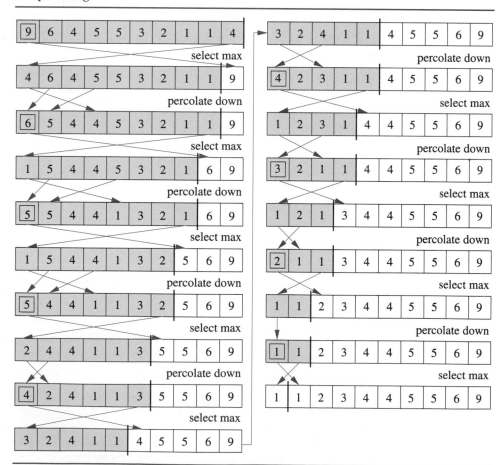

---

**PROGRAM 15.15**

`HeapSorter<T>` class `DoSort` member function definition

---

```
1  template <class T>
2  void HeapSorter<T>::DoSort (Array<T>& array)
3  {
4      array.SetBase (1);
5      BuildHeap (array);
6      for (unsigned int i = n; i >= 2; --i)
7      {
8          Swap (array [i], array [1]);
9          PercolateDown (array, i - 1U, 1);
10     }
11 }
```

---

no longer required by the max-heap. However, the next element of the sorted sequence belongs in position $k$!

So, the sorting phase of heapsort works like this: We repeatedly swap the largest element in the heap (always in position 1) into the next position of the sorted sequence. After each such swap, there is a new value at the root of the heap and this new value is pushed down into the correct position in the heap using the `PercolateDown` routine.

Program 15.15 gives the `DoSort` routine of the `HeapSorter<T>` class. The `DoSort` routine embodies both phases of the heapsort algorithm. However, before it starts the first phase of the algorithm, `DoSort` sets the array base to one. This modification of the array base simplifies the coding of the algorithms. As discussed in Section 15.2 the array base will have been set to zero by the `Sort` member function of the `Sorter<T>` base class and will be restored to the original base by that routine.

In the first phase of heapsort the `BuildHeap` routine is called to transform the array into a max-heap. As discussed above, this is done in $O(n)$ time.

The second phase of the heapsort algorithm builds the sorted list. Altogether, $n - 1$ iterations of the loop on lines 6–10 are required. Each iteration involves one swap followed by a `PercolateDown` operation. Since the worst-case running time for `PercolateDown` is $O(\log n)$, the total running time of the loop is $O(n \log n)$. The running time of the second phase asymptotically dominates that of the first phase. As a result, the worst-case running time of heapsort is $O(n \log n)$.

## 15.6 Merge Sorting

The fourth class of sorting algorithm we consider comprises algorithms that sort by *merging*. Merging is the combination of two or more sorted sequences into a single sorted sequence.

Figure 15.9 illustrates the basic, two-way merge operation. In a two-way merge, two sorted sequences are merged into one. Clearly, two sorted sequences each of length $n$

**FIGURE 15.9**
Two-way merging.

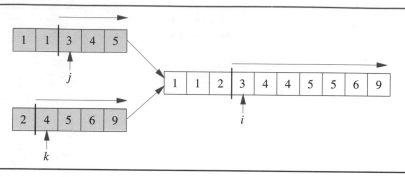

can be merged into a sorted sequence of length $2n$ in $O(2n) = O(n)$ steps. However, in order to do this, we need space in which to store the result. That is, it is not possible to merge the two sequences *in place* in $O(n)$ steps.

Sorting by merging is a recursive, divide-and-conquer strategy. In the base case, we have a sequence with exactly one element in it. Since such a sequence is already sorted, there is nothing to be done. To sort a sequence of $n > 1$ elements,

1.  divide the sequence into two sequences of length $\lfloor n/2 \rfloor$ and $\lceil n/2 \rceil$;
2.  recursively sort each of the two subsequences; and then,
3.  merge the sorted subsequences to obtain the final result.

Figure 15.10 illustrates the operation of the two-way merge sort algorithm.

### Implementation

Program 15.16 declares the **TwoWayMergeSorter<T>** class template. A single member variable, **tempArray**, is declared. This variable is a pointer to an **Array<T>** instance. Since merge operations cannot be done in place, a second, temporary array is needed. The **tempArray** variable keeps track of that array. The **TwoWayMerge-Sorter** constructor simply sets the **tempArray** pointer to zero.

In addition to the constructor, three protected member functions are declared, **Merge** and two versions of **DoSort**. The purpose of the **Merge** function is to merge sorted subsequences of the array to be sorted. The two **DoSort** routines implement the sorting algorithm itself.

### Merging

The **Merge** function of the **TwoWayMergeSorter<T>** class is defined in Program 15.17. Altogether, this function takes four parameters: The first is a reference to the array to be sorted. The remaining three, **left**, **middle**, and **right**, are unsigned integers. It is assumed that

$$\text{left} \leq \text{middle} < \text{right}.$$

**FIGURE 15.10**
Two-way merge sorting.

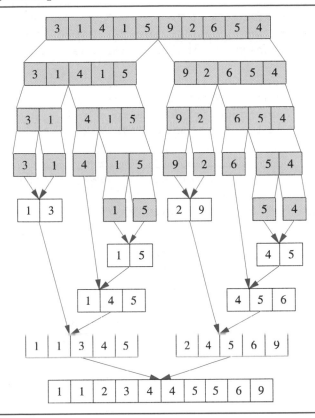

**PROGRAM 15.16**
`TwoWayMergeSorter<T>` class definition

```
1   template <class T>
2   class TwoWayMergeSorter : public MergeSorter<T>
3   {
4   protected:
5       Array<T>* tempArray;
6
7       void Merge (Array<T>&,
8           unsigned int, unsigned int, unsigned int);
9       void DoSort (Array<T>&, unsigned int, unsigned int);
10      void DoSort (Array<T>&);
11  public:
12      TwoWayMergeSorter () : tempArray (0) {}
13  };
```

**PROGRAM 15.17**
TwoWayMergeSorter<T> class `Merge` member function definition

```
1   template <class T>
2   void TwoWayMergeSorter<T>::Merge (Array<T>& array,
3       unsigned int left, unsigned int middle, unsigned int right)
4   {
5       unsigned int i = left;
6       unsigned int j = left;
7       unsigned int k = middle + 1;
8       while (j <= middle && k <= right)
9       {
10          if (array [j] <= array [k])
11              (*tempArray) [i++] = array [j++];
12          else
13              (*tempArray) [i++] = array [k++];
14      }
15      while (j <= middle)
16          (*tempArray) [i++] = array [j++];
17      while (k <= right)
18          (*tempArray) [i++] = array [k++];
19      for (i = left; i <= right; ++i)
20          array [i] = (*tempArray) [i];
21  }
```

Furthermore, it is assumed that the two subsequences of the array,

$$\texttt{array[left], array[left+1],}\ldots,\texttt{array[middle],}$$

and

$$\texttt{array[middle+1], array[middle+2],}\ldots,\texttt{array[right],}$$

are both sorted. The `Merge` routine merges the two sorted subsequences using the temporary array specified by `tempArray`. It then copies the merged (and sorted) sequence into the array at

$$\texttt{array[left],array[left+1],}\ldots,\texttt{array[right].}$$

In order to determine the running time of the `Merge` routine it is necessary to recognize that the total number of iterations of the three loops (lines 8–14, lines 15–16, and lines 17–18) is `right` − `left` + 1. The total number of iterations of the fourth loop (lines 19–20) is the same. Since all the loop bodies do a constant amount of work, the total running time for the `Merge` routine is $O(n)$, where $n = $ `right` − `left` + 1 is the total number of elements in the two subsequences that are merged.

---

**PROGRAM 15.18**

`TwoWayMergeSorter<T>` class `DoSort` member function definitions

---

```
1  template <class T>
2  void TwoWayMergeSorter<T>::DoSort (Array<T>& array)
3  {
4      tempArray = new Array<T> (n);
5      DoSort (array, 0, n - 1U);
6      delete tempArray;
7      tempArray = 0;
8  }
9
10 template <class T>
11 void TwoWayMergeSorter<T>::DoSort (Array<T>& array,
12     unsigned int left, unsigned int right)
13 {
14     if (left < right)
15     {
16         unsigned int const middle = (left + right) / 2;
17         DoSort (array, left, middle);
18         DoSort (array, middle + 1, right);
19         Merge (array, left, middle, right);
20     }
21 }
```

---

### Two-Way Merge Sorting

Program 15.18 gives the code for the two `DoSort` member functions of the **TwoWay-MergeSorter** class. The main `DoSort` routine takes as its lone argument a reference to the array to be sorted (line 2). First, it allocates a temporary array, the length of which is equal to the length of the array to be sorted (line 4). Then it calls the second, recursive `DoSort` routine which sorts the array (line 5). After the array has been sorted, the main `DoSort` deletes the temporary array (line 6).

The second `DoSort` routine implements the recursive, divide-and-conquer merge sort algorithm described above. The routine takes three parameters—**array**, **left**, and **right**. The first is a reference to the array to be sorted, and the latter two specify the subsequence of the array to be sorted. If the sequence to be sorted contains more than one element, the sequence is split in two (line 16), each half is recursively sorted (lines 17–18), and then two sorted halves are merged (line 19).

### Running Time Analysis

The running time of merge sort is determined by the running time of the recursive `DoSort` routine. (The main `DoSort` only adds a constant amount of overhead.) The running time of the recursive `DoSort` routine is given by the following recurrence:

$$T(n) = \begin{cases} O(1) & n = 1, \\ T(\lfloor n/2 \rfloor) + T(\lceil n/2 \rceil) + O(n) & n > 1, \end{cases} \qquad (15.10)$$

where $n = \texttt{right} - \texttt{left} + 1$.

In order to simplify the solution of Equation 15.10 we shall assume that $n = 2^k$ for some integer $k \geq 0$. Dropping the $O(\cdot)$s from the equation we get

$$T(n) = \begin{cases} 1 & n = 1, \\ 2T(n/2) + n & n > 1, \end{cases}$$

which is easily solved by repeated substitution:

$$\begin{aligned} T(n) &= 2T(n/2) + n \\ &= 4T(n/4) + 2n \\ &= 8T(n/8) + 3n \\ &\;\;\vdots \\ &= 2^k T(n/2^k) + kn \\ &\;\;\vdots \\ &= nT(1) + n\log_2 n \\ &= n + n\log_2 n \end{aligned}$$

Therefore, the running time of merge sort is $O(n \log n)$.

## 15.7  A Lower Bound on Sorting

The preceding sections present three $O(n \log n)$ sorting algorithms—quicksort, heapsort, and the two-way merge sort. But is $O(n \log n)$ the best we can do? In this section we answer the question by showing that any sorting algorithm that sorts using only binary comparisons must make $\Omega(n \log n)$ such comparisons. If each binary comparison takes a constant amount of time, then running time for any such sorting algorithm is also $\Omega(n \log n)$.

Consider the problem of sorting the sequence $S = \{a, b, c\}$ comprised of three distinct items, that is, $a \neq b \wedge a \neq c \wedge b \neq c$. Figure 15.11 illustrates a possible sorting algorithm in the form of a *decision tree*. Each node of the decision tree represents one binary comparison. That is, in each node of the tree, exactly two elements of the sequence are compared. Since there are exactly two possible outcomes for each comparison, each non-leaf node of the binary tree has degree 2.

For example, suppose that $a < b < c$. Consider how the algorithm shown in Figure 15.11 discovers this. The first comparison compares $a$ and $b$ which reveals that $a < b$. The second comparison compares $a$ and $c$ to find that $a < c$. At this point it has been determined that $a < b$ and $a < c$—the relative order of $b$ and $c$ is not yet known. There-

**FIGURE 15.11**

A decision tree for comparison sorting.

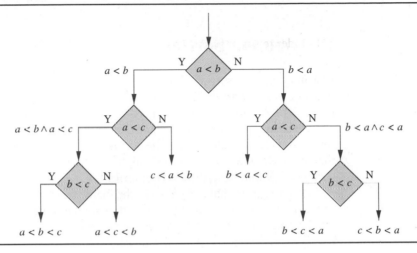

fore, one more comparison is required to determine that $b < c$. Notice that the algorithm shown in Figure 15.11 works correctly in all cases because every possible permutation of the sequence $S$ appears as a leaf node in the decision tree. Furthermore, the number of comparisons required in the worst case is equal to the height of the decision tree!

Any sorting algorithm that uses only binary comparisons can be represented by a binary decision tree. Furthermore, it is the height of the binary decision tree that determines the worst-case running time of the algorithm. In general, the size and shape of the decision tree is a function of the sorting algorithm and the number of items to be sorted.

Given an input sequence of $n$ items to be sorted, every binary decision tree that correctly sorts the input sequence must have *at least* $n!$ leaves—one for each permutation of the input. Therefore, it follows directly from Theorem 9.3 that the height of the binary decision tree is *at least* $\lceil \log_2 n! \rceil$:

$$\lceil \log_2 n! \rceil \geq \log_2 n!$$

$$\geq \sum_{i=1}^{n} \log_2 i$$

$$\geq \sum_{i=1}^{n/2} \log_2 n/2$$

$$\geq n/2 \log_2 n/2$$

$$= \Omega(n \log n).$$

Since the height of the decision tree is $\Omega(n \log n)$, the number of comparisons done by any sorting algorithm that sorts using only binary comparisons is $\Omega(n \log n)$. Assuming each comparison can be done in constant time, the running time of any such sorting algorithm is $\Omega(n \log n)$.

## 15.8 Distribution Sorting

The final class of sorting algorithm considered in this chapter consists of algorithms that sort by *distribution*. The unique characteristic of a distribution sorting algorithm is that it does *not* make use of comparisons to do the sorting.

Instead, distribution sorting algorithms rely on a priori knowledge about the universal set from which the elements to be sorted are drawn. For example, if we know a priori that the size of the universe is a small, fixed constant, say $m$, then we can use the bucket sorting algorithm described in Section 15.8.1.

Similarly, if we have a universe the elements of which can be represented with a small, finite number of bits (or even digits, letters, or symbols), then we can use the radix sorting algorithm given in Section 15.8.2.

### 15.8.1 Bucket Sort

Bucket sort is possibly the simplest distribution sorting algorithm. The essential requirement is that the size of the universe from which the elements to be sorted are drawn is a small, fixed constant, say $m$.

For example, suppose that we are sorting elements drawn from $\{0, 1, \ldots, m - 1\}$, i.e., the set of integers in the interval $[0, m - 1]$. Bucket sort uses $m$ counters. The $i$th counter keeps track of the number of occurrences of the $i$th element of the universe. Figure 15.12 illustrates how this is done.

In Figure 15.12, the universal set is assumed to be $\{0, 1, \ldots, 9\}$. Therefore, ten counters are required—one to keep track of the number of zeroes, one to keep track of the number of ones, and so on. A single pass through the data suffices to count all of the el-

**FIGURE 15.12**
Bucket sorting.

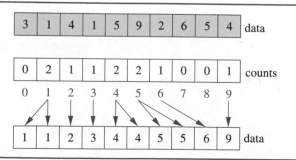

---

**PROGRAM 15.19**
BucketSorter class definition

---

```
1  class BucketSorter : public DistributionSorter<unsigned int>
2  {
3  protected:
4      unsigned int const m;
5      Array<unsigned int> count;
6
7      void DoSort (Array<unsigned int>&);
8  public:
9      BucketSorter (unsigned int _m) : m (_m), count (_m) {}
10 };
```

---

ements. Once the counts have been determined, the sorted sequence is easily obtained. For example, the sorted sequence contains no zeroes, two 1s, one 2, and so on.

### Implementation

Program 15.19 gives the declaration of the **BucketSorter** class. Notice that the **BucketSorter** class is not a template. This bucker sorter is designed to sort specifically an array of **unsigned int**s. The **BucketSorter** class contains two member variables, **m** and **count**. The unsigned integer **m** simply keeps track of the size of the universe. The **count** variable is an array of unsigned integers used to count the number of occurrences of each element of the universal set.

The constructor for the **BucketSorter** class takes a single argument which specifies the size of the universal set. The variable **m** is set to the specified value, and the **count** array is initialized to have the required size.

The **DoSort** routine of the **BucketSorter** is defined in Program 15.20. This routine is passed a reference to the array of data to be sorted. **DoSort** begins by setting all of the counters to zero (lines 3–4). This can clearly be done in $O(m)$ time.

Next, a single pass is made through the data to count the number of occurrences of each element of the universe (lines 5–6). Since each element of the array is examined exactly once, the running time is $O(n)$.

In the final step, the sorted output sequence is created (lines 7–9). Since the output sequence contains exactly $n$ items, the body of the inner loop (line 9) is executed exactly $n$ times. During the $i$th iteration of the outer loop (line 7), the loop termination test of the inner loop (line 8) is evaluated $count[i] + 1$ times. As a result, the total running time of the final step is $O(m + n)$.

Thus, the running time of the bucket sort routine is $O(m+n)$. Note that if $m = O(n)$, the running time for bucket sort is $O(n)$. That is, the bucket sort algorithm is a *linear-time* sorting algorithm! Bucket sort breaks the $\Omega(n \log n)$ bound associated with sorting algorithms that use binary comparisons because bucket sort does not do any binary comparisons. The cost associated with breaking the $\Omega(n \log n)$ running time bound is the $O(m)$ space required for the array of counters. Consequently, bucket sort is practical only for small $m$. For example, to sort 16-bit integers using bucket sort requires the use of an array of $2^{16} = 65\,536$ counters.

---

**PROGRAM 15.20**
BucketSorter class DoSort member function definition

```
 1   void BucketSorter::DoSort (Array<unsigned int>& array)
 2   {
 3       for (unsigned int i = 0; i < m; ++i)
 4           count [i] = 0;
 5       for (unsigned int j = 0; j < n; ++j)
 6           ++count [array [j]];
 7       for (unsigned int i = 0, j = 0; i < m; ++i)
 8           for ( ; count [i] > 0; --count [i])
 9               array [j++] = i;
10   }
```

---

### 15.8.2 Radix Sort

This section presents a sorting algorithm known as *least-significant-digit-first radix sorting*. Radix sorting is based on the bucket sorting algorithm discussed in the preceding section. However, radix sorting is practical for much larger universal sets than it is practical to handle with a bucket sort.

Radix sorting can be used when each element of the universal set can be viewed as a sequence of digits (or letters or any other symbols). For example, we can represent each integer between 0 and 99 as a sequence of two, decimal digits (e.g., the number five is represented as "05").

To sort an array of two-digit numbers, the algorithm makes two sorting passes through the array. In the first pass, the elements of the array are sorted by the *least significant* decimal digit. In the second pass, the elements of the array are sorted by the *most significant* decimal digit. The key characteristic of the radix sort is that the second pass is done in such a way that it does not destroy the effect of the first pass. Consequently, after two passes through the array, the data contained therein are sorted.

Each pass of the radix sort is implemented as a bucket sort. In the example we base the sort on *decimal* digits. Therefore, this is called a *radix-10* sort and ten buckets are required to do each sorting pass.

Figure 15.13 illustrates the operation of the radix-10 sort. The first radix sorting pass considers the least significant digits. As in the bucket sort, a single pass is made through the unsorted data, counting the number of times each decimal digit appears as the least-significant digit. For example, there are no elements that have a 0 as the least-significant digit; there are two elements that have a 1 as the least-significant digit; and so on.

After the counts have been determined, it is necessary to permute the input sequence so that it is sorted by the least-significant digits. To do this permutation efficiently, we compute the sequence of *offsets* given by

$$\text{offset}[i] = \begin{cases} 0 & i = 0, \\ \sum_{j=0}^{i-1} \text{count}[i] & 0 < i < R, \end{cases} \tag{15.11}$$

**FIGURE 15.13**
Radix sorting.

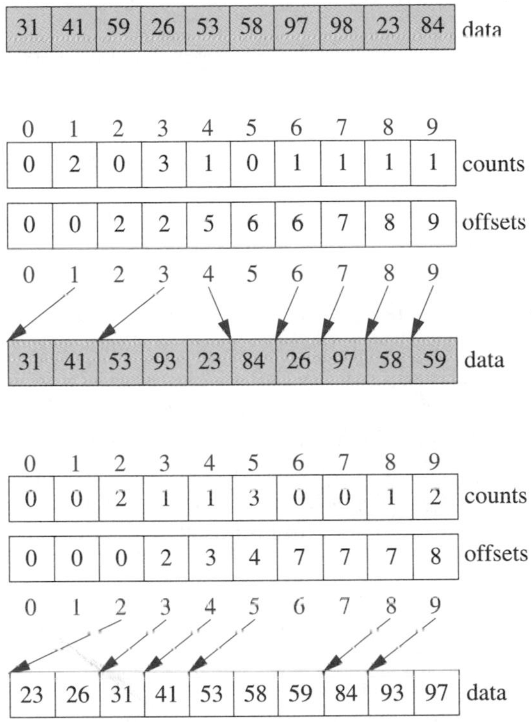

where $R$ is the sorting radix. Note that `offset[`$i$`]` is the position in the permuted sequence of the first occurrence of an element whose least significant digit is $i$. By making use of the offsets, it is possible to permute the input sequence by making a single pass through the sequence.

The second radix sorting pass considers the most significant digits. As above, a single pass is made through the permuted data sequence counting the number of times each decimal digit appears as the most-significant digit. Then the sequence of *offsets* is computed as above. The sequence is permuted again using the offsets producing the final, sorted sequence.

In general, radix sorting can be used when the elements of the universe can be viewed as $p$-digit numbers with respect to some radix, $R$. That is, each element of the universe has the form

$$\sum_{i=0}^{p-1} d_i R^i,$$

where $d_i \in \{0, 1, \ldots, R - 1\}$ for $0 \leq i < p$. In this case, the radix sort algorithm must make $p$ sorting passes from the least significant digit, $d_0$, to the most significant digit, $d_{p-1}$, and each sorting pass uses exactly $R$ counters.

Radix sorting can also be used when the universe can be viewed as the cross-product of a finite number of finite sets. That is, when the universe has the form

$$U = U_1 \times U_2 \times U_3 \times \cdots \times U_p,$$

where $p > 0$ is a fixed integer constant and $U_i$ is a finite set for $1 \leq i \leq p$. For example, each card in a 52-card deck of playing cards can be represented as an element of $U = U_1 \times U_2$, where $U_1 = \{\clubsuit, \diamondsuit, \heartsuit, \spadesuit\}$ and $U_2 = \{A, 2, 3, 4, 5, 6, 7, 8, 9, 10, J, Q, K\}$.

Before we can sort over the universe $U$, we need to define what it means for one element to precede another in $U$. The usual way to do this is called *lexicographic ordering*. For example, in the case of the playing cards we may say that one card precedes another if its suit precedes the other suit or if the suits are equal but the face value precedes that of the other.

In general, given the universe $U = U_1 \times U_2 \times U_2 \times \cdots \times U_p$, and two elements of $U$, say $x$ and $y$, represented by the $p$-tuples $x = (x_1, x_2, \ldots, x_p)$ and $y = (y_1, y_2, \ldots, y_p)$, respectively, we say that $x$ *lexicographically precedes* $y$ if there exists $1 \leq k \leq p$ such that $x_k < y_k$ and $x_i = y_i$ for all $1 \leq i < k$.

With this definition of precedence, we can radix sort a sequence of elements drawn from $U$ by sorting with respect to the components of the $p$-tuples. Specifically, we sort first with respect to $U_p$, then $U_{p-1}$, and so on down to $U_1$. Notice that the algorithm does $p$ sorting passes and in the $i$th pass it requires $|U_i|$ counters. For example, to sort a deck of cards, two passes are required. In first pass the cards are sorted into 13 piles according to their face values. In the second pass the cards are sorted into four piles according to their suits.

## Implementation

Program 15.21 gives the declaration of the **RadixSorter** class. Notice that the **RadixSorter** class is not a template. This radix sorter is designed to sort specifically an array of **unsigned ints**.

---

**PROGRAM 15.21**
RadixSorter class definition

```
1    class RadixSorter : public DistributionSorter<unsigned int>
2    {
3    protected:
4        static unsigned int const r;
5        static unsigned int const R;
6        static unsigned int const p;
7
8        Array<unsigned int> count;
9
10       void DoSort (Array<unsigned int>&);
11   public:
12       RadixSorter () : count (R) {}
13   };
```

---

Three constants are declared as static members of the **RadixSorter** class—**R**, **r**, and **p**. The constant $R$ represents the radix, and $r = \log_2 R$. The constant $p$ is the number sorting passes needed to sort the data.

The **RadixSorter** class contains one member variable—**count**. The **count** variable is an array of unsigned integers used to implement the sorting passes. The **RadixSorter** constructor simply initializes the **count** array with length $R$.

Program 15.22 defines the constants **R**, **r**, and **p**, and gives the code for the **DoSort** member function of the **RadixSorter** class. In this case $r = 8$ and $R = 2^r = 256$.

---

**PROGRAM 15.22**
**RadixSorter** class **DoSort** member function definition

```
1   unsigned int const RadixSorter::r = 8;
2   unsigned int const RadixSorter::R = 1 << r;
3   unsigned int const RadixSorter::p =
4       (bitsizeof (unsigned int) + r - 1U) / r;
5
6   void RadixSorter::DoSort (Array<unsigned int>& array)
7   {
8       Array<unsigned int> tempArray (n);
9       for (unsigned int i = 0; i < p; ++i)
10      {
11          for (unsigned int j = 0; j < R; ++j)
12              count [j] = 0;
13          for (unsigned int k = 0; k < n; ++k)
14          {
15              ++count [(array [k] >> (r * i)) & (R - 1U)];
16              tempArray [k] = array [k];
17          }
18          unsigned int pos = 0;
19          for (unsigned int j = 0; j < R; ++j)
20          {
21              unsigned int const tmp = count [j];
22              count [j] = pos;
23              pos += tmp;
24          }
25          for (unsigned int k = 0; k < n; ++k)
26          {
27              unsigned int j =
28                  (tempArray [k] >> (r * i)) & (R - 1U);
29              array [count [j]++] = tempArray [k];
30          }
31      }
32  }
```

---

Therefore, a radix-256 sort is being done. We have chosen $R$ as a power of 2 because that way the computations required to implement the radix sort can be implemented efficiently using simple bit shift and mask operations. In order to sort $b$-bit unsigned integers, it is necessary to make $p = \lceil \log_R 2^b \rceil = \lceil b/r \rceil$ sorting passes. The constants $r$, $R$, and $p$ are initialized accordingly.

`DoSort` begins by creating a temporary array of `unsigned int`s of length $n$. Each iteration of the main loop corresponds to one pass of the radix sort (lines 9–30). In all $p$ iterations are required.

During the $i$th pass of the main loop the following steps are done: First, the $R$ counters are all set to zero (lines 11–12). This takes $O(R)$ time. Then a pass is made through the input array during which the number of occurrences of each radix-$R$ digit in the $i$th digit position are counted (lines 13–17). This pass takes $O(n)$ time. Notice that during this pass all the input data is copied into the temporary array.

Next, the array of counts is transformed into an array of offsets according to Equation 15.11. This requires a single pass through the counter array (lines 18–24). Therefore, it takes $O(R)$ time. Finally, the data sequence is permuted by copying the values from the temporary array back into the input array (lines 25–30). Since this requires a single pass through the data arrays, the running time is $O(n)$.

After the $p$ sorting passes have been done, the array of data is sorted. The running time for the `DoSort` routine of the `RadixSorter` class is $O\big(p(R + n)\big)$. If we assume that the size of an integer is 32 bits and given that $R = 256$, the number of sorting passes required is $p = 4$. Therefore, the running time for the radix sort is simply $O(n)$; that is, radix sort is a linear-time sorting algorithm.

## 15.9 Performance Data

In order to better understand the actual performance of the various sorting algorithms presented in this chapter, it is necessary to conduct some experiments. Only by conducting experiments is it possible to determine the relative performance of algorithms with the same asymptotic running time.

To measure the performance of a sorting algorithm, we need to provide it with some data to sort. To obtain the results presented here, random sequences of unsigned integers were sorted, that is, for each value of $n$, the `RandomNumberGenerator` class defined in Section 14.5.1 was used to create a sequence of $n$ integers. In all cases (except for bucket sort) the random numbers are uniformly distributed in the interval $[1, 2^{31} - 1]$. For the bucket sort the numbers are uniformly distributed in $[0, 2^{10} - 1]$.

Figures 15.14, 15.15, and 15.16 show the actual running times of the sorting algorithms presented in this chapter. These running times were measured on a Sun SPARC-station 5, Model 85, which has an 85 MHz clock, and 32MB RAM. The programs were compiled using the SPARCompiler C++ 4.1 compiler, and run under the Solaris 2.3 operating system. The times shown are user CPU times, measured in seconds.

Figure 15.14 shows the running times of the $O(n^2)$ sorts for sequences of length $n$, $100 \le n \le 20\,000$. Notice that the bubble sort has the worst performance and that

**FIGURE 15.14**
Actual running times of the $O(n^2)$ sorts.

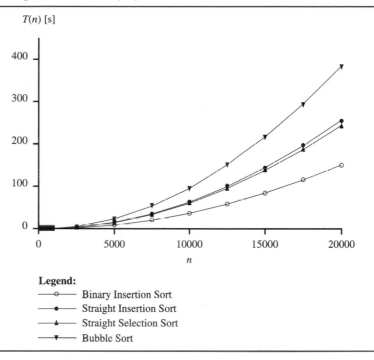

Legend:
—○— Binary Insertion Sort
—●— Straight Insertion Sort
—▲— Straight Selection Sort
—▼— Bubble Sort

**FIGURE 15.15**
Actual running times of the $O(n \log n)$ sorts.

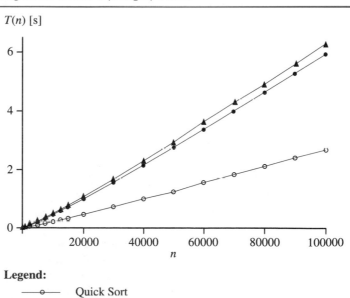

Legend:
—○— Quick Sort
—●— Heap Sort
—▲— Merge Sort

**FIGURE 15.16**
Actual running times of the $O(n)$ sorts.

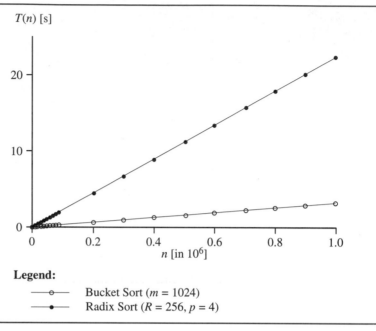

Legend:

—o— Bucket Sort ($m = 1024$)
—•— Radix Sort ($R = 256, p = 4$)

the binary insertion sort has the best performance. Figure 15.14 clearly shows that, as predicted, binary insertion is better than straight insertion. Notice too that all of the $O(n^2)$ sorts require in excess of 2 minutes of execution time to sort an array of 20 000 integers.

The performance of the $O(n \log n)$ sorts is shown in Figure 15.15. In this case, the length of the sequence varies between $n = 100$ and $n = 100\,000$. The graph clearly shows that the $O(n \log n)$ algorithms are significantly faster than the $O(n^2)$ ones. All three algorithms sort 100 000 integers in under 6 seconds. Clearly, quick sort is the best of the three, whereas the two-way merge sort and heap sort have similar running times.

Figure 15.16 shows the actual running times for the bucket sort and radix sort algorithms. Both these algorithms were shown to be $O(n)$ sorts. The graph shows results for $n$ between 100 and 1 000 000. The universe used to test bucket sort was $\{0, 1, \ldots, 1023\}$; that is, a total of $m = 1024$ counters (buckets) were used. For the radix sort, 32-bit integers were sorted by using the radix $R = 256$ and doing $p = 4$ sorting passes.

Clearly, the bucket sort has the best running time. For example, it sorts 1 million 10-bit integers in about 5 seconds. Radix sort performs extremely well too. It sorts 1 million 32-bit integers in about 20 seconds. This is a factor of 4 slower than the bucket sort due largely to the fact that radix sort does four sorting passes whereas bucket sort requires only one.

# Exercises

**15.1** Consider the sequence of integers

$$S = \{8, 9, 7, 9, 3, 2, 3, 8, 4, 6\}.$$

For each of the following sorting algorithms, draw a sequence of diagrams that traces the execution of the algorithm as it sorts the sequence $S$: straight insertion sort, binary insertion sort, bubble sort, quick sort, straight selection sort, heapsort, merge sort, and bucket sort.

**15.2** Draw a sequence of diagrams that traces the execution of a radix-10 sort of the sequence

$$S = \{89, 79, 32, 38, 46, 26, 43, 38, 32, 79\}.$$

**15.3** For each of the sorting algorithms listed in Exercise 15.1 and 15.2 indicate whether the sorting algorithm is *stable*.

**15.4** Consider a sequence of three distinct keys $\{a, b, c\}$. Draw the binary decision tree that represents each of the following sorting algorithms: straight insertion sort, straight selection sort, and bubble sort.

**15.5** Devise an algorithm to sort a sequence of exactly three elements. Make your algorithm as efficient as possible.

**15.6** Prove that the swapping of a pair of adjacent elements removes at most one inversion from a sequence.

**15.7** Consider the sequence of elements $\{s_1, s_2, \ldots, s_n\}$. What is the maximum number of inversions that can be removed by swapping a pair of distinct elements $s_i$ and $s_j$? Express the result in terms of the *distance* between $s_i$ and $s_j$: $d(s_i, s_j) = j - i + 1$.

**15.8** Devise a sequence of keys such that *exactly* 11 inversions are removed by the swapping of one pair of elements.

**15.9** Prove that *binary insertion sort* requires $O(n \log n)$ comparisons.

**15.10** Consider an arbitrary sequence $\{s_1, s_2, \ldots, s_n\}$. To sort the sequence, we determine the permutation $\{p_1, p_2, \ldots, p_n\}$ such that

$$s_{p_1} \leq s_{p_2} \leq \cdots \leq s_{p_n}.$$

Prove that *bubble sort* requires at least $p$ passes where

$$p = \max_{1 \leq i \leq n} (i - p_i).$$

**15.11** Modify the bubble sort algorithm (Program 15.6) so that it terminates the outer loop when it detects that the array is sorted. What is the running time of the modified algorithm? **Hint**: See Exercise 15.10.

**15.12**   A variant of the bubble sorting algorithm is the so-called *odd-even transposition sort*. Like bubble sort, this algorithm requires a total of $n-1$ passes through the array. Each pass consists of two phases: The first phase compares `array[i]` with `array[i + 1]` and swaps them if necessary for all the odd values of of $i$. The second phase does the same for the even values of $i$.

   **a.**   Show that the array is guaranteed to be sorted after $n - 1$ passes.

   **b.**   What is the running time of this algorithm?

**15.13**   Another variant of the bubble sorting algorithm is the so-called *cocktail shaker sort*. Like bubble sort, this algorithm a total of $n - 1$ passes through the array. However, alternating passes go in opposite directions. For example, during the first pass the largest item bubbles to the end of the array and during the second pass the smallest item bubbles to the beginning of the array.

   **a.**   Show that the array is guaranteed to be sorted after $n - 1$ passes.

   **b.**   What is the running time of this algorithm?

**15.14**   Consider the following algorithm for selecting the $k$th largest element from an unsorted sequence of of $n$ elements, $S = \{s_1, s_2, \ldots, s_n\}$.

   **1.**   If $n \leq 5$, sort $S$ and select directly the $k$th largest element.

   **2.**   Otherwise, $n > 5$: Partition the sequence $S$ into subsequences of length 5. In general, there will be $\lfloor n/5 \rfloor$ subsequences of length 5 and one of length $n$ mod 5.

   **3.**   Sort by any means each of the subsequences of length 5. (See Exercise 15.5.)

   **4.**   Form the sequence $M = \{m_1, m_2, \ldots, m_{\lfloor n/5 \rfloor}\}$ containing the $\lfloor n/5 \rfloor$ median values of each of the subsequences of length 5.

   **5.**   Apply the selection procedure recursively to find the median element of $M$. Let $m$ be the median of the medians.

   **6.**   Partition $S$ into three subsequences, $S = \{L, E, G\}$, such that all the elements in $L$ are less than $m$, all the elements in $E$ are equal to $m$, and all the elements of $G$ are greater than $m$.

   **7.**   If $k \leq |L|$ then apply the procedure recursively to select the $k$th largest element of $L$; if $|L| < k \leq |L| + |E|$, the result is $m$; otherwise apply the procedure recursively to select the $(k - (|L| + |E|))$th largest element of $G$.

   **a.**   What is the running time of this algorithm?

   **b.**   Show that if we use this algorithm to select the pivot the worst-case running time of *quick sort* is $O(n \log n)$.

**15.15**   Show that the sum of the heights of the nodes in a complete binary tree with $n$ nodes altogether is $n - b(n)$, where $b(n)$ is the number of ones in the binary representation of $n$.

# Programming Projects

**15.1**   Design and implement an algorithm that finds all the duplicates in a random sequence of keys.

15.2 Suppose that instead of an **Array<T>** instance we wish to sort a sequence of data represented using the linked-list class **LinkedList<T>**. Which of the sorting algorithms described in this chapter is the most appropriate for sorting a linked list? Design and implement a linked-list sorter class that implements this algorithm.

15.3 Replace the **DoSort** routine of the **MergeSorter** class with a nonrecursive version. What is the running time of the nonrecursive merge sort?

15.4 Replace the **DoSort** routine of the **QuickSorter** class with a nonrecursive version. What is the running time of the nonrecursive quick sort? **Hint:** Use a stack.

15.5 Design and implement a radix-sorter class that sorts an array of **string** class instances.

15.6 Design and implement a **RandomPivotQuickSorter** class that uses a random number generator (see Section 14.5.1) to select a pseudorandom pivot. Run a sequence of experiments to compare the running times of random pivot selection with median-of-three pivot selection.

15.7 Design and implement a **MeanPivotQuickSorter** class that partitions the sequence to be sorted into elements that are less than the mean and elements that are greater than the mean. Run a sequence of experiments to compare the running times of the mean pivot quick sorter with median-of-three pivot selection.

15.8 Design and implement a **MedianPivotQuickSorter** class that uses the algorithm given in Exercise 15.14 to select the median element for the pivot. Run a sequence of experiments to compare the running times of median pivot selection with median-of-three pivot selection.

15.9 Design and implement a sorter class that sorts using a **PriorityQueue** instance. (See Chapter 11.)

# 16 | Graphs and Graph Algorithms

A graph is simply a set of points together with a set of lines connecting various points. Myriad real-world application problems can be reduced to problems on graphs.

Suppose you are planning a trip by airplane. From a map you have determined the distances between the airports in the various cities that you wish to visit. The information you have gathered can be represented using a graph, as shown in Figure 16.1(*a*). The points in the graph represent the cities and the lines represent the distances between them. Given such a graph, you can answer questions such as "What is the shortest distance between LAX and JFK?" or "What is the shortest route that visits all of the cities?"

An electric circuit can also be viewed as a graph, as shown in Figure 16.1(*b*). In this case the points in the graph indicate where the components are connected (i.e., the wires) and the lines represent the components themselves (e.g, resistors and capacitors). Given such a graph, we can answer questions such as "What are the mesh equations that describe the circuit's behavior?"

Similarly, a logic circuit can be reduced to a graph, as shown in Figure 16.1(*c*). In this case the logic gates are represented by the points and arrows represent the signal flows from gate outputs to gate inputs. Given such a graph, we can answer questions such as "How long does it take for the signals to propagate from the inputs to the outputs?" or "Which gates are on the critical path?"

Finally, Figure 16.1(*d*) illustrates that a graph can be used to represent a *finite state machine*. The points of the graph represent the states and labeled arrows indicate the allowable state transitions. Given such a graph, we can answer questions such as "Are all the states reachable?" or "Can the finite state machine deadlock?"

This chapter is a brief introduction to the body of knowledge known as *graph theory*. It covers the most common data structures for the representation of graphs and introduces some fundamental graph algorithms.

**FIGURE 16.1**
Real-world examples of graphs.

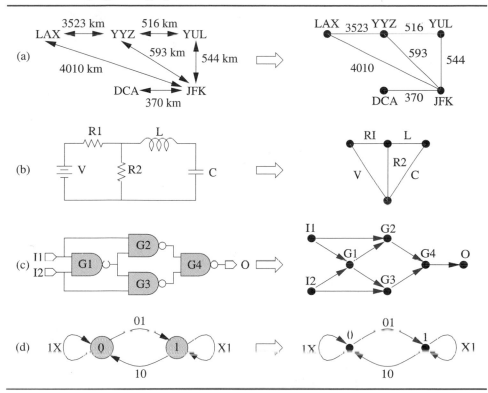

## 16.1 Basics

### Directed Graphs

We begin with the definition of a directed graph.

### Definition 16.1 (Directed Graph)
*A* directed graph, *or* digraph, *is an ordered pair* $G = (\mathcal{V}, \mathcal{E})$ *with the following properties:*

1. *The first component,* $\mathcal{V}$*, is a finite, non-empty set. The elements of* $\mathcal{V}$ *are called the vertices of G.*

2. *The second component,* $\mathcal{E}$*, is a finite set of ordered pairs of vertices. That is,* $\mathcal{E} \subseteq \mathcal{V} \times \mathcal{V}$*. The elements of* $\mathcal{E}$ *are called the edges of G.*

**FIGURE 16.2**
A directed graph.

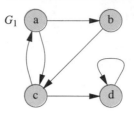

For example, consider the directed graph $G_1 = (\mathcal{V}_1, \mathcal{E}_1)$ comprised of four vertices and six edges:

$$\mathcal{V}_1 = \{a, b, c, d\}$$
$$\mathcal{E}_1 = \{(a, b), (a, c), (b, c), (c, a), (c, d), (d, d)\}.$$

The graph $G$ can be represented *graphically*, as shown in Figure 16.2. The vertices are represented by appropriately labeled circles, and the edges are represented by arrows that connect associated vertices.

Notice that because the pairs that represent edges are *ordered*, the two edges $(a, c)$ and $(c, a)$ are distinct. Furthermore, since $\mathcal{E}_1$ is a mathematical set, it cannot contain more than one instance of a given edge. And finally, an edge such as $(d, d)$ may connect a node to itself.

## Terminology

Consider a directed graph $G = (\mathcal{V}, \mathcal{E})$ as given by Defintion 16.1.

- Each element of $\mathcal{V}$ is called a *vertex* or a *node* of $G$. Hence, $\mathcal{V}$ is the set of *vertices* (or *nodes*) of $G$.

- Each element of $\mathcal{E}$ is called an *edge* or an *arc* of $G$. Hence, $\mathcal{E}$ is the set of *edges* (or *arcs*) of $G$.

- An edge $(v, w) \in \mathcal{E}$ can be represented as $v \rightarrow w$. An arrow that points from $v$ to $w$ is known as a *directed arc*. Vertex $w$ is called the *head* of the arc because it is found at the arrow head. Conversely, $v$ is called the *tail* of the arc. Finally, vertex $w$ is said to be *adjacent* to vertex $v$.

- An edge $e = (v, w)$ is said to *emanate* from vertex $v$. We use notation $\mathcal{A}(v)$ to denote the set of edges emanating from vertex $v$, that is, $\mathcal{A}(v) = \{(v_0, v_1) \in \mathcal{E} : v_0 = v\}$.

- The *out-degree* of a node is the number of edges emanating from that node. Therefore, the out-degree of $v$ is $|\mathcal{A}(v)|$.

- An edge $e = (v, w)$ is said to be *incident* on vertex $w$. We use notation $\mathcal{I}(w)$ to denote the set of edges incident on vertex $w$, that is, $\mathcal{I}(w) = \{(v_0, v_1) \in \mathcal{E} : v_1 = w\}$.

**TABLE 16.1**
Emanating and Incident Edge Sets for Graph $G_1$ in Figure 16.2

| Vertex $v$ | $\mathcal{A}(v)$ | Out-Degree | $\mathcal{I}(v)$ | In-Degree |
|---|---|---|---|---|
| $a$ | $\{(a, b), (a, c)\}$ | 2 | $\{(c, a)\}$ | 1 |
| $b$ | $\{(b, c)\}$ | 1 | $\{(a, b)\}$ | 1 |
| $c$ | $\{(c, a), (c, d)\}$ | 2 | $\{(a, c), (b, c)\}$ | 2 |
| $d$ | $\{(d, d)\}$ | 1 | $\{(c, d), (d, d)\}$ | 2 |

- The *in-degree* of a node is the number of edges incident on that node. Therefore, the in-degree of $w$ is $|\mathcal{I}(w)|$.

For example, Table 16.1 enumerates the sets of emanating and incident edges and the in- and out-degrees for each of the vertices in graph $G_1$ shown in Figure 16.2. In order to introduce more terminology, we need the following definition:

**Definition 16.2 (Path and Path Length)**
*A path in a directed graph $G = (\mathcal{V}, \mathcal{E})$ is a non-empty sequence of vertices*

$$P = \{v_1, v_2, \ldots, v_k\},$$

*where $v_i \in \mathcal{V}$ for $1 < i < k$ such that $(v_i, v_{i+1}) \in \mathcal{E}$ for $1 \le i < k$. The length of path $P$ is $k - 1$.*

For example, consider again the graph $G_1$ shown in Figure 16.2. Among the paths contained in $G_1$ there is the path of length zero, $\{a\}$; the path of length 1, $\{b, c\}$; the path of length 2, $\{a, b, c\}$; and so on. In fact, this graph generates an infinite number of paths! (To see how this is possible, consider that $\{a, c, a, c, a, c, a, c, a, c, a, c, a\}$ is a path in $G_1$.) Notice too the subtle distinction between a path of length zero, say $\{d\}$, and the path of length 1 $\{d, d\}$.

**More Terminology**
Consider the path $P = \{v_1, v_2, \ldots, v_k\}$ in a directed graph $G = (\mathcal{V}, \mathcal{E})$.

- Vertex $v_{i+1}$ is the *successor* of vertex $v_i$ for $1 \le i < k$. Each element $v_i$ of path $P$ (except the last) has a *successor*.

- Vertex $v_{i-1}$ is the *predecessor* of vertex $v_i$ for $1 < i \le k$. Each element $v_i$ of path $P$ (except the first) has a *predecessor.*

- A path $P$ is called a *simple* path if and only if $v_i \ne v_j$ for all $i$ and $j$ such that $1 \le i < j \le k$. However, it *is* permissible for $v_1$ to be the same as $v_k$ in a simple path.

- A *cycle* is a path $P$ of nonzero length in which $v_1 = v_k$. The *length of a cycle* is just the length of the path $P$.

- A *loop* is a cycle of length 1, that is, it is a path of the form $\{v, v\}$.
- A *simple cycle* is a path that is both a *cycle* and *simple*.

Referring again to graph $G_1$ in Figure 16.2 we find that the path $\{a, b, c, d\}$ is a simple path of length 3. Conversely, the path $\{c, a, c, d\}$ also has length 3 but is not simple because vertex $c$ occurs twice in the sequence (but not at the ends). The graph contains the path $\{a, b, c, a\}$ which is a cycle of length 3, as well as $\{a, c, a, c, a\}$, a cycle of length 4. The former is a simple cycle but the latter is not.

### Directed Acyclic Graphs
For certain applications it is convenient to deal with graphs that contain no cycles. For example, a tree (see Chapter 9) is a special kind of graph that contains no cycles.

### Definition 16.3 (Directed Acyclic Graph (DAG))
*A directed, acyclic graph is a directed graph that contains no cycles.*

Obviously, all trees are DAGs. However, not all DAGs are trees. For example, consider the two directed, acyclic graphs, $G_2$ and $G_3$, shown in Figure 16.3. Clearly $G_2$ is a tree but $G_3$ is not.

### Undirected Graphs
An undirected graph is a graph in which the nodes are connected by *undirected arcs*. An undirected arc is an edge that has no arrow. Both ends of an undirected arc are equivalent—there is no head or tail. Therefore, we represent an edge in an undirected graph as a set rather than an ordered pair.

### Definition 16.4 (Undirected Graph)
*An undirected graph is an ordered pair $G = (\mathcal{V}, \mathcal{E})$ with the following properties:*

1. *The first component, $\mathcal{V}$, is a finite, non-empty set. The elements of $\mathcal{V}$ are called the vertices of G.*

---

**FIGURE 16.3**
Two directed, acyclic graphs.

---

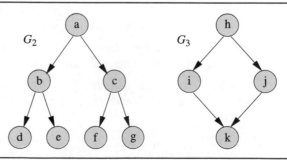

**FIGURE 16.4**
An undirected graph.

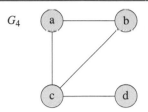

$G_4$

2.  *The second component, $\mathscr{E}$, is a finite set of sets. Each element of $\mathscr{E}$ is a set that is comprised of exactly two (distinct) vertices. The elements of $\mathscr{E}$ are called the edges of G.*

For example, consider the undirected graph $G_4 = (\mathcal{V}_4, \mathscr{E}_4)$ comprised of four vertices and four edges:

$$\mathcal{V}_4 = \{a, b, c, d\}$$
$$\mathscr{E}_4 = \{\{a, b\}, \{a, c\}, \{b, c\}, \{c, d\}\}$$

The graph $G_4$ can be represented *graphically* as shown in Figure 16.4. The vertices are represented by appropriately labeled circles, and the edges are represented by lines that connect associated vertices.

Notice that because an edge in an undirected graph is a set, $\{a, b\} \equiv \{b, a\}$, and since $\mathscr{E}_4$ is also a set, it cannot contain more than one instance of a given edge. Another consequence of Defintion 16.4 is that there cannot be an edge from a node to itself in an undirected graph because an edge is a set of size 2 and a set cannot contain duplicates.

### Terminology
Consider an undirected graph $G = (\mathcal{V}, \mathscr{E})$ as given by Definition 16.4.

- An edge $\{v, w\} \in \mathscr{E}$ *emanates from* and is *incident on* both vertices $v$ and $w$.
- The set of edges emanating from a vertex $v$ is the set $\mathscr{A}(v) = \{(v_0, v_1) \in \mathscr{E} : v_0 = v \lor v_1 = v\}$. The set of edges incident on a vertex $w$ is $\mathscr{I}(w) \equiv \mathscr{A}(w)$.

### Labeled Graphs
Practical applications of graphs usually require that they be annotated with additional information. Such information may be attached to the edges of the graph and to the nodes of the graph. A graph which has been annotated in some way is called a *labeled graph*. Figure 16.5 shows two examples of this.

For example, we can use a directed graph with labeled vertices such as $G_5$ in Figure 16.5 to represent a finite state machine. Each vertex corresponds to a state of the machine, and each edge corresponds to an allowable state transition. In such a graph

**FIGURE 16.5**
Labeled graphs.

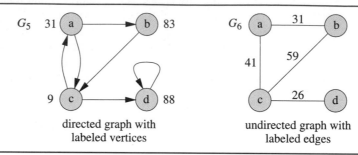

directed graph with
labeled vertices

undirected graph with
labeled edges

we can attach a label to each vertex that records some property of the corresponding state such as the latency time for that state.

We can use an undirected graph with labeled edges such as $G_6$ in Figure 16.5 to represent geographic information. In such a graph, the vertices represent geographic locations and the edges represent possible routes between locations. In such a graph we might use a label on each edge to represent the distance between the end points.

## 16.1.1   Representing Graphs

Consider a directed graph $G = (\mathcal{V}, \mathcal{E})$. Since $\mathcal{E} \subseteq \mathcal{V} \times \mathcal{V}$, graph $G$ contains at most $|\mathcal{V}|^2$ edges. There are $2^{|\mathcal{V}|^2}$ possible sets of edges for a given set of vertices $\mathcal{V}$. Therefore, the main concern when designing a graph representation scheme is to find a suitable way to represent the set of edges.

### Adjacency Matrices
Consider a directed graph $G = (\mathcal{V}, \mathcal{E})$ with $n$ vertices, $\mathcal{V} = \{v_1, v_2, \ldots, v_n\}$. The simplest graph representation scheme uses an $n \times n$ matrix $A$ of zeroes and ones given by

$$A_{i,j} = \begin{cases} 1 & (v_i, v_j) \in \mathcal{E}, \\ 0 & \text{otherwise.} \end{cases}$$

That is, the $(i, j)$th element of the matrix, is a one only if $v_i \to v_j$ is an edge in $G$. The matrix $A$ is called an *adjacency matrix*.

For example, the adjacency matrix for graph $G_1$ in Figure 16.2 is

$$A_1 = \begin{bmatrix} 0 & 1 & 1 & 0 \\ 0 & 0 & 1 & 0 \\ 1 & 0 & 0 & 1 \\ 0 & 0 & 0 & 1 \end{bmatrix}.$$

Clearly, the number of 1's in the adjacency matrix is equal to the number of edges in the graph.

One advantage of using an adjacency matrix is that it is easy to determine the sets of edges emanating from or incident on a given vertex. For example, consider vertex $v_i$. Each 1 in the $i$th row corresponds to an edge that emanates from vertex $v_i$. Conversely, each 1 in the $i$th column corresponds to an edge incident on vertex $v_i$.

We can also use adjacency matrices to represent undirected graphs. That is, we represent an undirected graph $G = (\mathcal{V}, \mathcal{E})$ with $n$ vertices, using an $n \times n$ matrix $A$ of zeroes and 1's given by

$$A_{i,j} = \begin{cases} 1 & \{v_i, v_j\} \in \mathcal{E}, \\ 0 & \text{otherwise.} \end{cases}$$

Since the two sets $\{v_i, v_j\}$ and $\{v_j, v_i\}$ are equivalent, matrix $A$ is symmetric about the diagonal. That is, $A_{i,j} = A_{j,i}$. Furthermore, all of the entries on the diagonal are zero. That is, $A_{i,i} = 0$ for $1 \le i \le n$.

For example, the adjacency matrix for graph $G_4$ in Figure 16.4 is

$$A_4 = \begin{bmatrix} 0 & 1 & 1 & 0 \\ 1 & 0 & 1 & 0 \\ 1 & 1 & 0 & 1 \\ 0 & 0 & 1 & 0 \end{bmatrix}$$

In this case, there are twice as many 1s in the adjacency matrix as there are edges in the undirected graph.

A simple variation allows us to use an adjacency matrix to represent an edge-labeled graph. For example, given numeric edge labels, we can represent a graph (directed or undirected) using an $n \times n$ matrix $A$ in which the $A_{i,j}$ is the numeric label associated with edge $(v_i, v_j)$ in the case of a directed graph, and edge $\{v_i, v_j\}$, in an undirected graph.

For example, the adjacency matrix for the graph $G_6$ in Figure 16.5 is

$$A_6 = \begin{bmatrix} \infty & 31 & 41 & \infty \\ 31 & \infty & 59 & \infty \\ 41 & 59 & \infty & 26 \\ \infty & \infty & 26 & \infty \end{bmatrix}$$

In this case, the array entries corresponding to nonexistent edges have all been set to $\infty$. Here $\infty$ serves as a kind of *sentinel*. The value to use for the sentinel depends on the application. For example, if the edges represent routes between geographic locations, then a route of length $\infty$ is much like one that does not exist.

Since the adjacency matrix has $|\mathcal{V}|^2$ entries, the amount of space needed to represent the edges of a graph is $O(|\mathcal{V}|^2)$, *regardless of the actual number of edges* in the graph. If the graph contains relatively few edges, e.g., if $|\mathcal{E}| \ll |\mathcal{V}|^2$, then most of the elements of the adjacency matrix will be zero (or $\infty$). A matrix in which most of the elements are zero (or $\infty$) is a *sparse matrix*.

### Sparse versus Dense Graphs

Informally, a graph with relatively few edges is *sparse,* and a graph with many edges is *dense.* The following definition defines precisely what we mean when we say that a graph "has relatively few edges":

### Definition 16.5 (Sparse Graph)

*A sparse graph is a graph* $G = (\mathcal{V}, \mathcal{E})$ *in which* $|\mathcal{E}| = O(\mathcal{V})$.

For example, consider a graph $G = (\mathcal{V}, \mathcal{E})$ with $n$ nodes. Suppose that the out-degree of each vertex in $G$ is some fixed constant $k$. Graph $G$ is a *sparse graph* because $|\mathcal{E}| = k|\mathcal{V}| = O(|\mathcal{V}|)$.

A graph that is not sparse is said to be *dense.*

### Definition 16.6 (Dense Graph)

*A dense graph is a graph* $G = (\mathcal{V}, \mathcal{E})$ *in which* $|\mathcal{E}| = \Theta(|\mathcal{V}|^2)$.

For example, consider a graph $G = (\mathcal{V}, \mathcal{E})$ with $n$ nodes. Suppose that the out-degree of each vertex in $G$ is some fraction $f$ of $n$, $0 < f \leq 1$. For example, if $n = 16$ and $f = 0.25$, the out-degree of each node is 4. Graph $G$ is a *dense graph* because $|\mathcal{E}| = f|\mathcal{V}|^2 = \Theta(|\mathcal{V}|^2)$.

---

**FIGURE 16.6**
Adjacency lists.

---

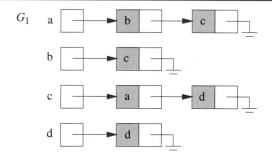

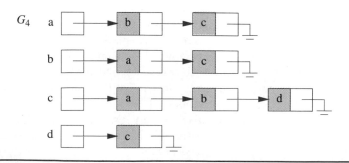

**Adjacency Lists**

One technique that is often used for a sparse graph, say $G = (\mathcal{V}, \mathcal{E})$, uses $|\mathcal{V}|$ linked lists—one for each vertex. The linked list for vertex $v_i \in \mathcal{V}$ contains the elements of $\{w : (v_i, w) \in \mathcal{A}(v_i)\}$, the set of nodes adjacent to $v_i$. As a result, the lists are called *adjacency lists.*

Figure 16.6 shows the adjacency lists for the directed graph $G_1$ of Figure 16.2 and the directed graph $G_4$ of Figure 16.4. Notice that the total number of list elements used to represent a directed graph is $|\mathcal{E}|$ but the number of lists elements used to represent an undirected graph is $2 \times |\mathcal{E}|$. Therefore, the space required for the adjacency lists is $O(|\mathcal{E}|)$.

By definition, a sparse graph has $|\mathcal{E}| = O(|\mathcal{V}|)$. Hence, the space required to represent a sparse graph using adjacency lists is $O(|\mathcal{V}|)$. Clearly this is asymptotically better than using adjacency matrices which require $O(|\mathcal{V}|^2)$ space.

## 16.2 Implementing Graphs

In keeping with the design framework used throughout this text, we view graphs as specialized containers. Formally, the graph $G = (\mathcal{V}, \mathcal{E})$ is an ordered pair comprised of two sets—a set of vertices and a set of edges. Informally, we can view a graph as a container with two compartments, one which holds vertices and one which holds edges. Therefore, there are three kinds of objects—vertices, edges, and graphs. Accordingly, we need three object classes: **Vertex**, **Edge**, and **Graph**. (See Figure 16.7.)

### 16.2.1 Implementing Vertices

What exactly is a vertex? The answer to this question depends on the application. At the very minimum, every vertex in a graph must be distinguishable from every other vertex in that graph. We can do this by numbering consecutively the vertices of a graph.

**FIGURE 16.7**
Object class hierarchy.

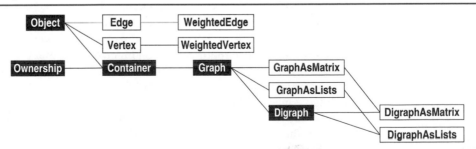

---

**PROGRAM 16.1**
Vertex class definition

---

```
1    class Vertex : public Object
2    {
3    public:
4        typedef unsigned int Number;
5    protected:
6        Number number;
7    public:
8        Vertex (Number);
9        virtual operator Number () const;
10       // ...
11   };
```

---

Program 16.1 defines the concrete class **Vertex**. Since we intend to insert instances of this class into containers, the **Vertex** class is derived from the **Object** base class. The **Vertex** class declares a single member the single member variable **number**. Each vertex inserted into a graph is required to have a different number.

A single **Vertex** constructor is declared. This constructor takes as its lone argument the number that is to be assigned to the vertex. In addition, the cast-to-**Number** member function (**operator Number**) is also declared. This allows the programmer to use a vertex wherever an integer is expected. The cast returns the value of the **number** member variable.

## 16.2.2 Implementing Edges

An edge in a directed graph is an ordered pair of vertices; an edge in an undirected graph is a set of two vertices. Because of the similarity of these concepts, we use the same class for both—the context in which an edge is used determines whether it is directed or undirected.

Program 16.2 declares the concrete class **Edge**. Since we intend to insert instances of this class into containers, the **Edge** class is derived from the **Object** base class.

The **Edge** class contains two member variables—**v0** and **v1**. Each is a reference to a vertex. When an instance of this class is used to represent a directed edge, then the edge represented shall be **v0** $\rightarrow$ **v1**. That is, **v1** is the head and **v0** is the tail. Alternatively, when an **Edge** instance represents an undirected edge, that edge is simply **{v0,v1}**.

Program 16.2 declares a constructor which takes two arguments, both of them references to **Vertex** instances. The effect of this constructor is to initialize the two corresponding member variables accordingly.

In addition to the constructor, there are three public member functions: **v0**, **v1**, and **Mate**. All three of them are accessors. The first two are used to access the member variables **v0** and **v1**, respectively.

**PROGRAM 16.2**
**Edge** class definition.

```
1   class Edge : public Object
2   {
3   protected:
4       Vertex& v0;
5       Vertex& v1;
6   public:
7       Edge (Vertex&, Vertex&);
8       virtual Vertex& V0 () const;
9       virtual Vertex& V1 () const;
10      virtual Vertex& Mate (Vertex const&) const;
11      // ...
12  };
```

For every instance **e** of the **Edge** class, the **Mate** member function satisfies the following identities:

$$e.Mate(e.V0()) \equiv e.V1()$$
$$e.Mate(e.V1()) \equiv e.V0().$$

Therefore, if we know that a vertex **v** is one of the vertices of **e**, then we can find the other vertex by calling **e.Mate(v)**.

### 16.2.3   Abstract Graphs and Digraphs

Directed graphs and undirected graphs have many common characteristics. Therefore, it seems reasonable to make use of inheritance in the implementation of graph classes. However, there are several possible ways in which to organize the class hierarchy:

**Option A** We could use a common abstract base class **Graph** to encapsulate the common attributes of all graphs and then derive two different classes **UndirectedGraph** and **DirectedGraph** from the common base class.

**Option B** Use **DirectedGraph** as the base class and derive the class **UndirectedGraph** from it. In this scenario we view an undirected graph as a directed graph that has its arrows removed.

**Option C** Use **UndirectedGraph** as the base class and derive the class **DirectedGraph** from it. In this scenario we view a directed graph as an undirected graph with arrows added.

As shown in Figure 16.7, we have chosen option C. We have chosen this approach because many algorithms for undirected graphs can also be used with directed graphs.

On the other hand, it is often the case that algorithms for directed graphs cannot be used with undirected graphs.

Program 16.3 declares two abstract classes, **Graph** and **Digraph**. The **Graph** class is the base class from which concrete classes that represent *undirected* graphs are derived. The **Digraph** abstract class extends the **Graph** class. The **Digraph** class is the base class from which concrete classes that represent *directed* graphs are derived.

The **Graph** class is an abstract base class since it contains pure virtual member functions. The graph class adds two member variables to those inherited from the base classes—**numberOfEdges** and **numberOfVertices**. A default constructor for the **Graph** class is also declared. The effect of this constructor is to initialize both member variables with the value zero. Therefore, a graph is initially empty—it contains neither vertices nor edges.

A number of **Graph** class member functions are declared in Program 16.3. There are essentially three groups of member functions: accessors and mutators, iterators, and traversals. The operations performed by the member functions are explained in the following sections.

### Accessors and Mutators

The **Graph** class declares the following accessor and mutator member functions:

**NumberOfEdges**  This accessor returns the number of edges contained by the graph.

**NumberOfVertices**  This accessor returns the number of vertices contained by the graph.

**AddVertex**  This mutator inserts a given vertex into a graph. For simplicity, we shall assume that a given vertex is inserted into exactly one graph. All the vertices contained in a given graph must have a unique vertex number. Furthermore, if a graph contains $n$ vertices, those vertices shall be numbered $0, 1, \ldots, n - 1$. Therefore, the next vertex inserted into the graph shall have the number $n$.

**SelectVertex**  This accessor takes an integer, say $i$ where $0 \leq i < n$, and returns reference to the $i$th vertex contained in the graph.

**operator[]**  This subscript operator takes an integer-valued subscript expression. We shall assume that the default behavior of this operator is to call **SelectVertex**.

**AddEdge**  This mutator inserts a given edge into a graph. For simplicity, we shall assume that a given edge is inserted into exactly one graph. Both vertices referenced by the edge must be vertices in the given graph.

**IsEdge**  This Boolean-valued accessor takes two **Vertex::Number** arguments. It returns **true** if the graph contains an edge that connects the corresponding vertices.

**SelectEdge**  This accessor takes two **Vertex::Number** arguments. It returns a reference to the edge instance (if it exists) that connects the corresponding vertices. The behavior of this routine is undefined when the edge does not exist. (An implementation will typically throw an exception.)

**IsCyclic**  This Boolean-valued accessor returns **true** if the graph is *cyclic*.

**PROGRAM 16.3**
Graph and Digraph class definitions

```
1   class Graph : public Container
2   {
3   protected:
4       unsigned int numberOfVertices;
5       unsigned int numberOfEdges;
6
7       void DepthFirstTraversal (
8           PrePostVisitor&, Vertex&, Array<bool>&) const;
9   public:
10      Graph ();
11
12      virtual unsigned int NumberOfEdges () const;
13      virtual unsigned int NumberOfVertices () const;
14      virtual void AddVertex (Vertex&) = 0;
15      virtual Vertex& SelectVertex (Vertex::Number) const = 0;
16      virtual Vertex& operator [] (Vertex::Number) const;
17      virtual void AddEdge (Edge&) = 0;
18      virtual Edge& SelectEdge (
19          Vertex::Number, Vertex::Number) const = 0;
20      virtual bool IsEdge (
21          Vertex::Number, Vertex::Number) const = 0;
22      virtual bool IsConnected () const;
23      virtual bool IsCyclic () const;
24
25      virtual Iterator& Vertices () const = 0;
26      virtual Iterator& Edges () const = 0;
27      virtual Iterator& IncidentEdges (Vertex const&) const = 0;
28      virtual Iterator& EmanatingEdges (Vertex const&) const = 0;
29
30      virtual void DepthFirstTraversal (
31          PrePostVisitor&, Vertex const&) const;
32      virtual void BreadthFirstTraversal (
33          Visitor&, Vertex const&) const;
34      // ...
35  };
36
37  class Digraph : public virtual Graph
38  {
39  public:
40      virtual bool IsConnected () const;
41      virtual bool IsCyclic () const;
42      virtual void TopologicalOrderTraversal (
43          Visitor&) const;
44  };
```

**IsConnected**    This Boolean-valued accessor returns **true** if the graph is *connected*. Connectedness of graphs is discussed in Section 16.3.4.

### Iterators

All the other container classes considered in this text have only one associated iterator. When dealing with graphs, it is convenient to have at least four iterators: The first two are used to enumerate the sets $\mathcal{V}$ and $\mathcal{E}$, and the last two are used to enumerate the sets $\mathcal{A}(v)$ and $\mathcal{I}(v)$ associated with a given vertex $v$.

Each of the following member functions allocates dynamically a new iterator instance as follows:

**Vertices**    This member function of the **Graph** class returns an iterator that can be used to traverse the elements of $\mathcal{V}$.

**Edges**    This member function of the **Graph** class returns an iterator that can be used to traverse the elements of $\mathcal{E}$.

**IncidentEdges**    This member function takes a reference to a vertex, say $v$, and returns an iterator that can be used to traverse the elements of $\mathcal{I}(v)$. The vertex $v$ must be contained by the graph.

**EmanatingEdges**    This member function takes a reference to a vertex, say $v$, and returns an iterator that can be used to traverse the elements of $\mathcal{A}(v)$. The vertex $v$ must be contained by the graph.

### Graph Traversals

These graph traversal functions are analogous to the **Accept** member function of the container class (see Section 5.2.5). Each of these functions takes a reference to a **Visitor** and performs a traversal. That is, all the *vertices* of the graph are visited systematically. When a vertex is visited, the **Visit** function of the visitor is applied to that vertex.

**DepthFirstTraversal** and **BreadthFirstTraversal**    Both of these functions accept two arguments—a reference to a **Visitor** and a reference to a vertex. The vertex specifies the starting node for either a depth-first traversal or a breadth-first traversal of the graph.

**TopologicalOrderTraversal**    A topological sort is an ordering of the nodes of a directed graph. This traversal visits the nodes of a directed graph in the order specified by a topological sort. Therefore, it is a member function of the **Digraph** class.

The graph traversal algorithms are discussed in Section 16.3.

## 16.2.4    Implementing Undirected Graphs

This section describes two concrete classes—**GraphAsMatrix** and **GraphAsLists**. These classes both represent *undirected graphs*. The **GraphAsMatrix** class represents the edges of a graph using an adjacency matrix. The **GraphAsLists** class represents the edges of a graph using adjacency lists.

---

**PROGRAM 16.4**
GraphAsMatrix class definition

```
1  class GraphAsMatrix : public virtual Graph
2  {
3  protected:
4      Array<Vertex*> vertices;
5      Array2D<Edge*> adjacencyMatrix;
6  public:
7      GraphAsMatrix (unsigned int);
8      // ...
9  };
```

---

### Using Adjacency Matrices

The **GraphAsMatrix** class is declared in Program 16.4. The **GraphAsMatrix** class is a concrete class derived from the base class **Graph**, which is shown in Program 16.3. Since **GraphAsMatrix** is a concrete class, it must provide implementations for all the member functions declared as pure virtual functions in the base classes—the function prototypes have been elided for the sake of brevity.

Each instance of the **GraphAsMatrix** class represents an undirected graph, say $G - (\mathcal{V}, \mathcal{E})$. The two member variables, **vertices** and **adjacencyMatrix**, are used to represent the sets $\mathcal{V}$ and $\mathcal{E}$, respectively.

The set of vertices, $\mathcal{V}$, is represented using a one-dimensional array of pointers to **Vertex** instances. The implementation uses the **Array<T>** class given in Section 4.1. The set of edges, $\mathcal{E}$, is represented using a two-dimensional matrix of pointers to **Edge** instances. The implementation uses the **Array2D<T>** class given in Section 4.3.

The **GraphAsMatrix** constructor takes a single argument of type **unsigned** that specifies the maximum number of vertices that the graph may contain. This quantity specifies the length of the array of vertices and the dimensions of the adjacency matrix. The implementation of the **GraphAsMatrix** class is left as programming project for the reader (Project 16.3).

### Using Adjacency Lists

Program 16.5 declares the **GraphAsLists** concrete class. The **GraphAsLists** class is derived from the abstract base class **Graph**. The **GraphAsLists** class represents the edges of a graph using adjacency lists.

Two member variables are declared—**vertices** and **adjacencyLists**. The former is an array of pointers to **Vertex** instances. This array is used to represent the elements of the vertex set $\mathcal{V}$.

The second member variable is an array of linked lists of pointers to edges. The $i$th linked list, **adjacencyLists[i]**, represents the set $\mathcal{A}(v_i)$ which is the set of edges emanating from vertex $v_i$. The implementation uses the **LinkedList<T>** class given in Section 4.2.

The **GraphAsLists** constructor takes a single argument of type **unsigned int** that specifies the maximum number of vertices that the graph may contain. This quantity specifies the lengths of the array of vertices and the array of adjacency lists. The

---

**PROGRAM 16.5**
GraphAsLists class definition

```
1   class GraphAsLists : public virtual Graph
2   {
3   protected:
4       Array<Vertex*> vertices;
5       Array<LinkedList<Edge*> > adjacencyLists;
6   public:
7       GraphAsLists (unsigned int);
8       // ...
9   };
```

---

implementation of the **GraphAsLists** class is left as programming project for the reader (Project 16.4).

### 16.2.5   Edge-Weighted and Vertex-Weighted Graphs

An *edge-weighted graph* is a graph in which each edge has been assigned a *weight*. Similarly, a *vertex-weighted graph* is a graph in which each vertex has been assigned a *weight*. In such graphs, the quantity represented by a weight depends on the application.

Since a graph is a container that contains specifically vertices and edges, it is not necessary to introduce new graph classes to represent edge-weighted and vertex-weighted graphs. Instead, we introduce two classes, **WeightedVertex** and **WeightedEdge**. By using instances of these new classes together with the existing graph classes, we can create arbitrary edge-weighted and vertex-weighted graphs. Program 16.6 contains the declarations of the **WeightedVertex** and **WeightedEdge** classes.

Since the **WeightedVertex** class is derived from the **Vertex** class, instances of the former can be used wherever the latter is expected. Therefore, we can create a vertex-weighted graph simply by inserting weighted vertices into an instance of one of the graph implementations discussed in the preceding section.

The **WeightedVertex** class contains a single member variable called **weight** which is a pointer to an **Object** instance. Therefore, any object type can be used as the weight. The constructor sets the weight to a given value, and the member function **Weight** is used to access the weight.

The **WeightedEdge** class is implemented similarly. That is, weighted edge instances can be used wherever an edge is expected. By inserting weighted edges into a graph, we get an edge-weighted graph. Clearly, if the application demands it, it is possible to use both weighted vertices and weighted edges in the same graph.

### 16.2.6   Comparison of Graph Representations

In order to make the appropriate choice when selecting a graph representation scheme, it is necessary to understand the time/space trade-offs. Although the details of the im-

---

**PROGRAM 16.6**
`WeightedVertex` and `WeightedEdge` class definitions

```
1   class WeightedVertex : public Vertex
2   {
3       Object* weight;
4   public:
5       WeightedVertex (Vertex::Number, Object&);
6       virtual Object& Weight () const;
7       // ...
8   };
9
10  class WeightedEdge : public Edge
11  {
12      Object* weight;
13  public:
14      WeightedEdge (Vertex&, Vertex&, Object&);
15      virtual Object& Weight () const;
16      // ...
17  };
```

---

plementations have been omitted, we can still make meaningful conclusions about the performance that we can expect from those implementations. In this section we consider the space required as well as the running times for basic graph operations.

### Space Comparison

Consider the representation of a directed graph $G = (\mathcal{V}, \mathcal{E})$. In addition to the $\mathcal{V}$ `Vertex` class instances and the $|\mathcal{E}|$ `Edge` class instances contained by the graph, there is the storage required by the adjacency matrix. In this case, the matrix is a $|\mathcal{V}| \times |\mathcal{V}|$ matrix of pointers to `Edge` instances. Therefore, the amount of storage required by an adjacency matrix implementation is

$$|\mathcal{V}| \times \texttt{sizeof(Vertex)} + |\mathcal{E}| \times \texttt{sizeof(Edge)} \qquad (16.1)$$
$$+ |\mathcal{V}|^2 \times \texttt{sizeof(Edge*)} + O(1).$$

On the other hand, consider the amount of storage required when we represent the same graph using adjacency lists. In addition to the vertices and the edges themselves, there are $|\mathcal{V}|$ linked lists. If we use the `LinkedList` class defined in Section 4.2, each such list has a `head` and `tail` pointer. Altogether there are $\mathcal{E}$ linked lists elements, each of which consists of a pointer to the next element of the lists and a pointer to an edge. Therefore, the total space required is

$$|\mathcal{V}| \times \texttt{sizeof(Vertex)} + |\mathcal{E}| \times \texttt{sizeof(Edge)} \qquad (16.2)$$
$$+ |\mathcal{V}| \times \texttt{sizeof(ListElement<Edge*>)}$$
$$+ |\mathcal{E}| \times (\texttt{sizeof(ListElement<Edge*>)} + \texttt{sizeof(Edge*)}) + O(1).$$

Notice that the space for the vertices and edges themselves cancels out when we compare Equation 16.1 with Equation 16.2. If we assume that all pointers require the same amount of space, we can conclude that adjacency lists use less space than adjacency matrices when

$$|\mathcal{E}| < \frac{|\mathcal{V}|^2 - |\mathcal{V}|}{2}.$$

For example, given a 10-node graph, the adjacency lists version uses less space when there are fewer than 45 edges. As a rough rule of thumb, we can say that adjacency lists use less space when the average degree of a node, $\bar{d} = |\mathcal{E}|/|\mathcal{V}|$, satisfies $\bar{d} \lessapprox |\mathcal{V}|/2$.

## Time Comparison

The following four operations are used extensively in the implementations of many different graph algorithms:

**find edge** $(v, w)$   Given vertices $v$ and $w$, this operation locates the corresponding **Edge** instance. When using an adjacency matrix, we can find an edge in constant time. When adjacency lists are used, the worst-case running time is $O(|\mathcal{A}(v)|)$, since $|\mathcal{A}(v)|$ is the length of the adjacency list associated with vertex $v$. This is the operation performed by the **SelectEdge** member function of the **Graph** class.

**enumerate all edges**   In order to locate all the edges in when using adjacency matrices, it is necessary to examine all $|\mathcal{V}|^2$ matrix entries. Therefore, the worst-case running time needed to enumerate all the edges is $O(|\mathcal{V}|^2)$.

On the other hand, to enumerate all the edges when using adjacency lists requires the traversal of $|\mathcal{V}|$ lists. In all there are $|\mathcal{E}|$ edges. Therefore, the worst-case running time is $O(|\mathcal{V}| + |\mathcal{E}|)$.

This operation is performed using the iterator returned by the **Edges** member function of the **Graph** class.

**enumerate edges emanating from** $v$   To enumerate all the edges that emanate from vertex $v$ requires a complete scan of the $v$th row of an adjacency matrix. Therefore, the worst-case running time when using adjacency matrices is $O(|\mathcal{V}|)$.

Enumerating the edges emanating from vertex $v$ is a trivial operation when using adjacency lists—just traverse the $v$th list. This takes $O(|\mathcal{A}(v)|)$ time in the worst case.

This operation is performed using the iterator returned by the **EmanatingEdges** member function of the **Graph** class.

**enumerate edges incident on** $w$   To enumerate all the edges are incident on vertex $w$ requires a complete scan of the $w$th column of an adjacency matrix. Therefore, the worst-case running time when using adjacency matrices is $O(|\mathcal{V}|)$.

Enumerating the edges incident on vertex $w$ is a non-trivial operation when using adjacency lists. It is necessary to search every adjacency list in order to find all

**TABLE 16.2**

Comparison of Graph Representations

| | Representation Scheme | |
|---|---|---|
| Operation | Adjacency Matrix | Adjacency List |
| Find edge $(v, w)$ | $O(1)$ | $O(|\mathcal{A}(v)|)$ |
| Enumerate all edges | $O(|\mathcal{V}|^2)$ | $O(|\mathcal{V}| + |\mathcal{E}|)$ |
| Enumerate edges emanating from $v$ | $O(|\mathcal{V}|)$ | $O(|\mathcal{A}(v)|)$ |
| Enumerate edges incident on $w$ | $O(|\mathcal{V}|)$ | $O(|\mathcal{V}| + |\mathcal{E}|)$ |

the edges incident on a given vertex. Therefore, the worst-case running time is $O(|\mathcal{V}| + |\mathcal{E}|)$.

This operation is performed using the iterator returned by the **IncidentEdges** member function of the **Graph** class.

Table 16.2 summarizes these running times.

## 16.3 Graph Traversals

There are many different applications of graphs. As a result, there are many different algorithms for manipulating them. However, many of the different graph algorithms have in common the characteristic that they systematically visit all the vertices in the graph. That is, the algorithm walks through the graph data structure and performs some computation at each vertex in the graph. This process of walking through the graph is called a *graph traversal*.

While there are many different possible ways in which to systematically visit all the vertices of a graph, certain traversal methods occur frequently enough that they are given names of their own. This section presents three of them—depth-first traversal, breadth-first traversal and topological sort.

### 16.3.1 Depth-First Traversal

The *depth-first traversal* of a graph is like the depth-first traversal of a tree discussed in Section 9.4. A depth-first traversal of a tree always starts at the root of the tree. Since a graph has no root, when we do a depth-first traversal, we must specify the vertex at which to begin.

A depth-first traversal of a tree visits a node and then recursively visits the subtrees of that node. Similarly, depth-first traversal of a graph visits a vertex and then recursively visits all the vertices adjacent to that node. The catch is that the graph may contain cycles, but the traversal must visit every vertex at most once. The solution to the problem is to keep track of the nodes that have been visited, so that the traversal does not suffer the fate of infinite recursion.

**FIGURE 16.8**
Depth-first traversal.

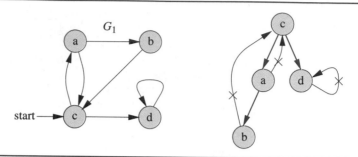

For example, Figure 16.8 illustrates the depth-first traversal of the directed graph $G_1$ starting from vertex $c$. The depth-first traversal visits the nodes in the order

$$c, a, b, d.$$

A depth-first traversal only follows edges that lead to unvisited vertices. As shown in Figure 16.8, if we omit the edges that are not followed, the remaining edges form a tree. Clearly, the depth-first traversal of this tree is equivalent to the depth-first traversal of the graph.

### Implementation

Program 16.7 gives the code for the two **DepthFirstTraversal** routines of the **Graph** class. One of them accepts two arguments, the other, three. As indicated in Program 16.3, the two-argument routine is declared **public** whereas the three-argument one is **protected**.

The user of the **Graph** class only sees the two-argument **DepthFirstTraversal** routine. This routine takes a reference to a **Visitor** instance and a reference to a **Vertex** instance. The idea is that the **Visit** function of the visitor is called once for each vertex in the graph and the vertices are visited in depth-first traversal order starting from the specified vertex.

In order to ensure that each vertex is visited at most once, an array of length $|\mathcal{V}|$ of Boolean values called **visited** is used (line 4). That is, **visited**[$i$] = **true** only if vertex $i$ has been visited. All the array elements are initially **false** (lines 5–6). After initializing the array, the two-argument routine calls the three-argument one, passing it a reference to the array as the third argument.

The three-argument routine returns immediately if the visitor is done. Otherwise, it visits the specified node, and then it follows all the edges emanating from that node and recursively visits the adjacent vertices *if those vertices have not already been visited.*

### Running Time Analysis

The running time of the depth-first traversal routine depends on the graph representation scheme used. The traversal visits each node in the graph at most once. When a node is visited, all the edges emanating from that node are considered. During a complete traversal the algorithm enumerates every edge in the graph.

**PROGRAM 16.7**
Graph class `DepthFirstTraversal` member function definition

```
1   void Graph::DepthFirstTraversal (
2       PrePostVisitor& visitor, Vertex const& start) const
3   {
4       Array<bool> visited (numberOfVertices);
5       for (Vertex::Number v = 0; v < numberOfVertices; ++v)
6           visited [v] = false;
7       DepthFirstTraversal (
8           visitor, const_cast<Vertex&> (start), visited);
9   }
10
11  void Graph::DepthFirstTraversal (PrePostVisitor& visitor,
12      Vertex& vertex, Array<bool>& visited) const
13  {
14      if (visitor.IsDone ())
15          return;
16      visitor.PreVisit (vertex);
17      visited [vertex] = true;
18      Iterator& p = EmanatingEdges (vertex);
19      while (!p.IsDone ()) {
20          Edge& edge = dynamic_cast<Edge&> (*p);
21          Vertex& to = edge.Mate (vertex);
22          if (!visited [to])
23              DepthFirstTraversal (visitor, to, visited);
24          ++p;
25      }
26      delete &p;
27      visitor.PostVisit (vertex);
28  }
```

Therefore, the worst-case running time for the depth-first traversal of a graph represented using an adjacency matrix is

$$|\mathcal{V}| \times (\mathcal{T}\langle\text{PreVisit()}\rangle + \mathcal{T}\langle\text{PostVisit()}\rangle) + O(|\mathcal{V}|^2).$$

When adjacency lists are used, the worst-case running time for the depth-first traversal routine is

$$|\mathcal{V}| \times (\mathcal{T}\langle\text{PreVisit()}\rangle + \mathcal{T}\langle\text{PostVisit()}\rangle) + O(|\mathcal{V}| + |\mathcal{E}|).$$

Recall that for a sparse graph $|\mathcal{E}| = O(|\mathcal{V}|)$. If the sparse graph is represented using adjacency lists and if $\mathcal{T}\langle\text{PreVisit()}\rangle = O(1)$ and $\mathcal{T}\langle\text{PostVisit()}\rangle = O(1)$ the worst-case running time of the depth-first traversal is simply $O(|\mathcal{V}|)$.

## 16.3.2  Breadth-First Traversal

The *breadth-first traversal* of a graph is like the breadth-first traversal of a tree discussed in Section 9.4. The breadth-first traversal of a tree visits the nodes in the order of their depth in the tree. Breadth-first tree traversal first visits all the nodes at depth zero (i.e., the root), then all the nodes at depth 1, and so on.

Since a graph has no root, when we do a breadth-first traversal, we must specify the vertex at which to start the traversal. Furthermore, we can define the depth of a given vertex to be the length of the shortest path from the starting vertex to the given vertex. Thus, breadth-first traversal first visits the starting vertex, then all the vertices adjacent to the starting vertex, and then all the vertices adjacent to those, and so on.

Section 6.2.3 presents a nonrecursive breadth-first traversal algorithm for $N$-ary trees that uses a queue to keep track of the vertices that need to be visited. The breadth-first graph traversal algorithm is very similar.

First, the starting vertex is enqueued. Then, the following steps are repeated until the queue is empty:

1. Remove the vertex at the head of the queue and call it **vertex**.
2. Visit **vertex**.
3. Follow each edge emanating from **vertex** to find the adjacent vertex and call it **to**. If **to** has not already been put into the queue, enqueue it.

Notice that a vertex can be put into the queue at most once. Therefore, the algorithm must somehow keep track of the vertices that have been enqueued.

Figure 16.9 illustrates the breadth-first traversal of the directed graph $G_1$ starting from vertex $a$. The algorithm begins by inserting the starting vertex, $a$, into the empty

---

**FIGURE 16.9**
Breadth-first traversal.

---

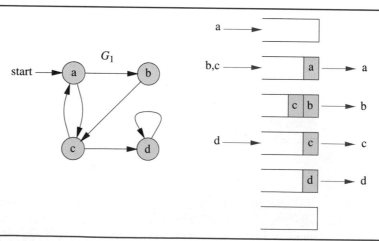

queue. Next, the head of the queue (vertex $a$) is dequeued and visited, and the vertices adjacent to it (vertices $b$ and $c$) are enqueued. When, $b$ is dequeued and visited we find that there is only adjacent vertex, $c$, and that vertex is already in the queue. Next vertex $c$ is dequeued and visited. Vertex $c$ is adjacent to $a$ and $d$. Since $a$ has already been enqueued (and subsequently dequeued) only vertex $d$ is put into the queue. Finally, vertex $d$ is dequeued an visited. Therefore, the breadth-first traversal of $G_1$ starting from $a$ visits the vertices in the sequence

$$a, b, c, d.$$

### Implementation

Program 16.8 gives the code for the **BreadthFirstTraversal** routine of the **Graph** class. This routine takes a reference to a **Visitor** instance and a reference to a **Vertex** instance. The **Visit** function of the visitor is called once for each vertex in the graph and the vertices are visited in breadth-first traversal order starting from the specified vertex.

A Boolean-valued array, **enqueued**, is used to keep track of the vertices that have been put into the queue. The elements of the array are all initialized to **false** (lines 4–6).

Next, a new queue instance is allocated dynamically (line 8). The queue is used to contain only vertices. Since the vertices are owned by the graph, they cannot also be owned by the queue. Therefore, the **RescindOwnership** function of the queue is called (line 9). This way, when the queue destructor is called, it will not attempt to delete any of the its contained objects.

The second argument of the **BreadthOrderTraversal** function is a reference to a **const** vertex. Therefore, the routine must not modify the start vertex. However, we need to push the vertex onto the queue and since the **Enqueue** function takes a non-**const Object** reference, it is necessary to cast away the **const**ness using a **const_cast** (line 12). This is not an unsafe cast in this context, because the queue is a local variable of the **BreadthOrderTraversal** routine and because the routine does not modify anything which it later dequeues from the queue.

The main loop of the **BreadthFirstTraversal** routine comprises lines 13–30. This loop continues as long as there is a vertex in the queue and the visitor is willing to do more work (line 13). In each iteration exactly one vertex is dequeued and visited (lines 15–17). After a vertex is visited, all the successors of that node are examined (lines 18–21). Every successor of the node that has not yet been enqueued is put into the queue, and the fact that it has been enqueued is recored in the array **enqueued** (lines 22–26).

### Running Time Analysis

The breadth-first traversal enqueues each node in the graph at most once. When a node is dequeued, all the edges emanating from that node are considered. Therefore, a complete traversal enumerates every edge in the graph.

The actual running time of the breadth-first traversal routine depends on the graph representation scheme used. The worst-case running time for the traversal of a graph represented using an adjacency matrix is

$$|\mathcal{V}| \times \mathcal{G}\langle \texttt{visit()}\rangle + O(|\mathcal{V}|^2).$$

---

**PROGRAM 16.8**
Graph class `BreadthFirstTraversal` member function definition

```
1   void Graph::BreadthFirstTraversal (
2       Visitor& visitor, Vertex const& start) const
3   {
4       Array<bool> enqueued (numberOfVertices);
5       for (Vertex::Number v = 0; v < numberOfVertices; ++v)
6           enqueued [v] = false;
7
8       Queue& queue = *new QueueAsLinkedList ();
9       queue.RescindOwnership ();
10
11      enqueued [start] = true;
12      queue.Enqueue (const_cast<Vertex&> (start));
13      while (!queue.IsEmpty () && !visitor.IsDone ())
14      {
15          Vertex& vertex =
16              dynamic_cast<Vertex&> (queue.Dequeue ());
17          visitor.Visit (vertex);
18          Iterator& p = EmanatingEdges (vertex);
19          while (!p.IsDone ()) {
20              Edge& edge = dynamic_cast<Edge&> (*p);
21              Vertex& to = edge.Mate (vertex);
22              if (!enqueued [to])
23              {
24                  enqueued [to] = true;
25                  queue.Enqueue (to);
26              }
27              ++p;
28          }
29          delete &p;
30      }
31      delete &queue;
32  }
```

---

When adjacency lists are used, the worst-case running time for the breadth-first traversal routine is

$$|\mathcal{V}| \times \mathcal{T}\langle \texttt{visit()} \rangle + O(|\mathcal{V}| + |\mathcal{E}|).$$

If the graph is sparse, then $|\mathcal{E}| = O(|\mathcal{V}|)$. Therefore, if a sparse graph is represented using adjacency lists and if $\mathcal{T}\langle \texttt{visit()} \rangle = O(1)$, the worst-case running time of the breadth-first traversal is just $O(|\mathcal{V}|)$.

**FIGURE 16.10**
A directed acyclic graph.

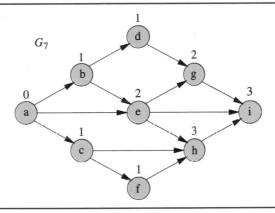

### 16.3.3   Topological Sort

A topological sort is an ordering of the vertices of a *directed acyclic graph* given by the following definition.

**Definition 16.7 (Topological Sort)**
*Consider a directed acyclic graph $G = (\mathcal{V}, \mathcal{E})$. A topological sort of the vertices of G is a sequence $S = \{v_1, v_2, \ldots, v_{|\mathcal{V}|}\}$ in which each element of $\mathcal{V}$ appears exactly once. For every pair of distinct vertices $v_i$ and $v_j$ in the sequence S, if $v_i \rightarrow v_j$ is an edge in G, i.e., $(v_i, v_j) \in \mathcal{E}$, then $i < j$.*

Informally, a topological sort is a list of the vertices of a DAG in which all the successors of any given vertex appear in the sequence after that vertex. Consider the directed acyclic graph $G_7$ shown in Figure 16.10. The sequence $S = \{a, b, c, d, e, f, g, h, i\}$ is a topological sort of the vertices of $G_7$. To see that this is so, consider the set of vertices:

$$\mathcal{E} = \{(a, b), (a, c), (a, e), (b, d), (b, e), (c, f), (c, h),$$
$$(d, g), (e, g), (e, h), (e, i), (f, h)(g, i), (h, i)\}.$$

The vertices in each edge are in alphabetical order, and so is the sequence $S$.

It should also be evident from Figure 16.10 that a topological sort is not unique. For example, the following are also valid topological sorts of the graph $G_7$:

$$S' = \{a, c, b, f, e, d, h, g, i\}$$
$$S'' = \{a, b, d, e, g, c, f, h, i\}$$
$$S''' = \{a, c, f, h, b, e, d, g, i\}$$

$$\vdots$$

One way to find a topological sort is to consider the *in-degrees* of the vertices. (The number above a vertex in Figure 16.10 is the in-degree of that vertex). Clearly the first vertex in a topological sort must have in-degree zero and every DAG must contain at least one vertex with in-degree zero. A simple algorithm to create the sort goes like this:

Repeat the following steps until the graph is empty:

1. Select a vertex that has in-degree zero.

2. Add the vertex to the sort.

3. Delete the vertex and all the edges emanating from it from the graph.

## Implementation

Instead of implementing an algorithm that computes a topological sort, we have chosen to implement a traversal that visits the vertices of a DAG in the order given by the topological sort. The topological order traversal can be used to implement many other graph algorithms. Furthermore, given such a traversal, it is easy to define a visitor that computes a topological sort.

In order to implement the algorithm described in the preceding section, an array of integers of length $|\mathcal{V}|$ is used to record the in-degrees of the vertices. As a result, it is not really necessary to remove vertices or edges from the graph during the traversal. Instead, the effect of removing a vertex and all the edges emanating from that vertex is simulated by decreasing the apparent in-degrees of all the successors of the removed vertex.

In addition, we use a queue to keep track of the vertices that have not yet been visited, but whose in-degree is zero. Doing so eliminates the need to search the array for zero entries.

Program 16.3 defines the **TopologicalOrderTraversal** routine of the **Digraph** class. This routine takes as its lone argument a reference to a visitor instance. The **Visit** function of the visitor is called once for each vertex in the graph. The order in which the vertices are visited is given by a topological sort of those vertices.

The algorithm begins by computing the in-degrees of all the vertices. An array of unsigned integers of length $\mathcal{V}$ called **inDegree** is used for this purpose. First, all the array elements are set to zero. Then, for each edge $(v_0, v_1) \in \mathcal{V}$, array element **inDegree**$(v_1)$ is increased by one (lines 3–12).

Next, a queue to hold vertices is created. Since the vertices are owned by the graph, the **RescindOwnership** member function of the queue is called. That way, the queue will not attempt to delete any contained vertices when its destructor is called. After the queue has been initialized, all vertices with in-degree zero are enqueued (lines 14–18).

The main loop of the **TopologicalOrderTraversal** routine comprises lines 19–33. This loop continues as long as the queue is not empty and the visitor is not finished. In each iteration of the main loop exactly one vertex is dequeued and visited (lines 21–23).

Once a vertex has been visited, the effect of removing that vertex from the graph is simulated by decreasing by 1 the in-degrees of all the successors of that vertex. When the in-degree of a vertex becomes zero, that vertex is enqueued (lines 24–30).

**PROGRAM 16.9**
Digraph class `TopologicalOrderTraversal` member function definition

```
1    void Digraph::TopologicalOrderTraversal (Visitor& visitor) const
2    {
3        Array<unsigned int> inDegree (numberOfVertices);
4        for (Vertex::Number v = 0; v < numberOfVertices; ++v)
5            inDegree [v] = 0;
6        Iterator& p = Edges ();
7        while (!p.IsDone ()) {
8            Edge& edge = dynamic_cast<Edge&> (*p);
9            ++inDegree [edge.V1 ()];
10           ++p;
11       }
12       delete &p;
13
14       Queue& queue = *new QueueAsLinkedList ();
15       queue.RescindOwnership ();
16       for (Vertex::Number v = 0; v < numberOfVertices; ++v)
17           if (inDegree [v] == 0)
18               queue.Enqueue (SelectVertex (v));
19       while (!queue.IsEmpty () && !visitor.IsDone ())
20       {
21           Vertex& vertex =
22               dynamic_cast<Vertex&> (queue.Dequeue ());
23           visitor.Visit (vertex);
24           Iterator& q = EmanatingEdges (vertex);
25           while (!q.IsDone ()) {
26               Edge& edge = dynamic_cast<Edge&> (*q);
27               Vertex& to = edge.V1 ();
28               if (--inDegree [to] == 0)
29                   queue.Enqueue (to);
30               ++q;
31           }
32           delete &q;
33       }
34       delete &queue;
35   }
```

### Running Time Analysis

The topological-order traversal enqueues each node in the graph at most once. When a node is dequeued, all the edges emanating from that node are considered. Therefore, a complete traversal enumerates every edge in the graph.

The worst-case running time for the traversal of a graph represented using an adjacency matrix is

$$|\mathcal{V}| \times \mathcal{T}\langle \texttt{visit()}\rangle + O(|\mathcal{V}|^2).$$

When adjacency lists are used, the worst-case running time for the topological-order traversal routine is

$$|\mathcal{V}| \times \mathcal{T}\langle \text{visit}() \rangle + O(|\mathcal{V}| + |\mathcal{E}|).$$

## 16.3.4   Graph Traversal Applications: Testing for Cycles and Connectedness

This section presents several graph algorithms that are based on graph traversals. The first two algorithms test undirected and directed graphs for connectedness. Both algorithms are implemented using the depth-first traversal. The third algorithm tests a directed graph for cycles. It is implemented using a topological-order traversal.

### Connectedness of an Undirected Graph

### Definition 16.8 (Connectedness of an Undirected Graph)
*An undirected graph* $G = (\mathcal{V}, \mathcal{E})$ *is* connected *if there is a path in G between every pair of vertices in* $\mathcal{V}$.

Consider the undirected graph shown in Figure 16.11. It is tempting to interpret this figure as a picture of two graphs. However, the figure actually represents the undirected graph $G_8 = (\mathcal{V}, \mathcal{E})$, given by

$$\mathcal{V} = \{a, b, c, d, e, f\}$$
$$\mathcal{E} = \{\{a, b\}, \{a, c\}, \{b, c\}, \{d, e\}, \{e, f\}\}.$$

Clearly, the graph $G_8$ is not connected. For example, there is no path between vertices $a$ and $d$. In fact, the graph $G_8$ consists of two, unconnected parts, each of which is a connected subgraph. The connected subgraphs of a graph are called *connected components*.

A traversal of an undirected graph (either depth-first or breadth-first) starting from any vertex will only visit all the other vertices of the graph if that graph is connected. Therefore, there is a very simple way to test whether an undirected graph is connected: count the number of vertices visited during a traversal of the graph. Only if all the vertices are visited is the graph connected.

---

**FIGURE 16.11**
An unconnected, undirected graph with two (connected) components.

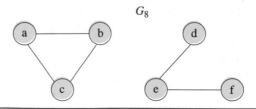

**PROGRAM 16.10**
Graph class IsConnected member function definition

```
1   class CountingVisitor : public Visitor
2   {
3       unsigned int count;
4   public:
5       CountingVisitor () : count (0)
6           {}
7       void Visit (Object&)
8           { ++count; }
9       unsigned int Count () const
10          { return count; }
11  };
12
13  bool Graph::IsConnected () const
14  {
15      CountingVisitor visitor;
16      DepthFirstTraversal (PreOrder (visitor), SelectVertex (0));
17      return visitor.Count () == numberOfVertices;
18  }
```

Program 16.10 shows how this can be implemented. The IsConnected member function of the Graph class is a Boolean-valued accessor that returns true if the graph is connected. The routine is implemented using a CountingVisitor and the DepthFirstTraversal routine.

A CountingVisitor is a visitor that simply counts the number of vertices it visits. It has a single member variable, count, which is initialized to zero in the constructor. The Visit routine adds one the count each time it is called and the Count accessor returns the value of the count.

The worst-case running time of the IsConnected routine is determined by the time taken by the DepthFirstTraversal. Clearly in this case $\mathcal{T}\langle\text{visitor()}\rangle = O(1)$. Therefore, the running time of IsConnected is $O(|\mathcal{V}|^2)$ when adjacency matrices are used to represent the graph and $O(|\mathcal{V}| + |\mathcal{E}|)$ when adjacency lists are used.

### Connectedness of a Directed Graph
When dealing with directed graphs, we define two kinds of connectedness, *strong* and *weak*. Strong connectedness of a directed graph is defined as follows:

### Definition 16.9 (Strong Connectedness of a Directed Graph)
*A directed graph $G = (\mathcal{V}, \mathcal{E})$ is strongly connected if there is a path in G between every pair of vertices in $\mathcal{V}$.*

For example, Figure 16.12 shows the directed graph $G_9 = \{\mathcal{V}, \mathcal{E}\}$ given by

$$\mathcal{V} = \{a, b, c, d, e, f\}$$
$$\mathcal{E} = \{(a, b), (b, c), (b, e), (c, a), (d, e), (e, f), (f, d),\}$$

Notice that the graph $G_9$ is *not* connected! For example, there is no path from any of the vertices in $\{d, e, f\}$ to any of the vertices in $\{a, b, c\}$. Nevertheless, the graph "looks" connected in the sense that it is not made up of separate parts in the way that the graph $G_8$ in Figure 16.11 is.

This idea of "looking" connected is what *weak connectedness* represents. To define weak connectedness we need to introduce first the notion of the undirected graph that underlies a directed graph: Consider a directed graph $G = (\mathcal{V}, \mathcal{E})$. The underlying undirected graph is the graph $\widehat{G} = (\mathcal{V}, \widehat{\mathcal{E}})$ where $\widehat{\mathcal{E}}$ represents the set of undirected edges that is obtained by removing the arrowheads from the directed edges in $G$:

$$\widehat{\mathcal{E}} = \left\{ \{v, w\} : (v, w) \in \mathcal{E} \lor (w, v) \in \mathcal{E} \right\}.$$

Weak connectedness of a directed graph is defined with respect to its underlying, undirected graph:

### Definition 16.10 (Weak Connectedness of a Directed Graph)
*A directed graph $G = (\mathcal{V}, \mathcal{E})$ is weakly connected if the underlying undirected graph $\widehat{G}$ is connected.*

For example, since the undirected graph $\widehat{G_9}$ in Figure 16.12 is connected, the directed graph $G_9$ is *weakly connected.* Consider what happens when we remove the edge $(b, e)$ from the directed graph $G_9$. The underlying undirected graph that we get is $G_8$ in Figure 16.11. Therefore, when we remove edge $(b, e)$ from $G_9$, the graph that remains is neither strongly connected nor weakly connected.

---

**FIGURE 16.12**
A weakly connected directed graph and the underlying undirected graph.

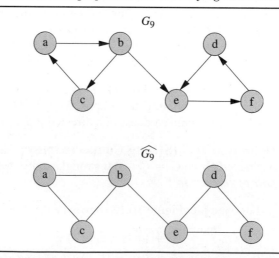

A traversal of a directed graph (either depth-first or breadth-first) starting from a given vertex will only visit all the vertices of an undirected graph if there is a path from the start vertex to every other vertex. Therefore, a simple way to test whether a directed graph is strongly connected uses $|\mathcal{V}|$ traversals—one starting from each vertex in $\mathcal{V}$. Each time the number of vertices visited is counted. The graph is strongly connected if all the vertices are visited in each traversal.

Program 16.11 shows how this can be implemented. It shows the **IsConnected** member function of the **Digraph** class which returns the Boolean value **true** if the graph is *strongly* connected.

The routine consists of a loop over all the vertices of the graph. Each iteration does a **DepthFirstTraversal** using the **CountingVisitor** given in Program 16.10. The running time for one iteration is essentially that of the **DepthOrderTraversal** since $\mathcal{T}\langle \text{visit()} \rangle = O(1)$ for the counting visitor. Therefore, the worst-case running time for the **IsConnected** routine is $O(|\mathcal{V}|^3)$ when adjacency matrices are used and $O(|\mathcal{V}|^2 + |\mathcal{V}| \cdot |\mathcal{E}|)$ when adjacency lists are used to represent the graph.

## Testing for Cycles in a Directed Graph

The final application of graph traversal that we consider in this section is to test a directed graph for cycles. An easy way to do this is to attempt a topological-order traversal using the algorithm given in Section 16.3.3. This algorithm only visits all the vertices of a directed graph if that graph contains no cycles.

To see why this is so, consider the directed cyclic graph $G_{10}$ shown in Figure 16.13. The topological traversal algorithm begins by computing the *in-degrees* of the vertices. (The number shown below each vertex in Figure 16.13 is the in-degree of that vertex.)

At each step of the traversal, a vertex with in-degree of zero is visited. After a vertex is visited, the vertex and all the edges emanating from that vertex are removed from the graph. Notice that if we remove vertex $a$ and edge $(a, b)$ from $G_{10}$, all the remaining vertices have in-degrees of 1. The presence of the cycle prevents the topological-order traversal from completing.

---

**PROGRAM 16.11**
Digraph class IsConnected member function definition

---

```
1   bool Digraph::IsConnected () const
2   {
3       for (Vertex::Number v = 0; v < numberOfVertices; ++v)
4       {
5           CountingVisitor visitor;
6           DepthFirstTraversal (
7               PreOrder (visitor), SelectVertex (v));
8           if (visitor.Count () != numberOfVertices)
9               return false;
10      }
11      return true;
12  }
```

---

**FIGURE 16.13**
A directed cyclic graph.

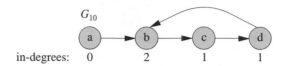

in-degrees:    0       2       1       1

**PROGRAM 16.12**
**Digraph** class **IsCyclic** member function definition

```
1   bool Digraph::IsCyclic () const
2   {
3       CountingVisitor visitor;
4       TopologicalOrderTraversal (visitor);
5       return visitor.Count () != numberOfVertices;
6   }
```

Therefore, a simple way to test whether a directed graph is cyclic is to attempt a topological traversal of its vertices. If all the vertices are not visited, the graph must be cyclic.

Program 16.12 gives the implementation of the **IsCyclic** member function of the **Digraph** class. This Boolean-valued accessor returns **true** if the graph is cyclic. The implementation simply makes use of a **CountingVisitor** to count the number of vertices visited during a **TopologicalOrderTraversal** of the graph.

The worst-case running time of the **IsCyclic** routine is determined by the time taken by the **TopologicalOrderTraversal**. Since $\mathcal{T}\langle\texttt{visit()}\rangle = O(1)$, the running time of **IsCyclic** is $O(|\mathcal{V}|^2)$ when adjacency matrices are used to represent the graph and $O(|\mathcal{V}| + |\mathcal{E}|)$ when adjacency lists are used.

## 16.4 Shortest-Path Algorithms

In this section we consider edge-weighted graphs, both directed and undirected, in which the weight measures the *cost* of traversing that edge. The units of cost depend on the application.

For example, we can use a directed graph to represent a network of airports. In such a graph the vertices represent the airports and the edges correspond to the available flights between airports. In this scenario there are several possible cost metrics: If we are interested in computing travel time, then we use an edge-weighted graph in which the weights represent the flying time between airports. If we are concerned with the financial cost of a trip, then the weights on the edges represent the monetary cost of a ticket. Finally, if we are interested in the actual distance traveled, then the weights represent the physical distances between airports.

If we are interested in traveling from point $A$ to $B$, we can use a suitably labeled graph to answer the following questions: What is the fastest way to get from $A$ to $B$? Which route from $A$ to $B$ has the least expensive airfare? What is the shortest possible distance traveled to get from $A$ to $B$?

Each of these questions is an instance of the same problem: Given an edge-weighted graph, $G = (\mathcal{V}, \mathcal{E})$, and two vertices, $v_s \in \mathcal{V}$ and $v_d \in \mathcal{V}$, find the path that starts at $v_s$ and ends at $v_d$ that has the smallest weighted path length. The weighted length of a path is defined as follows.

### Definition 16.11 (Weighted Path Length)

*Consider an edge-weighted graph $G = (\mathcal{V}, \mathcal{E})$. Let $C(v_i, v_j)$ be the weight on the edge connecting $v_i$ to $v_j$. A path in $G$ is a non-empty sequence of vertices $P = \{v_1, v_2, \ldots, v_k\}$. The weighted path length of path $P$ is given by*

$$\sum_{i=1}^{k-1} C(v_i, v_{i+1}).$$

The *weighted* length of a path is the sum of the weights on the edges in that path. Conversely, the *unweighted* length of a path is simply the number of edges in that path. Therefore, the *unweighted* length of a path is equivalent to the weighted path length obtained when all edge weights are 1.

## 16.4.1 Single-Source Shortest Path

In this section we consider the *single-source shortest path* problem: Given an edge-weighted graph $G = (\mathcal{V}, \mathcal{E})$ and a vertex $v_s \in \mathcal{V}$, find the shortest weighted path from $v_s$ to every other vertex in $\mathcal{V}$.

Why do we find the shortest path to every other vertex if we are interested only in the shortest path from, say, $v_s$ to $v_d$? It turns out that in order to find the shortest path from $v_s$ to $v_d$, it is necessary to find the shortest path from $v_s$ to every other vertex in $G$!

Clearly, when we search for the shortest path, we must consider all the vertices in $\mathcal{V}$. If a vertex is ignored, say $v_i$, then we will not consider any of the paths from $v_s$ to $v_d$ that pass through $v_i$. But if we fail to consider all the paths from $v_s$ to $v_d$, we cannot be ensured of finding the shortest one.

Furthermore, suppose the shortest path from $v_s$ to $v_d$ passes through some intermediate node $v_i$, that is, the shortest path is of the form $P = \{v_s, \ldots, v_i, \ldots, v_d\}$. It must be the case that the portion of $P$ between $v_s$ to $v_i$ is also the shortest path from $v_s$ to $v_i$. Suppose it is not. Then there exists another shorter path from $v_s$ to $v_i$. But then, $P$ would not be the shortest path from $v_s$ to $v_d$, because we could obtain a shorter one by replacing the portion of $P$ between $v_s$ and $v_i$ by the shorter path.

Consider the directed graph $G_{11}$ shown in Figure 16.14. The shortest *weighted* path between vertices $b$ and $f$ is the path $\{b, a, c, e, f\}$, which has the weighted path length 9. On the other hand, the shortest *unweighted* path from $b$ to $f$ is the path of length 3, $\{b, c, e, f\}$.

---

**FIGURE 16.14**
Two edge-weighted directed graphs.

---

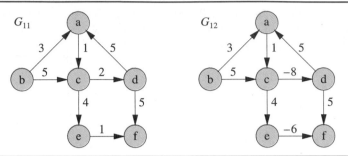

As long as all the edge weights are non-negative (as is the case for $G_{11}$), the shortest-path problem is well defined. Unfortunately, things get a little tricky in the presence of negative edge weights.

For example, consider the graph $G_{12}$ shown in Figure 16.14. Suppose we are looking for the shortest path from $d$ to $f$. Exactly two edges emanate from vertex $d$, both with the same edge weight of 5. If the graph contained only positive edge weights, there could be no shorter path than the direct path $\{d, f\}$.

However, in a graph that contains negative weights, a long path gets "shorter" when we add edges with negative weights to it. For example, the path $\{d, a, c, e, f\}$ has a total weighted path length of 4, even though the first edge, $(d, a)$, has the weight 5.

But negative weights are even more insidious than this: For example, the path $\{d, a, c, d, a, e, f\}$, which also joins vertex $d$ to $f$, has a weighted path length of 2 but the path $\{d, a, c, d, a, c, d, a, e, f\}$ has length zero. That is, as the number of edges in the path increases, the weighted path length decreases! The problem in this case is the existence of the cycle $\{d, a, c, d\}$ the weighted path length of which is less than zero. Such a cycle is called a *negative cost cycle*.

Clearly, the shortest-path problem is not defined for graphs that contain negative cost cycles. However, negative edges are not intrinsically bad. Solutions to the problem do exist for graphs that contain both positive and negative edge weights, as long as there are no negative cost cycles. Nevertheless, the problem is greatly simplified when all edges carry non-negative weights.

## Dijkstra's Algorithm

*Dijkstra's algorithm* is a greedy algorithm for solving the single-source, shortest-path problem on an edge-weighted graph in which all the weights are non-negative. It finds the shortest paths from some initial vertex, say $v_s$, to all the other vertices one-by-one. The essential feature of Dijkstra's algorithm is the order in which the paths are determined: The paths are discovered in the order of their weighted lengths, starting with the shortest, proceeding to the longest.

For each vertex $v$, Dijkstra's algorithm keeps track of three pieces of information, $k_v$, $d_v$, and $p_v$:

$k_v$    The Boolean-valued flag $k_v$ indicates that the shortest path to vertex $v$ is *known*. Initially, $k_v = $ **false** for all $v \in \mathcal{V}$.

$d_v$  The quantity $d_v$ is the length of the shortest known path from $v_s$ to $v$. When the algorithm begins, no shortest paths are known. The distance $d_v$ is a *tentative* distance. During the course of the algorithm candidate paths are examined and the *tentative* distances are modified.

Initially, $d_v = \infty$ for all $v \in \mathcal{V}$ such that $v \neq v_s$, while $d_{v_s} = 0$.

$p_v$  The predecessor of vertex $v$ on the shortest path from $v_s$ to $v$. That is, the shortest path from $v_s$ to $v$ has the form $\{v_s, \ldots, p_v, v\}$.

Initially, $p_v$ is unknown for all $v \in \mathcal{V}$.

Dijkstra's algorithm proceeds in phases. The following steps are performed in each pass:

1.  From the set of vertices for which $k_v = $ **false**, select the vertex $v$ having the smallest tentative distance $d_v$.

2.  Set $k_v \leftarrow$ **true**.

3.  For each vertex $w$ adjacent to $v$ for which $k_w \neq$ **true**, test whether the tentative distance $d_w$ is greater than $d_v + C(v, w)$. If it is, set $d_w \leftarrow d_v + C(v, w)$ and set $p_w \leftarrow v$.

In each pass exactly one vertex has its $k_v$ set to **true**. The algorithm terminates after $|\mathcal{V}|$ passes are completed at which time all the shortest paths are known.

Table 16.3 illustrates the operation of Dijkstra's algorithm as it finds the shortest paths starting from vertex $b$ in graph $G_{11}$ shown in Figure 16.14.

Initially all the tentative distances are $\infty$, except for vertex $b$ which has tentative distance zero. Therefore, vertex $b$ is selected in the first pass. The mark $\sqrt{}$ beside an entry in Table 16.3 indicates that the shortest path is *known* ($k_v = $ **true**).

Next we follow the edges emanating from vertex $b$, $b \rightarrow a$ and $b \rightarrow c$, and update the distances accordingly. The new tentative distance for $a$ becomes 3 and the new tentative distance for $c$ is 5. In both cases, the next-to-last vertex on the shortest path is vertex $b$.

**TABLE 16.3**
Operation of Dijkstra's Algorithm

| Vertex | Initially | Passes | | | | | |
| --- | --- | --- | --- | --- | --- | --- | --- |
| | | 1 | 2 | 3 | 4 | 5 | 6 |
| $a$ | $\infty$ | $3\,b$ | $\sqrt{}\,3\,b$ | $\sqrt{}\,3\,b$ | $\sqrt{}\,3\,b$ | $\sqrt{}\,3\,b$ | $\sqrt{}\,3\,b$ |
| $b$ | $0\,-$ | $\sqrt{}\,0\,-$ | $\sqrt{}\,0\,-$ | $\sqrt{}\,0\,-$ | $\sqrt{}\,0\,-$ | $\sqrt{}\,0\,-$ | $\sqrt{}\,0\,-$ |
| $c$ | $\infty$ | $5\,b$ | $4\,a$ | $\sqrt{}\,4\,a$ | $\sqrt{}\,4\,a$ | $\sqrt{}\,4\,a$ | $\sqrt{}\,4\,a$ |
| $d$ | $\infty$ | $\infty$ | $\infty$ | $6\,c$ | $\sqrt{}\,6\,c$ | $\sqrt{}\,6\,c$ | $\sqrt{}\,6\,c$ |
| $e$ | $\infty$ | $\infty$ | $\infty$ | $8\,c$ | $8\,c$ | $\sqrt{}\,8\,c$ | $\sqrt{}\,8\,c$ |
| $f$ | $\infty$ | $\infty$ | $\infty$ | $\infty$ | $11\,d$ | $9\,e$ | $\sqrt{}\,9\,e$ |

In the second pass, vertex $a$ is selected and its entry is marked with √ indicating the shortest path is known. There is one edge emanating from $a$, $a \rightarrow c$. The distance to $c$ via $a$ is 4. Since this is less than the tentative distance to $c$, vertex $c$ is given the new tentative distance 4 and its predecessor on the shortest path is set to $a$. The algorithm continues in this fashion for a total of $\mathcal{V}$ passes until all the shortest paths have been found.

The shortest-path information contained in the right-most column of Table 16.3 can be represented in the form of a vertex-weighted graph, as shown in Figure 16.15.

This graph contains the same set of vertices as the problem graph $G_{11}$. Each vertex $v$ is labeled with the length $d_v$ of the shortest path from $b$ to $v$. Each vertex (except $b$) has a single emanating edge that connects the vertex to the next-to-last vertex on the shortest path. By following the edges in this graph from any vertex $v$ to vertex $b$, we can construct the shortest path from $b$ to $v$ in reverse.

### Data Structures for Dijkstra's Algorithm

The implementation of Dijkstra's algorithm described below uses the **TableEntry** structure declared in Program 16.13. Each **TableEntry** instance has three fields, **known**, **distance**, and **predecessor**, which correspond to the variables $k_v$, $d_v$, and $p_v$, respectively.

In each pass of its operation, Dijkstra's algorithm selects from the set of vertices for which the shortest path is not yet known the one with the smallest tentative distance. Therefore, we use a *priority queue* to represent this set of vertices.

The priority assigned to a vertex is its tentative distance. The class **Assoc** defined in Program 16.13 is used to associate a priority with a given object instance. The **Assoc** class is derived from the **Association** class given in Section 5.2.11. Notice that the **Assoc** constructor calls **RescindOwnership** to prevent the destructor from deleting the associated object instance.

### Implementation

A version of Dijkstra's algorithm is shown in Program 16.14. The **Dijkstras-Algorithm** function takes two arguments. The first is a **const** reference to a directed

---

**FIGURE 16.15**
The shortest-path graph for $G_{11}$.

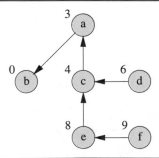

**PROGRAM 16.13**
Data structures for Dijkstra's algorithm

```
1   struct TableEntry
2   {
3       bool known;
4       int distance;
5       Vertex::Number predecessor;
6
7       TableEntry () : known (false),
8           distance (numeric_limits<int>::max ()) {}
9   };
10
11  class Assoc : public Association
12  {
13      Int priority;
14  public:
15      Assoc (int p, Object& object) :
16          Association (priority, object), priority (p)
17          { RescindOwnership (); }
18  };
```

graph instance. It is assumed that the directed graph is an edge-weighted graph in which the weights are instances of the **Int** class defined in Program 5.8. The second argument is a **const** reference to the start node.

The **DijkstrasAlgorithm** routine returns its result in the form of a shortest-path graph. Therefore, the return value is a reference to a **Digraph** instance. The function allocates the storage, constructs the shortest-path graph, and returns a reference to that graph.

The main data structures used are called **table** and **queue** (lines 4–5). The former is an array of $n = |\mathcal{V}|$ **TableEntry** elements. The latter is a reference to a priority queue. In this case, a **BinaryHeap** of length $|\mathcal{E}|$ is used. (See Section 11.2.)

The algorithm begins by setting the tentative distance for the start vertex to zero and inserting the start vertex into the priority queue with priority zero (lines 7–8).

The main loop of the routine comprises lines 8–35. In each iteration of this loop the vertex with the smallest distance is dequeued (lines 10–12). The vertex is processed only if its table entry indicates that the shortest path is not already known (line 13).

When a vertex **v0** is processed, its shortest path is deemed to be *known* (line 15). Then each vertex **v1** adjacent to vertex is considered (lines 16–19). The distance to **v1** along the path that passes through **v0** is computed (lines 20–23). If this distance is less than the tentative distance associated with **v1**, entries in the table for **v1** are updated, and the **v1** is given a new priority and inserted into the priority queue (lines 24–29).

The main loop terminates when all the shortest paths have been found. The shortest-path graph is then constructed using the information in the table (lines 38–45).

**PROGRAM 16.14**
Dijkstra's Algorithm.

```
1   Digraph& DijkstrasAlgorithm (Digraph const& g, Vertex const& s)
2   {
3       unsigned int const n = g.NumberOfVertices ();
4       Array<TableEntry> table (n);
5       PriorityQueue& queue = *new BinaryHeap (g.NumberOfEdges ());
6       table [s].distance = 0;
7       queue.Enqueue (*new Assoc (0, const_cast<Vertex&> (s)));
8       while (!queue.IsEmpty ())
9       {
10          Assoc& assoc =
11              dynamic_cast<Assoc&> (queue.DequeueMin ());
12          Vertex& v0 = dynamic_cast<Vertex&> (assoc.Value ());
13          if (!table [v0].known)
14          {
15              table [v0].known = true;
16              Iterator& p = g.EmanatingEdges (v0);
17              while (!p.IsDone ()) {
18                  WeightedEdge& edge =
19                      dynamic_cast<WeightedEdge&> (*p);
20                  Vertex& v1 = edge.V1 ();
21                  Int& weight =
22                      dynamic_cast<Int&> (edge.Weight ());
23                  int const d = table [v0].distance + weight;
24                  if (table [v1].distance > d)
25                  {
26                      table [v1].distance = d;
27                      table [v1].predecessor = v0;
28                      queue.Enqueue (*new Assoc (d, v1));
29                  }
30                  ++p;
31              }
32              delete &p;
33          }
34          delete &assoc;
35      }
36      delete &queue;
37
38      Digraph& result = *new DigraphAsLists (n);
39      for (Vertex::Number v = 0; v < n; ++v)
40          result.AddVertex (*new WeightedVertex (
41              v, *new Int (table [v].distance)));
42      for (Vertex::Number v = 0; v < n; ++v)
43          if (v != s)
44              result.AddEdge (*new Edge (
45                  result [v], result [table [v].predecessor]));
46      return result;
47  }
```

### Running Time Analysis

The running time of the `DijkstrasAlgorithm` routine is dominated by the running time of the main loop (lines 8–35). (It is easy to see that lines 3–7 run in constant time, and lines 38–45 run in $O(|\mathcal{V}|)$ time.)

To determine the running time of the main loop, we proceed as follows: First, we ignore temporarily the time required for the **Enqueue** and **Dequeue** operations in the priority queue. Clearly, each vertex in the graph is processed exactly once. When a vertex is processed all the edges emanating from it are considered. Therefore, the time (ignoring the priority queue operations) taken is $O(|V| + |E|)$ when adjacency lists are used and $O(|V|^2)$ when adjacency matrices are used.

Now, we add back the worst-case time required for the priority queue operations. In the worst case, a vertex is enqueued and subsequently dequeued once for every edge in the graph. Therefore, the length of the priority queue is at most $|\mathcal{E}|$. As a result, the worst-case time for each operation is $O(\log |\mathcal{E}|)$.

Thus, the worst-case running time for Dijkstra's algorithm is

$$O(|\mathcal{V}| + |\mathcal{E}| \log |\mathcal{E}|),$$

when adjacency lists are used, and

$$O(|\mathcal{V}|^2 + |\mathcal{E}| \log |\mathcal{E}|),$$

when adjacency matrices are used to represent the input graph.

## 16.4.2 All-Pairs Source Shortest Path

In this section we consider the *all-pairs, shortest path* problem: Given an edge-weighted graph $G = (\mathcal{V}, \mathcal{E})$, for each pair of vertices in $\mathcal{V}$ find the *length* of the shortest weighted path between the two vertices.

One way to solve this problem is to run Dijkstra's algorithm $|\mathcal{V}|$ times in turn using each vertex in $\mathcal{V}$ as the initial vertex. Therefore, we can solve the all-pairs problem in $O(|\mathcal{V}|^2 + |\mathcal{V}||\mathcal{E}| \log |\mathcal{E}|)$ time when adjacency lists are used, and $O(|\mathcal{V}|^3 + |\mathcal{V}||\mathcal{E}| \log |\mathcal{E}|)$ when adjacency matrices are used. However, for a dense graph ($|\mathcal{E}| = \Theta(|\mathcal{V}|^2)$) the running time of Dijkstra's algorithm is $O(|\mathcal{V}|^3 \log |\mathcal{V}|)$, regardless of the representation scheme used.

### Floyd's Algorithm

*Floyd's algorithm* uses the dynamic programming method to solve the all-pairs shortest-path problem on a dense graph. The method makes efficient use of an adjacency matrix to solve the problem. Consider an edge-weighted graph $G = (\mathcal{V}, \mathcal{E})$, where $C(v, w)$ represents the weight on edge $(v, w)$. Suppose the vertices are numbered from 1 to $|\mathcal{V}|$, that is, let $\mathcal{V} = \{v_1, v_2, \ldots, v_{|\mathcal{V}|}\}$. Furthermore, let $\mathcal{V}_k$ be the set comprised of the first $k$ vertices in $\mathcal{V}$, that is, $\mathcal{V}_k = \{v_1, v_2, \ldots, v_k\}$, for $0 \le k \le |\mathcal{V}|$.

Let $P_k(v, w)$ be the shortest path from vertex $v$ to $w$ that passes only through vertices in $\mathcal{V}_k$, if such a path exists, that is, the path $P_k(v, w)$ has the form

$$P_k(v, w) = \{v, \underbrace{\ldots}_{\in \mathcal{V}_k}, w\}.$$

Let $D_k(v, w)$ be the *length* of path $P_k(v, w)$:

$$D_k(v, w) = \begin{cases} |P_k(v, w)| & P_k(v, w) \text{ exists,} \\ \infty & \text{otherwise.} \end{cases}$$

Since $\mathcal{V}_0 = \varnothing$, the $P_0$ paths correspond to the edges of $G$:

$$P_0(v, w) = \begin{cases} \{v, w\} & (v, w) \in \mathcal{E}, \\ \text{undefined} & \text{otherwise.} \end{cases}$$

Therefore, the $D_0$ path lengths correspond to the weights on the edges of $G$:

$$D_0(v, w) = \begin{cases} C(v, w) & (v, w) \in \mathcal{E}, \\ \infty & \text{otherwise.} \end{cases}$$

Floyd's algorithm computes the sequence of matrices $D_0, D_1, \ldots, D_{|\mathcal{V}|}$. The distances in $D_i$ represent paths with intermediate vertices in $\mathcal{V}_i$. Since $\mathcal{V}_{i+1} = \mathcal{V}_i \cup \{v_{i+1}\}$, we can obtain the distances in $D_{i+1}$ from those in $D_i$ by considering only the paths that pass through vertex $v_{i+1}$. Figure 16.16 illustrates how this is done.

For every pair of vertices $(v, w)$, we compare the distance $D_i(v, w)$, (which represents the shortest path from $v$ to $w$ that does not pass through $v_{i+1}$) with the sum $D_i(v, v_{i+1}) + D_i(v_{i+1}, w)$ (which represents the shortest path from $v$ to $w$ that does pass through $v_{i+1}$). Thus, $D_{i+1}$ is computed as follows:

$$D_{i+1}(v, w) = \min\{D_i(v, v_{i+1}) + D_i(v_{i+1}, w), D_i(v, w)\}.$$

## Implementation

An implementation of Floyd's algorithm is shown in Program 16.14. The **Floyds-Algorithm** function takes as its lone argument a **const** reference to a directed graph instance. The directed graph is assumed to be an edge-weighted graph in which the weights are instances of the **Int** class defined in Program 5.8.

---

**FIGURE 16.16**
Calculating $D_{i+1}$ in Floyd's algorithm.

---

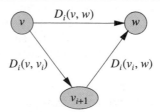

**PROGRAM 16.15**
Floyd's algorithm

```
1   Digraph& FloydsAlgorithm (Digraph const& g)
2   {
3       using numeric_limits<unsigned int>::max;
4
5       unsigned int const n = g.NumberOfVertices ();
6       Array2D<unsigned int> distance (n, n);
7       for (Vertex::Number v = 0; v < n; ++v)
8           for (Vertex::Number w = 0; w < n; ++w)
9               distance [v][w] = max ();
10      Iterator& p = g.Edges ();
11      while (!p.IsDone ())
12      {
13          WeightedEdge& edge =
14              dynamic_cast<WeightedEdge&> (*p);
15          Int& weight = dynamic_cast<Int&> (edge.Weight ());
16          distance [edge.V0 ()][edge.V1 ()] = weight;
17          ++p;
18      }
19      delete &p;
20
21      for (Vertex::Number i = 0; i < n; ++i)
22          for (Vertex::Number v = 0; v < n; ++v)
23              for (Vertex::Number w = 0; w < n; ++w)
24                  if (distance [v][i] != max () &&
25                      distance [i][w] != max ())
26                  {
27                      int const d =
28                          distance [v][i] + distance [i][w];
29                      if (distance [v][w] > d)
30                          distance [v][w] = d;
31                  }
32
33      Digraph& result = *new DigraphAsMatrix (n);
34      for (Vertex::Number v = 0; v < n; ++v)
35          result.AddVertex (*new Vertex (v));
36      for (Vertex::Number v = 0; v < n; ++v)
37          for (Vertex::Number w = 0; w < n; ++w)
38              if (distance [v][w] != max ())
39                  result.AddEdge (*new WeightedEdge (
40                      result [v], result [w],
41                      *new Int (distance [v][w])));
42      return result;
43  }
```

The `FloydsAlgorithm` routine returns its result in the form of an edge-weighted directed graph. Therefore, the return value is a reference to a `Digraph` instance. The function allocates the storage, constructs the graph and returns a reference to that graph.

The principal data structure used by the algorithm is a $|\mathcal{V}| \times |\mathcal{V}|$ matrix of unsigned integers called `distance`. All the elements of the matrix are initially set to $\infty$ (lines 6–9). Next, an edge iterator is used to visit all the edges in the input graph in order to transfer the weights from the graph to the `distance` matrix (lines 10–19).

The main work of the algorithm is done in three nested loops (lines 21–31). The outer loop computes the sequence of distance matrices $D_1, D_2, \ldots, D_{|\mathcal{V}|}$. The inner two loops consider all possible pairs of vertices. Notice that as $D_{i+1}$ is computed, its entries overwrite those of $D_i$.

Finally, the values in the `distance` matrix are transferred to the result graph. The result graph contains the same set of vertices as the input graph. For each finite entry in the `distance` matrix, a weighted edge is added to the result graph.

### Running Time Analysis

The worst-case running time for Floyd's algorithm is easily determined. Creating and initializing the `distance` matrix is $O(|\mathcal{V}|^2)$ (lines 6–9). Transferring the weights from the input graph to the `distance` matrix requires $O(|\mathcal{V}| + |\mathcal{E}|)$ time if adjacency lists are used, and $O(|\mathcal{V}|^2)$ time when an adjacency matrix is used to represent the input graph (lines 10–19).

The running time for the three nested loops is $O(|\mathcal{V}|^3)$ in the worst case. Finally, constructing the result graph and transferring the entries from the `distance` matrix to the result requires $O(|\mathcal{V}|^2)$ time. As a result, the worst-case running time of Floyd's algorithm is $O(|\mathcal{V}|^3)$.

## 16.5 Minimum-Cost Spanning Trees

In this section we consider undirected graphs and their subgraphs. A *subgraph* of a graph $G = (\mathcal{V}, \mathcal{E})$ is any graph $G' = (\mathcal{V}', \mathcal{E}')$ such that $\mathcal{V}' \subseteq \mathcal{V}$ and $\mathcal{E}' \subseteq \mathcal{E}$. In particular, we consider *connected* undirected graphs and their *minimal subgraphs*. The minimal subgraph of a connected graph is called a *spanning tree:*

### Definition 16.12 (Spanning Tree)
*Consider a* connected, undirected *graph* $G = (\mathcal{V}, \mathcal{E})$. *A spanning tree of G is a subgraph of G, say* $T = (\mathcal{V}', \mathcal{E}')$, *with the following properties:*

1. $\mathcal{V}' = \mathcal{V}$.
2. *T is connected.*
3. *T is acyclic.*

Figure 16.17 shows an undirected graph, $G_{13}$, together with three of its spanning trees. A spanning tree is called a *tree* because every *acyclic* undirected graph can be viewed as a general, unordered tree. Because the edges are undirected, any vertex may

**FIGURE 16.17**
An undirected graph and three spanning trees.

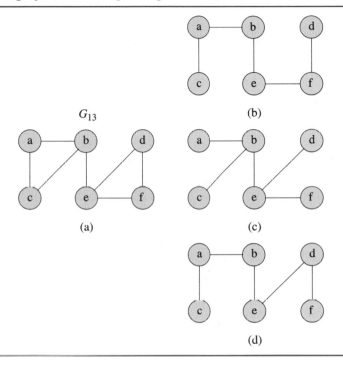

$G_{13}$

(a)

(b)

(c)

(d)

be chosen to serve as the root of the tree. For example, the spanning tree of $G_{13}$ given in Figure 16.17(c) can be viewed as the general, unordered tree

$$\{b, \{a\}, \{c\}, \{e, \{d\}, \{f\}\}\}.$$

According to Definition 16.12, a spanning tree is connected. Therefore, as long as the tree contains more than one vertex, there can be no vertex with degree zero. Furthermore, the following theorem guarantees that there is always at least one vertex with degree 1.

**Theorem 16.1**
*Consider a connected, undirected graph $G = (\mathcal{V}, \mathcal{E})$, where $|\mathcal{V}| > 1$. Let $T = (\mathcal{V}, \mathcal{E}')$ be a spanning tree of $G$. The spanning tree $T$ contains at least one vertex of degree 1.*

**Proof**    (By contradiction)    Assume that there is no vertex in $T$ of degree 1. That is, all the vertices in $T$ have degree 2 or greater. Then by following edges into and out of vertices we can construct a path that is cyclic. But a spanning tree is acyclic— a contradiction. Therefore, a spanning tree always contains at least one vertex of degree 1.

According to Definition 16.12, the edge set of a spanning tree is a subset of the edges in the spanned graph. How many edges must a spanning tree have? The following theorem answers the question.

### Theorem 16.2

*Consider a connected, undirected graph $G = (\mathcal{V}, \mathcal{E})$. Let $T = (\mathcal{V}, \mathcal{E}')$ be a spanning tree of G. The number of edges in the spanning tree is given by*

$$|\mathcal{E}'| = |\mathcal{V}| - 1.$$

**Proof** (By induction) We can prove Theorem 16.2 by induction on $|\mathcal{V}|$, the number of vertices in the graph.

**Base Case** Consider a graph that contains only one node, that is, $|\mathcal{V}| = 1$. Clearly, the spanning tree for such a graph contains no edges. Since $|\mathcal{V}| - 1 = 0$, the theorem is valid.

**Inductive Hypothesis** Assume that the number of edges in a spanning tree for a graph with $|\mathcal{V}|$ has been shown to be $|\mathcal{V}| - 1$ for $|\mathcal{V}| = 1, 2, \ldots, k$.

Consider a graph $G_{k+1} = (\mathcal{V}, \mathcal{E})$ with $k + 1$ vertices and its spanning tree $T_{k+1} = (\mathcal{V}, \mathcal{E}')$. According to Theorem 16.1, $G_{k+1}$ contains at least one vertex of degree 1. Let $v \in \mathcal{V}$ be one such vertex and $\{v, w\} \in \mathcal{E}'$ be the one edge emanating from $v$ in $T_{k+1}$.

Let $T_k$ be the graph of $k$ nodes obtained by removing $v$ and its emanating edge from the graph $T_{k+1}$, that is, $T_k = (\mathcal{V} - \{v\}, \mathcal{E}' - \{v, w\})$.

Since $T_{k+1}$ is connected, so too is $T_k$. Similarly, since $T_{k+1}$ is acyclic, so too is $T_k$. Therefore, $T_k$ is a spanning tree with $k$ vertices. By the inductive hypothesis $T_k$ has $k - 1$ edges. Thus, $T_{k+1}$ has $k$ edges.

Therefore, by induction on $k$, the spanning tree for a graph with $|\mathcal{V}|$ vertices contains $|\mathcal{V}| - 1$ edges.

---

### Constructing Spanning Trees

Any traversal of a connected, undirected tree visits all the vertices in that tree, regardless of the node from which the traversal is started. During the traversal certain edges are traversed while the remaining edges are not. Specifically, an edge is traversed if it leads from a vertex that has been visited to a vertex that has not been visited. The set of edges which are traversed during a traversal forms a spanning tree.

The spanning tree obtained from a breadth-first traversal starting at vertex $v$ of graph $G$ is called the *breadth-first spanning tree* of $G$ rooted at $v$. For example, the spanning tree shown in Figure 16.17(c) is the breadth-first spanning tree of $G_{13}$ rooted at vertex $b$.

Similarly, the spanning tree obtained from a depth-first traversal is the *depth-first spanning tree* of $G$ rooted at $v$. The spanning tree shown in Figure 16.17(d) is the depth-first spanning tree of $G_{13}$ rooted at vertex $c$.

### Minimum-Cost Spanning Trees

The total *cost* of an edge-weighted undirected graph is simply the sum of the weights on all the edges in that graph. A minimum-cost spanning tree of a graph is a spanning tree of that graph that has the least total cost.

**FIGURE 16.18**
An edge-weighted, undirected graph and a minimum-cost spanning tree.

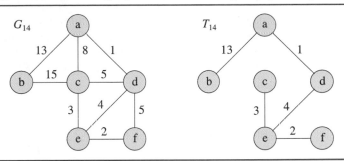

### Definition 16.13 Minimal Spanning Tree

*Consider an* edge-weighted, *undirected, connected graph* $G = (\mathcal{V}, \mathcal{E})$, *where* $C(v, w)$ *represents the weight on edge* $\{v, w\} \in \mathcal{E}$. *The* minimum spanning tree *of G is the spanning tree* $T = (\mathcal{V}, \mathcal{E}')$ *that has the smallest total cost,*

$$\sum_{\{v,w\}\in\mathcal{E}'} C(v, w).$$

Figure 16.18 shows edge-weighted graph $G_{14}$ together with its minimum-cost spanning tree $T_{14}$. In general, it is possible for a graph to have several different minimum-cost spanning trees. However, in this case there is only one.

The two sections that follow present two different algorithms for finding the minimum-cost spanning tree. Both algorithms are similar in that they build the tree one edge at a time.

### 16.5.1 Prim's Algorithm

*Prim's algorithm* finds a minimum-cost spanning tree of an edge-weighted, connected, undirected graph $G = (\mathcal{V}, \mathcal{E})$. The algorithm constructs the minimum-cost spanning tree of a graph by selecting edges from the graph one-by-one and adding those edges to the spanning tree.

Prim's algorithm is essentially a minor variation of *Dijkstra's algorithm* (see Section 16.4.1). To construct the spanning tree, the algorithm constructs a sequence of spanning trees $T_0, T_1, \ldots, T_{|\mathcal{V}|-1}$, each of which is a subgraph of G. The algorithm begins with a tree that contains one selected vertex, say $v_s \in \mathcal{V}$. That is, $T_0 = \{\{v_s\}, \varnothing\}$.

Given $T_i = \{\mathcal{V}_i, \mathcal{E}_i\}$, we obtain the next tree in the sequence as follows. Consider the set of edges given by

$$\mathcal{H}_i = \bigcup_{u\in\mathcal{V}_i} \mathcal{A}(u) - \bigcup_{u\in\mathcal{V}_i} \mathcal{I}(u).$$

The set $\mathcal{H}_i$ contains all the edges $\{v, w\}$ such that exactly one of $v$ or $w$ is in $\mathcal{V}_i$ (but not both). Select the edge $\{v, w\} \in \mathcal{H}_i$ with the smallest edge weight,

$$C(v, w) = \min_{\{v', w'\} \in \mathcal{H}_i} C(v', w').$$

Then $T_{i+1} = \{\mathcal{V}_{i+1}, \mathcal{E}_{i+1}\}$, where $\mathcal{V}_{i+1} = \mathcal{V}_i \cup \{v\}$ and $\mathcal{E}_{i+1} = \mathcal{E} \cup \{\{v, w\}\}$. After $|\mathcal{V}| - 1$ such steps we get $T_{|\mathcal{V}|-1}$, which is the minimum-cost spanning tree of $G$.

Figure 16.19 illustrates how Prim's algorithm determines the minimum-cost spanning tree of the graph $G_{14}$ shown in Figure 16.18. The circled vertices are the elements of $\mathcal{V}_i$, the solid edges represent the elements of $\mathcal{E}_i$ and the dashed edges represent the elements of $\mathcal{H}_i$.

## Implementation

An implementation of Prim's algorithm is shown in Program 16.16. This implementation is almost identical to the version of **Dijkstra's** algorithm given in Program 16.14. In fact, there are only four differences between the two algorithms. These are found on lines 1, 23, 38, and 40–41.

The **PrimsAlgorithm** function takes two arguments. The first is a **const** reference to a undirected graph instance. We assume that the graph is edge-weighted and that the weights are instances of the **Int** class defined in Program 5.8. The second argument is a **const** reference to the start node.

The **PrimsAlgorithm** routine returns a minimum-cost spanning tree represented as an undirected graph. Therefore, the return value is a reference to a **Graph** instance. The function allocates the storage, constructs the spanning tree, and returns a reference to that graph.

---

**FIGURE 16.19**
Operation of Prim's algorithm.

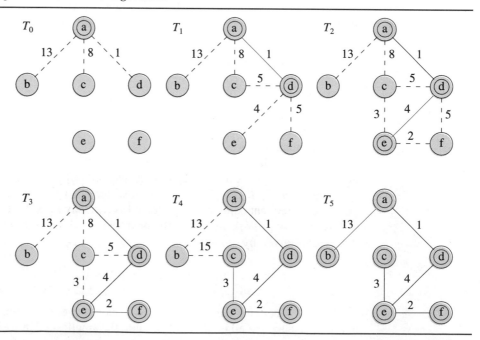

## PROGRAM 16.16
Prim's algorithm.

```
1   Graph& PrimsAlgorithm (Graph const& g, Vertex const& s)
2   {
3       unsigned int const n = g.NumberOfVertices ();
4       Array<TableEntry> table (n);
5       PriorityQueue& queue = *new BinaryHeap (g.NumberOfEdges ());
6       table [s].distance = 0;
7       queue.Enqueue (*new Assoc (0, const_cast<Vertex&> (s)));
8       while (!queue.IsEmpty ())
9       {
10          Assoc& assoc =
11              dynamic_cast<Assoc&> (queue.DequeueMin ());
12          Vertex& v0 = dynamic_cast<Vertex&> (assoc.Value ());
13          if (!table [v0].known)
14          {
15              table [v0].known = true;
16              Iterator& p = g.EmanatingEdges (v0);
17              while (!p.IsDone ()) {
18                  WeightedEdge& edge =
19                      dynamic_cast<WeightedEdge&> (*p);
20                  Vertex& v1 = edge.V1 ();
21                  Int& weight =
22                      dynamic_cast<Int&> (edge.Weight ());
23                  int const d = weight;
24                  if (table [v1].distance > d)
25                  {
26                      table [v1].distance = d;
27                      table [v1].predecessor = v0;
28                      queue.Enqueue (*new Assoc (d, v1));
29                  }
30                  ++p;
31              }
32              delete &p;
33          }
34          delete &assoc;
35      }
36      delete &queue;
37
38      Graph& result = *new GraphAsLists (n);
39      for (Vertex::Number v = 0; v < n; ++v)
40          result.AddVertex (*new Vertex (v));
41
42      for (Vertex::Number v = 0; v < n; ++v)
43          if (v != s)
44              result.AddEdge (*new Edge (
45                  result [v], result [table [v].predecessor]));
46      return result;
47  }
```

The running time of Prim's algorithm is asymptotically the same as Dijkstra's algorithm. That is, the worst-case running time is

$$O(|\mathcal{V}| + |\mathcal{E}| \log |\mathcal{E}|),$$

when adjacency lists are used, and

$$O(|\mathcal{V}|^2 + |\mathcal{E}| \log |\mathcal{E}|),$$

when adjacency matrices are used to represent the input graph.

## 16.5.2   Kruskal's Algorithm

Like Prim's algorithm, *Kruskal's algorithm* also constructs the minimum spanning tree of a graph by adding edges to the spanning tree one-by-one. At all points during its execution the set of edges selected by Prim's algorithm forms exactly one tree. On the other hand, the set of edges selected by Kruskal's algorithm forms a forest of trees.

Kruskal's algorithm is conceptually quite simple. The edges are selected and added to the spanning tree in increasing order of their weights. An edge is added to the tree only if it does not create a cycle.

The beauty of Kruskal's algorithm is the way that potential cycles are detected. Consider an undirected graph $G = (\mathcal{V}, \mathcal{E})$. We can view the set of vertices, $\mathcal{V}$, as a *universal set* and the set of edges, $\mathcal{E}$, as the definition of an *equivalence relation* over the universe $\mathcal{V}$. (See Definition 12.1.) In general, an equivalence relation partitions a universal set into a set of equivalence classes. If the graph is connected, there is only one equivalence class—all the elements of the universal set are *equivalent*. Therefore, a *spanning tree* is a minimal set of equivalences that result in a single equivalence class.

Kruskal's algorithm computes, $P_0, P_1, \ldots, P_{|\mathcal{V}-1|}$, a sequence of *partitions* of the set of vertices $\mathcal{V}$. (Partitions are discussed in Section 12.4.) The initial partition consists of $|\mathcal{V}|$ sets of size one:

$$P_0 = \{\{v_1\}, \{v_2\}, \ldots, \{v_{|\mathcal{V}|}\}, \}.$$

Each subsequent element of the sequence is obtained from its predecessor by *joining* two of the elements of the partition. Therefore, $P_i$ has the form

$$P_i = \{S_0^i, S_1^i, \ldots, S_{|\mathcal{V}|-1-i}^i\},$$

for $0 \le i \le |\mathcal{V}| - 1$.

To construct the sequence the edges in $\mathcal{E}$ are considered one-by-one in increasing order of their weights. Suppose we have computed the sequence up to $P_i$ and the next edge to be considered is $\{v, w\}$. If $v$ and $w$ are both members of the same element of partition $P_i$, then the edge forms a cycle and is not part of the minimum-cost spanning tree.

On the other hand, suppose $v$ and $w$ are members of two different elements of partition $P_i$, say $S_k^i$ and $S_l^i$ (respectively). Then $\{v, w\}$ must be an edge in the minimum-cost

**FIGURE 16.20**
Operation of Kruskal's algorithm.

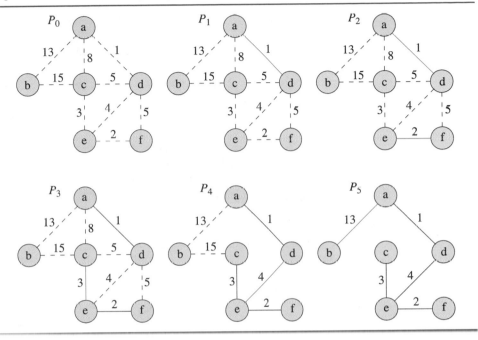

spanning tree. In this case, we compute $P_{i+1}$ by *joining* $S_k^i$ and $S_l^i$. That is, we replace $S_k^i$ and $S_l^i$ in $P_i$ by the *union* $S_k^i \cup S_l^i$.

Figure 16.20 illustrates how Kruskal's algorithm determines the minimum-cost spanning tree of the graph $G_{14}$ shown in Figure 16.18. The algorithm computes the following sequence of partitions:

$$P_0 = \{\{a\}, \{b\}, \{c\}, \{d\}, \{e\}, \{f\}\}$$
$$P_1 = \{\{a, d\}, \{b\}, \{c\}, \{e\}, \{f\}\}$$
$$P_2 = \{\{a, d\}, \{b\}, \{c\}, \{e, f\}\}$$
$$P_3 = \{\{a, d\}, \{b\}, \{c, e, f\}\}$$
$$P_4 = \{\{a, c, d, e, f\}, \{b\}\}$$
$$P_5 = \{\{a, b, c, d, e, f\}\}$$

## Implementation

An implementation of Kruskal's algorithm is shown in Program 16.17. The **Kruskals-Algorithm** function takes as its lone argument a **const** reference to an edge-weighted, undirected graph. This implementation assumes that the edge weights are instances of the **Int** class defined in Program 5.8. The routine computes the minimum-cost spanning tree and returns it in the form of an edge-weighted undirected graph. The function allocates the storage, constructs the graph, and returns a reference to a **Graph** instance.

**PROGRAM 16.17**
Kruskal's algorithm

```
1   Graph& KruskalsAlgorithm (Graph const& g)
2   {
3       unsigned int const n = g.NumberOfVertices ();
4
5       Graph& result = *new GraphAsLists (n);
6       for (Vertex::Number v = 0; v < n; ++v)
7           result.AddVertex (*new Vertex (v));
8
9       PriorityQueue& queue = *new BinaryHeap (g.NumberOfEdges ());
10      Iterator& p = g.Edges ();
11      while (!p.IsDone ()) {
12          WeightedEdge& edge =
13              dynamic_cast<WeightedEdge&> (*p);
14          Int& weight = dynamic_cast<Int&> (edge.Weight ());
15          queue.Enqueue (*new Assoc (weight, edge));
16          ++p;
17      }
18      delete &p;
19
20      Partition& partition = *new PartitionAsForest (n);
21      while (!queue.IsEmpty () && partition.Count () > 1)
22      {
23          Assoc& assoc =
24              dynamic_cast<Assoc&> (queue.DequeueMin ());
25          Edge& edge = dynamic_cast<Edge&> (assoc.Value ());
26          Vertex::Number const v0 = edge.V0 ();
27          Vertex::Number const v1 = edge.V1 ();
28          Set& s = partition.Find (Set::Element (v0));
29          Set& t = partition.Find (Set::Element (v1));
30          if (s != t)
31          {
32              partition.Join (s, t);
33              result.AddEdge (*new Edge (result[v0], result[v1]));
34          }
35          delete &assoc;
36      }
37      delete &partition;
38      delete &queue;
39      return result;
40  }
```

The main data structures used by the routine are a priority queue to hold the edges, a partition to detect cycles and a graph for the result. This implementation uses a **BinaryHeap** (Section 11.2) for the priority queue, a **PartitionAsForest** (Section 12.4) for the partition, and a **GraphAsLists** for the spanning tree.

### Running Time Analysis

The **KruskalsAlgorithm** routine begins by creating a graph to hold the result spanning tree (lines 3–7). Since a spanning tree is a sparse graph the **GraphAsLists** class is used to represent it. Initially the graph contains $|\mathcal{V}|$ vertices but no edges. The running time for lines 3–7 is $O(|\mathcal{V}|)$.

Next all of the edges in the input graph are inserted one-by-one into the priority queue (lines 9–18). Since there are $|\mathcal{E}|$ edges, the worst-case running time for a single insertion is $O(\log |\mathcal{E}|)$. Therefore, the worst-case running time to initialize the priority queue is

$$O(|\mathcal{V}| + |\mathcal{E}| \log |\mathcal{E}|),$$

when adjacency lists are used, and

$$O(|\mathcal{V}|^2 + |\mathcal{E}| \log |\mathcal{E}|),$$

when adjacency matrices are used to represent the input graph.

The main loop of the routine comprises lines 21–36. This loop is done at most $|\mathcal{E}|$ times. In each iteration of the loop, one edge is removed from the priority queue (lines 23–25). In the worst-case this takes $O(\log |\mathcal{E}|)$ time.

Then, two partition *find* operations are done to determine the elements of the partition that contain the two end-points of the given edge (lines 26–29). Since the partition contains at most $|\mathcal{V}|$ elements, the running time for the find operations is $O(\log |\mathcal{V}|)$. If the two elements of the partition are distinct, then an edge is added to the spanning tree and a *join* operation is done to unite the two elements of the partition (lines 30–34). The join operation also requires $O(\log |\mathcal{V}|)$ time in the worst-case. Therefore, the total running time for the main loop is $O(|\mathcal{E}| \log |\mathcal{E}| + |\mathcal{E}| \log |\mathcal{V}|)$.

Thus, the worst-case running time for Kruskal's algorithm is

$$O(|\mathcal{V}| + |\mathcal{E}| \log |\mathcal{E}| + |\mathcal{E}| \log |\mathcal{V}|),$$

when adjacency lists are used, and

$$O(|\mathcal{V}|^2 + |\mathcal{E}| \log |\mathcal{E}| + |\mathcal{E}| \log |\mathcal{V}|),$$

when adjacency matrices are used to represent the input graph.

## 16.6 Application: Critical Path Analysis

In the introduction to this chapter, it is stated that there are myriad applications of graphs. In this section we consider one such application—*critical path analysis*. Critical path analysis crops up in a number of different contexts, from the planning of construction projects to the analysis of combinational logic circuits.

For example, consider the scheduling of activities required to construct a building. Before the foundation can be poured, it is necessary to dig a hole in the ground. After the building has been framed, the electricians and the plumbers can rough in the electrical and water services and this rough-in must be completed before the insulation is put up and the walls are closed in.

We can represent the set of activities and the scheduling constraints using a vertex-weighted, directed acyclic graph (DAG). Each vertex represents an activity and the weight on the vertex represents the time required to complete the activity. The directed edges represent the sequencing constraints. That is, an edge from vertex $v$ to vertex $w$ indicates that activity $v$ must complete before $w$ may begin. Clearly, such a graph must be *acyclic*.

A graph in which the vertices represent activities is called an *activity-node graph*. Figure 16.21 shows an example of an activity-node graph. In such a graph it is understood that independent activities may proceed in parallel. For example, after activity $A$ is completed, activities $B$ and $C$ may proceed in parallel. However, activity $D$ cannot begin until *both B and C* are done.

Critical path analysis answers the following questions:

1. What is the minimum time needed to complete all activities?
2. For a given activity $v$, is it possible to delay the completion of that activity without affecting the overall completion time? If yes, by how much can the completion of activity $v$ be delayed?

The activity-node graph is a vertex-weighted graph. However, the algorithms presented in the preceding sections all require edge-weighted graphs. Therefore, we must convert the vertex-weighted graph into its edge-weighted *dual*. In the dual graph the edges represent the activities, and the vertices represent the commencement and termination of activities. For this reason, the dual graph is called an *event-node graph*.

Figure 16.22 shows the event-node graph corresponding to the activity node graph given in Figure 16.21. Where an activity depends on more than one predecessor it is necessary to insert *dummy* edges.

---

**FIGURE 16.21**
An activity-node graph.

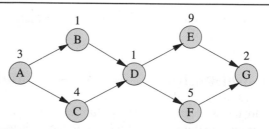

**FIGURE 16.22**
The event-node graph corresponding to Figure 16.21.

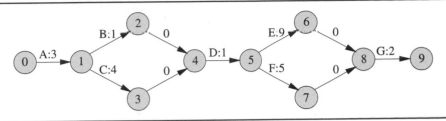

For example, activity $D$ cannot commence until both $B$ and $C$ are finished. In the event-node graph vertex 2 represents the termination of activity $B$ and vertex 3 represents the termination of activity $C$. It is necessary to introduce vertex 4 to represent the event that *both* $B$ and $C$ have completed. Edges $2 \rightarrow 4$ and $3 \rightarrow 4$ represent this synchronization constraint. Since these edges do not represent activities, the edge weights are zero.

For each vertex $v$ in the event node graph we define two times. The first $E_v$ is the *earliest event time* for event $v$. It is the earliest time at which event $v$ can occur assuming the first event begins at time zero. The earliest event time is given by

$$E_w = \begin{cases} 0 & w = v_i, \\ \min_{(v,w) \in \mathcal{I}(w)} E_v + C(v, w) & \text{otherwise,} \end{cases} \qquad (16.3)$$

where $v_i$ is the *initial* event, $\mathcal{I}(w)$ is the set of incident edges on vertex $w$, and $C(v, w)$ is the weight on vertex $(v, w)$.

Similarly, $L_v$ is the *latest event time* for event $v$. It is the latest time at which event $v$ can occur. The latest event time is given by

$$L_v = \begin{cases} E_{v_f} & w = v_f, \\ \max_{(v,w) \in \mathcal{A}(w)} E_w - C(v, w) & \text{otherwise,} \end{cases} \qquad (16.4)$$

where $v_f$ is the *final* event.

Given the earliest and latest event times for all events, we can compute time available for each activity. For example, consider an activity represented by edge $(v, w)$. The amount of time available for the activity is $L_w - E_v$, and the time required for that activity is $C(v, w)$. We define the *slack time* for an activity as the amount of time by which an activity can be delayed without affecting the overall completion time of the project. The slack time for the activity represented by edge $(v, w)$ is given by

$$S(v, w) = L_w - E_v - C(v, w). \qquad (16.5)$$

Activities with zero slack are *critical*. That is, critical activities must be completed on time—any delay affects the overall completion time. A *critical path* is a path in the event-node graph from the initial vertex to the final vertex comprised solely of critical activities.

**TABLE 16.4**
Critical Path Analysis Results for the Activity-Node Graph in Figure 16.21

| Activity | $C(v, w)$ | $E_v$ | $L_w$ | $S(v, w)$ |
|----------|-----------|-------|-------|-----------|
| $A$ | 3 | 0 | 3 | 0 |
| $B$ | 1 | 3 | 7 | 3 |
| $C$ | 4 | 3 | 7 | 0 |
| $D$ | 1 | 7 | 8 | 0 |
| $E$ | 9 | 8 | 17 | 0 |
| $F$ | 5 | 8 | 17 | 4 |
| $G$ | 2 | 17 | 18 | 0 |

Table 16.4 gives the results obtained from the critical path analysis of the activity-node graph shown in Figure 16.21. The tabulated results indicate the critical path is

$$\{A, C, D, E, G\}.$$

## Implementation

Given an activity-node graph, the objective of critical path analysis is to determine the slack time for each activity and thereby to identify the critical activities and the critical path. We shall assume that the activity node graph has already been transformed to an edge-node graph. The implementation of this transformation is left as a project for the reader (Project 16.10). Therefore, the first step is to compute the earliest and latest event times.

According to Equation 16.3, the earliest event time of vertex $w$ is obtained from the earliest event times of all its predecessors. Therefore, we must compute the earliest event times *in topological order*. To do this, we define the **EarliestTimeVisitor** shown in Program 16.18.

The **EarliestTimeVisitor** has three member variables—**graph, earliest-Time**, and **startTime**. The first is a reference to the event-node graph; the second refers to an array used to record the $E_v$ values; and the third is the time at which the initial activity starts.

The **Visit** member function of the **EarliestTimeVisitor** class implements directly Equation 16.3. It uses an **IncidentEdges** iterator to determine all the predecessors of a given node and computes $\min_{(v,w)\in\mathcal{I}(w)} E_v + C(v, w)$.

In order to compute the latest event times, it is necessary to define also a **LatestTimeVisitor**. This visitor must visit the vertices of the event-node graph in *reverse topological order*. Its implementation follows directly from Equation 16.4 and Program 16.18.

Program 16.19 defines the routine called **CriticalPathAnalysis** that does what its name implies. This routine takes as its lone argument a reference to a **Digraph** instance that represents an event-node graph. This implementation assumes that the edge weights are instances of the **Int** class defined in Program 5.8.

**PROGRAM 16.18**
Critical path analysis—computing earliest event times

```
1  class EarliestTimeVisitor : public Visitor
2  {
3      Graph& graph;
4      Array<unsigned int>& earliestTime;
5  public:
6      EarliestTimeVisitor (Graph& g, Array<unsigned int>& e) :
7          graph (g), earliestTime (e)
8          {}
9      void Visit (Object& object)
10     {
11         Vertex& w = dynamic_cast<Vertex&> (object);
12         unsigned int max = earliestTime [0];
13         Iterator& p = graph.IncidentEdges (w);
14         while (!p.IsDone ()) {
15             WeightedEdge& edge =
16                 dynamic_cast<WeightedEdge&> (*p);
17             Int& weight =
18                 dynamic_cast<Int&> (edge.Weight ());
19             Vertex& v = edge.V0 ();
20             unsigned int const t =
21                 earliestTime [v] + weight;
22             if (t > max)
23                 max = t;
24             ++p;
25         }
26         delete &p;
27         earliestTime [w] = max;
28     }
29 };
```

The routine first uses the `EarliestTimeVisitor` in a topological order traversal to compute the earliest event times which are recored in the `earliestTime` array (lines 5–8). Next, the latest event times are computed and recorded in the `latestTime` array. Notice that this is done using a `LatestTimeVisitor` in a *postorder* depth-first traversal (lines 10–13). This is because a postorder depth-first traversal is equivalent to a topological order traversal in reverse!

Once the earliest and latest event times have been found, we can compute the slack time for each edge. In the implementation shown, an edge-weighted graph is constructed that is isomorphic with the the original event-node graph, but in which the edge weights are the slack times as given by Equation 16.5 (lines 15–31). By constructing such a graph we can make use of Dijkstra's algorithm to find the shortest path from start to finish since the shortest path must be the critical path (line 34).

```
1   Digraph& CriticalPathAnalysis (Digraph& g)
2   {
3       unsigned int const n = g.NumberOfVertices ();
4
5       Array<unsigned int> earliestTime (n);
6       earliestTime [0] = 0;
7       g.TopologicalOrderTraversal (
8           EarliestTimeVisitor (g, earliestTime));
9
10      Array<unsigned int> latestTime (n);
11      latestTime [n - 1U] = earliestTime [n - 1U];
12      g.DepthFirstTraversal (PostOrder (
13          LatestTimeVisitor (g, latestTime)), g[0]);
14
15      DigraphAsLists slackGraph (n);
16      for (Vertex::Number v = 0; v < n; ++v)
17          slackGraph.AddVertex (*new Vertex (v));
18      Iterator& p = g.Edges ();
19      while (!p.IsDone ()) {
20          WeightedEdge& edge =
21              dynamic_cast<WeightedEdge&> (*p);
22          Int& weight =
23              dynamic_cast<Int&> (edge.Weight ());
24          Vertex& v0 = edge.V0 ();
25          Vertex& v1 = edge.V1 ();
26          unsigned int const slack =
27              latestTime [v1] - earliestTime [v0] - weight;
28          slackGraph.AddEdge (*new WeightedEdge (
29              slackGraph [v0], slackGraph [v1], *new Int(slack)));
30          ++p;
31      }
32      delete &p;
33
34      return DijkstrasAlgorithm (slackGraph, slackGraph [0]);
35  }
```

**FIGURE 16.23**
The critical path graph corresponding to Figure 16.22.

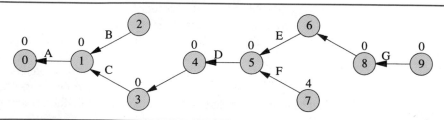

The `DijkstrasAlgorithm` routine given in Section 16.4.1 returns its result in the form of a shortest-path graph. The shortest-path graph for the activity-node graph of Figure 16.22 is shown in Figure 16.23. By following the path in this graph from vertex 9 back to vertex 0, we find that the critical path is {A, C, D, E, G}.

## Exercises

**16.1**  Consider the *undirected graph* $G_A$ shown in Figure 16.24. List the elements of $\mathcal{V}$ and $\mathcal{E}$. Then, for each vertex $v \in \mathcal{V}$ do the following:

   **a.**  Compute the in-degree of $v$.

   **b.**  Compute the out-degree of $v$.

   **c.**  List the elements of $\mathcal{A}(v)$.

   **d.**  List the elements of $\mathcal{I}(v)$.

**16.2**  Consider the directed graph $G_A$ shown in Figure 16.24.

   **a.**  Show how the graph is represented using an adjacency matrix.

   **b.**  Show how the graph is represented using adjacency lists.

**16.3**  Repeat Exercises 16.1 and 16.2 for the *directed graph* $G_B$ shown in Figure 16.24.

**16.4**  Consider a *depth-first traversal* of the undirected graph $G_A$ shown in Figure 16.24 starting from vertex $a$.

   **a.**  List the order in which the nodes are visited in a preorder traversal.

   **b.**  List the order in which the nodes are visited in a postorder traversal.

   Repeat this exercise for a depth-first traversal starting from vertex $d$.

**16.5**  List the order in which the nodes of the undirected graph $G_A$ shown in Figure 16.24 are visited by a *breadth-first traversal* that starts from vertex $a$. Repeat this exercise for a breadth-first traversal starting from vertex $d$.

---

**FIGURE 16.24**
Sample graphs.

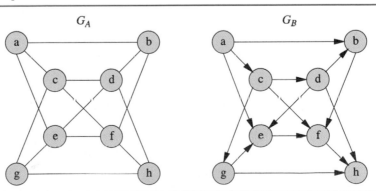

**16.6**   Repeat Exercises 16.4 and 16.5 for the *directed graph* $G_B$ shown in Figure 16.24.

**16.7**   List the order in which the nodes of the directed graph $G_B$ shown in Figure 16.24 are visited by a *topological order traversal* that starts from vertex $a$.

**16.8**   Consider an undirected graph $G = (\mathcal{V}, \mathcal{E})$. If we use a $|\mathcal{V}| \times |\mathcal{V}|$ adjacency matrix $A$ to represent the graph, we end up using twice as much space as we need because $A$ contains redundant information. That is, $A$ is symmetric about the diagonal and all the diagonal entries are zero. Show how a one-dimensional array of length $|\mathcal{V}|(|\mathcal{V}| - 1)/2$ can be used to represent $G$. **Hint:** consider just the part of $A$ above the diagonal.

**16.9**   What is the relationship between the sum of the degrees of the vertices of a graph and the number of edges in the graph?

**16.10**   A graph with the maximum number of edges is called a *fully connected graph*. Draw fully connected, undirected graphs that contain 2, 3, 4, and 5 vertices.

**16.11**   Prove that an undirected graph with $n$ vertices contains at most $n(n - 1)/2$ edges.

**16.12**   Every tree is a directed, acyclic graph (DAG), but there exist DAGs that are not trees.

   **a.**   How can we tell whether a given DAG is a tree?

   **b.**   Devise an algorithm to test whether a given DAG is a tree.

**16.13**   Consider an acyclic, connected, undirected graph $G$ that has $n$ vertices. How many edges does $G$ have?

**16.14**   In general, an undirected graph contains one or more *connected components*. A connected component of a graph $G$ is a subgraph of $G$ that is *connected* and contains the largest possible number of vertices. Each vertex of $G$ is a member of exactly one connected component of $G$.

   **a.**   Devise an algorithm to count the number of connected components in a graph.

   **b.**   Devise an algorithm that labels the vertices of a graph in such a way that all the vertices in a given connected component get the same label and vertices in different connected components get different labels.

**16.15**   A *source* in a directed graph is a vertex with zero in-degree. Prove that every DAG has at least one source.

**16.16**   What kind of DAG has a unique topological sort?

**16.17**   Under what conditions does a *postorder* depth-first traversal of a DAG visit the vertices in *reverse* topological order?

**16.18**   Consider a pair of vertices, $v$ and $w$, in a directed graph. Vertex $w$ is said to be *reachable* from vertex $v$ if there exists a path in $G$ from $v$ to $w$. Devise an algorithm that takes as input a graph, $G = (\mathcal{V}, \mathcal{E})$, and a pair of vertices, $v, w \in \mathcal{V}$, and determines whether $w$ is reachable from $v$.

**16.19**   An *Eulerian walk* is a path in an undirected graph that starts and ends at the same vertex *and traverses every edge* in the graph. Prove that in order for such a path to exist, all the nodes must have even degree.

**FIGURE 16.25**
Sample weighted graphs.

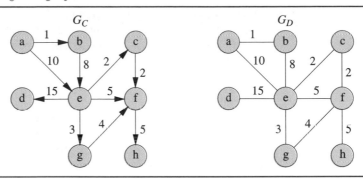

**16.20** Consider the binary relation $<$ defined for the elements of the set $\{a, b, c, d\}$ as follows:

$$\{a < b, a < c, b < c, b < d, c < d, d < a\}.$$

How can we determine whether $<$ is a *total order?*

**16.21** Show how the *single-source shortest path* problem can be solved on a DAG using a topological-order traversal. What is the running time of your algorithm?

**16.22** Consider the directed graph $G_C$ shown in Figure 16.25. Trace the execution of *Dijkstra's algorithm* as it solves the single-source shortest path problem starting from vertex $a$. Give your answer in a form similar to Table 16.3.

**16.23** Dijkstra's algorithm works as long as there are no negative edge weights. Given a graph that contains negative edge weights, we might be tempted to eliminate the negative weights by adding a constant weight to all of the edge weights to make them all positive. Explain why this does not work.

**16.24** Dijkstra's algorithm can be modified to deal with negative edge weights (but not negative cost cycles) by eliminating the *known* flag $k_v$ and by inserting a vertex back into the queue every time its *tentative distance* $d_v$ decreases. Explain why the modified algorithm works correctly. What is the running time of the modified algorithm?

**16.25** Consider the directed graph $G_C$ shown in Figure 16.25. Trace the execution of *Floyd's algorithm* as it solves the *all-pairs shortest path problem.*

**16.26** Prove that if the edge weights on an undirected graph are *distinct*, there is only one minimum-cost spanning tree.

**16.27** Consider the undirected graph $G_D$ shown in Figure 16.25. Trace the execution of *Prim's algorithm* as it finds the *minimum-cost spanning tree* starting from vertex $a$.

**16.28** Repeat Exercise 16.27 using *Kruskal's algorithm.*

**16.29** Do Exercise 14.7.

## Programming Projects

**16.1**  Devise a graph description language. Implement a routine that reads the description of a graph and constructs a graph object instance. Your routine should be completely generic—it should not depend on the graph implementation used.

**16.2**  Extend Project 16.1 by writing a routine that prints the description of a given graph object instance.

**16.3**  Complete the implementation of the **GraphAsMatrix** class declared in Program 16.4 by providing suitable definitions for the following member functions: **GraphAsMatrix** (constructor), **~GraphAsMatrix** (destructor), **Purge**, **AddVertex**, **SelectVertex**, **AddEdge**, **SelectEdge**, **IsEdge**, **Vertices**, **Edges**, **IncidentEdges**, and **EmanatingEdges**. Write a test program and test your implementation.

**16.4**  Repeat Project 16.3 for the **GraphAsLists** class.

**16.5**  The **DigraphAsMatrix** class can be implemented using multiple inheritance:

```
class DigraphAsMatrix : public Digraph, public GraphAsMatrix
{
...
};
```

Implement the **DigraphAsMatrix** class by providing suitable definitions for the following member functions: **DigraphAsMatrix** (constructor), **~DigraphAsMatrix** (destructor), **Purge**, **AddEdge**, **SelectEdge**, **IsEdge**, and **Edges**. You must also have a complete implementation of the base class **GraphAsMatrix** (see Project 16.3). Write a test program and test your implementation.

**16.6**  Repeat Project 16.5 for the **DigraphAsLists** class.

**16.7**  Add a member function to the **Digraph** class abstract interface that creates an instance of and returns a reference to an undirected graph which underlies the given digraph.

**16.8**  Devise an approach using an iterator and a stack to perform a topological-order traversal by doing a postorder depth-first traversal in reverse.

**16.9**  The single-source shortest path problem on a DAG can be solved by visiting the vertices in topological order. Write a visitor for use with the **TopologicalOrderTraversal** routine that solves the single-source shortest path problem on a DAG.

**16.10**  Devise and implement a routine that transforms a vertex-weighted *activity-node graph* into an edge-weighted *event-node graph*.

**16.11**  Complete the implementation of the critical path analysis routines. In particular, you must implement the **LatestTimeVisitor** along the lines of the **EarliestTimeVisitor** defined in Program 16.18.

# A | C++ and Object-Oriented Programming

This appendix is a brief review of the fundamentals of programming in C++. It identifies and describes the features of C++ that are used throughout this text. This appendix is *not* a C++ tutorial—if you are not familiar with C++, you should read one of the myriad C++ programming books.

## A.1  Variables, Pointers, and References

A *variable* is a programming language abstraction that represents a storage location. A variable has the following *attributes*:

**name**  The *name* of a variable is the label used to identify a variable in the text of a program.

**address**  The *address* of a variable is the memory address of the storage location(s) occupied by that variable. The address attribute of a variable is also known as the *l-value* because the *l*-value of a variable is required when a variable name is used on the *left* side of an assignment statement.

**size**  The *size* of a variable is the amount of storage (in bytes) occupied by that variable.

**type**  The *type* of a variable determines the set of values that the variable can have *and* the set of operations that can be performed on that variable.

**value**  The *value* of a variable is the content of the memory location(s) occupied by that variable. (How the contents of the memory locations are interpreted is determined by the *type* of the variable.) The value attribute of a variable is also known as the *r-value* because the *r*-value of a variable is required when a variable name is used on the *right* side of an assignment statement.

**619**

**lifetime** The *lifetime* of a variable is the interval of time in the execution of a program during which a variable is said to exist. Some variables exist for the entire execution of a program; some are created and destroyed automatically during the execution of a program; and others are explicitly created and destroyed by the programmer.

**scope** The *scope* of a variable is the range of statements in the text of a program in which that variable can be referenced.

Consider the C++ variable declaration statement:

```
int i = 57;
```

This statement defines a variable and *binds* various attributes with that variable. The name of the variable is `i`, the type of the variable is `int`, its size is `sizeof(int)` (typically two or four bytes), and its initial value is 57.

Some attributes of a variable, such as its name, type and size, are bound at compile time. This is called *static binding*. Other attributes of a variable, such as its address and value, may be bound at run time. This is called *dynamic binding*.

## A.1.1 Pointers Are Variables

The C++ statement

```
int* p;
```

declares a *pointer*. A pointer is a variable the type of which has the form $T*$, where $T$ is an arbitrary type. In this case, $T = $ `int` and we say that `p` is a *pointer* to `int`.

Since a pointer is a variable, it has all the attributes of a variable. In particular, it has both an *address* (*l*-value) and a *value* (*r*-value).

Consider a C++ program that contains the following global variable declarations:

```
int i = 57;
int j = 31;
int* p = 0;
int* q = (int*) 1004;
```

Suppose the four variables, `i`, `j`, `p`, and `q`, are stored in contiguous memory locations starting at address 1000, as shown in Figure A.1. (We assume that `sizeof(int)=` `sizeof(int*)=4`.) Note that the variable named `j` has the value 31 and is found at address 1004. Similarly, the variable named `q` has the value 1004 and is found at address 1012.

An assignment statement such as

```
i = j;
```

**FIGURE A.1**
Memory layout of C++ variables and pointers.

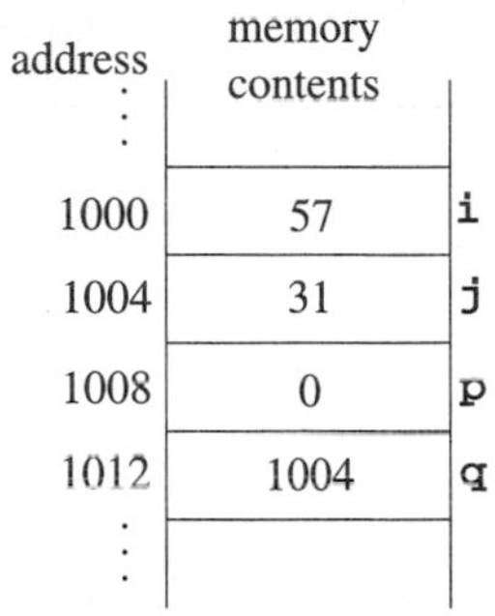

| address | memory contents | |
|---------|-----------------|---|
| ⋮ | | |
| 1000 | 57 | i |
| 1004 | 31 | j |
| 1008 | 0 | p |
| 1012 | 1004 | q |
| ⋮ | | |

takes the value (*r*-value) of j, in this case 31, and stores it in memory at the address (*l*-value) of i, in this case 1000. Similarly, the assignment

```
p = q;
```

takes the value of q, in this case 1004, and stores it in memory at the address of p, in this case 1008.

### Dereferencing Pointers

A variable of type $T*$ is said to *point* at an object of type $T$. What this really means is that the *value* of the $T*$ variable is the address of another variable of type $T$. For example, in Figure A.1 the variable q is has type int*, i.e., it is a *pointer* to an int. The *value* of q is 1004, which is the *address* of the variable j.

To access the variable to which a pointer points, we must *dereference* the pointer. For example, to dereference the pointer q we write *q. Whereas q denotes the pointer variable itself, *q denotes the int to which the pointer points.

If we use *q in a context where an *r*-value is expected, then we get the *r*-value of the variable to which q points. For example, since q points to the variable j, the assignment

```
i = *q;
```

takes the *r*-value of j (31) and assigns it to i.

Similarly, if we use *q in a context where an *l*-value is required, then we get the *l*-value of the variable to which q points. For example, since q points to the variable j, the assignment

```
*q = 31;
```

takes the *l*-value of j (1004) and stores 31 at that location. Notice that the *l*-value of *q is identical to the *r*-value of q.

### A.1.2 References Are Not Variables

In C++, a *reference* is an alternative name for a variable. The declaration of a reference looks very much like the declaration of a variable. However, a reference is not a variable. The notation *T&* denotes a reference to a variable of type *T*. For example, the code sequence

```
int i = 57;
int& r = i;
```

defines one variable, **i**, and one reference, **r**.

In C++ all references must be initialized. In this case the reference **r** *refers* to the variable **i**. A reference can be used in a program everywhere that a variable can be used. In particular, if the reference **r** is used where a *r*-value is required, it is the *r*-value of **i** that is obtained. Similarly, if the reference **r** is used where an *l*-value is required, it is the *l*-value of **i** that is obtained.

Is it important to note that in C++, despite appearances, there are no operators that operate on references. In particular, it is not possible to change the variable to which a reference refers. And since every reference must be initialized by associating it with a variable, there is no such thing as a *null* reference. References are mainly used in C++ programs to specify the arguments and return values of functions.

## A.2 Parameter Passing

Parameter passing methods are the ways in which parameters are transfered between functions when one function calls another. C++ provides two parameter passing methods—*pass-by-value* and *pass-by-reference*.

### A.2.1 Pass By Value

Consider a pair of C++ functions defined in Program A.1. The function **One** calls the function **Two**. In general, every function call includes a (possibly empty) list of arguments. The arguments specified in a function call are called *actual parameters*. In this case, there is only one actual parameter—**y**.

The method by which the parameter is passed to a function is determined by the function definition. In this case, the function **Two** is defined as accepting a single argument of type **int** called **x**. The arguments which appear in a function definition are called *formal parameters*. If the type of a formal parameter is *not* a reference (see Section A.1.2), then the parameter passing method is *pass-by-value*.

The semantics of pass-by-value work like this: The effect of the formal parameter definition is to create a local variable of the specified type in the given function. For

---

**PROGRAM A.1**
Example of pass-by-value parameter passing

---

```
1   void Two (int x)
2   {
3       x = 2;
4       cout << x << endl;
5   }
6
7   void One ()
8   {
9       int y = 1;
10      Two (y);
11      cout << y << endl;
12  }
```

---

example, the function **Two** has a local variable of type **int** called **x**. When the function is called, the *values* (*r*-values) of the *actual parameters* are used to initialize the *formal parameters* before the body of the function is executed.

Since the formal parameters give rise to local variables, if a new value is assigned to a formal parameter, that value has no effect on the actual parameters. Therefore, the output obtained produced by the function **One** defined in Program A.1 is:

```
2
1
```

## A.2.2   Pass By Reference

Consider the pair of C++ functions defined in Program A.2. The only difference between this code and the code given in Program A.1 is the definition of the formal parameter of the function **Two**: In this case, the parameter **x** is declared to be a *reference* to an **int**. In general, if the type of a formal parameter is a reference, then the parameter passing method is *pass-by-reference*.

A reference formal parameter is not a variable. When a function is called that has a reference formal parameter, the effect of the call is to associate the reference with the corresponding actual parameter. That is, the reference becomes an alternative name for the corresponding actual parameter. Consequently, this means that the actual parameter passed by reference must be a variable.

A reference formal parameter can be used in the called function everywhere that a variable can be used. In particular, if the reference formal parameter is used where an *r*-value is required, it is the *r*-value of the actual parameter that is obtained. Similarly, if the reference parameter is used where an *l*-value is required, it is the *l*-value of actual

---

**PROGRAM A.2**
Example of pass-by-reference parameter passing

```
1   void Two (int& x)
2   {
3       x = 2;
4       cout << x << endl;
5   }
6
7   void One ()
8   {
9       int y = 1;
10      Two (y);
11      cout << y << endl;
12  }
```

---

parameter that is obtained. Therefore, the output obtained produced by the function **One** defined in Program A.2 is

2
2

### The Trade-off

Clearly, the parameter passing method used constrains the functionality of the called function: When pass-by-value is used, the called function cannot modify the actual parameters; when pass-by-reference is used, the called function is able to modify the actual parameters. In addition, the two methods have different time and space requirements that need to be understood in order to make the proper selection.

Pass-by-value creates a local variable and initializes that local variable by copying the value of the actual parameter. This means that space is used (on the stack) for the local variable and that time is taken to initialize that local variable. For small variables these penalties are insignificant. However, if the variable is large, the time and space penalties may become prohibitive.

On the other hand, pass-by-reference does not create a local variable nor does it require the copying of the actual parameter. However, because of the way it must be implemented, every time a reference formal parameter is used to access the corresponding actual parameter, a small amount of extra time is taken to dereference the reference. As a result, it is typically more efficient to pass small variables by value and large variables by reference.

### Constant Parameters

In general, pass-by-reference parameter passing allows the called function to modify the actual parameters. However, sometimes it is the case that the programmer does not want the actual parameters to be modified. Nevertheless, pass-by-reference may be the preferred method for performance reasons.

In C++ we can use the `const` keyword to achieve the performance of pass-by-reference while at the same time ensuring that the actual parameter cannot be modified. Consider the following definition of the function `Two`:

```
void Two (int const& x)
{
    x = 2; // Not allowed.
    cout << x << endl; // This is ok.
}
```

The `const` keyword modifies the type `int`. It says that the `int` to which `x` refers is a constant. The value of `x` can be used without impunity. However, `x` cannot be used as the target of an assignment statement. In fact, the variable `x` cannot be used in any context where it might be modified. Any attempt to do so is an error that is detected by the compiler.

## A.3  Objects and Classes

"An *object* is a region of storage[12]." The *type* of the object determines how that region of storage is interpreted and how it can be manipulated. C++ provides *built-in types*, such as `char`, `int`, and `float`, and it supports the creation of *user-defined types* using the `class` construct.

The `class` construct is what makes C++ an *object-oriented* language. A C++ class definition groups a set of values with a set of operations. Classes facilitate modularity and information hiding. The user of a class manipulates object instances of that class only through a well-defined interface.

It is often the case that different classes possess common features. Different classes may share common values; they may perform the same operations; they may support common interfaces. In C++ such relationships are expressed using *derivation* and *inheritance*.

### A.3.1  Member Variables and Member Functions

A class groups a set of values and a set of operations. The values and the operations of a class are called its *members*. *Member variables* implement the values and *member functions* implement the operations.

Suppose we wish to define a class to represent *complex numbers*. The `Complex` class definition shown in Program A.3 illustrates how this can be done. Two member variables, `real` and `imag`, are declared. These represent the real and imaginary parts of a complex numbers (respectively).

---

**PROGRAM A.3**
Complex class definition

---

```
1   class Complex
2   {
3       double real;
4       double imag;
5   public:
6       Complex ();
7       Complex (double);
8       Complex (double, double);
9       Complex (Complex const&);
10      ~Complex ();
11
12      double Real () const;
13      double Imag () const;
14      double R () const;
15      double Theta () const;
16      void Put (ostream&) const;
17
18      void SetReal (double);
19      void SetImag (double);
20      Complex& operator = (Complex  const&);
21  };
```

---

Every object instance of the **Complex** class contains its own member variables. Consider the following variable declarations:

```
Complex c;
Complex d;
```

Both **c** and **d** are instances of the complex class. Therefore, each of them has a **real** and **imag** member variable. The member variables of an object are accessed using the *dot* operator. For example, **c.real** refers to the **real** member variable of **c**, and **d.imag** refers to the **imag** member of **d**.

The **Complex** class definition also contains a list of function prototypes which declare the *member functions* of the class. In general, a member function performs some operations on an instance of the class. Again, the *dot* operator is used to specify the object on which the operation is performed. For example, **c.SetReal(1.0)** invokes the **SetReal** function on **c**, and **d.Put(cout)** invokes the **Put** function on **d**.

## A.3.2 Constructors and Destructors

A *constructor* is a member function that has the same name as its class (and which has no return value). For example, there are four constructors declared in Program A.3

(lines 6–9). The purpose of a constructor is to *initialize* an object. In fact, C++ makes the following promise: If a class has a constructor, all objects of that class will be initialized.

Consider the following sequence of variable declarations:

```
Complex c;        // calls Complex ()
Complex d = 2.0;  // calls Complex (double)
Complex i(0, 1);  // calls Complex (double, double)
Complex j(i);     // calls Complex (Complex const&)
```

Each variable declaration *implicitly* causes the appropriate constructor to be invoked. In particular, the equal sign in the declaration of **d** denotes *initialization* not assignment and, therefore, is accomplished by calling the constructor.

### Default Constructor

The constructor which takes no arguments is called the *default constructor*. For example, the default constructor is invoked when a variable is declared like this:

```
Complex c;
```

In fact, the compiler will generate its own default constructor for a class provided that no other constructors have been defined by the programmer. The compiler generated default constructor initializes the member variables of the class using their respective default constructors.

Program A.4 gives the implementation of the default constructor of the **Complex** class. Because the implementation the member function is given outside of the class definition, the name of the function is prefixed with the class name followed by `::`.

The default constructor explicitly invokes the constructors for the member variables **real** and **imag** (line 2). After the member variables have been initialized, the body of the constructor runs. In this case, the body of the constructor is empty (line 3).

### Copy Constructor

The *copy constructor* for class **T** is a member function of the form `T(T&)` or `T(T const&)`. The purpose of a copy constructor is to initialize a new object of a given class by copying an existing object of that class. Consider this sequence of declarations:

```
Complex c;
Complex d(c);
```

The variable **c** is initialized using the default constructor, whereas **d** is initialized by calling the copy constructor. In effect, the value of **c** is copied into **d**.

The compiler will generate its own copy constructor for any class in which no copy constructor has been defined by the programmer. The compiler-generated copy constructor initializes the member variables of the class using their respective copy constructors.

---

**PROGRAM A.4**
Complex class constructors and destructor

---

```
1    Complex::Complex () :
2        real (0), imag (0)
3        {}
4
5    Complex::Complex (double x) :
6        real (x), imag (0)
7        {}
8
9    Complex::Complex (double x, double y) :
10       real (x), imag (y)
11       {}
12
13   Complex::Complex (Complex const& c) :
14       real (c.real), imag (c.imag)
15       {}
16
17   Complex::~Complex ()
18       {}
```

---

### The Copy Constructor, Parameter Passing, and Function Return Values

The copy constructor plays a special rôle in pass-by-value parameter passing. As discussed in Section A.2.1, the semantics of pass-by-value stipulate that the values of the actual parameters are used to *initialize* the formal parameters when a function is called. The compiler achieves this by using the copy constructor to copy the value of the actual parameter to the formal parameter.

The copy constructor plays a similar rôle when a value is returned from a function using the **return** statement. The copy constructor is used to copy the value from the called function back to the point where the calling function makes use of the result.

Program A.4 gives an implementation for the copy constructor of the **Complex** class. The copy constructor initializes the member variables **real** and **imag** by calling explicitly their respective copy constructors (line 14). After the member variables have been initialized, the body of the constructor runs. In this case, the body of the copy constructor is empty (line 15).

### Destructors

A *destructor* is a special member function used to *finalize* an object. The name the destructor for class **T** is **~T()** and, like constructors, it has no return value. The destructor takes no arguments and, therefore, there is only one destructor per class.

It is normally not necessary to call a destructor explicitly. The destructor for an object is automatically invoked at the end of the lifetime of that object. In particular, this means that the destructors for global variables run after the **main** routine exits, and that the destructors for local and temporary variables run when the program exits the scope containing those variables.

If the programmer does not define a destructor explicitly, the C++ compiler generates one. The compiler-generated destructor simply invokes the destructors for the member variables of the class. The members of a class are always destroyed in the reverse of the order in which they were constructed.

Program A.4 defines explicitly a destructor for the class `Complex` (lines 17–18). In this case, the body of the destructor is empty. When the destructor runs, the body of the destructor is run first. After the body of the destructor has completed, the destructors for the member variables run (automatically).

### A.3.3 Accessors and Mutators

An *accessor* is a member function that accesses the contents of an object but does not modify that object. In the simplest case, an accessor just returns the value of one of the member variables. In general, an accessor performs some computation using the member variables as long as that computation does not modify any of the member variables.

Program A.5 defines the five accessor member functions of the `Complex` class—`Real`, `Imag`, `R`, `Theta`, and `Put`. The fact that these functions are accessors is indicated by the `const` keyword at the end of the function declarator. The `const` signifies that this member function is not permitted to modify the object on which it operates. In fact, the C++ compiler will not allow any operations that could modify any of the member variables of the object.

---

**PROGRAM A.5**
`Complex` class accessors

---

```
1   double Complex::Real () const
2       { return real; }
3
4   double Complex::Imag () const
5       { return imag; }
6
7   double Complex::R () const
8       { return std::sqrt (real * real + imag * imag); }
9
10  double Complex::Theta () const
11      { return atan2 (imag, real); }
13
14  void Complex::Put (ostream& s) const
15      { s << real << "+" << imag << "i"; }
```

By defining suitable accessors, it is possible to hide the implementation of the class from the user of that class. Consider the following statements:

```
cout << c.real << endl;
cout << c.Real() << endl;
```

The first statement depends on the implementation of the **Complex** class. If we change the implementation of the class from the one given (which uses rectangular coordinates) to one that uses polar coordinates, then the first statement above must also be changed. On the other hand, the second statement does not need to be modified, provided we reimplement the **Real** member function when we switch to polar coordinates.

## Mutators

A *mutator* is a member function that can modify an object. Every non-**const** member function of a class is a mutator. In the simplest case, a mutator just assigns a new value to one of the member variables. In general, a mutator performs some computation and modifies any number of member variables.

Program A.6 defines three mutators for the **Complex** class. The first two, **SetReal** and **SetImag**, simply assign new values to the **real** and **imag** member variables, respectively.

Program A.6 also shows how the assignment operator, **operator=**, can be *overloaded*. By overloading the assignment operator in this way the function is called whenever a complex number is assigned to another like this:

```
c = d;
```

If the programmer does not define an assignment operator explicitly, the C++ compiler generates one. The compiler-generated assignment operator simply assigns

---

**PROGRAM A.6**
**Complex** class mutators

```
1   void Complex::SetReal (double x)
2       { real = x; }
3
4   void Complex::SetImag (double y)
5       { imag = y; }
6
7   Complex& Complex::operator = (Complex  const& c)
8   {
9       real = c.real;
10      imag = c.imag;
11      return *this;
12  }
```

one-by-one the member variables of the class by invoking their respective assignment operators.

### Member Access Control

Every member of a class, be it a variable or a function, has an *access control attribute* which affects the manner in which that member can be accessed. The members of a class can be `private`, `public`, or `protected`.

By default, the members of a `class` are private. For example, the member variables `real` and `imag` declared in Program A.3 are both `private`. `Private` members can be used only by member functions and friends of the class in which the member is declared.

On the other hand, `public` members of a class can be used by any function. In Program A.3 the keyword `public` on line 5 indicates that all the following member functions are publicly accessible.

In effect, the public part of a class defines the interface to that class and the private part of the class encapsulates the implementation of that class. By making the implementation of a class private, we ensure that the code which uses the class depends only on the interface and not on the implementation of the class. Furthermore, we can modify the implementation of the class without affecting the code of the user of that class.

`Protected` members are similar to `private` members. That is, they can be used by member functions and friends of the class in which the member is declared. In addition, `protected` members can also be used by member functions and friends of all the classes derived from the class in which the member is declared. The `protected` category is discussed again in Section A.4.1.

## A.4   Inheritance and Polymorphism

### A.4.1   Derivation and Inheritance

This section reviews the concept of a derived class. Derived classes are an extremely useful feature of C++ because they allow the programmer to define new classes by extending existing classes. By using derived classes, the programmer can exploit the commonalities that exist among the classes in a program. Different classes can share values, operations, and interfaces.

*Derivation* is the definition of a new class by extending one or more existing classes. The new class is called the *derived class*, and the existing classes from which it is derived are called the *base classes*. Usually there is only one base class. However, C++ allows there to be more than one base class (*multiple inheritance*).

Consider the classes `Person` and `Parent` defined in Program A.7. Because parents are people too, the `Parent` class is derived from the `Person` class.

A derived class *inherits* all the members of all its base classes. That is, the derived class contains all the member variables contained in the base classes and the derived class supports all the same operations provided by the base classes. For example,

---

**PROGRAM A.7**
Derivation and inheritance in C++

---

```
1    class Person
2    {
3    public:
4        enum Sex { male, female };
5    protected:
6        string name;
7        Sex sex;
8    public:
9        std::string Name () const
10           { return name; }
11       void Put (ostream& s) const
12           { s << name; }
13       //...
14   };
15
16   class Parent : public Person
17   {
18   protected:
19       unsigned int numberOfChildren;
20       Person* child;
21   public:
22       Person& Child (unsigned int i) const
23       {
24           if (i >= numberOfChildren)
25               throw out_of_range ("invalid child number");
26           return child [i];
27       }
28       void Put (ostream& s)
29       {
30           //...
31       }
32       //...
33   };
```

---

consider the following variable declarations:

```
Person p;
Parent q;
```

Since **p** is a **Person**, it has the member variables **name** and **sex** and member function **Name**. Furthermore, since **Parent** is derived from **Person**, then the object **q** also has the member variables **name** and **sex** and member function **Name**.

A derived class can *extend* the base class(es) in several ways: New member variables can be defined, new member functions can be defined, and existing member functions can be *overridden*. For example, the `Parent` class adds the member variables `numberOfChildren` and `child` and the member function `Child`.

If a function is defined in a derived class that has exactly the same *signature* (name and types of arguments) as a function in a base class, the function in the derived class *overrides* the one in the base class. For example, the `Put` function in the `Parent` class overrides the `Put` function in the `Person` class. Therefore, `p.Put(...)` invokes `Person::Put`, whereas `q.Put(...)` invokes `Parent::Put`.

An instance of a derived class can be used anywhere in a program where an instance of the base class may be used. For example, this means that a `Parent` may be passed as an actual parameter to a function (either by value or by reference) in which the formal parameter is a `Person`.

It is also possible to assign the address of a derived class object to a pointer to a base class object like this:

```
Person* ptr = new Parent;
```

However, having done so, it is not possible to call `ptr->Child(...)`, because `ptr` is a pointer to a `Person` instance and a `Person` is not necessarily a `Parent`.

Similarly, we can use a reference to a `Person` to refer to a parent:

```
Person& p = *new Parent;
```

For the same reasons as explained above, it is not possible to use the reference `p` to invoke `p.Child(...)`.

### Derivation and Access Control

Members of a class can be `private`, `public`, or `protected`. As explained in Section A.3.3, private members are accessible only by member functions and friends of the class in which the member is declared. In particular, this means that the member functions of a derived class cannot access the private members of the base classes even though the derived class has inherited those members! On the other hand, if we make the members of the base classes public, then all classes can access those members directly, not just derived classes.

C++ provides a third category of access control—`protected`. `Protected` members can be used by member functions and friends of the class in which the member is declared as well as by member functions and friends of all the classes derived from the class in which the member is declared.

A derived class *inherits* all the members of its base class(es). The accessibility of the members inherited by a derived class depends on whether the derivation is `private` or `public`:

```
class B {... };
class D1 : public B {... };
class D2 : private B {... };
```

Here **B** is a public base class of **D1**. This means that the public members of **B** are also public in **D1** and that the protected members of **B** are also protected in **D1**. On the other hand, **B** is a private base class of **D2**. This means that the public and protected members of **B** are private in **D2**.

## A.4.2 Polymorphism

*Polymorphism* literally means "having many forms." Polymorphism arises when a set of distinct classes share a common interface because they are all derived from the same base class(es). Because the derived classes are distinct, their implementations may differ. However, because the derived classes share a common interface, instances of those classes are used in exactly the same way.

Consider a program for creating simple drawings. Suppose the program provides a set of primitive graphical objects, such as circles, rectangles, and squares. The user of the program selects the desired objects, and then invokes commands to draw, to erase, or to move them about. Ideally, all graphical objects support the same set of operations. Nevertheless, the way that the operations are implemented varies from one object to the next.

We implement this as follows: First, we define a **GraphicalObject** class which represents the common interface shared by all graphical objects. Then, we derive from **GraphicalObject** classes to represent circles, rectangles, and squares.

Consider the **GraphicalObject** class declared in Program A.8. This class has a single member variable, **center**, which is an instance of the **Point** class and which represents the position in the drawing of the center-point of the graphical object. The constructor for the **GraphicalObject** class takes as its lone argument a reference to a **Point** and initializes the **center** member variables accordingly.

In addition to the constructor and destructor, three member functions are declared. The **Draw** routine draws the object, the **Erase** routine erases the object, and the **MoveTo** routine moves the object to a new position.

Program A.9 shows a possible implementation for the **Erase** function: In this case we assume that the image is drawn using an imaginary pen. Assuming that we know how to draw a graphical object, we can erase the object by changing the color of the pen so that it matches the background color and then redrawing the object.

Once we can erase an object as well as draw it, then moving it is easy. Just erase the object, change its **center** point, and then draw it again. This is how the **MoveTo** function shown in Program A.9 is implemented.

We have seen that the **GraphicalObject** class provides implementations for the **Erase** and **MoveTo** member functions. However, the **GraphicalObject** class does not provide an implementation for the **Draw** function. Why not? Because until we know what kind of object it is, we cannot possibly know how to draw it!

Consider the **Circle** class defined in Program A.10. This class is derived from **GraphicalObject**. Therefore, it inherits the member variable **center** and the member functions **Erase** and **MoveTo**. The **Circle** class adds an additional member variable, **radius**, and it overrides the **Draw** routine. The body of the **Draw** routine is

**PROGRAM A.8**
`Point` and `GraphicalObject` class definitions

```
1   class Point
2   {
3       int x;
4       int y;
5   public:
6       Point (int, int);
7       //...
8   };
9
10  class GraphicalObject
11  {
12  protected:
13      Point center;
14
15      GraphicalObject (Point const& p) :
16  center (p) {}
17  public:
18      virtual ~GraphicalObject ();
19      virtual void Draw () const = 0;
20      virtual void Erase () const;
21      virtual void MoveTo (Point const&);
22  };
```

**PROGRAM A.9**
`GraphicalObject` class `MoveTo` and `Erase` member function definitions

```
1   void GraphicalObject::Erase () const
2   {
3       SetPenColour (backgroundColour);
4       Draw ();
5       SetPenColour (foregroundColour);
6   }
7
8   void GraphicalObject::MoveTo (Point const& p)
9   {
10      Erase ();
11      center = p;
12      Draw ();
13  }
```

---

**PROGRAM A.10**
Circle, Rectangle and Square class definitions

```
1   class Circle : public GraphicalObject
2   {
3       int radius;
4   public:
5       Circle (Point const& p, int r) :
6           GraphicalObject (p), radius (r) {}
7
8       void Draw () const;
9   };
10
11  class Rectangle : public GraphicalObject
12  {
13      int height;
14      int width;
15  public:
16      Rectangle (Point const& p, int ht, int wid) :
17          GraphicalObject (p), height (ht), width (wid) {}
18
19      void Draw () const;
20  };
21
22  class Square : public Rectangle
23  {
24  public:
25      Square (Point const& p, int wid) :
26          Rectangle (p, wid, wid) {}
27  };
```

---

not shown in Program A.10. However, we shall assume that it draws a circle with the given radius and center point.

Using the `Circle` class defined in Program A.10 we can write code like this:

```
Circle c (Point (0, 0), 5);
c.Draw ();
c.MoveTo (Point (10, 10));
c.Erase ();
```

This code sequence declares a circle object with its center initially at position (0, 0) and radius 5. The circle is then drawn, moved to (10, 10), and then erased.

Program A.10 also defines the classes `Rectangle` and `Square`. The `Rectangle` class is also derived from `GraphicalObject`. Therefore, it inherits the member variable **center** and the member functions **Erase** and **MoveTo**. The `Rectangle` class adds two additional member variables, `height` and `width`, and it overrides the `Draw` routine. The body of the `Draw` routine is not shown in Program A.10. However, we shall assume that it draws a rectangle with the given dimensions and center point.

The `Square` class is derived from the `Rectangle` class. No new member variables or functions are declared—those inherited from `GraphicalObject` or from `Rectangle` are sufficient. The constructor simply arranges to make sure that the `height` and `width` of a square are equal!

### Virtual Member Functions

In Program A.8 `Draw`, `Erase`, and `MoveTo` are all declared as `virtual` member functions of the `GraphicalObject` class. Declaring a member function `virtual` changes the way in which the compiler determines the member function to call.

Consider the following sequence of instructions:

```
GraphicalObject& g1 = *new Circle (Point (0,0), 5);
GraphicalObject& g2 = *new Square (Point (0,0), 5);
g1.Draw ();
g2.Draw ();
```

If the `Draw` function was not declared virtual, then both `g1.Draw()` and `g2.Draw()` would invoke `GraphicalObject::Draw`. However, because `Draw` is a `virtual` function, `g1.Draw()` calls `Circle::Draw` and `g2.Draw()` calls `Rectangle::Draw`.

It is as if every object of a class contains a pointer to the actual routine to be invoked when a virtual function is called on that object. For example, `Circle` objects carry pointers to `Circle::Draw`, `GraphicalObject::Erase`, and `Graphical-Object::MoveTo`, whereas `Square` objects carry pointers to `Rectangle::Draw`, `GraphicalObject::Erase` and `GraphicalObject::MoveTo`.

Virtual functions ensure that the "correct" member function is actually called, regardless of how the object is accessed. Consider the following sequence:

```
Square s (Point (0,0), 5);
Rectangle& r = s;
GraphicalObject& g = r;
```

Here `s`, `r`, and `g` all refer to the same object, even though they are all of different types. However, because `Draw` is `virtual`, `s.Draw()`, `r.Draw()`, and `g.Draw()` all invoke `Rectangle::Draw`.

### Abstract Classes and Concrete Classes

In C++ an *abstract class* is one which defines an interface, but does not necessarily provide implementations for all its member functions. An abstract class is meant to be used as the base class from which other classes are derived. The derived class is expected to provide implementations for the member functions that are not implemented in the base class. A derived class that implements all the missing functionality is called a *concrete class*.

For example, the `GraphicalObject` class defined in Programs A.8 and A.9 is an abstract class. In particular, no implementation is given for the virtual member function `Draw`. The fact that no implementation is given is indicated by the `=0` attached to the `Draw` function prototype in the class definition (Program A.8, line 19). Recall that an object carries a pointer to the appropriate routine for every virtual member function it supports. The `=0` says that the pointer for the `Draw` function is not defined in the `GraphicalObject` class and, therefore, it must be defined in a derived class.

A virtual member function for which no implementation is given is called a *pure virtual function*. If a C++ class contains a pure virtual function, it is an *abstract class*. In C++ it is not possible to instantiate an abstract class; for example, the following declaration is illegal:

```
GraphicalObject g (Point (0,0)); // Wrong.
```

If we were allowed to declare `g` in this way, then we could attempt to invoke the nonexistent member function `g.Draw()`.

In fact, there is a second reason why the declaration of `g` is an error: The `GraphicalObject` constructor is not `public` (see Program A.8, lines 15–16). So, even if the `GraphicalObject` class was a concrete class, we are still prevented from instantiating it. Since the constructor is `protected`, it can be called by a derived class. Therefore, it is possible to instantiate `Circle`, `Rectangle`, and `Square`.

### Algorithmic Abstraction

Abstract classes can be used in many interesting ways. One of the most useful paradigms is the use of an abstract class for *algorithmic abstraction*. The `Erase` and `MoveTo` functions defined in Program A.9 are examples of this.

The `Erase` and `MoveTo` functions are implemented in the abstract class `GraphicalObject`. The algorithms implemented are designed to work in any concrete class derived from `GraphicalObject`, be it `Circle`, `Rectangle`, or `Square`. In effect, we have written algorithms that work regardless of the actual class of the object. Therefore, such algorithms are called *abstract algorithms*.

Abstract algorithms typically invoke virtual member functions. For example, the `MoveTo` function invokes `Erase` and `Draw` to do most of the actual work. In this case, the derived classes are expected to inherit the abstract algorithm `MoveTo` and to override the pure virtual function `Draw`. Thus, the derived class customizes the behavior of the abstract algorithm by overriding the appropriate member functions. The virtual function resolution mechanism ensures that the "correct" member function is always called.

## A.4.3  Multiple Inheritance

In C++ a class can be derived from one or more base classes. However, all the base classes must be distinct, that is, the following declaration is not allowed:

```
class D : public B, public B {... }; // Wrong.
```

**FIGURE A.2**
Multiple derivation and virtual base classes.

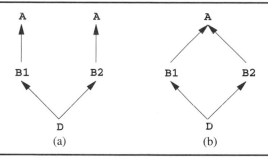

Nevertheless, it is possible for a class to be *indirectly derived* from the same base class more than once, for example, consider the following class definitions:

```
class A {... };
class B1 : public A {... };
class B2 : public A {... };
class D : public B1, public B2 {... };
```

The derived class **D** inherits two instances of the base class **A**—one indirectly via **B1**, the other indirectly via **B2**. In particular, this means that **D** contains two copies of each member variable of class **A**. It also means that when a member function of **A** is called, it is necessary to specify which of the two instances of **A** is to be used—the one from which **B1** is derived or the one from which **B2** is derived. This scenario is shown in Figure A.2(*a*).

Sometimes it makes more sense for the derived class **D** to contain only one instance of the base class **A**. In C++ this is accomplished using *virtual base classes*:

```
class A {... };
class B1 : virtual public A {... };
class B2 : virtual public A {... };
class D : public B1, public B2 {... };
```

In this case, the derived class **D** contains only one instance of the base class **A**. Therefore, **D** contains only one copy of the member variables declared in **A** and there is not ambiguity when invoking the member functions of **A**. This corresponds to the situation shown in Figure A.2(*b*).

## A.4.4   Run-Time Type Information and Casts

Consider the following declarations which make use of the **Rectangle** and **Square** classes defined in Program A.10:

```
Rectangle r (Point (0,0), 5, 10);
Square s (Point (0,0), 15);
```

Clearly, the assignment

```
r = s;
```

is valid because **Square** is derived from **Rectangle**. That is, since a **Square** is a **Rectangle**, we may assign **s** to **r**.

On the other hand, the assignment

```
s = r;
```

is not valid because a **Rectangle** instance is not necessarily a **Square**.

Consider now the following declarations:

```
Rectangle& r = *new Square (Point (0,0), 20);
Square s;
```

The assignment **s=r** is still invalid because **r** is a reference to a **Rectangle**, and a **Rectangle** instance is not necessarily a **Square**, despite the fact that in this case it actually is!

In order to do the assignment, it is necessary to convert the type of **r** from a reference to a **Rectangle** to a reference to a **Square**. This is done in C++ using a *cast operator*:

```
s = (Square&) r;
```

However, a conversion like this is unchecked. Neither the compiler nor the run-time system can determine whether **r** actually refers to a **Square**.

To determine the actual type of the object to which **r** refers, we must make use of *run-time type information*. In C++, every object instance of a class that has virtual functions keeps track of its type. We can test the type of such an object explicitly using the C++ **typeid** operator like this:

```
if (typeid (r) == typeid (Square))
    s = (Square&) r;
```

This code is type-safe because the cast is only done when the object to which **r** refers actually is a **Square**.

C++ also provides a type-safe cast operator called **dynamic_cast<T>()**. In this case, **T** must be either a pointer type or a reference type. The **dynamic_cast** operator combines the run-time type-compatibility check with the type cast operation. For example, the statement

```
s = dynamic_cast<Square&> (r);
```

succeeds if **r** is found at run-time to be is an instance of the **Square** class. If it is not, the **dynamic_cast** operator throws a **bad_cast** exception. (Exceptions are discussed in Section A.6.)

## A.5 Templates

In C++, *templates* are used to define generic functions and classes. A *generic* function or class is one which takes a *type* as an actual parameter. As a result, a single function or class definition gives rise to a family of functions or classes that are compiled from the same source code, but operate on different types.

For example, consider the following function definition:

```
int Max (int x, int y)
    { return x > y ? x : y; }
```

The **Max** function takes two arguments of type **int** and returns the larger of the two. To compute the maximum value of a pair doubles, we require a different **Max** function.

By using a template, we can define a generic **Max** function like this:

```
template <class T>
T Max (T x, T y)
    { return x > y ? x : y; }
```

The template definition gives rise to a family of **Max** functions, one for every different type **T**. The C++ compiler automatically creates the appropriate **Max** functions as needed. For example, the code sequence

```
int i = Max (1, 2);
double d = Max (1.0, 2.0);
```

causes the creation of two **Max** functions, one for arguments of type **int** and the other for arguments of type **double**.

Templates can also be used to define generic classes. For example, consider the following class definition:

```
class Stack
{
    //...
public:
    void Push (int);
    int Pop ();
};
```

---

**PROGRAM A.11**
Stack template definition

```
1    template <class T>
2    class Stack
3    {
4        //...
5    public:
6        void Push (T);
7        T Pop ();
8    };
9
10   template <class T>
11   void Stack<T>::Push (T arg)
12   {
13       //...
14   }
15
16   template <class T>
17   T Stack<T>::Pop ()
18   {
19       //...
20   }
```

---

This `Stack` class represents a stack of integers. The member functions `Push` and `Pop` are used to insert and to withdraw an `int` from the stack (respectively). If instead of `int`s a stack of `double`s is required, we must write a different `Stack` class. By using a template as shown in Program A.11 we can define a generic `Stack` class.

The required classes are created automatically by the C++ compiler as needed. For example, the code sequence

```
Stack<int> s1;
s1.Push (1);
Stack<double> s2;
s2.Push (1.0);
```

causes the creation of two stack classes, `Stack<int>` and `Stack<double>`. This example also illustrates that the name of the class includes the actual type parameter used to create it.

## A.6   Exceptions

Sometimes unexpected situations arise during the execution of a program. Careful programmers write code that detects errors and deals with them appropriately. However, a simple algorithm can become unintelligible when error-checking is added because the error-checking code can obscure the normal operation of the algorithm.

*Exceptions* provide a clean way to detect and handle unexpected situations. When a program detects an error, it *throws* an exception. When an exception is thrown, control is transferred to the appropriate *exception handler*. By defining a function that *catches* the exception, the programmer can write the code to handle the error.

In C++, an exception is an object. Typically exceptions are derived (directly or indirectly) from the base class called **exception**, which is defined in the C++ standard library header file called **<exception>**.

A function throws an exception by using the **throw** statement:

```
class domain_error : public exception {};

void f ()
{
    //...
    throw domain_error ();
}
```

The **throw** statement is similar to a **return** statement. A **return** statement represents the normal termination of a function, and the object returned matches the return value of the function. A **throw** statement represents the abnormal termination of a function, and the object thrown represents the type of error encountered.

Exception handlers are defined using a **try** block:

```
void g ()
{
    try {
        f ();
    }
    catch (domain_error) {
        // exception handler
    }
    catch (range_error) {
        // exception handler
    }
}
```

The body of the **try** block is executed either until an exception is thrown or until it terminates normally.

One or more exception handlers follow a **try** block. Each exception handler consists of a **catch** clause which specifies the exceptions to be caught, and a block of code, which is executed when the exception occurs. When the body of the **try** block throws an exception for which an exception is defined, control is transferred to the body of the exception handler.

In this example, the exception was thrown by the function `f()` and caught by the function `g()`. In general when an exception is thrown, the chain of functions called is searched in reverse (from caller to callee) to find the closest matching `catch` statement. As the stack of called functions unwinds, the destructors for the local variables declared in those functions are automatically executed. When a program throws an exception that is not caught, the program terminates.

# B | Class Hierarchy Diagrams

FIGURE B.1
Key for the class hierarchy diagrams.

| Abstract Class | Concrete Class |
|:---:|:---:|
| base class | derived class |

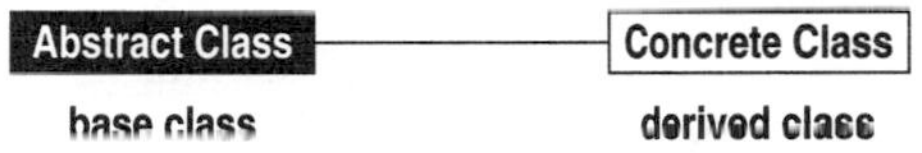

**FIGURE B.2**
Complete class hierarchy diagram.

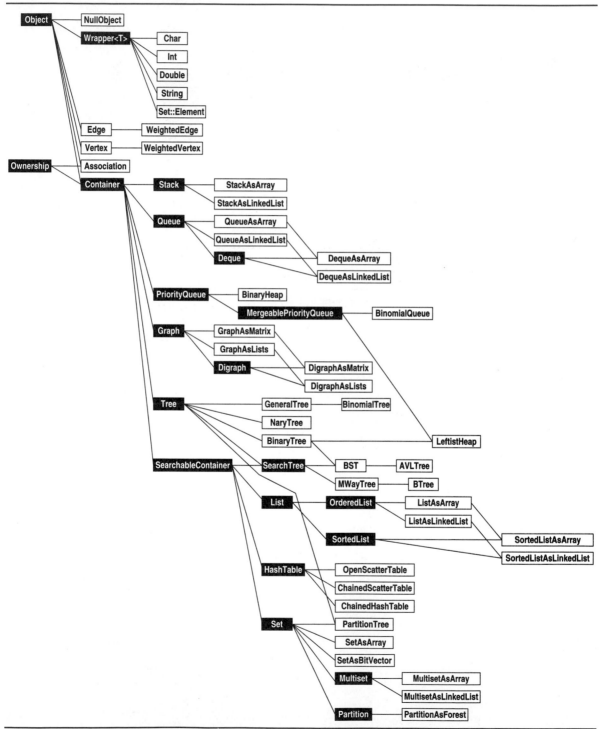

# C | Character Codes

**TABLE C.1**
Seven-bit ASCII Character Set

| Bits 6-3 | Bits 2-0 | | | | | | | |
|---|---|---|---|---|---|---|---|---|
| | 0 | 1 | 2 | 3 | 4 | 5 | 6 | 7 |
| 0 | NUL | SOH | STX | ETX | EOT | ENQ | ACK | BEL |
| 1 | BS | HT | NL | VT | NP | CR | SO | SI |
| 2 | DLE | DC1 | DC2 | DC3 | DC4 | NAK | SYN | ETB |
| 3 | CAN | EM | SUB | ESC | FS | GS | RS | US |
| 4 | SP | ! | " | # | $ | % | & | ' |
| 5 | ( | ) | * | + | , | – | . | / |
| 6 | 0 | 1 | 2 | 3 | 4 | 5 | 6 | 7 |
| 7 | 8 | 9 | : | ; | < | = | > | ? |
| 010 | @ | A | B | C | D | E | F | G |
| 011 | H | I | J | K | L | M | N | O |
| 012 | P | Q | R | S | T | U | V | W |
| 013 | X | Y | Z | [ | \ | ] | ^ | _ |
| 014 | ' | a | b | c | d | e | f | g |
| 015 | h | i | j | k | l | m | n | o |
| 016 | p | q | r | s | t | u | v | w |
| 017 | x | y | z | { | \| | \| | ~ | DEL |

# Bibliography

[1] Alfred V. Aho and John E. Hopcropft and Jeffrey D. Ullman. *Data Structures and Algorithms*. Addison-Wesley, Reading, MA, 1983.

[2] Alfred V. Aho and Jeffrey D. Ullman. *Foundations of Computer Science*. Computer Science Press, New York, NY, 1992.

[3] ANSI Accredited Standards Committee X3, Information Processing Systems. *Working Paper for Draft Proposed International Standard for Information Systems—Programming Language C++*. December 1996. Document Number X3J16/96-0225 WG21/N1043.

[4] Ken Arnold and James Gosling. *The Java™ Programming Language*. The Java™ Series. Addison-Wesley, Reading, MA, 1996.

[5] Borland International. *Borland C++ Version 3.0 Programmer's Guide*. 1991.

[6] Timothy A. Budd. *Classic Data Structures in C++*. Addison-Wesley, Reading, MA, 1994.

[7] Computational Science Education Project, Mathematical Optimization. Virtual book, 1995. `http://csep1.phy.ornl.gov/CSEP/MO/MO.html`.

[8] Computational Science Education Project, Random Number Generators. Virtual book, 1995. `http://csep1.phy.ornl.gov/CSEP/RN/RN.html`.

[9] Galean Dodds de Wolf, Robert J. Gregg, Barbara P. Harris, and Matthew H. Scargill, editors. *Gage Canadian Dictionary*. Gage Educational Publishing Company, Toronto, Canada, 1997.

[10] Rick Decker and Stuart Hirshfeld. *Working Classes: Data Structures and Algorithms Using C++*. PWS Publishing Company, Boston, MA, 1996.

[11] Adam Drozdek. *Data Structures and Algorithms in C++*. PWS Publishing Company, Boston, MA, 1996.

[12] Margaret A. Ellis and Bjarne Stroustrup. *The Annotated C++ Reference Manual*. Addison-Wesley, Reading, MA, 1990.

[13] James A. Field. MakeGraph User's Guide. Technical Report 94-04, Department of Electrical and Computer Engineering, University of Waterloo, Waterloo, Ontario, 1994.

[14] Erich Gamma, Richard Helm, Ralph Johnson, and John Vlissides. *Design Patterns: Elements of Reusable Object-Oriented Software.* Addison-Wesley, Reading, MA, 1995.

[15] Michel Goosens, Frank Mittelbach, and Alexander Samarin. *The L^ATEX Companion.* Addison-Wesley, Reading, MA, 1994.

[16] Irwin Guttman and S. S. WIlks and J. Stuart Hunter. *Introductory Engineering Statistics,* 2nd ed. John Wiley & Sons, New York, 1971.

[17] Gregory L. Heileman. *Data Structures, Algorithms, and Object-Oriented Programming.* McGraw-Hill, New York, 1996.

[18] Ellis Horowitz and Sartaj Sahni. *Data Structures in Pascal,* 3rd ed. W. H. Freeman and Company, New York, 1990.

[19] Ellis Horowitz, Sartaj Sahni, and Dinesh Mehta. *Fundamentals of Data Structures in C++.* W. H. Freeman and Company, New York, 1995.

[20] Brian W. Kernighan and Dennis M. Ritchie. *The C Programming Language.* Prentice Hall, Englewood Cliffs, New Jersey, 1978.

[21] Leonard Kleinrock. *Queueing Systems, Volume I: Theory.* John Wiley & Sons, New York, 1975.

[22] Donald E. Knuth. *Fundamental Algorithms,* volume 1 of *The Art of Computer Programming,* 2nd ed. Addison-Wesley, Reading, MA, 1973.

[23] Donald E. Knuth. *Sorting and Searching,* volume 3 of *The Art of Computer Programming.* Addison-Wesley, Reading, MA, 1973.

[24] Donald E. Knuth. *Seminumerical Algorithms,* volume 2 of *The Art of Computer Programming,* 2nd ed. Addison-Wesley, Reading, MA, 1981.

[25] Donald E. Knuth. *The* METAFONT*book.* Addison-Wesley, Reading, MA, 1986.

[26] Donald E. Knuth. *The TEXbook.* Addison-Wesley, Reading, MA, 1986.

[27] Elliot B. Koffman, David Stemple, and Caroline E. Wardle, Recommended Curriculum for CS2, 1984. *Communications of the ACM,* 28(8):815–818, August 1985.

[28] Leslie Lamport. *L^ATEX: A Document Preparation System,* 2nd ed. Addison-Wesley, Reading, MA, 1994.

[29] Yedidyah Langsam, Moshe J. Augenstein, and Aaron M. Tenenbaum. *Data Structures Using C and C++,* 2nd ed. Prentice Hall, Englewood Cliffs, NJ, 1996.

[30] Kenneth McAloon and Anthony Tromba. *Calculus,* volume 1BCD. Harcourt Brace Jovanovich, Inc., New York, NY, 1972.

[31] Thomas L. Naps. *Introduction to Program Design and Data Structures.* West Publishing, St. Paul, MN, 1993.

[32] Stephen K. Park and Keith W. Miller, Random Number Generators: Good Ones Are Hard To Find. *Communications of the ACM,* 31(10):1192–1201, October 1988.

[33] P. J. Plauger. *The Draft Standard C++ Library.* Prentice Hall, Englewood Cliffs, NJ, 1995.

[34] Stephen R. Schach. *Classical and Object-Oriented Software Engineering,* 3rd ed. Irwin, Chicago, IL, 1996.

[35] G. Michael Schneider and Steven C. Bruell. *Concepts in Data Structures and Software Development.* West Publishing, St. Paul, MN, 1991.

[36] Bjarne Stroustrup. *The C++ Programming Language,* 2nd ed. Addison-Wesley, Reading, MA, 1991.

[37] Bjarne Stroustrup. *The Design and Evolution of C++.* Addison-Wesley, Reading, MA, 1994.

[38] Allen B. Tucker, Bruce H. Barnes, Robert M. Aiken, Keith Barker, Kim B. Bruce, J. Thomas Cain, Susan E. Conry, Gerald L. Engel, Richard G. Epstein, Doris K. Lidtke, Michael C. Mulder, Jean B. Rogers, Eugene H. Spafford, A. Joe Turner. *Computing Curricula 1991: Report of the ACM/IEEE-CS Joint Curriculum Task Force.* ACM/IEEE, 1991.

[39] Larry Wall and Randal L. Schwartz. *Programming perl.* O'Reilly & Associates, Sebastopol, CA,1991.

[40] Mark Allen Weiss. *Data Structures and Algorithm Analysis,* 2nd ed. Benjamin/Cummings, Redwood City, CA, 1995.

[41] Mark Allen Weiss. *Algorithms, Data Structures and Problem Solving with C++.* Addison-Wesley, Reading, MA, 1996.

[42] Geoff Whale. *Data Structures and Abstraction Using C.* Thomson Nelson Australia, Melbourne, Australia, 1996.

# Index

$O$, *see* big oh
$\Omega$, *see* omega
$\Theta$, *see* theta
$\gamma$, *see* Euler's constant
$\lambda$, *see* lambda
$o$, *see* little oh

abstract algorithms, 269
abstract class, 97, 637
abstract data type, 66, 96
abstract solver, 470
abstract sorter, 510
access path, 320
accessor, 71, 629
activation record, 9, 432
activity-node graph, 610
actual parameter, 622
acyclic
    directed graph, 562
adapter, 271
address, 95, 619
address arithmetic, 88
adjacency lists, 567
adjacency matrix, 564
adjacent, 560
ADT, *see* abstract data type
algorithmic abstraction, 638
ancestor, 256
    proper, 256
and, 397
annealing, 503
annealing schedule, 503
arc
    directed, 560
    undirected, 562
arithmetic series, 23
arithmetic series summation, 23

arity, 281
array, 66
**Array2D<T>**, **88**
**Array2D<T>::**
    **Array2D**, 88, **89**
    **operator[]**, 88, **89**
    **Row::**
        **operator[]**, **88**
        **Row**, **88**
    **Row**, **88**
    **Select**, 88, **89**
**Array<T>**, **68**
**Array<T>::**
    **~Array**, 68, **71**
    **Array**, 68, **69**, **70**
    **Base**, 68, **71**
    **Data**, 68, **71**
    **Length**, 68, **71**
    **operator[]**, 68, **72**
    **SetBase**, 68, **73**
    **SetLength**, 68, **73**
ASCII, 212
**Assoc**, **595**
**Association**, **118**
**Association::**
    **~Association**, 118, **120**
    **Association**, 118, **120**
    **CompareTo**, 118, **121**
    **Hash**, 118, **218**
    **Key**, 118, **121**
    **Put**, 118, **121**
    **Value**, 118, **121**
asymptotic behavior, 34
attributes, 95
AVL balance condition, 316
AVL rotation, 320
AVL tree, 352

**AVLTree**, **318**
**AVLTree::**
    **AdjustHeight**, 318, **319**
    **AttachKey**, 318, **326**
    **AVLTree**, 318
    **Balance**, 318, **326**
    **BalanceFactor**, 318, **319**
    **DetachKey**, 318, **326**
    **Height**, 318
    **Left**, 318
    **LLRotation**, 318, **324**
    **LRRotation**, 318, **325**
    **Right**, 318
    **RLRotation**, 318
    **RRRotation**, 318

B-Tree, 335
B-tree, 335
Bachmann, P., 34
backtracking algorithms, 467
**bad_cast**, 104
**bad_cast**, 641
bag, 124, 401
balance condition, 315, 335
    AVL, 316
base class, 97, 631
best-fit allocation strategy, 436, 460
big oh, 34
    tightness, 43, 49
    transitive property, 40
binary digit, 375
binary heap, 533
binary operator, 139
binary search, 189, 477
binary search tree, 299, 300
binary tree, 246, 261
    complete, 353

`BinaryHeap`, 358
`BinaryHeap::`
  `~BinaryHeap`, 358,
    359
  `BinaryHeap`, 358, **359**
  `DequeueMin`, **363**
  `Enqueue`, **360**
  `FindMin`, **361**
  `Purge`, **359**
`BinaryInsertion-`
`Sorter<T>::`
  `DoSort`, **517**
`BinarySearch`, **477**
`BinaryTree`, **287**
`BinaryTree::`
  `~BinaryTree`, 287, **289**
  `AttachKey`, 287
  `AttachLeft`, 287
  `AttachRight`, 287
  `BinaryTree`, 287, **288**
  `CompareTo`, **291**
  `DepthFirstTraversal`,
    **289**
  `DetachKey`, 287
  `DetachLeft`, 287
  `DetachRight`, 287
  `Key`, 287
  `Left`, 287
  `Purge`, **289**
  `Right`, 287
binding, 96, 620
`Binom`, **490**
binomial, 373
binomial coefficient, 373
`BinomialQueue`, **379**
`BinomialQueue::`
  `~BinomialQueue`, 379
  `AddTree`, 379, **379**
  `BinomialQueue`, 379
  `Carry`, 379, **382**
  `DequeueMin`, **384**
  `Enqueue`, **383**
  `FindMin`, **380**
  `FindMinTree`, 379, **380**
  `Merge`, **381**
  `RemoveTree`, 379, **379**
  `Sum`, 379, **382**
`BinomialTree`, **377**
`BinomialTree::`
  `Add`, 377, **377**
  `BinomialTree`, 377
  `Subtree`, **377**
bit, 375
`bitsizeof`, **206**
bitwise exclusive-or, 450

Boolean
  and, 397
  or, 397
bound, 96
branch-and-bound, 474
breadth-first spanning tree, 602
breadth-first traversal, 150, 254,
  468, 580
`BreadthFirstSolver`, **472**
`BreadthFirstSolver::`
  `DoSolve`, 472, **473**
brute-force algorithms, 463
`BST`, **309**
`BST::`
  `AttachKey`, **312**
  `Balance`, **312**
  `BST`, 309
  `DetachKey`, **314**
  `Find`, **311**
  `FindMin`, **311**
  `Insert`, **312**
  `Left`, 309, **310**
  `Right`, 309, **310**
  `Withdraw`, **314**
`BTree`, **337**
`BTree::`
  `AttachKey`, 337
  `AttachLeftHalfOf`, 337
  `AttachRightHalfOf`, 337
  `AttachSubtree`, 337
  `BTree`, 337
  `Insert`, 337, **342**
  `InsertKey`, 337
  `InsertPair`, **343**
  `InsertSubtree`, 337
  `Withdraw`, 337
bubble sort, 518
`BubbleSorter<T>::`
  `DoSort`, **520**
bucket sort, 59
buckets, 59
`BucketSort`, **59**
`BucketSorter::`
  `DoSort`, **548**
`BucketSorter<T>`, **547**
`BucketSorter<T>::`
  `BucketSorter`, **547**
  `DoSort`, 547
buddy system, 448
`BuddyPool`, **452**
`BuddyPool::`
  `~BuddyPool`, 452, **453**
  `Acquire`, 452, **454**
  `Block::`
    `Links`, **452**

  `Block`, **452**
  `Buddy`, **452**
  `BuddyPool`, 452, **453**
  `Header`, **452**
  `InsertAfter`, 452
  `Release`, 452, **456**
  `Unlink`, 452
built-in types, 625

C programming language, 95
C++ programming language, 95
carry, 381
cast operator, 640
ceiling function, 18
central limit theorem, 506
chained scatter table, 225
`ChainedHashTable`, **221**
`ChainedHashTable::`
  `~ChainedHashTable`,
    221
  `ChainedHashTable`,
    221, 221
  `Find`, **223**
  `Insert`, **222**
  `Purge`, **221**
  `Withdraw`, **222**
`ChainedScatterTable`, **226**
`ChainedScatterTable::`
  `~ChainedScatterTable`,
    228
  `ChainedScatterTable`,
    226, **228**
  `Entry::`
    `Entry`, 226, **228**
  `Entry`, **226**
  `Find`, **229**
  `Insert`, **229**
  `Purge`, **228**
  `Withdraw`, **231**
`Char`, **106**
child, 150, 255
`Circle`, **636**
`Circle::`
  `Circle`, **636**
  `Draw`, **636**
circular list, 74, 160
clock frequency, 22
clock period, 22
coalesce, 225
cocktail shaker sort, 556
coefficient
  binomial, 373
coercion, 91
collapsing find, 416
column-major order, 94

commensurate
    elements, 187, 509
    functions, 44
complement, 423
complete *N*-ary tree, 356
complete binary tree, 353, 533
`Complex`, **626**
complex numbers, 625
`Complex::`
    `~Complex`, 626, **628**
    `Complex`, 626, **628**
    `Imag`, 626, **629**
    `operator=`, 626, **630**
    `Put`, 626, **629**
    `R`, 626, **629**
    `Real`, 626, **629**
    `SetImag`, 626, **630**
    `SetReal`, 626, **630**
    `Theta`, 626, **629**
component
    connected, 586
compound statement, 50
concrete class, 97, 637
conditional execution, 52
conjunction, 392
connected
    directed graph
        strongly, 587
        weakly, 588
    undirected graph, 586
connected component, 586, 616
conquer, *see* divide
`const` member functions, 71
constant, 45
constructor, 626
    copy, 69
    default, 68
`Container`, **106**
`Container::`
    `Accept`, 106
    `Container`, 106, **107**
    `Count`, 106, **107**
    `Hash`, 106, **217**
    `IsEmpty`, 106, **107**
    `IsFull`, 106, **107**
    `NewIterator`, 106, **115**
    `Put`, 106, **111**
copy constructor, 69
counted do loop, 51
critical activity, 611
critical path, 611
critical path analysis, 609
`CriticalPathAnalysis`,
    **614**
cubic, 45

cycle, 561
    negative cost, 592
    simple, 562

data ordering property, 299
database, 119
decision tree, 544
default constructor, 68, 627
default copy constructor, 93
degree, 150
    in, 561
    out, 560
dense graph, 566
depth, 256
depth-first spanning tree, 602
depth-first traversal, 468, 577
`DepthFirstBranchAnd-`
    `BoundSolver::`
        `DoSolve`, 475
`DepthFirstSolver`, **471**
`DepthFirstSolver::`
    `DoSolve`, 471, **472**
`Deque`, **153**
deque, 126, 152
`Deque::`
    `Dequeue`, **153**, 153
    `DequeueHead`, 153
    `DequeueTail`, 153
    `Enqueue`, 153, **153**
    `EnqueueHead`, 153
    `EnqueueTail`, 153
    `Head`, 153
    `Tail`, 153
`DequeAsArray`, **155**
`DequeAsArray::`
    `DequeAsArray`, 155
    `DequeueHead`, **155**
    `DequeueTail`, **156**
    `EnqueueHead`, **156**
    `EnqueueTail`, **155**
    `Head`, **155**
    `Tail`, **156**
`DequeAsLinkedList`, **157**
`DequeAsLinkedList::`
    `DequeAsLinkedList`,
        157
    `DequeueHead`, **157**
    `DequeueTail`, **158**
    `EnqueueHead`, **158**
    `EnqueueTail`, **157**
    `Head`, **157**
    `Tail`, **158**
dereference, 621
derivation, 97, 631
derivative, 183

derived class, 631
descendant, 256
    proper, 256
destructor, 628
difference, 392, 393, 404
    symmetric, 423
differentiation, 183
digit
    binary, 375
`Digraph`, **571**
digraph, *see* directed graph
`Digraph::`
    `IsConnected`, 571, **589**
    `IsCyclic`, 571, **590**
    `TopologicalOrder-`
        `Traversal`, 571, **585**
Dijkstra's algorithm, 592
`DijkstrasAlgorithm`, **596**
direct containment, 116
directed acyclic graph, 562
directed arc, 560
directed graph, 559
discrete event simulation, 385
disjunction, 392
distribution sorting, 546
distribution sorts, 512
`DistributionSorter<T>`, **512**
divide and conquer, 476
division method of hashing, 204
`domain_error`, 80
`Double`, **106**
double construction, 429
double hashing, 237
double rotation, 322
double-ended queue, 152
doubly-linked list, 159
`DoublyLinkedPool`, **444**
`DoublyLinkedPool::`
    `~DoublyLinkedPool`,
        444, **445**
    `Acquire`, 444, **446**
    `Block::`
        `Links`, **444**
    `Block`, **444**
    `DoublyLinkedPool`,
        444, **445**
    `Header`, **444**
    `InsertAfter`, **444**
    `Release`, 444, **445**
    `Unlink`, **444**
dual, 610
dynamic binding, 96
`dynamic_cast`, 104, 120
dynamic programming, 486
`dynamic_cast`, **640**

earliest event time, 611
**EarliestTimeVisitor,
613**
**EarliestTimeVisitor::
EarliestTimeVisitor,
613
Visit, 613**
**Edge, 569**
edge, 150, 560
emanate, 560
incident, 560
edge-weighted graph, 574
**Edge::
Edge, 569
Mate, 569
V0, 569
V1, 569**
element, 392
emanate, 560
enumeration, 124
equivalence classes, 421
equivalence of trees, 290
equivalence relation, 421, 606
Euler's constant, 19, 305, 528
Euler, Leonhard, 373
Eulerian walk, 616
evaluation stack, 267
**Event, 458**
event-node graph, 610
exception, 72, 80
exception handler, 643
exceptions, 643
exchange sorting, 518
exchange sorts, 511
**ExchangeSorter<T>,
512**
exclusive or, 214
exclusive-or, 450
exponent, 211
exponential, 45
exponential cooling, 503
exponential distribution, 501
**ExponentialRV, 500**
**ExponentialRV::
ExponentialRV,
500, 500**
expression tree, 265
external node, 258
external path length, 305

**Factorial, 13**
factorial, 12
feasible solution, 464
**Fibonacci, 54, 55, 479, 487**
Fibonacci hashing method, 207

Fibonacci number, 208, 316
Fibonacci numbers, 54, 478
closed-form expression, 56
generalized, 486
FIFO, 142
fifo-in, first-out, 142
find
collapsing, 416
**FindMaximum, 15**
first-fit allocation strategy, 436, 460
floor function, 18
Floyd's algorithm, 597
**FloydsAlgorithm, 599**
forest, 370, 375, 410
formal parameter, 622
Fortran, 95
foundational data structure, 66
free, 433
free list, 433
free store, 69
**frexp, 211**
friend, 91, 132
fully connected graph, 616

Gauss, Karl Friedrich, 373
generalization, 154
generalized Fibonacci numbers, 486
**GeneralTree, 278**
**GeneralTree::
~GeneralTree, 278, 279
AttachSubtree,
278, 280
DetachSubtree,
278, 280
GeneralTree, 278, 279
Key, 278, 280
Purge, 279
Subtree, 278, 280**
generic, 641
geometric series, 25
geometric series summation, 22, 24,
25, 29
**GeometricSeriesSum,
22, 25, 30**
golden ratio, 207
**Graph, 571**
graph
connectedness, 586
dense, 566
directed, 559
directed acyclic, 562
edge-weighted, 574
labeled, 563
sparse, 566
traversal, 577

undirected, 562
vertex-weighted, 574
graph theory, 558
**Graph::
AddEdge, 571
AddVertex, 571
BreadthFirst-
Traversal, 571, 582
DepthFirstTraversal,
571, 579
Edges, 571
EmanatingEdges, 571
Graph, 571
IncidentEdges, 571
IsConnected, 571, 587
IsCyclic, 571
IsEdge, 571
NumberOfEdges, 571
NumberOfVertices, 571
operator[], 571
SelectEdge, 571
SelectVertex, 571
Vertices, 571**
**GraphAsLists, 574**
**GraphAsLists::
GraphAsLists, 574**
**GraphAsMatrix, 573**
**GraphAsMatrix::
GraphAsMatrix, 573**
**GraphicalObject, 635**
**GraphicalObject::
~GraphicalObject, 635
Draw, 635
Erase, 635, 635
GraphicalObject, 635
MoveTo, 635, 635**

harmonic number, 17, 18, 246, 305, 528
harmonic series, 18
**Hash, 210, 212, 214**
hash function, 203
hash table, 218
hashing
division method, 204
Fibonacci method, 207
middle-square method, 205
multiplication method, 206
**HashingVisitor, 217**
**HashingVisitor::
HashingVisitor, 217
Visit, 217**
**HashTable, 219**
**HashTable::
H, 219, 219
HashTable, 219, 219**

head, 73
heap, 69, 352, 432
heapify, 533
heapsort, 533
**HeapSorter<T>**, 533
**HeapSorter<T>::**
    **BuildHeap**, 533, **535**
    **DoSort**, 533, **539**
    **PercolateDown**,
      533, **535**
height
    of a node in a tree, 256
    of a tree, 256
heuristic, 475
hierarchy, 253
**Horner**, **12**, **50**
Horner's rule, 11, 24, 213

idempotent, 100
if-then-else, 52
in-degree, 561, 584
in-place sorting, 513, 530
incident, 560
increment, 496
indirect containment, 116, 277
infix, 139
infix notation, 266
**InfixVisitor**, **295**
inheritance, 631
initialized static variables, 432
**InOrder**, **270**
inorder traversal, 254, 307
    *M*-way tree, 307
**InOrder::**
    **InOrder**, **270**
    **Visit**, **270**
insertion sorting, 513
    straight, 513
insertion sorts, 511
**InsertSorter<T>**, **512**
**Int**, **106**
integral type, 210
interface, 97
internal node, 258
internal path length, 305
    complete binary tree, 355
internal path length of a tree, 302
Internet domain name, 214
intersection, 392, 393, 404
inverse modulo *W*, 207
inversion, 513
isomorphic, 257
isomorphic trees, 296
iteration, 51
iterative algorithm, 54

**Iterator**, **112**
**Iterator::**
    **~Iterator**, 112
    **IsDone**, 112
    **operator***, 112
    **operator++**, 112
    **Reset**, 112

Java, 124

key, 119, 203
keyed data, 217
knapsack problem, 465
Kruskal's algorithm, 606
**KruskalsAlgorithm**,
  **608**

L'Hôpital's rule, 42
l-value, 95, 619
labeled graph, 563
lambda, *see* load factor
last-in, first-out, 128
latest event time, 611
leaf, 255
leaf node, 259
least-significant-digit-first radix
    sorting, 548
left subtree, 261, 299
leftist tree, 364
**LeftistHeap**, **366**
**LeftistHeap::**
    **DequeueMin**, **369**
    **Enqueue**, **369**
    **FindMin**, **369**
    **Left**, 366
    **LeftistHeap**, 366
    **Merge**, 366, **366**
    **Right**, 366
    **SwapContents**, 366
level, 256
level-order, 356
level-order traversal, 150
lexicographic order, 87
lexicographic ordering, 550
lexicographically precede, 550
lifetime, 95, 620
LIFO, 128
limit, 37
linear, 45
linear congruential random
    number generator, 495
linear probing, 234
linear search, 15
linked list, 66
**LinkedList<T>**, **77**

**LinkedList<T>::**
    **~LinkedList**, 77, 79
    **Append**, 77, **82**
    **Extract**, 77, **84**
    **First**, 77, **81**
    **Head**, 77, **80**
    **InsertAfter**, 77, **86**
    **InsertBefore**, 77, **86**
    **IsEmpty**, 77, **80**
    **Last**, 77, **81**
    **LinkedList**, 77, **79**, **83**
    **operator=**, 77, **83**
    **Prepend**, 77, **81**
    **Purge**, 77, **79**
    **Tail**, 77, **80**
**List**, 166
list, 164
**List::**
    **FindPosition**, 166
    **operator[]**, 166
    **Withdraw**, 166
**ListAsArray**, 167
**ListAsArray::**
    **Find**, 168
    **FindPosition**, 172
    **Insert**, 167
    **InsertAfter**, 173
    **IsMember**, 168
    **ListAsArray**, 167, **167**
    **operator[]**, 167, 172
    **Pos**, 171
    **Withdraw**, 170, **174**
**ListAsLinkedList**, 175
**ListAsLinkedList::**
    **Find**, 177
    **FindPosition**, 179
    **Insert**, 176
    **InsertAfter**, 180
    **IsMember**, 177
    **ListAsLinkedList**,
      175, **176**
    **operator[]**, 176, **179**
    **Pos**, 178
    **Withdraw**, 178, **181**
**ListElement<T>**, 77
**ListElement<T>::**
    **Datum**, 77, **78**
    **ListElement**, 77, **78**
    **Next**, 77, **78**
little oh, 49
LL rotation, 321
    in a B-tree, 344
load factor, 224
log squared, 45
logarithm, 45

loop, 562
loose asymptotic bound, 49
LR rotation, 322
Lukasiewicz, Jan, 139

*M*-way search tree, 298
mantissa, 211
many-to-one mapping, 203
matrix
    adjacency, 564
    sparse, 565
**Matrix<T>, 91**
**Matrix<T>::**
    **Matrix**, 91
    **operator***, 91, **92**
    **operator+**, 91
    **operator[]**, 91
max-heap, 533
median, 529
median-of-three pivot selection, 529
**MedianOfThreeQuick-**
**Sorter<T>, 530**
**MedianOfThreeQuick-**
**Sorter<T>::**
    **SelectPivot**, 530, **530**
member variable accessor, 71
memory map, 426
merge sort, 480
merge sorting, 539
merge sorts, 512
mergeable priority queue, 351
**MergeablePriorityQueue,**
**351**
**MergeablePriorityQueue::**
    **Merge**, 351
**MergeSort, 481**
**MergeSorter<T>, 512**
merging nodes in a B-tree, 344
Mersenne primes, 497
middle-square hashing method, 205
min heap, 352
minimal subgraph, 600
minimum spanning tree, 603
mixed linear congruential random number
    generator, 496
modulus, 495
Monte Carlo methods, 501
multi-dimensional array, 85
multiple inheritance, 106, 631
multiplication hashing method, 206
multiplicative linear congruential random
    number generator, 496
**Multiset, 402**
multiset, 401
**MultisetAsArray, 403**

**MultisetAsArray::**
    **Insert, 404**
    **IsMember, 404**
    **MultisetAsArray**, 403, **404**
    **Withdraw, 404**
**MultisetAsLinkedList, 406**
**MultisetAsLinkedList::**
    **MultisetAsLinkedList,**
    406
mutator, 630
**MWayTree, 328**
**MWayTree::**
    **~MWayTree**, 328
    **DepthFirstTraversal,**
    **330**
    **Find, 330, 332**
    **FindIndex**, 328, **332**
    **Insert, 333**
    **Key**, 328
    **MWayTree**, 328
    **Subtree**, 328
    **Withdraw, 334**

N-ary tree
    *N*-ary tree, 258
N-queens problem
    *N*-queens problem, 505
name, 95, 619
**name()**, 111
**Nary tree, 356**
**NaryTree, 282**
**NaryTree::**
    **~NaryTree**, 282
    **AttachKey**, 282, **284**
    **AttachSubtree,**
    282, **285**
    **DetachKey**, 282, **284**
    **DetachSubtree,**
    282, **285**
    **IsEmpty, 283**
    **Key**, 282, **284**
    **NaryTree**, 282, **283**
    **Subtree**, 282, **285**
negative cost cycle, 592
Newton, Isaac, 373
next-fit allocation strategy, 460
node, 150, 254, 258, 261, 560
non-recursive algorithm, 54
normalize, 496
null path length, 363
null-terminated sequence, 212
**NullIterator, 114**
**NullIterator::**
    **IsDone**, 114, **115**
    **NullIterator**, 114, **115**

    **operator***, 114, **115**
    **operator++**, 114, **115**
    **Reset**, 114, **115**
**NullObject, 103**
**NullObject::**
    **CompareTo**, 103, 103
    **Hash**, 103, **103**
    **Instance**, 103, **103**
    **IsNull**, 103, **103**
    **NullObject**, **103**, 103
    **Put**, **103**, 103

**Object, 99**
object, 625
object-oriented programming, 92
object-oriented programming language,
    96
**Object::**
    **~Object**, 99, **101**
    **Compare**, 99, **101**
    **CompareTo**, 99
    **Hash**, 99
    **IsNull**, 99, **101**
    **Put**, 99
objective function, 464
odd-even transposition sort, 556
omega, 45
open addressing, 234
**OpenScatterTable, 238**
**OpenScatterTable::**
    **~OpenScatterTable**, 239
    **C**, 238, **240**
    **Entry::**
        **Entry**, 238, **239**, 239
    **Entry, 238**
    **Find, 242**
    **FindInstance**, 238
    **FindMatch**, 238, **242**
    **FindUnoccupied**, 238, **240**
    **Insert, 240**
    **OpenScatterTable,**
    238, **239**
    **Purge, 239**
    **Withdraw**, 243, **244**
**operator delete, 431**
**operator new, 431**
operator overloading, 266, 630
operator precedence, 139
**operator***, 395, **398**, **402**, **405**, **408**
**operator+**, 395, **398**, **402**, **405**, **407**
**operator-**, 395, **398**, **402**, **405**
**operator::**
    **!=, 100**
    **<, 100**
    **<<, 100**

`<=`, **100**
`==`, **100**
`>`, **100**
`>=`, **100**
`operator<=`, 395, **399**
`operator==`, 395, **399**
optimal binary search tree, 506
or, 397
ordered list, 164
ordered tree, 259, 261
`OrderedList`, **166**
`OrderedList::`
   `InsertAfter`, 166
   `InsertBefore`, 166
ordinal number, 178
oriented tree, 259
`out_of_range`, **72**
out-degree, 560
overloading
   operator, 630
override, 633
`Ownership`, **117**
ownership, 116
`Ownership::`
   `AssertOwnership`,
     117
   `IsOwner`, 117
   `Ownership`, 117
   `RescindOwnership`,
     117

parameter passing, 622
`Parent`, **632**
parent, 150, 255
`Parent::`
   `Child`, **632**
parentheses, 139
partial order, 398
`Partition`, **410**
partition, 408, 606
`Partition::`
   `Find`, 410
   `Join`, 410
`PartitionAsForest`, **412**
`PartitionAsForest::`
   `~PartitionAsForest`,
     412, **413**
   `CheckArguments`, **415**
   `Find`, **414**, **417**
   `Join`, **415**, **418**, **420**
   `PartitionAsForest`,
     412, **413**
`PartitionTree`, **412**
`PartitionTree::`
   `PartitionTree`, 412, **413**

Pascal, 95
Pascal's triangle, 489
Pascal, Blaise, 489
pass-by-reference, 622, 623
pass-by-value, 622
path, 561
   access, 320
path length
   external, 305
   internal, 305
   weighted, 591
perfect binary tree, 302, 315
period, 495
`Person`, **632**
`Person::`
   `Name`, **632**
`Pi`, **504**
pivot, 521
placement syntax, 430
`Point`, **635**
`Point::`
   `Point`, 635
pointer, 620
Polish notation, 139
polymorphism, 97, 634
`Polynomial`, **196**
polynomial, 40, 47
`Polynomial::`
   `operator+`, 196
position, 165
`PostOrder`, **270**
postorder traversal, 263
`PostOrder::`
   `PostOrder`, **270**
   `PostVisit`, **270**
`Power`, **27**
power set, 395
precede lexicographically, 550
predecessor, 158, 561
prefix notation, 266, 267
`PrefixSums`, **52**
`PreOrder`, **270**
preorder traversal, 263
`PreOrder::`
   `PreOrder`, **270**
   `PreVisit`, **270**
prepend, 80
`PrePostVisitor`, **270**
`PrePostVisitor::`
   `PostVisit`, 270
   `PreVisit`, 270
Prim's algorithm, 603
primary clustering, 236
prime
   relatively, 207

`PrimsAlgorithm`, **605**
priority queue
   mergeable, 351
`PriorityQueue`, **351**
`PriorityQueue::`
   `DequeueMin`, 351
   `Enqueue`, 351
   `FindMin`, 351
probability density function, 503
probe sequence, 234
processor stack, 432
proper subset, 397
proper superset, 397
protected, 91
pruning a solution space, 474
pseudorandom, 495
pure virtual function, 638
pure virtual member function, 97
`PuttingVisitor`, **111**
`PuttingVisitor::`
   `PuttingVisitor`, **111**
   `Visit`, **111**

quadratic, 45
quadratic probing, 236
`Queue`, **143**
queue, 126
`Queue::`
   `Dequeue`, 143
   `Enqueue`, 143
   `Head`, 143
`QueueAsArray`, **143**
`QueueAsArray::`
   `~QueueAsArray`,
     **143**, **145**
   `Dequeue`, **146**
   `Enqueue`, **146**
   `Head`, **146**
   `Purge`, **145**
   `QueueAsArray`, **143**, **145**
`QueueAsLinkedList`, **147**
`QueueAsLinkedList::`
   `~QueueAsLinkedList`,
     147, **148**
   `Dequeue`, **149**
   `Enqueue`, **149**
   `Head`, **149**
   `Purge`, **148**
   `QueueAsLinkedList`,
     147, **148**
quicksort, 520
`QuickSorter<T>`, **523**
`QuickSorter<T>::`
   `DoSort`, 523, **524**
   `SelectPivot`, 523

r-value, 95, 619
radix sorting, 548
**RadixSorter::**
 **DoSort, 551**
**RadixSorter<T>, 550**
**RadixSorter<T>::**
 **DoSort**, 550
 **RadixSorter, 550**
random number generator
 linear congruential, 495
 mixed linear congruential, 496
 multiplicative linear congruential, 496
random numbers, 495
random variable, 499
**RandomNumberGenerator, 498**
**RandomNumberGenerator::**
 **Next, 498**, 498
 **SetSeed, 498**, 498
**RandomVariable, 500**
**RandomVariable::**
 **Sample**, 500, **500**
rank, 420
read-only access, 71
record, 96
**Rectangle, 636**
**Rectangle::**
 **Draw**, 636
 **Rectangle, 636**
recurrence relation, 14
recursive algorithm, 12, 55
reference, 622
reflexive, 421
relation
 equivalence, 421
relatively prime, 207
repeated substitution, 14
reserved, 433
Reverse-Polish notation, 139
right subtree, 261, 299
RL rotation, 322
root, 254
rotation
 AVL, 320
 double, 322
 LL, 321, 344
 LR, 322
 RL, 322
 RR, 322, 344
 single, 322
row-major order, 87
RPN, *see* Reverse-Polish notation
RR rotation, 322
 in a B-tree, 344

RTTI, *see* run-time type information
run-time type information, 102, 111, 640

scales, 467
scatter tables, 225
scope, 95, 96, 620
search tree
 *M*-way, 298
 binary, 300
**SearchableContainer, 121**
**SearchableContainer::**
 **Find**, 121
 **Insert**, 121
 **IsMember**, 121
 **Withdraw**, 121
**SearchTree, 309**
**SearchTree::**
 **FindMax**, 309
 **FindMin**, 309
seed, 495
selection sorting, 529
selection sorts, 512
**SelectionSorter<T>, 512**
sentinel, 73, 565
separate chaining, 220
sequence, 165
sequential composition, 51
**Set, 394**
set, 392
**Set::**
 **Element, 394**
 **Set**, 394
**SetAsArray, 395**
**SetAsArray::**
 **Insert, 396**
 **IsMember, 396**
 **SetAsArray**, 395, **396**
 **Withdraw, 396**
**SetAsBitVector, 400**
**SetAsBitVector::**
 **Insert, 400**
 **IsMember, 400**
 **SetAsBitVector, 400**, 400
 **Withdraw, 400**
sibling, 255
significant, 211
simple cycle, 562
**SimpleRV, 500**
**SimpleRV::**
 **Sample**, 500, **500**
simulated annealing, 503
simulation time, 386
single rotation, 322
single-ended queue, 142
singleton, 102, 424, 497

singly-linked list, 158
**SinglyLinkedPool, 434**
**SinglyLinkedPool::**
 **~SinglyLinkedPool**, 434, **435**
 **Acquire**, 434, **437**
 **Block, 434**
 **Header, 434**
 **Release**, 434, **438**
 **SinglyLinkedPool**, 434, **435**
size, 95, 619
slack time, 611
**Solution, 469**
solution space, 467
**Solution::**
 **Bound**, 469
 **Clone**, 469
 **IsComplete**, 469
 **IsFeasible**, 469
 **Objective**, 469
 **Successors**, 469
**Solver, 470**
solver, 470
**Solver::**
 **DoSolve**, 470
 **Solve**, 470, **471**
 **UpdateBest**, 470, **471**
sort
 topological, 583
sorted list, 164, 186, 351
**SortedList, 187**
**SortedListAsArray, 188**
**SortedListAsArray::**
 **Find**, 191
 **FindOffset**, 188, **190**
 **FindPosition**, 191
 **Insert**, 189
 **SortedListAsArray**, 188
 **Withdraw**, 191
**SortedListAsLinkedList, 192**
**SortedListAsLinkedList::**
 **Insert**, 193
 **SortedListAsLinked-List**, 192
sorter, 510
**Sorter<T>, 510**
**Sorter<T>::**
 **DoSort**, 510
 **Sort**, 510, **511**
 **Swap**, 510, **511**
sorting
 in place, 530
 in-place, 513

sorting algorithm
    bucket sort, 59
sorting by distribution, 546
sorting by exchanging, 518
sorting by insertion, 513
sorting by merging, 539
sorting by selection, 529
source, 616
spanning tree, 600
    breadth-first, 602
    depth-first, 602
    minimum, 603
sparse graph, 566
sparse matrix, 565
specialization, 154
**Square**, **636**
**Square::**
    **Square**, **636**
stable sorts, 510
**Stack**, **128**
stack, 127
stack frame, 9
**Stack::**
    **Pop**, 128
    **Push**, 128
    **Top**, 128
**Stack<T>**, **642**
**Stack<T>::**
    **Pop**, **642**
    **Push**, **642**
**StackAsArray**, **129**
**StackAsArray::**
    **~StackAsArray**, 129
    **Accept**, 131
    **Iter::**
        **IsDone**, 133
        **Iter**, 129, 133
        **operator***, 133
        **operator++**, 133
        **Reset**, 133
    **Iter**, 129
    **Pop**, 130
    **Purge**, 129
    **Push**, 130
    **StackAsArray**, 129, 129
    **Top**, 130
**StackAsLinkedList**, 133
**StackAsLinkedList::**
    **~StackAsLinkedList**,
    134
    **Accept**, 137
    **Iter::**
        **IsDone**, 137
        **Iter**, 133, 137

**operator***, 137
**operator++**, 137
**Reset**, 137
**Iter**, 133
**Pop**, 135
**Purge**, 134
**Push**, 135
**StackAsLinkedList**,
133, **134**
**Top**, 135
state, 385
static binding, 96
static member, 497
Stirling numbers, 409
**StoragePool**, **428**
**StoragePool::**
    **~StoragePool**, 428
    **Acquire**, 428
    **Release**, 428
**StoragePoolTest**, **459**
straight insertion sorting, 513
straight selection sorting, 530
**StraightInsertion-**
**Sorter<T>::**
    **DoSort**, **515**
**StraightSelection-**
**Sorter<T>::**
    **DoSort**, 532
**String**, **106**
**string**, 212
strongly connected, 587
subgraph, 600
    minimal, 600
subset, 397
    proper, 397
subtraction, 392
subtree, 150
successor, 158, 561
**Sum**, **10**
superset, 397
    proper, 397
symbol table, 201, 247
symmetric, 421
symmetric difference, 423

**TableEntry**, **595**
tail, 73
telescoping, 304, 482
temperature, 505
template, 641
**Term**, **185**, **195**
**Term::**
    **Coefficient**, 195, **195**
    **CompareTo**, 185, **185**

**Differentiate**, 185, **185**
**Exponent**, **195**, 195
**operator+**, **195**, 195
**Term**, 185, **185**
tertiary tree, 258
theta, 49
throw, 643
tight asymptotic bound, 43
time
    simulation, 386
topological sort, 583
total order, 509
    binary trees, 290
transitive, 187, 421, 509
traversal, 262, 468, 577
    breadth-first, 254, 580
    depth-first, 577
    inorder, 254, 307
    postorder, 263
    preorder, 263
**Tree**, **268**
tree, 254
    *N*-ary, 258
    binary, 261
    equivalence, 290
    expression, 265
    height, 256
    internal path length, 302
    leftist, 364
    ordered, 259, 261
    oriented, 259
    search, *see* search tree
    tertiary, 258
    traversal, 262
tree traversal, 150
**Tree::**
    **Accept**, 268, **273**
    **BreadthFirstTraversal**,
    268, **272**
    **Degree**, 268
    **DepthFirstTraversal**,
    268, **269**
    **Height**, 268
    **IsEmpty**, 268
    **IsLeaf**, 268
    **Iter::**
        **IsDone**, 274, **276**
        **Iter**, 274, 275
        **operator***, 274, **276**
        **operator++**, 274, **276**
        **Reset**, 275
    **Iter**, 274
    **Key**, 268
    **Subtree**, 268

`TwoWayMergeSorter<T>`, **541**
`TwoWayMergeSorter<T>::`
   `DoSort`, 541, **543**
   `Merge`, 541, **542**
   `TwoWayMergeSorter`,
   **541**
type, 95, 619
`typeid`, 111
`typeinfo.h`, 111
`Typeset`, **494**

undirected arc, 562
undirected graph, 562
uniform distribution, 204
uniform hashing model, 245
`UniformRV`, **500**
`UniformRV::`
   `Sample`, 500, **500**
   `UniformRV`, 500, **500**
union, 136, 392, 393, 403
union by rank, 420
union by size, 418

universal set, 392, 606
unsorted list, 351

value, 95, 119, 619
variable, 619
Venn diagram, 256, 392
`Vertex`, **568**
vertex, 560
vertex-weighted graph, 574
`Vertex::`
   `operator[]`, 568
   `Vertex`, 568
virtual, 97
virtual base class, 639
visibility, 95
`Visitor`, **108**
`Visitor::`
   `IsDone`, 108
   `Visit`, 108

weakly connected, 588
weighted path length, 591

`WeightedEdge`, **575**
`WeightedEdge::`
   `Weight`, 575
   `WeightedEdge`, 575
`WeightedVertex`, **575**
`WeightedVertex::`
   `Weight`, 575
   `WeightedVertex`, 575
word size, 205
worst-fig allocation strategy, 460
wrapper, 102
`Wrapper<T>`, **104**
`Wrapper<T>::`
   `CompareTo`, 104, **105**
   `Hash`, 104, **105**, **216**
   `operator T const&`,
   104, **105**
   `operator=`, 104, **105**
   `Put`, 104, **105**
   `Wrapper`, 104, **105**